Life and Death Planning
for Retirement Benefits

The Essential Handbook for Estate Planners

Fourth Edition, Completely Revised
2002

Natalie B. Choate

Ataxplan Publications, Boston, Massachusetts

For future updates of this book, visit our website:

www.ataxplan.com

Life and Death Planning for Retirement Benefits

The Essential Handbook for Estate Planners
Fourth edition, completely revised

By Natalie B. Choate

Published by: Ataxplan Publications
                  Post Office Box 1093-K
                  Boston, Massachusetts 02103-1093

Publisher's Cataloging-in-Publication Data
Choate, Natalie B.
        Life and Death Planning for Retirement Benefits: The Essential Handbook for Estate Planners— 4th ed. / Natalie B. Choate
        p.   cm.
Includes bibliographical references and index.

ISBN 0-9649440-5-7

        1. Estate planning - United States. 2. Tax planning - United States. 3. Retirement income - Taxation - United States. 4. Inheritance and transfer tax - United States. I. Choate, Natalie B. II. Title

KF 6585 .C43 2001

To my mother

Jhan English Choate

who has had to put up with a lot

Warning and Disclaimer

The rules applicable to qualified retirement plan benefits and IRAs are among the most complex in the tax code. I have read few works on this subject that were, in my view, completely accurate; in fact most that I have seen, including, unfortunately, earlier incarnations of this work, contain errors. Furthermore, even accurate information can become outdated quickly as IRS or Congressional policy shifts. Despite my best efforts, it is likely that this book, too, contains errors. Citations are provided so that estate planning practitioners can check any statements made in this book and reach their own conclusions regarding what the law is.

This book is intended to provide general information regarding the tax and other laws applicable to retirement benefits, and to provide suggestions regarding appropriate estate planning actions for different situations. It is not intended as a substitute for the practitioner's own research, or for the advice of a qualified estate planning specialist. The author and publisher shall have neither liability nor responsibility to any person or entity with respect to any loss or damage caused, or alleged to be caused, directly or indirectly by the information contained in this book.

If you do not wish to be bound by the above, you may return this book to the publisher for a full refund.

Summary of Contents

Table of Contents

NOTES

Introduction

The purpose of this book is to explain, for the benefit of my fellow estate planning lawyers, and all other tax and financial services professionals involved in helping individuals plan for distribution of their retirement benefits, as many of the applicable rules as I can fit into almost 600 pages. I hope the book will serve as both a handy reference source for the expert and a basic guide for the novice.

Limitations of this Book

Many important aspects of planning for retirement distributions are *not* covered in this book, such as annuity payouts, investment alternatives and financial planning considerations generally. This book also does not cover: § 457 plans; qualified domestic relations orders (QDROs); stock options and other non-qualified forms of deferred compensation; ESOPs; creditors' rights; state tax issues; and community property. Other sources for some of these topics are mentioned in the Bibliography.

This book is designed to explain estate planning and tax planning issues for the benefit of estate and financial planners who are counseling individuals (and their beneficiaries) who have assets in retirement plans. It does not cover plan distribution issues which are of concern to plan administrators, but which do not have a significant impact on planning decisions for the individual participant, such as distribution notice requirements.

This book deals with the *federal* tax law applicable to retirement benefits, but in a few instances state law has a bearing on the subject. When state law has a significant impact, planners will need to determine the law applicable to their clients.

Prior Publication

Parts of the text were previously published in the following articles by the author:

"How to Create Separate Accounts Within a Single IRA for Purposes of the Minimum Distribution Rules," Trusts & Estates, Vol. 139, No. 9 (Sept. 2000), page 38.

"The 'Estate' As Beneficiary Of Retirement Benefits," <u>Trusts & Estates</u>, Vol. 138, No. 10 (Sept. 1999), p. 41.

"When a 'Trust for the Spouse' Is Treated the Same as the 'Spouse,'" <u>Trusts & Estates</u>, Vol. 140, No. 9 (Sept. 2001), p. 36.

"A Practical Guide to the Spousal Consent Requirements," <u>Insights & Strategies</u>, Vol. 14, No. 7 (July 2001).

"How to Advise Beneficiaries," <u>Ed Slott's IRA Advisor</u> (see Appendix D), Oct. 2001.

"Required and Permitted Elections Under the Minimum Distribution Rules," NY State Bar Association <u>Trusts and Estates Law Section Newsletter</u>, Vol. 33, No. 3, p. 4 (Fall 2000).

Terminology Used in this Book

The Glossary at the end of the book contains definitions of estate planning and retirement plan terms used throughout this book, including descriptions of the various types of retirement plans discussed in this book. If confronted with an unfamiliar term in the text be sure to check the Glossary; also see ¶ 1.2.02. In this book:

<u>Section numbers</u> refer to the Internal Revenue Code of 1986, as amended through September 2001, unless otherwise specified. <u>Reg.</u> stands for "Treasury Regulation" unless otherwise specified. <u>P.R.</u> and <u>Prop. Reg.</u> mean "Proposed Treasury Regulation."

<u>Retirement plan</u> means a corporate or self-employed ("Keogh") pension, profit sharing and stock bonus plan that is "qualified" under § 401(a), an individual retirement account (IRA) created under § 408, a Roth IRA established under § 408A, or a tax-sheltered annuity (or mutual fund) arrangement established under § 403(b). The narrower term <u>qualified plan</u> or <u>qualified retirement plan</u> (QRP) includes only 401(a) plans. For more description of these plan types see the Glossary at the end of the book.

The "<u>Participant</u>" is the person whose benefits we are dealing with: the employee who has benefits in a pension or profit sharing plan, or for whom a tax-sheltered annuity was purchased; or the account-holder in the case of an IRA. For ease of understanding, throughout this book, except in some specific examples and case studies, "Participant" is male and the feminine pronoun refers to Participant's spouse. Of course any statement would apply equally to a female Participant and her male spouse. There are certain matters (lump sum distributions.

¶ 2.3; plan-owned life insurance, ¶ 8.3) that apply only to qualified plans; in discussing these matters, sometimes "employee" is used instead of Participant. When discussing an issues particularly from the point of view of advising an individual what to do I sometimes refer to the Participant as "the client," and in Chapter 4 (and maybe elsewhere) the Participant is sometimes called the "Decedent."

Abbreviations Used in this Book
(And where to find definitions)

Code	Internal Revenue Code of 1986.
COLA	Cost-Of-Living Adjustment.
CRT	Charitable Remainder Trust; ¶ 7.5.04.
DNI	Distributable Net Income; ¶ 6.1.03.
EGTRRA	Economic Growth and Tax Relief Reconciliation Act of 2001 (P.L. 107-16)
ERISA	Employee Retirement Income Security Act of 1974 (P.L. 93-406).
GST tax	Generation Skipping Transfer tax; "Estate Plan" Glossary.
IRA	Individual Retirement Account; "Plan Types" Glossary.
IRD	Income in Respect of a Decedent; ¶ 2.2.
IRS	Internal Revenue Service.
IRT	Individual Retirement Trust; "Plan Types" Glossary.
LSD	Lump Sum Distribution; ¶ 2.3.
MRD	Minimum Required Distribution; ¶ 1.2.02.
PLR	IRS private letter ruling.
Prop. Reg.	Proposed Treasury Regulation
QDRO	Qualified Domestic Relations Order; § 414(p).
QJSA	Qualified Joint and Survivor Annuity; ¶ 3.4.02.
QPSA	Qualified Pre-retirement Survivor Annuity; ¶ 3.4.02.
QRP	Qualified Retirement Plan; "Plan Types" Glossary.
RBD	Required Beginning Date; ¶ 1.3.00.
REA	Retirement Equity Act of 1984 (P. L. 98-397); ¶ 3.4.
TAMRA '88	The Technical and Miscellaneous Revenue Act of 1988 (P. L. 100-647).
TAPRA '97	Taxpayer Relief Act of 1997 (P. L. 105-34).
TEFRA '82	The Tax Equity and Fiscal Responsibility Act of 1982 (P. L. 97-248).
TRA '84	The Tax Reform Act of 1984 (P. L. 98-369).
TRA '86	The Tax Reform Act of 1986 (P. L. 99-514).
UCA '92	Unemployment Compensation Amendments of 1992 (P. L. 102-318).

How to Use Cross References

The book is divided into numbered Chapters. Chapters are divided into *sections* (which are numbered "x.y"), and sections are divided into *subsections* (which are numbered "x.y.zz'). "X" is the number of the Chapter, "y" is the number of the section, and "zz" is the number of the subsection. Cross references to other parts of the book, indicated by the "¶" symbol, are liberally provided. A cross reference to "¶ 1.7.04" refers to Chapter 1, section 7, subsection 1.7.04.

Case studies in Chapter 11 illustrate some of the planning principles and real life issues created by the labyrinth of rules discussed in the earlier Chapters. Throughout the book, the text contains cross references to related case studies in Chapter 11.

Appendix B provides beneficiary designation forms for some common situations, along with some related trust provisions and other miscellaneous forms suggested in the text. Whenever a drafting suggestion or planning idea in the text is illustrated by a form in Appendix B, that form is cross-referenced. If there is no form reference, you can assume no form is provided.

Other Hints for Using this Book

There are many "gray areas" in the tax treatment of retirement benefits—questions the regulations do not answer; points of law subject to different interpretations; or regulatory positions that seem contrary to law or for some other reason likely to be changed in the future. When a practitioner encounters one of these in practice, the response may differ depending on whether he is doing advance planning for a client, or is dealing with a *fait accompli*. For this reason, from time to time in this book, in suggesting ways to deal with an issue, I distinguish between "planning mode" and "cleanup mode."

"Planning mode" deals with advance planning, and suggests a "safe harbor" course of action—the steps that should produce a predictable result and offer peace of mind. "Cleanup mode" deals with the *fait accompli* situation, when it is too late for advance planning, usually because Participant has already died. In cleanup mode, a more aggressive position may be appropriate on the issue, since there is often nothing to lose.

At the end of each Chapter, there is a summary of the planning principles developed in that Chapter. Bear in mind that most of these are general guidelines which do not apply to every case. The more detailed discussion in the Chapter provides the basis for these principles, and points out limitations and exceptions.

Acknowledgments

Reviewers and contributors

I am most grateful to those who took the time to read sections of the book and send me their thoughtful comments, almost all of which were incorporated into the book. For this edition, these "peer reviewers" were Alan S. Acker, Esq., of Columbus, Ohio; Barry S. Picker, CPA, of Brooklyn, NY; Ed Slott, CPA, of Rockville Centre, NY; Steven E. Trytten, Esq., Calleton & Trytten, LLP, Pasadena, CA; and Mark W. Worthington, Esq., of Worcester, MA. I know that their material reward for this effort (free copies of the book) is trivial in view of the time and effort they expended to help me improve the accuracy and readability of the work.

I also thank, most especially, my personal in-house Harvard Law Review editor, Ian M. Starr, Esq., who pitched in to proofread, cite check and edit several chapters, and who is also my booking agent, tour-arranger and husband, and who makes it all worth it.

I am grateful too to the many other professionals who on countless occasions have willingly shared their expertise in person, by phone, letter and email, including Jonathan Blattmachr, Don DiCarlo, Dave Foster, Seymour Goldberg, Chris Hoyt, Mike Jones, Bob Keebler, Stephen J. Krass, Steve Leimberg, and Lou Mezzullo.

The work of many who helped with earlier editions is still evident in this one:

From the 1999 edition: "Above and beyond the help one could reasonably hope to receive from volunteer "peer reviewers," Guerdon T. Ely, MBA, CFP, of Silver Oak Advisory Group (fee-only financial advisors), Chico, California, and Michael Jones, CPA, of Monterey, California, re-ran number-intensive case studies and examples throughout the book, and thereby killed a number of bugs; and Ellen K. Harrison, Esq., of Washington, DC, made major contributions to Chapter 4.

" I am very grateful to the lawyers and others who took the time to review parts of the 1999 or 1996 edition and give me their comments, most of which led directly to improvements in the work (though I retain responsibility for all deficiencies in the finished product): Virginia Coleman, Esq., Boston; Paul Frimmer, Esq., Los Angeles; Randall J. Gingiss, Esq., Chicago; Zoe M. Hicks, Esq., Atlanta; Jerold I. Horn, Esq., Peoria; Larry Katzenstein, Esq., St. Louis; James H. Landon, Esq., Atlanta; my Bingham Dana LLP colleague George Mair, Esq.; Al Martin, Esq., Overland Park, KS; Ronald T. Martin, Esq.; David W. Polstra, CFP, Norcross, GA; Michael G. Riley, Esq., Cleveland; Kathleen R. Sherby, St. Louis; Lee Slavutin, M.D., C.P.C., New York; and Mark W. Worthington, Esq., Worcester."

In over thirty years of consciously or unknowingly gathering material for this book, I have talked with, listened to, or read the work of hundreds of estate planners, actuaries, accountants, lawyers, financial planners, retirees, trust officers, mutual fund personnel, plan administrators, IRS and DOL staffers, plan participants and writers who have studied the subject matter. Since almost everyone who spends time thinking about these issues or working with the actual problems of real life employers and employees has some interesting and new insight into the subject, I have learned from almost every encounter. In earlier editions I have listed the names of those whose questions and insights had led to something new or better in the book. It is no longer possible to do that, partly because the number of my "contributors" has become too large, and partly because so often I learn something from a seminar attendee whose name I never get. To all who have shared thoughts, questions, comments and suggestions for improvement, thank you!

I used to wonder why authors thanked their typists. Now having had first hand experience with the fantastic dedication and skill of the principal "word processor" of this book, Maureen Cash, I know. I relied heavily on her problem-solving ability and perfectionism, as well as the skills, professionalism and hard work of the others who worked on the production of the manuscript: in chronological order, Jeri Arbo, Sheila Irvine, Pat Longo and Joan Breen.

The Minimum Distribution Rules

The minimum distribution rules of § 401(a)(9) dictate how quickly (or slowly) benefits come out of retirement plans. Understanding these rules is key to successful tax planning for retirement benefits. These rules have changed radically since the 1999 edition of this book.

1.1 Introduction, Where to Find What

1.1.01 § 401(a)(9); importance of minimum distribution rules

Congress wants tax-favored retirement plans to be *retirement* plans—not estate-building, wealth transfer vehicles. To that end, Congress enacted § 401(a)(9), which compels certain annual "minimum required distributions" (MRDs) from plans beginning generally at age 70½ or, if earlier, death. Failure to distribute the required minimum results in a 50% penalty tax on amounts that should have been distributed but were not. § 4974; ¶ 1.9.06. § 401(a)(9) and its related regulations are called the "minimum distribution rules."

Despite the apparent goal of these rules (assuring that tax-favored retirement plans are used primarily to provide retirement income), § 401(a)(9) permits tax deferral to continue long past the death of the participant whose work created the benefit—*if* the participant leaves his retirement benefits to the right kind of beneficiary. If various requirements (described in this Chapter) are met, Congress allows the retirement benefits to be paid out gradually, after the worker's death, over the life expectancy of the worker's beneficiary. The financial benefit of the long-term tax deferral permitted by the minimum distribution rules (see ¶ 1.2.01) puts a premium on naming a beneficiary who will qualify for (and make best use of) this "life expectancy payout method."

The IRS's simplification of the minimum distribution rules in 2001 (¶ 1.1.03) has lulled some practitioners into thinking that favorable tax treatment is now assured for everyone, without the need for careful planning. As the length and complexity of this Chapter attest, this impression is false. Tax and estate planning professionals still need to study these rules, for both planning and compliance reasons.

Planning has become easier, but maximizing the value of the retirement benefits still depends on naming the right beneficiary. Changes in the Internal Revenue Code in 2001 permit larger contributions to retirement plans, and the 2001 minimum distribution rule changes allow participants to leave money in their retirement plans longer; together, these changes mean that clients will be able to pass larger sums on to their chosen beneficiaries in the form of tax-favored retirement plans. The new regulations also give older participants more flexibility to change beneficiaries to achieve a favorable estate planning result. Thus, there will be *more money* riding on the "right" choice of beneficiary and *less excuse* for not making the best choice.

What about compliance? It seems likely (see ¶ 1.9.06) that the IRS, post-2001, will be less forgiving of errors in computing minimum distributions and more stringent in enforcing the 50% penalty tax. Paying this penalty would be a painful experience for any client (and for any advisor held responsible for the mistake).

The rest of this ¶ 1.1 gives the background of the minimum distribution rules and tells where to find the law and related information.

1.1.02 *What this Chapter covers and does not cover*

This Chapter covers, throughout, both *planning* and *compliance* issues regarding the minimum distribution rules. Of particular interest from a planning perspective, the Chapter discusses the advantages of the life expectancy payout method (¶ 1.2.01); explains what the participant must do to qualify for the most favorable treatment the rules allow (¶ 1.7); and summarizes planning principles (¶ 1.10). Regarding compliance, this Chapter explains how the life expectancy payout system works generally (¶ 1.2.02-¶ 1.2.08); and how to compute required distributions in all situations, so that participants and beneficiaries can comply with the rules and avoid the 50% penalty

(¶ 1.3-¶ 1.6). This Chapter also covers various planning opportunities and pitfalls under, and fascinating facts about, the minimum distribution rules and the 50% penalty (throughout, plus ¶ 1.8-¶ 1.09).

The minimum distribution system discussed in this Chapter applies to "individual account plans," including money purchase pension plans, profit sharing plans, 401(k) plans, 403(b) plans and IRAs. (See Glossary.) If benefits are paid in the form of an *annuity*, different rules apply. See P.R. § 1.401(a)(9)-6. This book does not cover annuity payouts.

See ¶ 5.1.03 for explanation of which rules in this Chapter do, and which do not, apply to Roth IRAs.

This Chapter discusses certain distribution options that are available to "individual beneficiaries and qualifying trusts" (see ¶ 1.7); the definition of what constitutes a qualifying trust is in a different Chapter (¶ 6.2).

This Chapter discusses only the rules applicable to 2001 and later years under the IRS's 2001 proposed minimum distribution regulations (¶ 1.1.03). For a complete explanation of the old rules (under the 1987/1997 proposed regulations) consult Chapter 1 of the 1999 edition of this book (see Bibliography). Those rules will apply only in rare situations, such as catch-up distributions for individuals who failed to take required distributions for pre-2001 years (¶ 1.9.06), or for individuals who revoke "TEFRA 242(b) designations" (¶ 8.5.02).

While this Chapter's discussion of the minimum distribution rules applies to most qualified retirement plans and IRAs, there are grandfather rules and exceptions which exempt some individuals and plans from some or all of the requirements. ¶ 8.5.

1.1.03 *The proposed minimum distribution regulations*

Congress established the minimum distribution system of § 401(a)(9) in substantially its present form in the Tax Reform Act of 1986. In 1987, the IRS issued proposed regulations § 1.401(a)(9)-1 and 2, and § 54.4974-2, interpreting and implementing the minimum distribution rules. One section of these "old proposed regs." was amended in December 1997.

In January 2001, the IRS issued new proposed minimum distribution regulations (published in the Federal Register January 17, 2001), replacing the 1987/1997 version, and issued a corrected version March 12, 2001 (2001-11 I.R.B. 865). These "new proposed regs" are numbered § 1.401(a)(9)-0 through § 1.401(a)(9)-8; § 1.403(b)-2; § 1.408-8; and § 54.4974-2. The proposed regulations begin with an explanation (called in this book the "Preamble"), which contains important material. Unfortunately many publications of the proposed regulations do not include the Preamble. One place to find it is in the 2001 CCH Standard Federal Tax Reporter ¶ 49,393 ("U.S. Tax Cases Advance Sheets" volume).

> Boxed text throughout this Chapter points out rules considered most likely to be modified when the IRS issues final minimum distribution regulations. The text boxes contain a place for you to mark whether the IRS did or did not make the anticipated modification when it issues final regulations. When the IRS issues final regulations, the author expects to post a description of each change from the proposed regulations (whether or not such change was given a "box") at the website www.ataxplan.com.

References in this Chapter to "proposed regulations" (P.R.) refer to the 2001 proposed minimum distribution regulations unless the "old proposed regs." are specified.

Proposed regulations § 1.401(a)(9)-0 through § 1.401(a)(9)-8 are addressed to qualified plans, but the same rules apply (with certain variations) also to IRAs and 403(b) plans, consistent with the Congressional mandate that rules "similar to" the rules of § 401(a)(9) shall apply to IRAs (§ 408(a)(6)) and 403(b) plans (§ 403(b)(10)). P.R. § 1.408-8, A-1(a) (IRAs) and § 1.403(b)-2, A-1(a) (403(b) plans).

1.1.04 *Effective dates of the old and new proposed regulations*

Although the 2001 proposed regulations completely restate and will replace the old proposed regulations, both sets apply in varying degrees in 2001. See ¶ 1.1.06 regarding the right to rely on proposed regulations.

The IRS proposes that the final version of the 2001 proposed regulations (which IRS expects to issue by 2002) will apply (for all plans and all participants and beneficiaries, with no "grandfathering" and no ability to opt out) for calendar years beginning on or after January 1, 2002. P.R., Preamble, "Proposed Effective Date."

The IRS says that taxpayers may not "rely on" the new proposed regulations in computing distributions required for years prior to 2001; they "may rely" only on the old proposed regulations for pre-2001 years. IRS Announcement 2001-23, 2001-10 I.R.B. 791. For example, an individual is instructed by the IRS in Announcement 2001-23 not to use the new rules to compute his year-2000 MRD, even if part or all of that MRD was paid in calendar 2001.

In determining minimum distributions for the year 2001, "taxpayers may rely on" either the new or the old proposed regulations. P.R., Preamble, "Proposed Effective Date." So, 2001 is a transition year, in which both sets of proposed regulations are in effect (to the extent proposed regulations can be said to be in effect).

See ¶ 10.4.06 for how the change in the regulations affects beneficiaries taking distributions from plans inherited from decedents who died before 2001.

1.1.05 *Effective date: by type of plan*

Traditional and Roth IRAs: IRA providers eventually will have to amend their documents to reflect the new rules. IRA sponsors are to wait before amending their documents until the IRS issues new model IRAs, which will not occur until the regulations are finalized. P.R., Preamble, "Amendment of IRAs and Effective Date."

However, IRA owners don't have to wait until the IRA provider takes action to take advantage of the new rules. "IRA owners are permitted, but not required, to follow" the new proposed regulations "for the 2001 calendar year," regardless of whether the underlying documents are amended. P.R., Preamble, "Amendment of IRAs and Effective Date." IRA owners include IRA beneficiaries; see IRS Announcement 2001-23, 2001-10 I.R.B. 791, supplementing IRS Publication 590 (2000 edition) ("Individual Retirement Arrangements").

So, the IRA owner determines his required distribution for 2001 under either the old or the new proposed regulations, whichever provides the smaller required distribution. The IRA owner does not have to file any election with the IRA provider or the IRS. As long as he takes the amount required by whichever set of rules produces the smallest MRD, he will not be liable for a penalty.

Qualified Plans: Qualified plans will have to be amended to reflect the new rules. A qualified plan may, but is not required to, implement the new rules prior to the effective date of final regulations, by adopting the model amendment in the new proposed regulations. IRS Announcement 2001-18, 2001-10 I.R.B. 791. The IRS will not issue determination, opinion or advisory letters regarding plan qualification based on the proposed regulations until final regulations are issued. P.R., Preamble, "Amendment of Qualified Plans." The plan administrator of a QRP that is not amended to adopt the new rules until 2002 must use the old rules to calculate MRDs for 2001. IRS Announcement 2001-18; see P.R. Preamble, "Amendment of Qualified Plans."

A Participant who is receiving required distributions from a qualified plan that is *not* amended prior to 2002 may nevertheless use the new method for computing his required distribution for 2001. In IRS Announcement 2001-23, 2001-10 I.R.B. 791 (amending IRS Publication 575, "Pension and Annuity Income"), the IRS tells retirees, "Use the new rules for figuring the required distribution for 2001 that must be made by the end of 2001." There is no mention anywhere in the Announcement of any exception to this direction. The author concludes from this that the IRS has given individuals permission to use the new rules for 2001 regardless of whether the plan is amended.

This means that if Participant receives a larger distribution from the plan in 2001 than the new rules would require (because the plan is still using the old rules), Participant can roll over the excess to an IRA within 60 days, because the excess is not a minimum required distribution (MRDs cannot be rolled over; ¶ 2.5.05). (Note: a non-spouse beneficiary who received a larger-than-required distribution *cannot* use a "rollover" to avoid tax on the excess distribution, because non-spouse beneficiaries cannot roll over distributions from an inherited plan. ¶ 2.5.04.)

The various IRS pronouncements, read together, lead to the conclusion that a QRP administrator can write a check that *is* an MRD when it leaves his office, but that same check is *not* an MRD when it arrives in the recipient's mailbox.

403(b) plans: The proposed regulations have no transition rule for 403(b) plan Participants. By analogy to IRAs and qualified plans, a 403(b) Participant or beneficiary presumably may use the new method of calculating distributions for 2001 regardless of whether the underlying plan is amended to reflect the new rules prior to 2002.

1.1.06 *Legal status of proposed regulations*

The purpose of this Chapter is to assist planners looking for "safe harbor" answers for their clients. Accordingly, most of this Chapter is about how to comply with the IRS's pronouncements, especially the proposed regulations. Compliance with the proposed regulations protects the taxpayer against later changes in the law, because if "future guidance is more restrictive than the guidance in these proposed regulations, the future guidance will be issued without retroactive effect." P.R., Preamble, "Proposed Effective Date."

Furthermore, if the taxpayer's actions are later prohibited by final regulations, but at the time taken constituted "a reasonable interpretation of the statute and proposed regulations," the taxpayer cannot be penalized. See, *e.g.*, discussion in PLR 9506001. If a particular interpretation of the law has been explicitly adopted by the IRS in one or more letter rulings, it is presumably safe to conclude that interpretation is "reasonable." See, *e.g.*, PLR 9311037.

On the other hand, if the taxpayer's actions are clearly *not* in compliance with the proposed regulations, his status is less favorable. Proposed regulations *theoretically* have a rather lowly status. They "are not entitled to judicial deference," Natomas North America, Inc. v. Comm'r, 90 T.C. 710, at 718, n. 11, (1988), and "are given no greater weight than a position advanced by the Commissioner on brief." Van Wyk v. Comm'r, 113 T.C. 441 (1999). However, when the IRS ultimately issues final regulations, these may be made effective retroactively.

Final regulations pertaining to statutory provisions enacted on or after July 30, 1996, can be made effective retroactive to taxable periods ending on or after the date the proposed regulations "to which they relate" were filed with the Federal Register, or even earlier in some cases. § 7805(b)(1)(B). For statutes enacted *before* that date (including the minimum distribution rules, enacted for the most part in 1986), there is no statutory limit on the retroactive effectiveness of final regulations. Therefore, the fact that a taxpayer's actions are based on a "reasonable interpretation of the statute" will be little consolation if his actions are contrary to a proposed regulation and the IRS later adopts the proposed regulation in question as a final regulation with a retroactive effective date.

For more discussion of the taxpayer's right (or lack thereof) to rely on IRS pronouncements of all types, see 2001 CCH *Standard*

Federal Tax Reporter ¶ 43,282.0211.

1.2 Overview of the "Life Expectancy Payout Method"

1.2.01 How "life expectancy method" works; economics of MRDs

The minimum distribution rules dictate when a retirement plan participant ("Participant"), or a beneficiary, must begin taking money out of the plan, and, once required distributions begin, how much must be taken out of the plan each year. Under most methods of computing required distributions (see ¶ 1.5.04 for exception), the annual "minimum required distribution" (MRD) is calculated by dividing an annually-revalued account balance by a life expectancy factor.

The basic idea is that, during retirement, Participant must take annual withdrawals from his retirement plans (except Roth IRAs; ¶ 5.1.03), thus subjecting the distributed amounts to income taxes (¶ 2.1.01). These mandated withdrawals are designed to reduce the retirement plan balance to zero over the joint life expectancy of Participant and a hypothetical beneficiary. The way the formula works (¶ 1.4.01), if Participant takes only the MRD each year, the account will have a positive balance for his entire lifetime (unless it is wiped out by investment losses).

In fact, depending on the rate of investment return, there may well be more in the account when Participant dies than there was when required distributions began. For example, if Participant takes only the MRD starting at age 70½, and the account has a 6% annual investment return, the account will have more dollars in it at his death than it did when he started taking required distributions if he dies at age 88 or younger. If investment returns are higher than 6%, the account value will stay above its age-70½ value to an even later age.

Once Participant dies, the rules become more restrictive. *If* the account is payable to the right type of beneficiary (individuals or qualifying trusts; see ¶ 1.7), *and* the life expectancy payout method is available under the plan in question (see ¶ 1.5.09), the rules require the beneficiary to take annual withdrawals designed to reduce the retirement plan account balance to zero over the life expectancy of the beneficiary. More favorable payout options are available if the beneficiary is Participant's spouse; see ¶ 1.6.

Again depending on the rate of investment return, if the beneficiary is young, and takes no more than the required minimum each year, the value of the inherited plan can double or triple, under the life expectancy payout method, by the time the *beneficiary* reaches retirement age.

Example: Two brothers died. Both were younger than age 70½. Each brother left his entire estate, including a $500,000 IRA, to his daughter. Both daughters, Lena and Tina, turned age 38 in the year following the year of the brothers' deaths. Each of the daughters, after taking a round-the-world cruise, buying a new house, and paying the estate taxes on her father's estate, was left with just one asset, the $500,000 IRA. Each daughter resolved to: withdraw from the inherited IRA only the minimum amount required by law; invest the after-tax proceeds of the withdrawals; and regard the inherited IRA plus the accumulated after-tax distributions as her retirement fund.

Each daughter kept her resolve, investing both in-plan and out-of-plan assets in 8% bonds, and paying income taxes at the rate of 36% on all plan withdrawals and bond interest, but there was one difference: Tina's father had named Tina as his "designated beneficiary" (¶ 1.7), so Tina was entitled to withdraw her father's IRA in installments over her 44.4-year life expectancy. ¶ 1.5.06. Lena's father had named no beneficiary; he never got around to filling out a designation of beneficiary form. Under the terms of the account agreement governing his IRA, since he had not named any beneficiary, his "beneficiary" was his estate. In minimum distribution rule jargon, he had "no designated beneficiary" (see ¶ 1.7.04). Lena, the sole beneficiary of the estate, had to withdraw all money from her father's IRA within five years after his death.

After 30 years, Lena has a $1.5 million investment portfolio, not in any IRA. Tina has an investment portfolio of $1.4 million outside the IRA. She also has $1.5 million still *inside* the IRA she inherited from her father. Tina still has 14.4 years left in her "life expectancy" over which to withdraw the remaining IRA balance. After 30 years, the daughter who used the life expectancy payout method (¶ 1.5.06) has almost twice as much money as the daughter who withdrew benefits under the 5-year rule (¶ 1.5.04).

The most valuable feature of retirement plans is the ability to invest without current taxation of the investment profits. In most cases, investing through a retirement plan defers income tax not only on the investment profits but also on Participant's compensation income that was originally contributed to the plan. This income tax is deferred until the date the money is distributed out of the plan to Participant or beneficiary. ¶ 2.1.01. The longer this deferral continues, the better, because, generally, the deferral of income tax increases the ultimate value of the benefits. (See ¶ 10.1.01 for discussion of when deferral may be less attractive than other alternatives.)

So long as assets stay in the retirement plan, Participant is investing not just "Participant's own" money, but also "Uncle Sam's share" of Participant's compensation and investment profits, i.e., the money that Participant otherwise would have had to pay to the IRS (and will eventually have to pay to the IRS) in income taxes. Keeping the money in the retirement plan enables Participant to reap a profit from investing "the IRS's money" along with his own. Once funds are distributed from the plan, they are included in the gross income of Participant or beneficiary (see ¶ 2.1.03 for exceptions), and Participant or beneficiary pays the IRS its share. Thereafter Participant (or beneficiary) will no longer enjoy any investment profits from the government's share of the plan.

Congress allows this tax-deferred investing to continue past the death of the worker whose "retirement plan" this is supposed to be—and even past the death of the worker's surviving spouse—but only if the account is left to a "designated beneficiary" (¶ 1.7). Congress allows the tax-deferred investing to continue over the life expectancy of a "designated beneficiary" regardless of how young that beneficiary may be.

The maximum theoretical duration of a retirement plan account is almost two full life-spans. Consider a 16-year old who contributes $2,000 from his summer job earnings to an IRA in 2001, lives to be 102 and then dies leaving the account to his newborn great grandchild, who has a life expectancy of 80+ years. If Participant and beneficiary take only minimum required distributions, the last dollar of the 2001 summer job earnings may not be taxed until 2167. If you add in the possibility of a rollover by Participant's surviving spouse (¶ 3.2) the final distribution could occur even later than that.

Calculating minimum distributions by dividing an annually-revalued account balance by the beneficiary's life expectancy tends to produce gradually increasing installments over the years, so long as the plan has a positive investment return. As long as the beneficiary's remaining life expectancy is greater than [100 ÷ the plan's annual growth rate], the plan balance will be growing faster than the beneficiary is withdrawing it. For example, if the plan is growing at 8% per year, and the beneficiary's life expectancy is 20 years, the first year's required distribution (1/20, or 5%), is less than the plan's earnings for the year (1/12.5, or 8%).

Eventually the beneficiary's life expectancy is reduced to the point that he is withdrawing more than the year's investment return. If the plan is growing at 8% per year, this crossover point would be reached 12.5 years before the end of the payout period. Even after this crossover point, the annual required minimum distributions tend to keep getting larger; though the plan balance is now shrinking, the fraction applied to it grows larger.

Note: the discussion above assumes a fixed, unwavering, investment return, which is impossible to achieve in real life. See Appendix D for discussion of software products available to help make this type of financial projection.

1.2.02 *Minimum distribution terminology*

The most important term in the minimum distribution dictionary is **"designated beneficiary."** The favorable "life-expectancy-of-the-beneficiary" payout method is available only if Participant's death benefits pass to a "designated beneficiary." A designated beneficiary is one or more individuals or qualifying trusts; see ¶ 1.7 for details. Since not every beneficiary is a *designated* beneficiary, the planner must understand what a designated beneficiary is, how to go about getting one and why and when it matters. ¶ 1.7 explains all of those points.

Other minimum distribution terms are less mysterious, and less crucial to proper planning (though important for understanding and complying with the rules).

A year for which a minimum distribution is required is called a "distribution calendar year" in the proposed regulations (in this book, **"distribution year"** for short). P.R. § 1.401(a)(9)-5, A-1(b).

The life expectancy period over which distributions must be made is called the "applicable distribution period" in the proposed regulations (**"Applicable Distribution Period"** in this book). P.R. § 1.401(a)(9)-5, A-1(a). The life expectancy factor used to determine required distributions is called the **"applicable divisor"** in the IRS's life expectancy tables. P.R. § 1.401(a)(9)-2, A-4(a)(1).

In this book, "**MRD**" stands for **minimum required distribution**. What is called in this book an MRD is sometimes called (by others) a "required minimum distribution" or "RMD."

"**RBD**" stands for required beginning date; the concept of the "**required beginning date**" is explained at ¶ 1.3.

For the meaning of abbreviations used in this Chapter that are not explained here see the Introduction. For definitions of types of retirement plans, see the Glossary at the end of the book.

1.2.03 Basic rules of MRDs and life expectancy payout method

MRDs (except in the case of the "5-year rule"; ¶ 1.5.04) are computed by dividing an annually-revalued account balance by a declining life expectancy factor. The first step in calculating MRDs, therefore, is to figure out the correct account balance and life expectancy factor to use. You also need to figure out when the distributions must start, the deadline for taking each year's distribution, and who is the right person to take the distribution. This Chapter provides all those details. In the meantime, here are some overall guidelines explaining how the life expectancy payout method works:

1.   Annual distributions required: Once required distributions begin, Participant (or beneficiary) must take a distribution every calendar year. P.R. § 1.401(a)(9)-5, A-1. The 5-year rule (¶ 1.5.04) is the only "minimum distribution rule" that does not require annual distributions.

2.   No maximum distribution: The formula (account balance divided by life expectancy factor) tells you the *minimum required* distribution. The rules impose no maximum distribution; Participant (or beneficiary) is always free, as far as the IRS is concerned, to take more than the minimum.

3.   Each year stands on it own: Taking more than the required amount in one year does not give you a "credit" you can use to reduce distributions in a later year. P.R. § 1.401(a)(9)-5, A-2. (Taking larger distributions in one year indirectly reduces later required distributions by reducing the account balance.)

4.   The "Law of the Plan": Just because a Participant or beneficiary qualifies for the life expectancy payout method under the law does not mean he will actually get to use it; the plan must allow it too. See ¶ 1.5.09.

5.   Deadline is December 31 (except...): The final date for taking each year's required distribution is December 31 of the year in question. P.R. § 1.401(a)(9)-5, A-1(c). The only exception is that, in the case of certain lifetime required distributions, the distribution for the first "distribution year" can be postponed until April 1 of the following year. ¶ 1.3.07. For unusual situations in which an MRD can be delayed beyond these deadlines, see ¶ 1.9.06.

6.   Distributions before RBD irrelevant: Whatever distributions Participant may have taken, elections he may have made or beneficiaries he may have named prior to his RBD have no effect on how his required distributions are calculated when he reaches the RBD. There is neither an advantage nor a disadvantage (in terms of what the MRD formula will be) to taking distributions prior to the RBD. P.R. § 1.401(a)(9)-2, A-4, A-6. For whether there is some *other* advantage to taking distributions prior to the RBD, see ¶ 10.1.01-¶ 10.1.02.

7.   Divisors are not percentages: The divisors in the applicable life expectancy table are divided into the account balance to produce the MRD; the divisor is not a percentage amount. For example, in the year a person turns age 70, his "divisor" under the Uniform Table is 26.2. That means his MRD is 1/26.2 times the account balance (about 4%)—not *26.2%* times the account balance.

1.2.04 *How to determine a person's life expectancy*

Calculating MRDs requires you to look up a life expectancy ("applicable divisor") in an IRS-supplied table. The three tables currently in use are:

1.   The table at P.R. § 1.401(a)(9)-5, A-4(a)(2), which this book

calls the "Uniform Table," is normally used for determining lifetime required distributions to the Participant (¶ 1.4.01). This table is reproduced in Appendix A of this book and in Appendix E of IRS Publication 590 (where it is called, in the 2000 edition, the "Table for Determining Applicable Divisor for MDIB");

2.   The IRS's Joint Life and Last Survivor Expectancy table, Table VI, is used for determining lifetime required distributions of a Participant whose sole beneficiary is his much-younger spouse (¶ 1.4.02). P.R. § 1.401(a)(9)-5, A-6(a). This table comes from Reg. § 1.72-9, and is reproduced in Appendix E of IRS Publication 590 (where it is called "Table II"). It is not reproduced in this book; and

3.   The IRS's Single Life Expectancy table, Table V, is used for determining post-death required distributions to an individual designated beneficiary or qualifying trust (¶ 1.5.06). P.R. § 1.401(a)(9)-5, A-6(a). It is also used for determining the remaining life expectancy of a Participant who dies after his RBD with no designated beneficiary (¶ 1.5.05). This table comes from Reg. § 1.72-9. It is reproduced in Appendix A of this book, and in Appendix E of IRS Publication 590 (where it is called "Table I").

The current IRS tables were promulgated in 1986. They are "unisex" (life expectancy for men and women is the same). The IRS updated its actuarial tables used for estate and gift tax valuations in May 1999, as required by § 7520, but this change did not affect the minimum distribution tables.

Congress, in § 634 of EGTRRA 2001, mandated that the IRS update its actuarial tables to reflect more recent mortality experience. When the IRS gets around to carrying out Congress's mandate, the new tables should reflect longer life expectancies, which will have the effect of reducing required distributions.

1.2.05 *What is a person's "age" for MRD purposes*

A person's "age" for purposes of the life expectancy tables (¶ 1.2.04) means the age he will attain on his birthday in the "distribution year." Stated another way, it is the age he will be at the end of the distribution year. P.R.§ 1.401(a)(9)-5, A-4, A-5(c).

Example: Clark turns age 70½ in 2002. 2002 is the first "distribution year" for his IRA, even though he does not actually have to take this first year's distribution until April 1, 2003. ¶ 1.3.07. To compute the 2002 required distribution, he looks up the "applicable divisor" for his age in the Uniform Table. The age he will use is the age he will attain on his 2002 birthday, which will be 70 if he was born before July 1, 71 if he was born after June 30.

Example: Bonnie died in 2001 and left her IRA to Diane as designated beneficiary (¶ 1.7). Diane plans to use the life expectancy payout method to take distributions from the IRA. To determine the Applicable Distribution Period, she finds her life expectancy in IRS Table V as of the first distribution year, which is 2002 (the year after the year in which Bonnie died; ¶ 1.5.06). The age she looks up in that table is her age as of her birthday in 2002 (i.e., her age as of the end of 2002).

Example: Josephine, surviving spouse of Napoleon, was sole beneficiary of Napoleon's 401(k) plan. She is taking annual MRDs as Napoleon's beneficiary; she did not roll over the benefits to her own retirement plan (see ¶ 3.2). Each year, the plan sends a required distribution to Josephine based on her life expectancy in that year. The life expectancy the plan uses each year (from Table V) is that for Josephine's attained age on her birthday *in the year of the distribution* (i.e., her age as of the end of each distribution year). ¶ 1.6.06.

1.2.06 *Recalculation of life expectancy vs. fixed term method*

There are two methods of computing life expectancy for minimum distribution purposes. The Participant or beneficiary taking the distribution has no choice in this matter—the proposed regulations tell you which method must be used in which situation.

Under the "fixed term method," you determine the applicable life expectancy in the first distribution year; then in each subsequent year, you just deduct one year from that initial number. (Some people call this the "reduce-by-one" method.) The fixed term method is used to determine required distributions to non-spouse beneficiaries, including a qualifying trust of which the spouse is not the sole beneficiary. ¶ 1.5.06, ¶ 1.5.08.

Example: Bonnie died in 2001 and left her IRA to Diane as designated beneficiary. Diane plans to use the life expectancy payout method to take distributions from the IRA. The Applicable Distribution Period is Diane's single life expectancy (¶ 1.2.04) as of the first distribution year, which is 2002 (the year after Bonnie's death). Diane turns 46 on her birthday in 2002, so her life expectancy from Table V is 36.8. For calculating her required distributions for 2003 (and later years), Diane just deducts one from the prior year's life expectancy (so her 2003 "divisor" is 35.8, 2004 is 34.8, and so on). She never goes "back to the table" again after the first distribution year.

When the fixed term method applies, the distribution period runs out eventually. In the case of Bonnie and Diane, the final required distribution will occur in the 37th year after Bonnie's death and it will wipe out the remaining balance of the account. Thus, even though Diane may well live more than 36.8 years after Bonnie's demise, her inherited IRA will run out of money no later than 2039. If Diane dies before her 36.8-year life expectancy runs out, her death does not change the calculation of MRDs: required distributions to whoever succeeds to the account at that point will still be based on what's left of Diane's original 36.8-year life expectancy (¶ 1.5.07).

Under the "recalculation" method, the life expectancy is "redetermined" every year. Instead of just deducting one from last year's life expectancy, you go back to the applicable table and look up the new life expectancy or "divisor" based on the new age. Recalculation is used for determining *all* lifetime required distributions to Participant (¶ 1.4.01, ¶ 1.4.02), and for determining post-death required distributions to a surviving spouse who is sole beneficiary (¶ 1.6.06). Under the recalculation method, life expectancy never runs out as long as the person is alive.

Example: Josephine, surviving spouse of Napoleon and sole beneficiary of Napoleon's 401(k) plan, is taking required distributions based on her life expectancy. She turned 46 in the year after Napoleon's death, so her "divisor" for the first distribution year was 36.8, just like Diane's first year divisor in the preceding example. For the second distribution year, however, Josephine's divisor is not 35.8 (36.8 minus one—as it would be if she were using the fixed term method); instead Josephine's second year divisor is 35.9 (the single life expectancy of a person age 47). The fixed term method doesn't apply when the surviving spouse is the sole beneficiary. Josephine, as a surviving spouse-sole beneficiary, determines her divisor each year by going back to the life expectancy table and determining her new life expectancy based on her new age (recalculation method).

1.2.07 *What account balance the "divisor" applies to*

Each year (except under the 5-year rule; ¶ 1.5.04) the MRD is determined by dividing the prior year-end account value by the applicable life expectancy factor (divisor). Exactly which "account value" is used depends on the type of retirement plan involved; and once the account value is ascertained, it may require certain adjustments (¶ 1.2.08) before it is ready to be used in the MRD formula.

In the case of a *qualified plan*, the account value used is "the account balance as of the last valuation date in the calendar year immediately preceding" the distribution year. P.R. § 1.401(a)(9)-5, A-3(a). A plan might have only one valuation date per plan year (such as "the last day of the plan year"), or it might have more than one. If the plan's last valuation date in the prior calendar year was December 31, you just use the account value as of that date and move on to ¶ 1.2.08.

On the other hand, if the plan's last valuation date in the prior calendar year was earlier than December 31, the last-valuation-date account balance must be *increased* by any contributions or forfeitures that were allocated to the account on any date that is after the valuation date but is still within the "valuation calendar year"; and then *decreased* by any distributions from the account made after the valuation date but before the end of the valuation calendar year. P.R. § 1.401(a)(9)-5, A-3(b), (c)(1).

Example: Tana is taking MRDs from a profit sharing plan. The plan operates on a November 30 fiscal year, and has only one annual valuation date, namely, November 30. To calculate Tana's MRD for 2002, you would start with her November 30, 2001, account balance. This account balance is then increased by any contributions or forfeitures that are allocated to the account on any date that is after the valuation date but is still within the "valuation calendar year"; in this example, that would mean the account balance is increased, for purposes of performing the MRD calculation, by contributions or forfeitures (but not investment profits) allocated to Tana's account as of any date in December, 2001. Second, assume Tana took a distribution of $10,000 in December, 2001. This $10,000 distribution is deducted from her November 30, 2001, account balance for purposes of calculating her 2002 required distribution.

If the plan in question is an *IRA*, the account balance is "the value of the IRA upon close of business" on December 31 of the calendar year immediately preceding the distribution year. P.R. § 1.408-8, A-6. No adjustment is required for contributions or distributions occurring between the plan's "last valuation date" and the end of the calendar year, because the last valuation date of an IRA *is* the end of the calendar year.

1.2.08 *Required adjustments to the account balance*

Once you have the correct "prior year-end account balance" (ascertained as provided in ¶ 1.2.07) two further adjustments may be required.

First, in computing the required distribution for a living Participant's second distribution year, the prior year-end account balance is reduced by the amount of any MRD for the first distribution year that had not yet been taken as of the close of the first distribution year—provided Participant actually takes that first-year MRD no later than the RBD. P.R. § 1.401(a)(9)-5, A-3(c)(2).

Example: Ramsey turned age 70½ in 2001. The MRD for her IRA for that year was $5,000. As permitted by law (¶ 1.3.07), she did not take that distribution until January 2002. The December 31, 2001, value of the IRA was $140,000, but that value includes the not-yet-distributed 2001 MRD of $5,000. To calculate her 2002 MRD, the account value she will use is $140,000 minus $5,000, or $135,000. (If she had failed to take the first year MRD of $5,000 by April 1, 2002, then she would lose the right to deduct that amount from her 12/31/01 account balance for purposes of computing the 2002 MRD.)

Second, you must *increase* the prior year-end balance by any amount that was added to the account in the distribution year ("Year 2") but which represented a rollover from another plan or IRA, if the amount in question was distributed from such other plan or IRA in the *prior* calendar year ("Year 1"). For purposes of MRDs from the *receiving* plan, such a rollover amount is *deemed* to have been received in the prior calendar year (i.e., Year 1) and not the year it was *actually* received (Year 2). P.R. § 1.401(a)(9)-7, A-2 (last sentence). If this rule did not exist, people could cheat on their MRDs by moving money around from account to account at the end of the year, so as to avoid having the funds count as part of the year-end account balance of *either* plan.

P.R. § 1.401(a)(9)-7 contains other lengthy rules regarding the effect of rollovers and plan-to-plan transfers on the calculation of required distributions, but (with the exception noted in the preceding paragraph) a rollover *into* a plan or IRA has no effect on MRDs *from* that plan or IRA until the year after the rollover is received. P.R. § 1.401(a)(9)-7, A-2. The rollover contribution has the effect of increasing the plan balance of the receiving plan, which affects the calculation of the MRD for the year *following* the rollover.

1.3 The Required Beginning Date (RBD)

1.3.00 *RBD: definition and significance*

The date on which Participant must begin taking distributions from his retirement plan is called his "required beginning date" (RBD). § 401(a)(9)(A). The RBD is not the same for every type of retirement plan. Thus, Participant could be required to begin distributions from his IRA in one year (¶ 1.3.01), from his pension plan in another year (¶ 1.3.03) and from his Roth IRA never (¶ 1.3.01).

The RBD matters mainly for *compliance* purposes. The Participant must start taking out the required distributions by that date to avoid penalty, and (after Participant's death) the calculation of required distributions is somewhat different depending on whether death occurred before, or on or after, the RBD; compare ¶ 1.5.02 with ¶ 1.5.03. The RBD has no special significance in *planning* beyond the fact that its arrival means income tax deferral is "beginning to end," as Participant must start drawing down his benefits.

In the Code, "required beginning date" refers only to the required commencement date of lifetime distributions to Participant. The date by which post-death distributions to the *beneficiary* must begin (¶ 1.5.02, ¶ 1.5.03, ¶ 1.6.06) does not have an official name; compare § 401(a)(9)(A) and (C) with § 401(a)(9)(B). In this chapter, "required commencement date" is used for the date by which a beneficiary must start taking distributions.

1.3.01 *RBD for IRAs and Roth IRAs*

Roth IRAs have NO RBD. A living Participant is *never* compelled to take distributions from his Roth IRA. ¶ 5.1.03. Minimum distribution requirements do not apply to a Roth IRA until after Participant's death; see ¶ 1.5.02.

For "traditional" (i.e., non-Roth) IRAs, the RBD is generally April 1 of the calendar year following the year in which Participant reaches age 70½. § 401(a)(9)(C)(i)(I), (ii)(II). See ¶ 1.3.08 for an exception for certain rollover contributions. With a traditional IRA, there is no possibility of postponing required distributions until after a post-age 70½ retirement as there is for qualified plans and 403(b) plans (¶ 1.3.02).

1.3.02 *Certain plans: RBD can be postponed until retirement*

The RBD for a non-5% owner (¶ 1.3.05) in a QRP or 403(b) plan is generally "April 1 of the calendar year following the *later of* the calendar year in which the employee attains age 70½, or the calendar year in which the employee retires from employment with the employer maintaining the plan." § 401(a)(9)(C); P.R. § 1.401(a)(9)-2, A-2(a).

The ability to postpone the RBD until a late (i.e., post-age 70½) retirement is of no interest to workers who retire before age 70½; or to the business owner who owns more than 5% of his company and thus is not eligible. The typical Participants making use of the postponed RBD are high-level executives and service professionals who work for large firms, own either no interest or just a small interest—5% or less—in the sponsoring employer, and want to keep working past age 70½.

Note: the above definition of RBD applies for 1997 and later years. Under the definition that was in effect between 1986 and 1997, postponing the RBD until after a post-age 70½ retirement was not an option unless a "grandfather rule" applied; see ¶ 8.5.03.

1.3.03 *RBD for qualified plans*

A qualified plan (QRP) is not required to recognize the postponed RBD authorized by § 401(a)(9)(C)(i). (¶ 1.3.02.) A QRP may choose to require *all* employees (even those who are not 5% owners) to commence distributions by April 1 of the calendar year following the year they reach age 70½. P.R. §§ 1.401(a)(9)-2, A-2(e); 1.401(a)(9)-8, A-9. If the plan *does* require all employees to commence distributions by April 1 of the calendar year following the year they reach age 70½, then (notwithstanding § 401(a)(9)(C)(i)!) that date becomes the employee's RBD. An employee in such a plan is treated as dying "after his RBD" if he dies after April 1 of the calendar year following the year in which he reached age 70½, even if he owned 5% or less of the sponsoring employer and had not yet retired. P.R. § 1.401(a)(9)-2, A-6(b).

The RBD for a Participant in a qualified plan is therefore:

1.   If the plan does not require all employees to commence distributions by April 1 of the calendar year following the year they reach age 70½, and Participant is not a 5-percent owner, Participant's RBD, effective in 1997 and later years, is April 1 of the calendar year following the later of the calendar year in which Participant attains age 70½, or the calendar year in which Participant retires. § 401(a)(9)(C)(i).

2.   If the plan *does* require all employees to commence distributions by April 1 of the calendar year following the year they reach age 70½, the RBD is April 1 of the calendar year following the calendar year in which Participant attains age 70½. P.R. § 1.401(a)(9)-2, A-6(b).

3.   If Participant is a 5-percent owner (¶ 1.3.05), his RBD is April 1 of the calendar year following the year in which he reaches age 70½. § 401(a)(9)(C)(ii)(I).

4.   If Participant was born before June 30, 1917, or has a valid pre-1984 "TEFRA 242(b) designation" in effect, there may be a later RBD; see ¶ 8.5.

1.3.04 *RBD for 403(b) plans*

The proposed regulations state that the RBD for all 403(b) plans is April 1 of the calendar year following the later of the year Participant reaches age 70½ and the year Participant retires. There is no possibility of a different rule for "5% owners" because all 403(b) plans are maintained by tax-exempt charitable organizations that have no "owners." P.R. § 1.403(b)-2, A-1(c)(1).

It is not clear whether a 403(b) plan that is not a qualified plan is permitted (as qualified plans are; ¶ 1.3.03) to impose April 1 of the calendar year following the age-70½-year as the RBD for all employees; compare P.R. § 1.401(a)(9)-2, A-2(e) with P.R. § 1.403(b)-2, A-1(c)(1).

A "grandfather rule" applies to certain pre-1987 balances in 403(b) plans if separately identified. See ¶ 8.5.03 and P.R. § 1.403(b)-2, A-2, A-3.

1.3.05 *Definition of "5% owner"*

The ability to postpone the RBD under a QRP until after a post-age 70½ retirement is not available for "an employee who is a 5-percent owner (as defined in section 416) with respect to the plan year ending in the calendar year in which the employee attains age 70½." § 401(a)(9)(C)(ii)(I).

§ 416(i)(1)(B)(i) defines 5-percent owner as someone who owns *"more than* 5 percent of the outstanding stock of the corporation or stock possessing more than 5 percent of the total combined voting power of all stock of the corporation, or (II) if the employer is not a corporation, any person who owns more than 5 percent of the capital or profits interest in the employer" (emphasis added). Note that someone who owns exactly 5% is not a 5% owner—you have to own more than 5% to be a 5% owner.

In determining ownership percentages under § 416, a modified version of the "constructive ownership" rules of § 318 applies. Under these very complicated rules, Participant could be deemed, for purposes of the 5% test, to own stock held by various family members, trusts, estates, partnerships or corporations; and stock options must be taken into account. When advising an employee regarding his eligibility for the postponed RBD, the advisor needs to identify not only ownership interests held by the employee himself but also those held by these related individuals and entities. Explanation of the constructive ownership rules is beyond the scope of this book.

1.3.06 *What does "retirement" mean?*

How many hours must Participant work, in what time frame, in order to be considered not "retired?" The author has found no definition of "retirement" in any IRS publication. Although they purport to define RBD, the proposed minimum distribution regulations say nothing on this point. For what guidance the IRS has provided to employers and plans, see IRS Notice 97-75, 1997-51 I.R.B. 18.

Another problem with respect to the definition of "retirement" is whether a Participant may be considered "retired" as to some assets in a plan (e.g., assets rolled over from the plan of a prior employer or from an IRA) but *not* retired as to some other assets in the very same plan (contributions of the current employer).

Another unsolved mystery: can a person retire more than once?

Example: Carmen retires from the Royal Cigar Company at age 72 and starts receiving MRDs from the RCC plan. She is in the Palm View Senior Condo Development and hates it. She is bored and the Company needs her back because business is booming. So at age 73 she goes back to work for RCC. Can her required distributions be suspended until she retires *again*? The statute reads as though there is only one "retirement" per employee.

1.3.07 *"RBD" versus "first distribution year"*

When the RBD is April 1 of the calendar year following the year Participant reaches age 70½ (or retires, if that is the applicable event), the distribution required on that date is actually the required distribution for the *preceding* year—the year in which Participant reached age 70½ (or retired, whichever is applicable). Participant's "first distribution year" is the year he reaches age 70½ (or retires, whichever is applicable). Any distributions he takes on or after January 1 of the "first distribution year" count towards the distribution that is required to be taken by the RBD.

The fact that the first distribution year is actually the year *before* the RBD is significant for several rules; see "Rollovers" (¶ 2.5), Roth IRA conversions (¶ 5.4.07) and how to calculate the required distribution for the second distribution year (¶ 1.2.08).

Normally the deadline for taking a distribution that is required "for" a particular distribution year is December 31 *of that year*. However, in the case of lifetime required distributions, when the requirement of taking distributions is triggered by attaining age 70½ or retirement, the deadline for the first distribution year is postponed to April 1 of the *following* year. P.R. § 1.401(a)(9)-5, A-1(c). This postponement of the required distribution for the first year does not apply to death benefits (¶ 1.5), or to the first required distribution triggered by a rollover contribution (¶ 1.3.08.)

If Participant takes advantage of the postponement, and delays his first required distribution until April 1 of the following year, he will have two required distributions from that plan in the second distribution year:

Example: Bernie turns age 70½ in 2001. 2001 is the "first distribution year" for his IRA. He can take the 2001 required distribution at any time in calendar 2001, or in 2002 (on or before April 1, 2002). There will be another required distribution for the year 2002, for which the deadline is December 31, 2002. He decides to postpone the 2001 distribution until March 2002, to gain additional income tax deferral in his IRA. Although this will mean his required distributions are "bunched up" in 2002 (because he will receive and pay tax on two years' distributions in that one year), Bernie doesn't care because his *other* income will be much lower in 2002, so the bunching of MRDs will not increase his income taxes.

The difference between the "first distribution year" and the "RBD" also creates a confusing situation if Participant happens to die during the "limbo period"(January 1 of the first distribution year to April 1 of the following year):

Example: Otto, who is retired, reaches age 70½ in June 2001. The minimum distribution rules have already started to affect him, beginning back in January of the year he reached age 70½; for example, he cannot roll over a distribution from his company's retirement plan in the year 2001 until after he has taken out that plan's MRD for 2001. ¶ 2.5.05. January 2002 rolls around. Now another MRD (the one for 2002) is triggered, and still Otto has taken nothing out of the plan, but there is no rush because he has until April 1, 2002. He dies on March

31, 2002. He has died *before* his RBD. The requirement of taking MRDs for 2001 and 2002 is simply erased, because he never reached the RBD. P.R. § 1.401(a)(9)-2, A-4, A-6.

1.3.08 *First required distribution date for rollover contributions*

If a rollover contribution (¶ 2.5) is made into a brand new IRA (an account which contained nothing at the time it received the rollover), there is no distribution required for the year in which the rollover contribution comes into the new account, because the prior year-end account balance was zero (see ¶ 1.2.08 for possible exception). The rollover will be part of the plan balance that determines the required distribution for the *following* year. The RBD for the new account is the later of (i) April 1 of the year after the year Participant reaches age 70½ or (2) December 31 of the year after the year of the rollover. PLRs 2001-23070; 1999-31049;1999-30052.

Example: Matt works for Lowden Tree. He is not a 5% owner. He turns 70½ in 2001. He has not retired yet. He is a participant in the Lowden Tree Profit Sharing Plan and also has an IRA (IRA # 1) which has been in existence for many years. The Lowden Tree Plan does not require all employees to commence distributions by April 1 of the calendar year following the year in which they reach 70½, so Matt does not yet have any required distributions from that plan (see ¶ 1.3.03). In July 2001, he takes an in-service distribution from the Lowden Tree Plan. He rolls half the distribution into his pre-existing IRA (IRA # 1) (for which his RBD is April 1, 2002, by which date he must take the 2001 required distribution). He rolls the other half into a *new* IRA (created just to receive this contribution) (IRA # 2). Although normally the RBD for an IRA is April 1 of the calendar year following the year Participant reaches age 70½, the RBD for this newly-created rollover IRA (IRA # 2) is December 31, 2002, i.e., the end of the calendar year following the rollover contribution, because the account balance was zero as of the December 31 preceding the rollover (i.e., December 31, 2000, when IRA # 2 did not exist).

In terms of *the amount Participant is required to take out as an MRD*, it doesn't matter whether the rollover is made to a new or a pre-existing IRA. In either case the rollover contribution will form part of the year-end account balance for the year in which the rollover occurred, and the dollars will have the same effect on the next year's required distribution. However, it does make a difference for *determination of the RBD*. If the amount is rolled to a pre-existing account, the RBD for that account may have already past (or could occur earlier than December 31 of the following year, as in the case of Matt's IRA # 1). If the amount is rolled to a new account, the RBD for that account does not occur until December 31 of the following year.

The exact RBD makes little or no difference in terms of planning considerations, but can be significant for compliance purposes. Compare ¶ 1.5.04 and ¶ 1.5.05. In the above example, if Matt dies after April 1, 2002, but before December 31, 2002, he has died *after* his RBD for his pre-existing IRA # 1 but *before* his RBD for IRA # 2.

1.4 Computing Required Lifetime Distributions

Once Participant reaches his RBD, § 401(a)(9) forces him to start taking money out of his retirement plans (except for Roth IRAs; the lifetime distribution requirements do not apply to Roth IRAs. ¶ 5.1.03). This ¶ 1.4 explains how to compute those distributions. Although the computation of post-death required distributions can be radically different depending who is the beneficiary of the plan (¶ 1.5), lifetime required distributions are computed the same way for most people.

1.4.01 *"Uniform table" to determine lifetime MRDs*

Once Participant reaches his RBD, how much does he have to take out of his retirement plan each year?

As usual, minimum distributions are determined by dividing Participant's prior year-end account balance (revalued annually) by a life expectancy factor (divisor). The proposed regulations allow two choices of "divisor": one that applies only to a Participant whose sole beneficiary is his spouse who is more than 10 years younger than he is (¶ 1.4.02); and the other, called in this outline the "Uniform Table" (¶ 1.2.04; see Appendix A) to be used by everyone else. P.R.§ 1.401(a)(9)-5, A-4(a).

The Uniform Table is the same table that was called the "MDIB rule table" under the 1987/1997 proposed regulations. The divisors in the Uniform Table represent the joint life expectancy of a Participant age 70 (or older) and a hypothetical beneficiary who is ten years younger than Participant. Thus, the initial divisor under this table (for a Participant age 70) is 26.2 years (the joint life expectancy of someone age 70 and someone age 60).

To calculate lifetime MRDs under the Table, first determine Participant's age on his birthday in the distribution year (¶ 1.2.05). Then divide the prior year-end account balance (¶ 1.2.07) by the divisor in the Uniform Table that corresponds to that age.

Example: Kenny, a widower, turns age 73 on his birthday in the year 2001. Under the Uniform Table, the applicable divisor for age 73 is 23.5. On December 31, 2000, the value of his IRA was $750,000. Divide $750,000 by 23.5; the result ($31,915) is Kenny's MRD for 2001 for that IRA.

The joint life expectancy factors in the Uniform Table are redetermined annually (¶ 1.2.06). In other words, the table does not start with a 26.2-year life expectancy (divisor) and then reduce it by one each year. If the table used such a "fixed term method," then all money would have to be distributed out of the plan by the time Participant reached age 96 (70 + 26). Instead, the table's factors are recomputed annually, so the divisor decreases by less than one each year. At age 75, the divisor is 21.8 (not 21.2), at age 89 it is 11.1 (not 7.2). The divisor never goes below 1.8 (age 115 and older). This means that, if Participant takes only the MRD, the account balance will never go down to zero, regardless of how long Participant lives. Even at age 114 the required distribution is only half the account (divisor is 2).

The Code requires that benefits be distributed either in full on the RBD, or, "beginning not later than the required beginning date...over the life of such employee or over the lives of such employee and a designated beneficiary (or over a period not extending beyond the life expectancy of such employee or the life expectancy of such employee and a designated beneficiary)." § 401(a)(9)(A)(ii). The IRS states that the proposed regulations' lifetime distribution method described above carries out this Code provision, because the Uniform Table "reflects the fact that an employee's beneficiary is subject to change until the death of the employee and *ultimately may be* a beneficiary more than 10 years younger than the employee"! P.R., Preamble, "The uniform distribution period"; emphasis added.

1.4.02 *Lifetime MRDs if sole beneficiary is much-younger spouse*

"If the sole designated beneficiary of an employee is the employee's surviving spouse, for required minimum distributions during the employee's lifetime, the Applicable Distribution Period is *the longer of* the distribution period determined in accordance with [the Uniform Table] or the joint life expectancy of the employee and spouse using the employee's and spouse's attained ages as of the employee's and the spouse's birthdays in the distribution calendar year." P.R. § 1.401(a)(9)-5, A-4(b) (emphasis added).

Note that this formulation mandates annual recalculation (¶ 1.2.06) of Participant's and Spouse's life expectancies.

The joint life expectancy table (¶ 1.2.04) will produce larger "divisors" and smaller required distributions than the Uniform Table if the spouse-beneficiary was born in a year more than ten years later than the year of Participant's birth.

Example: Tallula was born February 25, 1925. Her spouse Irving was born August 25, 1945. In 2002, Tallula turns 77 and Irving turns 57. If Tallula names Irving as sole beneficiary of her IRA for the entire 2002 distribution year, Tallula's MRD for 2002 will be calculated using Table VI and the joint life expectancy of one person age 77 and one person age 57. The resulting "divisor" (27.5; about 3.64%) produces a smaller required distribution than the Uniform Table divisor (20.1; about 4.98%) for a person Tallula's age, because the Uniform Table is based on the joint life expectancy of one person age 77 and one person age 67—a shorter life expectancy.

Example: Johnny's date of birth was February 25, 1925. His spouse Evelyn's date of birth was August 25, 1935. Even though in "real life" Evelyn is more than 10 years younger than Johnny (she is 10 years and six months younger to be exact), she is *not* more than 10 years younger for minimum distribution purposes. For MRD purposes, she is exactly 10 years younger (i.e., she turns 67 in the year he turns 77). Use of the true joint life expectancy of Johnny and Evelyn will not produce smaller MRDs than use of the Uniform Table.

1.4.03 *Spouse-as-sole-beneficiary determined yearly*

The spouse is "sole designated beneficiary" for purposes of

determining Participant's required distributions "if the spouse is the sole beneficiary of the employee's entire interest at all times during the distribution calendar year." P.R. § 1.401(a)(9)-5, A-4(b).

Box 1.4.03: The way the proposed regulation is written, if the spouse ceases to be the spouse (or ceases to be the sole beneficiary), at any time during the distribution year, the joint life expectancy of husband and wife cannot be used to measure required distributions. This could impose hardship or at least great administrative inconvenience if a much-younger spouse lost her status as such due to death or divorce. Comments suggested that the regulation be revised to provide that, if the spouse ceases to be the sole beneficiary because of death or divorce during the distribution year, she would still be considered "sole beneficiary" for the rest of that distribution year. This would be consistent with the overall approach of making changes in status effective in the year following the change.

Final regs: The IRS (did not modify this rule) (did modify this rule as follows:)

1.5 MRDs After Participant's Death

1.5.01 *Overview of post-death required distributions*

When Participant dies, distributions must commence (or continue) after his death. The determination of required distributions after Participant's death depends on several factors:

1. Did Participant die before or after his RBD? This factor is not significant for planning purposes, but the calculation of required distributions is somewhat different depending on whether death occurred before (¶ 1.5.02) or after (¶ 1.5.03) the RBD. Since the RBD can be different for different plans (¶ 1.3), it is possible that Participant's death occurred before the RBD for some retirement plans and after the RBD for other plans. In case of any difficulty in deciding whether Participant died

before or after the RBD, re-read ¶ 1.3, especially ¶ 1.3.07. Neither the Code nor the proposed regulations specifically states what rule applies in the case of a Participant who dies *on* his RBD, nor that the post-RBD rules apply when the Participant dies after the RBD *without having taken the distribution that is required to be taken by that date*. It is believed that the rules for death "after the RBD" apply in any case of death *on or* after the RBD, regardless of whether Participant actually took his MRD on or before the RBD.

2.   Are there are *multiple beneficiaries*? If yes, then you need to determine whether the "separate accounts" rule (¶ 1.7.06) applies. If the retirement benefit is payable to multiple beneficiaries, but as of the Designation Date (see ¶ 1.8) their interests constitute "separate accounts payable to different beneficiaries," then the rules in ¶ 1.5.02 or ¶ 1.5.03 may be applied separately to each such "separate account." See full explanation at ¶ 1.7.06. The distribution options described in ¶ 1.5.02 and ¶ 1.5.03 either apply to Participant's *entire benefit under the plan*, or (if the separate accounts rule is to be used) apply to *each separate account*.

3.   Do the benefits pass to a "designated beneficiary," and if so who is that designated beneficiary? See ¶ 1.7 for explanation of how to determine who is Participant's "beneficiary" and whether there is a "*designated* beneficiary"; this Code-defined term does not simply mean any beneficiary who is designated by Participant! Understanding the meaning of designated beneficiary is crucial to both planning and compliance with the minimum distribution rules. Also, the identity of Participant's beneficiary is not fixed, for purposes of these rules, until the end of the year following the year of Participant's death (the "Designation Date"; ¶ 1.8). The rules in ¶ 1.5.02 or ¶ 1.5.03 apply *once the identity of the beneficiary is finalized on the Designation Date*.

4.   Does the plan put limits on distribution options? See ¶ 1.5.09.

In most cases these rules are nowhere near as complicated as the following description makes them appear; it's just that there are enough little variations and possible exceptions to make it impossible to state the rules simply.

The Code has two sets of post-death required distribution rules. If Participant dies after the RBD, "the remaining portion of such interest will be distributed at least as rapidly as under the method of distributions being used" to calculate Participant's MRDs during his life. § 401(a)(9)(B)(i). This is called the "at-least-as-rapidly rule."

If Participant dies before the RBD, on the other hand, benefits must be distributed within five years after Participant's death (the 5-year rule; ¶ 1.5.04) (§ 401(a)(9)(B)(ii)), unless the benefits are left to a "designated beneficiary" (¶ 1.7), in which case the benefits can be distributed over the life expectancy of the designated beneficiary. § 401(a)(9)(B)(iii), (iv).

In the proposed regulations, the IRS, in the interest of simplification, wisely bypassed the statutory scheme, jettisoning the "at-least-as-rapidly" rule (which was pretty much irrelevant even under the old version of the proposed regulations), and minimizing (to the extent possible given statutory limits) the differences between death before versus death after the RBD.

1.5.02 *Required distributions if Participant dies before RBD*

This ¶ 1.5.02 tells what distributions are required after Participant's death (a) for all of Participant's Roth IRAs (regardless of how old Participant was when he died; see ¶ 5.1.03); and (b) for all of Participant's other retirement plans as to which Participant died *before* his RBD (¶ 1.3).

There is no required distribution for the year of Participant's death. See ¶ 1.3.07. Required distributions begin, at the earliest, in the year after the year of Participant's death. The exact required commencement date, like the calculation of the distribution itself, depends on the identity of the beneficiary.

A.   If there is only one beneficiary, and that beneficiary is Participant's surviving spouse, the distribution options and required commencement date are described in ¶ 1.6.

B.   If there is only one beneficiary, and that beneficiary is an individual (¶ 1.7.03) who is not Participant's surviving spouse, then that individual is Participant's "designated beneficiary."

The designated beneficiary may take required distributions in annual instalments (beginning no later than the end of the year after the year in which Participant died) over a period not longer than the designated beneficiary's life expectancy, if that option is permitted by the plan (¶ 1.5.09). For how to compute that life expectancy, see ¶ 1.5.06. Alternatively, the designated beneficiary may take distributions using the 5-year rule (¶ 1.5.04), if that option is permitted by the plan. P.R. § 1.401(a)(9)-3, A-1.

C.   If a qualifying trust (¶ 6.2) is the sole beneficiary, then the individual beneficiary(ies) of the trust are Participant's "designated beneficiary(ies)." If the sole beneficiary of the trust is Participant's spouse, see ¶ 6.3.13 for applicable rules; otherwise, the trust may take required distributions in annual instalments (beginning no later than the end of the year after the year in which Participant died) over a period not longer than the life expectancy of the oldest beneficiary of the trust (or of the sole beneficiary of the trust, if the trust has only one beneficiary), if that option is permitted by the plan (¶ 1.5.09). For how to compute that life expectancy, see ¶ 1.5.06 (if the trust has only one beneficiary) or ¶ 1.5.08 (if the trust has more than one beneficiary). Alternatively, the trust may take distributions using the 5-year rule (¶ 1.5.04), if that option is permitted by the plan. P.R. § 1.401(a)(9)-4, A-5(a).

D.   If there is only one beneficiary, and that beneficiary is neither an individual (¶ 1.7.03) nor a qualifying trust (¶ 6.2), then Participant is treated as having "no designated beneficiary." The benefits must be distributed under the 5-year rule (¶ 1.5.04). P.R. § 1.401(a)(9)-3, A-4(a)(2). Distributions do not have to commence in the year after death, as long as all benefits are distributed by the end of the year that contains the fifth anniversary of the Participant's date of death, as explained at ¶ 1.5.04. See also ¶ 1.5.09.

E.   If there are two or more beneficiaries, and they are all either individuals (¶ 1.7.03) or qualifying trusts (¶ 6.2), then all of the individual beneficiaries (and all beneficiaries of the qualifying trusts) are Participant's "designated beneficiaries." If the only beneficiaries are the spouse individually and one or more qualifying trusts of which the spouse is the sole beneficiary, see ¶ 6.3.13 for applicable rules; otherwise, the beneficiaries (including any trusts that are beneficiaries) may take distributions in annual instalments over a period not longer than the life expectancy of the oldest designated beneficiary, if that option is permitted by the plan (¶ 1.5.09). P.R. § 1.401(a)(9)-5, A-7(a). This rule applies even if one of the individual beneficiaries (or one of the beneficiaries of any qualifying trust) is Participant's surviving spouse, because she is not the sole designated beneficiary; however, she may still have the option to roll over the portion payable to her (¶ 3.2; ¶ 3.2.09). For how to compute the oldest designated beneficiary's life expectancy, see ¶ 1.5.08. Distributions must begin no later than the end of the year after the year in which Participant died. P.R. § 1.401(a)(9)-3, A-3(a). Alternatively, the beneficiaries may take distributions using the 5-year rule (¶ 1.5.04), if that option is permitted by the plan. P.R. § 1.401(a)(9)-3, A-1.

F.   If there are two or more beneficiaries, but any beneficiary is neither an individual (¶ 1.7.03) nor a qualifying trust (¶ 6.2), then Participant is treated as having "no designated beneficiary." P.R. § 1.401(a)(9)-5, A-7(a). The benefits must be distributed under the 5-year rule (¶ 1.5.04). P.R. § 1.401(a)(9)-3, A-4(a)(2). This rule applies even if one of the beneficiaries is Participant's surviving spouse; however, she may still have the option to roll over the portion payable to her (¶ 3.2, ¶ 3.2.09). Distributions do not have to commence at any particular time, as long as all benefits are distributed by the end of the year that contains the fifth anniversary of the Participant's date of death, as explained at ¶ 1.5.04.

1.5.03 *Required distributions if Participant dies after RBD*

Here are the requirements for post-death distributions if Participant dies after his RBD. These rules apply to all types of retirement plans covered by this book (except Roth IRAs, as to which Participant's death is always "before" the RBD; see ¶ 1.5.02).

When Participant dies on or after his RBD, the required distribution for the year of Participant's death is still based on whatever method Participant was using prior to death—the Uniform Table or the joint life expectancy of Participant and Spouse, whichever is applicable (see ¶ 1.4). P.R. § 1.401(a)(9)-5, A-4(a)(1). If Participant had not yet taken the full required distribution for the year of death, the balance must be taken by the end of that year by the *beneficiary* of the account, *not* by Participant's estate. See, e.g., PLR 1999-30052. The beneficiary owns the account once Participant dies, and the estate has no right to take any distribution from it (unless of course the estate is the beneficiary). If the estate were entitled to take the balance of the year-of-death required distribution, then the estate would be a "beneficiary" of the account, with potentially disastrous consequences under the minimum distribution rules. See P.R. § 1.401(a)(9)-4, A-1, third sentence (definition of "beneficiary") and ¶ 1.7.04.

Beginning with the year after the year of Participant's death, required distributions depend on who is the beneficiary; in all cases, a distribution must be taken in the year following the year of Participant's death and every year thereafter, until the account has been entirely distributed.

A.   If Participant's surviving spouse is the sole beneficiary, the distribution options are described in ¶ 1.6.

B.   If there is one beneficiary, and that beneficiary is an individual (¶ 1.7.03) but is *not* Participant's surviving spouse, then the beneficiary must take required distributions in annual instalments (beginning no later than the end of the year after the year in which Participant died) over a period not longer than the beneficiary's life expectancy, if that option is permitted by the plan. For how to compute that life expectancy, see ¶ 1.5.06. P.R. § 1.401(a)(9)-5, A-5(a)(1).

C.   If a qualifying trust (¶ 6.2) is the sole beneficiary, then the individual beneficiaries of the trust are Participant's "designated beneficiary(ies)." ¶ 6.2.04. If the sole beneficiary of the trust is Participant's spouse, see ¶ 6.3.13 for applicable rules; otherwise, the trust must take required distributions in annual instalments over a period not longer than the life expectancy of the oldest beneficiary of the trust (or of the sole beneficiary of the trust, if the trust has only one beneficiary), if that option is permitted by the plan (see ¶ 1.5.09). For how to compute that life expectancy, see ¶ 1.5.06 (if the trust has only one beneficiary) or ¶ 1.5.08 (if the trust has more than one beneficiary). P.R. § 1.401(a)(9)-4, A-5(a).

D.   If there is only one beneficiary, and that beneficiary is neither an individual nor a qualifying trust (¶ 6.2), then Participant is treated as having "no designated beneficiary." ¶ 1.7.03. The Applicable Distribution Period is Participant's remaining life expectancy. P.R. § 1.401(a)(9)-5, A-5(a)(2). See ¶ 1.5.05 for how to compute this.

E.   If there are two or more beneficiaries, and they are all either individuals (¶ 1.7.03) or qualifying trusts (¶ 6.2), then all of the individual beneficiaries and all beneficiary(ies) of the qualifying trust(s) are Participant's "designated beneficiaries." If the only beneficiaries are the spouse individually and one or more qualifying trusts of which the spouse is the sole beneficiary, see ¶ 6.3.13; otherwise, the beneficiaries (including any trusts that are beneficiaries) may take required distributions in annual instalments over a period not longer than the life expectancy of the oldest designated beneficiary, if that option is permitted by the plan (¶ 1.5.09). This rule applies even if Participant's surviving spouse is one of the beneficiaries or is the oldest beneficiary, because she is not the sole designated beneficiary; however, she may still have the option to roll over the portion payable to her (see ¶ 3.2; ¶ 3.2.09). For how to compute the life expectancy, see ¶ 1.5.08. P.R. § 1.401(a)(9)-5, A-7(a).

F.   If there are two or more beneficiaries, but any of the beneficiaries is neither an individual (¶ 1.7.03) nor a qualifying trust (¶ 6.2), then Participant is treated as having "no designated beneficiary." ¶ 1.7.03. P.R. § 1.401(a)(9)-5, A-7(a). The Applicable Distribution Period is Participant's remaining life expectancy. P.R. § 1.401(a)(9)-5, A-5(a)(2). See ¶ 1.5.05 for how to compute this. This rule applies even if one of the beneficiaries is Participant's surviving spouse; however, she may still have the option to roll over the portion payable to her (¶ 3.2, ¶ 3.2.09).

1.5.04 *Death before RBD: the 5-year rule*

The 5-year rule is the only distribution method available if Participant dies before his RBD (¶ 1.3) with no designated beneficiary (unless the lack of a designated beneficiary can be "cured" before the Designation Date; see ¶ 1.8). It *may* be available as an option in other cases of death before the RBD; see the last two paragraphs of this ¶ 1.5.04.

The 5-year rule ceases to have any application once Participant reaches his RBD. The 5-year rule is never available as an option in case of death on or after the RBD. (Since Roth IRAs have no RBD, however, the 5-year rule may apply to a Roth IRA even after Participant has passed his RBD on all his other retirement plans.)

The 5-year rule operates differently from the rest of the MRD rules. Under the 5-year rule, there is no annual required distribution. The only requirement is that the entire plan balance must be distributed by December 31 of the year that contains the fifth anniversary of Participant's date of death. P.R. §§ 1.401(a)(9)-3, A-2; 54.4974-2, A-3(c). Thus, a beneficiary taking distributions under this rule could spread them over all the years in the period (which could be up to six *taxable* years), or could wait until the end of the period and take out all the money on that date. However, as with other legally allowed distribution options, the terms of the particular retirement plan might require distribution in one lump sum, with no option even to spread the distributions over five years; see ¶ 1.5.09.

There are two basic options under the tax law if Participant dies before his RBD leaving benefits to a designated beneficiary (benefits must be paid out either under the 5-year rule or over the life expectancy of the designated beneficiary; ¶ 1.5.02). How do you know which one applies? (If there is no designated beneficiary it's easy—only the 5-year rule is available.)

A retirement plan may allow its participants and/or their beneficiaries to elect irrevocably which method will apply (P.R. § 1.401(a)(9)-3, A-4(b)), or may provide that one or the other method *must* be used in some or all situations. For example, a plan could provide that the 5-year rule is not available if there is a designated beneficiary. P.R. § 1.401(a)(9)-3, A-4(c). Under such a plan, a designated beneficiary would have to take annual distributions based on his life expectancy to avoid the 50% penalty (¶ 1.9.06), and could not just wait until the end of the fifth year and withdraw the entire balance on the last day of the 5-year period. He would have to take annual distributions in years 1-4 (and then take the balance on the last day of the 5-year period, if that was his goal).

If the plan permits participants and/or beneficiaries to choose between the 5-year rule and the life expectancy payout, the plan can provide a default rule that will apply if Participant and beneficiary fail to elect a method. If the plan does not contain a default rule, the default rule is the life expectancy of the designated beneficiary. P.R. § 1.401(a)(9)-3, A-4(c) (last two sentences). (This is a change from the old proposed regs., under which the default rule was the 5-year rule.)

1.5.05 *Death after RBD with no DB: Participant's life expectancy*

The Applicable Distribution Period is the remaining years of *Participant's* single life expectancy if Participant dies after his RBD with no designated beneficiary (unless the lack of a designated beneficiary can be "cured" by the Designation Date; see ¶ 1.8). This method NEVER applies in cases of death before the RBD (and NEVER applies to Roth IRAs, as to which death is always "before the RBD").

To calculate Participant's remaining life expectancy, use the IRS's single life expectancy table (¶ 1.2.04) and find the expectancy factor based on the age Participant had attained (or would have attained had he lived long enough) on his birthday in the year of his death. The life expectancy for the year of Participant's death, *reduced by one year*, is used as the "divisor" for the first distribution year (i.e., the year *after* Participant's death). The divisor is reduced by one each year thereafter (fixed-term method; ¶ 1.2.06). P.R. § 1.401(a)(9)-4, A-3(b) and § 1.401(a)(9)-5, A-5(c)(3).

The largest divisor that could apply under this rule is 14.3. If Participant turned 70 in the year he reached age 70½, then died in the following year (but after his RBD), his age on his year-of-death birthday would be 71, for which the single life expectancy is 15.3 years, meaning the "divisor" for the non-designated-beneficiary's first distribution year (year after Participant's death) would be 14.3. If Participant dies later than the year he turns 103, the beneficiary will have to take out the entire balance in the year after Participant's death (because after age 103 the single life expectancy declines to less than 2, meaning the divisor for the year after Participant's death in the age-104-year would be less than one).

1.5.06 *How to compute distributions: one non-spouse beneficiary*

If there is one, individual, designated beneficiary, who is not Participant's spouse, the Applicable Distribution Period is the designated beneficiary's (single) life expectancy (¶ 1.2.04), determined based on his age on his birthday in the year after the year in which Participant died (¶ 1.2.05), and reduced by one each year thereafter ("fixed-term method"; ¶ 1.2.06). This method applies regardless of whether Participant died before, on or after his RBD. See ¶ 1.5.02, B, and ¶ 1.5.03, B. These post-death required distributions begin the year after the year of death; in other words, the beneficiary's first "distribution year" is the year after Participant's death.

Example: Jack dies in 2002. Dennis, who is not Jack's spouse, is sole beneficiary of Jack's IRA as of the Designation Date (¶ 1.8), 12/31/03. Dennis turns 65 on his birthday in 2003. The single life expectancy of a person age 65 is 20.0. By the end of 2003, Dennis must withdraw from the IRA at least 1/20th of the 12/31/02 account balance. If Jack died on or after April 1 of the year following the year in which he reached age 70½, and Jack had not withdrawn the MRD for 2002 by the time of his death, Dennis *also* must withdraw the balance of the 2002 MRD (computed using the Uniform Table and Jack's age as of Jack's birthday in 2002) prior to the end of 2002 (¶ 1.5.03).

Box 1.5.06: If Participant dies on or after his RBD, leaving his benefits to a designated beneficiary, and the designated beneficiary was born in a year earlier than the year of Participant's birth, the life expectancy of the designated beneficiary will produce a faster payout than would have been required if Participant had left no designated beneficiary (because the beneficiary's life expectancy is shorter than Participant's life expectancy). Perhaps the IRS will change the rules to permit Participant's remaining life expectancy to be used instead of the designated beneficiary's life expectancy, in other words, establishing Participant's remaining life expectancy as a "floor."

Final regs: The IRS (did not modify this rule) (did modify this rule as follows:)

1.5.07 *Effect of subsequent death of designated beneficiary*

Once the Applicable Distribution Period has been established based on the life expectancy of Participant's non-spouse designated beneficiary, the subsequent death of the designated beneficiary prior to the end of the Applicable Distribution Period has no effect on required distributions. Distributions can continue to be made over the remaining life expectancy of the now-deceased designated beneficiary. P.R. § 1.401(a)(9)-5, A-7(c)(2) and (c)(3) (Example 1).

Example: In the preceding example, assume Dennis dies in 2013, 10 years into his 20-year Applicable Distribution Period. At Dennis's death, ownership of the remaining IRA balance passes to Regis, a successor beneficiary named by Dennis (see ¶ 1.9.02). Required distributions to Regis continue to be calculated based on Dennis's life expectancy; he uses what's left of the 20-year Applicable Distribution Period established on Jack's "Designation Date" (12/31/03).

For different rules that apply on the designated beneficiary's death if the designated beneficiary was the spouse of the Participant (i.e., if Dennis were Jack's spouse), see ¶ 1.6.05 and ¶ 1.6.06.

1.5.08 *How to compute distributions: multiple beneficiaries*

Before applying the following rule, be sure to read the caveats at ¶ 1.5.01 regarding whether there really are "multiple beneficiaries" (as opposed to "separate accounts payable to different beneficiaries," ¶ 1.7.06). The following multiple beneficiary rule usually applies when determining required distributions to qualifying trusts (¶ 6.2), because most trusts have more than one beneficiary. This rule also applies whenever (i) there are multiple individual beneficiaries of the account and (ii) the separate accounts rule does not apply.

If there are multiple beneficiaries as of the Designation Date, and all are individuals, the Applicable Distribution Period is the life expectancy of the oldest beneficiary, determined based on his age on his birthday in the year after the year in which Participant died, and reduced by one each year thereafter. This method applies regardless of whether Participant died before, on or after his RBD, and regardless of whether the surviving spouse is one of the beneficiaries or is the oldest designated beneficiary. P.R. § 1.401(a)(9)-5, A-7(a)(1). The oldest beneficiary's life expectancy is calculated as described in ¶ 1.5.06.

Example: Natalie leaves her IRA to her sister and brother-in-law, Cindy and John. Cindy and John prefer to leave the IRA intact as a single account. This is more convenient for them for investment purposes and also for "dispositive" purposes since they both want the survivor of them to own the account solely if one of them dies. They are close in age, so there would be no great advantage, in terms of reducing required distributions, to treating the IRA as two separate accounts payable to each of them individually. They want the convenience of having to compute only one required distribution annually, and of not having to track "separate accounts" within the IRA. They decide to compute distributions by treating the inherited IRA as a single account that is payable to multiple beneficiaries. Their required distributions will be based on the life expectancy of whichever one of them is the older.

Example: Percy dies in 2002. As of the Designation Date (December 31, 2003), the beneficiary of Percy's IRA is Percy's testamentary trust, which is a trust for the benefit of Percy's wife Olivia for life, with remainder to Percy's children at Olivia's death. The trust complies with the "trust rules" (¶ 6.2), and Olivia (who turns 65 on her 2003 birthday) is the oldest beneficiary of the trust as of the Designation Date. The single life expectancy of a person age 65 is 20.0. By the end of 2003, the trust must withdraw from the IRA at least 1/20th of the 12/31/2002 account value.

1.5.09 *Plan is not required to offer life expectancy payout*

As has already become apparent (¶ 1.5.04), a retirement plan is not required to offer all the payout options that the law allows. While most IRAs permit the life expectancy payout, the situation is just the opposite with qualified plans. Most qualified retirement plans offer death benefits only in the form of lump sum distributions (or in some cases annuities), and do not offer the "life expectancy payout method." A plan is not even required, when the 5-year rule (¶ 1.5.04) applies, to allow the beneficiary to spread out distributions over the five years. See Fallon case study, Chapter 11, for one possible response to the problem of a plan that does not permit the life expectancy payout.

1.6 Special Rules for the Surviving Spouse

This section describes the special rules that apply when Participant's sole beneficiary is his spouse.

1.6.01 Overview of the special spousal rules

The Code provides special rules that apply when Participant's spouse ("Spouse") is named as Participant's beneficiary. One of the many positive features of the 2001 proposed minimum distribution regulations is greater clarity regarding application of these special spousal rules, including an explanation of when a "trust for the benefit of the spouse" may take advantage of certain tax provisions available to "the spouse" (¶ 6.3.13).

Note: the proposed regulations often refer to the spouse as Participant's "surviving spouse" even while they are both alive. See, e.g., P.R. § 1.401(a)(9)-5, A-4(b). Of course, while Participant is alive his spouse is not yet (and may never become) the "surviving" spouse. In this book, as in the proposed regulations, "spouse" and "surviving spouse" are used interchangeably.

There are four special provisions that may apply when Participant's surviving spouse is named as beneficiary:

1.   The calculation of lifetime required distributions using Table VI rather than the Uniform Table, if Participant's sole beneficiary is his much-younger spouse. This rule is discussed at ¶ 1.4.02.

2.   Use of the special recalc/fixed-term combo method for calculating Spouse's life expectancy after Participant's death if Spouse is the sole beneficiary; see ¶ 1.6.06.

3.   The postponed commencement date for required distributions (and related rules) when Participant dies before his RBD leaving benefits to Spouse as sole beneficiary; see ¶ 1.6.04 and ¶ 1.6.05.

4.   Spouse's right to roll over to another retirement plan, tax-free, benefits inherited from a deceased spouse (or treat an IRA inherited from a deceased spouse as her own IRA). For this

right, unlike numbers 1-3, Spouse does not have to be "sole" beneficiary. The spouse's rollover and election rights are covered at ¶ 3.2.

1.6.02 Definition of "sole beneficiary"

For purposes of the special minimum distribution rules applicable to a spouse-beneficiary, Spouse must be the "sole" beneficiary. Spouse is the sole beneficiary if she, alone, will inherit all of the benefits if she survives Participant; in other words if she is the sole *primary* beneficiary. The fact that other beneficiaries are named as *contingent* beneficiaries (who will take if Spouse does not survive Participant, or does not survive him for some specified period of time) does not impair her status as "sole" beneficiary.

Example: The beneficiary designation form for Bud's IRA provides: "I name my spouse, Louise Clark, as my sole primary beneficiary, to receive 100% of all benefits payable under this Plan on account of my death if she survives me by 30 days. If she does not survive me by 30 days, or if she is not married to me at my death, the benefits shall instead be paid to my sister Gladys Williams." The spouse, Louise, is Bud's sole beneficiary so long as both spouses are alive and married to each other. She is Bud's sole beneficiary at his death if she is married to him at his death, survives him by 30 days and does not disclaim the benefits. The fact that Gladys is named as a contingent beneficiary does not impair Louise's status as sole beneficiary.

Extremely important note: If the retirement benefit in question is divided into "separate accounts" payable to different beneficiaries (¶ 1.7.06), then the test of whether Spouse is the "sole beneficiary" is applied only to the separate account of which Spouse is the beneficiary. P.R. § 1.401(a)(9)-8, A-2. If Spouse is one of several beneficiaries of Participant's retirement plan, but the beneficiaries' respective interests constitute "separate accounts payable to different beneficiaries," the minimum distribution rules can apply separately to each of the separate accounts. Spouse may be entitled to "sole beneficiary" status with regard to a fractional share payable to her, even if there are other beneficiaries who are entitled to the rest of the benefit. See PLR 2001-21073 and further discussion at ¶ 1.7.06.

1.6.03 *When Spouse's status as sole beneficiary is determined*

The applicable time for determining whether Spouse is the sole beneficiary differs depending on which tax provision is being considered.

For purposes of computing *required distributions during Participant's life*, see ¶ 1.4.02.

For purposes of the *post-death minimum distribution rules* (¶ 1.6.04 though ¶ 1.6.06), it is not essential that Spouse be the sole beneficiary at the time of the decedent's death, only that she be sole beneficiary on December 31 of the year after the year in which Participant died (the "Designation Date") (¶ 1.8). Thus, in some cases, if Spouse is just one of several beneficiaries on the date of death, and therefore is not the "sole" beneficiary, it will be possible to "remove" the other beneficiaries (by means of disclaimer or distribution) so that Spouse can become the sole beneficiary by the Designation Date. See ¶ 1.8.

Spouse's rights to roll over non-required distributions she receives from the retirement plan of her deceased spouse, and to elect to treat an IRA inherited from the deceased spouse as her own IRA, are not part of the "minimum distribution rules." These derive from § 402 and § 408, not § 401(a)(9). See ¶ 3.2. Therefore these rights do not depend on Spouse's surviving until the Designation Date; she can exercise these rights at any time before the Designation Date (provided, in the case of the election, that she is sole beneficiary on the election date). She also can exercise these rights at any time *on or after* the Designation Date (provided, in the case of the election, that she was the sole beneficiary of the IRA on the Designation Date). See P.R. § 1.408-8, A-5(a).

1.6.04 *Required commencement date for distributions to Spouse*

If Participant dies on or after his RBD (¶ 1.3), the required commencement date for distributions to Spouse is the same as the required commencement date for distributions to any other designated beneficiary: December 31 of the year after the year of Participant's death.

If Participant dies *prior* to his RBD, and Spouse is the *sole* designated beneficiary, however, the annual distributions to Spouse over her life expectancy do not have to begin until the end of the *later* of: the year following the year in which Participant died, or the year in which Participant would have reached age 70½. § 401(a)(9)(B)(iv)(I); P.R. § 1.401(a)(9)-3, A-3(b). Non-spouse beneficiaries must commence distributions by the end of the year after Participant's death. § 401(a)(9)(B)(iii); P.R. § 1.401(a)(9)-3, A-3(a).

This rule theoretically applies whenever Participant dies before his RBD, but it has no effect (i.e., it does not provide a special late commencement date for Spouse) unless Participant dies before the year he would have reached age 69½. If he dies in the age-69½ year or later, spouse's required commencement date is the same as the required commencement date of any other beneficiary, i.e., the end of the year after the year of Participant's death.

1.6.05 *Spouse treated as "Participant" if both die young*

If Participant died before his RBD, and Spouse is the sole designated beneficiary as of the Designation Date, § 401(a)(9)(B)(iv)(II) provides an additional rule for what happens on Spouse's later death. This additional rule, translated into English, is:

If: (1) Participant died before the year in which he would have reached age 69½, leaving his benefits to Spouse as sole beneficiary and (2) Spouse is still the sole beneficiary as of the Designation Date, but (3) Spouse, although she survived until the Designation Date, later dies before the end of the year in which Participant would have reached age 70½, then: required distributions after Spouse's death will not be based on Spouse's remaining life expectancy (even though her life expectancy was the "Applicable Distribution Period" that would have applied for required distributions to her had she lived). Rather, a new distribution period starts: benefits must be distributed either by the end of the year that contains the fifth anniversary of *Spouse's* death or (if the benefits are payable to a designated beneficiary *of Spouse*) in annual instalments over the life expectancy of Spouse's designated beneficiary, commencing no later than December 31 of the year following the year in which *Spouse* died. P.R. § 1.401(a)(9)-3, A-6, A-5.

The "designated beneficiary" to whom the benefits are paid on the death of Spouse could be an individual named as beneficiary by Spouse or by the plan; see P.R. § 1.401(a)(9)-5, A-7(d) (last sentence). Unfortunately, if Spouse does not get around to designating a successor beneficiary for her interest, under most plans and IRAs the benefits will pass to Spouse's estate meaning that, upon Spouse's death during the time this rule applies, the benefits will not pass to a "designated beneficiary" and the 5-year rule will apply (¶ 1.7.04).

Theoretically this rule applies if Participant dies before his RBD, but once you work out all the possibilities it cannot *actually* apply unless he dies before the year he would have reached age 69½ for the following reason. If he dies in the age-69½ year or later, Spouse's required commencement date is the same as Participant's Designation Date, i.e., the end of the year after the year of Participant's death. If she survives to that date, the rule ceases to apply (because she didn't die before distributions were required to commence to her). If she *fails* to survive until that date, then she is not the designated beneficiary (¶ 1.8) so the rule doesn't apply.

1.6.06 *How to determine Spouse's life expectancy*

⁰   If Participant's benefits are left to a single "designated beneficiary" (determined as of the Designation Date), and that beneficiary is *not* Spouse, the Applicable Distribution Period is the life expectancy of the designated beneficiary, determined based on his or her age on his or her birthday in the year after the year in which Participant died, and reduced by one each year thereafter ("fixed-term method"). ¶ 1.5.06.

In contrast to this, if Spouse is Participant's *sole* beneficiary on the Designation Date, Spouse's life expectancy is determined by a combination of recalculation and fixed-term (¶ 1.2.06) methods: During Spouse's lifetime, Spouse must take distributions over her life expectancy, *recalculated annually*, beginning in whatever year she is required to begin distributions (¶ 1.6.04). Her life expectancy is determined using the single life expectancy table (¶ 1.2.04) based on her age on her birthday in the year for which a distribution is required. ¶ 1.2.05. P.R. § 1.401(a)(9)-5, A-5(c)(2) (first sentence) and A-6. See "Josephine" example at ¶ 1.2.06. Remember, this rule will not apply to benefits Spouse has rolled over to her own retirement plan, or, in the case of an inherited IRA, elected to treat as her own. See ¶ 3.2.

When Spouse later dies (i.e., dies after she was required to commence taking distributions), the required distribution for the year of her death must be paid out to the beneficiary to the extent Spouse had not already taken it by the time of her death. Any remaining benefits must be paid out over the remaining *fixed term* life expectancy of Spouse, computed as of her age on her birthday in the year of her death. P.R. § 1.401(a)(9)-5, A-5(c)(2). Spouse's life expectancy as of her age on her birthday in the year of her death (whether or not she actually survived until such birthday) is the "applicable divisor" for the successor beneficiaries' first distribution year, which is the year after the year of Spouse's death. For the rule if Spouse dies before she was required to commence taking distributions, see ¶ 1.5.07 (if she dies before the Designation Date) or ¶ 1.6.05.

Box 1.6.06: Note: It would appear that the divisor for the year after the year of Spouse's death should be the life expectancy as of the year of death *reduced by one* (as is the case in computing the remaining life expectancy of a deceased Participant; see ¶ 1.5.05), but this is not what the proposed regulations provide. This discrepancy could be the subject of a change when the regulations are finalized.

Final regs: The IRS (did not modify this rule) (did modify this rule as follows:)

This convoluted rule gives Spouse and her heirs the advantage of recalculation during Spouse's lifetime (distributions stretch out over her lifetime) and the advantage of a fixed-term payout after her death. However, it is not as favorable, in most cases, as the spousal rollover (¶ 3.2). With the spousal rollover, distributions during Spouse's life are computed using the Uniform Table (¶ 1.2.04), which, because its factors are based on joint life expectancies, produces smaller required distributions than Spouse's single life expectancy. Also, distributions from a rollover account after Spouse's death are based on the life expectancy of Spouse's designated beneficiary, which (depending on the age of the designated beneficiary and of Spouse) could be a much longer distribution period than the remaining years of Spouse's life expectancy.

Example: Harry dies in 2003 at age 75 leaving his 401(k) plan entirely to his wife Grace. Harry had taken his MRD for 2003 prior to his death. Grace does not roll over the 401(k) plan to her own IRA; she leaves it in Harry's name. As long as it stays in Harry's name, Grace's required distributions each year (beginning with the year 2004) are computed based on Grace's life expectancy as of her birthday in such year (recalculation method). Her age on her 2006 birthday will be 76. The single life expectancy of someone age 76 (¶ 1.2.04) is 11.9, so her 2006 required distribution from the 401(k) plan for the year is the 2005 year-end account value (¶ 1.2.07) divided by 11.9.

Now Grace dies in 2007. Even though she died before reaching her year-2007 birthday, we look at the age she *would have attained* in 2007 (which is not necessarily her age at her death) to calculate required distributions for the year of her death and later. She would have attained age 77 on her birthday in the year 2007 had she lived. The MRD for the year of her death is based on the single life expectancy of someone age 77 (11.2 years). Her life expectancy is then fixed at 11.2 years because of her death. MRDs to her successor beneficiaries thereafter will be based on this 11.2-year life expectancy, using the fixed-term method.

Assume Grace had not taken the year-2007 MRD before she died. Her successor beneficiaries must now take the 2007 distribution, which is the 2006 year-end account value divided by 11.2; and in 2008 they will take the 2008 MRD, which is the 2007 year-end account value also divided by 11.2. In other words, the first year after the year of her death the MRD divisor is the same as the MRD divisor for the year in which she died, namely, 11.2 in this example. For the second year after her death, the divisor will be 10.2.

If Grace had rolled over the inherited account to her own IRA, she could have named her own designated beneficiaries, and they would have been able to use their own life expectancies for required distributions, instead of being limited to using the rest of Grace's life expectancy.

If, on the Designation Date, Spouse is not the sole beneficiary, but all beneficiaries are individuals and Spouse is the *oldest* beneficiary, her life expectancy is computed in the same fixed-term manner as that of any other beneficiary (see ¶ 1.5.06); the recalc/fixed term combination method described above does not apply.

1.7 Designated Beneficiary: What, Who and Why

1.7.01 *Significance of having a "designated beneficiary"*

The value of the "life expectancy payout method" has been

explained. ¶ 1.2.01. While any Participant can use this method for calculating his lifetime required distributions (¶ 1.4.01), availability of this valuable tool is sharply limited once Participant dies. § 401(a)(9) allows Participant's death benefits to be distributed over the life expectancy of a *"designated* beneficiary," which is a defined term. If there is no "designated beneficiary," the payout options will generally be less favorable, as explained in ¶ 1.5. Therefore, estate planners must understand the meaning of this term and in most cases will want to take steps to assure that clients have a "designated beneficiary" to maximize the value of their retirement plans for the benefit of their family members or other chosen beneficiaries. (However, see ¶ 1.7.07 for cases in which it doesn't matter whether there is a "designated beneficiary.")

This ¶ 1.7 explains what a "beneficiary" is (¶ 1.7.02); the difference between a "beneficiary" and a "designated beneficiary" (¶ 1.7.03); the problems when an "estate" is a beneficiary (¶ 1.7.04 and ¶ 1.7.05); and the vital "separate accounts" rule (¶ 1.7.06). See ¶ 1.8 for discussion of how to modify the selection of beneficiary after Participant's death.

1.7.02 *Who is Participant's "beneficiary"*

Like life insurance proceeds, retirement benefits generally pass, as non-probate property, by contract, to the beneficiary named on the Participant's beneficiary designation form. Most retirement plans and IRAs have a printed form they expect Participant to use to name a beneficiary for his death benefits; some plans and IRA providers will accept attachments to the printed form, or a separate instrument in place of the printed form, designating a beneficiary.

Beneficiary designations offer a vast field for exploration by someone other than this author. Someone (else) really should write about such issues as: the problems created when participants file contradictory, ambiguous and otherwise ineffective beneficiary designations; how an IRA custodial account may be considered a probate asset in some jurisdictions; and which state's law governs the interpretation of a beneficiary designation form. This ¶ 1.7.02 discusses naming a beneficiary *only* from the perspective of the minimum distribution rules.

For purposes of the minimum distribution rules, the "beneficiary" means the person or persons who inherit the plan on

Participant's death. In most cases, that means only the "primary beneficiary(ies)." In the standard type of beneficiary designation, a contingent beneficiary would take a share of the benefits only if the primary beneficiary (or all of the primary beneficiaries) failed to survive Participant. When Participant dies, if the primary beneficiary *does* survive Participant, the contingent beneficiary ceases to have any relevance to the determination of who is Participant's beneficiary for minimum distribution purposes (although, under the proposed regulations, this could change—the contingent beneficiary could *become* a beneficiary for minimum distribution purposes—as a result of a disclaimer during the period between the date of death and the Designation Date; see ¶ 1.8).

Example: Jan leaves her IRA to Jon as primary beneficiary, with Kate as contingent beneficiary. Jan dies and Jon survives her. Unless Jon disclaims all or part of the benefits (¶ 8.2.01) before the Designation Date, or dies before the Designation Date (¶ 1.8.08), Jon is Jan's sole beneficiary.

If the primary beneficiary does not survive Participant, the "beneficiary" is the contingent beneficiary, because that is who inherits Participant's benefits.

Example: Regina leaves her IRA to her children A, B and C, with the proviso that if any child predeceases her that child's issue take the share such child would have taken if living. B predeceases Regina, leaving two children and no other issue, so at Regina's death her beneficiaries are A, C and the two children of B.

If the contingent beneficiary's rights are contingent on something other than the primary beneficiary's failure to survive Participant (or disclaimer), however, the question becomes more complicated. Normally this could not happen except in the context of a trust, because normally an IRA provider or plan administrator would not accept a beneficiary designation that had additional post-death conditions in it, unless the conditions were contained in a trust. When such a contingent beneficiary can be disregarded is discussed under the trust rules (¶ 6.3.04).

1.7.03 *The definition of "designated beneficiary"*

In order for benefits to be distributable over "the life expectancy of the designated beneficiary," there must be a "designated beneficiary." Not every "beneficiary" is a *designated* beneficiary." The Code defines designated beneficiary as "any individual designated as a beneficiary by the employee." § 401(a)(9)(E).

The proposed regulations substantially expand this definition:

"A designated beneficiary is an individual who is designated as a beneficiary under the plan. An individual may be designated as a beneficiary under the plan either by the terms of the plan or, if the plan so provides, by an affirmative election by the employee...specifying the beneficiary. A beneficiary designated as such under the plan is an individual who is entitled to a portion of an employee's benefit, contingent on the employee's death or another specified event....A designated beneficiary need not be specified by name in the plan or by the employee to the plan in order to be a designated beneficiary so long as the individual who is to be the beneficiary is identifiable under the plan as of [the Designation Date; see ¶ 1.8.01]. The members of a class of beneficiaries capable of expansion or contraction will be treated as being identifiable if it is possible, as of the date the beneficiary is determined, to identify the class member with the shortest life expectancy. The fact that an employee's interest under the plan passes to a certain individual under applicable state law does not make that individual a designated beneficiary unless the individual is designated as a beneficiary under the plan." P.R. § 1.401(a)(9)-4, A-1.

"Must an employee (or the employee's spouse) make an affirmative election specifying a beneficiary for a person to be a designated beneficiary under section 40l(a)(9)(E)?"

"A-2. No. A designated beneficiary is an individual who is designated as a beneficiary under the plan whether or not the designation under the plan was made by the employee." P.R. § 1.401(a)(9)-4, A-2.

So, there are several key elements to achieving "designated beneficiary" status:

1.   Only "individuals" can be designated beneficiaries. An "estate" does not qualify; ¶ 1.7.04. A trust is not an individual, but, if

some tricky rules are complied with, you can look through the trust and treat the individual trust beneficiaries as if Participant had named them directly as his beneficiaries; see ¶ 6.2. A partnership, corporation or LLC is not an "individual" for this purpose, even if under some tax rules it is not treated as an entity separate from its individual owners.

2.   If there are multiple beneficiaries, all must be individuals and it must be possible to identify the oldest member of the group. ¶ 6.2.07. You also must determine, in the case of multiple beneficiaries, whether the separate accounts rule applies. ¶ 1.7.06.

3.   Finally, the beneficiary must be designated either "by the terms of the plan" or (if the plan allows it) by the employee. See ¶ 1.7.05.

If Participant fills out his beneficiary form and names only "my spouse," or "my children," or "my friends Larry, Moe and Curly," as his death beneficiaries, and the named individual(s) survive Participant, there is no problem. We have individual beneficiaries who have been "affirmatively elected" by Participant, so there is a "designated beneficiary" whose life expectancy can be used to measure required distributions after Participant's death.

If Participant does not fill out a beneficiary designation form; or if all the beneficiaries he named fail to survive him, there is *still* no problem—*if* the plan fills the gap by specifying individuals to whom the benefits pass. Most qualified retirement plans, for example, provide that all benefits will be paid to Participant's surviving spouse if Participant fails to designate another beneficiary (or maybe even regardless of whether Participant designates some other beneficiary; see ¶ 3.4).

However, in many cases, if Participant fails to fill out the beneficiary form (or his named beneficiaries fail to survive him), the plan or IRA will provide that the benefits are paid to Participant's "estate." This will normally mean loss of the ability to use the life expectancy payout method, as explained in ¶ 1.7.04.

1.7.04 *Estate cannot be a "designated beneficiary"*

According to the IRS, if benefits are payable to Participant's "estate," Participant has "no designated beneficiary," even if all beneficiaries of the estate are individuals. P.R. § 1.401(a)(9)-4, A-3(a); PLR 2001-26041.

In this author's opinion, the IRS's position that the life expectancy method is not available if an "estate" is a beneficiary is incorrect. The Code provides that any portion of the employee's benefit payable "to (*or for the benefit of*)" a designated beneficiary may be distributed over that beneficiary's life expectancy. § 401(a)(9)(B)(iii) (emphasis added). Benefits paid to an estate are paid "for the benefit of" the estate's beneficiaries, and if the beneficiaries of the estate are all individuals (or qualifying trusts; ¶ 6.2), they should be recognized as "designated beneficiaries" and allowed to use the life expectancy method.

However, it is unquestionably the IRS's position that if any part of Participant's benefits is payable to Participant's "estate," participant has no designated beneficiary. Accordingly, this book follows that rule. For more on the contrary view, see Choate, N., "The 'Estate' As Beneficiary Of Retirement Benefits," Trusts & Estates, Vol. 138, No. 10 (Sept. 1999), p. 41.

See ¶ 1.8.06 for discussion of whether this problem can be solved post-mortem by distributing the account out of the estate. See ¶ 3.2.09 for whether spousal rollover may still be available. See ¶ 8.2.07 regarding disclaimers in this situation. For ways a retirement plan could be drafted to avoid this problem, see ¶ 1.7.05.

1.7.05 *Drafting retirement plan to avoid "estate" as beneficiary*

As explained at ¶ 1.7.04, the IRS has drawn a line in the sand on the question of whether the individual beneficiaries of an estate can be considered "designated beneficiaries." Some IRA providers are attempting to respond to this problem (and provide better results for their careless customers who don't fill out beneficiary designations) by designating individual beneficiaries (rather than simply "Participant's estate") who will take benefits Participant has not effectively disposed of in his beneficiary designation form. Here are several approaches IRA providers may consider, with the pros and cons of each:

1.   One approach is to try to guess who the Participant would have selected as his beneficiary had he gotten around to it. Such an IRA might provide that benefits not effectively disposed of by Participant's beneficiary designation form will pass to Participant's surviving spouse, if any, otherwise to Participant's issue, if any. This approach will work well in some cases, but will create problems in other cases, for example when the spouse is estranged, or when Participant's will disinherited some of his issue. It was to avoid such problems that most IRA agreements pay defaulted benefits to Participant's estate; but since the IRS has a vendetta against "estates," IRA providers are encouraged to try to create estate plans by guesswork.

2.   Another approach is to provide that benefits not effectively disposed of by Participant's beneficiary designation form will pass to the individuals who would have been Participant's heirs at law had Participant died intestate and had this account been an asset of Participant's probate estate. This approach successfully transforms the heirs-at-law into "designated beneficiaries." The drawback of this approach is that it requires the IRA provider to figure out the law of Participant's state of domicile, and, like approach #1, it risks running contrary to Participant's wishes as demonstrated in Participant's duly allowed will.

3.   Another approach is to name Participant's estate as the default beneficiary, but provide *in the retirement plan* that, if the executor or administrator of Participant's estate distributes the account to the individual estate beneficiaries before the Designation Date (¶ 1.8), those individual beneficiaries will be considered the Participant's beneficiaries "under the plan." For example, an IRA provider whose agreement names Participant's estate as the default beneficiary could add the following clause to its agreement: "If the Account is payable under the terms of this Agreement to Participant's estate, and if, before the final date for determination of the designated beneficiary of the Account as provided in P.R. § 1.401(a)(9)-4, A-4, the executor or administrator of Participant's estate has transferred the Account (or directed the IRA provider to transfer the Account) or any part thereof to the beneficiary or

beneficiaries of Participant's estate in a transfer described in Reg. § 1.691(a)-4(b)(2), then Participant's 'beneficiary,' with respect to the Account (or the part so transferred), shall mean such transferee(s) and not Participant's estate." This clause adds nothing to the rights of the executor or duties of the IRA custodian, because the executor is already entitled to direct the IRA custodian to transfer the account to the estate beneficiaries. ¶ 6.1.06. This clause does not in any way change the rights to the benefits (which, under the stipulated default-of-beneficiary clause, already belong to the estate beneficiaries). This clause does not take away the rights of the Participant to choose his own beneficiary because whether he left a will or chose to die intestate he "chose" the beneficiaries of his estate. All this clause does is change the status of the estate beneficiary from being (arguably) nothing more than an individual who receives the benefits merely because the benefits pass to him "under applicable state law" (a no-no in the proposed regulations) to being "designated as a beneficiary under the plan...by the terms of the plan."

If Participant failed to name a beneficiary, can the executor or administrator of his estate name one for him? Probably not. See PLR 2001-26036, in which daughter, as executrix of mother's estate, attempted to establish an IRA in mother's name and named herself as beneficiary. The IRS ruled that "a beneficiary must be designated either by a plan participant, an IRA holder or, in limited circumstances, the surviving spouse of said participant or IRA holder. Neither the Code nor the proposed [regulations] provide that the executrix of the estate of a surviving spouse who elected to treat IRAs of her deceased husband as her own may designate herself as the beneficiary of the surviving spouse's IRAs."

1.7.06 *Multiple beneficiary rules and "separate accounts"*

Under the IRS's multiple beneficiary rules, if the Participant has more than one beneficiary, Participant has "no designated beneficiary" unless all of the beneficiaries are individuals; and if all of the beneficiaries are individuals, they all must use the oldest beneficiary's life expectancy to calculate required distributions. ¶ 1.5.08.

There is an exception to these rules. If Participant's benefit under a plan is divided into separate accounts, *and* "the beneficiaries with respect to a separate account...differ from the beneficiaries with respect to the other separate accounts...such separate account...*need not be* aggregated with other separate accounts" for purposes of the applying § 401(a)(9). "Instead, the rules in section 401(a)(9) *may* separately apply to such separate account." P.R. § 1.401(a)(9)-8, A-2(a), (b) (emphasis added). This is one of the most useful provisions in planning for retirement benefits. It means, for example, that when an IRA is left to several beneficiaries each one can use his or her own life expectancy to measure required distributions.

Example: Zachary dies, leaving his IRA in equal shares to his sister DeeDee (age 30) and his brother Willy (age 5). If the two beneficiaries' shares are not treated as separate accounts for purposes of § 401(a)(9), then required distributions to both beneficiaries will be measured by the life expectancy of the sister (52.2 years) because she is the oldest beneficiary. If each sibling's portion is treated as a separate account, required distributions to each beneficiary may be measured by his or her own life expectancy. Since the younger brother's life expectancy at age 5 is 76.6 years, treating the beneficiaries' respective shares as "separate accounts" gives Willy another 24 years of potential income tax deferral.

A "separate account" within a single IRA (or other defined contribution plan account) "is a portion of an employee's benefit determined by an acceptable separate accounting including allocating investment gains and losses, and contributions and forfeitures, on a pro rata basis in a reasonable and consistent manner between such portion and any other benefits." P.R. § 1.401(a)(9)-8, A-3(a). Note that "separate accounts" is basically a bookkeeping concept. "Physical" separation of assets is not required. All that is required is that someone is tracking the allocation of profits, losses and distributions among the various beneficiaries, and that the allocation of gains and losses must be "proportionate" among the separate accounts.

A beneficiary designation that leaves the IRA in fractional or percentage shares to multiple beneficiaries is sufficient to establish separate accounts for those beneficiaries as of the date of death within the meaning of the proposed regulation. For example, if the IRA is left "in equal shares to my three children," then each of the children would be entitled to a pro rata share of the account's gains and losses occurring between the date of death and the date of distribution. See, e.g., PLR 9809059, in which 50% of an IRA was left to Trust K. The IRS ruled that Trust K's 50% interest constituted a separate account. Therefore, MRDs to Trust K under § 401(a)(9)(iii) were measured by the life expectancy of the oldest beneficiary *of Trust K*, not by the life expectancy of the oldest beneficiary *of the entire IRA*.

In PLR 1999-31049, Taxpayer B died leaving his six children as equal beneficiaries of his seven rollover IRAs. The IRS ruled that each child's share was a separate account. The IRAs involved in PLR 1999-31049 were actually "physically" transferred into six equal separate IRAs, one payable to each of the six beneficiaries, after the participant's death and before the end of the year in which death occurred and before any post-death distributions had occurred.

However, "physical" division is not a prerequisite of separate account treatment, as illustrated by PLR 2001-21073, in which two inherited IRAs were owned by three beneficiaries: Spouse owned 45% of each and Taxpayers C and D owned 55%. Although the three beneficiaries' interests in each inherited IRA were held in a commingled account, "documentation submitted with this ruling request indicates that [Spouse's] 45% interest(s) in such IRAs have been allocated gains and losses distinct from the gains and losses allocated to the remaining 55% interests in the IRAs, and, where applicable, charged with its appropriate share of expenses incurred by the IRAs." Spouse was ruled to be the sole beneficiary of her 45% share, and as such entitled to all the special breaks allowed when the surviving spouse is sole beneficiary (¶ 1.6).

Since separate account treatment is optional under the proposed regulations, not mandatory, it may be important to take some step, over and above simply leaving the benefits in fractional or percentage shares, indicating that the parties want to have § 401(a)(9) applied separately to the separate accounts. For ways to do this after Participant's death, see ¶ 10.4.02.

In planning mode, one way to assure separate account treatment is for Participant to specify that separate account treatment will be used. If Participant knows that separate account treatment would be beneficial, this approach may be preferable to making this desirable outcome dependant on the beneficiaries' post mortem actions. See Section 3.05, Forms 2.1, 2.2, Appendix B. Another approach is to have all the separate account language set up in the beneficiary designation form or account agreement, but leave it up to the beneficiaries themselves to elect whether they want separate application of § 401(a)(9) to their respective portions.

An IRA provider could facilitate either of these approaches by having the appropriate language in the IRA account agreement, so Participant (or beneficiaries as the case may be) simply have to check boxes rather than draft lengthy beneficiary designation forms or post-mortem agreements. Because creating separate accounts within a single IRA normally will involve some custom drafting, and complexities beyond the standard type of IRA account agreement used by most IRA providers, the separate account approach will probably be permitted only by those IRA providers that cater to larger investment accounts.

Another way to accomplish the objective is for Participant to divide his IRA into actual separate IRAs payable to the respective beneficiaries. For example, a Participant leaving his IRA partly to charity and partly to an individual beneficiary could create two totally separate IRAs, one payable to each of the respective beneficiaries. Some clients and planners find this approach simpler, or at least easier to understand, than the separate-accounts-within-a-single-IRA approach. Also, this approach may be the only one available if the IRA provider in question does not allow separate-accounts-within-a-single-IRA. Actual separate IRAs have the non-tax advantage of not requiring the beneficiaries to interact with each other after Participant's death.

The disadvantages of having multiple IRAs (as opposed to one IRA that contains separate accounts) include the additional paperwork (multiple monthly statements from the IRA provider instead of just one monthly statement), the difficulty of keeping the IRAs in the same relative proportion to each other when each contains different investments, and possibly increased investment management fees applicable to multiple smaller accounts compared with one larger account.

It is not clear whether separate account treatment can be used for a pecuniary gift. For example, suppose Participant wants his IRA benefits paid at his death "$50,000 to My Favorite Charity, Inc., and the balance to my daughter Gretchen." The proposed regulation talks about "allocating investment gains and losses, and contributions and forfeitures, *on a pro rata basis*" (emphasis added), which suggests that the IRS had only a fractional-type bequest in mind. In Planning Mode, it should not be difficult to rework a pecuniary gift into a fractional gift as of the date of death, which should solve the problem.

For *lifetime* MRDs, the separate accounts would have to exist throughout the distribution year in question. Reminder: Separate accounts make no difference in the computation of lifetime distributions unless Participant's more-than-10-years-younger spouse is sole beneficiary of one of the accounts; see ¶ 1.4.01-¶ 1.4.02. For post-death distributions, the separate accounts should be established no later than the Designation Date (¶ 1.8), but see ¶ 1.8.04.

1.7.07 *When having a designated beneficiary doesn't matter*

While having a "designated beneficiary" is vital to obtaining the advantages of a payout of death benefits over the life expectancy of a beneficiary, there are situations in which this goal is unimportant. For example, when Participant's chosen beneficiary is a charity (see Chapter 7): charities are exempt from income tax and therefore have no need to try to defer income taxes after Participant's death.

Also, when the money will come out of the retirement plan immediately after Participant's death regardless of whether the benefits pass to a designated beneficiary, either because the plan doesn't offer any form of benefit other than a lump sum (¶ 1.5.09), or a lump sum distribution is the most attractive distribution form for tax reasons (see ¶ 2.3, ¶ 2.4 for certain tax advantages for certain lump sum distributions), or the beneficiaries plan to cash out the plan and spend it as soon as possible after Participant's death whether they qualify for life expectancy payout or not.

If Participant is past his RBD, and his chosen beneficiary is close to him in age (or older) there is little or no advantage to using the life expectancy of the beneficiary as an Applicable Distribution Period (compare ¶ 1.5.05 and ¶ 1.5.06). In all of these situations, there is no need to jump through hoops to try to qualify for a life expectancy payout method that will not be available, or will not be advantageous, or for some other reason will not be used.

1.8 The "Designation Date"

Beneficiaries of a deceased employee or IRA owner have until December 31 of the year after the year of death to "finalize" the decedent's choice of beneficiary for purposes of determining required distributions, through disclaimers or distributions or possibly other means. This means that post-mortem planning can have a significant effect on required distributions. This ¶ 1.8 looks at ways to improve the beneficiary designation post mortem, including methods the IRS specifically blesses in the proposed regulations and other methods.

1.8.01 *Designated beneficiary fixed at end of year after death*

The proposed regulations specify that the date for determining Participant's beneficiary is not the date of death. Rather, "the employee's designated beneficiary will be determined based on the beneficiaries designated as of the last day of the calendar year following the calendar year of the employee's death." P.R. § 1.401(a)(9)-4, A-4(a).

This does not mean that post-death planning can somehow designate a new crop of beneficiaries. Rather, it means that "...any person who was a beneficiary as of the date of the employee's death, but is not a beneficiary as of that later date (e.g., because the person disclaims entitlement to the benefit in favor of another beneficiary or because the person receives the entire benefit to which the person is entitled before that date), *is not taken into account* in determining the employee's designated beneficiary for purposes of determining the distribution period for required minimum distributions after the employee's death." P.R. § 1.401(a)(9)-4, A-4(a) (emphasis added). In other words, *if* there are "good" beneficiaries (e.g., individual beneficiaries with long life expectancies) who are *already named* by the deceased Participant (e.g., as contingent beneficiaries, or among a group of multiple beneficiaries), it is possible (by disclaimer, distribution or possibly other means) to eliminate other (e.g., older or non-individual) beneficiaries, so that by December 31 of the year after the year of death only the "good" beneficiaries are left.

1.8.02 *New problem: Designation Date same as distribution date*

The fact that the date for *determining who is the designated beneficiary* (which determines the amount of the required distribution) is now also the deadline for *starting the required distributions* can create such problems for plan administrators that the IRS will probably have to modify this approach.

Example: Corey dies in 2002 leaving his IRA to his three children, Flora, Dora and Laura. Flora disclaims her share and as a result her share passes to the contingent beneficiary, a trust for her children, the trustee of which drags his feet in supplying the required documentation to the IRA provider. The trustee and Dora want separate accounts established, but Laura won't go along with the idea because she doesn't like Dora. Finally, on December 30, 2003, the trustee (bringing the required documentation) and Laura (having finally signed the separate account agreement) come in to see the IRA provider, but say they can't find Dora anywhere. The IRA provider now has 24 hours to compute the separate accounts, review the trust documentation, calculate MRDs to the trust and Laura, figure out whether Dora is dead (and if so calculate the required distribution to her estate) or alive (and if so calculate the MRD based on Dora's life expectancy), and cut three checks to make the distributions. Obviously, this won't work!

Box 1.8.02: Perhaps the IRS, in final regulations, will allow a postponement of the first post-death required distribution until the April 1 following the Designation Date, or provide an automatic waiver of the excise tax (¶ 1.9.06) for failure to take the first post-death distribution if it is made within a certain amount of time after the Designation Date.

       Final regs: The IRS (did not modify this rule) (did modify this rule as follows:)

1.8.03 *Changing the designated beneficiary by disclaimer*

       The proposed regulations clarify that disclaimers made before the Designation Date are given effect in determining who is the designated beneficiary. P.R. § 1.401(a)(9)-4, A-4(a); Preamble, "Determination of the Designated Beneficiary." Thus, an older beneficiary (such as a surviving spouse or child) can disclaim the benefits and allow them to pass to a younger contingent beneficiary (such as a child or grandchild) and the younger beneficiary will then be "the" designated beneficiary whose life expectancy becomes the Applicable Distribution Period. See ¶ 8.1-¶ 8.2. As a reminder, the deadline for making a "qualified disclaimer" is considerably *earlier* than the Designation Date generally, nine months after Participant's death. ¶ 8.1.11. The fact that the Designation Date is not until

December 31 of the year after the year of death does *not* extend the deadline for making a qualified disclaimer.

1.8.04 *Establishing separate accounts after death*

A retirement plan account that is left to multiple beneficiaries can be divided into separate accounts for them after Participant's death. If the separate accounts are established by the Designation Date, then each separate account stands on its own for purposes of determining required distributions to the beneficiary of that account. ¶ 1.7.06.

This can be helpful for: assuring that the existence of non-individual beneficiaries does not prevent individual beneficiaries from using the life expectancy payout method; assuring that each designated individual beneficiary can use his or her own life expectancy (rather than the life expectancy of the oldest beneficiary) to measure required distributions; and applying the special spousal rules (¶ 1.6).

Box 1.8.04: In case of death after the RBD, the proposed regulations, read literally, either require that "separate accounts" be established on or before the RBD in order to be recognized for post-death distributions or do not allow separate accounts at all. See P.R. § 1.401(a)(9)-8, A-2(a), which states that separate accounts are aggregated "except as otherwise provided in" subparagraph (b), and subparagraph (b) does not provide any specific contrary rule for *post-death* distributions where death occurs after the RBD.

The Preamble ("Determination of Designated Beneficiary") says that the proposed regulations provide "the same rules for distributions after the employee's death, regardless of whether such death occurs before or after" the RBD. The Preamble also states that "If, as of the end of the year following the year of the employee's death, the employee has more than one designated beneficiary and the account or benefit has not been divided into separate accounts or shares for each beneficiary, the beneficiary with the shortest life expectancy is the designated beneficiary," which suggests that the separate accounts determination is made on the Designation Date and does not suggest that this result applies only if death occurred before the RBD.

In view of these statements in the Preamble, it appears that P.R. § 1.401(a)(9)-8, A-2(a) is a technical glitch and that the IRS intends that "separate accounts" can be established during the post-death

---

cleanup period whether death occurred before or after the RBD. Hopefully, this reading will be confirmed in final regulations.

Final regs: The IRS (did not modify this rule) (did modify this rule as follows:)

1.8.05 *Eliminating beneficiaries by distributing their benefits*

Another way to cure the multiple beneficiary problem is to distribute, to any non-individual (or older) beneficiaries, the shares payable to them. If the amounts payable to the non-individual (or older) beneficiaries are entirely distributed to them by the Designation Date, then only the remaining (younger, individual) beneficiaries who still have an interest in the benefit will "count" for purposes of determining who is the designated beneficiary. P.R. § 1.401(a)(9)-4, A-4(a). This could be very helpful if the separate account rule (¶ 1.7.06) is not available.

Example: Frank's beneficiary designation for his $1 million IRA reads "I leave $10,000 to Charity X and the rest of my IRA to my son." If the charity's share is paid out by the Designation Date, the son is left as the sole beneficiary. The multiple beneficiary rule (¶ 1.7.06) does not apply. Since the son is an individual, he is a "designated beneficiary," and required distributions will be determined based on the son's life expectancy.

1.8.06 *Distributing the account itself out of an estate*

The IRS states emphatically, twice, that an estate cannot be a "designated beneficiary." P.R. §§ 1.401(a)(9)-4, A-3(a), 1.401(a)(9)-8, A-11. See ¶ 1.7.04. It is not clear under the proposed regulations whether this problem can be cured by distributing the retirement plan itself (intact) out of the estate to the individual beneficiaries of the estate before the Designation Date. (See ¶ 6.1.06 for discussion of a fiduciary's ability to transfer a retirement benefit account to the beneficiaries of an estate or trust.)

Example: Jane dies without having named a beneficiary for her $1 million IRA. Under the terms of the IRA agreement, the IRA is payable to her estate in this case, so she does not have a "designated beneficiary" at the time of death. The only beneficiaries of her estate are her children Gray and Seymour. Before the Designation Date, the executor of her estate, before taking any distributions from the IRA, transfers the IRA account to Gray and Seymour. This transfer does not trigger any income tax, because it is an assignment of the right-to-receive-IRD to the persons entitled to receive the IRD under the decedent's will (¶ 2.2.04). On the Designation Date, the children are the sole owners of the account. Since they are individuals, do they qualify as "designated beneficiaries" and can they use the life expectancy payout method?

The proposed regulations do not discuss this situation. Perhaps it works; the Preamble indicates that the examples in the proposed regulations are not intended to be the only ways the identity of the designated beneficiary can be modified. For example, the Preamble states that the proposed regulation "allows...the beneficiary to be changed after the employee's death, *such as* [sic] by one or more beneficiaries disclaiming or being cashed out" ("Overview") (emphasis added), and "any beneficiary eliminated by distribution of the benefit or through disclaimer (*or otherwise*) during the period between the employee's death and the end of the year following the year of death is disregarded..." ("Determination of the designated beneficiary") (emphasis added).

On the other hand, the Proposed Regulations' definition of designated beneficiary is "an individual who is designated as a beneficiary *under the plan*...." The individual must be "identifiable *under the plan*" as of the Designation Date. "The fact that an employee's interest under the plan passes to a certain individual under applicable state law does not make that individual a designated beneficiary unless the individual is designated as a beneficiary *under the plan*." P.R. § 1.401(a)(9)-4, A-1 (emphasis added). This language suggests that the residuary beneficiaries of an estate could not be "designated beneficiaries" if the plan merely provides that benefits are payable to the "estate"of the deceased participant. See ¶ 1.7.05 for a plan provision to avoid this problem.

1.8.07 *Powers of appointment*

What if Participant's beneficiary designation form gives Participant's executor (or spouse, or some other person), a power to appoint the benefits to any person the power-holder chooses (other than the power-holder himself)? If the power-holder exercises the power irrevocably prior to the Designation Date by appointing the benefits to an individual, would the beneficiary so selected be a "designated beneficiary?"

The proposed regulations discuss only eliminating (by means of disclaimer or distribution) beneficiaries chosen by Participant, as opposed to adding new beneficiaries or choosing beneficiaries at random from a huge amorphous class. However, as noted (¶ 1.8.06), the Preamble says that the examples provided are not intended to be exclusive. Furthermore, P.R. § 1.401(a)(9)-5, A-7(d)(1), provides that an employee is deemed to have no designated beneficiary if the plan permits any person to "have the discretion to change the beneficiaries of the employee" "*after the end of the calendar year following the calendar year in which the employee died*" (emphasis added). This implies that granting someone the power to change the employee's beneficiaries *prior* to the Designation Date is not a problem.

P.R. § 1.401(a)(9)-4, A-1, provides that "An individual may be designated as a beneficiary under the plan either by the terms of the plan or, if the plan so provides, by an affirmative election by the employee *(or the employee's surviving spouse)* specifying the beneficiary." P.R. § 1.401(a)(9)-4, Q-2, asks "Must an employee *(or the employee's spouse)* make an affirmative election specifying a beneficiary for a person to be a designated beneficiary?" (Emphasis added.) Some practitioners have wondered whether these parenthetical references to Spouse's designating a beneficiary are intended to allow Spouse (but not other beneficiaries or fiduciaries) to exercise a broad power of appointment during the post-death clean-up period. That seems unlikely because these references to a designation by the employee's spouse were carried over verbatim from the old proposed regulations (old P.R. § 1.401(a)(9)-1, D-1 and D-2), which did not allow any post-death cleanup period. Probably the phrase is merely referring to the § 401(a)(9)(B)(iv)(II) situation (¶ 1.6.05; designated beneficiary is determined as of Spouse's death, if Participant died before his RBD leaving benefits to Spouse as sole beneficiary and she then died before the required commencement of distributions to her).

1.8.08 *Effect of beneficiary's death prior to Designation Date*

Under the proposed regulations, the death of the primary beneficiary after Participant's death but prior to the Designation Date apparently causes the primary beneficiary to lose his status as "designated beneficiary." Participant's beneficiary will then be whoever happens to succeed to the interest of the primary beneficiary at that point.

If the plan permits the original beneficiary to name his own beneficiary (a successor beneficiary; ¶ 1.9.02), *and* the original beneficiary got around to doing that before he died, *and* the successor beneficiary is an individual who then does manage to survive until the Designation Date, then the successor beneficiary presumably becomes *Participant's* designated beneficiary, and the successor beneficiary's life expectancy is used to measure MRDs.

However, it often happens that either the plan does not permit beneficiaries to name successor beneficiaries, or the plan permits it but the beneficiary dies without doing so. In either case, the "successor beneficiary" is likely to be the original beneficiary's *estate*...meaning that all of a sudden Participant has "no designated beneficiary," because an estate is not an individual. ¶ 1.7.04. If the beneficiary's executor can make a timely disclaimer of the benefits (¶ 8.1) that may solve the problem in some cases.

What steps can practitioners take in drafting beneficiary designation forms to head off this problem?

If the original beneficiary dies simultaneously with, or shortly after, Participant, the problem can be avoided by including standard simultaneous death or requirement-of-survival clauses in the beneficiary designation form. For example, Participant's beneficiary designation can specify that, in case of simultaneous deaths of Participant and primary beneficiary, the primary beneficiary is deemed to predecease Participant and the contingent beneficiary takes the benefits; or that any named beneficiary must survive Participant by some period of time (such as 30 days) to be entitled to the benefits.

However, in order for a bequest to the surviving spouse to qualify for the estate tax marital deduction (¶ 3.3), it cannot be subject to a survivorship requirement longer than six months. § 2056(b)(3). A requirement that the surviving spouse survive until the Designation Date would cause the gift to the spouse not to qualify for the marital deduction for Participant's estate, even if the spouse does in fact survive that long.

Even if marital deduction qualification is not of concern (for example, if the beneficiaries are Participant's children rather than the spouse), it creates hardships on the beneficiaries to require them to survive until the Designation Date to be entitled to any benefits. They might need the money sooner—to pay estate taxes for example.

Another approach is for Participant to provide for an individual default beneficiary to take the benefits if the original beneficiary, having survived Participant, dies before taking out the benefits and without having named his own successor beneficiaries. Some IRA providers will not allow this, on the grounds that once Participant has died the beneficiary owns the account absolutely and it is not possible for Participant to exercise further control over it. There should be no objection, however, if the IRA is already in the form of a trust (§ 408(a)) rather than the more common custodial account (§ 408(h)). The only other sure way around the problems is for Participant, instead of naming (e.g.) child as beneficiary, to name a trust as beneficiary, and give child the unlimited right to withdraw from the trust. The trust can provide suitable contingent beneficiaries if child dies before having withdrawn all of the benefits.

Box 1.8.08: Perhaps the IRS will respond to comments requesting that the beneficiary's survival until the Designation Date not be required as a condition of "designated beneficiary" status.

Final regs: The IRS (did not modify this rule) (did modify this rule as follows:)

1.9 Other Important MRD Rules

1.9.01 *Taking distributions from multiple plans: IRS Notice 88-38*

If the client participates in more than one qualified retirement plan, the MRD must be calculated separately for each such plan, and each such plan must distribute the MRD calculated for that plan. P.R. § 1.401(a)(9)-8, A-1. Thus if the client participates in two pension plans and a 401(k) plan, he will receive three separate MRDs, one from each of these plans.

A different rule applies for IRAs. The MRD must be calculated separately for each IRA, but (subject to the exception noted below) Participant is not required to take each IRA's calculated amount from that IRA. He can total up the MRDs required from all of his IRAs, and then take the total amount all from one of the IRAs, or from any combination of them. Notice 88-38, 1988-1 C.B. 524; P.R. § 1.408-8, A-9.

This rule applies also to 403(b) accounts. The MRD must be calculated separately for each 403(b) account, but (subject to the exception noted below) Participant is not required to take each 403(b) account's calculated amount from that 403(b) account. He can total up the MRDs required from all of his 403(b) arrangements, and then (with the exception noted below) take the total amount all from one of them, or from any combination of them. Notice 88-38, 1988-1 C.B. 524; P.R. § 1.408-8, A-9.

Here is the exception: Notice 88-38 stated that an individual could combine inherited IRAs with non-inherited IRAs. The proposed regulations modify Notice 88-38 (without mentioning that this is a modification) by providing that: an individual's IRAs held as *owner* may not be aggregated with IRAs held as *beneficiary of another person*; an individual's 403(b) plans held as *employee* may not be aggregated with such individual's 403(b) plans held as *beneficiary of another person* (P.R. § 1.403(b)-2, A-4); and an individual's IRAs (or 403(b) plans) held as beneficiary of one decedent may not be aggregated with IRAs (or 403(b) plans) held as beneficiary of another decedent. P.R. § 1.408-8, A-9.

Note that IRAs can be combined only with other IRAs, not with 403(b)s. 403(b)s can be combined only with other 403(b)s, not with IRAs.

Note also that Notice 88-38 allows the *taxpayer who must take distributions* to combine multiple IRAs he must take distributions from (see Notice 88-38, Example 4); it does not allow IRAs inherited by multiple beneficiaries *from a single participant* to be "pooled" so that required distributions paid to one beneficiary can fulfill the distribution requirement applicable to another beneficiary.

Example: Jeffrey dies, leaving two IRAs. One is payable to a marital deduction trust, the other to a credit shelter trust. The "trust rules" (¶ 6.2) are complied with, so the beneficiaries of the respective trusts are treated as Jeffrey's designated beneficiaries, and the life expectancy of the oldest beneficiary of each trust is used to measure the post-death MRDs to that trust. Assume the credit shelter trust permits accumulation of income. To maximize income tax deferral and minimize estate taxes, the family would like to compute one single MRD for both trusts and take it entirely from the IRA payable to the marital trust. This way, the credit shelter trust would get the maximum available income tax deferral and what income taxes had to be paid would be paid by the marital trust, where at least they could reduce Spouse's future taxable estate. Notice 88-38 does NOT appear to allow this maneuver.

1.9.02 *A beneficiary can name his/her own successor beneficiary*

The proposed regulations confirm that allowing a beneficiary to "designate a subsequent beneficiary for distributions of any portion of the employee's benefit after the beneficiary dies" does not violate the rule that no person may "have the discretion to change the beneficiaries of the employee" after the Designation Date (¶ 1.8). P.R. § 1.401(a)(9)-5, A-7(d)(1). See example at ¶ 1.5.07.

1.9.03 *Tax-free distributions count towards the MRD*

Nothing in the Code says that only taxable distributions fulfill the distribution requirement. PLR 9840041 confirmed that a tax-free distribution can be used to satisfy the requirement. In that ruling, an employee took a distribution of his entire balance from an employer plan, rolled over the taxable portion of the distribution and did not roll over the non-taxable amounts. The IRS ruled that the non-taxable distribution, which exceeded the MRD, satisfied the MRD requirement.

Certain types of retirement plans accept, or used to accept, non-deductible employee contributions. Such plans typically maintain two "accounts" on the books for each employee, the "employer contribution account" and the "employee contribution account." The employee would typically have no "basis" in the employer contribution account, but would have some basis in the employee contribution account. Distributions from the employee contribution account would therefore be partly tax-free (as a distribution of basis). ¶ 2.1.04.

Even though the two accounts are maintained as "separate accounts" on the employer's books, they must be treated as one account for MRD purposes unless they are payable to different beneficiaries; and even if they are payable to different beneficiaries, separate account treatment is optional. ¶ 1.7.06. Thus, an employee who has made non-deductible contributions to a qualified retirement plan can, if he wishes, use distributions from the employee contribution account to fulfill the MRD requirement with regard to both the employer and employee contribution accounts.

Unfortunately, an IRA owner cannot use the same approach (take out non-deductible amounts first), because (a) all IRA distributions generally are deemed to come proportionately from taxable and after-tax amounts, and (b) all IRAs are treated as one single account for this purpose; for detailed explanation of this rule, see ¶ 5.4.10-¶ 5.4.12.

1.9.04 *Distributions in kind*

Participant or beneficiary can take required distributions in kind as well as in cash. Plans are permitted to distribute property as well as cash. See instructions for IRS form 1099-R (2000), Box 1, where the payer is instructed "If you distribute employer securities or other property, include in box 1 the FMV of the securities or other property on the date of distribution." There is nothing in the Code, proposed regulations, or form 1099-R instructions that indicates distributions in kind could not be used to satisfy the minimum distribution requirement.

1.9.05 *Who enforces the minimum distribution rules*

Compliance with the minimum distribution rules is one of the more than 30 requirements a "qualified retirement plan" must meet to stay "qualified." § 401(a). Accordingly, in the case of qualified plans, the plan administrator is the enforcer of the minimum distribution rules. Since disqualification of the plan would be a disaster for all concerned (the plan would lose its income tax exemption for example), the plan administrator is extremely concerned to make sure required distributions are distributed—even though the penalty for failing to make a required distribution is imposed on the "payee" (non-payee?) rather than on the plan. § 4974.

An IRA does not have to be "qualified" in the same way as qualified plans have to be qualified; the IRS does not issue individual "determination letters" for IRAs. Rev. Proc. 87-50, 1987-2 C.B. 647,

§ 4.03. Furthermore, the IRA provider typically does not have sufficient information to enforce the minimum distribution rules; for example, the IRA provider has no way of knowing whether Participant satisfied the MRD requirement for that IRA by taking a larger distribution from another IRA held by a different provider (¶ 1.9.01). The penalty for failure to take the MRD falls on the payee, not on the IRA provider.

The proposed regulations impose a new burden on IRA providers: reporting to the IRS annually, not only the year-end account value of each IRA (as they already do), but also the amount of the MRD for the year in question. P.R. § 1.408-8, A-10. For example, if the reporting requirement is in effect for 2003, the IRA provider will have to report the 12/31/2003 balance, and will also have to report the 2003 required distribution (which is based on the 12/31/*2002* balance). This will enable the IRS more easily to police compliance with the minimum distribution rules. The IRS can compare the individual's 1040 with the IRA providers' reports, and see if the total IRA distributions reported by the taxpayer match the total MRDs reported by all his IRA providers.

The effective date for this new reporting requirement has not been established. P.R., Preamble, "IRA reporting of required minimum distributions." The IRS is considering whether to extend the MRD reporting requirement to 403(b) plans. P.R., Preamble, "IRA reporting of required minimum distributions."

> The proposed regulations' requirement that IRA providers report MRD amounts to the IRS was the subject of major objections by the IRA provider industry. This feature of the proposed regulations may change in the final version.
>
> Final regs: The IRS (did not modify this rule) (did modify this rule as follows:)

1.9.06 *50% penalty for failure to take MRD*

§ 4974 imposes a penalty for failure to take a required distribution. The penalty is 50% of the amount that was supposed to be, but was not, distributed. Based on anecdotal evidence, the IRS has made little or no attempt to collect this penalty from anyone since 1986. Presumably enforcement will become more vigorous once final minimum distribution regulations are issued.

Minimum distributions can be delayed beyond the normal deadline (¶ 1.2.03) in only two situations: a review period for QDROs and (in the case of insured plans) delay caused by receivership of the insurance company. P.R. § 1.401(a)(9)-8, A-7, A-8.

There are two provisions for waiver of the penalty. In the case of a Participant who dies before his RBD, *if there is only one individual beneficiary*, the penalty is automatically waived if Participant's entire benefit is distributed by the end of the fifth calendar year following the calendar year in which Participant died. P.R. § 54.4974-2, A-8(b). It is not clear why the IRS would limit this reasonable provision to the situation in which there is only one individual beneficiary.

The 50% penalty tax can be waived by the IRS on a case-by-case basis (§ 4974(d)) "if the payee described in section 4974(a) establishes to the satisfaction of the Commissioner" that "(1) The shortfall...in the amount distributed in any taxable year was due to reasonable error; and (2) Reasonable steps are being taken to remedy the shortfall." P.R. § 54.4974-2, A-8(a). If you want to request a waiver of the penalty then presumably "to remedy the shortfall" you would have to take a distribution of not only the distribution that was missed but also the income the undistributed MRD earned between December 31 of the year in which you should have taken the MRD out of the plan and the date you actually take it out of the plan. There is no guidance on how to calculate this.

Although the proposed regulation doesn't say so, the IRS wants you to pay the penalty first and then request a refund. See IRS Publication 590 (2000), p. 35, "Excess Accumulations (Insufficient Distributions)," and instructions for Form 5329 (2000), Part VII. The form to file to report the penalty is 5329. It is supposed to be attached to Form 1040 for the year the distribution was missed. Instructions for Form 5329 (2000), "When and Where to File." According to Publication 590 and the instructions to Form 5329, you are supposed to file amended 1040's for each year in which the MRD was not taken just to add the Form 5329 for each year.

Reminder: The point of filing amended returns is *not* to add the missed distributions back in to your income for those years. The minimum distribution rules do not create "constructive distributions" of the MRD amounts; you actually have to take the distribution in order to have income to report. The income is properly reported in the later year, when the (late) distribution is actually taken. The amended 1040 will show the same income, but a new higher tax (because of the 50% penalty).

For how to compute the penalty, see Reg. § 54.4974-1.

1.10 Summary of Planning Principles

1.   The opportunity for continued income tax deferral on plan contributions and investment income is the most valuable feature of qualified retirement plans and IRAs. Preserving the option of continued tax deferral is an important goal of estate planning for retirement benefits. The minimum distribution rules set the outer limits on deferral and establish the requirements for reaching those limits. Planning for retirement benefits therefore requires familiarity with these rules.

2.   Naming a beneficiary for retirement benefits does more than determine who will receive the benefits after Participant's death; it also determines the maximum period of income tax deferral that will be available for those benefits.

3.   Naming Participant's "estate" as beneficiary generally reduces the opportunities for continued income tax deferral compared with naming an individual beneficiary.

4.   Naming a trust as beneficiary has the same effect as naming an estate, unless the "trust rules" (¶ 6.2) are complied with.

5.   Naming a young beneficiary will produce the longest possible income tax deferral.

6.   If Participant is naming more than one beneficiary, consider structuring the benefits as "separate accounts payable to different beneficiaries" (¶ 1.7.06), especially if the beneficiaries are substantially apart in age, or if the group includes both individual beneficiaries (or qualifying trusts; ¶ 6.2) and non-individual beneficiaries (such as a charity), to enable each individual beneficiary (and qualifying trust) to use his or her own life expectancy (or the life expectancy of the trust beneficiary) to measure required distributions after Participant's death.

2

Income Taxes:
IRD; LSD; NUA; Rollovers

*The impact of federal income taxes on
estate planning for retirement benefits*

This Chapter examines the federal income tax treatment of retirement benefits: how benefits are taxed (as "income in respect of a decedent" or "IRD") after the death of the participant; the special tax treatment given to certain lump sum distributions and distributions of employer stock; and deferring income taxes with "rollovers."

2.1 Income Tax Treatment: In General

This ¶ 2.1 explains the federal income tax treatment of non-annuity distributions from QRPs, IRAs and 403(b) plans. This book does not cover state or local income taxes.

2.1.01 *Plan distributions includible in gross income*

Income taxation of distributions from qualified retirement plans ("QRPs") is governed by § 402(a), which provides that, except as otherwise provided in § 402, "any amount actually distributed to any distributee by any employees' trust described in section 401(a) which is exempt from tax under section 501(a) shall be taxable to the distributee, in the taxable year of the distributee in which distributed, under section 72 (relating to annuities)." § 408(d)(1) provides similarly for distributions from IRAs, as § 403(b)(1) does for 403(b) plans. See ¶ 5.2 regarding distributions from Roth IRAs.

If the distribution occurs after Participant's death § 691 also applies; see ¶ 2.2.

§ 72 is one of the most complicated sections of the Code. It has lengthy rules dealing with: taxation of distributions (and deemed distributions) from annuity contracts, employer plans, life insurance contracts and modified endowment contracts; how the "investment in the contract" (basis) is apportioned among distributions; and various penalties. Since this ¶ 2.1 covers only non-annuity distributions from QRPs, IRAs and 403(b) plans, there is no need to tackle most of the intricacies of § 72. Suffice it to say that all distributions (¶ 2.1.02) from a QRP, IRA or 403(b) plan are includible in the distributee's gross income as ordinary income unless an exception applies. The exceptions are listed in ¶ 2.1.03.

The only two parts of § 72 covered in depth in this book are the penalty for certain distributions before age 59½ (§ 72(t), covered in Chapter 9), and how to compute the non-taxable portion of distributions received from a plan to which Participant has made non-deductible contributions (¶ 2.1.04).

2.1.02 Actual distributions and deemed distributions

Generally, a Participant or beneficiary is taxable on QRP, IRA or 403(b) benefits only if, as and when such benefits are "actually distributed." §§ 402(a), 408(d)(1), 403(b)(1). The doctrine of "constructive receipt" (that income becomes taxable when it is "made available," not just when it is paid) does not apply to these benefits. Compare § 402(b), dealing with tax treatment of distributions from "nonexempt" employee benefit plans, providing that the employee is taxed on amounts "actually distributed *or made available.*"

However, there are certain events that can cause a Participant or beneficiary to be currently taxable on retirement benefits without an actual distribution. For example:

1.   After Participant's death, certain "assignments" of Participant's retirement plan benefits can trigger immediate realization of the underlying income as explained at ¶ 2.2.05.

2.   If a QRP ceases to be "qualified" under § 401(a), income taxation would cease to be governed by § 402(a); the results of this event are beyond the scope of this book.

3.   Under § 72(p) certain loans made by a QRP to the Participant may be treated as distributions at the time made or if the loan is defaulted. This book does not cover plan loans.

4.   § 408(e)(2) provides that "[I]f, during any taxable year of the individual for whose benefit any [IRA] is established, that

individual or his beneficiary engages in any transaction prohibited by section 4975 with respect to such account, such account ceases to be an individual retirement account as of the first day of such taxable year," and the individual will be taxed "as if there were a distribution on such first day in an amount equal to the fair market value (on such first day) of all assets in the account (on such first day)." This book does not cover prohibited transactions.

5.   "If, during any taxable year of the individual for whose benefit an individual retirement account is established, that individual uses the account or any portion thereof as security for a loan, the portion so used is treated as distributed to that individual." § 408(e)(4).

6.   The acquisition by any IRA (or by a self-directed account in a QRP) of a "collectible" (as defined in § 408(m)(2)) is treated as a distribution of the cost of the "collectible." § 408(m)(1).

7.   Lifetime assignment of a Roth IRA to "another individual" causes a deemed distribution of the account to Participant; see ¶ 5.5.07. Presumably the IRS would apply the same rule to traditional IRAs.

2.1.03 *Catalogue of no-tax or low-tax distributions*

As noted (¶ 2.1.01), retirement plan distributions are generally taxable to the recipient as ordinary income. Here is a list of all the exceptions to that general rule, with a cross reference telling where to find more information about each:

1.   "Qualified distributions" from a Roth IRA are tax-free. ¶ 5.2.01.

2.   Distributions "rolled over" to another retirement plan are tax-free if various requirements are met. Tax-free rollovers are discussed at ¶ 2.5 and ¶ 3.2.

3.   Distributions of life insurance proceeds from a QRP are partly tax-free; see ¶ 8.3.05. Distribution of a life insurance policy on

an employee's life to that employee may be partly tax-free as a return of basis. ¶ 8.3.03.

4.   See ¶ 2.1.04 regarding tax-free return of Participant's non-deductible contributions.

5.   Certain distributions of "employer stock" from a QRP are eligible for deferred taxation at capital gains rates rather than immediate taxation at ordinary income rates. See ¶ 2.4.

6.   Certain lump sum distributions from QRPs to individuals born before 1936 are eligible for reduced tax; see ¶ 2.3.06-¶ 2.3.12.

7.   While a distribution to a Participant's beneficiary after Participant's death is taxable just as it would have been if made to Participant during life, the beneficiary is entitled to an income tax deduction for federal estate taxes paid on the benefits; see ¶ 2.2.08.

8.   If Participant's beneficiary is income tax-exempt, the beneficiary will not have to pay income tax on the distribution. See generally Chapter 7 and in particular ¶ 7.5.01.

2.1.04 *Recovery of Participant's basis (investment in the contract)*

A Participant's non-deductible contributions to a QRP, traditional IRA or Roth IRA are not subject to income tax when distributed by the plan. In the lingo of § 72, these contributions are considered Participant's "investment in the contract," or what might be more familiarly called his "basis." The tricky part is knowing, for any particular distribution, how much of that distribution can be treated as a tax-free return of Participant's investment in the contract (also called "recovery of Participant's basis"). The rules are different depending on the type of plan.

See ¶ 5.4.10-¶ 5.4.12 for explanation of how much of a distribution from a traditional IRA is treated as recovery of basis.

See ¶ 5.2.03 for explanation of how much of a non-qualified distribution from a Roth IRA is tax-free as recovery of basis (qualified distributions from Roth IRAs are 100% tax-free; ¶ 5.2.01).

Regarding after-tax contributions to QRPs, usually the employer maintains a separate accounting for the employ*ee* contribution account (meaning the employee's after-tax contributions and the earnings thereon) and the employ*er* contribution account (meaning the employer's contributions and the earnings thereon). If the employee were to take an instalment or annuity payout of the employee contribution account as well as the employer contribution account, recovery of the after-tax contributions would be determined under § 72 and is beyond the scope of this book.

To avoid the complications of § 72, typically the employee takes a lump sum distribution of the employee contribution account. That distribution is non-taxable to the extent it represents the employee's non-deductible (after-tax) contributions; the employee may choose to roll over the taxable part of that distribution tax-free to an IRA. See, e.g., PLR 9840041. The employee then takes a lump sum distribution or instalment or annuity payout of the employer contribution account, all distributions from which are fully taxable. This typical scenario may change as a result of EGTRRA 2001, which permits non-taxable as well as taxable portions of the employee's account to be rolled over to another retirement plan; see ¶ 5.4.12.

2.1.05 *Withholding of federal income taxes*

Retirement plan distributions are subject to withholding of federal income taxes. § 3405. This fact creates problems and planning opportunities. This book does not cover state or local withholding requirements.

The withholding requirement distinguishes between "periodic payments," "non-periodic" payments, and "eligible rollover distributions." Periodic payments from all types of retirement plans are subject to withholding of taxes at the same rate as wages. Non-periodic payments are subject to withholding at a flat rate of 10%. The recipient can elect out of having anything withheld from either a periodic or a non-periodic payment, so the withholding is voluntary.

"Eligible rollover distributions" from qualified retirement plans (QRP) are subject to withholding at a 20% rate, and the recipient can*not* elect out. The only way to avoid the 20% withholding is to have the distribution paid directly to an eligible retirement plan ("direct rollover").

This ¶ 2.1.05 discusses the details of each type of withholding, and the planning opportunities and pitfalls. Exceptions and special cases are discussed at ¶ 2.1.06.

The Code defines "periodic payment" as a distribution that is "an annuity or similar periodic payment." § 3405(e)(2). The IRS says "periodic payments are pension or annuity payments made for more than 1 year that are not eligible rollover distributions," and include "substantially equal payments made at least once a year over the life of the employee and/or beneficiaries or for 10 years or more." IRS Publication 15A, "Employer's Supplemental Tax Guide" (§ 9, Pensions and Annuities). An "annuity" is "a series of payments payable over a period greater than one year and taxable under section 72...whether or not the payments are variable in amount." Reg. § 35.3405-1T, A-9.

The distinction between periodic payments and non-periodic payments is a little vague, but is not terribly important. Both types are subject to withholding by all types of plans, and with both types the recipient can elect out of having anything withheld. The only difference is the rate of withholding, but since the recipient can arrange to have either more or less withheld from either type of payment the statutorily prescribed rate of withholding is not terribly important.

The significant distinction is between "eligible rollover distributions" and the other types of payments, because withholding from an eligible rollover distribution is mandatory unless the distribution is sent by direct rollover to another retirement plan. An "eligible rollover distribution" is basically any distribution from a qualified plan (§ 402(c)(1)(A)) or (after 2001) 403(b) plan that is eligible to be rolled over. § 3405; § 402(f)(2)(A). For list of distributions eligible or not eligible to be rolled over, see ¶ 2.5.02.

The mandatory withholding on eligible rollover distributions does not pose a problem if someone simply wants to get the money out of the QRP without paying any income tax until the following April 15. All such person has to do is have his distribution transferred directly (a "direct rollover") into an IRA, so the qualified plan doesn't have to withhold anything; and then take the money out of the IRA (electing out of withholding on the IRA distribution).

The person for whom mandatory withholding is truly mandatory is the person who wants to take a lump sum distribution and qualify for special averaging treatment (¶ 2.3.06). This person cannot roll over any part of the distribution, and so will be forced to pay 20% income tax on it through withholding. He can get a refund when he files his tax return for the year of the distribution, if his total tax payments (including this withholding) exceed his actual tax liability.

2.1.06 *Withholding: exceptions and special rules*

A retirement plan does not have to withhold taxes from a distribution to the extent it is "reasonable to believe" that the distribution is not includible in the payee's income. For some reason this exception is not applicable to a traditional IRA. § 3405(e)(1)(B)(ii); Reg. § 35.3405-1T, A-2.

If the entire distribution consists of securities of the employer corporation (as defined in § 402(e)(4)(E)) (and up to $200 cash "in lieu of financial shares," whatever that means), there is no withholding. If the distribution consists of securities of the employer corporation plus cash and other property, the maximum amount that may be withheld is the value of the cash and other property. § 3405(e)(8). In connection with that sort of mixed distribution, "it is reasonable to believe that all net unrealized appreciation from employer securities is not includible in gross income." Reg. § 35.3405-1T, A-30; see ¶ 2.4.

There is no withholding on dividends paid to participants on employer securities held in the plan. § 3405(e)(1)(B)(ii); § 404(k)(2).

2.2 Income in Respect of a Decedent (IRD)

For treatment of IRD payable to a charity or charitable remainder trust see Chapter 7.

2.2.01 *No stepped-up basis for IRD*

An individual who inherits property from someone who dies before 2010 does not simply take over the decedent's income tax basis in the property; rather, the inheritor's future gain or loss will be computed by reference to the value of that property as of the decedent's date of death (or as of the "alternate valuation date," if that date was used to compute the decedent's federal estate tax). § 1014(c). This tax rule is usually referred to as "stepped-up basis," on the assumption that the property appreciated between the time the decedent acquired it and the date of death, although of course it might have declined in value (in which case there is really a "stepped-down basis").

However, "property which constitutes a right to receive an item of income in respect of a decedent" (IRD) is an exception: IRD does not get a new basis at death. Instead of a stepped-up basis, an individual who inherits IRD takes over the decedent's basis ("carryover basis").

After 2009, § 1014(c) is repealed and "carryover basis" will apply generally to all assets. Therefore, generally, an individual who inherits an asset from someone who dies after 2009 will take over the decedent's basis. This change will *somewhat* "level the playing field" between IRD and non-IRD assets, but will not totally eliminate it for three reasons:

A.   Even after 2009, there will be a limited stepped-up basis: the decedent's executor will have the power to allocate $1 million of "basis step-up" among the decedent's appreciated assets. Even more "step-up" can be allocated among assets left to the surviving spouse. IRD will not be eligible for the allocation of basis step-up.

B.   Retirement plan distributions will be taxable as ordinary income, while the built-in gain in other inherited assets may be eligible for capital gain treatment.

C.   Section 901 of EGTRRA reinstates § 1014(c) (as in effect prior to EGTRRA) for deaths after 2010.

IRD is not defined in the Code, but may be generally defined as income earned by an individual that is not realized until after his death.

2.2.02 *When IRD is taxed*

§ 691 governs the income tax treatment of IRD. Under § 691(a)(1), IRD is includible (when received) in the gross income of the person or entity who acquired, from the decedent, the right to receive such income. This could be the estate (if the right to receive the income passes to the estate as a result of decedent's death); or a person who is entitled to receive the income directly as decedent's beneficiary under a retirement plan or similar arrangement; or a beneficiary who is entitled to receive the IRD by virtue of a bequest under the decedent's will.

§ 691(a)(2), in addition, imposes a tax on the transfer of the right-to-receive IRD by the person or entity who received the right-to-receive the IRD from the decedent. However, there is an exception: the tax is *not* imposed on a transfer of the right-to-receive IRD to the person who is *entitled* to the IRD by reason of the decedent's death or as a result of a bequest from the decedent.

So, § 691 makes a distinction between "IRD" and "the right-to-receive IRD." Generally, IRD is taxed to the recipient upon receipt; but if the right-to-receive the IRD is transferred, the transfer will trigger an income tax unless the exception applies.

Death benefits under qualified plans, 403(b) plans, and IRAs are IRD, and thus will be subject to income tax when distributed to the beneficiary (except to the extent such distribution is excludible from gross income; see ¶ 2.1.03).

Thus, retirement benefits are generally subject to *both* estate taxes and income taxes. This creates numerous planning considerations, one of which is the desirability of deferring the imposition of income taxes as long as possible; see Chapter 1.

Another planning consideration is, once distribution does occur, how to keep the income tax as low as possible, for example by leaving these benefits to beneficiaries in a low income tax bracket.

2.2.03 *Drawback of making IRD payable to a trust*

IRD paid to a trust is generally subject to trust income tax rates. A trust generally pays higher tax than an individual taxpayer on the same amount of income. See ¶ 6.1.03. Thus, making retirement benefits payable to a marital, credit shelter or other trust may result in the benefits' being taxed more heavily than if the benefits were paid to individual family members. See ¶ 10.5.

Note that IRD distributed from a retirement plan to a trust is generally "principal" for trust accounting purposes. However, for *income tax purposes*, it is "income." See ¶ 6.1.07.

2.2.04 *Tax treatment of IRD paid to an estate*

IRD items will be taxed to the estate if paid to the estate. However, if the estate, before actually receiving the income, distributes the *right* to receive the income, then:

(a)   the distributee will be taxable on the income, if he/she acquired it by specific bequest or as residuary legatee of the estate; Reg. § 1.691(a)-2(b), Examples (1) and (2); § 1.691(a)-4(b).

(b)   If the distribution is treated as a "sale," however, the estate is taxable (on the greater of the value of the right transferred, or the consideration—if any—received for the transfer). Reg. § 1.691(a)-4(a). See ¶ 2.2.05.

If the will leaves retirement benefits to a particular beneficiary, but the benefits are paid to the estate before the estate gets a chance to assign the "right-to-receive" the benefits to that beneficiary, distributing the benefits to the beneficiary upon receipt should carry out the taxable income to the beneficiary. See ¶ 6.1.03. Although normally all items of income are pro-rated proportionately among beneficiaries who receive distributions, a different allocation specified in the governing instrument is respected. Reg. § 1.661(b)-1; § 1.663. See ¶ 7.4.06.
The following examples illustrate these rules.

Example 1: Larry names Liz as beneficiary of his IRA. Liz is taxable on IRA distributions she receives after Larry's death.

Example 2: Mike names his estate as beneficiary of his IRA. His will provides that any IRA benefits are specifically bequeathed to Liz. After Mike's death, the estate assigns the IRA to Liz. Liz pays the tax on the IRA distributions.

Example 3: Eddie names his estate as beneficiary of his IRA. His will provides that any IRA benefits are specifically bequeathed to Liz. After Eddie's death, all property in the IRA is distributed to Eddie's estate. The executor immediate transfers the distributed property out to Liz in the same taxable year that the funds were received. Liz pays the tax on the IRA distributions.

If the right-to-receive IRD is distributed as a specific "bequest" from a *trust*, rather than an *estate*, the same principles should apply: the beneficiary who is entitled to the item, and not the trust, bears the income tax. Reg. § 1.691(a)-(4)(b); § 1.663.(c)-2(b)(3).
If the right-to-receive is distributed to the trust beneficiaries under a discretionary power to distribute principal, do the beneficiaries pay the income tax? Presumably the answer is yes, although the regulations provide only that if a trust *terminates* and distributes the right-to-receive to the beneficiaries, the beneficiaries pay the tax. Reg. § 1.691(a)-4(b)(3). Professor Jeffrey Pennell points out that possibly a discretionary distribution of principal would be considered a "partial

termination" of the trust and thus fit within the regulation cited.

2.2.05 *Assignment of the right-to-receive IRD*

The major planning pitfall of IRD has to do with "assignments" of the right-to-receive such income, which trigger immediate tax under § 691(a)(2). The problem of assignment of the right-to-receive IRD does not exist when IRD assets are divided up to fulfill fractional bequests; see, *e.g.,* PLR 9537005, Ruling 7. The pitfall comes when the right-to-receive IRD is used to satisfy a pecuniary bequest.

It is axiomatic among estate planners that a distribution of the right-to-receive IRD in fulfillment of a pecuniary bequest triggers immediate realization of income by the estate or other funding entity.[1] In view of the universality of this belief, it is surprising to learn that this result is not specified in any Code section, Treasury regulation or

---

[1]See, *e.g.*, Alan S. Acker, Income in Respect of a Decedent, 862 Tax Mgmt. (BNA), at A-11; Jonathan G. Blattmachr, "Income in Respect of a Decedent," 12 Probate Notes 47 (1986), 50; Natalie B. Choate, Life and Death Planning for Retirement Benefits, 1st ed., (Foundation for Continuing Education, 1993); CCH 1997 Standard Federal Tax Reporter, ¶25,306.0112; M. Carr Ferguson, *et al.*, Federal Income Taxation of Estates, Trust and Beneficiaries (2d ed. 1997) at 3:27; E. James Gamble, "Planning for Distributions from Retirement Plans," N.Y.U. Proceedings of the Forty-Fifth Institute on Federal Taxation, Vol. 1, Ch. 27, § 27.04[5] last paragraph (1987, p. 27-15); Norman H. Lane and Howard M. Zaritzky, Federal Income Taxation of Estates and Trusts, 2d Ed., (Warren Gorham & Lamont, 1988-1997) ¶15.08, pp.15-54,55; Alson Martin, Esq., "Recent Developments/Estate Planning/Post Mortem Planning for QRPs and IRAs," in course materials for ALI-ABA seminar Professional Organizations, Qualified Plans, etc., 2/98, at p. 103; Louis A. Mezzullo, Estate and Gift Tax Issues for Employee Benefit Plans, 378 Tax Mgmt. (BNA) A-31; Michael D. Mulligan, "Planning for Income in Respect of a Decedent Can Minimize Effects of Double Taxation," 57 J. Tax'n 22, pp. 106-112 (1982); Willard B. Thompson, "How to Structure a Trust as Beneficiary of a Qualified Plan or IRA Death Benefits," Estate Planning, January/February 1988 at p. 10.

Revenue Ruling, nor has any reported case ever so held.

However, this widely held belief does not spring out of thin air. It derives partly from the regulations under § 691(a)(2). The IRS, in its regulations, does not come right out and say that transferring the right-to-receive IRD in fulfilment of a pecuniary bequest is treated as a non-exempt transfer of the right-to-receive, but strongly implies it. Reg. § 1.691(a)-4(b)(2) says that, if the right-to-receive IRD is transferred to "a *specific* or *residuary* legatee" (emphasis added), only the legatee includes the IRD in income. The negative implication is that fulfilling a *pecuniary* bequest with the right-to-receive IRD does *not* carry out the income tax burden to the legatee. In other words, the regulation implies that satisfying a pecuniary bequest with the right-to-receive IRD should be treated as a "sale," just as (under Reg. § 1.661(a)-2(f)(1)) satisfying a pecuniary bequest with appreciated property is treated as a "sale."

Furthermore, the IRS has indicated in several private letter rulings that it considers the "sale" principle of §1.661(a)-2(f)(1) applicable to funding a pecuniary bequest with the right-to-receive IRD. PLRs 9123036 (using an installment obligation to fund a pecuniary credit shelter gift would trigger realization of gain); 9315016 and 9507008 (satisfying pecuniary legacies with Series E or H bonds triggers realization by the funding entity of the untaxed interest accruals on the bonds, which were IRD).

IRD, however, is taxed under § 691, not §§ 661-663. It is taxed only when § 691 says it is taxed. § 691's standards for carrying out the income tax burden to the beneficiaries are not the same as the "DNI" rules of §§ 661-663. Thus, it is quite logical, under the Code, that a pecuniary bequest funded with *IRD* could carry the income tax burden to the beneficiary when funding the same bequest with *appreciated property* would not.

Example: Ron dies, leaving his $1 million IRA payable to his trust as beneficiary. The trust contains a pecuniary formula marital bequest, under which the marital trust is entitled to $400,000. The trust holds no other assets except the IRA. Ron's trustee transfers $400,000 of the IRA to the marital trust and keeps the rest for the residuary credit shelter trust. In this example, surely the IRA is transferred to the marital trust "by bequest from the decedent." The funding trust is not "selling" or "exchanging" the IRA—it is fulfilling the pecuniary marital bequest, and a transfer in fulfillment of a bequest is not taxable under § 691(a)(2). The trust has no choice regarding which asset to use to fund the marital trust—the IRA is the only asset available.

Most commentators assume that transferring IRD in fulfillment of a pecuniary bequest is exactly the same as fulfilling such a bequest with appreciated property in kind, but the rationale for taxing the transfer of appreciated property in fulfillment of a pecuniary bequest does not exist in the case of Ron's IRA. When a pecuniary bequest is fulfilled by a transfer of appreciated property in kind, the transaction is treated as a "sale" of that property because the residuary estate has, by this transaction, realized the benefit of the appreciation that has occurred between the date of death and the date of funding the bequest. The residuary estate has an asset which has grown in value, and uses this to satisfy a fixed dollar liability, thereby in effect "cashing in" that appreciation to satisfy its obligation. The recipient of the pecuniary bequest did *not* benefit from the appreciation, because he would have received the same dollar value either way, whether in cash or in property.

IRD, however, is different. The right-to-receive IRD is not "appreciated property." In fact a retirement plan such as an IRA, which is a common form of "right-to-receive IRD," could easily have *depreciated* in value between the date of death and the date of funding particular bequests. The residuary estate has not necessarily realized any "profit" by funding the pecuniary bequest with IRD, or, if it has realized a gain, it is only to the extent there has been appreciation after the date of death, not to the extent of the entire value of the asset.

Although the precise question discussed here has never been decided, the principle that § 691 overrides the §§ 661-662 scheme is established in other contexts. On the question of whether an estate can take a distributions deduction (¶ 6.1.03) for distributing the right-to-receive IRD, the Tax Court (in holding that the estate can not take such a deduction despite the specific language of § 661(a), which appears to allow deduction) has stated that, "We hold as a general principle that section 691 overrides sections 661 and 662" (Edmund D. Rollert Residuary Trust, 85-1 USTC ¶ 9139 (C.A. 6); 752 F2d 112) and "...the transfer by an estate of section 691 property is treated as a neutral event, and is not subject to the distribution rules of section 661 and 662" (Estate of Jack Dean, 46 TCM 184 (1983)). As one source put it, "the general distribution rules of subchapter J...do not apply to distributions of rights to [IRD]...[the DNI] scheme is antagonistic to the rules of section 691...Section 691...prevails over the rules relating generally to distributions, and a transfer to a beneficiary of property representing [IRD] is treated as a neutral event." James J. Freeland, *et al.,* "Estate and Trust Distribution of Property in Kind After the Tax Reform Act of 1984," 38 Tax L. Rev. 449, 463 (1985).

2.2.06 *Letter rulings allow fulfilling pecuniary bequests with IRD*

Letter rulings indicate that the IRS *may* have recognized that transferring retirement benefits in fulfillment of a pecuniary marital bequest is not a § 691(a)(2) transfer. In PLR 9524020 an estate was allowed to transfer an IRA directly to a surviving spouse in fulfillment of a pecuniary spousal share under state statute.

PLR 9608036 involved the transfer of an IRA by a pourover trust in fulfillment of a pecuniary formula marital gift. The ruling treated the IRA, for purposes of the spousal rollover rules, as acquired by the spouse "from the decedent," not "from the trust." If the IRA were deemed acquired "from the trust" (a "third party") rather than "from the decedent," it would not have been eligible for rollover under § 408, according to the ruling. This logic is similar to that of § 691(a)(2), under which a transfer of the right-to-receive IRD to one who is entitled to it by bequest *from the decedent* is not a taxable event, while a transfer to any other person *is* taxable.

In PLR 9623056 the decedent's IRA was payable to a trust which was also the residuary beneficiary of his will. The trust created a marital trust by means of a pecuniary marital formula, and a residuary credit shelter trust. The IRA was not payable to either of these specific subtrusts. The IRS permitted a tax-free rollover by the spouse of the portion of the IRA allocated to the marital trust.

In PLR 9808043 an IRA was payable to Participant's estate. The will left a "pecuniary formula marital bequest outright to" the spouse, and left "the remainder" to a "credit shelter trust." Because the surviving spouse, as executrix, was entitled to and did use the IRA to fund the pecuniary marital bequest, and the bequest was outright, the IRS ruled that the surviving spouse was entitled to roll over the IRA proceeds distributed to her via the pecuniary bequest.

In none of these four rulings did the IRS say that the transfer of the IRA generated current income to the funding entity. Although the IRS did not mention IRD or § 691(a)(2) in any of these rulings, in view of the emphasis on the fact that pecuniary bequests were involved it is hard to believe the IRS is overlooking the § 691(a)(2) issue time after time.

A possible explanation, which would make these rulings consistent with the otherwise apparently inconsistent letter rulings (holding that Reg. § 661(a)-2(f)(1) applies to funding a pecuniary bequest with the right-to-receive IRD), *may* be found in the statutory conflict between §§ 402 and 408, on the one hand, and § 691(a)(2) on the other. The Code provides that the income represented by qualified plans and IRAs is included in gross income only when it is "actually distributed" (§ 402(a)) or "paid or distributed" (§ 408(d)(1)). These provisions override other normal income tax rules such as the doctrine of constructive receipt. (See ¶ 2.1.02). Perhaps they also override § 691(a)(2).

For more on this issue, see Choate, N., "Mysteries of IRD," Tax Management Memorandum, Vol. 38, No. 20, p. 235 (Tax Management Inc., Washington, D.C., 9/29/97). See also discussion at Acker, *supra*, at § VII(A)(1)(g),(h), p. A-27; and PLR 1999-25033 in which the IRS ruled that a non-pro rata division of community property, in which a surviving spouse took the decedent's IRA as part of the surviving spouse's share of the community property, did not constitute a § 691(a)(2) "assignment."

Planning mode: Because of the IRS' apparent position that funding a pecuniary bequest with IRD is a taxable transfer, planners are strongly advised to avoid having retirement benefits pass through a pecuniary funding formula. If benefits must pass to a trust, make them payable to a trust that is not going to have to be divided up. If the benefits are going to a trust which will be divided among various shares (*e.g.*, a marital and a family share), either specify clearly (in both the designation of beneficiary form and in the trust instrument) which trust share these retirement benefits go to (so that the benefits pass to the chosen share directly, rather than through the funding formula), or use a fractional formula (fulfillment of which does not trigger immediate realization of IRD) rather than a pecuniary formula (which may).

Cleanup mode: Although it is highly advisable to steer clear of funding a pecuniary bequest with qualified plan or IRA benefits, inevitably some participants will leave their benefits payable to a trust which contains a pecuniary funding formula. In these circumstances, first look into the possibility of using disclaimers to get the benefits payable to the "right" beneficiary (see Chapter 8). If that course is not available, and the retirement benefit must pass through the pecuniary funding formula, see if the benefits can be passed through the pecuniary formula to the spouse for a spousal rollover (see letter rulings cited above), and the other arguments cited above for why funding the pecuniary gift with this asset should not trigger tax.

2.2.07 *Income tax deduction for estate tax paid on IRD*

The federal estate tax paid on IRD is deductible for federal income tax purposes. § 691(c). To determine the amount of the deduction, first determine the estate tax actually due on the entire estate. Next, determine the net value of all items of IRD that were includible in the estate. For definition of net value see § 691(c)(2)(B). The estate tax attributable to the IRD is the difference between the actual federal estate tax due on the estate, and the federal estate tax that would have been due had all the IRD had been excluded from the estate.

Example: Harvey dies in 1999, leaving his $2 million taxable estate (including a $1 million pension plan) to his daughter Emma. The federal estate tax on a $2 million taxable estate, after deducting the unified credit and the maximum credit for state death taxes, is $469,900. If the $1 million IRA were excluded from the taxable estate, the taxable estate would be only $1 million, and the federal estate tax would be $101,300. Thus the amount of federal estate tax attributable to the IRA is $469,900 minus $101,300, or $368,600. Emma will be entitled to an income tax deduction of $368,600 which she can claim when she receives the $1 million pension distribution.

Note also the following:

1.   The deductible portion of the estate tax is computed at the marginal rate, not the average rate; this is favorable to the taxpayer. In the Harvey and Emma example above, even though the IRA constituted only 50% of the taxable estate, it accounted for 75% of the estate tax, so the IRD deduction equals 75% of the total estate tax.

2.   Under EGTRRA, federal estate taxes are scheduled to be reduced (through increasing exemptions and declining top rates)

for deaths in years 2002 through 2009; the federal estate tax is repealed for deaths in 2010; and the estate tax is reinstated (under EGTRRA's sunset provision, § 901) for deaths in 2011 and later. EGTRRA did not repeal or amend § 691, so if federal estate taxes are paid (because Participant died in a year in which the estate tax was in effect), they can be deducted when the beneficiary receives a distribution from the plan, even if the distribution comes in a year when the estate tax no longer exists.

3.   State estate taxes are *not* deductible. Under EGTRRA, the credit allowed against the federal estate tax for *state* death taxes paid by the estate, is phased out (for estates of decedents dying in 2002-2004) and then repealed (for deaths in 2005 or later). § 2011. The immediate effect of this change, for beneficiaries of decedents in "sponge tax" states, is to make a higher proportion of the total estate tax bill deductible for income tax purposes under § 691. "Sponge tax" states are those which impose no death tax other than the amount allowed as a credit against federal estate taxes under § 2011. In these states, the state death tax will automatically disappear as the credit disappears. These states may react by imposing new forms of death taxes, in which case the benefit beneficiaries receive from their increased § 691(c) deduction will presumably be taken away by other means.

4.   The computation of the § 691(c) deduction becomes more complex if a marital or charitable deduction is involved; this topic is beyond the scope of this book. See Westfall and Mair, *Estate Planning Law and Taxation* (3d ed., Warren, Gorham & Lamont, Boston, 1998), ¶ 14.02.

2.2.08 *Planning for client with short life expectancy*

There are times when an estate planner is called upon to advise a client who, due to accident or illness, has a severely shortened life expectancy. One suggestion to consider is cashing out retirement plan benefits that will have to be cashed out anyway shortly after the client's demise (either because of minimum distribution requirements, or to pay estate taxes, or just because the beneficiaries will want the money).

When an IRA or other tax-deferred retirement plan will have to be cashed out shortly after Participant's death, *and* the estate will be subject to estate taxes, there are several reasons why it is better to cash out the account immediately *before* death rather than immediately after:

First, if the plan is cashed out before death, the income taxes on the benefits are thereby removed from the estate for estate tax purposes—in effect, both the federal *and* state income taxes on the benefits become 100% deductible for estate tax purposes. If the plan is cashed out *after* death, the recipient of the benefits gets a federal income tax deduction under § 691(c) for the *federal* estate taxes paid on the benefits (¶ 2.2.07)—but *not* for the *state* estate taxes.

Second, the § 691(c) deduction is an itemized deduction, and as such may not be fully deductible; see ¶ 2.2.11. Finally, the recipient may not be able to take the § 691(c) deduction in determining his *state* income tax.

For all these reasons, paying the income taxes "first" and the estate taxes "second" may produce a lower tax burden overall than doing it the other way round. Another way to get the same advantages is to convert to a Roth IRA if the client is eligible; see ¶ 5.5.06.

On the other hand, if the death benefits are going to be paid to charity (so they will not be subject to income taxes—see Chapter 7), or will be paid to a designated beneficiary over a long life expectancy (so the income taxes can be deferred for a long time—see Chapter 1) this arbitrage advantage disappears. Similarly, if the beneficiary is in a lower income tax bracket than Participant, that may reduce the arbitrage advantage. Finally, if the estate will not be subject to estate tax, there is no known tax advantage to cashing out the plans before death.

2.2.09 *Who gets the § 691(c) deduction*

The § 691(c) deduction goes to the person who receives the IRD, not the person who paid the estate tax. If there are several beneficiaries who receive the IRD, the deduction is apportioned among them in proportion to the amounts of IRD each received.

Example: Jack dies with an estate of $3 million. He leaves his $1 million IRA (which is entirely IRD) to his daughters Jill and Holly. He leaves his $2 million probate estate (which is not IRD) to his son Alex. Alex pays the federal estate tax of $897,500. The § 691(c) deduction goes equally to Jill and Holly because they received the IRD, even though Alex is the one who paid the estate tax.

2.2.10 § 691(c) deduction for installment and annuity payouts

Calculating the § 691(c) deduction is easy when the beneficiary receives a distribution of the entire benefit all at once. What if the retirement benefit is not distributed as a lump sum but rather in installments over the life expectancy of the beneficiary? Clearly the deduction will also be spread out; but how much of the deduction is allocated to each payment? How much of each distribution represents "IRD" that was included in the gross estate, and how much represents income earned by the retirement plan after the date of death?

When IRD is in the form of a joint and survivor *annuity*, the Code requires that the § 691(c) deduction be amortized over the surviving annuitant's life expectancy and apportioned equally to the annuity payments received by the survivor. § 691(d). However, no Code section, regulation or other official source discusses the allocation of the deduction to non-annuity payouts, such as instalment payments. For a catalogue of several possible alternative methods, see Hoyt, C.R., "Inherited IRAs: When Deferring Distributions Doesn't Make Sense," Trusts & Estates, June 1998, p. 52. For possible future developments in this area, keep an eye on QDOT regulations and rulings, where deciding which retirement plan distributions constitute IRD and which constitute post-death earnings is critical to application of the deferred estate tax; see Chapter 4.

Meanwhile, the method used by many practitioners (based on an unscientific survey by the author) could be called the "IRD comes out first" method. All distributions from the retirement plan are assumed to be coming out of the IRD (rather than out of the post-death earnings of the plan) until the § 691(c) deduction has been entirely used up:

Example: In the Jack and Jill example above, the total § 691(c) deduction was $427,600, which is 42.76% of the total $1 million IRA. Suppose the IRA has grown to be worth $1.2 million by the time Jill and Holly, the beneficiaries, take their first withdrawal of $30,000 each. They assume the distributions come entirely from the $1 million original principal of the IRA (from the IRD, in other words) and none of it from the $200,000 post-death earnings, so each daughter takes a deduction equal to 42.76% of her $30,000 distribution, or $12,801.

Each daughter keeps doing this until she has received a total of $500,000 of distributions from the IRA, at which point she has used up all of her 50% share of the $427,600 § 691(c) deduction.

2.2.11 § 691(c) deduction on the income tax return

The § 691(c) deduction is reported as an "other miscellaneous deduction" on the beneficiary's income tax return. As such, it is not subject to the 2% "floor" applicable to "miscellaneous itemized deductions." § 67(b)(7); see line instructions to IRS Form 1040, Schedule A. However, it is an "itemized deduction," and as such it is subject to the reduction of itemized deductions by up to 3% of AGI in excess of $132,950 (as of 2001), if paid to an *individual*. § 68.

The impact of the 3% reduction rule will vary from beneficiary to beneficiary depending on the size of the distribution and the amount of the beneficiary's other income and deductions. In the case of a high-income taxpayer, with few itemized deductions, the benefit of the § 691(c) deduction could be substantially reduced by the § 68 adjustment.

Example: In 2001, Joyce receives a $500,000 distribution from her deceased mother's IRA. She is single. Assume the § 691(c) deduction allocable to this distribution is $200,000, and that Joyce has other AGI of $2 million in excess of the $132,950 § 68 threshold, and no other itemized deductions. If she did not receive the $500,000 IRA distribution, her taxable income would be $2,132,950.

With the distribution, her income is:

Gross:		$2,632,950
Less: itemized deduction	200,000	
Reduced by (3% x $2,500,000)	-75,000	
	125,000	-125,000
Taxable income		$2,507,950

In the above example, the § 691(c) deduction is chopped from $200,000 to $125,000. The fact that the 3% reduction rule does not apply to trusts tends to offset somewhat the higher income tax bracket generally applicable to trusts (¶ 2.2.03).

Under EGTRRA, the reduction applicable under present law to itemized deductions of high income taxpayers is *itself* reduced in the years 2006-2009, so in those years high-income taxpayers will be entitled to deduct a higher proportion of their itemized deductions. EGTRRA then repeals § 68 effective in 2010 (but EGTRRA's sunset provision reinstates it in 2011 at 2001 levels). A high-income beneficiary who inherits a retirement plan that was subject to a large estate tax may want to consider deferring receipt of the income from the plan until 2010, if that's possible under the plan terms and the minimum distribution rules; deferring receipt until the repeal of § 68 is effective may increase the amount of the § 691(c) deduction such person can take.

2.3 Lump Sum Distributions

2.3.01 *Introduction to lump sum distributions*

Through the years, the Code has provided a special gentle treatment for "lump sum distributions" (LSD) from qualified plans. A person who wishes to obtain this special treatment is confronted with some of the most convoluted requirements known to post-ERISA man.

Congress has changed the rules on LSD treatment so often that the IRS has been unable to keep pace with regulations. There are only assorted proposed and temporary regulations issued from 1975 through 1979 (under old Code § 402(c)), which became obsolete before they could be finalized. The instructions for IRS Forms 4972 and 1099-R are often the best indication of the IRS's interpretation of the LSD rules.

From 1992 through 1999, the definition of LSD was found in § 402(d); after 1999, it went back to its pre-1992 home, § 402(e).

For years prior to 2000, an LSD from a qualified plan, as defined in § 402(d), could be eligible for various special tax treatments, including "five year forward averaging" ("5YFA") (§ 402(d)(1)); "10-year averaging" (¶ 2.3.06); "20% capital gain tax" for benefits attributable to pre-1974 participation (¶ 2.3.09); and the postponement of tax on the "net unrealized appreciation" of employer securities distributed as part of the LSD (¶ 2.4). As a result of changes made by the Small Business Jobs Protection Act of 1996, *one* of these special deals, 5YFA, ceased to be available for distributions after 1999. The requirements applicable to 5YFA are not covered in this edition of this book. For full details regarding this subject see pages 101-106 of the

1999 edition of this book.

To achieve the favorable tax treatment, the taxpayer must clear various requirement "hurdles," many of which are surrounded by hidden issue "landmines." The requirements that must be met in order for a distribution to qualify as an LSD, under both pre-2000 and post-1999 law, are summarized in ¶ 2.3.02 through ¶ 2.3.05. If a distribution clears the three hurdles described in ¶ 2.3.02 through ¶ 2.3.05 it is an LSD. That doesn't mean much, however, unless it meets further tests necessary to qualify for particular favorable tax treatments. If the LSD includes employer stock, see ¶ 2.4. If it meets numerous *additional* tests, it can qualify for special averaging treatment; see ¶ 2.3.06 through ¶ 2.3.12.

This ¶ 2.3 does not exhaust the intricacies of § 402(d). The following aspects of LSDs are not treated here: LSDs under QDROs; interplay with the § 691(c) deduction; an LSD paid to multiple recipients; and distribution of annuity contracts as part of an LSD.

2.3.02 *First hurdle: type of plan*

Only distributions from § 401(a) "qualified plans" (pension, profit sharing or stock bonus) can qualify as LSDs. Both corporate plans and self-employed ("Keogh") plans can give rise to LSDs, but a distribution from an IRA, SEP-IRA or 403(b) plan can never qualify for LSD treatment. § 402(e)(4)(D)(i).

2.3.03 *Second hurdle: "reason" for distribution*

The distribution must be made either:

(i)   On account of the employee's death; or
(ii)   After the employee attains age 59½; or
(iii)   On account of the employee's "separation from service."

§ 402(e)(4)(D)(i)(I-III).

Reason (iii) is not available to the self-employed person; a distribution to a self-employed person is eligible for LSD treatment only under reasons (i) or (ii), or if he is "disabled," which for this purpose means "unable to engage in any substantial gainful activity by reason of any medically determined physical or mental impairment which can be expected to result in death or to be of long continued and indefinite duration." § 402(e)(4)(D)(i)(IV).

These LSD "triggering events" are of significance primarily for determining whether there has been a distribution of 100% of the balance to the credit of the employee (¶ 2.3.04).

(a)   Landmine: separation from service

A treatise could be written on the subject of what constitutes "separation from service." If the employee in question was fired, moved to another state and is now working for a competing company while engaged in bitter litigation with his former company, he has probably "separated from service." On the other hand, if the employer from which he "separated" sold all its assets to a new company, which rehired the employee the next day to do the same job at the same desk, you may need a ruling to determine whether there has been a "separation from service." See, *e.g.*, PLR 1999-27048. Defining "separation from service" is beyond the scope of this book.

The frustrating technicalities of the term "separation from service" caused Congress to change to a different term—"severance from employment"—in defining when an elective deferral account may properly be distributed from a 401(k) plan; see § 401(k)(2)(B)(k)(I), effective for distributions after 2001. Unfortunately, Congress did not make the same amendment in § 402(e), so "separation from service" is still the term applicable in the definition of lump sum distribution. All the cases and rulings generated in recent years on the meaning of separation of service came from 401(k) plans; note that future 401(k) rulings etc. will no longer be of use in the analysis of lump sum distribution issues, since the two Code sections now use different terms.

(b)   Landmine: "on account of"

Occasionally taxpayers have had problems asserting that a particular LSD was made "on account of" an LSD triggering event. For example, if an employee receives a distribution upon separation from service, but at the same time the plan is terminating and *everyone* is receiving a full distribution whether or not he separated from service, the IRS may say the distribution is "on account of" the plan termination (which is not an "LSD triggering event") and *not* "on account of" the separation from service.

2.3.04 *Third hurdle: distribution all in one taxable year*

The distribution, to qualify, must be a "distribution within one taxable year of the recipient of the balance to the credit of [the] employee... from the plan." § 402(e)(4)(D)(i). This hurdle is surrounded by landmines. The general guiding principle is that the employee's entire balance in all "aggregated plans," determined as of the most recent triggering event (¶ 2.3.03) must be distributed to him within one calendar year. For exceptions to this rule, see ¶ 2.3.05.

Clearly, if an employee takes out, say, one-third of his plan balance in 1997 and leaves two-thirds in the plan, the distribution of the one-third portion in 1997 does not qualify for LSD treatment because it is not a distribution of the entire balance. Now suppose the employee takes out the remaining two-thirds of his balance in 1998. He has taken out 100% of his (remaining) plan balance in 1998. Is the 1998 distribution an LSD?

It *would* be a distribution of 100% of the balance to his credit in one calendar year *if* the "balance to his credit" simply meant the entire balance as of the date of distribution—but that is not what it means. Rather, the rule means that, in order to qualify for LSD treatment, there can be distributions in only one taxable year following the most recent triggering event (¶ 2.3.03). See Prop. Reg. §1.402(e)-2(d)(1)(ii); Rev. Rul. 69-495, 1969-2 C.B. 100. The "balance to the credit" of the employee is determined as of the first distribution following the most recent triggering event. This is the balance that must be distributed "in one taxable year." IRS Notice 89-25, 1989-1 C.B. 662, A-6.

Example: After Elaine retired from Acme Widget in 1997 at age 64, she withdrew $60,000 from her $800,000 Acme Widget Profit Sharing Plan account in order to fulfill her lifelong dream of traveling around the world in a submarine. Returning to the U.S. in 1998, paler but wiser, she takes a distribution of the rest of her profit sharing account. This final distribution would not qualify for LSD treatment because the entire balance that existed on the date of the most recent triggering event (separation from service) was not distributed all in one calendar year.

In contrast to this, suppose that Elaine, upon returning from her cruise, died on her way to the Acme benefits office. Now there is a new triggering event, the death of the employee. Her beneficiary can elect

LSD treatment for her remaining plan balance even though Elaine, had she lived, could not have done so. Another alternative: suppose Elaine had withdrawn the $60,000 for her cruise *before* she retired. Then her later separation from service would have been a new triggering event, and the final distribution would qualify for LSD treatment.

The IRS instructions for Form 4972 (2000) make no reference to this requirement. Prior distributions from the same plan are referred to only in connection with the rule that if any prior distribution from the same plan was rolled over, subsequent distributions cannot receive special averaging treatment (¶ 2.3.07). These instructions give the impression that the IRS regards the triggering events as obsolete. However, unless the IRS has had an unpublicized change of heart, Notice 89-25 is still in effect. The Code's definition of LSD still includes the requirement that the distribution be of the "balance to the credit" of the employee which becomes payable "after the employee attains age 59½," or "on account of" Participant's death, separation from service (non-owner employees) or disability (owner-employees).

Here are other landmines surrounding this hurdle:

(a)   Landmine: Post year-end vesting and other adjustments

If you THINK you have withdrawn 100% of your plan balance, but then after the end of the year you receive a little extra due to a previous bookkeeping error, you have probably lost your LSD eligibility. However, if the post-year-end increase comes about because the employee is rehired, and prior forfeited amounts are reinstated, see ¶ 2.3.05.

Here is an example of how this requirement can unexpectedly pose a problem:

Example: Lewis terminated his Keogh plan and took a lump sum distribution of the entire balance in 1997. He diligently closed every account the plan had and distributed all the assets to himself before the end of the calendar year. Then in January 1998 he received a notice from a federal court: because of certain securities transactions that had occurred in his Keogh plan account in 1993, he (in his capacity as trustee of the plan) was a plaintiff in a class action suit against the Aging Bull Brokerage Firm. Enclosed with the notice is a check for $1.98, representing his share of the winnings in the now-settled class action suit. The check is payable to (and presumably constitutes an undistributed asset of) the Keogh plan. The balance of his plan, in other words, was NOT distributed all in one year.

To avoid this problem, when distributing all assets of an account (or when terminating the plan altogether), have the plan trustee sign a blanket assignment of all remaining assets, claims, etc., known and unknown, to the recipient (Participant or the beneficiary, as the case may be). Thus, the recipient, not the plan trustee, becomes the owner of the stray interest, dividends, and class action claims that seem inevitably to turn up after the plan is liquidated, and the newly-discovered dollars do not upset the LSD status of the terminating distribution.

(b)   Landmine: aggregation of plans

In determining whether the entire balance to the credit of an employee has been distributed, certain plans must be aggregated. Specifically all profit sharing plans of the same employer are considered to be one plan for this purpose; all pension plans of the employer are treated as one plan; and all stock bonus plans are treated as one. § 402(e)(4)(D)(ii).

Unfortunately it is not always easy to determine what type a particular retirement plan is. The employee is entitled to a summary plan description for each plan; that should tell what type it is. If not, you could request the answer from the company benefits office; or request a copy of the most recent IRS annual report (Form 5500 series) filed by the employer. Form 5500 requires the employer to check a box indicating whether the plan is a profit sharing, pension or stock bonus plan, and the employer is required to provide a copy of this form to the employee on request.

Finding out what type of plan a particular retirement plan is does not necessarily end the problems with this requirement. For one thing plans may have to be aggregated, even if they are *not* both of the same type, if they have interrelated benefit formulas. Also, it may be impossible to obtain distribution of 100% of all similar plans. For example, the employer may have two pension plans (a defined benefit and a money purchase), which must be aggregated for purposes of this requirement, but the employer may permit lump sum distributions from only one of them.

If the employer maintains more than one plan, and it is proposed to take an LSD from only one of them, it may require a legal opinion of an ERISA lawyer, or the employer's counsel, to be sure that this requirement is met for the proposed distribution.

(c) Landmine: employers under common control

When aggregating "plans of a similar type" of the "employer," who is the "employer"? Must we aggregate separate *employers*, too, if they are under common control?

When two employers are under common control (*e.g.*, a proprietorship and a corporation owned by the same person), § 414 says the two entities will be treated as one "employer" for purposes of certain Code sections relating to retirement plans. § 414(b),(c). § 402 is not among the listed sections. This would seem to imply that employers are *not* aggregated for purposes of § 402. However, the author is not aware of any authority one way or the other on this question.

If your client is taking an LSD from an employer's plan, while he still has a balance in a plan of "similar type" maintained by a different employer that is under common control, this question must be further investigated.

(d) One taxable year of the "recipient"

Here's a stumper: Richard wants to take an LSD of his $300,000 profit sharing plan in 1999. He withdraws $200,000 in May; but due to delays in selling some stock inside the plan, the rest of the distribution is delayed a bit. Richard dies in June and the remaining $100,000 is paid in July to Richard's estate, after the end of Richard's taxable year (which ended unexpectedly at his death). Clearly the estate's $100,000 payment qualifies as an LSD (because Richard's death was a new "triggering event"); but is there any way that the entire $300,000 can be aggregated and treated as an LSD?

2.3.05 *Exceptions to the all-in-one-year rule*

"Accumulated deductible employee contributions" can be ignored in determining whether the employee has received a distribution of his entire plan balance. § 402(e)(4)(D)(i). This type of contribution, which was permitted under § 72(o) only for the years

1982 to 1986, is rarely encountered.

Another exception: "Dividends to ESOP participants pursuant to section 404(k)(2)(B) of the Code are not treated as part of the balance to the credit of an employee for purposes of the lump sum distribution rules under section 402(e)(4)(A) of the Code. Thus, such distribution does not prevent a subsequent distribution of the balance to the credit of an employee from being a lump sum distribution." PLR 9024083.

Query: Can distributions from the employee's *after-tax contribution* account in one year be ignored in determining whether the distribution of the *employer-contribution* account in a later year qualifies for LSD treatment?

If the employee has terminated his service and withdrawn 100% of his plan balance, but then after the end of the year the employee is rehired, and prior forfeited amounts are reinstated, then technically the prior LSD is not "disqualified"; however, § 402(d)(6) (before 2000) provided a recapture provision under which the benefits received from the now defunct 5YFA treatment had to be paid back to the IRS in the year the increased vesting occurred. If the post-year-end increased vesting did not occur because of a rehire, but rather due to a plan termination (which sometimes causes 100% vesting of everyone retroactively), the status of the prior special averaging treatment is unknown.

2.3.06 *Special averaging method: Participants born before 1936*

If an LSD (as defined in ¶ 2.3.02-¶ 2.3.05) meets certain additional requirements, the LSD can receive certain tax breaks: it can be excluded altogether from the recipient's adjusted gross income and taxed separately, using "10-year averaging" (¶ 2.3.08), with or without some "20% capital gain" (¶ 2.3.09) thrown in. These two special tax deals are referred to collectively as the "special averaging method." An LSD for which a proper election is made to use these methods is excluded from the recipient's adjusted gross income (AGI). § 402(d)(3); § 62(a)(8). The fact that an LSD for which special averaging is elected is excluded from AGI can be beneficial, but it can also create additional problems.

On the good side, it means the distribution will not be included in AGI for purposes of: the income limit for obtaining a Roth IRA (¶ 5.4.04); the threshold for deducting medical expenses (7.5% of AGI)

(§ 213(a)); the threshold for reduction of itemized deductions by 3% of "excess" AGI (§ 68) ($132,950 in 2001; this deduction-reduction is phased down in 2006-2009 and repealed after 2009 by EGTRRA); the threshold for reducing personal exemptions (§151(d)(3)) ($199,450 for a married couple in 2001; this reduction is also phased down in 2006-2009 and repealed after 2009 by EGTRRA); or determining how much of the recipient's Social Security benefits for that year will be subject to income tax under § 86. On the negative side, the exclusion of the LSD from AGI may reduce the client's ability to make large charitable gifts (which are limited to a certain percentage of AGI) (§ 170(b)).

> Mike Jones, CPA extraordinaire, who has "dominion over palm and pine" (he practices in California and Minnesota), rattled off the following observations about the special averaging treatment of LSDs, when he reviewed this chapter prior to publication:
>
> 1.   Special averaging treatment for an LSD is the only occasion in the Code when a trust or estate gets to use the *individual* income tax rate schedule rather than trust rates.
>
> 2.   The exclusion from income means a client can receive (say) a $100,000 LSD, elect special averaging, pay roughly $15,000 of income tax, donate the $100,000 to charity, and take a deduction of $100,000 from his *ordinary* income (which saves roughly $40,000 of income tax).
>
> 3.   On the negative side, if the LSD is subject to state income tax, it may generate a large deduction for state income tax, which in turn may make the taxpayer subject to the alternative minimum tax if the LSD is excluded from AGI.

2.3.07 *Requirements for special averaging method*

The special averaging method is available only for individuals born before 1936. TRA '86 § 1122(h), as amended by TAMRA '88, § 1011A(b)(11), (13)-(15). Special averaging may be elected only once with respect to a taxpayer. It must be elected for all lump sum distributions in the same year that qualify for it. Other requirements are listed in Form 4972, which can be used as a checklist to determine qualification.

Only individuals, estates and trusts can elect the special averaging method. A distribution to a partnership or corporation will not qualify. § 402(d)(4)(B). If the distribution meets the requirements described above, special averaging treatment is not automatic; it is elected by filing Form 4972.

2.3.08 *How to calculate tax using 10-year averaging*

Here is how to determine the tax under the 10-year averaging method:

(i)   Divide the LSD by 10.

(ii)   Determine the tax on 10% of the LSD using 1986 rates applicable to single taxpayers (conveniently reproduced in the instructions to IRS Form 4972).

(iii)   Multiply the amount obtained in step (ii) by 10. The result is the 10-year averaging tax applicable to the distribution.

Although maximum tax rates were higher in 1986 than they are now, the effect of the 10-year averaging calculation is to tax the distribution as if it were 10 small distributions rather than one big distribution. The result can be dramatically lower-than-usual taxes, especially on smaller LSDs. See Table 2 in Appendix A.

Exceptions:

- There is a "minimum distribution allowance" which produces an even lower tax on distributions under $70,000. See Form 4972.
- No tax is paid currently on the value of certain annuity contracts included in the distribution, though it is still counted as part of the LSD.
- The above method determines the tax on the "ordinary income" portion of the LSD. See ¶ 2.3.09 for possible capital gain treatment of part of the distribution.

2.3.09 *20% capital gain rate for pre-1974 participation*

If the employee was born before 1936, and was a participant in the plan prior to 1974, part of the LSD for which the "special averaging method" (¶ 2.3.07) has been elected is eligible to be treated as a "capital gain" taxed at 20%. This 20% rate applies without regard to the actual tax rate on capital gain in any particular year.

Prop. Reg. § 1.402(e)-2(d) provides that the "capital gain" portion of the distribution is determined by deducting the "ordinary income portion" (OIP) from the "total taxable amount" (TTA). The OIP is determined by multiplying the TTA by the following fraction:

Numerator: Calendar years of active participation after 1973.
Denominator: Total calendar years of active participation.

In the case of pre-1974 years, the employee gets twelve months' credit for each calendar year or partial calendar year of participation. For post-1973 years a different rule applies: He gets one *month's* credit for each calendar month or part of a month in which he is an active participant.

It is possible, with smaller distributions, for the 20% "capital gain method" to produce a higher tax than would apply under 10-year averaging. In this case, Participant can elect to have his capital gain portion treated as ordinary income; or rather, technically, to "treat pre-1974 participation as post-1973 participation." See § 402(e)(4)(L) as it existed prior to repeal by TAMRA '88 § 1011A(b)(8)(G). If this election is made, the 20% treatment is waived and the entire distribution is taxed under 10-year averaging (¶ 2.3.08).

2.3.10 *Capital gain: what is an "active participant?"*

What is an "active participant" for purposes of the fraction described at ¶ 2.3.09? The regulations under § 219(g) (which limits the income tax deduction for IRA contributions by those who are "active participants" in various types of retirement plans) gives a very specific definition. Under Reg. § 1.219-2 a person is an "active participant" in a money purchase pension plan in a particular year *only* if some of the employer contribution was required to be allocated to his account for that year; or in a profit sharing plan *only* if any forfeiture or employer contribution was added to his account in that year. If this § 1.219-2 definition were applied for purposes of determining the capital gain portion of an LSD, the OIP/TTA fraction would become fixed, once and for all, when the plan discontinued contributions on behalf of the employee, since "active participation" (in the § 219 sense) ends then.

But the IRS apparently does not apply the § 219 definition of "active participation" to § 402 for this purpose. It appears that the IRS uses, for purposes of determining the "capital gain" portion of an LSD, a definition which makes no distinction between "participation" and "active participation," thus rendering nugatory the word "active" in the Code's phrase *active* participation." The IRS definition is in a 1975 proposed regulation, § 1.402(e)-2; and is repeated in the instructions to Form 1099-R, which is the tax form used (by the employer) to report how much of each distribution is ordinary income and how much is capital gain. From the 2000 "Instructions for Form 1099-R, Box 3," p. R-6: "Active participation begins with the first month in which the employee became a participant under the plan and ends with the earliest of –"

(i)   The month the employee receives the LSD.

(ii)   The month the employee dies.

(iii)   In the case of a common law employee, the month of separation from service.

(iv)   In the case of a self-employed person who receives the LSD on account of disability, the month in which he becomes disabled.

The effect of this definition is to gradually and inexorably reduce the capital gain portion of the distribution, even if the plan has been "frozen" since 1974, since the fraction keeps changing until events (i) - (iv) occur.

This definition appears arbitrary and capricious, first, because it ignores the word "active" in the Code, and second, because the IRS used the § 219 definition intact for *another* part of the LSD determinations under § 402 (namely the "five years of participation" requirement that formerly applied when determining eligibility for the now-repealed five-year averaging method) when to do so favored the Treasury.

2.3.11 *Tax on OIP when there is a capital gain portion*

Once you have determined how much of the total taxable amount (TTA) is the "ordinary income portion" (OIP) (to be taxed under 10-year averaging), and how much is capital gain (to be taxed at a flat 20%), how do you calculate the tax on the OIP? There are two possible methods:

(i)   Calculate the 10-year averaging tax on the TTA then multiply the result by the fraction OIP/TTA; or

(ii)   Calculate the 10-year averaging tax on the OIP only.

Method (i) was required by § 402(e)(1)(B) before it was repealed by TRA '86. However, the grandfather rule which continues 20% capital gain treatment for those born before 1936 appears to adopt method (ii): see § 1122(h)(3)(b) of TRA '86 as amended by TAMRA '88 § 1101A(b)(11), (13)-(15). IRS Form 4972 clearly uses method (ii) (see part III of form). Method (ii) produces a lower tax than method (i). Thus, the treatment of "grandfathered" individuals is more favorable than the treatment they would have received prior to the change in the law that they are being grandfathered from.

2.3.12 *Effect of EGTRRA 2001*

The 10-year averaging and 20% capital gain tax grandfather rules were not repealed by EGTRRA and thus will continue to be available indefinitely for LSDs of benefits of employees born before 1936; however, EGTRRA did put on one new limitation. EGTRRA substantially liberalized the rollover rules (see ¶ 2.5). Congress intends the liberalized rollover rules to increase the "portability" of pensions, not to increase the amounts eligible for ancient grandfather rules. Accordingly, EGTRRA § 641(f)(3) provides that the benefits of TRA '86 § 1122(h) "shall not apply" to a distribution from an otherwise-eligible retirement plan "if there was a rollover to such plan on behalf of such individual which is permitted solely by reason of any amendment made by this section."

2.4 Net Unrealized Appreciation of Employer Stock

This ¶ 2.4 describes the special favorable tax treatment available for "lump sum distributions" (and certain other distributions) of employer stock from a retirement plan.

For charitable giving with "NUA stock" see ¶ 7.6.04. For 10% penalty on distributions of stock prior to the employee's attaining age 59½, see ¶ 9.1.03.

2.4.01 *NUA: Tax deferral and long-term capital gain*

The Code gives special favorable treatment to distributions of "employer securities" from a qualified plan. Any growth in value of such securities which has occurred between the time the plan originally placed the securities in the employee's account and the time of the distribution is called "net unrealized appreciation" (NUA). Under certain circumstances, NUA is not taxed at the time of the distribution; rather, only the plan's cost basis in the stock is included in the employee's gross income at the time of the distribution. Taxation of the NUA is postponed until the stock is later sold. § 402(e)(4).

When the stock is later sold, the NUA is taxed as long term capital gain, regardless of how long the recipient (or the plan) actually held the stock. See Reg. § 1.402(a)-1(b)(1)(i) (sale of such stock shall be treated as sale of a capital asset "held for more than 6 months"). This regulation was written before the holding period for long-term capital gain was extended to, as of this writing, twelve months, but Notice 98-24, IRB 1998-17, 4/13/98, confirms that the actual holding period need not be calculated to qualify for the long-term capital gain tax rate.

Example: Joe Thomas, age 61, retires from Baby Bell Corp. and receives an LSD of his 401(k) plan, consisting entirely of 10,000 shares of Baby Bell stock. The plan's cost basis for that stock is $10 per share; the stock is worth $100 a share at the time of the distribution. Joe will receive a 1099-R from Baby Bell, indicating a gross distribution of $1 million and a taxable amount of $100,000. The NUA is $900,000. If Joe sells the stock immediately for $1 million, he will have long term capital gain of $900,000. Suppose instead he waits two months and sells the stock for $125 a share. Now he has a short term capital gain of $250,000 ($25 appreciation between date of distribution and date of sale, times 10,000 shares) in addition to his long term capital gain of $900,000. If he holds the stock for 12 months after receiving the distribution, all gain on any subsequent sale will be long term capital gain.

The tax deferral/capital gain treatment is not available for all distributions of employer securities. It applies in only two situations:

1.   If the securities are distributed as part of a "lump sum distribution" (see requirements described at ¶ 2.3.02-¶ 2.3.05) *all* the

NUA is non-taxable at the time of the distribution.

2.   If the distribution is *not* an LSD, then only the NUA attributable to the *employee's* contributions is excludable.

2.4.02 *Determining the amount of NUA*

The employer is supposed to determine how much of a distribution of employer securities constitutes NUA. The employer then reports this figure in Form 1099-R, box 6. For tax planning purposes the employee will probably want to know how much of the distribution is NUA no later than the date he receives the distribution, so it is to be hoped that the employer can provide this information then, rather than making the employee wait until January of the next year, when the 1099-R is prepared.

Reg. § 1.402(a)-1(b) and Notice 89-25, 1989-1 C.B. 662, A-1, tell the employer how to calculate the NUA. For example, if the employer contributed employer stock directly to the employee's account, then the NUA is the difference between the value of the stock when originally contributed to the employee's account and the value of the stock on the date of the distribution. These calculations can be complex—for example, if there have been prior distributions, or if there are both employer and employee contributions, or if the plan holds other investments besides employer securities, or if the plan has sold some of the employer securities.

2.4.03 *Distributions after the employee's death*

The favorable tax treatment of NUA also applies when employer stock is distributed to the employee's beneficiaries. So, even if the employee dies before taking a distribution of the employer securities, the beneficiary can exclude the NUA from income—*if* the beneficiary takes a lump sum distribution of the employee's balance. (If the beneficiary takes distribution of the benefits in some form other than an LSD, then the beneficiary can exclude only the NUA attributable to stock purchased with the employee's contributions.)

The IRS has held that the NUA, like other post-death retirement plan distributions, constitutes "IRD" (¶ 2.2). Rev. Rul. 69-297, 1969-1 C.B. 131. Accordingly, when Participant's beneficiaries sell the employer stock that is distributed to them from the plan in a qualifying distribution, they will pay long term capital gain on the NUA portion of the sale proceeds. They will get a § 691(c) deduction (¶ 2.2.07) for the estate taxes paid on the NUA; this deduction will reduce the capital gain.

2.4.04 *Basis of stock distributed during life and held until death*

When the employee receives an LSD of employer stock and the NUA is excluded from his income, his basis in the stock going forward is the value that *was* taxed upon distribution, *i.e.*, the plan's original cost basis of the stock.

If the employee still holds the stock at his death, does it receive a new basis equal to its date of death value—the so-called "stepped-up basis" of § 1014(c)? The IRS has ruled that such stock does *not* receive a stepped up basis, to the extent the employee benefitted from exclusion of NUA. According to the IRS, the NUA which the employee received upon distribution of the stock to him originally, and which was not taxed when distributed to him, retains its character as NUA even after the employee's death, and will constitute IRD to the employee's heirs when they eventually sell the stock. Only to the extent, if any, that the stock appreciated in value *after* it was distributed to the employee by the plan does it receive a stepped-up basis. Rev. Rul. 75-125, 1975-1 C.B. 254.

2.4.05 *Election to include NUA in income*

The recipient can elect *out* of the favorable tax treatment, *i.e.*, can elect to have the NUA taxed as income when the distribution is received rather than deferring tax until the stock is sold. This option could be attractive if (i) the distribution qualifies for special averaging (¶ 2.3.06) and (ii) the total distribution is small enough that the tax under the special averaging method is less than the capital gain tax that will otherwise eventually have to be paid. Of course this decision is based on some guesswork, since it involves comparing today's special averaging rate with tomorrow's capital gain rate.

2.4.06 *Rollovers and NUA*

For most retiring employees, rolling over (¶ 2.5) any large lump sum distribution received from an employer plan is the best tax-saving and financial planning strategy. The opportunity for continued tax-deferred growth of retirement assets inside an IRA offers the greatest financial value for *most* retirees.

An LSD which includes appreciated employer securities often provides an exception to this rule of thumb. Since the NUA is not taxed currently anyway, rolling it over does not defer tax on the NUA. The NUA, even if not rolled over, will not be taxed until the stock is sold. Furthermore, rolling over NUA will convert this unrealized long term capital gain into ordinary income, since IRA distributions are taxed as ordinary income (¶ 2.1.01). Thus, if the employee is planning to hold onto the employer stock, the rule of thumb would be: do *not* roll over NUA. (Note that NUA *can* be rolled over even in pre-2002 years, unlike other "tax-free" distributions. Reg. § 1.402(c)-2, A-3(b).)

The requirements that an LSD must meet to qualify for the favorable NUA treatment are more lenient than the requirements that must be met for an LSD to qualify for special averaging treatment. Although it is a requirement for special averaging (see ¶ 2.3.07) that no portion of the LSD be rolled over, and indeed that no other qualifying distribution received in the same year be rolled over, no such requirement applies to obtaining the exclusion from income of the NUA portion of an LSD.

Accordingly, if the employee receives a distribution that (i) meets the LSD requirements (¶ 2.3.02 - ¶ 2.3.05) and (ii) includes employer securities, the employee can exclude from his income the NUA inherent in the securities, while rolling over to an IRA the *rest* of the distribution, *i.e.*, the assets other than the employer securities, which otherwise would be included in gross income. PLR 9721036. If he rolls over some but not all of the employer stock, a ruling should be obtained to determine proper allocation of the NUA between the rolled and the non-rolled stock.

Another alternative, if the LSD also qualifies' for special averaging treatment (¶ 2.3.06), is not to roll over any part of the distribution, and pay tax on the taxable portion using the special averaging method. See IRS instructions for Form 4972. See ¶ 9.1.03 regarding the 10% "premature distributions" penalty (§ 72(t)) if the employee is under 59½.

2.4.07 *If the employee wants to sell the stock*

If the employee wants to sell the employer stock he is receiving, then more complex calculations are necessary. He can take his distribution of employer stock, not roll it over, and sell it; he will then pay tax at long-term capital gain rates, to the extent the sale proceeds consist of NUA.

Or, the employee can roll the stock over to an IRA and sell it inside the IRA and pay *no* current tax. This approach could be attractive if the taxation can be deferred, via the IRA, for a very long period of time. Even if the employee's ordinary income tax bracket at the time of ultimate future distribution will be higher than the capital gain tax he would have to pay today if he sells the stock outside the plan, the advantages of deferral may overcome the bracket differential.

For another approach that may be attractive if the employee wants to sell the stock see ¶ 7.6.04.

2.4.08 *Client with shortened life expectancy*

A client faced with imminent death may want to know what steps can be taken to increase the financial protection of his family if the anticipated event occurs. If such a client is a participant in a plan which holds appreciated employer stock, one point to consider is whether distribution should be taken before death. As with any retirement plan, distribution before death may have certain tax advantages (see ¶ 2.2.08), but distribution of a plan balance that includes appreciated employer securities, with a rollover of as much of the currently taxable portion as possible, may be attractive if it is desired to continue the tax deferral on retirement benefits after the client's death.

Example: Dagwood has six months to live. He is a participant in his company's retirement plan. One-third of his account in the plan consists of employer stock which has substantially appreciated; the other two-thirds consists of mutual funds. He has made no contributions to the plan. His beneficiaries are his children. If they inherit the plan, they are faced with a disagreeable choice: either they take an LSD of the entire benefit (in order to take advantage of the favorable treatment of the NUA portion of the distribution), thus forfeiting all possibility of continued tax deferral on the non-employer stock portion of the benefit; or, they opt for continued tax deferral by taking out all the plan benefits in instalments over their life expectancy (see Chapter 1)—and forfeit the favorable capital gain treatment of the NUA. They are faced with this choice because they do not have the option of rolling over the taxable portion (see ¶ 2.5.04).

If, on the other hand, Dagwood takes an LSD of the entire plan balance while he is still living, *he* can use the partial rollover strategy to get the best of both worlds. He rolls over the portion of the distribution that is not employer stock; and the children, when they inherit this rollover IRA, can benefit from continued tax deferral by gradually withdrawing the IRA over their life expectancy. He does *not* roll over the stock with its built-in NUA; when the children inherit this stock, they can sell it and pay only long term capital gains tax on the NUA portion of the proceeds.

2.5 Rollovers and Plan-to-Plan Transfers

2.5.01 *Definition of rollover and plan-to-plan transfer*

Under § 402, generally, retirement plan distributions are not taxed in the year received if they are "rolled over" to a different retirement plan or IRA. A "rollover" is generally a distribution from one plan or IRA to Participant, followed by a transfer of the distribution by Participant to another plan or IRA maintained for him.

A rollover differs from a "trustee-to-trustee transfer," "custodian-to-custodian transfer" or "plan-to-plan transfer." With these types of transfers (all of which are hereinafter referred to as "plan-to-plan transfers"), the money is never distributed to Participant—it goes straight from one IRA to another (or from one qualified retirement plan (QRP) to another). Over the years, Participants and the IRS learned that many of the technical rules that apply to rollovers (such as the one-per-year limit) do not apply to these transfers. Rev. Rul. 78-406, 1978-2 C.B. 157.

What has made things vastly more confusing, however, is that (since the "Unemployment Compensation Amendments of 1992, P.L. 102-318) ("UCA"), the direct transfer of a participant's benefits from a QRP to an IRA is called a "direct rollover" and it *is* considered a rollover at least in some respects; likewise (since TAPRA '97) the conversion of a traditional IRA to a Roth IRA (¶ 5.4.01), even if it is done by plan-to-plan transfer, must meet some (not all) requirements of a true "rollover."

Until 1992, the requirements for a valid rollover were almost as difficult and perilous as the LSD rules, but UCA (applicable to distributions after 1992) vastly liberalized the rules, making rollovers much easier to accomplish.

2.5.02 *Distributions that cannot be rolled over*

Any distribution from a qualified plan, IRA or 403(b) plan can be rolled over, with only the following exceptions:

1.   A required distribution under § 401(a)(9) (see Chapter 1) cannot be rolled over. See ¶ 2.5.05.

2.   "Any distribution which is one of a series of substantially equal periodic payments" made annually or more often (a) over the life or life expectancy of Participant, (b) over the joint life or life expectancy of Participant and a designated beneficiary, or (c) over a "specified period of 10 years or more" may not be rolled over. § 402(c)(4)(A). Reg. § 1.402(c)-2, A-5, explains how to determine whether a distribution is part of a series of "substantially equal installments" over 10 or more years.

3.   Certain corrective or "deemed" distributions cannot be rolled over (for example, the taxable cost of insurance in a plan (¶ 8.3.01), or a plan loan that is foreclosed, or the return of an excess 401(k) contribution).

4.   Non-taxable distributions (see ¶ 2.1.03) could not, prior to enactment of EGTRRA 2001, be rolled over. See § 402(c)(2) prior to amendment by EGTRRA, applicable to years before 2002; Reg. § 1.402(c)-2, A-3. For the ability to roll over after-tax amounts post-EGTRRA, see ¶ 5.4.12.

5.   Hardship distributions (from any type of plan; prior to 2002, this limitation applies only to hardship distributions from 401(k) plans) cannot be rolled over.

Another EGTRRA change is the broadening of the definition of "eligible retirement plan," i.e., the type of plan that can receive a rollover. Before 2002, a Participant may roll a QRP distribution over into only another QRP or an IRA. After 2001, § 402(c)(8)(B) also allows tax-free rollovers from QRPs to 457 and 403(b) plans.

2.5.03 *Deadline for rolling over; rollovers by executor*

A rollover generally must be completed no later than "the 60th day following the day on which the distributee received the property distributed." § 420(c)(3)(A).

What if Participant receives a distribution, and is planning to roll it over, but then dies before having completed the rollover. If the 60-day deadline is met, can Participant's executor complete the rollover? Here is a collection of the sparse authority on what an executor can do by way of making IRA contributions and related decisions for the deceased Participant:

1.   An executor may not make a $2,000 IRA contribution on a decedent's behalf. PLR 8439066.

2.   Where Participant had received a distribution, but then died before rolling it over, his executor could roll over the distribution to an IRA in the decedent's name, provided the rollover was completed within 60 days after the distribution was received by Participant. Gunther v. U.S., 573 F. Supp. 126, 127 (1982) (USDC MI, 51 AFTR 2d 83-1314). See AOD 1981-038 (11/10/83), in which the IRS announced it would not follow Gunther to the extent Gunther held that an executor can exercise a decedent's right to roll over a plan distribution.

3.   In a now-expired Temporary Regulation (dealing with the 15% excise tax on excess plan accumulations and distributions under since-repealed § 4981A) the IRS specifically recognized post-death rollovers. The Temp. Reg. explained the effect on the calculation of decedent's 15% excise tax in the following situation: "ROLLOVER AFTER DEATH. If any amount is distributed from a qualified employer plan or individual retirement plan within the 60-day period ending on the decedent's date of death and is rolled over to an IRA after such date but within 60 days of the date distributed...." Temp. Reg. § 54.4981A-1T (d-5)(c).

4.   The IRS does not allow a surviving spouse's executor to exercise Spouse's "personal" right to elect to treat the deceased Participant's IRA as Spouse's own IRA (see ¶ 3.2.06), but does

allow Participant's executor to elect to "recharacterize" a Roth IRA contribution as a traditional IRA contribution or vice versa (see ¶ 5.8.07).

The IRS will have to become more liberal in recognizing post-death rollovers in view of § 402(c)(3)(B), added by EGTRRA, effective for years after 2001. This section encourages the IRS to provide exceptions to the 60-day deadline for completing a rollover: "HARDSHIP EXCEPTION.--The Secretary may waive the 60-day requirement under subparagraph (A) where the failure to waive such requirement would be against equity or good conscience, including casualty, disaster, or other events beyond the reasonable control of the individual subject to such requirement."

The legislative history for this section states: "The conference agreement provides that the Secretary may waive the 60-day rollover period if the failure to waive such requirement would be against equity or good conscience, including cases of casualty, disaster, or other events beyond the reasonable control of the individual subject to such requirement. For example, the Secretary may issue guidance that includes objective standards for a waiver of the 60-day rollover period, such as waiving the rule due to military service in a combat zone or during a Presidentially declared disaster (both of which are provided for under present law), or for a period during which the participant has received payment in the form of a check, but has not cashed the check, or for errors committed by a financial institution, or in cases of inability to complete a rollover due to *death*, disability, hospitalization, incarceration, restrictions imposed by a foreign country, or postal error." Emphasis added.

Since Congress seems to want the IRS to allow executors an extension of time to complete rollovers for deceased Participants, presumably the IRS will have to allow such executor-completed rollovers in the first place (as they apparently once considered doing; see the Temp. Reg. cited above).

However, the fact that Congress seems to want the IRS to allow Participant's executor to *complete* a rollover does not mean the IRS will feel obliged to consider allowing Participant's executor to *initiate* a rollover. There is nothing in EGTRRA to provide hope to those planners who would like to see executors be permitted to remove a deceased Participant's benefits from a QRP and roll them over to an IRA in the name of the decedent (so as to obtain the more favorable payout options typically available under an IRA; see ¶ 1.5.09.

The major unexplored territory with post-death rollovers is who will be the beneficiary of the IRA that receives a post-death rollover, and who decides who will be the beneficiary of that IRA. Logically, if we assume the executor doesn't have authority to create an estate plan for the deceased Participant, the beneficiary of the rollover IRA should be Participant's estate (since that's who "owned" the distribution that Participant received before his death, that the executor wants to roll over to an IRA). But naming Participant's estate as beneficiary of the rollover IRA would defeat the purpose of the rollover, in view of the IRS's intransigence on the question of "looking through" the estate for purposes of determining the "designated beneficiary" for minimum distribution purposes. See ¶ 1.7.04.

2.5.04 *Rollovers of inherited benefits*

For rollovers by a surviving spouse named as beneficiary of Participant's benefits, see ¶ 3.205. Unfortunately, a non-spouse beneficiary is not allowed to roll over inherited benefits to his own plan; a non-spouse beneficiary is not even allowed to roll over benefits from a decedent's plan into an IRA in the name of the *decedent*. §§ 402(c)(9), 408(d)(3)(C).

A surviving spouse who inherits an IRA may elect to treat the decedent's IRA as her own; see ¶ 3.2.05. A non-spouse beneficiary cannot elect to treat the decedent's IRA as his or her own, with one "grandfather"-type exception: any beneficiary (even a non-spouse) of an IRA owner who died *before 1984* could elect to treat the decedent's IRA as his or her own IRA. See Prop. Reg. § 1.408-8, A-4.

2.5.05 *No rollover of minimum required distributions*

The rule that a minimum required distribution (MRD) cannot be rolled over (§§ 402(c)(4)(B), 408(d)(3)(E)) can take Participants by surprise.

For example, the first distribution received in any year for which a distribution is required will be considered part of the MRD for that year and thus cannot be rolled over. Reg. § 1.402(c)-2, A-7. Furthermore, Participant's first "Distribution Year" is not the year in which the required beginning date (RBD) (¶ 1.3) occurs; it is the year *before* the RBD. Thus the first Distribution Year is the year Participant reaches age 70½ (or retires as the case may be; see ¶ 1.3), even though the first MRD does not have to be taken until April 1 of the *following* year. Any distribution received on or after January 1 of the first Distribution Year will be considered part of the MRD for that year, and thus cannot be rolled over.

Example: Leonard turns 70½ in 2001. On 1/1/2001 he retires from his job at XYZ Corp. and asks the plan administrator of the retirement plan to distribute his benefits to his IRA in a "direct rollover." The administrator replies that it will make a direct rollover of everything except the MRD for 2001. Leonard replies, fine, he will take the 2001 MRD as a taxable distribution and roll over the rest. Since he has named his 40-year-old wife Louise as his designated beneficiary the MRD should be 1/42.9th of the account balance, based on their 42.9 year joint life expectancy (¶ 1.4.02). But the administrator says, "Louise is your wife and designated beneficiary now, but you are entitled to use your and Louise's joint life expectancy to measure required distributions only if she is your sole beneficiary for the entire Distribution Year. Since we don't know for sure that she will be your sole beneficiary for all of 2001, we will distribute to you the MRD calculated using the Uniform Table (¶1.4.01)—which is 1/26th of the account, not 1/42.9th."

For similar problems facing would-be Roth IRA converters, see ¶ 5.4.07.

2.6 Summary of Planning Principles

1.   In choosing among possible beneficiaries (including trusts) for retirement benefits, consider their respective income tax brackets along with other factors. Other things being equal, it is more tax-effective to leave retirement benefits (and other IRD assets) to lower-bracket beneficiaries, and non-IRD assets to higher bracket beneficiaries.

2.   Do not use retirement benefits to fund a pecuniary bequest under a will or trust. Do not arrange retirement benefits so that they will have to pass through a pecuniary formula in a will or trust.

3.   As between the marital and the credit shelter share, it is

generally better to use IRD to fund the marital share, so no part of the "credit shelter" is "wasted" paying income taxes. Income taxes paid out of the marital share will reduce the future taxable estate of the spouse. Exception: the advantages of long-term income tax deferral that are available for certain "credit shelter" dispositions may outweigh the drawbacks of funding a credit shelter gift with IRD.

4.   When determining what benefits each beneficiary will receive, consider the impact of the § 691(c) deduction for federal estate taxes paid on IRD. This deduction benefits the person who receives the IRD, not the person who pays the estate tax.

5.   If the client's retirement plan holds stock of the employer which sponsors the plan, evaluate the alternatives for treatment of the "NUA" before any distributions are taken from the plan (or before selling that stock inside the plan).

6.   Determine whether a client is eligible for "lump sum distribution" income tax treatment. Do not take steps (such as a rollover) which would eliminate eligibility for beneficial LSD treatment without carefully considering the alternatives.

3

Marital Matters

Rules and estate planning concerns for the married Participant and surviving Spouse

This Chapter deals with various rules that apply (and planning options available) to married Participants.

3.1 Considerations for Married Participants

3.1.01 *Checklist of considerations for married Participant*

Here is a list of factors that need to be considered when planning for disposition of retirement benefits of a married Participant, whether he is thinking of leaving those benefits to his spouse ("Spouse"), to a trust for her benefit, or to someone else entirely.

1. Determine what rights if any federal law ("REA") gives Spouse in Participant's retirement benefits, since REA may prevent Participant from naming whoever he wants to name, and/or from taking benefits out of his plan, without the consent of Spouse (which consent must meet various requirements). See ¶ 3.4.

2. State law may give Spouse rights in any of Participant's plans REA does not apply to. Community property and other state law spousal property rights are beyond the scope of this book.

3. Federal tax law gives Spouse (and no other beneficiary) a powerful option to defer income taxes, the "spousal rollover." See ¶ 3.2 for the advantages of and rules applicable to the spousal rollover.

4. The minimum distribution rules (Chapter 1) have a variety of special provisions (intended to be favorable, through they don't always operate favorably) that apply when Spouse is named as

Participant's beneficiary. These are discussed at ¶ 1.6.

5.   Whenever benefits are left to a marital trust (or even to Spouse outright; ¶ 3.3.14) special precautions must be taken to make sure the disposition qualifies for the marital deduction, if estate taxes are a concern. See ¶ 3.3.

6.   If Spouse is not a U.S. citizen, and estate taxes are a concern, read Chapter 4.

7.   Leaving benefits to a "QTIP" trust often results in substantially higher income taxes than leaving benefits to Spouse outright. See ¶ 3.3.10.

8.   Preparing the typical "credit shelter/marital share" estate plan poses special challenges when one or both spouses have no assets other than retirement plans to use to fund the "credit shelter" share. This problem is discussed at ¶ 10.5.

9.   For special rules regarding the Spouse and a Roth IRA, see ¶ 5.8.03.

10.   Review the "simultaneous death" issues at ¶ 3.1.02.

3.1.02 *Simultaneous death clauses*

If Participant names Spouse as his beneficiary, and they die simultaneously, it will be presumed under the Uniform Simultaneous Death Law that Spouse predeceased Participant. A presumption that Spouse *survived* Participant, if contained in Participant's will or trust, will NOT govern retirement plan death benefits payable directly to Spouse. To have an effective presumption that Spouse survives in that case, the presumption must be contained in the designation of beneficiary form itself. Such a presumption may be used, if Spouse's estate is smaller than Participant's, to equalize the estates for estate tax purposes.

Note: Before attempting to create a presumption of spousal survival in a designation of beneficiary form, check the plan to make sure it does not create an irrebuttable presumption that Participant survives the beneficiary in case of simultaneous deaths.

What is the effect of such a survivorship presumption under the minimum distribution rules? Participant's "designated beneficiary" (¶ 1.7) is not determined until the end of the year after the year of Participant's death (the "Designation Date"; ¶ 1.8.01) anyway. Therefore, the effect of a presumption that Spouse survived would be the same as if Spouse had actually survived Participant (and so become, as beneficiary, the owner of the benefits) but then died before the Designation Date. The critical question for determining post-death required distributions is, who owns the benefits on the Designation Date?

If the benefits have passed to *another* individual beneficiary by the Designation Date, that individual beneficiary would be entitled to take the benefits over his or her life expectancy (¶ 1.5.06) as the "designated beneficiary" of Participant. The minimum distribution rules "don't care" whether that individual became the owner of the benefits because he/she was *Participant's contingent beneficiary* or because he/she was *Spouse's successor beneficiary* (¶ 1.5.07), as long as he/she is entitled to the benefits as a beneficiary (primary, contingent or successor), i.e., he/she did *not* acquire the right to the benefits merely by virtue of being an "heir at law" of Participant or Spouse, or through an estate (¶ 1.7.04).

If Spouse survives Participant, or is presumed to survive as a result of a simultaneous death clause, but is not still living on the Designation Date, how can you assure that the benefits will pass to one or more individual beneficiaries in that case?

As previously noted (¶ 1.8.08), some plan administrators will not allow Participant to say, as part of Participant's beneficiary designation form, who will own the benefits if Participant's primary beneficiary survives Participant but dies before either withdrawing the benefits or naming a Successor Beneficiary. If Participant wants to (1) name Spouse as his Primary Beneficiary and (2) presume Spouse survives in case of simultaneous death, then Participant had better also be sure that either (3) the plan administrator will allow Participant to name a Successor Beneficiary under those circumstances or (4) the plan administrator will accept a designation of Successor Beneficiary from Spouse—while Participant is still living—to cover the possibility of her brief survival (or simultaneous death with presumption of survival), and then Participant must make sure that the proper designation (whether #3 or #4) is in place.

An easier way to deal with the issue is not to presume Spouse (or any other beneficiary) survives Participant in case of simultaneous or close-in-time deaths; then the benefits will pass directly to Participant's contingent beneficiary, and (assuming the contingent beneficiary is an individual and survives until the Designation Date) availability of the life expectancy payout method is assured.

One more point: there would be no minimum distribution rules advantage to trying to achieve a spousal rollover (¶ 3.2) in case of simultaneous or close-in-time deaths. The advantages of a spousal rollover don't matter if Spouse does not in fact survive, as long as a younger generation successor beneficiary can be installed by the Designation Date.

3.2 Spousal Rollover of Inherited Benefits; Election to Treat Inherited IRA as Spouse's IRA

This ¶ 3.2 deals with Spouse's option to roll over, tax-free, to another retirement plan distributions made to her from the retirement plan of her deceased spouse (Participant). ¶ 2.5 explains what a rollover is and the rules governing tax-free rollovers generally; this ¶ 3.2 discusses additional rules and considerations that apply to a rollover by a surviving spouse.

When Spouse inherits an IRA she has the option to elect to treat it as her own. The effect of such an election is the same as that of a tax-free rollover. Throughout this ¶ 3.2, "spousal rollover" means "spousal rollover (or, in the case of an inherited IRA, Spouse's election to treat the inherited IRA as her own)." For particular rules dealing with the IRA election, see ¶ 3.2.05.

3.2.01 *Advantages of spousal rollover*

The surviving spouse's ability to "roll over" (¶ 2. 5.01) inherited benefits to her own retirement plan gives her a powerful option to defer income taxes not available to other beneficiaries. By rolling over benefits to her own retirement plan, Spouse becomes the "Participant" with regard to those benefits under the minimum distribution rules. By rolling over the benefits to her own IRA (see ¶ 3.2.10 for other types of plans Spouse can roll into), or by electing to treat an inherited IRA as "her own" IRA (¶ 3.2.05), Spouse gains the following income tax deferral advantages compared with a beneficiary who must take the benefits solely "as beneficiary" (and even compared with taking the benefits herself as a "spouse-beneficiary," using the special options available only to a spouse-beneficiary; see ¶ 1.6):

1.   Other beneficiaries must commence distributions by the end of the year after Participant's death (¶ 1.5.02, ¶ 1.5.03). A Spouse who is under age 70½ can postpone distributions from the rollover IRA until she reaches her own RBD (¶ 1.3).

2.   The maximum deferral period for anyone (even Spouse) who takes inherited benefits as *beneficiary* is the beneficiary's *single* life expectancy. Spouse can take MRDs from a *rollover* IRA using the favorable "Uniform Table" (¶ 1.4.01), which is based on the *joint* life expectancy of Spouse (as Participant) and a hypothetical 10-years-younger beneficiary, and thus provides small required distributions than would use of Spouse's single life expectancy.

3.   Spouse can name her own designated beneficiary for the rollover IRA. After her death, MRDs will be based on the life expectancy of her designated beneficiary. In contrast, when a beneficiary (even Spouse) takes the inherited benefits merely "as beneficiary," distributions after such beneficiary's death will generally continue to be based solely on such beneficiary's life expectancy (see ¶ 1.5, ¶ 1.6); there is no ability for payments after a beneficiary's death to be extended over the life expectancy of *another* beneficiary (except in the rare case in which both spouses die young; ¶ 1.6.05).

This does not mean that naming Spouse as beneficiary is necessarily the way to achieve the longest income tax deferral on benefits. Nevertheless, the spousal rollover is still an extremely valuable deferral tool for three reasons: First, most participants want to name their spouses as beneficiaries, despite the longer income tax deferral that might be available if children or grandchildren were named, so the rollover becomes a way to revive the option of longer deferral if Spouse survives Participant. Second, once Participant has died, the spousal rollover shines as a way to correct problems that exist with Participant's beneficiary designation (¶ 3.2.09). Third, if the only form of distribution permitted by Participant's retirement plan is a lump sum distribution (see ¶ 1.5.09), the spousal rollover is the only way to preserve the possibility of a life expectancy payout (because Spouse, as beneficiary of the lump sum distribution, can roll the distribution to a retirement plan that permits the life expectancy payout while other beneficiaries could not).

The spousal rollover is so valuable that it is frequently the object of *post mortem* planning efforts. See ¶ 8.2.03 for the use of qualified disclaimers to redirect to Spouse retirement benefits that were left payable to the "wrong" beneficiary, so the spousal rollover can be used.

3.2.02 *Rollover if Spouse is under age 59½*

A drawback of the spousal rollover is its effect on the 10% penalty applicable to pre-age 59½, distributions (Chapter 9). If Spouse is named as beneficiary, she is entitled to withdraw benefits from the deceased Participant's plan or IRA without a penalty even if she is younger than age 59½ (and even if the deceased Participant was younger than age 59½) because the penalty does not apply to death benefits (¶ 9.3.01). If she rolls over the benefits to her own retirement plan, however, they lose their character as penalty-exempt-death benefits. She will not be able to withdraw them until she herself reaches age 59½, unless she either pays the 10% penalty or qualifies for one of the exceptions (¶ 9.2, ¶ 9.3) from that tax.

So what should a Spouse who inherits benefits while under age 59½ do? One approach is to leave the benefits in the decedent's plan until Spouse reaches age 59½. The advantage of this approach is that Spouse can draw money out of the decedent's plan, as beneficiary, penalty-free, whenever she needs it, and (once she reaches age 59½) roll over whatever is left to her own retirement plan. The *drawback* of this approach is what happens if Spouse dies before she does the rollover. There are three possibilities if that happens, each of which generally would result in less income tax deferral than if Spouse had rolled over the benefits prior to her death:

1. If Spouse died after she was required to commence taking distributions (see ¶ 1.6.04), the benefits remaining in the decedent's plan at her death will have to be distributed over Spouse's remaining single life expectancy (¶ 1.6.06).

2.   If Spouse died before the Designation Date, see ¶ 1.8.08.

3.   If Spouse died on or after Participant's Designation Date, but before her required commencement date, the 5-year rule and its exceptions will apply as if Spouse were the "participant." See ¶ 1.6.05.

Rather than leaving the benefits in the decedent's plan until she is over 59½, Spouse could choose to roll over the benefits to her own retirement plan. This option is best if she won't need any money from the account prior to age 59½. Even if she will need money after the rollover, however, she can withdraw from her rollover IRA penalty-free if she qualifies for an exception; for example, she could structure her withdrawals as a "series of substantially equal periodic payments" (¶ 9.2).

Finally, she could roll over some of the benefits and leave some of them (equivalent to what she thinks she might need before age 59½) in the decedent's plan.

An old letter ruling (PLR 9608042) suggested that, by withdrawing *any* benefits penalty-free before she herself attained age 59½, Spouse would be making an irrevocable election not to treat Participant's IRA as her own IRA. The IRS has abandoned this idea. See, e.g., Prop. Reg. § 1.408-8, A-5, which provides that "The surviving spouse of an individual may elect...to treat the spouse's entire interest as a beneficiary in an individual's IRA (*or the remaining part of such interest if distribution thereof has commenced to the spouse*) as the spouse's own IRA." Emphasis added. By specifying that the spousal election can be made even after Spouse has taken one or more distributions as beneficiary, the IRS confirms that taking a distribution as beneficiary does not constitute an election not to treat the remaining benefits as Spouse's own. See also PLR 2001-10033 (spouse not forced to elect between taking as beneficiary and taking as owner).

3.2.03 *Spousal rollover of QRP distribution*

§ 402(c)(9) allows Participant in a qualified retirement plan (QRP) to "roll over" certain plan distributions to another QRP, or to an individual retirement account (IRA), provided various requirements are met. ¶ 2.5. If death benefits are paid to Participant's surviving spouse, the rollover rules "apply to such distribution in the same manner as if

Spouse were" the Participant.

The distribution does not have to be a distribution of the entire account balance. Partial distributions are eligible for rollover, unless they are MRDs or part of a series of substantially equal payments (see ¶ 2.5.02). The tests for determining whether a distribution is an "eligible rollover distribution," and other rollover rules, are the same for the surviving spouse as they would have been for the deceased Participant, except that there are slightly different rules regarding what type of plan Spouse may roll the distribution into (see ¶ 3.2.10).

3.2.04 *Deadline for completing spousal rollover*

There is no deadline, as such, for making a spousal rollover. Of course, once any benefits are actually distributed to Spouse, they must be rolled over within 60 days or not at all. § 402(c)(3). But there is no specific time limit based on Participant's death after which it becomes "too late" to roll over distributions. The Code provides simply that a QRP distribution of death benefits to Spouse can be rolled over by Spouse if the deceased Participant could have rolled it over had it been paid to him. § 402(c)(9).

However, there are other rules which, as a practical matter, do create "deadlines" for completing the spousal rollover or otherwise function as limitations on Spouse's ability to roll over:

1.   If Spouse dies before completing the rollover, see ¶ 3.2.02 (for discussion of MRD drawbacks) and ¶ 3.2.07 (regarding whether Spouse's executor can complete a rollover).

2.   If Participant was already past his RBD when his death occurred, MRDs must continue until the rollover occurs; thus delay may waste deferral opportunities or even eliminate the possibility of a rollover. See ¶ 2.5.05.

3.2.05 *Rollover (or spousal election) for inherited IRA*

§ 408(d), in a backhanded way, permits a surviving spouse to treat an inherited IRA as if it were Spouse's *own* IRA, and to roll over distributions from decedent's IRA to her own IRA.

The Code provides that distributions from an "inherited IRA" may not be treated as tax-free rollovers; but then goes on to say that an "inherited IRA" means an IRA acquired by reason of the death of another individual, if the person who inherited the account is not the surviving spouse of the decedent. § 408(d)(3)(C). Thus an IRA inherited by Spouse is not subject to the restrictions applicable to an "inherited IRA" (¶ 2.5.04) and by negative implication Spouse may roll over distributions to her from the deceased Participant's IRA as if it were Spouse's own IRA.

Prop. Reg. § 1.408-8, A-5(a), provides that "The surviving spouse of an individual may elect...to treat the spouse's entire interest as a beneficiary in an individual's IRA (or the remaining part of such interest if distribution thereof has commenced to the spouse) as the spouse's own IRA." The effect of such an election is that Spouse's "interest in the IRA would then be subject to the distribution requirements of section 401(a)(9)(A) applicable to the spouse as the IRA owner rather than those of section 401(a)(9)(B) applicable to the surviving spouse as the decedent IRA owner's beneficiary."

The spousal election "is permitted to be made at any time after the distribution of the required minimum amount for the account for the calendar year containing the individual's date of death. In order to make this election, the spouse must be the sole beneficiary of the IRA and have an unlimited right to withdrawal [sic] amounts from the IRA." Note that the requirement that Spouse be "sole" beneficiary to make this election is satisfied (as to a "separate account" within the retirement plan benefit) if Spouse is sole beneficiary of such separate account, even if she is not sole beneficiary of Participant's entire interest in the retirement plan. See ¶ 1.7.06.

Prop. Reg. § 1.408-8, A-5(b) explains how Spouse makes this election. Ideally, with proper advice and planning, Spouse makes the election in an affirmative manner by "redesignating the account as the account in the name of the surviving spouse as IRA owner rather than as beneficiary." However, the election can get made automatically by Spouse's taking actions deemed inconsistent with "beneficiary" status. This can happen in either of two ways. One is Spouse makes a contribution to the account; since contributions to an inherited IRA are not allowed, Spouse is deemed to have elected to treat the account as her own if she contributes to it. Prop. Reg. § 1.408-8, A-5(b)(2).

The other way is if Spouse fails to take a MRD that would be required to be made to her as beneficiary. Prop. Reg. § 1.408-8, A-5(b)(1). See, e.g., PLR 2001-21073.

This provision of the proposed regulations needs additional

work by the IRS, since as written it does not work properly in all situations. For example, it appears to require Spouse to take two MRDs in one year (the year of Participant's death). Since further clarification is likely in final regulations, this topic will not be discussed further here.

3.2.06 *Rollover (but no election) for 403(b) plans*

The Code does not permit spousal rollovers or elections for 403(b) plans. § 403(b) has no provision comparable to § 408(d)(3)(C) (¶ 3.2.05) permitting Spouse to treat an inherited 403(b) plan as her own. The proposed regulations confirm that a surviving spouse as beneficiary of a 403(b) plan cannot elect to treat an inherited 403(b) account as her own; that option applies only to inherited IRAs. Prop. Reg. § 1.403(b)-2, A-1(c)(2).

§ 403(b)(8) permits rollovers by a 403(b) plan *Participant,* but has no provision for rollovers by Participant's *Spouse.* § 403(b)(8)(B) provides that "rules similar to" § 402(c)(2)-(c)(7) (dealing with rollovers of qualified plan distributions) shall apply to distributions from 403(b) plans, but § 403(b) does not "import" § 402(c)(9), the provision that allows *spousal* rollovers.

Nevertheless, the IRS thinks Congress meant to allow spousal rollovers of distributions from 403(b) plans, and allows such rollovers. Reg. § 1.403(b)-2, A-1 (last sentence) provides that various rollover rules in § 402, including § 402(c)(9), apply to rollovers from 403(b) plans, even though they were not specifically mentioned by Congress in § 403(b)(8)(B). See, e.g., PLRs 2001-01018, 9713018.

3.2.07 *Rollover or election by Spouse's executor*

The IRS has not allowed the executor of Spouse's estate to exercise Spouse's "personal" right to treat the deceased Participant's IRA as Spouse's own IRA. PLRs 2001-26036, 9237038. As one lawyer put it, "She can't roll over in her grave" (Colin S. Marshall, 1997).

Congress has authorized the IRS to liberalize its rollover rules, to allow (among other things) the rollover, after an employee's death, of a distribution made to the employee during life which he failed, due to his death, to complete within 60 days after the distribution. See § 402(c)(3) (effective after 2001). Presumably any such liberalized rule will *also* apply to a distribution made after Participant's death to a surviving spouse which she does not manage to roll over within 60 days because she dies before completing the rollover. As with any post-death rollovers that may be permitted a very thorny question is who will be the beneficiary of the rollover IRA; see discussion at ¶ 2.5.03.

However, nothing in EGTRRA requires the IRS to review its policy of not permitting the surviving spouse's executor to *initiate* a rollover. Therefore, after 2001 as well as before 2002, if it is desirable for Spouse to roll over amounts left to her by Participant, such rollovers should be initiated and completed as soon as possible after Participant's death.

3.2.08 *Required beginning date for rolled over benefits*

Once Spouse has completed a rollover, the minimum distribution rules apply to the rolled over amount as if she were the Participant (which she now is, with respect to the rolled over amounts). See ¶ 1.3.08 for the required beginning date for rolled over amounts.

3.2.09 *Rollover when Spouse inherits through an estate or trust*

The IRS, in letter rulings, has permitted a spousal rollover where Spouse was not named as the designated beneficiary, but the benefits were payable to Participant's estate and Spouse was the sole beneficiary of the estate. See, *e.g.*, PLRs 2001-29036, 8911006, and 9402023 (Spouse was sole beneficiary and personal representative).

In other rulings, Spouse was not the sole beneficiary, but was the residuary beneficiary and also was the executrix. As executrix, she distributed the right to receive Participant's retirement benefits (which were payable to the estate) to herself in partial fulfillment of the residuary bequest. The IRS allowed her to roll the benefits over. PLRs 2001-06047, 2001-01038, 9351041, 9545010.

In another ruling, Spouse claimed a statutory share of the estate. Under applicable state law, a surviving spouse who elected the statutory share could also specify which assets would be used to fund that share. Spouse exercised this right by directing the trustee of the decedent's QRP (which was payable to the estate) to transfer assets of the plan directly into an IRA in Spouse's own name. This was held to be a valid "direct rollover." PLR 9524020.

There have been letter rulings permitting a spousal rollover where benefits were payable to a trust under which Spouse had an unlimited right to withdraw the principal. Spouse exercised the power to withdraw the funds from the IRA into the trust, then out to herself and into her own IRA. PLRs 2001-30056, 1999-25033, 9302022, 9426049, and 9427035.

PLR 9426049 may be the most extreme of these favorable rulings. Participant's benefits were payable to a trust that was to be divided into two subtrusts at his death. Spouse and a bank were co-trustees, but Spouse had the right to remove the bank, and become sole trustee, one year after Participant's death. After the one-year period, the trustees allocated the benefits to one of the subtrusts, and caused them to be distributed to Spouse under a discretionary power to pay her principal "in her best interest." This was held to be a valid rollover because of Spouse's power to remove the co-trustee and distribute principal to herself, even though for the first year after Participant's death she had no such power (and even though she never did exercise this power).

Based on these rulings, it is clear that Spouse is entitled to roll over not only benefits that are paid to her directly as beneficiary, but also benefits that are paid to her as an estate or trust beneficiary *provided* that she is *entitled* to the benefits. She is entitled to the benefits if either:

1.   She is the sole beneficiary of the estate or trust;

2.   She is not the sole beneficiary of the estate or trust, but under the terms of the governing instrument the benefits must be paid to her (and not allocated to other beneficiaries' shares), for example because the will or trust requires that the retirement benefits be allocated to spouse, or because there are no assets available to fund her share other than the retirement plan. If under the terms of the will or trust only part of the assets would necessarily have to be allocated to her share, only that part qualifies for the rollover.

3.   If the benefits are allocated to Spouse's share as a result of the exercise of someone's discretion (rather than because the will or trust requires it) the rollover is still allowed if Spouse is the one who has the discretion (as beneficiary or as fiduciary).

These rulings can obviously be useful in cleanup mode. The

approach could also be useful for planning purposes. A client who wants to divide benefits between Spouse and a credit shelter trust by a formula could leave the benefits to a trust, have the trustee apply the formula to determine how much Spouse is entitled to, and then have the trustee direct the plan administrator to pay the marital portion of the benefits directly to Spouse. Spouse would be able to roll over the amount allocated to her share if, for example, the trustee had no discretion in applying the formula and was required to fulfill Spouse's formula share to the maximum extent possible with retirement benefits. See Form 3.2, Appendix B.

If payment of the benefits to Spouse depends on the discretion of some third party, such as a trustee who is not Spouse herself, the rollover will not be allowed. The rulings have denied rollovers for an IRA payable, for example, to a QTIP trust (¶ 3.3.04) where Spouse's power to withdraw principal was not immediate and unlimited. PLRs 9322005 (Spouse could receive principal only in discretion of a third party trustee), 9321032, and 9445029.

3.2.10 *Types of plan Spouse can roll benefits into*

1.   Spouse can roll benefits to a pre-existing IRA, or to a new IRA established to receive this rollover.

2.   After 2001, Spouse can roll over a post-2001 distribution into any type of plan a living Participant is permitted to roll into; see ¶ 2.5.02. § 402(c)(9).

3.   The IRS has permitted Spouse to roll over benefits from Participant's plan or IRA into another IRA *still in the name of the decedent.* PLRs 9418034, 9842058. This approach may be more attractive than a rollover to an IRA in Spouse's own name when Spouse wants to move the benefits to a different IRA provider, but wants the benefits to retain their status as "death benefits" exempt from the penalty on premature distributions (¶ 3.2.02).

3.3 Qualifying for the Marital Deduction

This ¶ 3.3 describes the requirements and effects of qualifying for the federal estate tax marital deduction for retirement benefits left to the surviving spouse (sometimes called "Spouse") of the retirement plan Participant (sometimes called the "decedent," the "client," or the "first spouse to die"), or to a trust for Spouse, if Spouse is a United States citizen. If Spouse is not a U.S. citizen, you must read Chapter 4 in addition to this ¶ 3.3; Chapter 4 contains additional requirements that must be met to qualify for the marital deduction in that case, and also describes the different way the marital deduction works in that case.

In reading this ¶ 3.3, keep in mind the difference between "trust accounting income," "taxable income" and "minimum required distributions" (¶ 6.1.07); and remember that there are different tests for whether a trust qualifies for the marital deduction (¶ 3.3.03 to ¶ 3.3.09), "passes" the minimum distribution trust rules (¶ 6.2), or is entitled to special options normally available only to the spouse under the minimum distribution (¶ 6.3.13) or rollover (¶ 3.2.09) rules.

The next two subsections are designed to provide a quick introduction to the marital deduction, not a complete exposition of its many intricacies. For complete discussion of estate planning techniques involving the marital deduction, and its requirements, see sources in the Bibliography. ¶ 3.3.03 through ¶ 3.3.14 then discuss how to make sure retirement benefits left to Spouse (or a marital trust) qualify for the deduction, and other marital deduction issues.

3.3.01 *What the marital deduction is and why planners care about it*

Federal estate tax law allows a decedent's estate a deduction, in computing the taxable estate, for the value of property left to the decedent's surviving spouse if various requirements are met. § 2056(a). As long as the federal estate tax is in effect (see § 2210(a), and § 901 of EGTRRA, repealing the estate tax for estates of decedents who die in 2010), qualifying for this "marital deduction" will be an important way to reduce estate taxes for a married client.

Example: It is 2002. Sonny has a $10 million profit sharing plan. Sonny has no other assets and no debts. If he dies in 2002 his estate will be subject to estate taxes because it is over the estate tax exemption amount ($1 million for deaths in 2002), unless some deduction or other technique for estate tax reduction can be applied. Sonny wants to leave his profit sharing plan benefits to his wife, Sally. Both are U.S. citizens. If he leaves the benefits to Sally in a way that qualifies for the marital deduction there will be no estate tax on Sonny's estate because the marital deduction ($10 million) reduced the taxable estate to $0.

Using the marital deduction to eliminate the estate tax on the estate of the first of the two spouses to die is a very popular estate planning technique. Even if not seeking to *eliminate* estate taxes on the first death, the first spouse to die normally wants whatever property he leaves to the surviving spouse to qualify for the estate tax marital deduction, to keep taxes as low as possible on the first death. Therefore estate planners must know how to make bequests qualify for the marital deduction.

Of course, the estate tax may not be actually eliminated (or even reduced) by leaving assets to Spouse and taking the marital deduction. Once Spouse receives the property from decedent's estate it is now part of *her* estate. Thus the property will be subject to estate tax on Spouse's subsequent death—unless Spouse makes the property vanish through spending, gifts and/or unsuccessful investing, or unless the estate tax itself vanishes through repeal or through increased exemptions. Barring such changes, however, the idea of the marital deduction is that the property is removed from the estate of the first spouse to die and added to the surviving spouse's estate, so the tax is merely deferred not eliminated. See, e.g., § 2044.

3.3.02 *The marital deduction requirements: quick tour*

§ 2056, which creates the marital deduction, provides a general rule (the deduction is allowed for the value of property "which passes or has passed from the decedent to his surviving spouse"; § 2056(a)), followed by an exception to the general rule (no deduction is allowed if the property that passes to the surviving spouse is a "life estate or other terminable interest"; § 2056(b)(1)), followed by several exceptions to the exception (certain terminable interests do qualify for the marital deduction after all). The key to qualifying for the marital deduction, therefore, is to make sure that any property left to the surviving spouse (1) is not a "terminable interest," or (2) if it is a terminable interest, it qualifies for one of the exceptions to the "terminable interest rule."

Here is the terminable interest rule: "Where, on the lapse of time, on the occurrence of an event or contingency, or on the failure of an event or contingency to occur, an interest passing to the surviving spouse will terminate or fail, no deduction shall be allowed under this section with respect to such interest--(A) if an interest in such property passes or has passed (for less than an adequate and full consideration in money or money's worth) from the decedent to any person other than such surviving spouse (or the estate of such spouse); and (B) if by reason of such passing such person (or his heirs or assigns) may possess or enjoy any part of such property after such termination or failure of the interest so passing to the surviving spouse...." § 2056(b)(1).

The classic "terminable interest" is a life estate:

Example: Howie leaves Blackacre to his wife Sandra for life, with remainder to Howie's children. Sandra's interest will "terminate or fail" upon her death; she has no power to control what happens to the property after her death, or to say who receives it after she is finished with it. An interest in Blackacre (i.e., the remainder interest) has passed from Howie to someone other than Sandra or her estate (i.e., Howie's children). Howie's children will "enjoy" Blackacre after Sandra's interest ends. Sandra's life estate in Blackacre is a "terminable interest."

One reason Congress is so concerned to make sure that Spouse doesn't get a terminable interest is that Congress wants to be sure the estate tax is merely deferred by the marital deduction, not eliminated. In the Howie and Sandra example, on Sandra's death there is nothing left to tax in Sandra's estate because all she owned was a life estate. On the death of a life tenant there is nothing to be taxed in the life tenant's estate. The life tenant has nothing she can transfer to others at her death, so the property is not includible in the gross estate of a life tenant—unless some special statutory provision applies to make it taxable. (There are two such special statutory provisions under which property is included in the estate of a life tenant. If the life tenant originally owned the entire property, gave it away and *retained* a life estate, as opposed to receiving the life estate from another person, see § 2036; the other is for "QTIP" property; see ¶ 3.3.04.)

To test a bequest for qualification for the marital deduction, therefore, you need determine (1) whether any interest in the property is passing from the decedent to someone other than Spouse or her estate (i.e., a third party), (2) if Spouse's interest in the same property will "terminate or fail" at some point and (3) whether the third party will have the property after termination of Spouse's interest. If the answer to these three questions is "yes," then the property is a terminable interest, and you need to determine (4) whether the property qualifies for any exception to the terminable interest rule.

The rest of this ¶ 3.3 looks at the most common forms of disposition of retirement benefits to Spouse and how these fit into the terminable interest rule and its exceptions. ¶ 3.3.03 through ¶ 3.3.12 look at leaving retirement benefits to a marital deduction trust ("marital trust"). ¶ 3.3.13 discusses the marital deduction rules for "survivor annuities." Finally, ¶ 3.3.14 discusses the marital deduction rules for benefits left outright to Spouse as named beneficiary under the plan.

The following discussion is merely an overview of the various methods of complying with the marital deduction; the practitioner needs to read the applicable statutory provisions and regulations for full details on the requirements before drafting an estate plan. In expert hands, the interaction of the marital deduction and minimum distribution rules could inspire creative solutions to planning problems; see, e.g., discussion at ¶ 3.3.11. Less experienced practitioners may wish to stay within the safe harbors of tried and true solutions; see, e.g., ¶ 3.3.07.

This book does not cover other forms of marital deduction disposition, such as the charitable remainder trust of which Spouse is the sole non-charitable beneficiary (§ 2056(b)(8)), insurance or annuity contracts with power of appointment (§ 2056(b)(6)), or the "estate trust" (trust of which Spouse is sole life beneficiary, and the remainder beneficiary is Spouse's estate).

3.3.03 "General power" marital trust

Under § 2056(b)(5), property qualifies for the marital deduction if Spouse (1) is "entitled for life to all income from" (¶ 3.3.06) the property, payable at least annually, and (2) has the power, exercisable by Spouse alone and in all events, to appoint the property to herself (or to her estate), and (3) there is no power in any other person to appoint any of the property to someone other than Spouse. This type of interest left to a surviving spouse is not a terminable interest because § 2056(b)(5) says that if these conditions are met no part of the property is considered to pass to someone other than Spouse. A trust that meets the requirements of § 2056(b)(5) is called a "general power marital trust" in this Chapter.

If Participant names a "general power marital trust" as

beneficiary of his retirement benefits, does he need to take any *other* steps to make sure the retirement benefits qualify for the marital deduction? Yes. See ¶ 3.3.05. For income tax effects of naming a general power marital trust as beneficiary of retirement benefits see ¶ 3.3.11.

3.3.04 *"QTIP" marital trust*

As explained in ¶ 3.3.03, § 2056(b)(5) defines a "general power marital trust" so that such a trust is not a terminable interest. Under § 2056(b)(7), Congress goes further and allows the marital deduction for a type of bequest to Spouse that definitely *is* a terminable interest, "qualified terminable interest property," or "QTIP."

Property qualifies for the estate tax marital deduction as QTIP if (1) Spouse is entitled for life to all of the income from the property (¶ 3.3.06), payable at least annually, and (2) no person has the power to appoint any of the property to someone other than Spouse during her lifetime, and (3) the decedent's executor irrevocably elects, on the decedent's estate tax return, to treat the property as QTIP. § 2056(b)(7). A trust that meets the requirements of § 2056(b)(7) is called a "qualified terminable interest property" marital trust, QTIP marital trust or simply "QTIP trust."

Since a QTIP trust really is a terminable interest, Congress needed to take one more step to insure that the estate tax would be merely deferred rather than eliminated when it allowed the marital deduction for QTIP trusts (see discussion at ¶ 3.3.02). Accordingly, § 2044 provides that the surviving spouse's estate includes any property for which the marital deduction was elected at the first spouse's death under § 2056(b)(7).

3.3.05 *Extra step required when benefits payable to marital trust*

Every estate planning lawyer should know how to draft a trust that complies with the marital deduction requirements described at ¶ 3.3.03 and ¶ 3.3.04. Many practitioners assume that, once the standard marital trust is drafted, and the trust is named as beneficiary of Participant's retirement benefits, qualification of those benefits for the estate tax marital deduction is assured (assuming Spouse survives Participant and doesn't disclaim her interest in the marital trust).

The IRS has a different view. The IRS's position is that, when a retirement plan benefit is payable to a marital trust, both the retirement plan benefit *and* the trust must meet the marital deduction requirements if the marital deduction is to be allowed. In the IRS's view, the retirement plan itself is an item of "terminable interest property" separate from the marital trust. Rev. Rul. 2000-2, 2000-31 I.R.B. 305 (1/4/2000).

Does this mean that all the marital deduction language must be recited in the beneficiary designation form as well as in the trust instrument? No. Although that would be one way to comply with the IRS's directive, Rev. Rul. 2000-2 says that the various "governing instrument" requirements are satisfied with respect to a retirement benefit payable to a marital trust if (1) the marital trust document contains the required language (e.g., giving the spouse the right to all income annually) and (2) the retirement plan document does not contain any provisions which would prevent the trustee of the marital trust from complying with the trust's provisions.

Note, however, that Rev. Rul. 2000-2 requires the executor, on the estate tax return, to elect QTIP treatment for *both* the retirement benefit *and* the marital trust when retirement benefits are payable to a marital trust, confirming the approach seen in PLR 9442032 as well as Rev. Rul. 89-89, 1989-2 C.B. 231.

3.3.06 *Meaning of "entitled for life to all of the income"*

One of the requirements for either type of marital trust (¶ 3.3.03-¶ 3.3.04) is that Spouse must be "entitled for life to all of the income" of the trust. There are several ways to comply with this requirement. This ¶ 3.3.06 discusses the general problems of meeting this requirement in connection with retirement benefits payable to a marital trust. Particular methods of compliance are discussed in ¶ 3.3.07 through ¶ 3.3.09.

Regardless of which method is used to comply with the entitled-to-all-income requirement, there are two perennial issues which make marital trust administration (and drafting) more difficult when the trust is funded with retirement benefits. One is, what is the "income" Spouse is entitled to when the asset in question is a retirement plan benefit? See ¶ 6.1.07 for discussion of that question.

The second problem is the minimum distribution rules (Chapter 1). Regardless of whether the trustee is or is not required to withdraw "income" from the retirement plan (see ¶ 3.3.07-¶ 3.3.09), the trustee must withdraw the minimum required distribution (MRD) annually. Thus, if the trust instrument requires the trustee to withdraw the "income" annually (¶ 3.3.07) what it is really requiring is that the trustee withdraw from the retirement plan each year the income or the MRD, whichever is the larger amount. The trustee must calculate both amounts each year in any case. The MRD may be more or less than the income. Spouse is entitled to the "income," but the marital deduction rules do not require that she receive the entire MRD (if that is larger than the income). Even though it is not a marital deduction requirement that the QTIP trustee distribute to Spouse the greater of the MRD or the income, it is sometimes appropriate to draft the trust that way; see ¶ 3.3.12.

This brings us to the crux of why it matters how a marital trust named as beneficiary of retirement benefits complies with the "entitled to all income" requirement. If the "income" of the retirement plan benefits is greater than the MRD, it would be desirable not to have to distribute the excess amount out of the retirement plan if such distribution would cause current taxation of that amount and that taxation that could have been deferred until later under the minimum distribution rules (Chapter 1). (As to why current distribution of such excess does not necessarily result in current *taxation* of such excess, see ¶ 3.3.07.) Therefore, if the current distribution of "all income" would result in significant acceleration of income taxation, the planner will look for a way to avoid such current distribution.

The planning process on this issue is quite complex, and it is not possible to review every possible factor and response here. A review of the following subsections will reveal that use of any method of compliance other than "distribute all income" (¶ 3.3.07) involves greater complication of the drafting and planning process. These complications are worth undertaking only if the result will be significantly improved income tax deferral (unless there is some other, non-tax, reason for incurring them). Therefore the planner needs to consider exactly what the difference will be between the amount of the "income" and the amount of the MRD; see further discussion at ¶ 3.3.09.

When the IRS updates its actuarial tables in compliance with EGTRRA (¶ 1.2.04), life expectancies will probably increase, resulting in smaller required distributions, and possibly a greater difference in amount between the (new, smaller) "MRD" and the "income" of a retirement plan payable to a QTIP trust. That change when it occurs could make the alternative method of compliance (¶ 3.3.09) beneficial in more cases.

Another factor to consider when deciding how to comply with the entitled-to-all-income requirement is how cooperative Spouse is likely to be. If Spouse is likely to exercise every demand right given to her (such as the right to require the trustee to invest in income-producing property, ¶ 3.3.08, or the right to demand distribution of income, ¶ 3.3.09), then nothing is likely to be achieved by substituting demand rights for the requirement of automatic current income distributions.

The next three subsections review three approaches to complying with the requirement that spouse be entitled for life to all income of a marital trust. The same rules apply to both QTIP and general power marital trusts for purposes of determining whether the spouse is entitled to all income. Reg. § 20.2056(b)-7(d)(2).

3.3.07 *Distribute all income to Spouse annually*

The easiest way to comply with the all-income requirement is to require the trustee to withdraw from the retirement plan each year, and distribute to Spouse, the "income" of the retirement plan. Reg. § 20.2056(b)-5(f)(8). This method was "blessed" by the IRS in Rev. Rul. 89-89, 1989-2 C.B. 231, and is believed to be the most commonly used by estate planners. See, *e.g.*, PLRs 9321035, 9321059, 9418026, and 9348025. For an example of a form using this method, see Form 7.4, Appendix B. Unless the "income" substantially exceeds the MRD (see ¶ 3.3.09) this method does not have significant tax drawbacks (beyond the usual drawbacks of leaving retirement benefits to a marital trust in the first place; see ¶ 3.3.10).

Even if use of this method does require distribution to Spouse of an amount significantly greater than the MRD (which would be the case if the "income" of the retirement plan substantially exceeds the MRD) that would not mean loss of deferral if Spouse is entitled to, and does, roll over the excess to her own retirement plan. See ¶ 3.2 for discussion of spousal rollovers generally. As explained in ¶ 3.2.09, the IRS has repeatedly ruled that a surviving spouse may roll over retirement plan distributions that are made to her through a trust if she was absolutely entitled to receive that amount from the plan via the trust. This rule would appear to allow spousal rollover of income distributions from a marital trust that is named as beneficiary of a retirement plan (to the extent the distribution exceeds the MRD; MRDs cannot be rolled over; ¶ 2.5.05), provided the trust requires the trustee to distribute those amounts to Spouse. However, the application of the rollover-through-trust rules in this specific context (for income distributions from a marital trust) has not been confirmed in any case or ruling.

Prior to 2000, the IRS's position was that the distribution from the plan of all income annually was the only method available for a retirement plan benefit payable to a trust to qualify for the marital deduction. Rev. Rul. 89-89. In Rev. Rul. 2000-2 the IRS reversed this position and acknowledged that a marital trust funded with retirement benefits can use other methods permitted in the regulations (see ¶ 3.3.08-¶ 3.3.09) for meeting the "entitled for life to all income" requirement. Rev. Rul. 2000-2 announced that it "obsoleted" Rev. Rul.89-89, which has led to some confusion among practitioners. The method "blessed" in Rev. Rul. 89-89 for complying with the entitled-to-all-income requirement (namely, requiring annual distribution of all income to Spouse) still works; Rev. Rul. 2000-2 obsoleted Rev. Rul. 89-89 only to the extent Rev. Rul. 89-89 said this was the *only* method that worked.

3.3.08 *Treat the retirement plan as "unproductive property"*

It wouldn't make sense for Congress to say Spouse must be "entitled to all income" of the trust, then allow the trust to invest in property that doesn't produce any income. The classic example of "unproductive property" (in the trust accounting sense) is a tree farm. As the trees grow, the property may be increasing in value but there are no sales proceeds, dividends, interest payments or other cash profits coming to the trust until the end of the line, when the trees are cut down and sold. Until the trees are cut down the asset generates no "income" to be distributed to Spouse.

Accordingly, to avoid leaving Spouse with a meaningless right, the law has to prevent the trustee from thwarting Spouse's income rights by investing the trust in non-income producing property against her wishes. A marital trust does not have to forbid the trustee to invest in non-income producing property, but if the trust is permitted to invest in unproductive property the trust must protect Spouse in one of two ways.

One way is to give Spouse the right to require the trustee to make any such property productive (she could require the trustee to cut down some trees for cash sale every year) or to convert it to productive property within a reasonable time (she could require the trustee to sell the tree farm and reinvest the proceeds in something that produces current income). Reg. § 20.2056(b)-5(f)(4).

If the trust corpus consists substantially of non-income producing property and Spouse does *not* have the power to compel the trustee to make it income producing, the trust will *still* qualify for the marital deduction if Spouse can "require that the trustee provide the required beneficial enjoyment, such as by payments to Spouse out of other assets of the trust." Reg. § 20.2056(b)-5(f)(5).

If a retirement plan from which annual MRDs are small or non-existent could be regarded as "unproductive property," current distribution of income could be avoided and income tax deferral enhanced, perhaps with fewer complications than are involved with giving Spouse an income demand right (¶ 3.3.09). Whether or how this could be done is beyond the scope of this discussion, but anyone trying it would need to deal with the following points.

First, unlike the other two methods (¶ 3.3.07, ¶ 3.3.09), there is no Revenue Ruling or other pronouncement from the IRS explaining how this method applies to retirement plans.

Second, since the IRS regards the retirement plan as a separate item of "terminable interest property" (see discussion of Rev. Rul. 2000-2 at ¶ 3.3.05), it is not clear that distributions to Spouse from other (non-retirement plan) assets held by the marital trust could be used to replace the missing income payments with regard to the "unproductive" retirement plan as permitted by Reg. § 20.2056(b)-5(f)(5). This issue can be avoided by giving Spouse the right to demand the property be made income-producing (Reg. § 20.2056(b)-5(f)(4)) rather than giving the trustee the right to substitute other distributions for the missing income payments.

Third, in view of the lack of authority regarding the definition of trust accounting income with respect to retirement benefits (see ¶ 6.1.07) it may not be clear that a retirement plan is "unproductive" just because it isn't distributing anything. If the trust instrument requires the trustee to distribute "all income" to Spouse, the trustee may not be complying with the trust document if the trustee doesn't distribute anything from the retirement plan, even if the trust allows the trustee to hold unproductive property with Spouse's consent, unless applicable state law or the governing instrument makes clear that a retirement plan has no "income" apart from what is distributed from the plan.

As to how MRDs could be non-existent, see ¶ 6.3.13: a marital trust for the benefit of the surviving spouse of a Participant who died before the year he would have reached age 70½ would not have to take any MRDs from the plan until the year the Participant would have reached age 70½, if the marital trust is a "conduit trust" as to Spouse. See further discussion at ¶ 3.3.11.

3.3.09 *Give Spouse the right to demand the income*

A surviving Spouse is entitled to all income of a trust if Spouse has "the right exercisable annually (or more frequently) to require distribution to herself of the trust income, and otherwise [*i.e.*, if she does not require such distribution in any year] the trust income [for such year] is to be accumulated...." Reg. § 20.2056(b)-5(f)(8).

In Rev. Rul. 2000-2, citing Reg. § 20.2056(b)-5(f)(8), the IRS ruled that an IRA payable to a marital trust qualified for the marital deduction where the trust gave the surviving spouse "the power, exercisable annually, to compel the trustee to withdraw from the IRA an amount equal to the income earned on the assets held by the IRA during the year and to distribute that amount through the trust to" the surviving spouse, and "[n]othing in the IRA instrument" prohibited the trustee from making such withdrawals.

Use of this method of complying with the entitled-to-all-income requirement involves substantial additional complications not discussed in Rev. Rul. 2000-2. Is Spouse's right to withdraw the income from the retirement plan to be lapsing or non-lapsing? If lapsing, will her failure to withdraw the income constitute a completed gift to the remainder beneficiaries of the trust? Whether her right is lapsing or not, her failure to withdraw current income could: change the income tax treatment of the trust (by causing it to become partially a "grantor trust" as to Spouse; see § 678(a)(2)); result in inclusion of the different portions of the trust in her estate under different Code sections (§ 2036 versus § 2044), which in turn could make different estate tax apportionment rules applicable to the different parts of the trust at her death (compare § 2207B(a)(1) and § 2207A(a)(1)); and (if a "reverse QTIP" election has been made for the trust; see § 2652(a)(3)) result in the trust's having two transferors for generation skipping transfer tax purposes. These questions are not relevant to marital deduction qualification, nor applicable only to retirement benefits, and are beyond the scope of this book, but need to be considered by a practitioner who uses this method of complying with the entitled-to-all-income requirement.

Before undertaking such additional complications, the practitioner should consider whether the effort will result in significant savings. For example, in a classic QTIP trust (income to Spouse, remainder to issue), the maximum period of income tax deferral for retirement benefits left to that trust is the life expectancy of the oldest trust beneficiary (¶ 1.5.08), who is (in most cases) Spouse. If Spouse is over age 50 at the time of Participant's death, the MRD based on her life expectancy will be more than 3% of the benefits. The "divisor" at age 50 under IRS Table V (see Appendix A) is 33.1, which translates to a MRD of just over 3% of the value of the plan; each year the divisor declines and the corresponding percentage increases (see ¶ 1.2.01 for more explanation). Unless the "income" rate of the retirement benefit is more than 3%, the MRD for a Spouse over age 50 will be more than the income—meaning the trustee will have to withdraw more than the "income" *regardless* of the fact that the trust allows income to be accumulated. If the MRD is close to or exceeds the amount of the "income" there is no advantage to allowing the trustee to accumulate income inside the retirement plan because the minimum distribution rules will prevent the trustee from doing so.

3.3.10 *Income tax drawbacks of leaving benefits to QTIP trust*

Even aside from the problems with the "all income" requirement, leaving retirement benefits to a QTIP trust is no tax bargain. Compared with leaving benefits outright to Spouse, the classic QTIP trust (income to Spouse, remainder to other beneficiaries) costs substantial extra income taxes, *even if* the trust qualifies for the marital deduction and *even if* the trust complies with the minimum distribution "trust rules" (¶ 6.2).

For example, if the retirement plan benefits were payable to Spouse personally and Spouse rolled them over to Spouse's own IRA, Spouse could defer distributions altogether until she reached age 70½. When the benefits are paid to a QTIP trust, in contrast, the minimum distribution rules require annual distributions to the trust beginning the year after Participant's death. ¶ 1.5.08.

Also, with a rollover IRA, when Spouse reaches her required beginning date (¶ 1.3), Spouse must start taking MRDs from the rollover IRA. These would be computed using the factors in the "Uniform Table" (¶ 1.4.01; see Appendix A), which represent the joint life expectancy of the IRA owner (Spouse in this case) and a hypothetical beneficiary who is 10 years younger. When the benefits are paid to a marital trust, in contrast, minimum distributions will be based (*at best*) on the single life expectancy of Spouse (if she is the oldest trust beneficiary, and the other requirements for "looking through" a trust for MRD purposes are met; ¶ 6.2.04). The use of the single life expectancy payout will produce a much more rapid depletion of the account than would use of the joint life expectancy factors in the Uniform Table.

With a rollover IRA, there can be a long period of deferral (over the life expectancy of Spouse's oldest designated beneficiary; ¶ 1.5.08) for any benefits remaining in the IRA at Spouse's death. When the benefits are paid to a marital trust, in contrast, MRDs will continue to be calculated based solely on Spouse's single life expectancy, even after Spouse's death. The opportunity to spread distributions over the long life expectancy of members of a younger generation is forever lost.

To the extent the retirement plan distributions are treated as "principal" for trust accounting purposes (¶ 6.1.07), they can be retained in the trust during Spouse's lifetime without jeopardizing the marital deduction. For income tax purposes, however, these distributions are taxable income (see §§ 402 and 691) regardless of their status for trust accounting purposes. Trust income tax rates reach the top federal bracket at a mere $8,901 of taxable income (2001 rates). A human does not hit her highest bracket until she has $297,351 of taxable income. Few surviving spouses will be in that high a bracket.

Thus, making benefits payable to a marital trust, as opposed to Spouse individually, often results in subjecting the benefits to income taxes sooner, and at a higher rate, than would be the case if Spouse personally were named as beneficiary. See the *Koslow* case study, Chapter 11, and more discussion at ¶ 10.5.05.

3.3.11 *Income tax treatment of other types of marital trust*

Can the QTIP trust drawbacks described in ¶ 3.3.10 be avoided by naming some other kind of marital trust as beneficiary?

A "general power marital trust" (¶ 3.3.03) has all the same drawbacks as a QTIP trust if it gives Spouse only the right to income, or if it gives Spouse the right to income plus limited rights to principal that fall short of allowing her unconditionally to withdraw the retirement plan from the trust. Examples of such limited principal rights would be the right to principal in the discretion of the trustee (who is someone other than herself), the right to principal based on an ascertainable standard relating to her health, education, maintenance and support (§ 2041(b)(1)(A)), or a "5-and-5 power" (see § 2514(e)). The fact that Spouse has a general power of appointment at death makes a difference in terms of what particular Code section the trust qualifies for the marital deduction under, but has no impact on the income tax problems discussed at ¶ 3.3.10.

If the trust gives Spouse the unconditional right to withdraw the retirement plan from the trust, and Spouse exercises that right, she can roll over the benefits to her own IRA; see ¶ 3.2.09. If she doesn't exercise the right, so the benefits stay in the trust, see ¶ 6.3.09 for tax treatment of a trust that is a "grantor trust" as to Spouse under § 678(a).

Finally, if the trust is a "conduit trust" as to Spouse (¶ 6.3.08), and Participant died many years before he would have reached age 70½, there are slightly more interesting planning possibilities. Such a trust would be entitled to exercise Spouse's right to defer the commencement of distributions until Participant would have reached age 70½. This right combined with a provision such as that used in Rev. Rul. 2000-2 (see discussion at ¶ 3.3.08) permitting accumulation of income in the retirement plan (with Spouse's consent) could substantially improve the income tax deferral compared with a standard QTIP trust. *All* plan distributions could be deferred until the year Participant would have reached age 70½. Since this approach makes a difference only for Participants who die relatively young (which most people don't), and since the conduit trust format requires all plan distributions (not just "income") to be distributed immediately to Spouse (which is not what most clients who leave benefits to a QTIP trust want), it seems unlikely this will be a widely used approach.

3.3.12 *Other considerations in naming a marital trust as beneficiary*

If the benefits are payable to a trust that is to be divided, at Participant's death, between a "marital trust" and a "credit shelter" (or bypass) trust, it is recommended that either the division be by means of a "fractional" (rather than a "pecuniary") formula, or, if a pecuniary formula is used, that the benefits be made payable directly to the marital trust so they don't become subject to the pecuniary formula for reasons explained at ¶ 2.2.05.

In addition to qualifying for the marital deduction, the practitioner will in many cases also want to be sure the trust complies with the minimum distribution "trust rules," so that benefits can be distributed to the trust over the life expectancy of the oldest trust beneficiary (¶ 6.2, ¶ 1.5.08). However, if Participant is past his required beginning date (¶ 1.3), and the oldest beneficiary of the trust (who typically is Spouse) is close in age to (or older than) Participant, compliance with the "trust rules" will make no difference: the payout period will be the same either way (compare ¶ 1.5.05 with ¶ 1.5.08).

If the client is determined not to leave any assets outright to Spouse, but is unhappy about the adverse income tax effects of a QTIP trust described at ¶ 3.3.10, consider making the retirement benefits payable to the credit shelter trust, and using other assets to fund the marital trust. Although this approach is contrary to the usual rule of thumb ("don't waste your credit shelter paying income taxes"; see ¶ 10.5), this move could substantially increase the potential income tax deferral if the only beneficiaries of the credit shelter trust are substantially younger than Spouse, because MRDs will be spread out over a longer life expectancy period (assuming the trust complies with the minimum distribution trust rules; ¶ 6.2).

3.3.13 Automatic QTIP election for "survivor annuities"

§ 2056(b)(7)(C) provides that "[i]n the case of an annuity included in the gross estate of the decedent under section 2039...where only the surviving spouse has the right to receive payments before the death of such surviving spouse--(i) the interest of such surviving spouse shall be treated as [QTIP], and (ii) the executor shall be treated as having made" a QTIP election for such property unless the executor elects *not* to have QTIP treatment apply.

Retirement plan benefits are considered annuities, includible in Participant's estate under § 2039, whether or not paid in the form of true annuities. Reg. § 20.2039-1(b).

The automatic QTIP treatment provided by § 2056(b)(7)(C) is a nice backup when benefits are left outright to Spouse (see ¶ 3.3.14). It can be helpful or not so helpful when retirement benefits are paid in the form of a true annuity and there is a possibility of payments continuing after Spouse's death:

Example: Mona is receiving a pension from her former employer's defined benefit plan. The form of distribution she elected (with spousal consent; see ¶ 3.4) is a monthly pension of $5,000 for her life, with a minimum guaranteed term of 10 years. She has named her husband Jeff as beneficiary to receive the balance of payments due under the guaranteed term if she dies before the guaranteed term is up. She has named her children Robin and Dana as successor beneficiaries to Jeff if he also does not survive until the end of the 10-year guarantee period. On her death the remaining value of the annuity is $400,000. Because this is included in Mona's estate under § 2039, and no one other than her spouse has the right to receive any payments until his death, the $400,000 is "qualified terminable interest property" under § 2056(b)(7)(C), unless her executor elects *not* to have it treated as QTIP. This treatment may be helpful if it eliminates unwanted estate taxes on Mona's estate.

It would have a negative effect, however, if Mona has few or no other assets (so her estate is not large enough to be taxable anyway), and Jeff has a substantial estate (large enough to be taxable), and Jeff (having survived Mona) also dies before the end of the 10-year guarantee period. If the automatic marital deduction applied to the annuity under § 2056(b)(7)(C) in Mona's estate then the remaining value of the payments will be includible in Jeff's estate under § 2044, resulting in estate taxes. These taxes could have been avoided if Mona's executor had elected out of QTIP treatment for the annuity on Mona's estate tax return.

3.3.14 *Marital deduction for benefits left outright to Spouse*

Death benefits payable directly to Spouse outright in a lump sum should qualify for the marital deduction, provided Spouse is a U.S. citizen and Spouse is entitled to withdraw all the benefits. See, *e.g.*, PLR 8843033. Where Spouse is named as sole beneficiary, with the unrestricted right to withdraw all the benefits from the plan, no part of Participant's interest in the plan passes to someone other than Spouse or her estate, so Spouse has not received a "terminable interest" (¶ 3.3.02).

There is one possible quibble with this conclusion. Suppose Participant has provided in his beneficiary designation form (or the plan documents provide) that, if Spouse dies before having withdrawn all the benefits, any benefits remaining in the account at Spouse's death pass to a "successor beneficiary" who is someone other than Spouse's estate. See ¶ 1.9.02.

Example: Jerry leaves his IRA outright to his wife Carol. However, Jerry's beneficiary designation form (or the account agreement governing the IRA) names his son Hanson as "successor beneficiary" to take the (remaining) benefits if Carol dies after Jerry but before she has withdrawn all the benefits. Since that successor beneficiary is someone other than Carol's own estate, Jerry asks you whether his IRA will qualify for the marital deduction for his estate, or whether it has been transformed into a nondeductible "terminable interest." He points out that an interest in the IRA (*i.e.*, the amount remaining in the account at Carol's death) will pass to someone other than Carol or her estate (*i.e.*, Hanson) upon the occurrence of an event or contingency (*i.e.*, Carol's failure to withdraw the benefits during her lifetime), which is the definition of a nondeductible terminable interest under § 2056(b)(1).

The author believes that this scenario does *not* create a nondeductible interest. For one thing, it meets the description of a deductible interest in § 2056(b)(5), which provides that an interest is deemed to pass to Spouse and only Spouse (and therefore is not a nondeductible terminable interest) if Spouse is entitled to all the income for life, at annual or more frequent intervals, and has the right (exercisable by her alone and in all events) to appoint the principal to herself with no person having the power to appoint it to someone other than her. Spouse has these rights with respect to a retirement plan benefits left outright to her, assuming there is nothing in the beneficiary designation form or plan documents that limits her right to withdraw the income or principal of the account.

The fact that the interest will pass to a successor beneficiary *if Spouse chooses not to withdraw the benefits* should not be deemed to transform this into a terminable interest. The situation is analogous to property left by wife to husband and child as joint tenants. After wife's death, husband can seek partition and take his share of the inherited joint property whenever he wishes, but *if he chooses not to withdraw his share*, it will automatically pass to child by right of survivorship on husband's death. This gift qualifies for the marital deduction. Reg. § 20.2056(b)-5(g)(2).

Furthermore, as explained at ¶ 3.3.13, § 2056(b)(7)(C) treats a surviving spouse's interest in a survivor annuity as "QTIP" property unless the decedent's executor elects otherwise, if Spouse is the sole beneficiary during her lifetime. Therefore, even if it were determined (wrongly, in the author's view) that Jerry's IRA in the example above *was* a terminable interest, the interest would qualify for the automatic QTIP marital deduction under § 2056(b)(7)(C).

To sidestep the issue altogether, one could include additional language such as that in Section 3.07, Forms 2.1, 2.2, Appendix B, when (1) Participant is naming Spouse outright as beneficiary and (2) either the plan document or the beneficiary designation form names a successor beneficiary (other than Spouse's estate) who will be entitled to receive the benefits that Spouse does not withdraw during her lifetime. This language explicitly recites that Spouse has the right to withdraw all income and principal of the benefits, tracking the wording of § 2056(b)(5) and Reg. § 20.2056(b)-5(f)(8).

For why it is desirable for Participant to name a successor beneficiary see ¶ 1.8.08 and ¶ 1.6.05.

3.4 REA '84 and Spousal Consent

3.4.01 *Introduction to the Retirement Equity Act of 1984*

This ¶ 3.4 describes the federal rights granted to spouses of retirement plan participants by the "Retirement Equity Act of 1984" ("REA" or "REACT") (P.L. 98-397), and discusses the estate planning implications of these rights. The applicable law is in IRC § 401(a)(11) and § 417, and the virtually identical ERISA § 205; and Treas. Regs. § 1.401(a)-20 and § 1.417(e)-1.

The purpose of this ¶ 3.4 is to provide estate planners with an overview of REA's requirements and exemptions, with emphasis on aspects that affect estate planning. This essay by no means exhausts REA's intricacies. Practitioners who have studied the spousal consent requirements are bedeviled by such problems as precisely when (relative to the distribution date) spousal consent must be obtained in order to be valid; whether a new spousal consent is required for every distribution if installments are being paid out prior to the RBD; and whether the consent requirements limit the ability of Participant and Spouse to change the form of benefits after the RBD.

This Chapter should not be relied upon for purposes of design or administration of a retirement plan. For an explanation of REA aimed at the plan designer or administrator, I recommend *The Pension Answer Book* by Stephen J. Krass (Panel Publications). See Bibliography for details on that Book and other recommended resources.

Retirement plans fall into three categories with respect to REA's requirements: plans that are subject to the full panoply of REA requirements (all pension plans, some profit sharing plans, some 403(b) plans; ¶ 3.4.02); plans that are subject to a modified version of the REA requirements (some profit sharing plans and some 403(b) plans; ¶ 3.4.03); and plans that are totally exempt from REA's requirements (IRAs, Roth IRAs and some 403(b) plans; ¶ 3.4.04).

3.4.02 *Plans subject to full-scale REA requirements*

If a plan is fully subject to REA, then, generally (for exceptions see ¶ 3.4.05), ANY benefits distributed by that plan to a married employee MUST be distributed in the form of a "qualified joint and survivor annuity" (QJSA), unless the employee has waived that form of benefit and the employee's spouse *consents* to the waiver. If a married employee covered by such a plan dies before retirement, then the plan MUST pay his surviving spouse a "qualified pre-retirement survivor annuity" (QPSA) unless she has *waived* the right to receive the QPSA. The spousal consent (to employee's waiver of QJSA) or spousal waiver (of right to QPSA) must meet specific requirements to be effective; see ¶ 3.4.07, ¶ 3.4.08.

A QJSA is an annuity (1) for the life of Participant with a survivor annuity for the life of Spouse which is not less than 50 percent of (and is not greater than 100 percent of) the amount of the annuity which is payable during the joint lives of Participant and Spouse, and (2) which is the actuarial equivalent of a single annuity for the life of Participant.

The definition of a QPSA is even more elaborate; basically, it is supposed to be the annuity Spouse would have received under the QJSA had the employee lived to retirement, retired with a QJSA, then died. In the case of a defined contribution plan (such as a money purchase pension plan, target benefit plan or "non-exempt" profit sharing plan), the value of the QPSA is defined as an annuity equal in value to 50% of the employee's account balance. § 417(d)(2).

All *pension plans* are subject to the QJSA/QPSA requirements that are described in this ¶ 3.4.02. Defined benefit plans, money purchase pension plans and target benefit plans are in this category. The Code's description is "all defined benefit plans and all defined contribution plans that are subject to the funding standards of § 412." § 401(a)(11)(B).

Other types of qualified retirement plans (profit sharing, stock bonus, 401(k) and ESOP) may or may not be subject to the rules described in this ¶ 3.4.02, depending on whether they fit into the "exemption" (which is not really an exemption, just a modified version of the requirements) described at ¶ 3.4.03.

3.4.03 REA requirements for "exempt" profit sharing plans

Certain qualified plans are exempt from the QJSA/QPSA requirements of REA described at ¶ 3.4.02. Although this type of plan could be any type of QRP other than a "pension" plan, i.e., it could be a profit sharing or stock bonus plan or ESOP, these plans are called here "exempt profit sharing plans." However, these plans are not exempt from *REA*, because (as a condition of being exempt from the QJSA/QPSA requirements) they still have to provide a spousal benefit. A qualified retirement plan that is not a pension plan (see ¶ 3.4.02) is not subject to the QJSA/QPSA requirements described at ¶ 3.4.02 if it meets tests A, B and C described below, and, most significantly for estate planning:

"The plan provides that the participant's nonforfeitable accrued benefit is payable *in full*, upon the participant's death, to the participant's surviving spouse (unless the participant elects, with spousal consent that satisfies the requirements of section 417(a)(2), that such benefit be provided instead to a designated beneficiary)." Emphasis added.

In other words, the only way a profit sharing plan can be "exempt" from the QJSA/QPSA requirements is by (among other requirements) providing a REA-type benefit, namely, distribution of 100% of Participant's account to Spouse at Participant's death unless Spouse consents to waive this right.

Despite the fact that an "exempt" profit sharing plan has to comply with REA, an exempt profit sharing plan is still critically different from a pension plan (or a non-exempt profit sharing plan). Under an exempt profit sharing plan, the employee can withdraw ALL his benefits from the plan whenever the plan permits him to do so (typically, upon separation from service, although some profit sharing plans permit in-service distributions) WITHOUT the consent of Spouse. He can then roll the distributed benefits over to an IRA (¶ 2.5) and continue to enjoy tax deferral without any further obligations to Spouse under federal law (¶ 3.4.04).

The trade-off is that, if the employee dies BEFORE having withdrawn the benefits from the exempt profit sharing plan, 100% of his benefits (including proceeds of any life insurance policy held in the plan) must be paid to the surviving spouse, unless Spouse has consented to waive this right. Reg. § 1.401(a)-20, A-12(b).

In addition to providing that 100% of Participant's benefits are paid to Spouse on Participant's death, a profit sharing plan must meet the following three tests in order to be exempt from QJSA/QPSA benefits for any particular Participant:

A.   The Participant does not elect to have his benefits under the plan paid in the form of a life annuity. As a practical matter, this means that the plan cannot *offer* annuities as a form of benefit if it wants to avoid the QJSA/QPSA requirements, because if the plan offers annuities some Participants will elect them, and then the plan will be in the QJSA/QPSA business. See Reg. § 1.401(a)-20, A-4. Many profit sharing plans choose not to offer any annuity form of benefit.

B.   The plan does not contain money transferred to it from a pension plan. This refers to direct transfers, for example, if an employer terminates its pension plan and transfers its funds into a profit sharing plan. Amounts rolled over into the profit sharing plan by employees are not consider transfers for this purpose even if the amount rolled over originally came from a pension plan. If a profit sharing plan *does* contain money that was transferred from a pension plan, there is a way of keeping the pension money (subject to REA) separate from the "pure" profit sharing plan money and avoiding the QPSA/QJSA requirements as to the latter. Reg. § 1.401(a)-20, A-5.

C.   The employees' benefits under the profit sharing plan are not taken into account as part of an interrelated benefit formula of a pension plan; Reg. § 1.401(a)-20, A-5(a)(3) (next to last sentence).

3.4.04 *IRAs, Roth IRAs and 403(b) plans*

IRAs and Roth IRAs are not subject to REA; neither ERISA § 205 nor IRC § 401(a)(11) applies to IRAs or Roth IRAs.

Finally, we come to the special case of 403(b) plans. Although 403(b) plans are subject to some of the same § 401(a) requirements as qualified plans (see § 403(b)(10), (12)), § 401(a)(11) is not one of the "401(a)" provisions "imported" into § 403(b), which would make it at first appear that 403(b) plans are not subject to REA. However, even though the Internal Revenue Code REA provisions don't apply, *some* 403(b) plans are subject to ERISA—which has its own set of QJSA/QPSA requirements. Therefore, "to the extent that section 205 [of ERISA] covers section 403(b) contracts and custodial accounts they are treated as section 401(a) plans" for purposes of the QJSA/QPSA requirements. Reg.§ 1.401(a)-20, A-3(d). Therefore, some 403(b) plans are subject to REA and some are not.

The 403(b) plans NOT covered by ERISA (and therefore not subject to REA) are those funded exclusively by means of elective employee deferrals (salary reduction agreements). 403(b) plans funded in whole or in part by employer contributions are subject to ERISA and therefore also to the REA requirements.

403(b) plans that are subject to ERISA and offer annuity benefits will be subject to REA's full QJSA/QPSA requirements, just like a pension plan (¶ 3.4.02). A 403(b) plan that is subject to ERISA but that does *not* offer annuity benefits (e.g., a plan funded exclusively with mutual fund custodial accounts pursuant to § 403(b)(7)) can use the alternative compliance procedure available to "exempt" profit sharing plans (¶ 3.4.03).

For full details on which 403(b) plans are covered by ERISA and which are exempt, see DOL Reg. § 2510.3-2(f).

3.4.05 *Various REA exceptions and miscellaneous points*

There are a few exceptions to the REA requirements, even for covered plans. These exceptions are rarely significant in estate planning, but are listed here in case they may be significant in your particular client's situation (but be sure to read ¶ 3.4.06).

A.   No spousal consent is required for distribution of benefits to Participant when the total value of Participant's benefits is under $5,000. Reg. § 1.411(a)-11(c)(3).

B.   REA does not require that a QPSA, or (in the case of an
       "exempt" profit sharing plan) the 100%-death-benefit-in-lieu-
       of-QPSA, be paid to a spouse who was married to the
       Participant for less than a year prior to the date of death.
       § 417(d); § 401(a)(11)(D).

C.   No spousal consent is required if "it is established to the
       satisfaction of a plan representative that the consent...may not
       be obtained because there is no spouse, because the spouse
       cannot be located, or because of such other circumstances as the
       Secretary may by regulations prescribe." § 417(a)(2)(B).

D.   There are special rules for using retirement plan benefits as
       security for a plan loan to the employee, under which Spouse
       must consent to the loan but then the loan can later be
       "foreclosed" without further spousal consent. § 417(a)(4).

E.   There are modified rules for ESOPs. § 401(a)(11)(C).

F.   There are exceptions for plans terminated (or employees retired)
       before REA's effective date.

G.   Spouse loses her rights upon divorce or legal separation or her
       "abandonment" of the Participant (except to the extent
       otherwise provided in a "qualified domestic relations order," or
       QDRO issued in connection with the divorce; see § 414(p)).
       Reg. § 1.401(a)-20, A-27.

3.4.06 *Plan may be more generous than REA requires*

       For reasons of administrative convenience or other reasons, a
retirement plan may give spouses more rights than REA requires. For
example, REA does not require that a QPSA, or (in the case of an
"exempt" profit sharing plan) the 100%-death-benefit-in-lieu-of-QPSA,
be paid to a spouse who was married to the Participant for less than a
year prior to the date of death. § 417(d); § 401(a)(11)(D). However,
many retirement plan designers decided it was easier to grant the same
rights to *all* spouses than to try to figure out exactly how long each

employee had been married, so many plans grant these rights to all surviving spouses, regardless of the length of the marriage.

Similarly, the value of the legally-required QPSA (which is supposed to be equivalent only to the survivor pension Spouse would have received under a joint and survivor annuity) is less than the total value of the employee's accrued benefit in the plan, but, again, it is administratively easier simply to award every non-consenting Spouse 100% of the value of the Participant's benefit than to figure out for each individual employee and spouse what would have been the relative values of their shares under a QJSA.

3.4.07 *Requirements for spousal consent or waiver*

Spouse's consent to waive any of these mandatory benefit forms cannot be in any old form done at any old time. § 417 contains elaborate rules for the spousal consent, including as to its form (¶ 3.4.08) and:

1.   Timing: Participant's waiver of a QPSA, and Spouse's consent to such waiver, must be given after the beginning of the plan year in which Participant reaches age 35, and prior to the employee's death. § 417(a)(6)(B). The IRS, unlike the Code itself, permits waiver of the QPSA even *before* Participant reaches age 35, provided that Participant goes through the waiver/consent process *again* after reaching age 35. Reg. § 1.401(a)-20, A-33. For "exempt" profit sharing plans (¶ 3.4.03), the spousal consent for waiver of the 100%-death-benefit-in-lieu-of-QPSA may be provided "at any time," including before Participant reaches age 35. Reg. § 1.401(a)-20, A-33(a).

2.   Disclosure: "No consent is valid unless [Participant] has received a general description of the material features, and an explanation of the relative values of, the optional forms of benefit available under the plan in a manner which would satisfy the notice requirements of section 417(a)(3)." Reg. § 1.417(e)-1(b)(2)(i). Although the statute requires that this disclosure be provided to *Participant* rather than Spouse, Spouse's consent to Participant's waiver of the QJSA or QPSA must "acknowledge the effect" of such waiver. This probably

means Spouse should see the same disclosures provided to Participant himself, in order that Spouse may understand the effect of the waiver.

3.4.08 *Form of spousal consent or waiver*

An election in proper form "designates a beneficiary (or a form of benefits) which may not be changed without spousal consent (or the consent of the spouse expressly permits designations by Participant without any requirement of further consent by the spouse), and...the spouse's consent acknowledges the effect of such election and is witnessed by a plan representative or a notary public." § 417(a)(2)(A). See Reg. § 1.401(a)-20, A-31 for more detail about the required form of spousal consent. Note that there are two ways Spouse can consent: the spousal consent can say "I am consenting to this *particular* beneficiary designation, but I do not consent in advance to any changes, so if you change the beneficiary designation hereafter you need to get a new consent from me"; or the spousal consent can expressly permit further changes ("designations") by Participant without the requirement of further spousal consents.

The IRS has published four sample spousal consent forms (IRS Notice 97-10 1997-2 I.R.B. 41). They are available on "Forms on Disk" (order form at end of this book).

3.4.09 *Key points for estate planners*

REA poses many challenges to estate planners, including:

1. REA creates serious, and sad, difficulties if Spouse is unable due to mental disability to consent to the desired estate plan. In that case the consent must be provided by Spouse's legal guardian. Reg. § 1.401(a)-20, A-27. The author has seen the following situation more than once: Participant has a mentally disabled spouse, whose life expectancy is shortened due to the disability. A survivor annuity would probably never provide a dime to the disabled spouse (because of his or her shortened life expectancy), but *would* reduce Participant's pension (because the plan's actuarial formula for determining the amount of benefits does not take into account the health of the individual Participant or Spouse). Through hard work and loving care

Participant has avoided the expense and humiliation of legal guardianship proceedings for the disabled spouse. Thanks to REA, and because of the importance to both spouses of maximizing the value of the pension, said expense and humiliation must be incurred when Participant reaches retirement age. Although the regulations say that Participant may be the guardian of a disabled spouse for the purpose of providing the needed consent, the court having jurisdiction either does not allow the employee to serve as guardian because the court perceives there is a conflict of interest, or requires appointment of a guardian ad litem with attendant expense.

2.   If there is any question about Spouse's willingness to consent, or to honor a consent once given, it becomes especially important to adhere strictly to the statutory requirements regarding the form of the consent. There is no guarantee that your client's plan's standard printed spousal consent form complies with REA. Consider supplying your own form, using the IRS-provided sample spousal consent forms (¶ 3.4.08).

3.   Waiver of the QJSA benefit must occur not more than 90 days prior to the annuity starting date, so it is impossible to lock in spousal consent in advance.

4.   The Supreme Court has held that REA preempts state spousal rights laws such as community property; Boggs v. Boggs, 117 S. Ct. 1754 (1997). The interrelation of REA and state spousal rights laws baffles the nation's estate planning gurus.

5.   Some defined benefit plans subsidize the annuity payments to Spouse (meaning that the employee's pension is not reduced to provide the survivor annuity; the married employee and the single employee receive the same pension), and do not permit Spouse to waive the survivor annuity. This type of plan typically would provide no death benefits at all other than the required spousal annuities, and would not allow an employee to cash out the value of his pension at retirement—the employee must take an annuity. § 417(a)(5).

6.   REA rights cannot be waived in a pre-nuptial agreement,

because the employee's affianced is not at that point the "spouse." "An agreement entered into prior to marriage does not satisfy the applicable consent requirements, even if the agreement is executed within the applicable election period." Reg. § 1.401(a)-20, A-28.

7. If Spouse is being asked to waive a QPSA or QJSA, consider whether Spouse needs to be advised of the option of retaining separate counsel. Spouse might for example wish to consent to a waiver of the QJSA (and allow Participant to roll over the benefits to an IRA) only if Participant agrees to name Spouse as beneficiary of the IRA.

8. If Spouse consents to Participant's naming a trust as beneficiary, later amendments to the trust do not require a subsequent spousal consent. Reg. § 1.401(a)-20, A-31(a).

3.5 Summary of Planning Principles

1. The tax laws generally, though not always, favor naming Spouse, personally, as designated beneficiary of retirement benefits and using other, non-IRD, assets to fund a credit shelter trust.

2. IRS rulings provide clear instructions for qualifying retirement benefits payable to QTIP trusts for the estate tax marital deduction. Although the method specified in these rulings is not the only way to obtain the marital deduction for benefits payable to a QTIP trust, many practitioners are choosing to use it.

3. Making benefits payable to a QTIP trust often results in a substantial loss of potential income tax deferral compared with leaving benefits to Spouse outright.

4. Upon Participant's death it is extremely important for Spouse to consider her options immediately, and to roll over the benefits if that is the chosen option.

4

Non-Citizen Spouse

If Participant's spouse is not a U.S. citizen, the usual marital deduction is not available. A modified marital deduction is available if certain requirements are met.

This Chapter explains the tax issues involved when the Participant's spouse is not a U.S. citizen (¶ 4.1, ¶ 4.2), then examines four alternatives for retirement benefits in this situation (¶ 4.3-¶ 4.6), and concludes with suggested investment and distribution strategies for a "Qualified Domestic Trust" (QDOT) (¶ 4.6) and a summary of planning principles (¶ 4.7). In this Chapter, the Participant is sometimes called the "Decedent" or "client." His spouse is called "Spouse."

4.1 Modified Marital Deduction for Non-Citizen Spouse

4.1.01 *Modified marital deduction and deferred estate tax*

Property passing to a surviving spouse who is not a United States citizen will not qualify for the normal estate tax marital deduction. § 2056(d)(1). However, if property left to Spouse in a form that would qualify for the marital deduction (but for the fact that Spouse is not a citizen) is placed in a certain kind of trust, called a qualified domestic trust ("QDOT"), either by Decedent or by Spouse, it will qualify for a *modified* version of the marital deduction. § 2056(d)(2).

Under this modified form of marital deduction, the property is not simply deducted from Decedent's estate and added to Spouse's estate, as normally occurs when the marital deduction is taken (¶ 3.3.01). Rather, the tax is merely deferred until one of three possible events triggers the requirement of paying estate tax: non-hardship distributions of principal to Spouse from the QDOT (§ 2056A(b)(1)(A), (3)(B)); QDOT's ceasing to meet the QDOT requirements

(§ 2056A(b)(4)); and Spouse's death (§ 2056A(b)(1)(B)). Any payment of deferred estate tax by the QDOT is treated as an additional distribution of principal to Spouse (resulting in more deferred estate tax). § 2056A(b)(11).

When a triggering event occurs, the deferred estate tax applies to the amount of the non-hardship principal distribution, or (in the case of Spouse's death or the disqualification of the QDOT) to the entire "principal" (¶ 4.7.03) of the QDOT. The amount of the tax is the amount of tax that would have been owed if the QDOT property (or amount distributed as the case may be) had been part of Decedent's estate back when Decedent died. § 2056A(b)(2). For example, if Spouse dies when the federal estate tax exemption is $3,500,000, but when Decedent died the exemption was only $1,000,000, the deferred estate tax is computed using the $1,000,000 exemption. Note that even though this is in effect a deferred estate tax, there is no requirement of paying interest on it.

The QDOT property will *also* be subject to U.S. estate tax as part of Spouse's estate upon her death, if she is a U.S. resident or citizen, under normal estate tax principles. In that case, her estate will receive a credit for the deferred estate tax paid on the property by the QDOT, and of course *her* estate will have the benefit of whatever estate tax exemption applies for the year of her death. § 2056(d)(3); § 2001(c). In effect, the estate tax payable on the QDOT at Spouse's death is going to be at Decedent's marginal rate, or at Spouse's marginal rate, whichever is higher.

Adding to the already-considerable complications of this setup are the scheduled repeal of the estate tax and the scheduled sunset of the repeal; see ¶ 4.1.03. But first, a way to avoid the whole mess:

4.1.02 *If Spouse becomes a citizen, or is or becomes a non-resident*

If Spouse becomes a *U.S. citizen* prior to the filing of the estate tax return for Decedent's estate, *and* if Spouse was a U.S. *resident* at all times after Decedent's death until she became a citizen, the normal marital deduction becomes available and it is not necessary to transfer property to a QDOT or worry about the deferred estate tax. § 2056(d)(4). This is often the simplest solution to the problem if Spouse intends to remain permanently in the U.S. This approach should be explored at the planning stage if possible, otherwise as soon as possible after Decedent's death, since becoming a citizen takes time.

If Spouse becomes a U.S. citizen *after* the filing of Decedent's estate tax return, all distributions to Spouse thereafter from the QDOT (or from non-assignable property subject to an agreement with the IRS; ¶ 4.6) are free of the deferred estate tax—provided Spouse was a U.S. *resident* at all times after Decedent's death until she became a citizen. The QDOT could terminate at that point and distribute its assets to Spouse free of the deferred estate tax. § 2056A(b)(12); Reg. § 20.2056A-10(a); see PLR 9848007.

If the non-citizen spouse is or becomes a non-U.S. *resident*, different considerations may apply. This situation is beyond the scope of this book.

The rest of this chapter assumes Spouse will remain a non-U.S. citizen.

4.1.03 *QDOTs, estate tax repeal and sunset*

Here is what happens to QDOT property under various scenarios, based on the Internal Revenue Code as it exists in September 2001 (including changes that have been enacted in 2001 that are to be effective after 2001). This ¶ 4.1.03 discusses what happens to *any* property left to a QDOT; the additional complications of *retirement plan benefits* left to a QDOT are discussed in subsequent sections.

§ 2056A(b), which imposes the deferred estate tax on QDOT property, is part of Chapter 11 (Subtitle B) of the Code (Estate and Gift Taxes). Chapter 11 "shall not apply to the estates of decedents dying after December 31, 2009." § 2210(a) This provision has no effect on the deferred estate tax on QDOTs established by decedents who died *prior* to 2010 that are still in existence in 2010.

§ 2210(b) deals with that situation. § 2210(b)(1) provides that the deferred estate tax on non-hardship distributions of principal from a QDOT "shall not apply to distributions made after December 31, 2020." However, since § 901 of EGTRRA repeals § 2210 effective after 2010, this provision will never apply.

§ 2210(b)(2) provides that the deferred estate tax imposed on a QDOT at Spouse's death "shall not apply" after December 31, 2009. § 2210 says nothing explicitly about the deferred estate tax imposed on a QDOT if the trust ceases to meet the requirements of § 2056A(a); however, since tax in that case is imposed "as if the surviving spouse died on the date" the trust ceased to qualify (§ 2056A(b)(4)), effectively the "cease to qualify" tax does not apply if the disqualification occurs in 2010 (since Spouse's death in 2010 would not trigger the deferred estate tax; § 2210(b)(2)). *Accordingly, the way the law is now written (but it's bound to be changed; see next paragraph) it would appear that all QDOTs still in existence on January 1, 2010, should take some step to make the trust disqualified in the year 2010,* and thereby eliminate all future concerns about the deferred estate tax.

There are two anomalies in § 2210. First, § 2210(a) says that the estate tax chapter will not apply to decedents dying after 2009 "except as provided in" § 2210(b); however, § 2210(b) applies *only* to estates of decedents who die *before* 2010, so it does not contain any exceptions to § 2210(a). Second, § 2210(b)(1) purports to continue to tax non-hardship distributions of principal from a pre-2010 QDOT until 2020, but seems to allow a QDOT to disqualify itself in 2010 without payment of deferred estate tax, which would make subsequent distributions non-taxable, which seems nonsensical and therefore presumably will be changed.

Here is a summary of possible results; it does not cover what happens if Decedent dies after 2009:

1. Decedent dies before 2010 and leaves property to a QDOT for the benefit of his non-citizen Spouse.

2. If Spouse dies before or after (but not during) 2210, and before the QDOT ceases to meet the requirements of § 2056A(a) (see #3), the property remaining in the QDOT at Spouse's death is subject to the deferred estate tax.

3. If, prior to Spouse's death, the QDOT ceases to meet the requirements of § 2056A(a), the deferred estate tax is imposed just as if Spouse had died when the disqualification occurs. § 2056A(b)(4).

4. If, prior to Spouse's death, prior to the disqualification of the QDOT, and prior to 2021, the QDOT distributes principal to Spouse, and the hardship exception (¶ 4.7.01) does not apply, the distribution is subject to the deferred estate tax.

5. If Spouse dies (or the QDOT ceases to qualify) in 2010 the deferred estate tax does not apply to the QDOT. § 2210(b)(2).

4.1.04 *Overview of ways to qualify for modified marital deduction*

If the surviving spouse is not a U.S. citizen (and will not become a U.S. citizen prior to filing the estate tax return), there are four possible ways to qualify for the modified marital deduction:

One is for Decedent to have arranged his estate plan so that property for which the marital deduction is sought will pass, on his death, directly to a QDOT. See ¶ 4.4.

If Decedent's estate plan failed to do this, the modified marital deduction is still available if Spouse herself, having inherited the property outright, transfers it to a QDOT prior to the filing of the estate tax return and no later than one year after the due date of the return. Reg. § 20.2056A-1(a)(iii). See ¶ 4.5 and ¶ 4.6.

Finally, ¶ 4.7 describes two other methods available for "non-assignable property"—that is, property (such as a non-assignable annuity) which passes to Spouse outright, but which cannot legally be transferred by Spouse to a QDOT. Spouse can get QDOT treatment for such "non-assignable property" by signing an agreement with the IRS that, when she receives a distribution from the non-assignable property, she will transfer the distributed amount to a QDOT, or, alternatively, by signing an agreement that she will pay the deferred estate tax on the distributed amount when she receives it. The regulations permit Spouse to elect to treat an individual retirement account (IRA) as non-assignable.

4.1.05 *Consider not qualifying for the marital deduction*

Any strategy that requires making retirement benefits qualify for the modified marital deduction involves loss of potential income tax deferral, or substantial complications and uncertainties, or all of the above (see ¶ 4.3-¶ 4.6). Decedent can avoid these difficulties by leaving his retirement benefits to his children or other non-spouse beneficiary, or to a trust that does not qualify for the marital deduction. The disadvantages of this approach are those that exist whenever retirement benefits are paid in a non-marital deduction disposition (see ¶ 10.5).

Another alternative is to make the benefits payable to Spouse individually but not claim the marital deduction. Scheduled Federal estate tax exemption increases from $675,000 to $3,500,000 over the years 2002-2009 (§ 2010(c)) will mean that more clients can leave 100% of their estates to their non-citizen surviving spouses and not incur an estate tax even *without* qualifying for the modified marital deduction; this much less complicated approach should appeal to an increasing number of clients. Even if an estate tax has to be paid on client's death, Spouse will get the benefit of the § 691(c) deduction. ¶ 2.2.07. This approach may be especially attractive if Spouse will probably return to her country of origin, so U.S. estate taxes will not apply to her estate (because she will be a non-citizen non-resident).

If Spouse is likely to remain a U.S. resident, whether leaving all retirement benefits outright to Spouse would be an attractive approach depends on the likely future estate tax Spouse faces. If federal estate taxes will apply on Spouse's death (e.g., because she is wealthy and dies when the estate tax is in effect), this approach will not be attractive, especially if estate taxes have to be paid at the first death, because the benefits, already reduced by income taxes, and by estate taxes at Decedent's death, would be subject to estate tax again at Spouse's death (though if Spouse dies within 10 years after Decedent the estate tax credit for tax on prior transfers would be available; § 2013). On the other hand, if estate taxes are not likely to apply at Spouse's death (either because her assets are under the exemption amount, or because estate taxes will have been repealed), this approach would be attractive.

4.1.06 *The requirements of a QDOT*

The distinguishing characteristics of a qualified domestic trust are set forth in § 2056A(a) and regulations. The principal requirements are:

(a)   At least one trustee of the QDOT must be an individual citizen of the United States or a United States domestic corporation. § 2056A(a)(1)(A).

(b)   The trust must be "maintained" under, and the administration of the trust must be governed by, the laws of a particular state or the District of Columbia. Reg. § 20.2056A-2(a).

(c)   No principal distribution may be made from the trust unless the U.S. trustee has the right to withhold from the distribution the deferred estate tax discussed at ¶ 4.1.01. § 2056A(a)(1)(B).

(d)   The trust must meet any additional requirements imposed by the Secretary of the Treasury by regulations to insure collection of the tax. § 2056A(a)(2). The IRS has imposed some such additional requirements, such as bonding for non-bank trustees and limits on non-U.S. real estate investments. Reg. § 20.2056A-2.

Note that there is no requirement that all of the QDOT income be distributable annually to Spouse, or even that Spouse be the sole beneficiary of the QDOT. The *QDOT* requirements are concerned *only* with the identity of the trustee, necessary elections, and security for collection of the deferred estate tax.

In summary, in order to qualify for the modified version of the marital deduction when Spouse is not a U.S. citizen, the property must be placed (by Decedent or by Spouse) in a trust which meets the above requirements; and *in addition* the property must pass from Decedent to Spouse (or to a trust for Spouse's benefit) in a way that qualifies for the marital deduction (aside from the QDOT requirements).

4.1.07 *Differences between QDOT created by Decedent, Spouse*

Regardless of whether Spouse is a U.S. citizen, the marital deduction is not allowed for property passing from Decedent to a trust for Spouse unless the trust meets certain requirements familiar to all estate planners: a "marital deduction trust" will be a nondeductible "terminable interest" unless it fits into one of the exceptions to the "terminable interest rule." ¶ 3.3.02. This Chapter assumes that any QDOT created by transfer from Decedent will be either a "general power marital trust" (¶ 3.3.03) or a "QTIP trust" (¶ 3.3.04), and so will qualify as an exception to that rule. (Two other categories of trust that qualify for the marital deduction, the rarely-used "estate trust," and the charitable remainder trust of which the spouse is the only non-charitable beneficiary, are not discussed in this Chapter.)

If property passes from Decedent to Spouse *outright*, it qualifies for the marital deduction (except for the QDOT requirements) under § 2056(a). An outright bequest is not a "terminable interest," and accordingly does not have to comply with the marital deduction *trust* rules. Therefore, when Spouse receives an outright bequest, and transfers the inherited property into a QDOT *she* creates, there is no requirement that the terms of that QDOT be similar to those of a "normal" marital deduction trust (unless the trust also contains property transferred to it directly by Decedent); only the QDOT requirements need be met. A "QTIP election" cannot be made for a QDOT established by Spouse. Reg. § 20.2056A-4(d), example 5.

A QDOT created by Spouse need not (and normally should not) be irrevocable. A QDOT created by Spouse need not (but probably should) require annual distribution of all income to Spouse. A QDOT created by Spouse could (but probably should not) allow distributions to people other than Spouse during her lifetime. For further suggestions regarding the terms of a QDOT created by Spouse, see ¶ 4.5.

Note: if the QDOT to which Spouse transfers property *also* contains any property transferred directly to it by Decedent then the *entire trust* must qualify for the marital deduction under § 2056. Reg. § 20.2056A-4(b)(1). In this chapter, a "QDOT funded by Spouse" means a QDOT *exclusively* so funded.

4.2 Income Tax vs. Deferred Estate Tax

4.2.01 *Statute suggests possibility of double tax*

Retirement benefits generally are subject both to income tax as "income in respect of a decedent" (IRD) (¶ 2.2) and estate tax. When the benefits are paid to a non-citizen Spouse or a QDOT it is not always clear how the income tax and the deferred estate tax relate to each other.

Under the statute, it appears possible that Spouse could be required to pay *both* income tax *and* deferred estate tax on the full amount of inherited retirement benefits, with neither tax deductible in determining the other. The regulations make it clear in a couple of situations (¶ 4.2.03, ¶ 4.2.04) that amounts used to pay income tax on IRD will not *also* be subject to the deferred estate tax; in other situations (¶ 4.2.05) we are left to assume that this result is allowed, without specific authority.

If the client's retirement plan is an IRA, one way to avoid all the complications described in this section is to convert the IRA to a Roth IRA during life, so that distributions post-death will generally not be subject to income tax; see Chapter 5.

4.2.02 § 691(c) deduction for deferred estate tax

Generally, the beneficiary of retirement benefits can deduct the federal estate taxes paid on the benefits in determining how much income tax the beneficiary must pay on those benefits, because § 691(c)(2)(A) allows an income tax deduction for estate taxes imposed on IRD *"under section 2001 or 2101...."* ¶ 2.2.07. Although the deferred estate tax is imposed by § *2056A* rather than by either of the two sections mentioned in § 691(c), the regulations provide that "The estate tax (net of any applicable credits) imposed under section 2056A(b)(1) constitutes an estate tax for purposes of section 691(c)(2)(A)." Reg. § 20.2056A-6(a).

While it is nice to know that the deferred estate tax qualifies for the 691(c) deduction, it is not clear how this will actually help Spouse. Normally, estate taxes are paid when a decedent dies, then the beneficiary collects the benefits, and the beneficiary can deduct the estate taxes paid when computing his income tax on the benefits. In the case of the *deferred* estate tax, however, Spouse (or the QDOT) normally collects the income-taxable benefits *first*, before the deferred estate tax has been "imposed" (at her death), so there is no estate tax to deduct because it hasn't been imposed yet. On the other hand, since any federal income taxes Spouse pays on the benefits are probably removed from the tax base for purposes of computing the deferred estate tax that will later be due (see the next three subsections), it makes sense that she does not also get a deduction in the other direction (i.e., deducting the estate tax for purposes of computing income tax).

In those situations (which planning will normally try to avoid) in which the deferred estate tax on retirement benefits has to be paid during Spouse's life (*e.g.*, if the QDOT ceases to qualify as a QDOT) Spouse will be able to take the § 691(c) deduction for the deferred estate tax with regard to subsequent distributions. Also, to the extent there are still some benefits inside the plan at Spouse's death, the next succeeding beneficiary can take a § 691(c) deduction for the deferred estate tax (and/or for the first spouse's original estate tax and/or the surviving spouse's estate tax). How to compute the deduction in these situations is beyond the scope of this book.

4.2.03 Income tax paid by Spouse on plan distributions

The Code exempts, from the deferred estate tax, distributions to Spouse from a QDOT made to reimburse Spouse for *federal* income taxes imposed on Spouse on any item of income of the QDOT "to which [Spouse] is not entitled under the terms of the trust." § 2056A(b)(15). The IRS in its regulations has interpreted this oddly worded Code provision in such a way as to alleviate the double taxation effect in some specific situations. Under the regulations, if Spouse receives a distribution from Decedent's retirement plan and then "assigns" that distribution to the QDOT, the QDOT can, without triggering deferred estate tax, reimburse Spouse for the federal income tax she pays on the distribution, including federal income taxes paid "through withholding." Reg. § 20.2056A-5(c)(3)(iv).

Example: The Acme Profit Sharing Plan distributes $100,000 to Spouse as a death benefit (and MRD) from Decedent's account in the plan. There is no withholding (see ¶ 2.1.05). Spouse assigns the $100,000 check to the QDOT pursuant to a "(c)(3)" agreement (¶ 4.6.01). At the end of the year, when the dust settles, it turns out that Spouse's income tax liability on the $100,000 distribution was $38,000. The QDOT can reimburse her for the $38,000 without having to pay deferred estate tax on the distribution. End result: QDOT holds $62,000 cash ($100,000 distribution minus $38,000 income tax reimbursement), Spouse holds $0 ($100,000 received from plan minus $100,000 paid to QDOT, $38,000 received from QDOT minus $38,000 paid to IRS).

Example: The Acme Profit Sharing Plan distributes a $100,000 lump sum distribution to Spouse as a death benefit from Decedent's account in the plan. $20,000 of the distribution is withheld for federal income taxes (¶ 2.1.05). Spouse assigns the distribution to the QDOT pursuant to a "(c)(3)" agreement (¶ 4.6.01). It's not clear how she can assign the *entire* distribution to the QDOT since she only received $80,000 of it, but that's what the regulation says is supposed to happen. Maybe she assigns to the QDOT her rights to the withheld taxes along with her rights to the net cash. At the end of the year, when the dust settles, it turns out that Spouse's income tax liability on the $100,000 distribution was $38,000. The QDOT can reimburse her for the $38,000 without having to pay deferred estate tax on the distribution; however, since the QDOT never received the withheld tax money ($20,000), it only reimburses Spouse $18,000. End result: QDOT holds $62,000 cash ($80,000 net distribution received minus $18,000 income tax reimbursement), Spouse holds $0 ($80,000 received from plan minus

$80,000 paid to QDOT, $18,000 received from QDOT minus $18,000 paid to IRS).

This estate-tax-free reimbursement is available only for taxes imposed by subtitle A, *federal* income taxes. It is not permitted for state income taxes. The reimbursable tax is calculated at the marginal rate, *i.e.*, the difference between Spouse's *actual* income tax for the year and what Spouse's tax *would* have been if the distribution had not been included in her gross income.

4.2.04 *Income taxes paid by the QDOT*

Assume Decedent left his IRA to a QTIP Trust (¶ 3.3.04) that is also a QDOT. The trust is to pay "income to Spouse for life, remainder to Decedent's issue." Because Spouse is only the income beneficiary, she is not treated as the "owner" of the trust *principal* for income tax purposes. Reg. § 1.671-3(b)(1). Accordingly, income taxes on distributions of IRD from the plan to the trust, to the extent such distributions are considered "principal" (see ¶ 6.1.07), are imposed directly on the trust. All income taxes (both federal and state, apparently) paid on any IRA distribution that is retained in the QDOT as principal are exempt from the deferred estate tax as "[p]ayments to applicable governmental authorities for income tax or any other applicable tax imposed on the QDOT" (other than the deferred estate tax itself). Reg. § 20.2056-5(c)(3)(ii).

In contrast, when benefits are payable to Spouse, and then transferred by Spouse to the QDOT, only the *federal* income taxes Spouse pays can be reimbursed by the QDOT free of deferred estate tax. § 2056A(b)(15); Reg. § 20.2056A-5(c)(3)(iv). This slight discrepancy in treatment of state income taxes argues in favor of leaving the benefits to a QTIP-QDOT, rather than outright to Spouse. The downside of leaving the benefits to a life income QTIP-QDOT is that the benefits will be taxed at trust rates, whereas income taxes might be lower if paid at Spouse's personal rate.

4.2.05 *QDOT income taxable to Spouse*

As noted (¶ 4.2.04), the regulations provide that if retirement benefits are distributed to, and taxable to, a QDOT, the income taxes paid by the QDOT are not subject to the deferred estate tax. What if, under § 678(a), Spouse, not the trust, is taxable on a plan distribution received by the trust, because she has the power to withdraw the distribution from the trust (see ¶ 4.3.02)? The regulations do not explicitly give relief here. The regulations explicitly exempt from the deferred estate tax only income taxes "imposed on the QDOT," or paid by Spouse on a plan distribution received by Spouse and assigned to the QDOT.

However, the non-taxable reimbursement of Spouse for income tax is "not limited to" the specific situations mentioned. § 20.2056A-5(c)(3)(iv). Presumably, reimbursement of Spouse by the QDOT for income tax paid by Spouse on trust income she *is* entitled to receive would also be allowed free of deferred estate tax, despite the fact that the Code allows tax-free reimbursement of Spouse only for taxes on trust income she is *not* entitled to.

The result should be the same when a distribution of IRD is made from the plan to the QDOT, and the trustee distributes the principal to Spouse under a discretionary power to distribute principal, if the principal distribution carries out "distributable net income" (DNI) to Spouse under § 661-§ 662 (¶ 6.1.03). The portion of such a principal distribution which Spouse is required to pay to the IRS as income taxes should not be subject to the deferred estate tax, but there is as yet no official confirmation on this.

4.3 Approach # 1: Decedent Leaves Benefits to Marital Trust-QDOT

4.3.01 *Advantage: safety, predictability*

At the planning stage, while the client is still living, the safest course is for the client to make his retirement benefits payable to a marital trust which will also qualify as a QDOT. With this approach, the client knows that, upon his death, the benefits will automatically pass in a manner that will qualify for the modified marital deduction; the success of the estate plan will not depend on Spouse's taking action after client's death to create a QDOT and assign assets to it (¶ 4.4, ¶ 4.5) or enter into an agreement with the IRS (¶ 4.6).

4.3.02 *Drawbacks; use of grantor trust to mitigate*

If Spouse is entitled only to annual income distributions, there all the usual disadvantages of leaving retirement benefits to a QTIP trust. See ¶ 10.5.05. A marital trust for the benefit of a *citizen* spouse could minimize the adverse effects of at least one of the drawbacks of the standard QTIP trust, namely, the high income tax rates applicable to a principal distribution from the retirement plan to the trust, by passing some or all of the distribution out to the spouse-beneficiary, if the trust permitted this. See ¶ 6.1.03. This safety valve is not helpful in the case of a marital trust-QDOT, however, because non-hardship distributions of principal from the QDOT to Spouse will attract the deferred estate tax. ¶ 4.1.01.

Possibly, giving Spouse the unlimited right to withdraw all of the principal from the trust at all times would cause the trust's income to be taxed at her (possibly lower) rate, rather than the trust's (often higher) rate, if she is a U.S. resident, thus eliminating at least one drawback; see discussion of § 678(a)(1) "grantor trusts" at ¶ 6.3.09 for more on this and other possible advantages of a § 678 grantor trust. Spouse is unlikely to exercise such withdrawal power under a QDOT because exercise would trigger the deferred estate tax.

One risk of using this approach is that the regulations do not explicitly permit the QDOT to reimburse Spouse for income tax she is required to pay on the trust's income under § 678, without paying the deferred estate tax on the reimbursement, although it appears *likely* that this is permitted; see ¶ 4.2.05. Another question is whether it is possible for the trust to be considered entirely subject to a right of withdrawal by Spouse (within the meaning of § 678(a)(1)) when the QDOT trustee has the right (as required by § 2056A(a)(1)(B)) to withhold the deferred estate tax from any distribution to her. See discussion at ¶ 4.5.01.

4.4 Approach # 2: Spouse Rolls Over Benefits to QDOT-IRT

As noted (¶ 4.1.01), if property passes outright to Spouse, the modified marital deduction can still be obtained if Spouse transfers the property to a QDOT. This option poses special problems in the case of retirement benefits that are paid to Spouse individually.

If Spouse is named personally as the beneficiary of Decedent's retirement plan, and she leaves the benefits in Decedent's plan, the benefits will not qualify for the marital deduction because the retirement plan is not a QDOT. If she withdraws the benefits from Decedent's plan, with the idea of transferring them to a QDOT, she will have to pay income tax on the benefits (unless the benefits are not subject to income tax; see ¶ 2.1.01,¶ 2.1.03).

4.4.01 *The combination QDOT-IRT*

One way out of this dilemma is for Spouse to take the benefits out of Decedent's retirement plan and roll them over tax-free (¶ 3.2) to a trust that is both a QDOT *and* an "individual retirement account" (IRA) under § 408(a). This will not merely salvage the marital deduction; it generally will provide income tax deferral opportunities that are superior, both during Spouse's life and after her death, to those available if Decedent had made his benefits payable directly to a marital trust-QDOT. ¶ 3.3.10 explains the income tax advantages of the spousal rollover compared with the treatment of a benefits paid to a marital trust as beneficiary.

There is no tax or legal obstacle in the way of combining an IRA and a QDOT. An IRA can be in the legal form of a trust (§ 408(a)) or a custodial account (§ 408(h)), though most IRAs are in the form of custodial accounts. The term "individual retirement trust" (IRT) is used here to distinguish the individual retirement account in the form of a trust from the more common custodial form of IRA.

The practical difficulties of this approach include drafting the document and finding a U.S. bank willing to serve as trustee (¶ 4.4.04). Unfortunately, this difficulty may be substantial in the case of a smaller retirement benefit. Larger banks' fee schedules make them good choices, usually, only for accounts worth $1 million or more. Smaller bank trust operations accept smaller trusts and IRAs, but in the author's experience smaller banks refuse to accept an *IRA* in the form of a trust because their IRAs are administered by an outside provider which furnishes all the forms and monitors compliance. A bank that does not have true in-house IRA capability will probably not be willing to take on a unique entity like a QDOT-IRT.

4.4.02 *Deferred estate tax on principal distributions*

There is a price to be paid for the greater income tax deferral that can be obtained with a QDOT-IRT. The price is paid when "principal" for which the marital deduction was taken in Decedent's estate is distributed from the QDOT-IRT to Spouse. At that time, the deferred estate tax, as well as income taxes, will have to be paid on the principal distribution.

Of course, deferred estate tax is due whenever principal is distributed to Spouse from *any* QDOT. But with a QTIP-QDOT (¶ 4.3), it is possible for the trust to exist for Spouse's entire lifetime without ever distributing principal. With a QDOT-IRT, the minimum distribution rules require certain amounts to be distributed every year after spouse reaches age 70½. See Chapter 1. "Principal" will have to be distributed out to Spouse when the minimum required distributions (MRDs) from the IRA exceed the "income" of the IRA (see ¶ 3.3.06, ¶ 6.1.07).

If (after age 70½) Spouse is taking out only the MRDs under the Uniform Table (¶ 1.4.01), *and* undistributed income inside the IRT retains its character as "income" for purposes of the deferred estate tax (see ¶ 4.7.03), then the distributions to Spouse will not be coming out of principal until very late in Spouse's life. The MRDs will be less than the annual income so long as the Uniform Table divisor expressed as a percentage (i.e., one, divided by the remaining life expectancy) is less than the rate of income, so for many years after Spouse's RBD the IRT will actually be accumulating some of its income.

Example: Suppose when Spouse reaches her RBD, the first year's divisor (see ¶ 1.4.01) is 26.2. Expressed as a percentage, the MRD for that year is 1/26.2, or 3.82%. If the QDOT-IRT earns more than 3.82% in income that year, the MRD will be less than the income. Even after the crossover point (where the current year's required distribution exceeds the current year's income), the excess distributions can be taken from accumulated income until that account is exhausted, before reaching the initial "principal" of the IRT. If Decedent died when Spouse was age 70, and the IRT consistently earns 8% annual income, and distributes only the MRD each year, the first distribution that would necessarily include principal (and therefore be subject to deferred estate tax) would not occur until Spouse was age 99. If Spouse dies before age 99, the deferred estate tax will obviously be due at the time of her death—but that is true under any QDOT disposition.

The point of this discussion is that rolling benefits over to a QDOT-IRT could be effective, despite the minimum distribution rules of § 401(a)(9), to defer the deferred estate tax on the retirement benefits until Spouse reaches a very advanced age. However, this conclusion depends on treating income accumulated inside the QDOT-IRT as "income" for purposes of the deferred estate tax. If the IRS decides that "principal" for this purpose includes accumulated income (see ¶ 4.7.03), however, the crossover point (when MRDs must necessarily include principal and therefore trigger deferred estate tax) will be reached much sooner. Accordingly, until further clarification of the IRS's position, accumulating income inside a QDOT-IRT is not recommended without obtaining a ruling on the status of undistributed income under § 2056A. In the absence of such a ruling, Spouse should (1) withdraw all income of the QDOT-IRT annually and (2) in any year in which the income exceeds the MRD, roll over the excess to her non-QDOT-IRA.

4.4.03 *No IRS ruling on QDOT-IRT qualification*

"Receipt of a favorable opinion letter on an IRA ... is not required as a condition of receiving favorable tax treatment." Rev. Proc. 87-50, 1987-2 C.B. 647, section 2.08. Although it will issue opinion letters on prototype IRAs, "The Service will not issue rulings or determination letters to individuals with respect to the status of their" IRAs. *Id.*, § 4.03. Fortunately, the IRS has supplied a "Model Trust Account" form for an IRA, known as Form 5305. "[I]ndividuals who adopt the Model Trust ... Account...will be treated as having an arrangement that meets the requirements of section 408(a)." *Id.*, § 5.01. By adopting Form 5305, and adding to it the provisions required for a QDOT (and other provisions deemed desirable for proper trust administration), Spouse has a QDOT-IRT. The IRT should be fully revocable by Spouse to avoid gift tax issues (see ¶ 4.5.01).

4.4.04 *Trustee of QDOT-IRT must be U.S. bank*

As a practical matter, the trustee of a QDOT-IRT must be a U.S. bank or other financial institution, for the following reasons:

First, in order for the trust to qualify as an IRA, the trustee must be a bank or such "other person who demonstrates to the satisfaction" of the IRS that "such other person will administer" the IRA in the required manner. § 408(a)(2). The procedure for a non-bank to seek IRS approval to serve as trustee of IRAs involves a filing fee of several thousand dollars, as well as demonstrating institutional soundness and continuity to the IRS. It is generally undertaken only by a firm which has plans to serve as trustee for many customers. It is hard to see how an individual could demonstrate the required permanence. Therefore, even though an individual can serve as trustee of a QDOT, an individual will *not* be able to be trustee (or even co-trustee) of a QDOT-IRT.

Second, in order to qualify as a QDOT, there must be at least one U.S. trustee. § 2056A(a)(1)(A). This leads to the conclusion that the trustee of a QDOT-IRT must be a U.S. bank.

4.5 Approach # 3:
Spouse Assigns IRA To A QDOT

4.5.01 *Assignment of inherited IRA to a QDOT*

Another approach is for Spouse to assign ownership of an inherited IRA to a revocable QDOT she creates. The QDOT would become the "owner" (account holder) of the IRA. If Spouse is treated as owner of all of the income and principal of the QDOT under the grantor trust rules (§ 676) then she should be able to elect to treat the IRA as her own IRA despite the fact that it is owned by a trust (see ¶ 6.3.13). Using a *revocable* trust avoids gift tax problems; Spouse's transfer of assets into a QDOT would be subject to gift tax if it put the property irrevocably beyond her control. Even if the initial transfer to the trust is structured so as not to trigger gift tax, distributions to someone other than Spouse during her life would constitute completed gifts, resulting in a gift tax payable by her. Reg. § 20.2056A-4(d), Example 5. Therefore typically a QDOT created by Spouse would be for her own sole life benefit and fully revocable by her.

The regulations also eliminate another possible problem with this approach, namely, the possible difference between assigning *the IRA* to a QDOT and transferring *the property held in the IRA* to the QDOT. Generally, property inherited outright by Spouse must be transferred to a QDOT by a certain deadline to qualify for the modified marital deduction. The regulations provide that the assignment of an IRA to a QDOT (provided various technical details are complied with) "is treated as a transfer of such property to the QDOT...." § 20.2056A-4(b)(7)(i).

Does this approach work? That depends on the answers to two interrelated questions: Does the assignment of the IRA violate the IRA rules, causing the IRA to lose its status as such? Can the QDOT trust be entirely a "grantor trust" as to Spouse despite the QDOT trustee's power and obligation to withhold the deferred estate tax from any distribution to Spouse?

The Code does not prohibit the assignment of an IRA; see § 408. The Code provides that *certain* assignments (to wit, pledging the IRA as security for a loan) will cause the IRA to lose its status as such (§ 408(e)(4)); this Code provision creating a negative tax effect for one specific type of assignment suggests that other types of assignments do not cause the IRA to lose its status as such. However, regardless of whether a living IRA owner might be able to make some other type of assignment of his IRA, an assignment by Spouse of an *inherited* IRA would trigger immediate realization of the income under a different Code section, § 691(a)(2), because the inherited IRA is a right to receive IRD (see ¶ 2.2.05)...unless, possibly, if the assignment is to a "grantor trust."

If the assignment is to a trust all of which is treated as owned by Spouse under § 676 (because she is a U.S. resident and has the unlimited right to revoke the trust), then, arguably, the transfer would not be a taxable assignment under the IRS's doctrine that Spouse and her grantor trust are one taxpayer, not two separate taxpayers. So we can't answer question # 1 (does the assignment of the IRA cause the IRA to lose its status as such?) until we have answered question # 2 (is the QDOT 100% revocable by Spouse, when her right to revoke is subject to the QDOT trustee's power to withhold?)

The IRS's pronouncements on this subject have been vague. In the Preamble to the QDOT regulations, § E, the IRS said: "In general, individual retirement accounts under section 408(a) are assignable.... However, if an [IRA] is assigned to a trust with respect to which [Spouse] is *not* treated as the owner under section 671 *et seq.* ...then the entire account balance is treated as a distribution... includible in [Spouse's] gross income" in the year of the assignment. (Emphasis added.) This implies that assignment of an IRA to a QDOT of which Spouse *is* treated as the owner (i) is possible and (ii) would *not* be treated as a distribution.

In the regulations, the IRS admits that IRAs "are assignable and subject to provisions of this paragraph (b)(7) [dealing with Spouse's assignment to a QDOT of assets she inherited outright]. *However,*" Spouse may elect to treat an inherited IRA as non-assignable (see ¶ 4.6.02). Reg. § 20.2056A-4(b)(7)(iii) (emphasis added). There is no hint in this statement why assignment to a QDOT would not be acceptable, but the "however" suggests that the IRS thinks the election to treat the IRA as non-assignable is preferable to the assignment approach.

It does not seem that the QDOT trustee's power and obligation to withhold deferred estate tax from any non-hardship principal distributions to Spouse should cause the trust to be considered less than fully "revocable" by Spouse (and thus ineligible for grantor trust status). By assigning inherited assets to the QDOT, Spouse was relieved of the obligation to pay the estate tax on those assets; in that sense the deferred estate tax is her obligation and its payment by the QDOT trustee is a payment "to" her, which supports the argument that this is a grantor trust. See discussion in Blattmachr, J., et al. *Income Taxation of Estates and Trusts*, 14th ed. (PLI Press, New York, NY 2000), § 3.3.7 (last paragraph, p. 3-32).

However, in view of the lack of precedent and clear authority on this approach, it would be advisable to get a ruling before using this approach (or use a different approach).

4.5.02 *Assignment of rollover IRA to a QDOT*

The regulations mention the assignment approach only in connection with an IRA owned by Decedent of which Spouse is named beneficiary and which Spouse then assigns to a QDOT she has created, with no rollover involved. The regulations do not specifically bless a rollover of Decedent's benefits by Spouse to her *own* IRA, followed by assignment of the *rollover* IRA to a QDOT. This procedure would be of interest, for example, to a Spouse who inherits a benefit under a QRP. Typically the deferral options are better if Spouse rolls the QRP benefit over to an IRA than if she leaves the benefits in the QRP and takes them as beneficiary (see ¶ 3.2.01).

However, there should not be any difference in result. The modified marital deduction is available if Spouse assigns to the QDOT *either* the asset inherited from Decedent *or* the "proceeds from the sale, exchange or conversion" of such asset. Reg. § 20.2056A-4(b)(3). If Spouse receives a distribution from Decedent's QRP, and rolls that distribution over to her own IRA, the rollover IRA presumably constitutes "proceeds" from the "conversion" of the inherited asset and thus is suitable for assignment to a QDOT to exactly the same extent an inherited IRA would be (see ¶ 4.5.01). See PLR 1999-18039 (surviving non-citizen spouse contributed inherited real estate to a wholly-owned corporation, then contributed 94.9% of the stock to the QDOT; stock ruled to be "proceeds" of the inherited property, marital deduction allowed for the 94.9% interest transferred to QDOT).

The IRS has, in connection with other provisions, allowed Spouse to use, for a rollover IRA, provisions that the regulations specifically authorize only for an inherited IRA; see ¶ 4.6.02.

4.5.03 *Advantages, drafting issues*

The "IRA assigned to a QDOT" has one advantage over the "combination QDOT-IRT" (¶ 4.4) arising out of the fact that principal distributions from the IRA at some point during Spouse's life are unavoidable under the minimum distribution rules (Chapter 1) if she lives long enough. With an "IRA assigned to a QDOT," the inevitable principal distributions come out of the IRA but stay in the QDOT, and accordingly the deferred estate tax can continue to be deferred. In contrast, principal distributions from a QDOT-IRT to Spouse individually will trigger deferred estate tax. ¶ 4.1.01

In order to preserve the option of income tax deferral as long as possible, the QDOT presumably must comply with the minimum distribution "trust rules" (¶ 6.2) after Spouse's death.

4.6 Approach # 4: Non-Assignable Annuities; IRAs Treated as Same

4.6.01 *Two alternatives for non-assignable assets*

The Code directs the IRS, by regulations, to permit the surviving non-citizen spouse to obtain QDOT treatment for assets, such as a life annuity, which Spouse cannot legally transfer to a QDOT before the estate tax return is filed. § 2056A(e). The regulations provide a method of obtaining QDOT-type marital deduction treatment for such annuities, as well as for any "plan, annuity or other arrangement" that cannot be transferred to a QDOT (whether because of applicable federal, foreign or state law, or because of the terms of the "plan or arrangement"). Reg. § 20.2056A-4(c)(1).

All qualified retirement plan ("QRP") benefits are considered "non-assignable" because QRP benefits cannot be assigned as a matter of federal law. § 401(a)(13); Reg. § 20.2056A-4(c)(1). A QRP benefit, therefore, is automatically a non-assignable annuity for purposes of § 2056A, even if Spouse has the option to take all the money out immediately.

For these and other "non-assignable" assets, Spouse is given a choice of two methods in lieu of immediately transferring the asset to a QDOT:

A.   Spouse can agree to pay, each year, the deferred estate tax on all non-hardship corpus distributions Spouse receives from the arrangement in that year. This right is granted in Reg. § 20.2056A-4(c)(2) and accordingly such an agreement is referred to in this Chapter as a "(c)(2) agreement."

B.   Alternatively, Spouse can agree that she will transfer to a QDOT all non-hardship corpus distributions she receives from the arrangement, as she receives them. This type of agreement is described in Reg. § 20.2056A-4(c)(3) and is referred to in this Chapter as a "(c)(3) agreement."

The advantage of the (c)(3) agreement compared with a (c)(2) agreement is that, under a (c)(3) agreement, Spouse can continue to defer estate taxes until her death (or other triggering event; ¶ 4.1.01), whereas under a (c)(2) agreement deferred estate taxes must be paid whenever principal is received. So why would anyone ever use a (c)(2) agreement? Its only advantage appears to be that it does not require drafting a QDOT. Perhaps the (c)(2) agreement would appear attractive if there is no QDOT already in existence created to receive other assets and either: Spouse expects to become a U.S. citizen in the near future and eliminate the deferred estate tax that way (¶ 4.1.02); or the asset in question is of small value. In most other cases, presumably, the (c)(3) agreement would be preferable.

In PLR 1999-04023, the spouse used some of each method in connection with a joint and survivor annuity inherited from Decedent's pension plan: she paid the deferred estate tax on the corpus portion of annuity distributions she received prior to the completion of reformation proceedings designed to bring Decedent's QDOT into conformity with final regulations and agreed under (c)(3) to pay over to the QDOT any such payments she received after reformation was complete.

Upon Spouse's death, the remaining value of the non-assignable asset is subject to the deferred estate tax. Reg. § 20.2056A-5(b)(2). The *QDOT trustee* is responsible for paying this tax with respect to other types of assets, i.e., assets that are assigned to the QDOT. With a non-assignable asset, *Spouse's estate* is responsible to report the death and pay the tax if (as can happen under a (c)(2) agreement) there is no QDOT in existence, or if (under either form of agreement) the remaining value of the asset passes at Spouse's death to beneficiaries other than the QDOT. If her estate has no assets the enforcement mechanism is not clear. Reg. § 25.2056A-4(c)(7).

4.6.02 *Election to treat IRA as non-assignable*

The (c)(2) and (c)(3) agreement scheme applies not only to a truly non-assignable benefit payable to Spouse, which she does not (or cannot) take out of the plan and roll over to an IRA; it also applies to an IRA established by Decedent and inherited by Spouse which Spouse elects to treat as a non-assignable benefit. Reg. § 20.2056A-4(c)(1).

Is the option to treat an IRA as non-assignable available for a *rollover* (as opposed to an inherited) IRA? The regulations say that "The Commissioner will prescribe by administrative guidance the extent, if any, to which" the election may be made for plan or IRA benefits which were distributed to Spouse and rolled over by her after Decedent's death. § 20.2056A-4(c)(1). As of August 2001, the Commissioner has issued no such administrative guidance, so there is no statutory or regulatory authority for a Spouse's electing to treat a rollover IRA as non-assignable.

The fact that there is no authority for such treatment, however, has not stopped the IRS from allowing surviving spouses, in at least two instances, to make the election and enter into a (c)(2) or (c)(3) agreement regarding a rollover IRA. See PLRs 9729040 (two QRPs rolled to IRA; (c)(2) agreement allowed) and 9713018 (rollover of 403(b) annuity to IRA; (c)(2) agreement allowed).

The (c)(2)- or (c)(3)-agreement approach puts substantial

responsibility on Spouse. She must make sure that her withdrawals do not exceed the "income" of the account (or, to the extent withdrawals do exceed income, i.e., to the extent such withdrawals constitute non-hardship distributions of "corpus"; ¶ 4.6.03) she must carry out the terms of her agreement with the IRS. With the other approaches (¶ 4.3-¶ 4.5), there is a third party trustee (the QDOT trustee) interposed between Spouse and the IRA who can monitor compliance with these points, but with an IRA Spouse has elected to treat as non-assignable she is on her own. The spouse's ability to understand and comply with these requirements should be considered when adopting this approach.

4.6.03 *How much of each distribution is "principal?"*

Under either a (c)(2) or (c)(3) agreement (¶ 4.6.01), Spouse is agreeing that she will do something whenever she receives a "corpus" (principal) distribution from the non-assignable annuity. The regulations require use of the following formula to determine how much of each distribution from an annuity is "corpus":

Corpus portion = PV/T

Under the formula, "PV" is the "total present value of the annuity," i.e., "the present value of the nonassignable annuity ... as of the date of [Decedent's] death, determined in accordance with interest rates and mortality data prescribed by section 7520." This should be same as the date of death value of Spouse's interest in the annuity as reported on Decedent's estate tax return, since the same method is used to value the annuity for estate tax purposes.

This "Present Value" is divided by the "expected annuity term" (T) to arrive at the "corpus amount" of the annual payment. The "expected annuity term" is "the number of years that would be required for the scheduled payments to exhaust a hypothetical fund equal to the present value of the scheduled payments." To determine *this* figure, you need IRS Publication 1457 (7-1999), "Book Aleph," (Actuarial Values for Remainder, etc., interests) which can be obtained from the Government Printing Office, and the § 7520 rate used to value the annuity as of the date of death. The IRS publishes the § 7520 rate monthly; it can be found at www.tigertables.com and CCH Standard Federal Tax Reporter (Index Volume), among other places. With Book Aleph and the § 7520 rate in hand, the steps are as follows: Divide PV by the amount of the annual payment under the annuity. Take the resulting quotient and match it up with an "annuity factor" from column 1 of Table B for the applicable § 7520 rate, in Book Aleph. If it falls between two factors, use the higher one (longer term). You now have "T." Reg. § 20.2056A-4(c)(4)(ii)(B).

Example 4 in Reg. § 20.2056A-4(d) illustrates the calculations. In the IRS's Example 4, a 60-year old surviving spouse is required to recover all of the corpus portion of a life annuity within 16 years after Decedent's death, even though her life expectancy is 24.2 years (according to IRS's Table V). Yet there is nothing in the regulation indicating that Spouse can *stop* paying taxes on (or sending to the QDOT) the annuity payments once the corpus has been fully recovered under the above formula. Accordingly, this approach would appear to be disadvantageous to Spouse.

4.6.04 *Determining "corpus" portion: individual account plan*

The wording of Reg. § 20.2056A-4(c)(4) suggests that the above formula is the *only* method which may be used to determine the corpus portion of plan distributions subject to a (c)(2) or a (c)(3) agreement. However, several letter rulings have confirmed that the formula applies only when benefits are in fact taken in the form of an annuity. For determining the corpus portion of distributions from an individual account plan (see Glossary) subject to a (c)(2) or (c)(3) agreement, the general (trust accounting) rules of Reg. § 20.2056A-5(c)(2) apply; see ¶ 4.7.05. See PLRs 9746049, 9729040 and 9713018.

4.7 QDOT Investment and Distribution Strategies

This section looks at various tax rules that have an effect on the administrative policies of a QDOT (including a QDOT-IRT), and the strategies suggested by these rules.

4.7.01 *Hardship exception to deferred estate tax*

An important exception to the general rule that principal distributions to Spouse from the QDOT are subject to the deferred estate tax is that distributions to Spouse on account of *hardship* are not subject to that tax. § 2056A(b)(3). "A distribution of principal is treated as made on account of hardship if the distribution is made to [Spouse] from the QDOT in response to an immediate and substantial financial need relating to [Spouse]'s health, maintenance, education, or support, or the health, maintenance, education, or support of any person that [Spouse] is legally obligated to support. A distribution is not treated as made on account of hardship if the amount distributed may be obtained from other sources that are reasonably available to [Spouse]; e.g., the sale by [Spouse] of personally owned, publicly traded stock or the cashing in of a certificate of deposit owned by [Spouse]. Assets such as closely held business interests, real estate and tangible personalty are not considered sources that are reasonably available to [Spouse]." Reg. § 20.2056A-5(c)(1).

This generous definition of hardship will make this exception a useful planning tool in many situations. The QDOT trustee should be on the lookout for possible hardship distribution opportunities. If Spouse keeps all her non-QDOT assets illiquid, more of her living expenses can be shifted to QDOT trust principal. If she needs money for living expenses, she should think of the QDOT trust as a resource first.

4.7.02 *Investment disincentives of a QDOT: capital growth*

The deferred estate tax problem can grow worse over the duration of the QDOT through capital growth and capital gains which augment the "corpus" of the QDOT, thus increasing the amount that will eventually be subject to the deferred estate tax. The structure of the deferred estate tax encourages investing for income and discourages investing for "growth" or capital gain.

Of course, all assets held by Spouse at her death (including QDOT income distributions she receives during life and does not spend) will be subject to estate tax if she is either a U.S. resident or a U.S. citizen at that time, so in many cases it will make no difference if the trust's investment gain is in the form of capital appreciation (subject to deferred estate tax) or income (subject to estate tax at Spouse's death if not spent by her). But if for any reason the estate tax rate on Spouse's estate will be significantly lower than the deferred estate tax rate applicable to the QDOT (*e.g.*, because Spouse ceases to be subject to U.S. estate tax), this factor becomes significant.

4.7.03 *How income can become principal*

Distributions of "income" from a QDOT are free of the deferred estate tax, whereas all (non-hardship) "principal" (or "corpus") dollars will be subject to that tax. Therefore "income" is very valuable. Unfortunately, as the following examples illustrate, it appears that the IRS wants to herd as many dollars as possible into the "principal" corral, where they can be branded with the deferred estate tax, and make it difficult for "income" dollars to escape tax-free onto the open range.

For example, whatever was in the retirement plan at Decedent's death *should* be considered the initial principal of the QDOT-IRT. However, the IRS may have refused to rule its agreement with this simple statement in PLR 9729040 (Ruling request 4, which was withdrawn; often, a taxpayer seeking a ruling will withdraw the request if the IRS indicates it will give a negative ruling). In another letter ruling, the initial principal of the QDOT was defined as *the amount rolled over to it*, with no stated exception for post-death income that had accumulated in the retirement plan. PLR 9623063. Although possibly there *was* no post-death accumulated income (and maybe that's why the ruling doesn't discuss this subject), it's also possible that this ruling means that any accumulated income rolled to a QDOT must be added to principal for deferred estate tax purposes.

Second example: Reg. § 20.2056A-5(c)(2) states that "income does not include capital gains." This rule seems unfair: If *income* is reinvested, and the reinvestment produces capital gain in the *income* account, that should be considered income for purposes of § 2056A, even if it is taxable as capital gain.

Third example: In PLR 9729040, the surviving non-citizen spouse did not intend to take distributions from a rollover IRA until she reached age 59½. The (c)(3) agreement she signed with the IRS stipulated that "any income accumulated in the IRAs prior to" Spouse's reaching that age would be considered principal. Since it is hard to imagine that she would have suggested this stipulation, one wonders if the IRS gave her the following choice: take your "income" distributions now and avoid deferred estate tax on them (but pay income taxes now, plus 10% penalty) (see Chapter 9); or defer income tax, and avoid the 10% penalty (but agree that the accumulated income becomes "principal" for purposes of the deferred estate tax). This could be called the "get tough on young widows" policy. (However, we don't need to feel too sorry for this Spouse, since she can presumably avoid both the 10% penalty and the deferred estate tax by not allowing the income to "accumulate inside the IRA." Instead, she could distribute the income to herself and roll those income distributions over tax-free *again*, to an IRA to which the (c)(3) agreement did not apply. See ¶ 4.7.04, ¶ 3.3.07.

Fourth example: On Spouse's death, the deferred estate tax can no longer be deferred. The deferred estate tax is imposed on "the value of the property remaining in a qualified domestic trust on the date of the death of the surviving spouse." § 2056(A)(b). It is not clear from this phrase that *undistributed income* held in the QDOT would be excluded from the tax base. The *proposed* regulations issued in 1992, § 20.2056A-5, specified that "the amount subject to tax is the value of the trust *corpus* on the date of Spouse's death" (emphasis added). The final regulations issued in August 1995 deleted this statement, retaining the ambiguity of the statute.

These examples suggest that the IRS intends to treat accumulated income as principal to the maximum extent possible for purposes of imposing the deferred estate tax. Therefore, the QDOT should distribute all income annually to Spouse, so the IRS cannot impose deferred estate tax on it.

4.7.04 *Rollover strategy for excess income distributions*

If the income distributed to Spouse in any particular year from a QDOT-IRT, or from an inherited or rollover IRA assigned to a QDOT, or from a rollover or inherited IRA that Spouse has elected to treat as non-assignable, is greater than the amount that would be required to be distributed to her under the minimum distribution rules (see Chapter 1), Spouse could establish a separate IRA (not a QDOT-IRT, and not an IRA held by a QDOT, and not an IRA subject to a (c)(2) or (c)(3) agreement) into which she rolls either the entire income distribution or the part of it that exceeds the MRD. See ¶ 3.3.07. This strategy would permit continued income tax deferral for the rolled amount while removing it from the reach of the deferred estate tax.

4.7.05 *What is income?*

The discussion at ¶ 4.7.03 shows how certain traditional items of "income" (capital gains in the income account; accumulated income) may be treated by the IRS as "principal" (and therefore subject to the deferred estate tax). Presumably the QDOT trustee will foil that IRS policy by promptly distributing all income to Spouse. Which leads to the question of how the trustee (and the IRS) determine whether an item (or distribution) is allocated to "income" earned after Decedent's death (not subject to the deferred estate tax), or "principal" (taxable)?

The regulations' pronouncements are all contained in Reg. § 20.2056A-5(c)(2). "Income" of the QDOT will mean income as it is defined in § 643(b), except that "income does not include capital gains....[or] any other item that would be allocated to corpus under applicable local law governing the administration of trusts irrespective of any specific trust provision to the contrary." Typically such "other items" allocated to corpus under local law would include the property originally contributed to the trust.

§ 643(b) defines "income" as "the amount of income of the estate or trust for the taxable year determined under the terms of the governing instrument and applicable local law." If local law has nothing to say on the subject, "the allocation...will be governed by general principles of law (including but not limited to any uniform state acts, such as the Uniform Principal and Income Act, or any Restatements of applicable law)."

Hopefully, "irrespective of any specific trust provision" means that the governing instrument's allocation will be respected, provided its method of determining principal and income is permitted under local law and provided it does not violate any specific QDOT rule. Or does it mean that income will be determined under local law, *without regard* to the specific provisions of the trust?

Regardless of what local law or the trust says, "income does not include items constituting" IRD unless otherwise provided in future administrative guidance. Reg. § 20.2056A-5(c)(2). Thus, a trust provision defining all retirement plan distributions as "income" will not change the character of such distributions (from taxable corpus to non-taxable income) for purposes of the deferred estate tax (because such distributions generally constitute "IRD"; see ¶ 2.2). Retirement plan distributions to a QDOT could bring to a head the never-resolved issue of which distributions from a retirement plan constitute IRD (i.e., funds that were in the plan as of the date of Decedent's death) and which distributions come from the plan's earnings and growth that occurred after the date of death; see ¶ 2.2.10.

The allocation of annuity payments between corpus and income by the method prescribed in the regulations (¶ 4.6.03) will be respected.

4.8 Summary of Planning Principles

As the discussion in this Chapter indicates, there is no problem-free way to dispose of retirement benefits when Spouse is not a U.S. citizen.

4.8.01 *Benefits that can be rolled over*

1.   If Spouse inherits QRP benefits outright, and wants to get both the income tax benefits of the spousal rollover (¶ 3.2.01) *and* the estate tax benefits of the modified marital deduction: either Spouse rolls over Decedent's benefits to a combination QDOT-IRT (¶ 4.4), or Spouse rolls over the benefits to a non-QDOT IRA that Spouse then "assigns" to a grantor-trust-type QDOT she establishes (¶ 4.5). A third choice (for which a ruling should be obtained, since "administrative guidance" is yet to be issued on this choice) is to roll over the benefits to a (non-QDOT) IRA, elect to treat the rollover IRA as non-assignable, and then sign an agreement with the IRS, agreeing either that Spouse will pay the deferred estate tax on the corpus portion of each payment as received or that Spouse will assign such corpus portion to a QDOT (¶ 4.6).

2.   If the inherited benefit is already in an IRA, things are a little easier: Spouse has all the same choices as for inherited QRP benefits, but does not need a ruling to treat the inherited IRA as non-assignable.

3.   In the planning stage, while Participant is still alive, the choice is even more complicated. The marital trust-QDOT (¶ 4.3) will appeal to the client who wants to control the ultimate disposition of the asset, or who simply wants his estate plan to be self-executing, without requiring Spouse to undertake additional steps after his death. However, making benefits payable directly to a QDOT probably eliminates the income tax benefits of a spousal rollover (but see ¶ 4.3.02). Making benefits payable outright to Spouse will appeal to the client who has no objection to giving Spouse control, desires maximum income tax deferral and is willing to adopt a plan which requires post-death action by Spouse in order to succeed.

4.   The client may be attracted to the income tax deferral

possibilities of the rollover, but reluctant to leave qualifying for the marital deduction entirely up to *post mortem* action. What this client might want, ideally, would be a plan which would have all the elements in place to automatically qualify for the modified marital deduction, without foreclosing the option of the spousal rollover. One way to achieve this result (for an IRA) would be for Decedent's IRA to be in the form of an IRT which will become a QDOT-IRT on his death (this is a variation of Alternative 2, not discussed in this book). Another possibility is to leave the benefits to a marital trust-QDOT (Alternative 1), but name Spouse as contingent beneficiary, so the trust can disclaim (see Chapter 8) the benefits and they will pass to Spouse who can roll them over, on the assumption that the trust would disclaim unless Spouse was disabled or for some other reason not able to carry out the rollover.

4.8.02 *Benefits that cannot be rolled over*

5.   If the benefits are non-assignable, and Spouse cannot roll them over, Spouse can agree to deposit the benefits into a QDOT as they are paid to her ("(c)(3) agreement"). Because this approach allows the longest deferral of the deferred estate tax it appears preferable to agreeing to pay the deferred estate tax on non-assignable benefits as they are received ("(c)(2) agreement"). However, agreeing to pay the deferred estate tax may be attractive for retirement benefits subject to income tax because the income tax can be deducted from the amount that will be subject to the deferred estate tax.

4.8.03 *Other comments*

6.   If using the marital trust-QDOT option (¶ 4.3), consider giving Spouse the unlimited right to withdraw principal, if that will cause distributions of IRD from the retirement plan to the trust to be taxed at Spouse's income tax rate and if Spouse's income tax rate will be lower than the trust's income tax rate. Unless there has been further guidance from the IRS, however, it might be advisable to get a ruling confirming that Spouse (assuming she is a U.S. resident) will be personally taxable on plan distributions to the trust because of her unlimited right to withdraw from the trust (despite the trustee's obligation to withhold from her withdrawals), and that principal distributions to Spouse to reimburse her for income taxes imposed *on*

her by virtue of § 678 on the distributions from the plan to the trust can be made free of the deferred estate tax before taking this route. Once the client has chosen to make the benefits payable either to Spouse or to a marital trust, consider making them "disclaimable" to the other (trust or Spouse) in case that option appears more attractive when death occurs (see Chapter 8).

7.   While the client is living, he should consider converting IRAs to Roth IRAs, if he is eligible to do so, to avoid many of these problems; see Chapter 5.

8.   In administering any QDOT, the trustee should take advantage of the hardship distribution exception whenever possible (to distribute principal to Spouse free of the deferred estate tax); and should consider investing so as to minimize growth of the original "principal," while maximizing "income." All income (whether earned inside or outside a retirement plan) should be distributed to the Spouse as soon as is practicable to avoid the risk that the IRS will say it has become "principal." If this income distribution includes retirement plan distributions in excess of the MRD, it may be that the excess can be rolled over by Spouse to her own non-QDOT-IRA.

5

Roth Retirement Plans

Roth retirement plans offer an intriguing opportunity for a limited number of people who are eligible, and can afford, to adopt them

5.1 Introduction to Roth Retirement Plans

5.1.01 *Roth retirement plans: background*

Prior to the debut of the Roth IRA in 1998, all retirement plans had the same basic tax structure: contributions to the plan might or might not be tax deductible; and all distributions from the plan (except to the extent attributable to after-tax contributions) would be includible in the recipient's gross income. Thus, income taxes on all of the plan's investment returns (and on some or all contributions to the plan) would be deferred until distributed from the plan (after retirement or after death, in most cases).

§ 408A established a new kind of IRA, called a "Roth IRA," effective in 1998. Reg. § 1.408A-9, A-1. The basic idea of the Roth IRA is that contributions are never deductible, but distributions are normally tax-free. Thus, the income tax on the plan's internal investment returns is not merely deferred, it is eliminated, at the cost of payment of income taxes up front on the plan contributions. Final regulations on Roth IRAs were issued by the IRS in February, 1999.

In 2001, EGTRRA added two more "Roth" retirement plans, the "deemed Roth IRA" (effective in 2003 and later years) (¶ 5.1.04) and the "Designated Roth Account" (beginning in 2006) (¶ 5.1.05).

5.1.02 *Overview of Roth IRAs*

Roth IRAs are treated just like traditional IRAs except where the Code specifies different treatment. § 408A(a); Reg. § 1.408A-1, A-1(b). Thus, if there is any question about Roth IRAs that is not specifically answered in § 408A or the Roth IRA regulations, the answer should be the same as for a traditional IRA.

In addition to tax-free distributions, the Roth IRA offers other attractions: no required distributions during life (¶ 5.1.03); and no maximum age for making contributions (¶ 5.3.04).

There are two ways to create a Roth IRA. One is by non-deductible contributions on behalf of an individual who has compensation income; the IRS calls these "regular contributions." Reg. § 1.408A-3, A-1; see ¶ 5.3. The other is by rolling over a distribution from a traditional IRA (or by conversion of a traditional IRA to a Roth IRA) (¶ 5.4). The rollover (or conversion) of a traditional IRA to a Roth IRA causes the full amount of the rollover (minus any applicable basis) to be currently taxed. ¶ 5.4.09.

Each of the two methods has its own rules and eligibility requirements.

5.1.03 How the minimum distribution rules apply to Roth IRAs

The lifetime minimum distribution rules (¶ 1.4) do not apply to Roth IRAs. § 408A(c)(5) provides that § 401(a)(9)(A) (which contains the lifetime minimum distribution rules) and the "incidental death benefit" rule (¶ 8.3.02) do not apply to Roth IRAs. Therefore, a person who reaches age 70½ does not have to start taking distributions from his Roth IRA as he does from his traditional IRA. There is no "required beginning date" (RBD) (¶ 1.3) for a Roth IRA. This is one of the two major advantages of the Roth IRA (the other being tax-free distributions; ¶ 5.2.01). A traditional IRA will eventually be diminished by required distributions to Participant if he lives long enough; the Roth IRA can keep growing larger as long as Participant lives.

Once death occurs, the minimum distribution rules do apply to Roth IRAs. The Roth IRA is not exempted from any minimum distribution rules other than § 401(a)(9)(A) and the incidental death benefit rule, both of which apply only during Participant's life, so distributions must begin coming out of the Roth IRA after Participant's death. Since there is no RBD for a Roth IRA, the post-death minimum distribution rules will be applied "as though the Roth IRA owner died before his" RBD, regardless of when he dies (i.e., regardless of whether he dies before or after reaching age 70½). Reg. § 1.408A-6, A-14(b). For how to compute required distributions from a Roth IRA after Participant's death, see ¶ 1.5.02.

Distributions from a Roth IRA cannot be used to fulfill a minimum distribution requirement arising from any other kind of IRA. Reg. § 1.408A-6, A-15.

5.1.04 *"Deemed" Roth IRAs (2003 and later)*

Under § 408(q), added by EGTRRA 2001, an employer that maintains a qualified retirement plan may (for plan years beginning after 2002) permit employees to make voluntary contributions to "a separate account or annuity established under the plan." The separate account must meet the requirements of § 408 (traditional IRA) or § 408A (Roth IRA). The separate account (the deemed traditional IRA or deemed Roth IRA) is then treated in all respects the same as a traditional IRA or Roth IRA, as the case may be, and is generally not subject to the qualified plan requirements.

Since a "deemed" Roth IRA is treated in all respects the same as a "real" Roth IRA, all the discussion in this Chapter about Roth IRAs applies equally to deemed Roth IRAs.

The purpose of deemed traditional IRAs and deemed Roth IRAs is, as with many of EGTRRA's provisions, to facilitate and encourage saving for retirement. The idea seems to be that the employee may find it convenient to make his annual IRA contribution right at the workplace. From the employer's perspective, adding yet another set of accounts to the company's retirement plan can only further complicate the already extremely complicated job of plan administration, especially since the deemed accounts are subject to an entirely different set of tax rules than the rest of the plan. Since employees who care about saving for retirement can easily contribute to traditional IRAs and Roth IRAs without employer involvement, it is hard to see what incentive an employer has to allow them to make deemed IRA contributions.

5.1.05 *Designated Roth Accounts (Roth 401(k)s) (2006 and later)*

The "designated Roth account" (also called the "Roth 401(k)") is another new type of retirement plan created by EGTRRA 2001. Under § 402A, effective for years after 2005, an employer can permit its employees to make "designated Roth contributions" to their "designated Roth accounts" under a 401(k) or 403(b) plan. § 402A(b). This option does not increase the amount that may be contributed to a 401(k) or 403(b) plan through salary reduction (elective deferral).

Rather, if the employer allows these designated Roth contributions, the employee may choose to have part or all of his normal elective deferrals to a 401(k) or 403(b) plan channeled into a designated Roth account (DRAC) in the plan rather than into a regular account.

The employer must maintain separate records for the Roth and non-Roth accounts. § 402A(b)(2).

Unlike normal 401(k) or 403(b) elective deferrals, the DRAC contribution is not excluded from the employee's income. Later "qualified" distributions from the Roth account are tax-free. § 402A(a)(1), (d)(1). The Five-Year Period necessary to qualify for the tax-free distribution feature begins, in the case of a DRAC, with the first year the employee made a designated Roth contribution *to that particular plan*. § 402A(d)(2)(B). With a Roth IRA, in contrast, the Five-Year Period begins with the first year of contribution to *any* Roth IRA; ¶ 5.2.02.

The only contributions that can go into the DRAC are the employee's elective deferrals, such as are permitted under a 401(k) or 403(b) plan. § 402A(e). § 402A contains no provision: for matching or other contributions by *employers* to DRACs of their employees; or for conversion of any other types of contributions or plan accumulations to DRACs.

Although the basic tax structure of the DRAC is similar to that of a Roth IRA (pay tax when money goes into the plan, and no tax when money comes out), the DRAC is a hybrid of a qualified plan and a Roth IRA. Note the following differences between DRACs and Roth IRAs:

1.   Anyone who is otherwise eligible to make elective contributions to the 401(k) or 403(b) plan can have his elective contribution designated as a Roth contribution, if the employer permits that feature in its plan, regardless of how much adjusted gross income that person has. § 402A(a)(1). In contrast, an individual may contribute to a Roth IRA only if his income is below a specified level (¶ 5.3.03, ¶ 5.4.03).

2.   Since the DRAC will be part of a qualified plan (or part of a 403(b) arrangement, as the case may be), it will apparently be subject to the requirement of lifetime minimum required distributions (see Chapter 1). Roth IRAs have no required distributions prior to the death of the participant (¶ 5.1.03).

Ed Slott, CPA, publisher of *Ed Slott's IRA Advisor*, and Barry Picker, CPA, author of *Barry Picker's Guide to Retirement Distribution Planning,* point out that, unless EGTRRA's provisions are further amended by Congress, no-one will ever receive a "qualified distribution" from a DRAC, because (a) the earliest year a DRAC can be established, under EGTRRA, is 2006, meaning that (b) the earliest year in which a qualified distribution could be received is 2011, but (c) under EGTRRA's "sunset" provision (§ 901) DRACs and the rest of EGTRRA's provisions are repealed for years after 2010.

Distributions from a DRAC may be rolled over subject to the same rules generally applicable to rollovers of distributions from the applicable type of plan, except that DRAC distributions may be rolled only to another DRAC or to a Roth IRA. § 402A(c)(3)(A). § 402A(d)(2)(B) specifies that if money is rolled into a DRAC from a DRAC in a different plan (e.g., with the employee's prior employer), the holding period for the transferee DRAC dates back to the date of establishment of the DRAC in the prior plan for purposes of calculating the Five-Year Period (¶ 5.2.02) necessary to have qualified distributions. However, § 402A says nothing about calculation of the Five-Year Period in case of a rollover from a DRAC to a Roth IRA, so this aspect will presumably require further clarification from Congress or the IRS.

Although the DRAC option does not increase the amount that employees can contribute to their 401(k) and 403(b) plans, it does offer employees something unique, namely the opportunity to have their salary deferral contributions place in a Roth-type retirement plan (no deduction now, tax-free distributions later) instead of a regular-type retirement plan (plan contribution excluded from income now, taxable distributions from plan later). Employees whose income is too high to allow them to contribute to a Roth IRA (see ¶ 5.3.03) cannot have a Roth retirement plan unless their employer offers DRACs. This makes DRACs different from deemed Roth IRAs, which add no new planning options, just (maybe, at best) greater convenience. Thus, presumably, employers will have an incentive to take on the additional burden of administering DRACs, as DRACs may be an attractive option for existing and potential employees.

The rest of this Chapter describes the rules and planning considerations applicable to Roth IRAs, emphasizing contrasts with traditional IRAs. Everything in this Chapter that applies to Roth IRAs applies equally to "deemed" Roth IRAs (¶ 5.1.04); however, the extent to which each rule will apply to "designated Roth accounts" remains to be seen. To make this Chapter easier to read, I have written simply about "Roth IRAs," rather than saying, every time, "Roth IRAs or deemed Roth IRAs."

5.1.06 *Roth IRA terminology*

In this Chapter: A "**traditional IRA**" refers to an individual retirement account or individual retirement trust established under § 408. A traditional IRA may contain deductible contributions, non-deductible contributions and/or rollovers from employer plans.

The term "**conversion**" of a traditional IRA to a Roth IRA includes a "rollover" from a traditional IRA to a Roth IRA. Conversion contributions and rollover contributions to Roth IRAs mean the same thing: a transfer, rollover or conversion of funds from a traditional IRA to a Roth IRA. See ¶ 5.4.

The "**Five-Year Period**" refers to the period of time after which distributions from a Roth IRA may be income tax-free. See ¶ 5.2.02.

The "**Ordering Rules**" are the rules which dictate which contribution (or earnings) a particular Roth IRA distribution is deemed to come from; see ¶ 5.2.04.

"The **regulations**" refers to the IRS's final regulations on Roth IRAs issued February 3, 1999, effective generally for taxable years beginning after December 31, 1997 (except that to the extent they replaced IRS Notice 98-50 (1998 C.B. 569) they were effective January 1, 2000). For more Roth IRA terms see ¶ 5.2.01 and ¶ 5.4.01.

5.1.07 *State law problems: creditors, taxes*

Many states' laws exempt IRAs from creditors' claims, but in many of these states the exemption refers to a specific Code section, namely § 408—which describes only traditional IRAs. Roth IRAs would presumably not be protected in such states without a legislative change. In states whose tax laws do not automatically follow federal Code changes, Roth IRAs may not receive favorable tax treatment without a legislative change. See also ¶ 5.4.09.

5.1.08 *Basis in property distributed from a Roth IRA*

The basis of property distributed from a Roth IRA is its fair market value on the date of the distribution. Reg. § 1.408A-6, A-16.

5.1.09 *Excess contributions: 6% penalty*

There is an excise tax of 6% imposed on contributions to Roth IRAs in excess of the applicable limits, just as there is for excess contributions to traditional IRAs. § 4973; Reg. § 1.408A-3, A-7. This excise tax would apply, for example, to a person who converted a traditional IRA to a Roth IRA but was not eligible to do so—for example, because he had more than $100,000 of income (see ¶ 5.4.03). This excise is imposed *annually* on the excess contribution. § 4973(a).

The "failed" conversion would be treated as a (taxable) distribution from the traditional IRA (subject to the 10% penalty under § 72(t) if the individual is under 59½; see Chapter 9), followed by an excess contribution to the Roth IRA. To avoid the penalty, the person would have to recharacterize the contribution (¶ 5.7).

5.2 Tax Treatment of Roth IRA Distributions

Not all Roth IRA distributions are automatically tax-free; only "qualified distributions" from a Roth IRA are income tax-free. ¶ 5.2.01. It is relatively easy to qualify for "qualified" distributions, and even non-qualified distributions from Roth IRAs (¶ 5.2.03) get favorable treatment compared with distributions from traditional IRAs (see ¶ 5.4.09-¶ 5.4.12).

5.2.01 *Definition and tax treatment of qualified distributions*

"Qualified distributions" from a Roth IRA are not included in the recipient's gross income for federal income tax purposes, regardless of whether the recipient is the Participant or a beneficiary. § 408A(d)(1). A qualified distribution is one made after the Five-Year Period (¶ 5.2.02); and which *in addition* (§ 408A(d)(2)(A)):

1.   Is made on or after the date on which Participant attains age 59½; or

2.   Is made to a beneficiary (or to Participant's estate) after Participant's death; or

3.   Is "attributable to" Participant's being totally disabled (as defined in § 72(m)(7)) (see ¶ 9.3.02); or

4.   Is a "qualified special purpose distribution." A qualified special purpose distribution is a distribution of up to $10,000 for certain purchases of a "first home" (see ¶ 9.3.09). § 408A(d)(5); § 72(t)(2)(F).

In general, these conditions for a qualified distribution from a Roth IRA resemble the requirements for avoiding the premature-distributions penalty of § 72(t) (Chapter 9), but are not identical. For example, withdrawals from a Roth IRA to pay "higher education expenses" are not qualified distributions, even though such withdrawals from a traditional IRA would be exempt from the 10% penalty. § 72(t)(2)(E).

5.2.02 *Computing Five-Year Period for qualified distributions*

The Five-Year Period (called in the statute the "nonexclusion period") for *all* of a Participant's Roth IRAs (with one exception applicable to certain surviving spouses; see ¶ 5.8.05) begins on January 1 of the first year for which a contribution was made to *any* Roth IRA maintained for that Participant. § 408A(d)(2)(B); Reg. § 1.408A-6, A-2.

Example: Fred puts $2,000 into his Roth IRA for 2001. He had never previously made any type of contribution to a Roth IRA and makes no further contributions in 2001. Fred's Five-Year Period starts January 1, 2001. The first year in which he can possibly have a qualified distribution is 2006. If he makes further contributions (either regular or rollover) to the same (or any other) Roth IRA in later years, those contributions do not start a new Five-Year Period running. This result appears to hold even if Fred cashes out the entire Roth IRA before the end of the Five-Year Period (otherwise than by means of a corrective distribution; ¶ 5.7.01).

However, if Fred *recharacterizes* his 2001 contribution (¶ 5.7.02), the Roth IRA is treated as if it never existed. Such an "unconversion" would extinguish the Five-Year Period, and he would have to start over in another year.

5.2.03 *Tax treatment of non-qualified distributions*

A non-qualified distribution is one made before the Five-Year Period is up; or which is made after expiration of the Five-Year Period but not for one of the specified reasons (age 59½, disability, death, etc.; ¶ 5.2.01). A non-qualified distribution is not *per se* excludible from gross income. However, even if a distribution is not "qualified" it receives favorable tax treatment compared with distributions from a traditional IRA.

A Roth IRA contains two types of money. First, it contains Participant's own regular contributions and/or conversion contributions; since these amounts were *already* included in Participant's gross income, these originally-contributed funds will not be included in his income *again* when they are later distributed. Thus, the amount of Participant's original contribution(s) to the Roth IRA (plus any after-tax contributions contained in a traditional IRA that was converted to a Roth IRA) constitutes Participant's basis (or "investment in the contract") in the Roth IRA. ¶ 2.1.04. If the account has grown to be worth more than this basis, the rest of the account value (which represents the earnings and growth that have occurred since the original contribution) has not yet been taxed (and may *never* be taxed if it is distributed in the form of a qualified distribution).

All distributions from a Roth IRA are deemed to come *first* out of Participant's contributions. § 408A(d)(4)(B); ¶ 5.2.04. Thus, if Participant needs to get money out of the Roth IRA, but the account has not been established long enough to generate qualified distributions, he can still take out money income tax-free, up to the amount he originally contributed.

In contrast to this favorable treatment afforded to Roth IRAs, all distributions from a *traditional* IRA are deemed to come *proportionately* from the "basis" (non-taxable) portion and the post-contribution earnings of all of Participant's aggregated IRAs. § 408(d)(1), (2); § 72(e)(2)(B), (5)(A), (5)(D)(iii), and (8). Thus, Participant's basis in a traditional IRA is recovered only gradually, as he makes withdrawals, and some part of every distribution is taxable. See ¶ 5.4.10 and ¶ 5.4.12.

See ¶ 5.4.09 and ¶ 5.6.03 for situations in which the distribution of Participant's own contributions may nevertheless accelerate taxation or result in a penalty.

5.2.04 *The Ordering Rules*

Any distribution from a Roth IRA (*except* a corrective distribution of an excess contribution; Reg. § 1.408A-6, A-9(e); ¶ 5.7.01) is deemed to come from the following sources, in the order indicated. § 408A(d)(4)(B); Reg. § 1.408A-6, A-9. These rules are referred to in this chapter as the "Ordering Rules."

1.   Any distribution is deemed to come, first, from Participant's *contributions* to his Roth IRA(s) (to the extent that all previous distributions from his Roth IRA(s) have not yet exceeded the contributions); and

2.   If Participant has made both "regular" (¶ 5.3) and "rollover" (conversion) (¶ 5.4) contributions, the distributions are deemed to come, first, from the regular contributions (with no rule specifying in what order contributions made in different years are deemed distributed), then from rollover contributions, on a first-in, first-out, basis; and

3.   Once it is thus determined that the distribution is deemed to come from a particular rollover contribution, the dollars that were includible in gross income by virtue of that rollover (¶ 5.4.09) are deemed distributed first, and non-taxable dollars last; and

4.   Finally, once all contributions have been distributed out, the balance of the distribution comes out of post-contribution earnings. Whew!

Fortunately, the Ordering Rules will have to be consulted only in certain unusual situations, namely:

1.   For most people, the Ordering Rules matter only for purposes of determining whether a non-qualified distribution is taxable; the Ordering Rules essentially mean that the distribution is NOT taxable until all contributions have been distributed out. See example at ¶ 5.8.01.

2.   The Ordering Rules mattered for someone who (A) converted

a traditional IRA to a Roth IRA in 1998 and (B) chose to spread the tax on the conversion over four years and (C) then took a distribution before 2001 (or died before 2002; ¶ 5.8.04.). The Ordering Rules will apply in determining whether the taxation is accelerated. See ¶ 5.4.09.

3.   The Ordering Rules matter also for someone who (A) converts a traditional IRA to a Roth IRA before reaching age 59½, and then takes a distribution (B) before reaching age 59½ and (C) within the five taxable years beginning with the year of the conversion. The Ordering Rules will apply in determining whether the 10% penalty applies to the distribution. See ¶ 5.6.03.

5.2.05 *Aggregation of Roth IRAs for income tax purposes*

§ 408A(d)(4)(A) provides that § "408(d)(2) shall be applied separately with respect to Roth IRAs and other individual retirement plans." This means that the taxation of distributions from *traditional* IRAs will be computed without regard to the existence of, or distributions from, *Roth* IRAs in the same year; and that all of Participant's Roth IRAs are treated as one single account for purposes of applying the Ordering Rules. § 408A(d)(4)(A).

5.3 "Regular Contributions" to a Roth IRA

One way to fund a Roth IRA is by making what the IRS calls "regular" (as opposed to "rollover"; ¶ 5.4) contributions. This ¶ 5.3 discusses the requirements for making a regular contribution to a Roth IRA, as contrasted with the rules governing regular contributions to a traditional IRA. See ¶ 5.7.04 for discussion of how to change your mind about which type of IRA you want to contribute to after you've already contributed.

5.3.01 *Definition of compensation*

Whether an individual is entitled to make a regular IRA contribution, and if so to *which type* of IRA (traditional or Roth), depends on various eligibility factors, the first of which is the necessity of having "compensation" income for the year in question.

"Compensation income" is partly defined in § 219(f)(1): it includes self-employment income (§ 401(c)(2)), and does *not* include pension, annuity or deferred compensation payments. It includes taxable alimony and separate maintenance payments (§ 71). It includes "wages, commissions, professional fees, tips, and other amounts received for personal services." Reg. § 1.408A-3, A-4. See Rev. Proc. 91-18, 1991-1 C.B. 522, for further detail on the definition.

Compensation income does not include gifts. If a parent decides to pay his toddler a salary for performing household chores, the IRS might maintain that the child has received a gift, not compensation, and that Roth IRA contributions based on this "compensation" are excess contributions subject to the 6% excise tax (§ 4973).

5.3.02 *How much may be contributed annually*

The maximum annual regular *Roth* IRA contribution derives from the maximum annual regular *traditional* IRA contribution.

The maximum amount that may be contributed to all of a person's traditional IRAs for a particular year is the lesser of the applicable dollar limit or the individual's compensation income (¶ 5.3.01) for the year. The maximum regular contribution for a particular year to all of a person's *Roth* IRAs is the exact same amount—minus the amount of regular contributions made to any traditional IRA(s) for that person for that year. § 408A(c)(2).

So, an individual who has compensation income (and who meets the other eligibility requirements; see ¶ 5.3.03, ¶ 5.3.04 for Roth IRAs, § 219 for traditional IRAs) may contribute to either a traditional IRA or a Roth IRA (whichever one or both he or she is eligible to contribute to), provided that the total contributed to both types of accounts for the year does not exceed the applicable dollar amount (or the individual's total compensation income for the year, if less).

Contributions to a "simplified employee pension" individual retirement account (SEP-IRA) (§ 408(k)) or a "simple retirement account" (SIMPLE IRA) (§ 408(p)) are *not* treated as "IRA contributions" for this purpose, so the maximum regular contribution by a person who is otherwise eligible to make a contribution to a Roth IRA in a particular year is not reduced by the amount of a contribution made for him to a SEP-IRA or SIMPLE IRA. § 408A(f).

The applicable dollar limit was $2,000 for the years 1998 through 2001. § 219(b)(1)(A), as in effect through 2001. § 219(b)(5), added by EGTRRA 2001, increases the applicable dollar limit for 2002 and later years to:

Year	Basic Applicable Dollar Limit	Add-on for Participant over 50
2002-2004	$3,000	$ 500
2005	$4,000	$ 500
2006-2007	$4,000	$1,000
2008-2010	$5,000	$1,000

The $500 or $1,000 add-on to the applicable dollar limit is available to a Participant who has attained age 50 by the end of the taxable year. § 219(b)(5)(B). After 2008, § 219(b)(5)(C) applies a COLA to the applicable dollar limit (but not to the over-50 add-on amount) in $500 increments. § 219(b)(5)(C). The sunset provision (§ 901(a)(2)) of EGTRRA would cause the dollar limit to revert to $2,000 for all individuals after 2010.

5.3.03 *Who may contribute to a Roth IRA: income limits*

Not just anyone who has compensation income may contribute to a Roth IRA. There is an income limit. A specially calculated version of "adjusted gross income" (see ¶ 5.4.04-¶ 5.4.06) cannot exceed the following levels. In order to be able to contribute the full dollar limit (e.g., $2,000 for 2001) to a Roth IRA, AGI may not exceed $95,000 for a single taxpayer, $150,000 for a married taxpayer filing a joint return, or zero for a married taxpayer filing a separate return.

The maximum dollar amount that may be contributed (e.g., in 2002, $3,500 for a person who had attained age 50 by the end of the year, or $3,000 for a younger person) is reduced if AGI exceeds these levels. The dollar contribution limit goes to zero at AGI of $110,000 (single), $160,000 (married filing jointly), or $10,000 (married filing separately). § 408A(c)(3)(A), (C)(ii). For this purpose, "a married individual who has lived apart from his or her spouse for the entire taxable year and who files separately is treated as not married." Reg. § 1.408A-3, A-3(b).

An individual who is prevented from making the maximum dollar contribution to a Roth IRA because of these income limits can contribute his reduced maximum to the Roth and the balance of the applicable dollar limit to a traditional IRA (assuming he otherwise

meets the requirements for contributing to a traditional IRA). Reg.
§ 1.408A-3, A-3(d), Example 4.

5.3.04 *Who may contribute: age, participation in workplace plan*

There is no maximum age limit for contributing to a Roth IRA,
as there is for contributions to a traditional IRA; a taxpayer can
contribute to a Roth IRA even after age 70½. § 408A(c)(4); compare
§ 219(d)(1); § 408(o)(2)(B)(i).
Participation in an employer plan is *irrelevant* for purposes of
determining whether (and how much) an individual may contribute to
a Roth IRA. A person who meets the income test and other
requirements (¶ 5.3.01-¶ 5.3.03) may contribute to a Roth IRA
regardless of whether he is or is not participating in a "workplace"
retirement plan in the same year.

5.3.05 *Deadline for contributions, and other rules*

As with traditional IRAs, only cash may be contributed.
§§ 408A(a), 408(a)(1). The trustee or custodian must be a bank (or
other entity that has gone through the IRS approval procedure for
serving in this capacity). § 408A(a); § 408(a)(2). The deadline for
making a regular Roth IRA contribution for a particular year is the
same as the deadline for traditional IRA contributions, i.e., the
unextended due date of the tax return for that year (Reg. § 1.408A-3, A-
2(b), in other words, for most people, April 15 following the year in
question. See ¶ 5.7.03 for exhaustive discussion of Roth IRA deadlines.

5.4 Conversion of Traditional IRA to Roth IRA

See ¶ 5.6 for interaction of Roth conversion and 10% penalty.
See ¶ 5.7.02 regarding the deadline for completing a Roth IRA
conversion.

5.4.01 *Rollover (conversion) contributions to a Roth IRA*

The second way to create a Roth IRA is to transfer funds to it
from a traditional IRA. The amount so transferred is included in
Participant's gross income ("treated as a distribution from" the
traditional IRA) (¶ 5.4.09); thereafter the account will enjoy the

favorable tax treatment afforded to Roth IRAs. § 408A(d)(3)(A), (B), (C). Since there is no limit on the amount that can be "converted" from a traditional IRA to a Roth IRA, a "conversion contribution" can be much a more substantial amount than the few thousand dollars per year maximum regular Roth IRA contribution (¶ 5.3.02).

Example: Manuel is 60 years old. He rolls over [or transfers, or converts—all these terms are used interchangeably] $300,000 from his traditional IRA to a Roth IRA in 2001. The entire $300,000 is included in his gross income for 2001. When he retires at age 65, in 2006, the Roth IRA has increased to $1.2 million. All subsequent distributions from the Roth IRA (whether made to Manuel or to his beneficiaries) will be income tax-free.

There are three ways to make this type of contribution to a Roth IRA:

1.   A distribution from a traditional IRA may be contributed (rolled over) to a Roth IRA within 60 days after the distribution is made. § 408(d)(3)(A)(i).

2.   Money in a traditional IRA may be transferred in a plan-to-plan transfer directly from the trustee (or custodian) of the traditional IRA to the trustee (or custodian) of the Roth IRA.

3.   All or part of a traditional IRA can simply be "redesignated" as a Roth IRA maintained by the same trustee or custodian. Reg. § 1.408A-4, A-1(b).

All three of these transactions are considered rollovers ("a distribution from the traditional IRA and a qualified rollover contribution to the Roth IRA"). Reg. § 1.408A-4, A-1(c). Prior to the arrival of Roth IRAs, "rollovers" were always tax-free, and most people still associate that word with tax-free transfers from one retirement plan to another (see ¶ 2.5). In contrast, the rollover of funds from a traditional IRA to a Roth IRA is taxable. The term "conversion" is often used (including in § 408A) for the rollover of funds from a traditional IRA to a Roth IRA, which is a taxable event, just as a handy way to distinguish that type of rollover from a "normal" rollover, which is non-taxable.

Both partial and total conversions are allowed. An individual may choose to convert all, part or none of his traditional IRA to a Roth IRA. There is no minimum or maximum dollar or percentage amount that must be converted.

Generally, there is no limit on the number of times an individual may convert traditional IRA funds to Roth IRA status. A person who converts part of his traditional IRA to a Roth IRA is free at any later time (in the same or a later year) to convert more of the same or another IRA to a Roth IRA. The one exception applies to someone who did a Roth IRA conversion, then later "unconverted"; see ¶ 5.7.07.

The one-rollover-per-year limitation in § 408(d)(3)(B) (which applies to tax-free rollover contributions to a traditional IRA) does not apply to a conversion to a Roth IRA, so such conversion may occur even if it is within 12 months of a tax-free rollover into a traditional IRA. Reg. § 1.408A-4, A-1(a).

5.4.02 *What type of plan may be converted to a Roth IRA*

An "individual retirement plan" may be converted to a Roth IRA. § 408A(d)(3) (B), (C); Reg. § 1.408A-4, A-5. "Individual retirement plans" include individual retirement accounts (IRAs) and individual retirement trusts (IRTs) under § 408(a), (h). However, an *inherited* traditional IRA may not be converted by the beneficiary to a Roth IRA. § 408(d)(3)(C).

A "simplified employee pension"-individual retirement account (SEP-IRA) (§ 408(k)) and a "simple retirement account" (SIMPLE IRA) (§ 408(p)) cannot be "redesignated" as Roth IRAs (§ 408A(f)). However, these types of IRAs can be rolled or converted into Roth IRAs, subject to one limit: a SIMPLE IRA distribution "is not eligible to be rolled over into" a Roth IRA "during the 2-year period...which begins on the date that the individual first participated in any SIMPLE IRA Plan maintained by the individual's employer...." Reg. § 1.408A-4, A-4(b). Once a SEP or SIMPLE IRA account has been converted to a Roth IRA, the account is not eligible to receive further contributions under the SEP or SIMPLE plan. Reg. § 1.408A-4, A-4(c).

There is no way to transfer funds directly from a qualified retirement plan or 403(b) plan to a Roth IRA, or to roll over a distribution from such a plan directly into a Roth IRA. § 408A(c)(6) says "No rollover contribution may be made to a Roth IRA unless it is a qualified rollover contribution"; and § 408A(e) defines a qualified rollover contribution as "a rollover contribution to a Roth IRA *from another such account, or from an individual retirement plan....*" (emphasis added). See also Reg. § 1.408A-4, A-5. However, a Participant in a qualified plan or 403(b) plan who receives a distribution eligible to be rolled to a traditional IRA can roll the distribution to a traditional IRA and then convert *that* to a Roth IRA.

Education IRAs cannot be converted to Roth IRAs. Reg. § 1.408A-6, A-18. Education IRAs are not covered in this book.

5.4.03 *Who may convert: income limit and filing status*

No conversion is permitted if "the taxpayer's adjusted gross income exceeds $100,000" for the taxable year. § 408A(c)(3)(B).

In the case of a *married couple filing jointly*, the $100,000 limit applies to the adjusted gross income (AGI) of the *couple*, not of each *spouse*. Reg. § 1.408A-4, A-2(b). Generally, no conversion is permitted if the taxpayer is *married filing a separate return* for the year. § 408A(c)(3)(B). However, if a "married individual has lived apart from his or her spouse for the entire taxable year, then such individual can treat himself or herself as not married for purposes of [the adjusted gross income test], file a separate return and be subject to the $100,000 limit on his or her separate modified AGI." Reg. § 1.408A-4, A-2(b).

The year you look at for applying this income limit is the year in which the distribution from the traditional IRA occurs (*i.e.*, the distribution that is rolled over to a Roth IRA), *not* the year that the contribution to the Roth IRA occurs. Reg. § 1.408A-4, A-2(a). Usually, the distribution from the traditional IRA and its recontribution to the Roth IRA occur simultaneously; this rule covers the case of a distribution from the traditional IRA that occurs in one taxable year, and is rolled over in the *next* taxable year (but still within 60 days of the distribution).

5.4.04 *Definition of AGI for both types of Roth IRA contributions*

The definition of adjusted gross income (AGI) discussed here (¶ 5.4.04-¶ 5.4.06) applies for purposes of determining eligibility for both regular Roth IRA contributions (¶ 5.3) and Roth IRA conversions (¶ 5.4) (although the *amount* of permitted AGI differs for purposes of eligibility for these different types of contributions).

For the years 1998 through 2004, the definition of "adjusted gross income" (AGI) is the same for purposes of determining a person's eligibility for both types of Roth IRA contributions (though the maximum permitted *amount* of AGI differs depending on which type of Roth IRA contribution you're talking about; compare ¶ 5.3.03 with ¶ 5.4.03). After 2004, there will be an additional adjustment required for purposes of the conversion eligibility test that does not apply for purposes of regular contribution eligibility; see ¶ 5.4.08.

"Adjusted gross income" is a defined term in the Code (§ 62); however, for purposes of determining Roth IRA eligibility you do not simply look at the "adjusted gross income" line on the person's Form 1040. Rather, the definition of AGI for purposes of the Roth IRA income limits starts with the modified definition of AGI used under § 219(g)(3) (income limits for making a deductible contribution to a traditional IRA when the individual is also a participant in an employer plan) and then makes one more adjustment (¶ 5.4.05) to arrive at the Roth IRA eligibility definition. § 408A(c)(3)(C).

The § 219(g)(3) definition of AGI includes the individual's taxable Social Security benefits (§ 86), and takes into account the disallowance of "passive activity losses" (§ 469) if applicable, then requires the following further adjustments:

1. Certain income that is normally *excluded* from AGI is added back in, namely: income resulting from redemption of U.S. savings bonds to pay higher education expenses (§ 135); qualified adoption expenses paid by the individual's employer (§ 137); and foreign earned income and housing costs (§ 911).

2. Certain deductions normally allowed for purposes of computing AGI are not allowed for this purpose, namely the deductions for: certain education loan interest expenses (§ 221); and certain tuition expenses (under § 222, effective after 2001). No deduction is allowed for IRA contributions (§ 219).

Once you have determined AGI as defined under § 219(g)(3), one further modification is required before you know what a person's "AGI" is for purposes of determining eligibility to contribute (or convert) to a Roth IRA; see ¶ 5.4.05. For years after 2004 see also ¶ 5.4.08.

5.4.05 *Conversion income does not count for purposes of AGI test*

For purposes of the income limits applicable to both regular Roth IRA contributions and Roth IRA conversions, AGI does *not* include any amount included in gross income because of the conversion of a traditional IRA to a Roth IRA. § 408A(c)(3)(C)(i).

So, if, in the year being tested, Participant does a conversion to a Roth IRA, resulting in the inclusion of some or all of the conversion amount in his gross income; or if the year being tested is 1999, 2000 or 2001 and gross income includes some income on account of a 1998 conversion for which Participant used the four-year spread; the gross income resulting from the conversion (¶ 5.4.09) is disregarded SOLELY FOR PURPOSE OF DETERMINING WHETHER THE TAXPAYER'S AGI IS LOW ENOUGH TO MAKE HIM ELIGIBLE TO CONTRIBUTE TO A ROTH IRA.

This aspect of Roth IRA conversions has been the downfall of many taxpayers and tax preparers, because it requires that the taxpayer's AGI be determined twice. Determining AGI is no easy task because it involves many interrelated computations, such as how much of the individual's Social Security payments are taxable, and how much "passive activity loss" is deductible. Yet all these computations must be done twice: First, for purposes of determining the individual's eligibility to contribute to a Roth IRA, all gross income resulting from traditional IRA-to-Roth IRA conversions is ignored (and all adjustments dependent on AGI are determined in accordance with this reduced income figure). This fictional AGI has *no relevance* to the taxpayer's actual tax burden—it is a pro forma number used solely to determine eligibility to contribute to a Roth IRA. Reg. § 1.408A-4, A-9.

Then, for purposes of determining the individual's *actual* tax owed, income resulting from conversions to a Roth IRA *is* included in gross income; and all computations dependent on the taxpayer's "AGI"—such as taxability of Social Security benefits, deductibility of medical expenses, etc.—are redetermined based on this true AGI figure.

5.4.06 *Income limit: effect of minimum required distribution*

What happens if Participant will be age 70½ or older by the end of the taxable year, and withdrawing his minimum required distribution (MRD) for the year would put his income over the $100,000 income limit?

Example: Jeanette is age 72. It is 2001 and she would like to convert her traditional IRA to a Roth IRA. Her AGI, before taking any IRA distributions, is $50,000, so based on this she meets the income limitation, but her MRD for 2001 from the traditional IRA is $75,000. If she has to take that much out of her IRA on a taxable basis she will be over the $100,000 income cap and cannot convert to a Roth IRA. Is there any way around this dilemma?

First question: Can the realization of deemed income that comes from converting to a Roth IRA count toward fulfilling her minimum distribution requirement for 2001? After all, the point of the minimum distribution rules is to make you pay some income tax on your retirement plan, and she will have paid tax on 100% of the traditional IRA value by converting it to a Roth. Unfortunately, there is no authority for the proposition that a Roth IRA conversion could be used, in place of an actual non-rolled-over cash distribution, to fulfill the minimum distribution requirement for the traditional IRA.

Second question: Since Jeanette is required to take an *actual* distribution in 2001, can she avoid the problem by first converting the traditional IRA to a Roth IRA, and THEN taking the distribution? The withdrawal from the brand new Roth IRA is non-taxable because it is deemed to be a return of her basis—it has already been included in her income by virtue of the conversion—and therefore the post-conversion distribution does not put her over the $100,000 income cap. Unfortunately, this maneuver is not possible either, because (1) MRDs may not be rolled over and (2) the first dollars distributed in any year are deemed to be part of the MRD for such year, until the MRD has been entirely distributed. ¶ 2.5.05. Also, a distribution from a Roth IRA does not count toward fulfilling the requirement of taking a MRD from a traditional IRA. Reg. § 1.408A-6, A-15.

Thus Jeanette must withdraw the MRD for the year from the traditional IRA, and not roll it over, before she can convert any of her *remaining* traditional IRA balance to a Roth IRA. Of course, once she withdraws the MRD of $75,000 her income will be over $100,000 and she cannot convert any part of the traditional IRA to a Roth IRA. Reg. § 1.408A-4, A-6(b). This result is not affected by the means through which the taxpayer effects the conversion, *i.e.*, whether by rollover or by trustee-to-trustee transfer, or by whether an amount greater than or equal to the year's MRD remains in the traditional IRA after the conversion.

If an amount is converted in violation of this principle, the amount is treated as a distribution to Participant, and (since it is not eligible for rollover) it would be treated as a regular contribution to the Roth IRA. Reg. § 1.408A-4, A-6(c). As such it will attract a 6% excess contribution penalty (imposed annually until the excess contribution is distributed) if it is in excess of the applicable limit on a regular Roth IRA contribution for that person for that year. Reg. § 1.408A-3, A-7.

5.4.07 *Trap for the unwary: conversions in the age 70½ year*

The rule that MRDs cannot be rolled over (¶ 2.5.05), and that the first dollars distributed in any year are deemed to come from the MRD until the MRD has been fully distributed, creates a trap for individuals in the year they turn age 70½.

Example: Jay, who is single, turns 70½ in 2001. His income (before taking any required distributions) is $80,000. He wants to convert his traditional IRA to a Roth IRA. His MRD from the traditional IRA for 2001 is $45,000, but he does not have to take that distribution until April 1, 2002 (¶ 1.3). Accordingly, he plans to defer that first distribution until January, 2002, so it will not count as part of his income for 2001 and therefore (he thinks) he is eligible to convert to a Roth IRA in 2001 because his income is under $100,000 (¶ 5.4.03). Unfortunately the no-conversion-until-after-taking-MRD rule applies to him just the same as it did to Jeanette in the preceding example. The $45,000 is a required distribution *for the year he turns 70½*, even though he is allowed to defer it until the next year. Therefore he cannot convert to a Roth IRA in 2001 until *after* he takes the $45,000 distribution (and once he takes the $45,000 distribution in 2001 he is ineligible to convert that year, because his income—$80,000 + $45,000—exceeds $100,000).

The moral of the story is: A person who wants to convert his IRA to a Roth IRA, and whose traditional IRA is large enough that minimum distributions could push him over the $100,000 limit, must act *before* the year he reaches age 70½.

Note that this rule does *not* preclude postponing MRDs for the age-70½-year from *other* (non-IRA) kinds of retirement plans until

April 1 of the following year, as a way of keeping income low enough to allow conversion of a traditional IRA to a Roth IRA:

Example: Justin, who is single and retired, turns 70½ in 2001. His income (before taking any required distributions) is $30,000. He wants to convert his traditional IRA to a Roth IRA. His MRD from the traditional IRA for 2001 is $45,000. His 2001 MRD from his 401(k) plan is $40,000. Although he must take the traditional IRA MRD of $45,000 in 2001 prior to converting the traditional IRA to a Roth IRA, that will bring his 2001 AGI up to only $75,000—still under the $100,000 eligibility ceiling. A $40,000 distribution from the 401(k) plan, if taken in 2001, would put his income over $100,000, but he does not have to take the 401(k) distribution for the age-70½-year until April 1, 2002. Accordingly, he defers the first 401(k) plan MRD until January, 2002, so it does not count as part of his income for 2001 and therefore he is eligible to convert the traditional IRA to a Roth IRA in 2001 because his income is under $100,000.

5.4.08 *Effect of required IRA distributions: after 2004*

For years after 2004, solely for purposes of applying the $100,000 limit that determines eligibility to convert a traditional IRA to a Roth IRA, AGI will NOT include any amount that is included in AGI by reason of a required minimum distribution from an IRA (including an inherited IRA). § 408A(c)(3)(C)(i)(II).

Example: In 2005, Lucy's MRD from her traditional IRA is $130,000. Her other income is $60,000. She will still be required to take, and pay tax on, the $130,000 distribution, and she cannot roll *that* distribution over to a Roth IRA (because it is a required distribution; ¶ 2.5.05); but she will be able to convert the *rest* of her IRA to a Roth IRA in that year, because her AGI (not counting the MRD of $130,000 from the traditional IRA, or the income caused the conversion; ¶ 5.4.05) is only $60,000, and thus under the $100,000 limit. Note that only the *required* distribution from the traditional IRA is ignored. Any amount Lucy withdraws from her traditional IRA in excess of the MRD *does* count as part of her AGI for purposes of determining her eligibility to convert to a Roth IRA.

Note also that only MRDs from IRAs (and from individual

retirement annuities) are disregarded under § 408A(c)(3)(C)(i)(II); required distributions from *other* types of retirement plans will still count for purposes of determining eligibility to convert a traditional IRA to a Roth IRA. This could be a good reason to roll money from a qualified plan or 403(b) plan into a traditional IRA—to increase the likelihood of qualifying for a Roth IRA conversion after 2004.

5.4.09 *Tax treatment of converting to a Roth IRA*

The rollover from a traditional IRA to a Roth IRA is treated as a distribution from the traditional IRA. § 408A(d)(3)(A), (B), (C). Thus, the rollover amount is included in Participant's gross income, to the extent an actual distribution of the same amount from his traditional IRA would have been taxable. ¶ 5.4.10 and ¶ 5.4.12 explain how to compute this amount. Note that the conversion may result in an increase in the taxpayer's required estimated tax payments for the year of the conversion (as well as in his safe harbor estimated tax levels for the following year).

For rollovers in 1998 ONLY, the inclusion in gross income could be spread equally over the four taxable years 1998, 1999, 2000 and 2001. This treatment occurred unless the taxpayer elected *not* to have it apply. § 408A(d)(3)(A)(iii). For full details on this election, and on the acceleration of taxation in case of actual distributions prior to 2001, see "1998 Conversions: The Four-Year Spread," in Chapter 5 of the 1999 edition of this book. See also ¶ 5.8.06.

State income tax effects should not be overlooked in planning a Roth IRA conversion. For example, if the individual will have to pay state income tax as well as federal income tax on the conversion, and he is planning to move to a state with no income tax, he may do better to defer the conversion until after the move.

5.4.10 *Conversion of non-taxable amounts: years prior to 2002*

Since conversion of a traditional IRA to a Roth IRA is treated (for income tax purposes) as a distribution of the converted amount (¶ 5.4.09), the amount converted is includible in Participant's gross income except to the extent it can be excluded from income as a return of Participant's basis (¶ 2.1.04). To the extent the amount converted represents Participant's basis in the traditional IRA it is non-taxable.

Example: Whit's only IRA is a traditional IRA worth $70,000. He has made a total of $6,000 of non-deductible contributions to his traditional IRA over the years and has never taken a distribution from the account. If he converts the entire traditional IRA to a Roth IRA in 2001, he will have to include only $64,000 in gross income on account of the conversion ($70,000 total IRA value minus $6,000 basis).

Once you have determined what the person's basis is in his traditional IRAs (see ¶ 5.4.11), how do you determine how much of that basis can be offset against income resulting from a Roth IRA conversion, if the person converts some, but not all, of his traditional IRA funds to a Roth IRA?

The extent to which a traditional IRA distribution (or conversion) is treated as a non-taxable return of basis (*i.e.*, the return of Participant's non-deductible contributions) is determined under § 408(d). Reg. § 1.408A-4, A-7(a). Under § 408(d)(2), for years prior to 2002, for purposes of determining how much of a traditional IRA distribution rolled over to a Roth IRA is non-taxable, all (traditional) IRAs are treated as one traditional IRA, and all distributions in one taxable year are treated as one distribution. This rule trips up some taxpayers:

Example: Each year for six years Gibbs has contributed the maximum amount permitted to his traditional IRA at X Mutual Fund. His contributions (cumulative total of $12,000) were not deductible. The traditional IRA that holds these contributions is now worth $30,000. He also has a traditional IRA worth $205,000 at Y Mutual Fund. The rollover IRA contains no after-tax contributions; it contains a rollover from a QRP maintained by Gibbs's former employer plus some deductible $2,000-per-year contributions Gibbs made years ago. He has no other IRAs. In 2001, he is eligible to convert to a Roth IRA and decides to convert the smaller, $30,000, IRA. He thinks that he will be taxable on only $18,000 by virtue of this conversion, because that particular account contains his $12,000 of non-deducted contributions, so he should be taxable on only $30,000-$12,000, or $18,000. Unfortunately for Gibbs, because of § 408(d)(2), his $30,000 conversion is *deemed* to come proportionately from *both* of his IRAs (valued as of year-end 2001), even though it *actually* came from only one of them. Therefore, the amount of the Roth IRA conversion that is deemed to come from his non-deducted contributions is A/B x C, where:

A = total amount of Gibbs's basis in both IRAs, i.e., $12,000 in this example;

B = total value of both of his traditional IRA accounts as of the end of 2001, with any amounts distributed out of either traditional IRA in 2001, including amounts rolled over to the Roth IRA, added back in for this purpose. Assume the 2001 year-end value of his remaining traditional IRA is $210,000, and there were no distributions from either traditional IRA in 2001 other than the conversion of the $30,000 traditional IRA to a Roth IRA, so B = $240,000 ($210,000 + $30,000); and

C = amount of 2001 distributions; in this case, the only 2001 "distribution" was the conversion of the smaller traditional IRA to a Roth IRA, so C is $30,000.

The amount of the $30,000 conversion Gibbs can exclude as representing his non-deductible contributions is $12,000/$240,000 x $30,000, or $1,500. The amount of income he must pay tax on as a result of the conversion is therefore $28,500 ($30,000 conversion minus $1,500 basis assigned to the conversion). His remaining basis in his traditional IRA is $10,500 ($12,000 total non-deducted contributions, less $1,500 used up in the Roth conversion).

Ed Slott has analogized this system to the "cream in the coffee." Once the cream has been poured into the coffee, there's no way to remove just the cream or just the coffee. Every "distribution" includes a proportionate amount of cream and coffee.

Note: If Participant has a traditional IRA that consists purely of distributions rolled over from a QRP (or purely of distributions rolled over from a 403(b) plan), and the Participant rolls that IRA back into the same or another QRP (or 403(b) plan), that rollover does not carry with it a proportionate amount of the Participant's basis. § 408(d)(3)(A)(ii), (iii). This type of traditional IRA is sometimes called a "conduit" IRA, because it holds money in transit from one QRP to another, or from one 403(b) plan to another.

5.4.11 *Determining basis in the traditional IRA (pre-2002)*

For years prior to 2002, the only possible "basis" a Participant could have in a traditional IRA was the cumulative amount of the Participant's non-deductible $2,000-per-year contributions. Prior to 2002, the only funds a traditional IRA could hold that would not be includible in income upon distribution would be these accumulated non-deductible "regular" contributions. There was just no other way for non-taxable money to get into a traditional IRA. For example:

1.   A Participant in a QRP could have made non-deductible contributions to that plan, and so could have a substantial basis in the QRP; however, those amounts could not be rolled over to a traditional IRA. § 401(a)(31) and § 402(c)(2), as applicable to years prior to 2002, limited rollovers from a QRP to an IRA to amounts that "would be includible in gross income" if not rolled over.

2.   Another type of non-taxable amount that can be contained in a QRP is life insurance proceeds (¶ 8.3.05). If a Participant died leaving his QRP benefits to his surviving spouse as beneficiary, and the benefits thus becoming payable to Spouse included life insurance proceeds, a distribution of all of Participant's benefits to Spouse would include the tax-free portion of the insurance proceeds. Spouse could roll over to a traditional IRA (¶ 3.2) everything *except* the tax-free insurance proceeds, because, again, § 401(a)(31) and § 402(c)(2) prevented rollover of non-taxable amounts. Income tax-free insurance proceeds could not be generated inside Participant's traditional IRA to start with because IRAs are forbidden to hold life insurance. § 408(a)(3).

The first year for which non-deductible $2,000 IRA contributions were permitted was 1987. § 408(o), added by § 1102 of TRA '86. As of the end of 2001, therefore, the most basis a person could have in a traditional IRA would be $30,000, the amount of basis a person would have if he made the maximum $2,000 IRA contribution every year for the years 1987-2001, and if in every year his contribution was non-deductible (see § 219(g)), and if he took no distributions during that time that diminished his basis.

A Participant who makes a non-deductible contribution to his

IRA is required to report the contribution to the IRS on Form 8606 (attached to Form 1040). Part of the information reported on Form 8606 is the cumulative total of such contributions. To determine a client's basis in his traditional IRAs, therefore, you need only look at his most recent Form 8606. (Whether everyone who is supposed to file this form has actually done so is another question.)

5.4.12 *Conversion of non-taxable amounts: years after 2001*

Three Code provisions that are effective for 2002 and later years change the rules regarding (1) rollover of non-taxable amounts to traditional IRAs (not previously allowed, now allowed); (2) rollovers from traditional IRAs to QRPs and 403(b) plans (allowed in more cases than previously); and (3) how certain rollovers are apportioned between taxable and non-taxable amounts. These changes are mainly significant because they make it easier for Participants to save for retirement, but they also incidentally create the opportunity for tax-free or lower-tax conversions of traditional IRAs to Roth IRAs.

First change: As noted (¶ 5.4.10), prior to 2002, § 401(a)(31) and § 402(c)(2) forbade the rollover of non-taxable amounts from a QRP to a traditional IRA. As amended by EGTRRA, these sections permit non-taxable as well as taxable amounts to be rolled over to a traditional IRA after 2001. Once non-taxable amounts are rolled over to a traditional IRA from a QRP, such amounts are then positioned to be converted to a Roth IRA. For an employee who has a substantial after-tax contribution account in his qualified plan, this process (rolling the amounts to a traditional IRA, then doing a Roth IRA conversion) represents a way to get the advantages of the Roth IRA (tax-free internal growth of the account, followed by tax-free distributions) with a lower price tag, since this employee already paid the "price" (income taxes) back when he made the non-deductible contribution to the QRP).

Second change: § 402(c)(8)(B) as amended by EGTRRA generally allows rollovers from any traditional IRA to a QRP or 403(b) plan for years after 2001—but only of the *taxable* money in the traditional IRA. Prior to this amendment, money could be rolled from a traditional IRA to a QRP (or 403(b) plan) only if the traditional IRA contained no contributions other than one or more distributions rolled from the same or another QRP (or 403(b) plan) (so-called "conduit

IRAs"; ¶ 5.4.10). Now funds can be rolled from *any* traditional IRA to *any* QRP or 403(b) plan that is willing to accept such contributions.

Third change: As noted above (see the "Gibbs" example at ¶ 5.4.10), § 408(d)(2) provides that (except in the case of rollovers of so-called "conduit IRAs") all of an individual's traditional IRAs are aggregated for purposes of allocating his basis to distributions from any particular traditional IRA (including a distribution that is converted to a Roth IRA), and any distribution (including a distribution that is converted to a Roth IRA) is deemed to come proportionately from the non-taxable and taxable portions of Participant's aggregated IRAs (the "cream in the coffee" rule). This method of determining the taxable and non-taxable portions of a distribution will still (after 2001) apply to Roth IRA conversions and to any distribution from the traditional IRA that is not rolled over to another retirement plan.

However, after 2001, the proportionate allocation rule will *not* apply to rollovers from a traditional IRA to a QRP or 403(b) plan (see "Second change"). Instead, after 2001, a distribution rolled from a traditional IRA to a QRP or 403(b) plan is deemed to come entirely out of the *taxable* portion of the traditional IRA (the non-taxable portion cannot be rolled to a QRP or 403(b) plan at all).§ 408(d)(3)(H)(ii).

This creates the possibility of the following sequence. In 2002, a retiring employee receives a QRP distribution that includes his after-tax contributions account. The employee rolls the distribution over to a traditional IRA. The IRA now contains $Z, consisting of the basis ($X) that would be non-taxable if distributed, plus the portion ($Y) that would be taxable upon distribution.

The employee participates in another QRP, maintained by the new business he started upon retirement from his former job. He rolls over $Y to the new QRP. Under § 408(d)(3)(H) the entire amount of this rollover is deemed to come from the *taxable* portion of the traditional IRA. After this rollover, the only money left in the traditional IRA is $X, which is all "basis." If he qualifies to convert the traditional IRA to a Roth IRA (¶ 5.4.03), he can convert the remaining traditional IRA funds to a Roth IRA tax-free. The conversion does not result in any amount being added to his gross income because the traditional IRA consisted of 100% non-taxable amounts at the time of the Roth IRA conversion, so he has gotten the benefits of a Roth IRA with no current income tax cost.

5.5 Planning Considerations for Roth IRAs

> *"Tax-free compounding is the best thing in the world."*
>
>   –Jonathan G. Blattmachr, Esq.

5.5.00 *The mathematics of the Roth retirement plan choice*

A Roth IRA is a nice asset to own. No other vehicle offers the ability to invest in the stock and (non-municipal) bond markets and generate totally tax-free investment accumulations you can spend in retirement.

The question is what price must be paid to acquire this wonderful asset. Generally, the price is payment of income taxes on the amount going *in* to the Roth retirement plan—taxes that could have been deferred (via a traditional retirement plan) until the money in question was taken *out* of the retirement plan. Is it more profitable to pay the taxes up front and get tax-free distributions later or to defer the taxes?

If you can duck that question by not paying taxes *either* when the money goes into the Roth plan *or* when it comes out, then you can get the advantages of a Roth retirement plan "free," so that has to be a good deal; see ¶ 5.4.12 and ¶ 5.5.01 for discussion of those unusual situations.

Assuming that's not an option, you are faced with doing a mathematical analysis of which alternative produces more dollars. See the Bibliography and software listed in Appendix D for resources that can help with this analysis.

One thing is sure however: if you take $A, pay income tax on it at B%, deposit the net after-tax amount in a Roth IRA, earn an investment return of C% and withdraw the accumulated funds ($D) on date E, the amount of money you will have ($D) will be *exactly the same* as if you had deposited $A in a traditional IRA, earned an investment return of C%, withdrawn the accumulated funds on date E, and paid income tax on that distribution at B%. In other words, there is nothing magic about paying taxes earlier rather than later.

For the Roth approach to be profitable, therefore, one or more of the factors in the equation must be different as between the Roth IRA option and the traditional IRA option. There are two factors in the equation that, for many of the people eligible to convert traditional

IRAs to Roth IRAs, can change enough to tilt the balance in favor of Roth IRAs. One of these factors is that the money in a Roth IRA does not have to be distributed at the same time money would have to be distributed out of a traditional IRA; it can stay in much longer, because of the different minimum distribution rules that apply to Roth IRAs (¶ 5.1.03). Thus tax-free compounding can occur to a greater extent in a Roth IRA during the owner's life than is possible with a traditional IRA (from which the owner must take lifetime distributions; ¶ 1.4).

The other factor is that the taxes on a Roth IRA conversion can be paid with money that is not in any retirement plan. Thus, the Roth IRA need not be depleted by the tax money, which can come from the non-retirement plan investment portfolio.

The complex mathematical computations that go into analyzing the Roth IRA option are beyond the scope of this book. The purpose of this ¶ 5.5 is to point out considerations that may make a Roth IRA contribution more or less attractive either purely as a financial proposition or for other reasons, and planning considerations that apply when dealing with a client who already has a Roth IRA.

5.5.01 *Choosing between traditional and Roth IRA contributions*

An individual who has compensation income and whose AGI is under the limits described at ¶ 5.3.03 has the option to contribute to a Roth IRA. If he is under age 70½ he also has the option to contribute to a traditional IRA instead of to a Roth IRA, or to contribute part of his maximum permitted "regular" contribution amount (¶ 5.3.02) to each type of IRA. Assuming he wants to contribute to a retirement plan, which type should he contribute to if he has a choice?

The decision is easy if the individual (or his spouse) is an active participant in an employer plan, and his (or their) AGI exceeds the amounts specified in § 219(g)(3)(B) (AGI limit for determining deductibility of traditional IRA contribution, where Participant or Spouse is a active participant in an employer plan); then his only choice is between a non-deductible traditional IRA and a Roth IRA. Since he can't get a tax deduction for his contribution no matter which kind of IRA he contributes to, he gives up nothing by contributing to the Roth IRA.

The decision is also easy if the individual's taxable income is so low he is not subject to income tax, since, again, he gives up nothing by opting to contribute to the Roth IRA (because the tax deduction he might get by contributing to a traditional IRA would not save him any income taxes).

If neither the individual (nor his spouse) is an active participant in an employer plan; or, if he (or his spouse) is an active participant in an employer plan, but his (or their) AGI is low enough that he can get a tax deduction for a contribution to a traditional IRA; *and* his (or their) tax bracket is higher than zero; then his choice is between a *deductible* traditional IRA contribution (which could save him some current income taxes) and the *non-deductible* Roth IRA contribution. Which is a better deal (save taxes now or save taxes later) is a very complicated question. This question will be faced by a much larger number of individuals when DRACs (¶ 5.1.05) come on stream in 2006. See further discussion in the next subsection.

5.5.02 *Risks of Roth IRA conversion*

This ¶ 5.5.02 lists risks that should be considered by anyone considering a Roth IRA conversion. Most clients considering a Roth IRA conversion will evaluate the financial impact using computer projections of one brand or another (see "Software," Appendix D). Computer projections of the benefits of converting an existing IRA to a Roth IRA are based on assumptions as to future tax rates, investment returns and withdrawal amounts. Most such projections assume a constant rate of investment return; that today's tax rates will last forever; and that participants and beneficiaries will withdraw from the account no more than required by today's minimum distribution rules. Other possible scenarios should be considered, such as a stock market decline; it would be a shame to pay income tax on today's stock values, only to find out later that this was the all-time market high. This exact scenario happened to many who converted to Roth IRAs in the halcyon investment era of 1998-1999, then endured the stock market declines of 2000-2001.

Under 2001 tax law changes, rates are scheduled to decline from 39.6% (as of 2000) to 35% (by 2006). The expectation of lower brackets will doubtless dampen enthusiasm for Roth conversions; why pay 39.6% to convert when one can wait a while and pay 35%? Of course, while the individual is waiting for new lower rates to kick in, something else (further law changes, a loss of eligibility, an increase in value that increases the cost of conversion, or death) could happen in the meantime that makes conversion more expensive or impossible.

Congress could make other changes that would make a Roth conversion less appealing. For example, Congress could decide to bring the minimum distribution rules back into line with the original purpose of tax-favored *retirement* plans, and require that all benefits be distributed within some much shorter period of time after the deaths of Participant and Spouse. Congress could decide that the Roth IRA was too good a deal, and take away some of its favorable tax features on a prospective basis. Of course future changes (such as higher income tax rates or a higher stock market) could also go the other way (and make a conversion at today's values and tax rates look good).

5.5.03 *Clients who may profit from Roth conversion*

The client most likely to profit from converting to a Roth IRA is one who: has sufficient other wealth that he will never need to draw from the account during life (not drawing anything out of the account is the way to maximize the tax-free accumulations of the Roth IRA); plans to leave the account to young generation beneficiaries, to be drawn down over their life expectancy after the client's death (¶ 1.2.01) (again, the long life expectancy payout available for distributions to a young designated beneficiary maximizes the tax-free build-up of the Roth IRA); and can afford to pay the income tax on the conversion, and the estate tax on the account's date of death value, from other assets, without sacrificing other goals such as his own financial security (so that the income tax-free Roth IRA is not depleted by paying tax bills). Add steady to rising income tax rates, no negative tax law changes and positive investment returns and the conversion is a definite winner.

Many clients who can afford to pay the taxes and take the risks will not qualify for the Roth conversion because of the $100,000 AGI limit (¶ 5.4.03). Most of the people who *are* eligible to convert simply cannot afford to write a check for the up-front tax on the conversion. Therefore, it may be that the Roth IRA conversion will mainly be of interest to: wealthy people who due to some fluke have income under $100,000 in a particular year; young people who face a long life expectancy and expect their tax bracket to rise; and those who see benefits in the Roth IRA conversion besides just the ultimate numerical payout, such as improvements in their cash flow options.

The IRS's 2001 minimum distribution rule changes (¶ 1.1.03) should increase the number of individuals who qualify to convert to a Roth IRA. Since MRDs from qualified plans and (until 2005) IRAs are included in gross income, anything that has the effect of reducing a Participant's MRDs should increase the number of Participants who will have gross income under $100,000. However, the longer deferral now available to traditional IRAs under the new rules (¶ 1.4.01) decreases the relative advantages of converting to a Roth IRA.

5.5.04 *Establishing Roth IRAs for low-income relatives*

Establishing a Roth IRA for teenage children, grandchildren, etc., has great appeal. Typically these young family members have summer or after-school jobs that generate compensation income on which an IRA contribution can be based, but have little enough income that they are in a low or zero tax bracket. The projections of what a humble $2,000 contribution will grow to by the time the 15-year-old child reaches age 65 can be staggering. What gives pause is that there is no way to prevent the donee from taking the money out of the account once he reaches the age of majority.

5.5.05 *Retiree with long life expectancy*

Roth IRAs have appeal for those retirees who do not need to withdraw any funds from their IRAs during life, especially those who expect to live well beyond the average life expectancy due to their genetic heritage and/or health. A traditional IRA Participant approaching age 70½ faces forced distributions that may substantially diminish the account over a long life span. ¶ 1.4.01. With a traditional IRA, the way to maximize tax deferral is to die prematurely (leaving benefits to a younger generation beneficiary) (¶ 1.2.01).

By converting the traditional IRA to a Roth IRA, this person can eliminate the forced lifetime distributions (¶ 5.1.03) and reverse the usual rule of thumb: The way to maximize tax deferral with a *Roth* IRA is to live as long as humanly possible, deferring the commencement of ANY distributions until that way-later-than-normal death (and then leave the benefits to a young beneficiary).

5.5.06 *Conversions to improve beneficiaries' tax situation*

Converting to a Roth IRA just before death can reduce *estate taxes* by removing the income taxes due on the Roth conversion from the gross estate. See ¶ 2.2.08.

A Participant may also choose to do a Roth conversion to save *income taxes* for his or her beneficiaries:

Example: Rhonda is a widow, age 65, living happily on her Social Security payments plus $25,000 a year withdrawn from a substantial traditional IRA representing a rollover of her late husband's pension plan. For the last several years, she has withdrawn sufficient extra dollars from the traditional IRA to use up the lower income tax brackets available to her. Even though she doesn't need this extra money for her living expenses, she knows that her children are all in the highest income tax bracket, and that some day those high brackets will apply to distributions the children take from the traditional IRA they inherit at her death. The Roth IRA conversion gives her another way to accomplish the same goal. She can convert some of the traditional IRA to a Roth IRA each year to use up her lower income tax brackets, and the high-bracket children will pay no income tax on distributions from the inherited Roth IRA.

Even if the pure economics indicate no substantial advantage to having Participant pay the income tax now rather than having the beneficiaries pay it later, it would be a convenience to the beneficiaries to inherit a Roth IRA (distributions from which are tax-free) rather than a traditional IRA, so they do not to have to wrestle with the valuable but complicated IRD deduction every year as they do their income tax returns (see ¶ 2.2.07).

5.5.07 *Estate planning with a Roth IRA*

See ¶ 10.5.03, "Solution G," for discussion of funding a credit shelter trust with a Roth IRA. See ¶ 10.5.05, "Solution E," for discussion of funding a QTIP trust with a Roth IRA.

A Roth IRA could substantially ease the problems of leaving retirement benefits to a non-citizen spouse (see Chapter 4), as compared with leaving traditional (taxable) retirement benefits to such spouse; many of the problems of leaving traditional retirement benefits to a non-citizen spouse arise from the fact that such benefits are taxable as income in respect of a decedent (¶ 2.2), and the Roth IRA eliminates this problem. See ¶ 4.2.

By funding the *generation skipping trust* (see Glossary) with Roth IRA death benefits (rather than traditional IRA death benefits),

Participant still gives his beneficiaries the advantage of long-term tax-free investment accumulations; *and* this approach has the additional advantages of totally tax-free distributions and not "wasting" any of the GST exemption paying income taxes. This use of a Roth IRA can be attractive if the oldest beneficiaries of the generation skipping trust are young (have a long life expectancy). If the oldest beneficiary of the generation skipping trust is not young, much of the potential advantage of the Roth IRA (stretching out tax-free distributions over a long life expectancy) is wasted.

According to the IRS, assigning a Roth IRA by *lifetime gift* "to another individual" causes the Roth IRA to be "deemed" distributed to the owner-donor, and accordingly it ceases to be a Roth IRA. Reg. § 1.408A-6, A-19. Needless to say, this treatment eliminates the advantages of such a gift. For a vigorous disagreement with the IRS's interpretation, see articles by Mervin Wilf cited in the Bibliography.

5.6 10% Penalty For Pre-Age 59½ Distributions

Full details on this penalty are contained in Chapter 9. This section discusses the penalty as it applies to Roth IRAs, and assumes you have read Chapter 9.

5.6.01 *Penalty does not apply to conversions*

The 10% penalty under § 72(t) (applicable to certain retirement plan distributions before age 59½) does not apply to the "deemed" distribution that results from converting a traditional IRA to a Roth IRA. § 408A(d)(3)(A)(ii); Reg. § 1.408A-4, A-7(b). Thus a young person who meets the eligibility requirements (¶ 5.4.03) may convert his traditional IRA to a Roth IRA without penalty. However, this does not mean he can forget about the 10% penalty; see ¶ 5.6.02-¶ 5.6.05.

5.6.02 *Penalty applies to certain distributions from the Roth IRA*

§ 72(t) imposes a 10% penalty on any distribution from a "qualified retirement plan (as defined in section 4974(c))" made while Participant is under age 59½ (see Chapter 9). The definition of "qualified retirement plan" in § 4974(c) includes traditional IRAs. The regulations confirm that the 10% penalty would apply to non-excepted pre-age 59½ distributions from Roth IRAs, the same as to traditional

IRAs, under the rule that Roth IRAs are treated the same as traditional IRAs unless § 408A provides otherwise. Reg. § 1.408A-6, A-5.

Since (regardless of the type of retirement plan) the 10% penalty applies only to the amount of a distribution that is includible in gross income (¶ 9.1.04), it would at first appear that it can only apply to *non-qualified* distributions from a Roth IRA (¶ 5.2.03), since qualified distributions (¶ 5.2.01) are not included in gross income; and basically this would be true—generally, for Roth IRAs, the penalty only applies to non-qualified distributions (see ¶ 5.6.04)—except for the two special rules dealing with the conversion of a traditional IRA to a Roth IRA by someone who takes distributions prior to age 59½ (¶ 5.6.03, ¶ 5.6.05).

5.6.03 *Conversion followed by distribution within five years*

A person who is under age 59½, although he can convert to a Roth IRA without penalty, has to come up with the money to pay the income tax on the conversion from some source *other* than the Roth IRA (or a traditional IRA), because he will owe the penalty to the extent he taps his traditional IRA or his newly-converted Roth IRA for this money.

If a Participant who is under age 59½ receives a distribution from a Roth IRA; and if "any portion" of that distribution is allocable under the Ordering Rules (¶ 5.2.04) to funds rolled over to the Roth from a traditional IRA that were includible in gross income; and "the distribution is made within the 5-taxable-year period beginning with the first day of the individual's taxable year in which the conversion contribution was made"; then the § 72(t) penalty shall apply to the distribution. § 408A(d)(3)(F); Reg. § 1.408A-6, A-5(b).

This provision was not included in the original Roth IRA legislation (TAPRA '97), but was added by the IRS Restructuring and Reform Bill of 1998, effective retroactively to January 1, 1998. This retroactive imposition of the penalty was held to be constitutional in Kitt v. U.S. (Fed. Cls. 2000, KTC 2000-490).

Note that this five-year period is *not the same* as the Five-Year Period for determining "qualified distributions" (¶ 5.2.02). The latter begins in the first year *any* contribution is made to any Roth IRA; the former begins, as to any conversion of a traditional IRA to a Roth IRA, with the year of that *particular* conversion. Reg. § 1.408A-6, A-5(c). Note also that this penalty applies regardless of whether the distribution is included in gross income in the year of the *distribution*.

Example: Rand, age 32, converts his $100,000 traditional IRA to a Roth IRA in 1999. He has no basis in the traditional IRA, so the entire $100,000 is includible in his gross income in 1999. He has no other Roth IRAs, and makes no other contributions to this one. In 2002, at age 35 (in other words, before the end of the five taxable years beginning with the year of the conversion, and while he is still under 59½) he takes $20,000 out of the Roth IRA to finance the purchase of a rare edition of *The Canterbury Tales*. Under the Ordering Rules, this distribution is deemed to come out of the portion of the 1999 conversion-contribution that was includible in gross income, and therefore it is subject to the 10% penalty.

"The exceptions under § 72(t) also apply to such a distribution," so there should be no penalty if the distribution is made after the death (or on account of the total disability) of Participant, for example. Reg. § 1.408A-6, A-5(b). But see discussion of Reg. § 1.408A-6, A-11, at ¶ 5.8.04.

5.6.04 *Taxable portion of non-qualified distributions*

If there is a distribution from a Roth IRA before Participant reaches age 59½, then, to the distribution is *not* allocable under the Ordering Rules (¶ 5.2.04) to money converted within the last five years from a traditional IRA, the penalty applies only to the portion of the distribution (if any) that is included in gross income (¶ 5.2.03). Reg. § 1.408A-6, A-5(a).

5.6.05 *Conversion while receiving "series of equal payments"*

The 10% penalty does not apply to IRA distributions that are part of a "Series of Substantially Equal Periodic Payments" (¶ 9.2). If an individual who is receiving such a series of payments from a traditional IRA converts the traditional IRA to a Roth IRA, the conversion is "not treated as a distribution for purposes of determining whether a modification" of the series (¶ 9.2.12) has occurred, so the conversion itself does not trigger the loss of the exempt status of the series. Reg. § 1.408A-4, A-12.

However, the conversion does not mean that the individual can stop taking his periodic payments. "If the original series...does not continue to be distributed in substantially equal periodic payments *from the Roth IRA* after the conversion, the series of payments will have been modified and, if this modification occurs within 5 years of the first payment or prior to the individual [sic] becoming disabled or attaining age 59½, the taxpayer will be subject to the recapture tax of § 72(t)(4)(A)." Reg. § 1.408A-4, A-12 (emphasis added); ¶ 9.2.12.

This statement in Reg. § 1.408A-4 seems to assume that the individual converted the entire traditional IRA to a Roth IRA. If he converted only part of the traditional IRA to a Roth IRA, it is not clear whether the rest of his "series" payments would have to come all from the Roth IRA, or proportionately from the new Roth IRA and the (now-diminished) traditional IRA; or whether Participant could take the payments from whichever of the two accounts he chooses.

5.7 Recharacterizations; Corrective Distributions

A taxpayer who is unhappy with the IRA contribution choices he made for a particular year, or who discovers that he was not eligible to contribute to the type of IRA he contributed to (¶ 5.3.03, ¶ 5.4.03), or who contributed more than he was entitled to contribute (¶ 5.3.02), has two ways to remedy the problem without incurring any penalty.

5.7.01 *Corrective distributions*

One way to correct mistakes (or simply act on a change of heart) is for Participant to distribute the contribution back to himself. If any Roth IRA contribution (together with its net income; ¶ 5.7.06) is distributed before the extended due date (¶ 5.7.04) of the tax return for the year for which the contribution was made, then (a) the contribution is treated, at least for purposes of the 6% penalty on excess IRA contributions (§ 4973(a)), as not having been contributed and (b) the net income on the contribution is "includible in gross income for the taxable year in which the contribution is made." Reg. §§ 1.408A-3, A-7, 1.408A-6, A-1(d); see also § 408(d)(4).

Example: Wayne contributed $2,000 to a new Roth IRA in 2001. By January 2002, the investments in the Roth IRA had earned $75 of interest, so the account was worth $2,075. Wayne then changed his mind and decided he would rather spend the money on a new gas grill. He closes the account, and the $2,075 is distributed out to him in

January 2002. The $75 of taxable income is included in his gross income for the year of the contribution (2001). If Wayne is under 59½, see ¶ 9.1.05 regarding the premature distributions penalty.

If Wayne has another change of heart before the due date of his 2001 tax return, can he still contribute $2,000 to an IRA for 2001 before the April 15, 2002 deadline? The answer to this is not clear. The maximum non-rollover contribution an IRA may accept for 2001 is $2,000. The IRS may say Wayne has used up his $2,000 dollar maximum for 2001 by making the original contribution to the Roth IRA (even though he unwound that contribution in early 2002).

If Wayne had a net loss inside the Roth IRA (instead of $75 of gain), is the loss treated as if it had been realized outside the Roth IRA; in other words, is there a way it can be used to offset other income? Barry Picker, CPA, points out that IRS Publication 590 may reveal the IRS's position on this. In Publication 590, on an analogous point, the IRS describes what happens when a taxpayer cashes out all of his traditional IRAs "and the total distributions are less than your unrecovered basis, if any. Your basis is the total amount of the nondeductible contributions in your traditional IRAs. You claim the loss as a miscellaneous itemized deduction, subject to the 2% limit, on Schedule A, Form 1040."

Once the grace period (extended due date of the tax return for the year the excess contribution is made; ¶ 5.7.04) has expired, if Participant did not withdraw the excess contribution and its associated income, Participant owes the penalty for that year. The penalty will continue to accrue annually until the excess contribution is either withdrawn from the account or treated as a proper contribution for a later year (to the extent Participant is eligible to make a contribution in a later year but does not do so; Reg. § 1.408A-3, A-7).

A timely corrective distribution can be useful for undoing *regular* Roth IRA contributions, but it is not much help for someone who has *converted* a traditional IRA to a Roth IRA and then wishes he hadn't (or who discovers after the fact that he wasn't eligible; ¶ 5.4.03). This person usually doesn't want to distribute the money out to himself, he just wants to restore the pre-conversion status quo. For this person, there is a second method of fixing the problem: an "unconversion," or "recharacterization."

5.7.02 *How to undo (recharacterize) a Roth IRA contribution*

The regulations provide broad relief to taxpayers who wish to "amend" their IRA contributions by switching the contribution from a Roth IRA to a traditional IRA or vice versa. This relief is for anyone who changes his mind about which type of IRA he wants his contribution to go to; it is not limited to (though it also helps) those who need to correct Roth IRA conversions for which they were ineligible (¶ 5.4.03). Reg. § 1.408A-5, A-10, Example 2.

A "regular" contribution made, for a particular taxable year, to either type of IRA may be transferred to the other type of IRA before the "extended due date" (¶ 5.7.04) of the person's tax return for such year. The contribution to a Roth IRA of a traditional IRA distribution made in a particular year may be transferred back to a traditional IRA before the "extended due date" (¶ 5.7.04) of the person's tax return for the year the distribution from the traditional IRA occurred. In either case, the contribution will be treated as a contribution to the *transferee* IRA for tax purposes. § 408A(d)(6), (7).

For example, if a person converts a traditional IRA to a Roth IRA in 2001, and then discovers that his income for 2001 exceeds the $100,000 limit so he is ineligible to do that conversion, he can move the money back to a traditional IRA before the extended due date of his tax return for 2001 and it will be treated as a rollover contribution to the traditional IRA. In effect, the Roth conversion is "undone," so the taxpayer does not realize income on account of the Roth conversion.

Here are the significant requirements for effecting a recharacterization:

1.   The transfer from the Roth IRA back to the traditional IRA (or vice versa) must be by trustee-to-trustee transfer (*not* by a rollover, which is a distribution to Participant followed by a recontribution to the other account). Reg. § 1.408A-5, A-1(a).

2.   Not only the original contribution but "any net income allocable to such contribution" must be retransferred. See ¶ 5.7.06.

3.   The election to recharacterize is made by providing notice and directions to the IRA trustee(s) involved. The election to recharacterize "cannot be revoked" after the transfer back to the traditional IRA has occurred. Reg. § 1.408A-5, A-6.

A recharacterized contribution will be treated for Federal income tax purposes as having been contributed to the transferee IRA (rather than the transferor IRA) "on the same date and (in the case of a regular contribution) for the same taxable year that the contribution was made to the transferor IRA." Reg. § 1.408A-5, A-3. A recharacterization is "never treated as a rollover for purposes of the one-rollover-per-year limitation of § 408(d)(3)(B), even if the contribution would have been treated as a rollover contribution by the [transferee] IRA if it had been made directly to the" transferee IRA in the first place. Reg. § 1.408A-5, A-8.

5.7.03 *Deadline for Roth IRA contributions and conversions*

The various deadlines for contributions, conversions, corrective distributions and recharacterizations are extremely confusing. Some deadlines are based on the calendar year end, some on the extended due date of the return, and some on the unextended due date; and some of the deadlines qualify for an "automatic" extension, though you don't get the automatic extension unless you ask for it.

Starting with the easiest one: A "regular" Roth IRA contribution (¶ 5.3) for a particular year must be made no later than the *unextended* due date of Participant's tax return for the year. For example, a $2,000 contribution "for" the year 2001 may be made at any time on or before April 15, 2002. When a participant sends in a contribution between January 1 and April 15, the IRA provider must ask which year it is for, since between those dates it could be for either the year in which the contribution occurs or the prior year. *There is no way to extend this April 15 deadline applicable to regular contributions.*

Conversions are slightly more complicated. Because the conversion is technically a "rollover" (¶ 2.5), a "conversion contribution" is tied to the traditional IRA "distribution" that is being "rolled over." Therefore a Roth IRA conversion that is supposed to be "for" the year 2001 must be tied to a *distribution* that occurred in the *calendar* year 2001. *The due date of the 2001 return is irrelevant.*

A distribution that is made from a traditional IRA in the calendar year 2001, if it is to be contributed to a Roth IRA, must be so contributed within 60 days after the date of the distribution. January 1, 2001, would be the first date in calendar 2001 on which an amount could be distributed out of a traditional IRA; therefore the earliest possible date for a "2001 Roth IRA conversion" would be January 1,

2001 (same-day conversion of a January 1 distribution). The last possible date in calendar 2001 on which an amount could be distributed out of a traditional IRA would be December 31, 2001; therefore the last possible date for a "2001 conversion" would be the 60th day after December 31, 2001 (the deadline for rolling over a traditional IRA distribution made on December 31, 2001; § 408(d)(3)(A)(i)).

Note that:

A.   Roth IRA conversions are usually accomplished by transferring sums directly from a traditional IRA to a Roth IRA. If both accounts are with the same IRA provider, the traditional IRA distribution and the Roth IRA contribution would normally occur simultaneously. Thus in this typical situation there would be no need to get involved with calculating the 60-day period.

B.   EGTRRA authorizes the IRS to come up with guidelines authorizing an extension of the 60-day rollover deadline in cases of hardship. ¶ 2.5.03. This would in effect also allow a longer period to complete a Roth IRA conversion in cases of hardship. See Reg. § 1.408A-4, A-1(b)(1).

5.7.04 *Recharacterization deadline: meaning of "extended due date"*

Generally, the deadline for recharacterizing an IRA contribution is the due date of the tax return for the year of the contribution that is being recharacterized, *including extensions.* § 408A(d)(6), (7). So:

1.   A regular contribution to either a Roth IRA or a traditional IRA for a particular year, that was made by the *unextended* due date of the return for that year, can be recharacterized by the *extended* due date of the return for that year.

2.   A conversion contribution to a Roth IRA that was made within 60 days after a distribution from a traditional IRA may be recharacterized by the (extended) due date of the return for the taxable year in which the distribution occurred.

"Due date including extensions" or "extended due date" has a special meaning under IRS regulations. The taxpayer does not actually have to get an extension of his income tax return in order to go beyond

April 15 for his recharacterization decision. Reg. § 301.9100-2(b) provides an automatic six-months extension (from the *unextended* due date of the return) for all "regulatory or statutory elections whose due dates are the...due date of the return including extensions *provided* the taxpayer timely filed its return for the year the election should have been made and the taxpayer takes" necessary corrective actions (such as filing an amended return if necessary). (Emphasis added.)

What's confusing is there are two different "automatic" extensions, for different periods of time, neither of which is totally automatic. Any taxpayer can obtain a *four-months'* "automatic" extension of time to file his income tax return (i.e., to August 15 instead of April 15)—but it's not truly automatic because to get this extension the taxpayer has to file Form 4868 by April 15. Then there's the "automatic" *six-months'* extension of time to recharacterize an IRA contribution. This extension *is* automatic in the sense that the taxpayer doesn't have to request it; but to qualify for this automatic extension he has to "timely" file his income tax return. "Timely" filing the income tax return means filing the return on or before April 15 (*or* getting an extension of time to file from the IRS and then filing the return on or before the extended due date).

Putting all these rules together, we find that if a taxpayer wants to recharacterize a Roth IRA contribution made in Year 1 he must complete the necessary actions (¶ 5.7.02) by whichever one of the following deadlines applies:

1. If he files his income tax return for Year 1 on or before its due date, he has until October 15 of Year 2 to complete the recharacterization. The "due date" of the Year 1 income tax return is April 15, Year 2, *unless* he obtained an extension of time to file the return, in which case the due date is whatever date the return was extended to. For example, if, on or before April 15, Year 2, he filed Form 4868 with the IRS requesting the "automatic" four months' extension of time (to August 15, Year 2), the due date of his Year 1 return is August 15, Year 2. However, *regardless* of whether he got an extension of time to file his income tax return, as long as he filed the income tax return by whatever date it was due, the deadline for recharacterizing his IRA contribution is October 15, Year 2, under the automatic extension rule of Reg. § 301.9100-2(b).

Example: Sandy files his income tax return on April 15, year 2. The deadline for recharacterizing his Year 1 IRA contribution is October 15, Year 2.

Example: On or before April 15, Year 2, Pearl files Form 4868 with the IRS requesting the automatic four months' extension of time (to August 15, Year 2) to file her Year 1 income tax return. She files her Year 1 tax return on August 10, Year 2. The deadline for recharacterizing her Year 1 IRA contribution is October 15, Year 2.

2.   If he does not file his income tax return for Year 1 on or before the date it is due (whether that due date is April 15 or a later date he qualified for by requesting an extension from the IRS), he must complete the recharacterization by April 15 of Year 2.

Example: Chad made a regular Roth IRA contribution in Year 1. On or before April 15, Year 2, he files form 4868 with the IRS requesting the automatic four months extension of time (to August 15, Year 2) to file his Year 1 income tax return. He does not apply for any further extensions. He does not file his Year 1 income tax return until August 20, Year 2, which is after the (extended) due date. Because he did not timely file his Year 1 tax return, his deadline for recharacterizing the Roth IRA contribution is April 15, Year 2.

For the purpose of recharacterizing 1998 conversions *only*, the deadline was extended to December 31, 1999, for a taxpayer who timely filed his 1998 return (and who files an amended return for 1998 if necessary to reflect the recharacterization). IRS Announcement 99-104, 1999-44 I.R.B. 555.

For the unfortunate taxpayer who discovers he was not eligible to convert to a Roth IRA, but misses all these deadlines for recharacterizing, there is still hope. There are procedures for applying to the IRS for relief in cases of good faith errors. See Reg. § 301.9100-1 *et seq.* The IRS has been generous in using these relief provisions to grant extensions for recharacterizations of erroneous Roth conversions, where the taxpayers requested relief before the IRS caught the mistake. See, e.g., PLRs 2001-16053 (taxpayer erroneously believed that due date of her return was October 15 and that capital gain did not count toward $100,000 Roth conversion income limit); 2001-16057 (recharacterization of improper Roth conversion was late due to financial institution error); 2001-16058, 2001-19059, 2001-20040, 2001-22050, 2001-28058 and 2001-30058 (taxpayers unaware they didn't qualify for Roth conversion and unaware of recharacterization deadline); 2001-26040 (taxpayers had been erroneously advised that the Roth IRA conversion income limit was $150,000, that the deadline for 1998 conversion was 4/15/99, etc.); and 2001-29040 (taxpayer ineligible to convert, and thought she had timely recharacterized all her Roth IRAs, but missed the deadline on one of them because she forgot about that account). In each of these PLRs, the IRS granted the taxpayers additional time, after the issuance of the ruling, to complete their recharacterizations.

5.7.05 *Confusion between "conversions" and "recharacterizations"*

While it is nice that taxpayers have been given a way to back out of Roth IRA conversions, so they need not be punished for (*e.g.*) making an incorrect prediction of their income, the addition of the recharacterization option is bound to create confusion among IRA owners and their advisors. Here are some points that will need to be constantly restated:

First, the ability to recharacterize a "Year 1"IRA contribution until October 15 of"Year 2" does *not* create a new extended right to do Roth IRA conversions between January 1 and October 15 of Year 2 that will count as Year 1 conversions. If, in Year 1, there was no traditional IRA distribution that was properly converted to a Roth IRA (¶ 5.4.01), there is nothing to "recharacterize."

Second, not every type of contribution to a *traditional* IRA may be recharacterized—only "regular" contributions, i.e., the $2,000-per-year (or other applicable dollar limit, depending on the year; ¶ 5.3.02) type. A tax-free rollover from an employer plan (or from another traditional IRA) to a traditional IRA may not be recharacterized as a Roth IRA conversion or contribution, because "an amount contributed to an IRA in a tax-free transfer cannot be recharacterized." Reg. § 1.408A-5, A-10, Example 4.

Similarly, employer contributions to a SEP or SIMPLE plan may not be recharacterized as contributions to a Roth IRA, because the employer could not have made direct contributions to a Roth IRA in the first place. Once the contribution has been made, the employee may be able to convert the account to a Roth IRA. Reg. § 1.408A-5, A-5; ¶ 5.4.02.

5.7.06 *Determining net income attributable to contribution*

In order to effect a recharacterization (unconversion), not only the original contribution but also any net income attributable to such contribution must be retransferred. Reg. § 1.408A-5, A-2(a). This requirement may be met in one of two ways. Note that "net income" may be a negative amount—a loss, in other words.

Method 1: If the contribution in question was made to a new, separate, Roth IRA that contained no other funds, *and* there have been no other contributions to or distributions from that separate Roth IRA, *and* the entire contribution is being recharacterized, then simply transferring the entire account balance back to a traditional IRA satisfies the requirement. Reg. § 1.408A-5, A-2(b). This method being so much simpler than Method 2, there is an advantage to keeping each year's contributions to a Roth IRA in a separate Roth IRA account (not commingled with any pre-existing Roth IRA), until the period has expired for recharacterizing such contributions.

Method 2: If Method 1 is not available, then the net income attributable to the contribution must be calculated by a formula that is contained in Reg. § 1.408-4(c)(2)(ii) (Reg. § 1.408A-5, A-2(c)), or IRS Notice 2000-39, 2000-30 I.R.B. 132.

5.7.07 *Same-year reconversions outlawed (2000 and later)*

The IRS since 1998 has imposed various limits on the ability to use the recharacterization rules to flip back and forth between traditional IRA and Roth IRA status. For the limits applicable to reconversions in 1998 and 1999, see *"Limit on the number of 'reconversions' in 1998 and 1999: IRS Notice 98-50"* at page 225 of the 1999 edition of this book.

In Reg. § 1.408A-5, A-9(a), the IRS banned same-year reconversions, effective in 2000 and later years. Once a recharacterization of a Roth IRA conversion occurs, the individual may not reconvert the amount to a Roth IRA until the taxable year following the taxable year of the original conversion, or until at least 30 days have elapsed since the recharacterization, *whichever is later*. If the individual defies this rule and attempts to reconvert before the prescribed time period ends, the result is a "failed conversion."

5.8 When the Roth IRA Owner Dies

This ¶ 5.8 collects the rules that come into play upon death of the Roth IRA owner.

5.8.01 *Five-Year Period: effect of Participant's death*

The Five-Year Period (¶ 5.2.02) does not start running over again just because the Roth IRA owner dies. The Five-Year Period applicable to distributions from an inherited Roth IRA is the Five-Year Period that applied to the account during the original owner's life. Reg. § 1.408A-6, A-7(a). Also, the Five-Year Period requirement is not *waived* simply because the original owner dies—even though in most cases the minimum distribution rules (¶ 5.1.03) require the beneficiaries to begin withdrawing from the account by the year following the year of death. Reg. § 1.408A-6, A-14(c).

Example: Agatha, age 83, converted her traditional IRA to a Roth IRA in 2001, shortly before her death. She had made no prior Roth IRA contributions, so the Five-Year Period for her Roth IRA starts January 1, 2001. Her designated beneficiary must begin taking required distributions in 2002 (the year after her death). Because the Five-Year Period has not elapsed, the required distributions for the years 2002-2005 are not "qualified distributions." However, all distributions to the beneficiary are deemed to come first out of Agatha's original rollover contribution (¶ 5.4.02). Since Agatha paid tax on that amount already (it was included in her gross income for the year of the conversion; ¶ 5.4.09), these distributions are still income-tax free so long as the distributions do not exceed the amount of Agatha's original contribution. See ¶ 5.2.03. Beginning in 2006 all distributions from Agatha's Roth IRA will be tax-free as "qualified distributions" (¶ 5.2.01).

5.8.02 *Income in respect of a decedent problem*

If Participant dies during the Five-Year Period, and the beneficiaries withdraw from the account before the Five-Year Period expires, and the total of their withdrawals during this period exceeds the total of Participant's contributions, the excess will constitute "income in respect of a decedent" (IRD) (see Chapter 2). However, any distribution made from the Roth IRA *after* the expiration of the Five-Year Period (and after Participant's death) will be an income tax-free qualified distribution (and so will *not* be IRD) (¶ 5.2.01). Since it is impossible to know at the time of Participant's death how much the beneficiaries will withdraw from the account prior to the end of the Five-Year Period, it is impossible to know, until the end of that period (or until total distribution of the account, if earlier), exactly how much IRD there is in the estate.

Recipients of IRD are entitled to an income tax deduction for federal estate taxes paid on IRD. The amount of the deduction depends on the amount of estate taxes paid on *all* of the IRD included in the estate and on what proportion of it each beneficiary received. § 691; ¶ 2.2.07. Thus, in an estate which pays a federal estate tax, the existence of a Roth IRA for which the Five-Year Period had not expired at death may make it impossible for tax preparers to finalize beneficiaries' IRD deductions until expiration of the Five-Year Period (or earlier distribution of the entire Roth IRA).

5.8.03 *Special rules for surviving spouses*

A surviving spouse as beneficiary of a Roth IRA can roll her share of the account over into a Roth IRA of her own, or (if she is the sole designated beneficiary) elect to treat the deceased spouse's Roth IRA as her own Roth IRA. The result of such rollover or election is that the minimum distribution rules (Chapter 1) and the 10% penalty for pre-age 59½ distributions (Chapter 9) are then applied to the surviving spouse as owner rather than as beneficiary. Reg. § 1.408A-2, A-4. For more on spousal rollovers, see ¶ 3.2.

The regulations provide a special favorable rule (not in the statute) for surviving spouses: if the beneficiary of a Roth IRA is the surviving spouse, and the "surviving spouse treats the Roth IRA as his or her own," and the surviving spouse also owns her own Roth IRA, the Five-Year Period (¶ 5.2.02) "with respect to any of the surviving spouse's Roth IRAs" (including the inherited one that the surviving spouse has elected to treat as her own) ends at the earlier of the end of either the Five-Year Period for the deceased spouse's Roth IRA or that applicable to the surviving spouse's own Roth IRAs. Reg. § 1.408A-6, A-7(b).

If the surviving spouse receives a distribution from: (i) a Roth IRA belonging to the surviving spouse into which she has rolled distributions from a Roth IRA she inherited from the deceased spouse; or (ii) a Roth IRA inherited from the deceased spouse that the surviving spouse has elected to treat as her own Roth IRA; such distribution is *not* as a distribution "made to a beneficiary on or after the owner's death." Reg. § 1.408A-6, A-3. Thus, even after expiration of the Five-Year Period, the spouse may not receive qualified distributions from the rollover (or elected) account until she herself reaches age 59½ (or is disabled). ¶ 5.2.01.

For another special rule regarding the surviving spouse, see ¶ 5.8.06.

5.8.04 *How the Ordering Rules apply to a decedent's Roth IRA*

If a Roth IRA owner dies, leaving his Roth IRA(s) to more than one beneficiary, and his death occurs at a time when the Ordering Rules (¶ 5.2.04) might matter (*i.e.*, before the end of the "Five-Year Period" necessary to have a qualified distribution; ¶ 5.2.01), the various components of the decedent's Roth IRA(s) that matter for purposes of the Ordering Rules are carried over and allocated pro rata among the beneficiaries who inherit the Roth IRA(s). Reg. § 1.408A-6, A-11.

This regulation also indicates that such carryover and allocation is necessary if the decedent died within five taxable years after doing a pre-age 59½ conversion (¶ 5.6.03), as if the 10% penalty (Chapter 9) could apply to distributions from such an account to the beneficiaries. However, distributions after death are excepted from the 10% penalty (§ 72(t)(2)(A)(ii); ¶ 9.3.01); and the regulations provide that the § 72(t) exceptions are available even for distributions within the five years following a conversion (Reg. § 1.408A-6, A-5(b), so the author does not see how the 10% penalty could apply to such distributions.

Is this carryover and allocation in case of death within the five years following a pre-age 59½ conversion important for a surviving spouse who inherits a Roth IRA and elects to treat it as her own (¶ 5.8.03)? Generally, the regulations provide that, when a surviving spouse elects to treat an inherited Roth IRA as her own, § 72(t) is applied as if the surviving spouse, *not* the decedent, were the owner of the account. Reg. § 1.408A-2, A-4. Does Reg. § 1.408A-6, A-11, suggest that, even though the surviving spouse is now treated as the owner for purposes of § 72(t), she still carries over the decedent's potential liability for the 10% penalty, if distributions occur within five years after the *decedent's* conversion? What if the surviving spouse is already over age 59½? Further clarification from the IRS is needed on this point.

5.8.05 *Other rules for tax treatment of inherited Roth IRAs*

Non-spouse beneficiaries cannot roll over an inherited Roth IRA (or convert an inherited traditional IRA to a Roth IRA), due to the prohibition (applicable to anyone other than the surviving spouse) on rolling over inherited IRAs. § 408(d)(3)(C).

Generally, if an individual (other than the surviving spouse; ¶5.8.03) inherits a Roth IRA, and also has a Roth IRA funded by his own contributions, the Five-Year Period runs separately ("is determined independently") for the two types. Reg. § 1.408A-6, A-7(b). A beneficiary cannot aggregate an inherited Roth IRA with his own Roth IRA for purposes of the minimum distribution rules (¶ 5.1.03). Reg. § 1.408A-6, A-15.

See ¶ 5.8.07 regarding who has the right to recharacterize Participant's contributions after Participant's death.

5.8.06 *1998 conversions: death during the four-year period*

If a person who made a 1998 conversion and chose to spread the tax on that conversion over four taxable years (see ¶ 5.4.09) dies before the end of 2001, all remaining income resulting from the 1998 conversion is accelerated onto the decedent's final return. § 408A(d)(3)(E)(ii)(I).

However, if Participant's surviving spouse is the sole beneficiary of all of his Roth IRAs, the spouse "may elect to treat the remaining amounts [that have not yet been included in the decedent's return for years prior to death] as includible in the spouse's gross income in the taxable years of the spouse ending with or within the taxable years of such [decedent] in which such amounts would otherwise have been includible." § 408A(d)(3)(E)(ii)(II). If the spouse makes this election, the instalment for the year of death is included on the decedent's final income tax return, and subsequent instalments are included on the surviving spouse's return. Reg. § 1.408A-4, A-11(b).

The spouse's election is made on Form 8606 or 1040, and may not be made (or changed) after the due date of the surviving spouse's tax return for the year of death. § 408A(d)(3)(E)(ii)(II); Reg. § 1.408A-4, A-11(b).

If the surviving spouse, having made the election, dies before the end of 2001, it appears that the remaining instalments are accelerated onto her return. See § 408A(d)(E)(ii)(I).

5.8.07 *Conversions, unconversions, by personal representative*

"The election to recharacterize a contribution...may be made on behalf of a deceased IRA owner by his or her executor, administrator, or other person responsible for filing the final Federal income tax return of the decedent under section 6012(b)(1)." Reg. § 1.408A-5, A-6(c).

Since the regulations give the Participant's personal representative—*not* the beneficiary who inherited the account—the right to "recharacterize" Roth IRA contributions (¶ 5.7.02), this raises the possibility that a beneficiary could inherit a recently established Roth IRA, only to have Participant's executor transform the account back into a traditional IRA. How the executor will persuade the Roth IRA provider to transfer the money back to a traditional IRA when the executor does not have title to the account is unclear.

5.9 Summary of Planning Principles

1.   Generally, it is easier to get money out of a Roth IRA tax-free than out of other retirement plans. Participant can withdraw his own contributions tax-free at any time (¶ 5.2.03); and (after expiration of the initial Five-Year Period; ¶ 5.2.02) *all* distributions are tax-free after Participant reaches age 59½ (or dies) (¶ 5.2.01). The only significant exception is that a person who converts to a Roth IRA while under age 59½ may have to pay a 10% penalty if he withdraws from the account within five years of the conversion (¶ 5.6.03).

2.   Funding a Roth IRA with annual contributions up to the annual dollar limit (¶ 5.3.02) is an excellent tax shelter for individuals who have "compensation income" but are in a low income tax bracket (¶ 5.5.01).

3.   Converting a traditional IRA to a Roth IRA (¶ 5.4) offers those who meet the income limit (¶ 5.4.03) a chance to eliminate required lifetime distributions (¶ 5.1.03) and (if they can pay the income tax on the conversion from other assets; ¶ 5.5.00) a way to

increase the relative portion of their investments that is inside a tax-favored retirement plan.

4.   For other reasons to convert a traditional IRA to a Roth IRA, see ¶ 5.5.06 and ¶ 5.5.07.

5.   A person under age 59½ can convert a traditional IRA to a Roth IRA without being liable for the 10% penalty (¶ 5.6.01), but must either pay the income tax on the conversion from other funds or pay a 10% penalty if he withdraws the needed money from the converted account (or from an unconverted IRA) within five years after the conversion (unless some other exception applies; see Chapter 9). ¶ 5.6.03.

6.   The decision to convert a traditional IRA to a Roth IRA is not irrevocable, since "recharacterization" (unconversion) offers a penalty-free way to back out of the conversion decision up until (if the Participant timely files his income tax return for the year of the conversion) October 15 of the year after the conversion. ¶ 5.7.02.

6

Trusts as Beneficiaries of Retirement Plans

The minimum distribution "trust rules," trust accounting, and other tax and non-tax concerns when naming a trust as beneficiary of retirement benefits.

This Chapter discusses issues that arise when retirement plan death benefits are payable to a trust, as the named beneficiary under a retirement plan, upon the death of the client ("Participant") who is the retirement plan participant.

6.1 Trust as Beneficiary: in General

This ¶ 6.1 lists the factors which (in addition to all other issues you need to consider in connection with any estate plan, or any disposition of retirement benefits) you need to review when it is proposed to name a *trust* as beneficiary of the client's retirement plan.

6.1.01 *Consider leaving benefits outright rather than in trust*

In preparing the estate plan, it may at first appear easier to have all the client's assets (including retirement benefits) "pour" into one trust, such as the client's "living" trust, so that a single fiduciary has control of all the assets and can then divide them up and distribute them according to a master formula and provisions contained in the trust. In view of the substantial complications and other disadvantages (explained in this Chapter and elsewhere; see, e.g., ¶ 10.5) involved in making *retirement benefits* payable to a trust, this rule of thumb does not apply to retirement benefits. With retirement benefits, the bias is in favor of leaving the benefits outright to the intended beneficiaries unless there is a compelling reason to leave them in trust.

Example: Anthony proposes to leave all his assets, including his retirement plan benefits, to his living trust. Upon his death, after payment of his debts, expenses, estate taxes and small bequests to various relatives, the trust is to terminate and be distributed outright to his three adult children. If a child predeceases Anthony, that child's share is instead held in trust for that child's issue until they reach age 35. Anthony has sufficient assets outside the retirement plans to enable his estate to pay all the debts, expenses, estate taxes and small bequests to various relatives without tapping the retirement plans for these purposes. Since it is not essential to the achievement of Anthony's estate plan goals that the retirement benefits pass to the trust, and since leaving the benefits to the trust would involve substantial additional complications (see all the issues discussed in this Chapter), Anthony decides to name his children, rather than the trust, as beneficiaries of his retirement plans.

If a child predeceases Anthony, however, that child's share will pass to that child's issue who are minors. Benefits left outright to a minor, though they could be kept in the control of a guardian or custodian until the minor reached the age of majority, would pass to the minor outright when he or she reached the age of majority. Anthony thinks that age is too young for his grandchildren to receive outright control of property, so in his beneficiary designation he provides that, if any child predeceases Anthony, that child's share is paid to Anthony's living trust to be held for such child's issue pursuant to the terms of the trust. Since leaving benefits outright to minor beneficiaries would be undesirable, there is a compelling reason to have the benefits pass to a trust in that case. See Form 1.1, Appendix B.

Example: Beth proposes to leave all her assets, including her retirement benefits, to a trust for the benefit of her son Ben, if he survives her, otherwise to Ben's minor children. Ben has problems with alcohol and gambling, has been married and divorced four times, and is frequently sued in connection with failed business deals. Any assets left to Ben outright are highly likely to be lost to one of his addictions, creditors or ill-conceived business ventures. Beth does not want that to happen to her hard-earned retirement money. Although it would be simpler to leave the retirement benefits to Ben outright, to avoid having to deal with all the issues discussed in this Chapter, there are compelling reasons to tie up Ben's inheritance in trust, so it is worth incurring the complications. A spendthrift trust will protect the trust's assets from claims of Ben's creditors, and put control of the assets in the hands of a trustee who can assure the assets are used wisely for Ben's benefit.

6.1.02 *Consider trust income tax issues*

Distributions to a trust after the client's death from the client's retirement plans (other than distributions from a Roth IRA; ¶ 5.2.01) will generally (for list of exceptions see ¶ 2.1.03) be included in the trust's gross income as "income in respect of a decedent" (¶ 2.2).

With the exception of "grantor trusts" (¶ 6.3.09), trusts generally are taxed as separate entities, subject to a separate rate schedule that applies only to trusts and estates. § 1(e). A trust goes into the highest tax bracket (39.6%) for taxable income in excess of $8,900 (2001 rates). For an individual, the top income tax bracket for 2001 is 39.1%, and it applies only to taxable income above $297,350. § 1(c). Thus, in all but the wealthiest families, income taxed to a trust will be taxed at a higher rate than would apply to the individual family members. See ¶ 10.5 and ¶ 3.3.10 for the estate planning implications of this fact in connection with leaving retirement benefits to a credit shelter trust or QTIP trust.

If the estate plan calls for the retirement benefits to be left to a trust, the planner needs to factor in the impact of the high trust tax rates, and also consider whether the high rates could be avoided or mitigated by one of the following means:

1.   A trust is entitled to an income tax deduction for distributions the trust makes from the trust's "distributable net income" (DNI) to individual trust beneficiaries, if various requirements are met. See ¶ 6.1.03.

2.   A trust is entitled to an income tax deduction for certain distributions the trust makes to charity, if various requirements are met. § 642(c). See ¶ 7.4.

3.   If the individual trust beneficiary is a U.S. citizen or resident, and has the unlimited right to take the retirement benefits out of the trust, the trust is considered a "grantor trust" as to that beneficiary, and the distributions from the retirement plan to the trust would be taxed at the beneficiary's rate not the trust's rate. § 678, § 672(f). See ¶ 6.3.09.

4.   If Participant's estate was liable for federal estate taxes the trust is entitled to an income tax deduction for the estate taxes paid

on the retirement benefits. § 691(c). See ¶ 2.2.07.

The fact that retirement plan distributions to the trust are "income in respect of a decedent" raises another concern, besides the issue of high trust income tax rates. If the trust's assets are to be divided into separate shares or trusts upon the client's death, and the division is to be on the basis of a "pecuniary" formula, there is a risk that the retirement benefits will be subjected to tax *immediately* (rather than upon distribution) if the retirement benefits are used to fund the "pecuniary" share. See ¶ 2.2.05 for details, and ¶ 6.1.05, Item 6.

6.1.03 *Trust passes out taxable income as part of "DNI"*

A trust may be able to reduce the income taxes payable on retirement plan distributions it receives by passing such distributions out to the individual trust beneficiaries. A trust gets an income tax deduction for distributions made from the trust's "distributable net income" (DNI) to individual trust beneficiaries. §§ 651, 661. The beneficiaries then include the distributions in their gross income. §§ 652, 662. If the distributions the trust receives from the retirement plan are passed out to the individual beneficiaries of the trust as part of DNI, the income tax burden is shifted to the individual beneficiaries, who may be in a lower tax bracket than the trust.

Computation of DNI and the allocation of DNI among beneficiaries' shares is a complex topic that is beyond the scope of this book. For details on the requirements and computations see § 663, regulations under applicable Code sections or the *Blattmachr* and *Zaritsky* books cited at the beginning of the Bibliography. See also discussion at ¶ 7.4. The purpose of this ¶ 6.1.03 is to point the way to successful drafting to take advantage of the DNI deduction. The following discussion uses the term "gross income" to refer to a retirement plan distribution that is received by a trust and is includible in the trust's gross income for the year of such receipt.

The fact that a trustee receives a retirement plan distribution and later makes a distribution to an individual trust beneficiary does *not* automatically mean that the distribution to the individual trust beneficiary carries with it the gross income arising from the retirement plan distribution. The trust might still be liable for the income tax on the retirement plan distribution it received. The question is (in trust administration lingo) whether such distribution "carries out DNI." For example:

The DNI deduction is available only for gross income that either is required to be distributed, or is actually distributed, to the individual beneficiary in the same taxable year it is received by the trust (or that is distributed within 65 days after the end of such taxable year, if the trustee elects under § 663(b) to have such distribution treated as made during such taxable year). §§ 651(a), 661(a).

Also, the DNI deduction is not available for distributions in fulfillment of a bequest of a specific sum of money ("straight" pecuniary bequest) (unless the governing instrument requires that such distribution is to be paid in more than three instalments). § 663(a)(1), Reg. § 1.663(a)-1. However, a "formula" pecuniary bequest is not considered a bequest of a specific sum of money for this purpose, and so can "carry out DNI." Reg. § 1.663(a)-1(b)(1). A formula pecuniary bequest for this purpose does not mean simply any pecuniary amount determined by a formula; it means a bequest of a sum of money determined by a formula where the amount of the bequest cannot be determined as of the date of death. Many marital deduction bequests are of this type; see, e.g., Form 3.4(B), Appendix B.

Finally, if there are two or more beneficiaries, and they have "substantially separate and independent shares," a distribution to one beneficiary will not carry out DNI that is allocated under the "separate shares" rule to a different beneficiary. § 663(c); ¶ 7.4.05.

With this background in mind, we look at some typical trust provisions and see whether these would cause or allow the gross income attributable to retirement plan distributions received by a trust to be "carried out" to individual trust beneficiaries (and therefore taxed to such beneficiaries rather than to the trust):

1.   A trust provides "income to spouse, remainder to issue." As explained at ¶ 6.1.07, Spouse is entitled under this provision only to "trust accounting income." Unless the trust instrument has a provision explicitly providing to the contrary, retirement plan distributions to the trust will be allocated wholly or partly to trust principal or "corpus" (¶ 6.1.07), and thus cannot be distributed to Spouse under this type of trust. Except for the portion that is properly attributable to trust accounting income (e.g., under UPIA 1997, 10% of MRDs; ¶ 6.1.07), which will be taxable to spouse as the income beneficiary, such distributions will be taxed to the trust. For comments on

including a provision that defines all retirement plan distributions as income in a QDOT, see ¶ 4.7.05.

2.   A trust provides "income to spouse, plus principal to spouse in the discretion of the independent trustee, remainder to issue." Under this trust the trustee could distribute to Spouse amounts the trust received from retirement plans, even if such amounts are allocable to trust principal, to the extent such distributions are permitted under whatever standards the trustee is given for exercise of its discretion to distribute principal to Spouse. If the trust says Spouse is entitled to principal only "if needed for her health, education and support," and she doesn't need any principal for those purposes, the trustee could not pass out to her the retirement plan distributions just to reduce income taxes. Accordingly, if it is desired to give the trustee discretion to distribute principal to Spouse for the purpose of reducing income taxes the trust instrument should so specify (or give the trustee broad discretion to distribute principal for any reason the trustee deems advisable). Assuming the distribution is authorized by the trust instrument, it will carry with it the gross income generated by the trustee's receipt of a retirement plan distribution in the same year; the retirement plan distribution received by the trust is included in DNI (see definition at § 643(a)), deductible by the trust (§ 661(a)), and includible in the beneficiary's income. § 662(a)(2), Reg. § 1.662(a)-3.

3.   If the trust instrument requires the trustee to distribute to the individual trust beneficiary all retirement plan distributions received by the trust (whether such plan distributions are considered "income" or "corpus" for trust accounting purposes), the plan distributions received by the trustee would be part of DNI and the DNI would be carried out and taxable to the beneficiary. § 643(a), 661(a)), 662(a)(2); Reg. § 1.662(a)-3. For further discussion of such "conduit trusts" see ¶ 6.3.08.

Accordingly, when drafting a trust that may receive retirement benefits, if you want the trust to be permitted to take advantage of the DNI deduction to reduce income taxes on distributions from the retirement plan, the trust instrument must give the trustee discretion to distribute principal (or at least the part of principal that consists of distributions from retirement plans) to the individual beneficiaries. If you want the trust to be *forced* to take advantage of this deduction, see discussion of "conduit trusts" at ¶ 6.3.08.

6.1.04 *Consider your client's particular retirement plans*

Part of what makes planning for retirement benefits difficult is the variety of arrangements that can be encompassed in the term "retirement benefits." The trustee of a trust that is named as sole beneficiary of a typical *self-directed IRA* simply owns an investment account with special tax characteristics; the trustee can freely trade assets "inside" the IRA, withdraw assets from the account at any time and in any amount, and even move the account to another IRA custodian (by means of a direct custodian-to-custodian transfer). The trustee's duties include directing the investments and making decisions regarding the timing of distributions.

In contrast to this, the trustee of a trust that is named as beneficiary of remaining payments under a *defined benefit plan* (for example, if the deceased participant was receiving a life annuity with a minimum term of years, and dies before the term of years is up, leaving the remaining payments to his trust), has no control over the underlying plan investments, has no control over the size or timing of distributions, and cannot move the "account" to another plan. With this type of traditional annuity-based retirement plan the trustee owns a mere contract right to receive the future payments. The trustee's only duty is to collect the payments.

In between the self-directed IRA (over which the trustee-named-as-beneficiary has complete control) and the defined benefit or annuity plan (over which the trustee-named-as-beneficiary has absolutely no control) are a variety of other types of qualified retirement plans where the trustee has some, but less than complete, control. For example, under a 401(k) plan, the trustee-named-as-beneficiary might have a limited menu of investment choices (among one "family" of mutual funds for example), and a limited menu of distribution options (such as lump sum or instalments over a term certain).

Despite the vast differences, in terms of the degree of the trustee's control, among the various types of retirement plans, Congress, the IRS, and the drafters of state laws often do not differentiate. In many cases the same rules apply both to self-directed IRAs and to more traditional annuity-based types of retirement benefits.

Many practitioners, like the drafters of legislation, would like to have a blanket trust form that will "work" for all clients' situations without further fine tuning. This approach can be hazardous when dealing with retirement benefits. The practitioner needs to think through exactly how the trust provisions will operate with regard to the particular client's major retirement plan assets, and adjust the estate plan accordingly.

Some retirement plans offer only a limited menu of payout options for death benefits. For example, many 401(k) plans offer a lump sum distribution as the only form of death benefit. See ¶ 1.5.09. A pension or 403(b) plan may offer only annuity payouts, or only fixed-instalment payouts. Some plans offer a variety of payout options to individual beneficiaries, but would not allow a trust the same choices. Some qualified plans refuse to honor disclaimers (¶ 8.2.08). Some plan administrators and IRA providers do not allow a terminating trust to pass the retirement benefit out to the trust beneficiary, but rather require the trust to cash out the plan (¶ 6.1.06).

Whenever a retirement plan constitutes a major asset of the client's estate, it is necessary to make sure that the proposed disposition of the retirement benefits will be permitted under the terms of the client's retirement plan.

6.1.05 Checklist of factors to consider when drafting trust

When drafting a trust that is to be named as beneficiary of a client's retirement plan benefits, consider the following points, in addition to those discussed at ¶ 6.1.01 through ¶ 6.1.04:

1.   If special provisions are to be included that deal with retirement plan benefits, you need to define "retirement benefits." See Form 7.5, Appendix B.

Example: Rita's retirement benefits are payable to a trust for the benefit of her elderly aunt and her young niece. Rita wants the retirement benefits allocated to the aunt's share and the rest of the trust assets allocated to the niece's share. The trust instrument needs to define "retirement benefits."

2.   If the trust is intended to qualify for the federal estate tax marital deduction, see ¶ 3.3.

3.   If the dispositive terms of the trust distinguish between "income" and "principal," consider how these terms will apply to the retirement plan and to distributions from it. See ¶ 6.1.07.

4.   The minimum distribution rules of § 401(a)(9) (Chapter 1) permit death benefits to be paid out over the life expectancy of individual beneficiary who inherits the benefits. The IRS's proposed regulations allow a trust that is named as beneficiary of retirement benefits to use this "life expectancy payout method" if various requirements are met. Compliance with these rules can be extremely important in certain situations. See ¶ 6.2.

5.   When Participant's spouse ("Spouse") is named as Participant's beneficiary, certain distribution options (including most importantly, but not limited to, the spousal rollover; ¶ 3.2) become available that are not available otherwise. These special options are usually *not* available when a trust is named as beneficiary, even if Spouse is the sole life beneficiary of the trust. If use of the special tax options available to a surviving spouse-beneficiary would be beneficial as part of the client's estate plan, consider whether it is feasible, in line with the client's other estate planning objectives, to name Spouse individually (instead of the trust) as beneficiary of the retirement plan; or if that is not feasible, consider whether the trust can be written so that it qualifies for some of the special spousal options; see ¶ 6.3.13.

6.   If the trust's assets are to be divided into shares or subtrusts upon the client's death, and the division is to be on the basis of a "pecuniary" formula (¶ 2.2.05), there is a risk that the retirement benefits will be subjected to tax *immediately* (rather than upon distribution) if the retirement benefits are used to fund the "pecuniary" share. To avoid this problem, either use a fractional (rather than a pecuniary) formula to divide the trust assets (see Form 3.2(B), Appendix B); or, either in the trust instrument (see Form 3.3(B), Appendix B) or the beneficiary designation form (see Form 3.4(A), Appendix B) or both, require that the retirement benefits be allocated to one particular

share or trust, so that the benefits do not become subject to the formula at all.

6.1.06 *Distributing a retirement plan out of a trust*

¶ 6.1.03 discussed the tax treatment of a trust's distribution to an individual trust beneficiary of a distribution the trust had received from a retirement plan. This ¶ 6.1.05 discusses distributing the retirement plan itself out of the trust to the beneficiary. The following are examples of the most common occasions for such distributions:

Example: Foster names the Foster Revocable Living Trust as beneficiary of his IRA. The Foster Revocable Living Trust provides that, upon Foster's death, the trustee is to divide all assets of the trust into two separate trusts, the Marital Trust and the Credit Shelter Trust, pursuant to a fractional formula. All retirement benefits are to be allocated to the marital trust. The trustee instructs the IRA provider to change the name of the owner of the IRA from "Foster Revocable Living Trust, as beneficiary of Foster, deceased," to "Marital Trust, as beneficiary of Foster, deceased." The trustee has distributed (transferred) the IRA from the Foster Revocable Living Trust to the Marital Trust.

Example: Stanley names the Stanley Revocable Trust as beneficiary of his IRA. The Stanley Revocable Trust provides that, after Stanley's death, the trustee is to pay income of the trust to Mrs. Stanley for life. On her death, the principal of the trust is to be paid outright to Stanley's two children, A and B. The trustee takes annual required distributions from Stanley's IRA. Because the Stanley Revocable Trust complies with the minimum distribution "trust rules" (¶ 6.2), these required distributions are computed using the life expectancy of Mrs. Stanley (the oldest trust beneficiary), which is 18 years. Mrs. Stanley dies 12 years later. There are seven years left to go in the life expectancy payout. The trustee instructs the IRA provider to divide the IRA into two separate equal IRAs and to change the name on these new IRAs from "Stanley Revocable Trust, as beneficiary of Stanley, deceased," to "Child A as beneficiary of Stanley, deceased" and "Child B as beneficiary of Stanley, deceased." The trustee has distributed (transferred) the IRA from the Stanley Revocable Living Trust to the to the two children equally.

Generally, the transfer of an inherited retirement plan after Participant's death would trigger immediate realization of the income represented by the retirement plan, because it is the transfer of a right to receive "income in respect of a decedent." § 691(a)(2); see ¶ 2.2.05. Thus, if Child A had inherited a retirement plan from Stanley, and Child A decided to give that IRA to Child B, Child A's gift-transfer of the IRA would trigger immediate realization of income by Child A, equal to the full value of the IRA. Reg. § 1.691(a)-4(a).

However, there is an exception to the § 691(a)(2) "trigger" rule: it does not apply to a "transfer to a person pursuant to the right of such person to receive such amount by reason of the death of the decedent or by bequest, devise, or inheritance from the decedent." § 691(a)(2). This exception applies to the transfer of the right to receive income in respect of a decedent by a terminating trust to the trust beneficiaries. Reg. § 1.691(a)-4(b)(3). Thus, the distribution of a retirement plan from a trust to the trust beneficiaries as in examples above does not cause realization of income. The same would be true in the case of distribution of a retirement plan by an estate to the estate's residuary beneficiaries.

PLR 2001-31033 (Rulings 5, 6 and 7) allowed the distribution of "IRA Y" from a terminating trust to Participant's children, C and D (although the ruling didn't mention § 691). From the ruling: "The provision of Trust X which provides for its termination does not change either the identity of the individuals who will receive the IRA Y proceeds or the identity of the designated beneficiary of IRA Y.... Furthermore, the Trust X termination language which results in distributions from IRA Y being made directly to Taxpayers C and D instead of initially to Trust X and then to Taxpayers C and D was language in Trust X approved by [Participant] during his lifetime which reflects [Participant's] intent to pay his children directly instead of through Trust X."

Although transfer of a retirement plan from a trust to the beneficiary who is entitled to it does not trigger income tax, some practitioners prefer to limit the times when such assignments will be necessary. For example, a typical trust provision for a minor child provides that the child will be entitled to outright distribution of his or her share in stages, such as one-third at age 25, one-third at age 30 and one-third at age 35. If a retirement plan will be a significant asset of the child's share, such a provision could require multiple divisions and assignments of the retirement plan, which may be administratively difficult. These difficulties could be avoided by requiring distribution of this particular asset at only one age rather than in stages.

6.1.07 *Trust accounting for retirement benefits*

There are three problems in applying traditional trust concepts of "principal" and "income" to retirement benefits payable to a trust. These are: the confusion between "trust accounting income" and "taxable income" or "federal gross income"; the confusion between "trust accounting income" and "minimum required distributions" (MRDs); and the difficulty of defining "trust accounting income" with respect to retirement benefits.

First, "income" as that term is generally used in a trust instrument means "trust accounting income," not income in the federal income tax sense. An asset can be "principal" (corpus) for trust accounting purposes and yet be "income" for purposes of the federal income tax law.

Example: Jorge dies leaving his $1 million 401(k) plan to a trust for his daughter. The trustee is to pay "income" to the daughter, and to distribute "principal" to the daughter if needed for her health, education and support until she reaches age 35, at which time the trust is to terminate and the remaining principal is to be distributed outright to the daughter. The trust instrument specifies that the date of death value of the 401(k) plan is the "principal" of this trust. The only form of death benefit allowed by the 401(k) plan is a lump sum in cash which is received by the trustee a few days after Jorge's death. Because the trust instrument defines this asset as "principal," the trustee holds the $1 million in the trust, invests it, and starts paying the income of the investments to the daughter. Then the trustee prepares the income tax return for the trust for its first year. He has to report as "income" the $1 million distribution from the 401(k) plan. This is "income" for federal income tax purposes even though it is "principal" for trust accounting purposes.

The second source of confusion is the difference between "trust accounting income" and "MRDs." The two are totally different concepts, though it is possible to have a definition of "income" that takes into account the minimum distribution concept.

Example: Belle dies leaving her $1 million IRA to a trust for her son Burt. The trustee is to pay "income" to Burt, and to distribute "principal" to Burt if needed for his health, education and support until he reaches age 35, at which time the trust is to terminate and the remaining principal is to be distributed outright to Burt. The trust instrument specifies that the date of death value of the IRA is the "principal" of this trust and that "income" with respect to the IRA means the income earned inside the IRA (i.e., interest and dividends on the IRA's investments) as if the IRA were itself a trust (see Form 7.6, Appendix B).   Each year, the trustee withdraws from the IRA the MRD based on Burt's life expectancy (see ¶ 6.2.04) and transfers that distribution to the trust's non-retirement plan investment account. In addition, because the trustee is required to pay Burt all "income" as that is defined in the trust, if the "income" of the IRA is larger than the MRD, the trustee has to withdraw the excess and distribute that also to Burt. If that outcome is considered undesirable, the trust could be drafted so that the trustee was required to withdraw and distribute to Burt the lesser of the "income" or the MRD (such a form could not be used for a marital trust; see ¶ 3.3.06).

Last but not least, there is no generally accepted definition of what "trust accounting income" means as applied to a retirement plan benefit payable to a trust. If the trust requires the trustee to pay all "income"of the trust to A for life and distribute the "principal" of the trust to B at A's death, and the trust's only asset is an IRA, or any other type of retirement plan, what is the "income" that A receives? We have seen that "trust accounting income" does not mean "federal gross income" and it does not mean "MRD"; so what does it mean?

State law will govern if the trust agreement does not cover this subject. Applicable state law may provide nothing at all on the subject, or may not provide a provision suitable for your client's situation.

For example, the Uniform Principal and Income Act (1997) ("UPIA 1997"), which has been adopted in some states, provides trust accounting rules for retirement plan *distributions*, but does not say how the trustee is to account for the retirement plan itself. Also, UPIA 1997 generally allocates 10% of any required distribution from a retirement plan to income. Amounts that are paid by the plan to the trust as dividends *per se* (for example, dividends distributed on stock held in an ESOP) are also allocated to income under UPIA 1997. All other distributions (i.e., 90% of required distributions, and 100% of non-required distributions) are generally allocated to principal. UPIA 1997, § 409. If a client whose trust would be governed by the law of a state that has adopted UPIA 1997 wants his trust beneficiary to receive the "income" of the trust, the 10% allocation rule may or may not reflect what the client means by "income."

For example, in the Belle/Burt example above, the UPIA 1997 definition would mean that Burt would receive only 10% of each year's MRD (plus income from the trust's non-retirement plan investments, including investments created by reinvestment of the "principal" portion of the required distributions).

UPIA 1997 also provides that a *larger* portion of any distribution is allocated to income to the extent such larger allocation is necessary for the trust to qualify for the federal estate tax marital deduction—but does not specify what that larger portion would be. UPIA 1997, § 409(e). Therefore, in a state that has adopted UPIA 1997, the state law definition of "income" with respect to a retirement plan payable to a marital deduction trust would be "at least 10% of any required distribution," with the upper limit not defined.

If you are drafting a trust under which important substantive rights of the beneficiaries depend on the distinction between "income" and "principal," and the trust may receive retirement benefits upon the client's death, it is advisable to include a provision explaining how retirement benefits are to be accounted for. Even if the applicable state law definition suits the client's needs perfectly, the state law could change before the trust becomes effective; for example, even the Uniform Principal and Income Act has evolved through three incarnations (1931, 1962 and 1997).

6.2 The Minimum Distribution Trust Rules

6.2.01 *Why complying with the trust rules matters*

§ 401(a)(9) generally requires that retirement benefits be entirely distributed out of the plan (and subjected to income tax) within five years after Participant's death (if he died before his required beginning date) (¶ 1.5.04), or over what would have been the remaining single life expectancy of the deceased participant (if he died on or after his required beginning date) (¶ 1.5.05). However, if the benefits are left to an individual (human) beneficiary, *or to a qualifying trust* (¶ 6.2.04), the benefits can be distributed, instead, in annual instalments over the individual beneficiary's life expectancy (or over the life expectancy of the oldest beneficiary of the trust; ¶ 1.5.08). See Chapter 1 for a full explanation of the minimum distribution rules.

In many cases, distribution over the life expectancy of a beneficiary provides substantially longer income tax deferral than does distribution over five years or over Participant's life expectancy. Since longer income tax deferral often translates into substantially more money for the family beneficiaries (¶ 1.2.01), it is important to consider whether the trust proposed to be named as beneficiary of retirement benefits "qualifies" under the IRS's minimum distribution trust rules.

Note, however, that the fact that a trust qualifies under the minimum distribution rules does not mean that the trust is a good choice as beneficiary of retirement benefits. Making benefits payable to a trust of which Spouse is the oldest (or even the sole) beneficiary results in substantially less income tax deferral than would be available (via the spousal rollover) for benefits left to Spouse outright *even if* the trust "passes" all the minimum distribution trust rules (see ¶ 3.3.10, ¶ 10.5.05). Also, complying with the "trust rules" does not solve the problem of high trust income tax rates (¶ 6.1.02).

6.2.02 *When complying with the trust rules doesn't matter*

Complying with the IRS's minimum distribution trust rules is not a requirement of making retirement benefits payable to a trust. If a trust named as beneficiary of a retirement plan "flunks" the rules, the trust still receives the benefits; it just does not get to use the life expectancy of the oldest trust beneficiary as the measuring period for required distributions.

There are cases in which it makes little or no difference whether the trust complies with the "trust rules." For example, many pension, profit sharing and 401(k) plans do not permit the "life expectancy" payout; they offer only the lump sum distribution form of death benefit. ¶ 1.5.09. If the client's retirement benefit is in this type of plan, then the life expectancy payout will not be available regardless of whether the trust "passes" the rules.

The identity of the trust beneficiary(ies) also may make qualification under the rules irrelevant. For example, if Participant is past his required beginning date (¶ 1.3), and the oldest beneficiary of the proposed trust is the same age as (or older than) Participant, then the payout period will be no longer if the trust "passes" the rules (the single life expectancy of the oldest trust beneficiary; ¶ 1.5.08) than if the trust "flunks" the rules (the single life expectancy of Participant; ¶ 1.5.05). Similarly, if the trust that is to be named as beneficiary of Participant's retirement plan is a charitable remainder trust that meets the requirements of § 664 (¶ 7.5.04) then the trust is income tax-exempt. An income tax-exempt entity does not need to take advantage of the income tax deferral potentially available under the life expectancy payout method, so passing the trust rules is irrelevant.

Finally, in some cases complying with the trust rules involves significant compromise with the client's other estate planning goals. It may be appropriate to sacrifice the income tax deferral possibilities of the life expectancy payout method in order to realize the client's other goals, especially if the retirement benefits are a relatively minor asset of the proposed trust. See the Joseph & Jennie case study, Chapter 11.

6.2.03 *Trust does not need to recite the MRD rules*

One thing the minimum rules do NOT require is that you specify in the trust instrument that the trustee must withdraw from the retirement plan the annual MRD. § 401(a)(9) requires the trustee to withdraw the MRD whether the trust instrument tells him to or not.

Nevertheless, practitioners frequently do mention the requirement of withdrawing the MRD for various reasons, such as: In a conduit trust (¶ 6.3.08), the minimum distribution rules are essentially incorporated into the substantive provisions of the trust, so they should be mentioned in that case. In other types of trusts it doesn't hurt to remind the trustee that he is supposed to comply with the minimum distribution rules. Finally, including language dealing with the minimum distribution rules makes it clear that the drafter was aware of these rules and that the dispositive terms of the trust are not meant to conflict with the minimum distribution rules. For example, in a marital deduction trust (¶ 3.3.07; Form 7.4, Appendix B) it is common to specify that the trustee must withdraw from the retirement plan "the greater of" the income (that Spouse is entitled to under the marital deduction rules) and the MRD.

6.2.04 *Trust beneficiaries can be "designated beneficiaries"*

Retirement plan death benefits generally may be distributed

over the life expectancy of Participant's "designated beneficiary." ¶ 1.5.06. A "designated beneficiary" means an individual (or group of individuals) who are to inherit the retirement benefits upon Participant's death. ¶ 1.7. Although the general rule is that a designated beneficiary must be an *individual*, the proposed regulations allow you to name a *trust* as beneficiary and still have a "designated beneficiary" for purposes of the minimum distribution rules. P.R. § 1.401(a)(9)-4, A-5. These rules permit you to look through a trust instrument, and treat the *trust beneficiaries* as if they had been named directly as Participant's beneficiaries, if the following four requirements are met:

1.   The trust must be valid under state law. ¶ 6.2.06.

2.   "The beneficiaries of the trust who are beneficiaries with respect to the trust's interest in the employee's benefit" must be "identifiable from the trust instrument." ¶ 6.2.07.

3.   "The trust is irrevocable or will, by its terms, become irrevocable upon the death of the" participant. ¶ 6.2.08.

4.   Certain documentation must be provided to "the plan administrator." ¶ 6.2.09-¶ 6.2.10.

If Participant dies leaving his retirement benefits to a trust, and the above four rules are satisfied, then, for purposes of § 401(a)(9), all beneficiaries of the trust "with respect to the trust's interest in [the] employee's benefit are treated as having been designated as beneficiaries of the employee under the plan." P.R. § 1.401(a)(9)-8, A-11.

However, just complying with these four rules does not in and of itself ensure that the "life expectancy" method will be available. For one thing, treating the trust beneficiaries as if they had been named as beneficiaries directly does not get you very far if the trust beneficiaries themselves do not qualify as "designated beneficiaries." Accordingly, the "fifth rule" is that:

5.   All beneficiaries of the trust must be individuals. ¶ 6.2.11.

Finally, there is another rule, not contained in the "trust" portion of the proposed regulations, but applicable to retirement benefits generally, which may affect the eligibility of a particular trust to use the life expectancy method:

6.   No person may have the power "to change the beneficiaries of the employee" after December 31 of the year after the year of Participant's death (that date is called the "Designation Date" in this Chapter; see ¶ 1.8). P.R. § 1.401(a)(9)-5, A-7(d)(1).

The implications of this "sixth rule" are not yet established; see ¶ 6.2.13.

The rules, though puzzling in several respects, are not terribly difficult to comply with in most typical estate planning situations, if that is an important goal. The obstacles to success are, first, that many practitioners are unaware of these rules and, second, that the application of the rules to several commonly used trust provisions is unclear at best and unfavorable at worst.

Examples of various trust provisions and how they fit into the rules discussed in this ¶ 6.2 can be found in the Trust Review Questionnaire, Appendix C.

6.2.05 *Date for testing trust's compliance with rules*

The relevant date for applying these questions is (except for the irrevocability requirement, which must be met as of the date of death; ¶ 6.2.08) the Designation Date. For example, if Participant died in 2001, the Designation Date is December 31, 2002. If the trust does not comply with the rules, but the Designation Date has not yet passed, then it may be possible to fix the problems so that the trust will comply by the Designation Date. For ideas on how to fix a trust see ¶ 10.2.

Once the Designation Date has passed, is there any requirement of ongoing compliance? The proposed regulations state that the trust must be in compliance with the trust rules "during any period during which required minimum distributions are being determined by treating the beneficiaries of the trust as designated beneficiaries." P.R. §1.401(a)(9)-4, A-5(b). Although this suggests that there must be some ongoing testing, the Applicable Distribution Period for post-death required distributions is irrevocably established on the Designation Date. P.R. §1.401(a)(9)-4, A-4; ¶ 1.5.07. If the trust meets all the requirements on the Designation Date it is not clear how, under the proposed regulations, the Applicable Distribution Period could change after the Designation Date even if the trust later fell out of compliance—for example, if the trust was in compliance with the rules on the Designation Date, but then later ceased to be a valid trust under state law.

6.2.06 *First Rule: trust must be valid under state law*

The first rule is that "The trust is a valid trust under state law, or would be but for the fact that there is no corpus."

For either a "living" trust or a testamentary trust, the question is not whether the trust is a valid existing trust when it is named as beneficiary, or as of the moment Participant dies, but whether it WILL BE a valid trust on the Designation Date. P.R. §1.401(a)(9)-4, A-5(b)(1). By that time, presumably, even a testamentary trust will be funded and operating.

A trust that would be *in*valid under state law should be rare; examples would include a trust that violates the rule against perpetuities, or a trust that violates public policy ("The trustee shall pay $1000 to my daughter every time she robs a bank"), or a trust that has no beneficiaries.

6.2.07 *Second Rule: beneficiaries must be identifiable*

The requirement that the beneficiaries of the trust be "identifiable" means that it must be possible, on the Designation Date, to determine who is the oldest person who could ever be a beneficiary of the trust. See P.R. § 1.401(a)(9)-4, A-1. You need to ascertain who the oldest beneficiary is because it is the oldest beneficiary (or, as the IRS puts it, the beneficiary "with the shortest life expectancy") whose life expectancy is used as the measuring period for required distributions after Participant's death. ¶ 1.5.08.

A beneficiary "need not be specified by name" so long as he is "identifiable." Thus, if the trust beneficiaries are "all my issue living from time to time," the beneficiaries are "identifiable" even though the class is not closed as of the applicable date, since no person with a shorter life expectancy can be added later. The oldest member of the class can be determined with certainty on the Designation Date. P.R. § 1.401(a)(9)-4, A-1.

Actually, there *is* theoretically a problem even with the common provision "the trust shall be distributed to my issue living at the time of my spouse's death." If people who are issue by virtue of legal adoption are to be included on the same basis as "natural" issue, there is a potential for violating the rule. After Participant's death, one of his issue could adopt someone who was born earlier than the person who was the oldest beneficiary of the trust at the Designation Date. It is not known whether the IRS would ever raise this "issue," but to avoid the problem, language can be included in the trust providing that older individuals cannot be later added to the class of trust beneficiaries by legal adoption. See Form 7.3, Appendix B.

The rule that the beneficiaries must be "identifiable" is similar to the rule against perpetuities, in that the mere *possibility* that an older beneficiary could be added to the trust after the applicable date is enough to make the trust flunk this rule, regardless of whether any such older beneficiary ever is *actually* added.

Example: Kit leaves his IRA to a trust that is to pay income to his daughter Julia for her life, and after her death is to pay income to her widower (if any) for his life, with remainder to Kit's grandchildren. Kit dies, survived by Julia and several grandchildren, all of whom are still living on the Designation Date. His trust flunks this Second Rule, because Julia, after the Designation Date, *could* marry a new husband who is older than she. Thus an older beneficiary *could* be added to this trust after the applicable date, and we cannot tell with certainty who is the oldest person who could ever be a beneficiary of the trust.

Any "power of appointment"or trustee "spray power" under which older beneficiaries *could* be added to the trust at a later date violates this rule. However, in certain cases you are permitted to disregard remainder beneficiaries of the trust. ¶ 6.3.04. In those cases you can also disregard any power of appointment that affects only the identity of remainder beneficiaries who could be disregarded.

6.2.08 *Third Rule: irrevocability requirement*

The third rule is: "The trust is irrevocable or will, by its terms, become irrevocable upon the death of the employee." Generally, any testamentary trust or "living trust" automatically becomes irrevocable upon the testator's or donor's death, and therefore passes this test. The proposed regulations specifically state that testamentary trusts can comply with the IRS's trust rules. P.R. § 1.401(a)(9)-5, A-7(c)(3),

Examples 2 and 3; Preamble, "Trust as beneficiary."

Unfortunately, it is not clear what the IRS is driving at with this rule. The IRS has never given an example of a trust that does not become irrevocable at Participant's death. Perhaps the regulation-writers are thinking of a situation where someone *other than* Participant has a power to "revoke" the trust after Participant's death. The word "revoke" implies that the donor is taking back a gift; so if the retirement benefits that pass to the trust come from Participant, a power held by someone else to remove all the assets from the trust would not really be a power to "revoke" the trust.

However, possibly the term "revoke" could apply to a trust even after Participant's death in the following situation: Participant owns an IRA that is community property. He leaves the IRA to a trust. Spouse has the power to "revoke" that trust with respect to Spouse's community property interest in any property in the trust, and that power would allow her to cancel the trust with respect to the IRA. It appears that the trust is not "irrevocable" as to the IRA proceeds up to the maximum amount that is subject to Spouse's power. If she exercises the power (removes the IRA from the trust), there is no problem; since the IRA is no longer part of the trust, we don't care whether the trust passes the trust rules. If Spouse does *not* exercise the power (for example, if she chooses to take out other assets, instead of the IRA, to satisfy her community property interest) the trust would presumably be considered revocable, as of Participant's death, with regard to the IRA. Since this is one test that must be met as of the date of death (rather than as of the Designation Date), presumably the only way to correct this problem would be by means of a qualified disclaimer (Chapter 8).

A trustee's power, after Participant's death, to amend administrative provisions of the trust should not be considered a power to "revoke," provided it is clear the trustee's power does not permit him to materially modify any beneficial interests. However, this point is not covered in the proposed regulations or any ruling.

Including in the trust the statement "This trust shall be irrevocable upon my death" is not necessary, since any testamentary trust or "living trust" automatically becomes irrevocable upon the testator's or donor's death, and therefore passes this test. On the other hand it does no harm to include this sentence, and inclusion may avoid the necessity of argument with possible future plan administrators and auditing IRS agents who may not be familiar with estate planning.

6.2.09 *Fourth Rule: documentation requirement (post-death)*

The trustee of the trust that is named as beneficiary must supply to the plan administrator (or, in the case of an IRA, to the IRA trustee, custodian, or issuer; P.R. § 1.408-8, A-1(b)) either a copy of the trust instrument or the alternative compliance information no later than the Designation Date. P.R. § 1.401(a)(9)-4, A-6(b).

Here is the information required to be supplied to the plan administrator in (lieu of a copy of the trust instrument) under the alternative method of compliance: the trustee must provide "...a final list of all beneficiaries of the trust (including contingent and remaindermen beneficiaries with a description of the conditions on their entitlement) as of the [Designation Date]; certify that, to the best of the trustee's knowledge, this list is correct and complete and that the [other three "trust rules"] are satisfied; and agree to provide a copy of the trust instrument to the plan administrator upon demand...." P.R. § 1.401(a)(9)-4, A-6(b)(1). An example of a certification intended to comply with this rule is provided at Form 6.2, Appendix B.

Supplying a copy of the trust itself would appear to be a simpler way of complying than providing a summary of the trust. However, some retirement plans may decide to require the alternative method of compliance, since the alternative method relieves the plan administrator of the burden of reading the trust and determining whether it complies with all the technical requirements of the trust rules.

6.2.10 *Documentation requirement for lifetime distributions*

For *lifetime* required distributions, Participant must supply a copy of the trust (or the alternative compliance information) to the plan administrator. However, the identity of the trust beneficiaries is irrelevant to the determination of lifetime distributions if Participant is using the Uniform Table (¶ 1.4.01). Therefore, Participant has no need to comply with the "trust documentation requirement" (or any other trust rules) for his lifetime distributions *unless*: (a) Participant has named a trust as Participant's sole beneficiary; and (b) Participant's spouse is the "sole" beneficiary of the trust (¶ 6.3.13); and (c) Spouse is sufficiently younger than Participant that required distributions are lower if computing using the joint life expectancy of husband and wife rather than the Uniform Table (¶ 1.4.02); and (d) Participant wants to use the actual joint life expectancy (rather than the Uniform Table) to measure his MRDs. P.R., Preamble, "Trust as beneficiary."

In this case Participant presumably must comply with the documentation requirement no later than the beginning of the distribution year in which he intends to use the spouses' joint life expectancy to calculate his MRDs, although it would be helpful if the IRS would spell out that deadline in the trust rule itself.

Note that in the case of lifetime required distributions the person who must fulfill this requirement is *Participant* (not the trustee, as is the case when Participant dies). P.R. § 1.401(a)(9)-4, A-6(a).

6.2.11 *Fifth Rule: all beneficiaries must be individuals*

The result of compliance with the first four rules is that the trust beneficiaries will be treated as if Participant had named them directly as beneficiaries. ¶ 6.2.04. The next step, therefore, is to make sure that these trust beneficiaries qualify as "designated beneficiaries," *i.e.*, that they are individuals. This requirement is much trickier than it appears. For one thing, some or all remainder beneficiaries count as beneficiaries for this purpose; see ¶ 6.3.

Another major pitfall in this rule is that, according to the proposed regulations, an "estate" is not an individual and therefore an "estate" cannot be a designated beneficiary. ¶ 1.7.04. Therefore, if any part of the trust's interest in the benefits will pass to an estate, Participant has "no designated beneficiary" (unless the estate can be disregarded; ¶ 6.3.04).

6.2.12 *Paying estate expenses, taxes, etc. from the trust*

Some IRS letter rulings suggest that even indirectly allowing benefits to pass to Participant's estate (as through a trust provision which allows or directs the use of trust property to pay Participant's debts or probate expenses) may be treated the same as naming the estate as a beneficiary and may result in having "no designated beneficiary." See, *e.g.*, PLR 9809059, in which part of an IRA was payable to "Trust K." In ruling that Trust K was entitled to use the "life expectancy method" for the IRA benefits payable to it, the IRS noted that "Trust K does *not* provide that trust assets shall be used to pay funeral costs," probate expenses or estate taxes (emphasis added). Although the ruling does not comment on the absence of such a provision, it merely recites the fact that the trust contained no such provision, one could conclude that the IRS ruled favorably on Trust K only because it did not contain the (forbidden?) clause.

The IRS, having apparently adopted this unfortunate position, then seems to bend over backwards in rulings to find a way around its own rule. In letter rulings regarding IRAs payable to trusts, the IRS has taken to reciting that state law exempted the IRAs from claims of creditors, without specifying what the relevance of such a state law provision is. This creates the impression that the state law exemption of the benefits from claims of creditors was significant, perhaps as "proof" that the trustee could not distribute retirement benefits to the estate to pay debts, expenses and taxes (although it doesn't prove that). See, e.g., PLR 2001-31033.

Planning mode: It would be highly advisable to amend the trust so it either prohibits this use of the retirement benefits, or requires that no such payments may be made from the retirement benefits on or after the Designation Date. See Form 7.2, Appendix B. (Note that this Form will not solve the problem if the trust has non-individual *remainder* beneficiaries; see ¶ 7.3.03.) If there are no assets available to pay debts, expenses and taxes other than retirement benefits, consider specifying that only certain retirement plans may be used for this purpose and other plans may not be, so that only the retirement plans authorized to be used to pay the debts and expenses will be "tainted," and the other(s) can be exempted from this problem; or have Participant take withdrawals during life so his estate will have sufficient non-plan assets to pay these items.

Cleanup mode: If the Designation Date has not yet passed, the trustee can withdraw from the retirement plan as much money as is expected to be needed from the plan to pay debts, expenses and taxes (if any will be so needed), then have all parties (trustee, executor, beneficiaries) agree that the estate will not claim any more funds from the retirement plan under this provision; or divide the plan into two separate accounts, and have all the parties agree that only one of them is allowed to be used to pay these items. If the agreement is binding under applicable state law on all future fiduciaries and beneficiaries of the estate, it should work to insulate the benefits from being considered payable to the estate after the Designation Date. If it is not feasible to eliminate the offending trust provision by one of these methods, the IRS may approve a fact-based argument (e.g., if you show that all realistically expected claims, debts and taxes have either been paid or provided for prior to the Designation Date, or that state law exempts retirement benefits from creditors' claims) and give a ruling.

6.2.13 *Sixth Rule: no changing beneficiaries after Designation Date*

The proposed regulations provide that "If the plan provides (or allows the employee to specify) that, after end of the calendar year following the calendar year in which the employee died, any person or persons have the discretion to change the beneficiaries of the employee, then for purposes of determining the distribution period after the employee's death, the employee will be treated as not having designated a beneficiary." P.R. § 1.401(a)(9)-5, A-7(d)(1). The intent and meaning of this provision are unclear. Might a "spray" power not limited by an ascertainable standard, or any other "power of appointment," be considered "the discretion to change the beneficiaries of the employee" after his death?

Judging by letter rulings approving trusts which contained powers to appoint principal among Participant's issue (1999-03050 ("Trust B"), 1999-18065 ("Trust 2")), the IRS apparently did not intend to prohibit this common estate planning device. Accordingly, it is commonly assumed that a power of appointment (or trustee spray power) that is *limited to a narrowly defined group* (such as Participant's "children" or "issue") does not violate the rule.

On the other hand, if the IRS intends to distinguish between these common estate planning devices (which are apparently permitted) and some broader category of "discretions" (which would be prohibited), the dividing line is not known. The IRS has never given any example of a beneficiary designation, plan provision or trust provision which would violate this "sixth rule." So, to err on the side of caution, until the IRS clarifies the boundaries, it would be wise to limit the potential appointees under a power of appointment to a narrow and clearly defined group, unless the power can be disregarded (¶ 6.3.04).

Also, under many states' laws, any power to appoint property to individuals includes the power to appoint in trust for such individuals. The IRS has never commented on the effect of such a state law in any private letter rulings or in the proposed regulations. Since the proposed regulations require that, if benefits are distributable under one trust to another trust, *both* trusts must comply with the rules (unless the distributee trust is "disregardable"; see ¶ 6.3.04), it would appear that any power of appointment that could be exercised by appointing in trust would cause a trust to flunk the trust rules unless the power is limited to appointing only to other trusts that comply with the rules. P.R. § 1.401(a)(9)-4, A-5(c).

Planning mode: Either do not use powers of appointment *at all* in trusts that are to receive retirement benefits, or be sure that such powers allow appointment of the benefits only to a small, clearly-defined group of individuals who are younger than the otherwise-oldest trust beneficiary, and specify that the power may be exercised only to appoint to such individuals outright or to a trust that complies with the minimum distribution trust rules.

Cleanup mode: Presumably § 1.401(a)(9)-5, A-7(d) is intended to interpret the statutory definition of "designated beneficiary" as "any individual designated as a beneficiary *by the employee.*" § 401(a)(9)(E) (emphasis added). It seems a reasonable interpretation of the statute that a narrowly defined group of individuals meets the statutory definition, even if Participant left it up to a beneficiary (holding a power of appointment) or a trustee (holding a spray power) to appoint the property among this group.

6.3 Who Are the Beneficiaries of a Trust?

6.3.01 *Post-death distributions; benefits and "proceeds" thereof*

This ¶ 6.3 deals only with ascertaining who are the beneficiaries of a trust for purposes of applying the minimum distribution rules to required distributions after the death of Participant. The trust rules apply to lifetime required distributions only in rare cases (see ¶ 6.2.10); that topic is not discussed directly here.

Also, note that whenever the proposed regulation discusses a trust's interest in a retirement plan that term includes not just the retirement plan itself and the distributions from the retirement plan, but also the "proceeds" resulting from the trust's reinvestment of the retirement plan distributions. Thus, the rules "care about" who is the beneficiary of the trust even after the retirement plan has ceased to exist (because 100% of it has been distributed to the trustee of the trust that was named as beneficiary of the retirement plan). The tests apply to that trust as long as the trust holds any distributions that were retained ("accumulated") in the trust even though they were reinvested in other forms of investment.

Example: Olga's retirement plan is payable to a trust. The trustee of the trust is instructed to withdraw all benefits from the retirement plan over a period of time not exceeding the life expectancy of Olga's husband Olaf, and to withdraw any remaining benefits from the plan upon Olaf's death. The trustee is to pay income of the trust to Olaf for his life, and after Olaf's death is to pay income to Olga's and Olaf's son Olaf Jr. for his life. On the death of Olaf Jr., the principal of the trust is to be paid to a remainder beneficiary. Under the minimum distribution trust rules we need to determine who that remainder beneficiary is, and include that remainder beneficiary when testing to see if (for example) all the trust beneficiaries are "individuals." Even though the retirement plan won't exist at that point (because it was all distributed to the trust no later than Olaf's death), the trust assets at that point will include the reinvested "proceeds" of the retirement plan distributions. Thus, if the remainder beneficiary who takes after Olaf Jr.'s death is not an individual the trust flunks the fifth rule (¶ 6.2.11).

6.3.02 Importance of definition of "trust beneficiary"

To apply the minimum distribution trust rules to a particular trust, we need to determine who are the "beneficiaries" of that trust. The trust beneficiaries who are "beneficiaries with respect to the trust's interest in" the retirement benefits must be "identifiable from the trust instrument." P.R. § 1.401(a)(9)-4, A-5(b)(3) (¶ 6.2.07). All beneficiaries of the trust must be individuals (¶ 6.2.11). Unfortunately the proposed regulations never define "trust beneficiary," leaving substantial doubt, in many cases, regarding whether a particular trust "passes" the rules or not.

This ¶ 6.3 discusses the question of which trust beneficiaries "count" for purposes of the minimum distribution trust rules, and which may be disregarded. If a trust has a non-individual beneficiary, the trust will "flunk" the rules—unless the rules allow that beneficiary to be disregarded. If it is not possible to identify the oldest person who could ever possibly be a beneficiary of the trust, then the trust again flunks, because its beneficiaries are not "identifiable"—unless the rules allow you to disregard the provision that creates the possibility of an "unidentifiable" beneficiary.

The first step in the process is to see whether certain beneficiaries may be disregarded because, even though they are beneficiaries of the overall trust, they cannot possibly receive any of the retirement benefits payable to that trust

6.3.03 *Beneficiaries with respect to "trust's interest in the benefits"*

In determining who are the "beneficiaries," we need be concerned only with beneficiaries who are such "with respect to the trust's interest in the employee's benefit." P.R. §§ 1.401(a)(9)-4, A-5(b)(3); 1.401(a)(9)-8, A-11 (last sentence).

Example 1: Calvin's IRA is payable to a trust. At his death the trust assets are divided between a marital trust and a credit shelter trust. However, Calvin's IRA is required to be paid to the marital trust (either because the plan beneficiary designation form names the marital trust directly as beneficiary, or because the trust requires that all retirement benefits are to be allocated to the marital trust). We need look only at the *beneficiaries of the marital trust* in applying the various tests and questions. However, if neither the beneficiary designation form nor the trust instrument requires (as of the applicable date) that all benefits be paid to one share or the other, then we need to look at all beneficiaries of both shares.

Example 2: Katerina's 401(k) plan benefits are payable to her living trust as beneficiary. The trust provides for distributions to be made to her husband Lou, various relatives and assorted charities. However, the trust contains a provision prohibiting use of retirement benefits to pay charitable bequests. Accordingly, the charities are not trust beneficiaries "with respect to the trust's interest in the employee benefit," and can be disregarded.

Note that this is not a "separate account" rule (see ¶ 1.7.06). Disregarding beneficiaries who are prohibited from sharing in the retirement benefit does not depend on the existence of "separate accounts" at the plan level or "separate shares" (¶ 7.4.04) in the usual tax or trust accounting sense. The conclusions in the above examples are based on the proposed regulations' statement that beneficiaries of the trust "with respect to the trust's interest in [the] employee's benefit are treated as having been designated as beneficiaries of the employee under the plan." P.R. § 1.401(a)(9)-8, A-11.

In the rest of this ¶ 6.3, "beneficiaries of the trust" means "beneficiaries of the trust with respect to the trust's interest in the employee's benefit."

Second, we must conclude that "all" trust beneficiaries ("current" beneficiaries, as well as those who have vested or contingent remainder interests) are considered "beneficiaries of the trust" for purposes of the proposed regulations—unless they can be excluded from consideration under the rules discussed below.

6.3.04 *Beneficiaries who may be disregarded ("not considered")*

If the trust rules are complied with, then all "trust beneficiaries" (except those who have no interest in the benefits because they are categorically excluded from sharing in them; ¶ 6.3.03) are treated as having been named directly as beneficiaries by Participant. If the trust has more than one beneficiary, then: "In the case of payments to a trust having more than one beneficiary, see A-7 of section 1.401(a)(9)-5 for the rules for determining the designated beneficiary whose life expectancy will be used to determine the distribution period." P.R. § 1.401(a)(9)-4, A-5(c). A-7 is *also* to be used for determining whether all beneficiaries are individuals. P.R. § 1.401(a)(9)-5, A-7.

Here is what A-7 says: "If a beneficiary (subsequent beneficiary) is entitled to any portion of an employee's benefit *only if another beneficiary dies before the entire benefit to which that other beneficiary is entitled has been distributed by the plan*, the subsequent beneficiary will not be considered a beneficiary for purposes of determining who is the designated beneficiary with the shortest life expectancy under paragraph (a) of this A-7 or whether a beneficiary who is not an individual is a beneficiary." P.R. § 1.401(a)(9)-5, A-7(c)(1).

As discussed at ¶ 6.3.10-¶ 6.3.11, this rule does not provide meaningful guidance in testing trusts for compliance with the rules, unless we are to conclude that many typical family trusts do not comply with the rules.

Do you need to understand the above rule? Only if you are trying to disregard some of the trust's beneficiaries. If all possible beneficiaries of the trust are individuals, and you know for sure which one is the oldest, you don't need to worry about the "A-7" rule. See example at ¶ 6.3.07. If, on the other hand, there are some contingent charitable remainder beneficiaries (for example), and you are hoping they don't count as "beneficiaries" of the trust at all (so your trust complies with the rule that all beneficiaries must be individuals), then you have to sit down and study the A-7 rule and see if you can come up with an interpretation of it that allows your trust to "pass."

The IRS has provided two examples of trusts that definitely comply with the rule. See ¶ 6.3.07 and ¶ 6.3.08. There are additional examples of trusts that are believed to comply with the rule; see ¶ 6.3.09 and ¶ 6.3.10. Finally, certain trusts definitely flunk the rule; see ¶ 6.3.05.

To understand the following discussion, it is essential to bear in mind the distinctions between "trust accounting income" and "MRDs" discussed at ¶ 6.1.07.

6.3.05 *Remainder beneficiaries generally do count*

If any distributions from the retirement plan to the trust made during the lifetime of the life beneficiary of the trust can be accumulated and held for the remainder beneficiaries, then the remainder beneficiaries must be counted as "beneficiaries." See P.R. § 1.401(a)(9)-5, A-7(c)(3), Example 2. Under the typical form of trust that provides income to one beneficiary remainder to another (such as a "QTIP" trust; ¶ 3.3.04) both the remainder beneficiary and the income beneficiary "count."

Example: Lou names a trust as beneficiary of his IRA. The trust is to pay all trust accounting income to Judy for life, and on Judy's death the principal goes to the Red Cross. Principal (that is, trust accounting principal) distributed from the retirement plan during Judy's life is "accumulated" in the trust, that is to say, it is held in the trust until Judy dies, and then it is turned over to the Red Cross. Accordingly, the Red Cross, as remainder beneficiary, *is* counted as a beneficiary of the trust, and therefore this trust "flunks" the rules because not all beneficiaries are individuals. See PLR 9820021 (a trust which provided income to spouse and remainder to charities; ruled, Participant had "no designated beneficiary"); see also, *e.g.*, PLR 9322005 (marital trust to a spouse for life, remainder to children; spouse *and children* regarded as beneficiaries).

Thus, if a trust with a vested charitable remainder is named as beneficiary of retirement plan death benefits, Participant "has no designated beneficiary." (See ¶ 1.5.04 and ¶ 1.5.05 for the result.)

If the remainder beneficiary is an individual, but is older than the life beneficiary the remainder beneficiary is the "oldest trust beneficiary" for purposes of measuring required distributions. Even though this result is illogical (because the remainder beneficiary will die before the life beneficiary, according to the IRS's actuarial tables, and so is not predicted to receive anything under the trust) it seems to be the IRS's position.

The same rule applies even if the trust is not *required* to "accumulate" the retirement plan distributions for the charitable (or older individual) remainder beneficiary, but *could* do so. In the Lou/Judy example above, giving the trustee discretion to distribute principal to Judy would not solve the problem; the charitable remainder beneficiary would still "count" as a trust beneficiary because the trustee also has discretion *not* to distribute principal to Judy but rather accumulate it for the charity.

If the remainder beneficiary is another trust, both trusts must comply with the trust rules (unless the remainder trust can be disregarded; see ¶ 6.3.04). P.R. § 1.401(a)(9)-4, A-5(c).

6.3.06 *Effect of powers of appointment*

It appears that if a "countable" remainder interest is subject to a power of appointment upon the death of the life beneficiary, all potential appointees are considered "beneficiaries." Thus (unless potential appointees can be ignored; see ¶ 6.3.04) potential appointees should be (i) identifiable (ii) individuals who are (iii) younger than the beneficiary whose life expectancy is the one that the parties want to use to measure distributions.

A provision such as "The trustee shall pay income to my spouse for life, and upon my spouse's death the principal shall be paid to such persons *among the class consisting of our issue* as my spouse shall appoint by her will" does not create a problem under this rule because the power is limited to a small, clearly-defined group of "identifiable" younger individuals. But "...upon my spouse's death the principal shall be paid to such members of *the class consisting of our issue and any charity* as my spouse shall appoint by her will" *does* create a problem: the benefits could pass under the power to a non-individual beneficiary, so this trust flunks this rule.

This does not necessarily mean that, so long as potential appointees are limited to younger individuals, a power of appointment is automatically "ok"; see ¶ 6.2.13.

Finally, if exercise of the power of appointment can affect the benefits only at a point where a contingent beneficiary could be ignored, the power can also be ignored. In other words, if you could disregard a contingent beneficiary, you can disregard a power of appointment that would determine the identity of that contingent beneficiary. See ¶ 6.3.04.

6.3.07 *Trust which cannot possibly pass to non-individuals*

One way to deal with the mystery of "which beneficiaries can be disregarded" is to draft the trust so there are no beneficiaries you *need* to disregard. If the trust property cannot under any circumstances be distributed to a non-individual beneficiary, then it passes the rule. For example, if the trust provides "income to spouse for life, remainder to our issue living at spouse's death; provided, if at any time during spouse's life there are no issue of ours living, the trust shall terminate and be distributed to spouse," it is impossible for the trust assets to pass to anyone other than spouse or issue, all of whom are individuals. Under the most conservative interpretation of the A-7 rule, this and the "conduit trust" described in the next subsection are the only trusts which pass the fifth rule.

6.3.08 *Conduit trusts (also called "MRD conduit trusts")*

A "conduit trust" is not an official term, but is a nickname for a trust which serves as a conduit for distributions from the retirement plan to the individual beneficiary of the trust. The trustee is required to withdraw the minimum distributions from the retirement plan over the life expectancy of the individual trust beneficiary (or of the oldest member of a group of individual trust beneficiaries) and distribute the distributions out to that beneficiary (or the members of the group).

The trustee does not have the power to hold and retain inside the trust any plan distributions made during the lifetime of the beneficiary (or of the oldest beneficiary). If the (oldest) trust beneficiary lives to his or her full life expectancy, 100% of the benefits will have been distributed out to individuals. With a conduit trust, the retirement benefits are deemed paid to the individual beneficiary for purposes of the minimum distribution rules, and the "all beneficiaries must be individuals" test is met. Remainder beneficiaries can be disregarded, because their entitlement to share in the benefits is dependant on the conduit-beneficiary dying before the plan has distributed all the benefits. See P.R. § 1.401(a)(9)-5, A-7(c)(3), Example 3, and examples under question 7 in the Trust Review Questionnaire, Appendix C.

The conduit trust could be useful in the following situations:

A.   Aunt Emily believes that leaving her IRA to her young nephews is a fine way to provide them with a retirement nest egg, but knows that, if she names them directly as beneficiaries, they will simply cash out the account immediately upon her death. So she leaves the IRA to a conduit trust for them. The purpose of the trust is to make sure that the nephews take advantage of the "life expectancy method," whether they want to or not, and to provide professional management for the undistributed portion of the IRA. The trustee is instructed to withdraw from the IRA, each year, the MRD (based on the life expectancy of the oldest nephew) and distribute it equally to the surviving nephews.

B.   Eli wants to leave his IRA to his wife Laura, but is concerned about her ability to handle a large sum of money that becomes subject to her control all at once. He is confident that she would handle wisely a stream of installment payments from the IRA. So he makes the IRA payable to a trust. The trustee will withdraw from the IRA and distribute to Laura each year the greater of the income of the IRA (see ¶ 3.3.07) or the MRD based on Laura's life expectancy.

Under the conduit trust approach, the primary trust beneficiary is in the same position as if he had been named directly, individually, as beneficiary of the benefits, but with a variation: it is as if Participant, instead of leaving it up to the beneficiary to decide when and how to take out the benefits, had specified a payout mode as well as a beneficiary. In this case, it is as if Participant had specified that distributions would be paid in instalments over the life expectancy of the designated beneficiary. If the designated beneficiary (or life beneficiary of the conduit trust) lives to his life expectancy, he will have received 100% of the benefits and the remainder beneficiary will receive nothing. If the designated beneficiary (or life beneficiary of the conduit trust) dies before the end of his life expectancy period, the remaining benefits will be paid to the remainder beneficiary of the trust (analogous to a contingent beneficiary).

The IRS has specified that under this type of trust the remainder beneficiary is not considered a beneficiary of the trust for purposes of the trust rules, and so can be disregarded. P.R. § 1.401(a)(9)-5, A-7(c)(3), Example 3.

Unfortunately, this type of trust is not useful in many situations. To work as intended it depends entirely the minimum distribution payout scheme staying exactly as it is under present law and being followed slavishly by the trustee. If changes in the law require or encourage faster distributions the trust beneficiary will receive the money much sooner than Participant intended.

For discussion of using conduit trusts in connection with a non-QDOT marital trust, see ¶ 10.5.05(C); in connection with a credit shelter trust, see ¶ 10.5.03(D).

Practice Note: The life expectancy payout period under a conduit trust could last longer than the Rule Against Perpetuities would permit the trust to last. Even though the maximum payout period for post-death MRDs is an individual beneficiary's single life expectancy, the beneficiary whose life expectancy is being used as a measuring period could die more than 21 years before the end of his IRS-defined life expectancy, in which case (if his was the only measuring life), the trust could (depending on exactly what the dispositive terms are at that point) be in existence more than 21 years after the termination of "lives in being" at the commencement of the trust. The trust drafter should take care that the payout period required by the trust does not exceed the "perpetuities" period under applicable state law.

6.3.09 § 678(a)(1) grantor trusts

Under the so-called "grantor trust rules" of the Code, a trust beneficiary who is a U.S. citizen or resident is treated for all purposes of the federal income tax as the "owner" of trust assets if such beneficiary has the sole unrestricted right to withdraw those assets from the trust. See §§ 678(a)(1), 672(f), as interpreted in regulations (see especially Reg. § 1.671-3(b)). See example at Question 6 of the Trust

Review Questionnaire, Appendix C. It would appear that if an individual beneficiary is deemed the owner of all of the trust's assets under § 678, then retirement benefits payable to such trust must be deemed paid "to" such individual beneficiary for purposes of the minimum distribution rules, and the "all beneficiaries must be individuals" test is met.

See, *e.g.*, PLR 1999-03050 ("Trust A"), in which the IRS ruled with respect to a marital trust under which the surviving spouse had the unlimited right to withdraw all principal and income: "You are the beneficiary of Trust A because the terms of Trust A provide that you may invade principal in your absolute discretion. Thus, the beneficiaries' entitlement to benefits after your death is essentially contingent upon your death within the meaning of...the proposed regulations and they are not considered." Note, however, that this ruling was under the old (1987-2000) proposed regulations and in any case did not mention § 678.

Treating the trust beneficiary as the owner of the benefits for income tax purposes has two significant results: income taxes on the trust's income will be imposed at the beneficiary's rate; and the remainder beneficiary will not be considered a beneficiary of the trust for purposes of the minimum distribution rules. Thus an estate, older individuals or charities can be named as remainder beneficiaries (to succeed to whatever part of the trust is not distributed to or withdrawn by the owner-beneficiary during his/her life) without loss of the use of the owner-beneficiary's life expectancy as the measuring period for required distributions. Similarly, a power of appointment that affects the trust property only after the death of the owner-beneficiary can be disregarded

Under this model, the trust beneficiary is given the unlimited right to withdraw the benefits (and any "proceeds" thereof; ¶ 6.3.01) from the trust at any time. Until the beneficiary chooses to exercise this right, the trustee exercises ownership rights and responsibilities on the beneficiary's behalf, for example, by investing the trust funds, choosing distribution options, and distributing income and/or principal to or for the benefit of the beneficiary.

This type of trust would be uncommon, since anyone wanting to give such broad rights to the beneficiary would presumably choose to leave the benefits outright to the beneficiary rather than in trust. However, there are two situations in which this model could be useful:

(a)   A marital deduction "qualified domestic trust" (QDOT) for the benefit of a non-citizen spouse (§ 2056A), where the only purpose of placing a trust between the surviving spouse and the retirement benefits is to qualify for the modified marital deduction available when the surviving spouse is not a U.S. citizen. See ¶ 4.3.02.

(b)   A trust to provide for a mentally handicapped beneficiary who can exercise the right of withdrawal only through a legal guardian. For this type of beneficiary, this type of trust provides the benefits of a discretionary trust without losing the benefits of the "life expectancy" method based on the life expectancy of the handicapped beneficiary. This can be particularly helpful where the primary beneficiary does not have and is not likely to have issue, and the only likely remainder beneficiaries are the primary beneficiary's older siblings, the beneficiary's own estate or charities.

Unfortunately, the IRS has never mentioned § 678(a)(1) either in the private letter rulings or in the proposed minimum distribution regulations, so the above conclusions are based on the author's analysis without the comforting assurance of any IRS pronouncements. See "Answer C" in the Trust Review Questionnaire, Appendix C, for more comments.

6.3.10 *Remainder contingent on premature death*

What if there is a charitable remainder interest that is not vested, but rather is contingent on all the family beneficiaries dying young, or dying "out of actuarial order" (what lawyers sometimes refer to as the "wipe-out clause")? The test for whether such a beneficiary can be disregarded is: A contingent remainder beneficiary does not count (i.e. is disregarded) if he, she or it will receive a share of the benefits only if the prior (individual) beneficiaries die before their share of the plan benefits "has been distributed by the plan." P.R. § 1.401(a)(9)-5, A-7(c)(1). Unfortunately, the meaning of this provision of the proposed regulations is subject to substantial doubt.

It seems *probable* that what the IRS means is this: Determine what happens to the retirement benefits (including "proceeds" thereof, i.e., amounts distributed from the plan and reinvested by the trust) if all the people who are living on the Designation Date and who are now (or may in the future be) beneficiaries of the trust live exactly to their IRS life expectancy and then die. If the retirement benefits (or proceeds thereof) *must* pass to individuals under those circumstances, then the trust passes the test, and any non-individual contingent remainder beneficiary can be disregarded because it will receive a share of the benefits only if the prior (individual) beneficiaries die otherwise than at the end of their IRS-defined life expectancy. This "hidden actuarial component" must be included in the test in order for many typical family trusts used in estate planning for pass the test. See examples at question 9 of the Trust Review Questionnaire, Appendix C.

However, the proposed regulations do not mention or endorse this "actuarial" test. If the proposed regulations are read literally the only trust under which the remainder beneficiaries can be disregarded is the conduit trust (¶ 6.3.08), the trust which requires the trustee to distribute all benefits to the individual trust beneficiaries as soon as such benefits have been distributed from the retirement plan to the trust. Accordingly, a trust which passes the trust rules only upon application of the "hidden actuarial component" is outside the safe harbor.

Example: Hunter leaves his IRA to a trust which provides "income to my wife Anita for life, and on her death the principal shall pass to our child, Peter, if he is then living, or, if he is then deceased, shall pass to Massachusetts Audubon Society." Massachusetts Audubon Society is not an individual. Does this trust "pass?"

To test the trust under the A-7 rule, you have to start with an assumption that the trust does "pass" the trust requirements and therefore the benefits will be distributed to the trust over the single life expectancy of Anita, the oldest beneficiary. (If, after we test the trust using that assumption, we find it doesn't "pass," then required distributions will be based on the schedule required if Hunter had "no designated beneficiary" rather than on Anita's life expectancy.) On Anita's death, the trust principal (including portions of the retirement plan that were distributed during Anita's life but which were treated as trust "principal" rather than trust "income" and so were not distributed to Anita) passes to son Peter. Therefore, son Peter definitely does count as a beneficiary because he is entitled to some of the IRA (or to some of the IRA proceeds) *regardless* of when Anita dies (not "only if [Anita] dies before the entire benefit to which [Anita] is entitled has been distributed by the plan").

The Audubon Society will receive something from this trust

only if Peter (the "other beneficiary") dies before his share of the benefits (the principal distributed during Anita's life, and the balance remaining in the IRA at Anita's death) has been distributed by the plan (i.e. before the end of *Anita's* life). However, this conclusion depends on the hidden actuarial component, for the following reason. If we are *not* entitled to assume that each individual lives exactly to his or her IRS-defined life expectancy and then dies, there are two scenarios in which both of the individual beneficiaries of this trust could die *after* "the benefits to which they are entitled" have been "distributed by the plan," and the charity could still get the money. Thus, this trust would flunk if we take the IRS's stated test as it is literally written, and if we are not entitled to assume that each beneficiary lives to his or her life expectancy. Here are the two scenarios:

1   If Anita lives past her IRS-defined life expectancy, the entire plan balance would have been distributed to the trust at that point. She's still alive; then Peter dies before Anita; and then Anita dies; and the Audubon Society gets the money.

2   Even if Anita does not live past her IRS-defined life expectancy, suppose the trustee decides to cash out the IRA before the end of her life expectancy for some reason (before he is required to in other words). Then Peter dies before Anita; and then Anita dies; and the Audubon Society gets the money.

Thus there are two scenarios under which the entire plan balance could be distributed *before* Anita's death; therefore it is possible that Peter could die AFTER the entire plan balance has been distributed by the plan but also before Anita's death. In that case the Audubon Society would be entitled to share in the benefits even though neither prior beneficiary died "before the benefits to which they were entitled were distributed by the plan." Both Anita and Peter died *after* all plan benefits were distributed and yet the Audubon Society got some money.

Unless the IRS permits use of the actuarial assumption described above, this trust flunks the rule—no matter how actuarially unlikely it is that the Audubon Society will receive anything under this trust.

The same fate would apply to the typical trust for young beneficiaries that calls for the trust to terminate and be distributed to them outright at a certain age. If the age for distribution is within the beneficiary's IRS-defined life expectancy, a remainder beneficiary who takes only if the individual beneficiary dies prematurely should not be considered a beneficiary. However, under the rule as the IRS has written it, which may or may not be as the IRS intended it, such a remainder beneficiary could not be disregarded, and accordingly would have to be a younger individual in order for the trust to "pass."

Example: Sheila leaves her IRA to a trust for the benefit of her child Harvey, age 6. The trustee is given discretion to use income and principal for Harvey's support and education. The trust is to terminate, with all remaining assets being distributed to Harvey outright, when Harvey reaches age 30. If Harvey dies before age 30, the Cornell Ornithological Laboratory receives the trust property. In determining whether all trust beneficiaries are individuals, Cornell should be "disregardable," because its interest does not take effect unless the individual beneficiary (Harvey) dies before age 30, *i.e.*, well before the end of his life expectancy.

However, if the IRS's test is applied literally, then this trust flunks, because the charity does not take "only" if Harvey dies before his interest in the plan is distributed by the plan. For example, suppose that a few years after Sheila's death the trustee cashes out the entire IRA because Congress passed a law repealing the federal income tax for one year. Harvey is only 9 when this occurs. The entire interest in the benefits to which Harvey is entitled has been distributed by the plan. Now Harvey dies at age 21. The charity gets the trust because Harvey did not live to age 30. Since under this hypothetically possible scenario the charity would get the money even though Harvey did NOT die before his interest "was distributed by the plan," the trust flunks—no matter how unlikely this hypothetically possible scenario may be.

6.3.11 *Regulation's Example 2 needs clarification*

The only example the IRS provides that has any bearing on this is in P.R. § 1.401(a)(9)-5, A-7(c)(3), Example 2. In this example, we are told that "Under the terms of Trust P, all trust income is payable annually to B [Spouse of the deceased participant, A], and no one has the power to appoint Trust P principal to any person other than B. A's children, who are all younger than B, are the sole remainder beneficiaries of Trust P. *No other person has a beneficial interest in Trust* P." (Emphasis added.) In this example, the IRS is making the point that B and the children of A are all considered "beneficiaries" of Trust P, so the surviving spouse is not the sole beneficiary, but her life expectancy is used to measure required distributions because she is the oldest beneficiary.

This example is defective, however, because it does not deal with the question of what happens if all of A's children predecease B. Either the trust document or state law must have something to say on that point, but the IRS's example is silent. Yet the only way we would be entitled to disregard the beneficiaries ("contingent beneficiaries") who take in that case is if their interests are contingent on all the named individual beneficiaries' dying before their interests are distributed by the plan. Since the plan could distribute 100% of the benefits to the trust immediately upon the death of A, and these distributions could be held in the trust until the death of B, and all the children of Participant could die before B, then under the IRS's test, read literally, without the "hidden actuarial component," we are not entitled to disregard these contingent beneficiaries.

Here are all the possibilities for what happens to "Trust P" in Example 2 if all A's children die before B, and the result under the IRS's test (and under the IRS's test as modified by the "hidden actuarial component"):

1.   Perhaps the trust provides for further younger individual beneficiaries (such as the issue of A's children) to take the remainder interest if A's children predecease B. But that doesn't resolve the question, because every human being in the whole world could predecease B, and the question is where does the trust principal go if *that* happens?

2.   Perhaps the trust provides for a charity (or for the children's own estates) to take the remainder interest if A's children predecease B. In that case the trust would flunk, because the charity (or the children's estates) could receive the benefits if the beneficiaries die "out of actuarial order" (but after all the benefits have been distributed by the plan), *unless* we are entitled to assume that the beneficiaries will not die "out of actuarial order." If we are entitled to assume that B will die at the end of her life expectancy period and that the children,

being younger than B, will outlive B, then the children (individuals) will inherit the trust at the end of B's life and the charity (or estates) will get nothing. If this assumption is made, the trust passes the rule.

3.   The only way that this trust can pass the IRS's literal test is if the trust provides that, if all the children predecease B, the trust terminates and is distributed *to B*. In that case, truly, there is no non-individual who has any interest in the trust because if the children survive B the children (who are individuals) get the benefits, and if B survives the children then B (who is an individual) gets the benefits, and there is no beneficiary we have to try to disregard. See ¶ 6.3.07. Since the IRS says that no one other than B and A's children has any beneficial interest in the trust maybe that is what they meant; but if so that would be an unusual trust provision.

The author hopes the IRS will provide further clarification of this point in final regulations. In the meantime, practitioners are left to draft trusts within the narrow confines of the guaranteed safe harbor trusts (¶ 6.3.07, ¶ 6.3.08), or to draft trusts that pass the rules based on common sense (¶ 6.3.09, ¶ 6.3.10) and hope that the IRS (or a court trying to interpret what the IRS has written) agrees with them.

6.3.12 *Trusts that last beyond current life expectancies*

While ¶ 6.3.10-¶ 6.3.11 argue that a trust should "pass" the trust rules if the trust will be distributed outright to now-living beneficiaries during their IRS-defined life expectancy, the minimum distribution rule status of perpetual dynasty trusts is in doubt, because such a trust will not necessarily be distributed to individuals who are living on the Designation Date even if all individual do live to their IRS-defined life expectancy. If the life expectancy payout is an important goal of the estate plan, it would be unwise to count on availability of the life expectancy of the oldest beneficiary of such a trust as a measuring period for MRDs without obtaining a ruling or legal opinion.

6.3.13 *When is 'a trust for Spouse' the same as 'Spouse'?*

Under the Code and proposed regulations, the surviving spouse as beneficiary is entitled to various special "deals" not available to other beneficiaries. See ¶ 1.6, ¶ 3.2. Participant similarly gets special treatment when he names Spouse as sole beneficiary. ¶ 1.4.02. This raises the question whether a trust for the sole or primary benefit of Spouse would be entitled to any of the special privileges that apply when Spouse individually is named as beneficiary. The answer to this varies. The following is a brief summary. For full details on this topic, see the article "When a 'Trust for Spouse' Is Treated the Same as 'Spouse'" by Natalie B. Choate, Trusts & Estates, Sept. 2001.

If Spouse is treated as owner of all of the trust property under the grantor trust rules (¶ 6.3.09), she should be considered the sole beneficiary of that trust; and the trust should be (although the proposed regulations do not discuss grantor trusts) entitled to all the privileges of Spouse individually so long as she has not made a completed transfer of the trust to anyone else (see "Answer C" of the Trust Review Questionnaire, Appendix C).

If Spouse is entitled to all income (i.e., trust accounting income; ¶ 6.1.07) of the trust for life, but she does NOT have the right to demand distribution to herself of the entire amount of Participant's retirement benefits payable to the trust, and she does NOT even have the right to demand distribution to herself of whatever amounts are distributed from the retirement plan to the trust during her lifetime, then the trust is a "classic QTIP trust." ¶ 3.3.04. Many "credit shelter trusts" also fall into this model. Even if distributions to such a trust will be measured by Spouse's life expectancy (because she is the oldest beneficiary of the trust), "some amounts distributed from...[the retirement plan] to [the QTIP trust] may be accumulated in [the QTIP trust] during [Spouse's] lifetime for the benefit of [the] remaindermen beneficiaries." Therefore the remainder beneficiaries are considered "beneficiaries" of the trust for purposes of the multiple beneficiary rule, and Spouse is not the sole beneficiary. This trust is not entitled to any of the privileges of Spouse.

As previewed by Rev. Rul. 2000-2, the proposed regulations confirm that a trust may use the delayed beginning date of § 401(a)(9)(B)(iv) (later of December 31 of the year after the year Participant died or December 31 of the year Participant would have reached age 70½; ¶ 1.6.04) for required distributions only if Spouse is the *sole* beneficiary of the trust. The example given is a trust which "provides that all amounts distributed from [Participant's] account in plan X to the trustee while [Spouse] is alive will be paid directly to

[Spouse] upon receipt by the trustee." P.R. § 1.401(a)(9)-5, A-7(c)(3), Example 3. Spouse is not the sole beneficiary of the trust if "some amounts distributed from [the retirement plan] to [the trust] may be accumulated in" the trust during Spouse's lifetime for the benefit of the remainder beneficiaries. P.R. § 1.401(a)(9)-5, A-7(c)(3), Example 2(iii). Therefore, the delayed commencement date (and related rules) of § 401(a)(9)(B)(iv) do not apply to benefits payable to a QTIP trust (¶ 3.3.04), but do apply to benefits payable to a conduit trust (¶ 6.3.08) or (presumably) to a trust of which Spouse is treated as sole owner under § 678 (¶ 6.3.09). P.R. § 1.408-8, A-5(a).

Required lifetime distributions to a Participant who has named a trust as beneficiary are determined under Table VI or the Uniform Table, whichever produces a lower MRD, in any particular distribution year, if Participant's sole beneficiary for such year is either Spouse, or a conduit trust for Spouse, or (presumably) a 100% grantor trust for Spouse, provided Participant complies with the documentation requirement (¶ 6.2.10) and other trust rules (¶ 6.2.04). A Participant who has named a QTIP Trust as beneficiary must use the Uniform Table (¶ 1.4.01).

The recalc/fixed term combo method of computing Spouse's life expectancy (¶ 1.6.06) is available to a trust only if the trust is the sole beneficiary of Participant, and Spouse is the sole beneficiary of the trust, i.e., the trust is a conduit trust (¶ 6.3.08) as to Spouse or (presumably) a 100% grantor trust (¶ 6.3.09) as to Spouse. P.R. § 1.401(a)(9)-5, A-5(c)(2). In the case of a QTIP Trust, or any other trust, the life expectancy of the oldest trust beneficiary applies and it is calculated on a fixed-term basis as described in P.R. § 1.401(a)(9)-5, A-5(c)(1).

6.3.14 "Separate accounts" vs. "separate trusts"

Under the "separate account" rule (¶ 1.7.06), the minimum distribution rules apply separately to different beneficiaries of a single retirement plan if the plan is divided into "separate accounts" payable respectively to such different beneficiaries. A common estate planning technique is to leave assets to a trust that will be divided, immediately upon Participant's death, into several trusts (such as a marital trust and credit shelter trust, or separate trusts for individual children).

It is clear from the Proposed Regulations that the separate account concept applies at the plan level, not at the trust level;

therefore, the overall or "funding" trust is considered "the" beneficiary of the retirement plan. The *plan benefit* is not considered divided into separate accounts merely because the *trust* is divided into separate trusts. See PLR 9809059.

However, if, after setting up the separate trusts (such as marital and credit shelter trusts, or separate trusts one for each child), the trustee of the trust that is named as beneficiary of the retirement plan causes the *retirement benefit* to be allocated into separate accounts, one payable to each of the separated trusts, before the Designation Date (¶ 1.8.01), that should be sufficient to allow each of the separate trusts to be recognized as a separate beneficiary for MRD purposes (and to be tested separately from each of the other trusts under all the rules discussed in this Chapter).

6.4 Summary of Planning Principles

1.   Because of the many potential drawbacks and complications of making retirement benefits payable to a trust, name a trust as beneficiary of retirement benefits only when there is an important reason to do so (rather than simply because it is convenient to have all assets "pour" into a single trust at the client's death).

2.   Despite the complications and drawbacks, naming a trust as beneficiary can facilitate such planning techniques as disclaimers and division of benefits using a tax-based formula, both of which may not be permitted in a beneficiary designation form but can be accomplished at the trust level.

3.   Review the trust drafting checklist (¶ 6.1.01-¶ 6.1.04) when considering naming a trust as beneficiary of retirement benefits.

4.   If "separate accounts" treatment (¶ 1.7.06) is an important goal, either make the benefits payable to separate trusts in the first place or verify that the plan administrator will recognize separate trusts as separate accounts even if the division does not occur until after Participant's death, provided that the division takes place prior to the Designation Date (see ¶ 6.3.14).

7

Charitable Giving

The pros, cons and pitfalls of funding
charitable gifts with retirement benefits

7.1 Introduction to Charitable Giving with Retirement Benefits

7.1.01 *What this Chapter covers*

This Chapter first explains the tax advantages of leaving retirement benefits to charity, then looks at the minimum distribution rule problems and income tax problems that arise when the charitable gift is paid from a trust that was named as beneficiary of the benefits (rather than being paid directly from the retirement plan to the charity). Next, this Chapter examines various types of charitable entities from the point of view of their suitability as recipients of retirement benefits, and looks at miscellaneous tax issues involved with charitable bequests of retirement benefits. The Chapter ends with a summary of planning principles.

This Chapter assumes the reader is generally familiar with the tax rules of charitable giving. For more information about charitable giving, see the sources cited in the Bibliography.

The planning principles discussed in this Chapter generally do not apply to Roth IRAs (Chapter 5). Since Roth IRA distributions are generally not subject to federal income tax, there is no income tax advantage to leaving such benefits to charity. The best planning strategies for Roth IRAs therefore generally do not include leaving such plans to charity. This Chapter deals only with traditional IRAs, qualified retirement plans ("QRPs") and 403(b) arrangements.

In this Chapter, "Charitable Remainder Trust" means a trust that meets the requirements of § 664; see ¶ 7.5.04.

7.1.02 Advantages of naming a charity as beneficiary

Because retirement plan death benefits are subject to income tax (¶ 2.1.01), there is an advantage to naming a charity as beneficiary of the benefits: charities are generally exempt from income taxes (¶ 7.5.01), and thus can collect the entire death benefit without paying income taxes. § 501(a), § 664(c). For the client who wants to leave some assets to charity at death, using the retirement benefits for that purpose is often the most tax-effective way to fund the gift.

Example: Helen wants to leave half of her $1.2 million estate to her favorite charity, the Salk Institute, and half to her nephew Achilles. Her assets are: a $600,000 IRA and $600,000 of cash. Achilles is in the 40% income tax bracket. If Helen simply leaves half of each asset to Achilles and half to the charity, Table 7.1 shows what each receives.

Table 7.1	Charity	Nephew
½ cash	300,000	300,000
½ IRA	300,000	300,000
Gross bequest	600,000	600,000
Less: income tax on ½ IRA	- 0	-120,000
Net bequest	600,000	480,000

If, instead, she leaves the entire IRA to the charity and all the cash to nephew Achilles, the charity receives the same amount it would have under the other approach, but the nephew receives more money than he would have received with the other approach, at the expense of the IRS, as shown in Table 7.2. This tax advantage of funding at-death charitable gifts with retirement benefits enables the client to fund his charitable gifts at a lower "cost" to the family beneficiaries.

Table 7.2	Charity	Nephew
IRA	600,000	0
Cash	<u>0</u>	<u>600,000</u>
Gross bequest	600,000	600,000
Less: income tax on IRA	-<u>0</u>	-<u>0</u>
Net bequest	600,000	600,000

Although it is generally desirable to use retirement benefits to fund at-death charitable gifts it is not necessarily easy to integrate this planning idea into a particular client's estate plan, as the discussion in this Chapter shows. Also, not every type of charitable organization receives the same favorable income tax treatment; see ¶ 7.5.01.

7.2 Pitfalls Under the Minimum Distribution Rules

7.2.01 *Relevance of minimum distribution rules*

Retirement plan benefits are generally subject to income taxes at the time of distribution, whether that distribution occurs before or after the participant's death. ¶ 2.1.01. Until distribution occurs, the investment growth inside the retirement plan incurs no income taxes and accordingly money inside a retirement plan can grow much faster than investments outside a retirement plan. Thus, a popular strategy for maximizing the value of retirement plan benefits is to keep the benefits inside the plan as long as possible. See ¶ 1.2.01.

Congress does not allow the deferral of taxation to go on forever. To avoid draconian penalties, and preserve the tax-favored status of the retirement plan, plan participants and administrators must comply with § 401(a)(9), which dictates when benefits must start to be distributed from retirement plans, and, once distribution begins, how fast distributions must be made. These "minimum distribution rules" can also be used positively, to continue deferral of income taxes for decades even after the participant's death. See Chapter 1.

In 2001, the IRS issued new proposed regulations interpreting and implementing the minimum distribution rules. ¶ 1.1.03. The 2001 proposed regulations substantially simplified the minimum distribution rules and eliminated some of the problems relating to naming a charity as beneficiary of retirement benefits. In this Chapter, "proposed regulations" (P.R.) means the 2001 proposed minimum distribution regulations unless otherwise specified.

When Participant reaches his "required beginning date" (RBD) (¶ 1.3; generally, April 1 following the year Participant reaches age 70½), Participant must begin to withdraw funds from his retirement plan. The computation of his annual "minimum required distributions" (MRDs) involves dividing the value of his plan account (revalued annually) by a life expectancy factor. Under the old proposed regulations, naming a charity as beneficiary caused these annual required distributions to be larger than they would be if an individual beneficiary was named. See pages 271-272 of the 1999 edition of this book. Under the new proposed regulations, it no longer matters, for purposes of determining Participant's required distributions *during life*, who is going to inherit Participant's retirement benefits after his death. Instead, all participants use a single "Uniform Table" to calculate their lifetime required distributions (with one exception—a Participant whose sole beneficiary is his spouse uses the joint life expectancy of himself and his spouse, rather than the Uniform Table, if the spouse is more than 10 years younger than Participant). ¶ 1.4. *Thus, the lifetime drawback of naming a charity as beneficiary of retirement benefits has been eliminated.*

When Participant dies, the beneficiary who inherits the benefits must begin to withdraw the benefits. If the benefits are inherited by an individual, group of individuals or qualifying trust (¶ 6.2), the payout period for the benefits is the life expectancy of that individual beneficiary (or the oldest member of the group, or oldest beneficiary of the trust). ¶ 1.5. Benefits payable to a non-individual beneficiary (such as a charity) must generally be paid out of the plan over a shorter period of time: within five years after Participant's death if he died before his RBD (¶ 1.5.04), or over Participant's remaining life expectancy if he died on or after his RBD (¶ 1.5.05).

As discussed in detail in Chapter 1, the key to long-term income tax deferral after Participant's death is the use of an individual beneficiary's life expectancy as the measuring period for required distributions. Because a charity is not an "individual" there can be a conflict between a Participant's goals of benefitting charity and maximizing income tax deferral for individual beneficiaries.

7.2.02 *Naming a charity as one of several beneficiaries*

For purposes of computing *post-death* minimum required distributions, there is no drawback or pitfall to leaving *all* of the client's retirement benefits under a particular plan to charity. The charity is not a "designated beneficiary," and therefore is not eligible to use the "life expectancy payout method," so all of Participant's benefits must be distributed within short order after his death; but this is not a problem, because the charity is income tax-exempt (generally speaking; see ¶ 7.5.01 for discussion of which charities are and which are not income tax-exempt). The income tax-exempt charity can receive the benefits in a lump sum or instalments or any which-way and still pay no income tax on the benefits, so the charitable beneficiary does not need the income tax deferral of a life expectancy payout to minimize taxes.

Naming a charity as beneficiary poses a problem in terms of post-death MRDs only if the client is not leaving the *entire* benefit to charity. If the client wants to leave part of the benefit to individuals and part to charity, and wants the individual beneficiaries to be able to use their life expectancies to compute their MRDs, the client has to overcome the IRS's "multiple beneficiary rule."

Under this rule (P.R. § 1.401(a)(9)-5, A-7(a)), ALL beneficiaries of a retirement plan death benefit must be individuals (or qualifying trusts; ¶ 6.2), if ANY of the benefits are to be paid out over the life expectancy of a beneficiary. See ¶ 1.7.06. Under this rule, a $1 million IRA payable at death "$1,000 to the United Way and the balance to my children" would have to be entirely distributed by the end of the fifth year after the death of a Participant who died before his RBD (or over Participant's remaining life expectancy, if he died on or after his RBD), because one of the beneficiaries is not an individual. These options will in most cases provide a shorter payout period (less income tax deferral) than the "life expectancy of the designated beneficiary."

Is the IRS's position correct? The proposed regulation appears to be harsher than the Code, which says that (at least in case of death before the RBD) if "*any portion* of the employee's interest is payable to (or for the benefit of) a designated beneficiary," *such portion* may be distributed over the life expectancy of the designated beneficiary. § 401(a)(9)(B)(iii) (emphasis added). Thus, the Code appears to permit a life expectancy payout to an individual designated beneficiary of his portion, even if some *other* "portion" of the benefit is payable to a non-individual.

Fortunately, it is easy in most cases, even under the proposed regulations, to have a life expectancy payout to an individual of part of the benefit, and distribute the rest of the benefit to a charity. The next four subsections explain four ways to achieve this. If a client is leaving benefits to both human and charitable beneficiaries and the "life expectancy of the beneficiary" payout method for the human beneficiaries is an important goal, read the next four subsections.

7.2.03 *Separate accounts for charitable, human, beneficiaries*

The multiple beneficiary rule does not apply if the respective shares of the individual and charitable beneficiaries constitute separate accounts payable to different beneficiaries as of the Designation Date. P.R. § 1.401(a)(9)-8, A-2, A-3. These "separate accounts" can be created by Participant (with appropriate language in the beneficiary designation form), or by the plan administrator (with appropriate language in the plan document), or by the beneficiaries themselves after Participant's death (and prior to the Designation Date). See ¶ 1.7.06 for full explanation of the separate accounts rule.

7.2.04 *If the spouse is the only non-charitable beneficiary*

The concern about multiple beneficiaries does not arise when the only beneficiaries are Spouse and one or more charities, if *Spouse in fact survives*, because Spouse does not need to take an installment payout of the benefits over her life expectancy in order to defer income taxes; she can simply roll over her share of the benefits to her own retirement plan. ¶ 3.2.

However, even when Spouse is named as the sole non-charitable beneficiary, it might be advisable to include the separate account language (¶ 7.2.03) to cover the possibility of Spouse's disclaimer, simultaneous death or predeceasing Participant *if* the contingent beneficiary in that case would be another non-charitable beneficiary. If the contingent beneficiary of the interest left to Spouse is another non-charitable beneficiary (such as Participant's child); *and* Spouse either (a) dies simultaneously with Participant, or (b) predeceases Participant (with Participant then failing to take steps to fix the beneficiary designation before he dies) or (c) disclaims the benefits; *and* the non-charitable contingent beneficiary would like to take his share of the benefits out over his life expectancy; then Participant may wish to include the "separate account" language in his beneficiary designation form.

7.2.05 *Separate account treatment for pecuniary gifts*

It is not clear that separate account treatment can be used for a pecuniary gift. For example, suppose Participant wants his IRA benefits to be paid at his death "$50,000 to My Favorite Charity, Inc., and the balance to my daughter Gretchen." P.R. § 1.401(a)(9)-8, A-2, talks about "allocating investment gains and losses, and contributions and forfeitures, *on a pro rata basis*" (emphasis added), which suggests that the IRS had only a fractional-type bequest in mind.

It should not be difficult, in planning mode (i.e. when drafting a beneficiary designation form for a living client) to rework a pecuniary gift into a fractional gift as of the date of death. If Participant is already deceased, the best approach is to pay out the pecuniary bequest prior to the Designation Date. ¶ 7.2.06.

7.2.06 *Distribute charity's share before Designation Date*

If the client has already died, and a retirement plan has been left to both charitable and individual beneficiaries, and it is not clear that the beneficiaries are entitled to "separate account" treatment (for example, because one or more beneficiaries' shares are defined as "pecuniary" amounts rather than on a fractional or percentage basis—¶ 7.2.05), the best way to deal with the multiple beneficiary problem is to pay out to any charitable beneficiary its share of the benefits prior to the Designation Date. Under P.R. § 1.401(a)(9)-4, A-4(a), as long as the charities have been totally paid out prior to the Designation Date, the beneficiaries who have not yet received a distribution of their shares (i.e., the individual beneficiaries) will be deemed to be the "only" beneficiaries for minimum distribution purposes. ¶ 1.8.05.

7.3 MRDs and Charitable Gifts Under Trusts

7.3.01 *Trust with charitable and human beneficiaries*

Suppose a client wants to name a trust as beneficiary of his retirement plan. His children are intended to be the primary beneficiaries of the trust, but the trust also has one or more charitable beneficiaries. He wants the plan benefits that pass to this trust to be paid out in installments over the life expectancy of his oldest child. To achieve the desired result, the various "trust rules" (¶ 6.2) must be complied with. One of these rules is that all trust beneficiaries must be individuals. This rule creates two problems in common estate planning situations involving charities.

First, *any* charitable gift to be paid from the trust at Participant's death, no matter how small, would cause the trust to flunk this requirement, unless the trustee is forbidden to use the retirement benefits to fund the charitable bequest. ¶ 6.3.03. Even the typical normally innocuous statement "this trust shall pay any bequests under my will, if my estate is not adequate to pay the same," could make the trust "flunk" if the will contains charitable bequests (however, the problem of payable-at-death charitable gifts can be easily cured by paying out all charitable bequests prior to the Designation Date; ¶ 6.2.05).

The second problem is that, generally, remainder beneficiaries are considered "beneficiaries" for this purpose. Thus, if the beneficiary of the client's retirement plan is a trust, and any part of the remainder interest in the trust passes to charity (or could be appointed to charity under a power of appointment), the trust will flunk (unless the charitable remainder beneficiary can be disregarded; ¶ 6.3.04). This is not a problem with a true "charitable remainder trust" that meets the requirements of § 664 (¶ 7.5.04), because such trusts are income tax-exempt. The problem is with a trust that is primarily a family trust but which happens to have charitable gifts that will be made after the family members' deaths.

Thus, when drafting a trust that is to make charitable gifts, or that may be used to fund charitable bequests under the will, it is important to determine whether any retirement benefits may be payable to that trust, and, if so, to draft appropriate language either:

1.   To forbid use of the retirement benefits to fund the charitable
       gifts, if you want the benefits to be paid out over the life
       expectancy of individual trust beneficiaries (¶ 7.3.02). This
       approach only works for charitable gifts to be paid upon
       Participant's death, not if there are charitable remainder
       interests, as explained at ¶ 7.3.02. Or,

2.   To match the retirement benefits to the charitable gifts, if the
       goal is to have the benefits pass to the charity free of income
       taxes (¶ 7.4.06). Under this approach you are giving up on using
       the life expectancy payout method for the benefits used to pay
       the charitable gifts.

The first step in analyzing a trust with both charitable and non-charitable beneficiaries is to determine whether the charitable gifts are to be made immediately upon the death of the Participant (¶ 7.3.02), or are remainder interests that do not vest until some later date (such as when an individual beneficiary dies) (¶ 7.3.03).

7.3.02 *If charitable gifts occur at death of Participant*

Example: Russ leaves his $3 million IRA to a trust. The trust provides that, upon Russ's death, the trustee is to pay $10,000 to Russ's favorite charity, and hold the rest of the funds in trust for the life of Russ's wife with remainder to Russ's issue. This trust has both charitable and non-charitable beneficiaries. Unless something is done to avoid the multiple beneficiary rule, the trust will not be able to use the life expectancy of the oldest trust beneficiary to measure required distributions from the IRA to the trust after Russ's death. ¶ 1.7.06.

Here is what can be done to solve this problem, i.e., achieve Russ's goal of paying $10,000 to the charity while still allowing the trust to qualify to use the life expectancy the oldest individual trust beneficiary to measure required distributions from the plan to the trust (see ¶ 6.2.04):

Planning mode: Include language in the trust agreement to prohibit use of the retirement plan to pay the charitable gift; this will work, assuming the trust has some other assets that can be used to fulfill Participant's charitable gifts. ¶ 6.3.03. See Form 7.2, App. B.

Cleanup mode: The trustee can "eliminate" the charitable beneficiary by paying to the charity its $10,000 bequest before the Designation Date. If the charity is paid in full prior to the Designation Date, then it is no longer a "beneficiary" of the trust as of the Designation Date, and (assuming that the one $10,000 bequest to a non-charitable beneficiary was the only "defect" of the trust under the minimum distribution trust rules) the trust has only individual beneficiaries and qualifies under the "trust rules." ¶ 6.2.05. If the trust does not contain a prohibition against paying retirement benefits to charity, and the trustee has authority to pay any asset to any beneficiary, the trustee could choose whether to use the IRA proceeds or other assets to pay the $10,000 bequest. It would make no difference, under the minimum distribution rules, which assets were used, as long as the charity has no further interest in the trust after the Designation Date.

7.3.03 *If charitable gifts are to occur after the Designation Date*

A prohibition against using retirement benefits to fund charitable gifts will not solve the multiple beneficiary rule problem if the charitable interest is not one that can be paid out or segregated at death.

Example: Heather's trust provides that, after Heather's death, the trust is divided into equal shares for her four children. Each child receives income for life from his or her share, plus principal in the trustee's discretion for the child's health, education and support. At death, each child can appoint the principal of such child's share among Heather's issue and any charity. If the child fails to exercise this power of appointment, such child's share is added to the shares of the other children. Assets coming to this trust at Heather's death include Heather's $2 million IRA and $3 million of other assets. The existence of potential charitable remainder beneficiaries (as appointees under the children's powers of appointment) would mean that, under the multiple beneficiary rule, this trust would flunk the IRS's minimum distribution trust rules, and would not be able to use the life expectancy of the oldest child to measure required distributions from the IRA to the trust after Heather's death.

Adding a blanket prohibition against paying retirement benefits to charity (such as Form 7.2, Appendix B) will *not* solve the problem in Heather's trust. Because the potential charitable gifts do not occur until each child dies, the trustee, in order to carry out a blanket prohibition against using retirement benefits to fund any charitable gift, would have to segregate the IRA (and all distributions from the IRA) from the other assets of the trust immediately upon Heather's death and keep them segregated for the duration of the trust. So instead of administering four trusts (one for each child) the trustee would end up administering eight trusts (one trust for each child's share of the IRA and IRA distributions, which could not be appointed to charity on the child's death, plus a separate trust for each child's share of the non-IRA assets, which *could* be appointed to charity on the child's death). That is the only way the trustee will be able to tell, when the child dies many years from now, which assets can be appointed to charity and which assets cannot be. The trust instrument would have to give the trustee authority to establish two separate trusts for each beneficiary (or, if that provision is not included, the trustee would probably have to go to court to get authority).

Suppose the trustee sets up the eight separate trust shares. Now Child A needs a discretionary distribution of principal. Does it come out of the retirement assets trust for Child A? or the non-retirement assets trust for Child A? Again, this is a question that must be covered in the trust instrument (or, if it is not, the trustee might have to go to court for authority to pay out of one share or the other).

Moral: Do not rely on a catchall prohibition against paying retirement benefits to non-individual beneficiaries to solve the problem of a charitable *remainder* interest in a trust that may receive retirement benefits.

If including a catchall paragraph does not solve the problem, what other solutions are there?

Planning mode: If there may be charitable remainder interests in a trust that is being created primarily for individual beneficiaries, and the trust may receive retirement benefits, here are the steps to go through and the options to consider:

A.   Determine which is a more important goal to the client, the charitable remainders or the life expectancy payout for the retirement benefits, then give up whichever one is less important. If the charitable gifts are high priority, for example, consider giving up the life expectancy payout over the life expectancy of the oldest trust beneficiary. In the Heather example above, if the total value of Heather's retirement plan had been $100,000 out of her total estate of $5 million, she might decide the life expectancy payout was not of significant value, and therefore not bother to take steps to try to preserve it.

B.   Consider creating separate trusts to receive the retirement benefits and the non-retirement assets. Returning to the Heather example, if Heather places high priority on *both* the life expectancy payout of her $2 million IRA over the life expectancy of her children, *and* on allowing the children to appoint their shares of the other $3 million of assets to charity, she could direct the trustee to establish two separate trusts for each child as above described, one for the child's share of the IRA proceeds and one for the child's share of the other assets. The power to appoint to charity would apply only to the trusts that held no retirement benefits. The drawback of this approach is the administrative inconvenience and cost of extra trust bookkeeping.

C.   Consider whether an income tax-exempt Charitable Remainder Trust (¶ 7.5.04) would be a better choice of beneficiary than the client's "regular" trust.

Example: Hilda, age 68, has a $3 million IRA. Her goal is to provide a life income to her sister (age 71) and remainder to a charitable foundation. Assuming the income stream from a Charitable Remainder Trust (¶ 7.5.04) would fulfill the non-charitable objective, it would make no sense to sacrifice her charitable objectives in order to get a life expectancy payout of the IRA (especially since her sister is elderly and does not have a multi-decade life expectancy). The CRT would provide far greater tax advantages: no income tax on distribution of the benefits from the IRA to the CRT, and an estate tax deduction for the value of the charitable remainder.

D.   Consider using a "conduit trust."

Example: Luigi wants his daughter Lavinia, age 41, to receive a stream of income from his $3 million IRA. A stream of minimum required IRA distributions over her life expectancy would be just right. However, he does not want her to have outright control of the entire IRA after his death. Although a stream of MRD payments from the IRA would not be guaranteed to last for Lavinia's entire life (it would last only until the end of her IRS-defined life expectancy), he thinks a stream of MRD payments probably *would* last for her lifetime because she has a below-average life expectancy due to her medical condition. If she does die prematurely, he wants to be sure that any money left in the IRA goes to the charity that funds research into Lavinia's medical condition. He could leave the benefits to a conduit trust (¶ 6.3.08) for Lavinia for life, with remainder to the charity. There would be no estate tax charitable deduction (because this is not a Charitable Remainder Trust; ¶ 7.5.04), but the trust would be able to use Lavinia's life expectancy to measure required distributions (because the charitable beneficiary can be disregarded; ¶ 6.3.04).

7.4 Income Tax Treatment of Charitable Gifts From a Trust or Estate

7.4.01 *Advantages of naming charity as beneficiary directly*

The way to leave retirement benefits to charity that involves the fewest difficulties and pitfalls is simply to name one or more existing "public" charities (¶ 7.5.02), private foundations (¶ 7.5.03), or Charitable Remainder Trusts (¶ 7.5.04), directly, as the beneficiary of 100% of the death benefit payable under the particular retirement plan, as in the following example:

"I name as my beneficiary, to receive 100% of the death benefits payable under the above-named retirement plan on account of my death, the Inner-City Scholarship Fund {address}."

Because the benefits are paid directly to the charity under the beneficiary designation form, income tax on the benefits is easily avoided: § 691 causes the benefits to be included directly in the income of the charitable recipient as named beneficiary (¶ 2.2.02), and the charity's tax exemption makes the distribution non-taxable (¶ 7.5.01(A)). The estate tax charitable deduction is available for the full value of the charity's interest. ¶ 7.5.01(B).

(As with any charitable gift, practitioners must consider such issues as the need to properly identify the intended recipient by using its correct legal name and adding such helpful information as the address and/or taxpayer identification number of the organization. Also, the practitioner needs to consider with the client whether to make the gift conditional on the recipient's meeting, at the time of the client's death, the applicable requirements under the Internal Revenue Code for income tax exemption and/or the estate tax charitable deduction. Since these considerations are the same for gifts of retirement benefits as for other gifts, these points will not be dealt with in this Chapter.)

7.4.02 *If benefits pass to charity through estate or trust, not directly*

Sometimes it is not feasible to name the intended charitable recipient directly as beneficiary of the retirement benefits. The most common reason for this is that some additional actions must be taken, after the client's death, to carry out the charitable gift.

For example, the intended charitable recipient may be a charitable foundation that has not been created yet; or the amount going to various charities may be based on a formula that depends on facts that cannot be determined until after the client's death, such as "Charity A shall receive an amount equal to 10% of my net estate, and the balance shall be paid to Charity B" (formula makes it impossible to determine how much Charity A receives until the estate is settled); or the client may want the charitable recipients to be selected after his death, with a designation such as "The benefits shall be distributed to such one or more educational institutions located in Massachusetts as my executor shall select from among those which are exempt from federal income taxes under § 501, and gifts to which qualify for the federal estate tax charitable deduction under § 2055."

In all of these examples, the retirement plan administrator may not be willing to accept a beneficiary designation that (for example) named a beneficiary that would not exist at the time of Participant's death, because the plan could find itself in the position of having to pay out a minimum required distribution with no one to pay it to. Similarly, a plan may not be willing to accept a beneficiary designation under which the plan administrator would not be able to tell, at Participant's death, who was entitled to the benefits.

In these situations, the benefits may have to be made payable to

Participant's estate or trust as beneficiary of the retirement plan, with the will (or trust instrument) specifying that the benefits are to be paid to the not-yet-created (or not-yet-selected) charitable beneficiaries. The executor of the will (or trustee of the trust) is then responsible for carrying out the post-death actions (such as forming the charitable foundation, or calculating the formula distributions, or selecting the charities), and the plan administrator can then simply follow the instructions of the executor (or trustee) in distributing the benefits. Unfortunately, this course introduces a substantial additional complexity, namely, the steps that must be taken to avoid having *income tax* imposed on the benefits at the estate (or trust) level.

The rest of this ¶ 7.4 discusses whether and how an estate or non-charitable trust can avoid income taxes on retirement plan benefits that are paid to it and used to fund charitable gifts under the instrument. (As to whether the ultimate charitable recipient then pays income tax on the retirement benefits so distributed to it, see ¶ 7.5.01.)

The following discussion assumes that the fiduciary receives a distribution from the retirement plan and, in the same year, funds a fractional or residuary gift to a "public" charity (¶ 7.5.02) or private foundation (¶ 7.5.03). If the charitable gift is not funded in the same year the distribution is received from the retirement plan, see ¶ 7.4.10. If, instead of taking a distribution from the plan and passing the distributed property out to the charity, the fiduciary assigns the retirement plan itself to the charity, see ¶ 7.4.09. If the bequest is a pecuniary bequest (as opposed to a fractional or residuary bequest) see ¶ 2.2.05. Gifts from an estate or non-charitable trust to a Charitable Remainder Trust (¶ 7.5.04), pooled income fund (¶ 7.5.06), or charitable lead trust (¶ 7.5.07) are beyond the scope of this discussion.

In the rest of this ¶ 7.4, "trust" means a trust that is not, itself, income tax-exempt (see ¶ 7.5.01).

7.4.03 *No DNI deduction for distributions to charity*

The income tax treatment of trusts is an extremely complex topic. This Chapter seeks only to highlight issues particularly involved when retirement plan benefits are paid to charity through a non-charitable trust, not to explain all the rules of trust income taxation. For full details, see the two sources described in the Bibliography, Blattmachr, J.G., et al., *Income Taxation of Estates and Trusts*, and Zaritsky, H., et al., *Federal Income Taxation of Estates and Trusts* (cited, in this Chapter as "Blattmachr" and "Zaritsky," respectively).

To vastly oversimplify a complex topic, the general scheme of income taxation of trusts and estates is as follows: All income items (including retirement plan distributions; ¶ 2.1.01) paid to an estate or trust are includible in its gross income just as such items would be included in the gross income of an individual if paid to such individual. A trust (unless its existence as a separate entity is ignored under the "grantor trust rules" of §§ 671-678; see ¶ 6.3.09) or estate is a separate taxpayer and pays tax on its taxable income at the rate prescribed for trusts and estates. §§ 641(a); 1(e).

However, the trust gets a unique deduction on its way from "gross income" to "taxable income": the trust can deduct certain distributions of income made to the trust's beneficiaries. §§ 651, 661. The beneficiaries then pay the income tax on these distributions. §§ 652, 662.

Needless to say there are complex rules governing this unique deduction. The first rule is that the amount the trust can deduct is limited to the amount of its "distributable net income" or "DNI." §§ 651, 661. Because of this limitation, the deduction is often called the "DNI deduction."

The second rule is that there is no DNI deduction allowed for a distribution from an estate or trust to a charity. §§ 651(a)(2), 663(a)(2). A distribution to a charity from an estate or trust is deductible, if at all, only as a charitable deduction under § 642(c). (Although the Code could be interpreted to mean that a trust can take a DNI deduction for distributions to charity that do not qualify for the deduction under § 642, the IRS has not interpreted it that way, and the courts have supported the IRS; see *Blattmachr*, § 2:6.1[J].) § 642(c) allows an estate or trust "a deduction in computing its taxable income [for] any amount of the gross income, without limitation, which pursuant to the terms of the governing instrument is, during the taxable year, paid for a" permitted charitable purpose. For meaning of "pursuant to the governing instrument" in this context, see *Zaritsky*, ¶ 4.07.

The third rule is the "separate share" rule of § 663(c). When the separate share rule applies, if a fiduciary distributes money to a beneficiary, that distribution will carry out DNI only to the extent there is DNI that is properly allocable to that particular beneficiary's "separate share." In December 1999, the IRS issued final regulations interpreting the separate share rules and these regulations specifically deal with the allocation of "income in respect of a decedent" (IRD)

(¶ 2.2) that is "corpus" (i.e., "principal" for trust accounting purposes; see ¶ 6.1.07) separately from other types of income that may make up DNI. The regulations' principles for dealing with IRD are different from the rules for "regular" DNI.

(Note: the "separate share rule" of § 663(c) governs the allocation of DNI among multiple beneficiaries *of a trust or estate,* and is not to be confused with the "separate account rule" of P.R. § 1.401(a)(9)-8, A-2, which dictates when multiple beneficiaries *of a retirement plan* are treated separately for purposes of the required distribution rules. ¶ 1.7.06. These are *completely* different and unrelated rules.)

Having in mind these various rules, we now look at what happens to a trust that (a) has both charitable and non-charitable beneficiaries and (b) is named as beneficiary of a retirement plan. In the following example, note that the bequests are in the form of fractional or percentage portions of the trust principal. The following discussion does not necessarily apply at all or in the same way to pecuniary bequests; see ¶ 2.2.05.

Example: Tom dies leaving his $1 million IRA, $1 million of real estate and $1 million of marketable securities to a trust. At Tom's death, the trust is to terminate and be distributed 50% to Charity and 50% to Tom's son Timmy, so each beneficiary is to receive a total of $1.5 million. The trust provides that Timmy has to pay all estate taxes, if there are any, out of his 50% share. Because Tom had no basis in the IRA (see ¶ 2.1.04), all distributions from the IRA after Tom's death are includible in the recipient's gross income as "income in respect of a decedent" (IRD). If the trustee takes $1 million out of the IRA (thereby generating $1 million of gross income to the trust) and distributes that $1 million to the charity in partial fulfillment of its 50% share, can the trust take an income tax deduction for the distribution to charity?

To answer this question, we first need to determine whether the separate share rules apply in this situation.

7.4.04 *Do the separate share rules allocate income to charity?*

The trust can take a charitable deduction under § 642(c) for a distribution to charity that is paid, pursuant to the governing instrument, out of the trust's gross income. If the gross income arising from the $1 million IRA distribution is not properly allocable to the charity's share the trust cannot deduct it.

The separate share rules generally tell us how much "gross income" is allocated to each beneficiary's share, but do those rules apply for purposes of determining how much is allocated to a *charitable* beneficiary's share? The separate share rule of § 663(c) applies "For the *sole* purpose of determining the amount of distributable net income in the application of sections 661 and 662" (emphasis added). It is not clear from this statement in § 663(c) whether the separate share rules apply in determining how much income is allocated to a *charity*'s share, since § 661 and § 662 generally don't apply to charitable distributions.

However, it appears probable that the separate share rules do apply to determine allocation of DNI among the separate shares allocable to charitable as well as non-charitable beneficiaries (even though, after all the allocating is done, there will be no DNI deduction for distributions to charity), because:

1.   The separate share rules apply if a trust or estate "has more than one beneficiary, and if different beneficiaries have substantially separate and independent shares...." Reg. § 1.663(c)-1(a). The regulation does not say the rules apply only if the entity has more than one *non-charitable* beneficiary.

2.   The IRS has not provided any other system for deciding how much of the trust's income is allocated to charitable shares.

3.   One of the examples in the separate share regulations includes allocation of DNI among both charitable and non-charitable beneficiaries, though noting that the "payments of income to the charitable organization are deductible by the estate to the extent provided in section 642(c) and are not subject to the distribution provisions of sections 661 and 662." Reg. § 1.663(c)-5, Example 11.

Having concluded that the separate share regulations apparently do apply in determining how much income is allocated to the charity's share, we next look at what those regulations say.

7.4.05 *Allocating IRD that is corpus under the separate share rule*

Retirement benefits paid to a trust are income in respect of a decedent (IRD). See ¶ 2.2. Here is what the separate share regulation says regarding the allocation of IRD among beneficiaries' separate shares:

"(3) Income in respect of a decedent. This paragraph (b)(3) governs the allocation of the portion of gross income includible in distributable net income that is income in respect of a decedent within the meaning of section 691(a) and is not [trust accounting income; see ¶ 6.1.07]. Such gross income is allocated *among the separate shares that could potentially be funded with these amounts...* The amount of such gross income allocated to each share is based on the relative value of each share that could potentially be funded with such amounts." Reg. § 1.663(c)-2(b)(3). (Emphasis added).

We next look at how this rule applies in three situations: if the governing instrument dictates which beneficiary's share is to receive the IRD (¶ 7.4.06); if the governing instrument is silent on which assets are allocated to which beneficiary's share and the applicable state law requires pro rata funding (¶ 7.4.07); and if the governing instrument allows the trustee to pick and choose which assets are to be used to fund which beneficiary's share (¶ 7.4.08).

7.4.06 *If governing instrument requires funding bequest with IRD*

Suppose Tom's trust (see "Example" at end of ¶ 7.4.03) contains the following provision: "The charity's share shall be funded to the maximum extent possible with retirement benefits, including any Individual Retirement Account or distribution therefrom (Retirement Assets). My son Timmy's share shall be funded to the maximum extent possible only with assets other than Retirement Assets."

The trustee withdraws $1 million from the IRA and distributes the $1 million to the charity in partial payment of its $1.5 million 50% share of the estate. On the same date, the trustee distributes Tom's real estate (also worth $1 million) to Timmy in partial fulfillment of his $1.5 million 50% share of the estate. Is the $1 million of gross income arising from the IRA distribution properly allocated to the charity's share under the separate share regulations?

Prior to the issuance of the final separate share regulations, it appeared that the IRS would not give effect to a trust provision (such as that in Tom's trust) that purports to assign *taxable income* to one beneficiary rather than another, where the provision in question has no "substantial economic effect." This principle is explained in *Zaritsky* at ¶ 2.04[4], pages 2-16 *et seq.* The provision in Tom's trust requiring the charity's share to be funded first with IRA proceeds has no "substantial economic effect" because the provision has no effect on *how much* the charity and Timmy will receive.

However, the separate share regulations indicate that a governing instrument provision that specifically allocates IRD to one beneficiary's share will be effective to cause the IRD to be allocated to that beneficiary's separate share for income tax purposes, even when such allocation has no economic effect. In Reg. § 1.663(c)-5, Example 9, the IRS tells us that "The will of Testator, who dies in 2000, directs the executor to divide the residue of the [$9 million] estate equally between Testator's two children, A and B. The will directs the executor to fund A's share first with the proceeds of Testator's individual retirement account....During 2000, the $900,000 balance in Testator's individual retirement account is distributed to the estate [and is allocated to corpus under local law and is IRD under § 691]. ...[F]or purposes of determining the distributable net income for each [child's] separate share, the $900,000 [IRA proceeds] must be allocated to A's share."

Accordingly, because Tom's trust directs that the retirement plan benefits must be used to fund the charity's share, the IRD resulting from cashing out the IRA is allocated to the charity's separate share. The fact that the governing instrument specifies that this income goes to the charity's share means that the charity's share is the only share that "could potentially be funded" with these proceeds. Thus, even if the trustee does not distribute anything to the charity that year, but does make a distribution to Timmy, the distribution to Timmy does not carry out any DNI attributable to the IRA distribution. (See ¶ 7.4.09 if the distribution to charity does not occur in the same year the IRA distribution is received.)

7.4.07 *If there is no authority to fund disproportionately*

Suppose Tom's trust requires that the beneficiaries's shares be funded pro rata with each trust asset; or Tom's trust is silent on the subject of which assets will be used to fund which beneficiary's share and applicable state law does not give the trustee authority to pick and choose which assets will be used to fund which beneficiary's share; state law requires that (unless the governing instrument specifically provides otherwise) each asset be distributed to each beneficiary proportionately.

Since "under the terms of the governing instrument or applicable local law" the fiduciary is required to allocate each asset proportionately, Timmy's share and the charity's share must be funded pro rata. Since each beneficiary's share can only "potentially be funded" with equal shares of each asset, the separate share regulations dictate that the $1 million IRA distribution received by the trust must be allocated equally for purposes of § 642(c) between the charity's share and Timmy's share.

Suppose the trustee takes a distribution of $1 million from the IRA and immediately distributes $1 million to Charity, then sells all the other estate assets (at a price which results in no gain or loss for the estate) and distributes $1 million of cash from the sale proceeds to Timmy, and makes no other distributions in that taxable year. The trust will get a charitable deduction of $500,000 under § 642(c), and a DNI deduction of $500,000 for the distribution to Timmy. Timmy will have to pay income tax on $500,000 of DNI, even though the IRA proceeds were actually distributed to the charity. As with the preceding example, there is no choice about which assets go to which beneficiary, so the only shares that can "potentially be funded" with the IRA distribution are Timmy's share (as to 50%) and the charity's share (as to 50%).

7.4.08 *If fiduciary has authority to pick and choose*

Suppose that Tom's trust, after specifying that the entire trust is to be distributed equally to Charity and Timmy, contains the following provision: "The Trustee shall not be obligated to distribute each asset equally to the two beneficiaries, but rather may make distributions in cash or in kind (including non pro rata distributions and distributions of undivided interests in property) or partly in cash and partly in kind, and may distribute different assets to each beneficiary, provided that the total amount distributed to each beneficiary is equal." In 2001, the trustee receives a $1 million cash distribution from the IRA, which it immediately distributes to Charity, and on the same date distributes Tom's real estate (also worth $1 million) to Timmy. There are no other distributions in 2001.

The trustee has exercised its authority to pick and choose which assets to use to fund each beneficiary's share. The question is, when the trustee goes to fill out the trust's income tax return for 2001, how does the trustee account for the $1 million of IRD the trust received from the IRA?

There are two possible interpretations of the separate share rule in this situation. The first interpretation, which is apparently the most widely accepted, is that, since the trustee *could* have elected to fund either beneficiary's share of the trust with the IRD, the trustee *must* (in computing its taxable income and DNI) allocate the IRD equally to the two shares. Under this interpretation, Timmy would have to pick up $500,000 of income even though the IRA proceeds were paid to the charity. While this is certainly the most obvious interpretation of the words "could potentially be funded," it has a defect, namely, that it overrides a specific provision of the governing instrument: in this example, there is specific authority in the governing instrument for the trustee to choose which assets are to be used to fund which share, and the trustee exercised that power.

A second possible interpretation of the regulation would be that, if the fiduciary has, and exercises, a power to allocate the IRD to a particular share, there is no longer an open question of which shares could "potentially be" funded, because one particular share *has* been funded with the IRD, and that is therefore the only share that can "potentially be" funded with the IRD. The argument in favor of this interpretation is that the regulations clearly permit the trust-donor to require (in the governing instrument) that IRD be used to fund certain shares, and provide that the income tax treatment will follow such a requirement (see Example 9 discussed at ¶ 7.4.06). If the donor's allocations in the governing instrument are controlling, then allocations made by the fiduciary pursuant to proper authority under the governing instrument should also be controlling.

If the second interpretation is correct, it remains to be explained what the IRS meant by shares that "could potentially be funded" with IRD when the fiduciary has a power to pick and choose which shares to allocate the asset to. The answer could be that, when the fiduciary has the authority (under state law or the governing instrument) to pick and choose which assets shall be used to fund which shares, the proportionate allocation rule of Reg. § 1.663(c)-2 applies if the fiduciary does not exercise the power, and the IRD is commingled with all other assets that could be used to fund each share.

Example: Tom's trust allows the trustee to pick and choose which assets will be used to fund which share. At the beginning of the year, the trustee holds the $1 million IRA, $1 million of real estate and $1 million of assorted other investments and cash. Early in the year the trustee withdraws $1 million cash from the IRA. As the months go by, the trustee pays some expenses, collects some interest, dividends and rental income, sells the real estate, pools all the cash in one account, sells some other investments, uses some of the commingled cash to buy short term notes that will mature shortly before estate taxes are due, and then, at the end of the year, makes a distribution of $200,000 cash to each beneficiary. The trustee has done nothing affirmative to allocate the IRA distribution to the charity or otherwise allocate any particular asset to a particular beneficiary; the IRD has been commingled with the rest of the trust assets. There is no way for the trustee now to identify the IRA proceeds and say "these are the IRA proceeds and I shall use them to pay the charity's share." In this case, the separate share regulations would clearly provide that the IRD is allocated equally to the two beneficiaries' shares because they *could* have been funded equally with the IRA proceeds.

7.4.09 *Avoiding deemed allocation by assigning the benefits*

As the discussion at ¶ 7.4.08 indicates, the meaning of § 1.663(c)-2(b)(3) is at best unclear and at worst negative (in the sense that the regulation may require pro rata allocation of IRD to beneficiaries' shares even when the fiduciary has, and exercises, authority for non-pro rata funding). Accordingly, planning should try to avoid the situation in which the trustee may not be able to get a charitable deduction for retirement plan distributions passed out to a charitable beneficiary. There are two ways to avoid the problem.

One way is for the governing instrument to specify that retirement plan benefits that are "IRD" shall be used to fund any bequest to charity that qualifies as a "separate share" under the regulations to the maximum extent possible (see ¶ 7.4.06).

If that approach is not available (for example, because Participant has already died, so it is too late to amend the trust to include that provision), the deemed allocation to non-charitable beneficiaries' shares of gross income arising from retirement plan distributions can still be avoided if:

1.   The trust gives the trustee authority to pick and choose which
        asset will be used to fund the charity's share; and

2.   The trust gives the trustee authority to distribute in kind; and

3.   The trustee, instead of taking distribution of the retirement
        benefits, instead assigns the retirement plan itself to the charity
        (see ¶ 6.1.06).

Following the assignment, the charity can take distributions
directly from the retirement plan. The distributions do not have to be
included in the gross income of the trust because the benefits are never
paid to the trust (¶ 2.1.01). The assignment itself does not trigger
realization of income; ¶ 2.2.04. The problem of Reg. § 1.663(c)-2(b)(3)
is avoided.

7.4.10 *Deduction if distribution to charity occurs in a later year*

The preceding discussion has dealt with retirement plan
distributions that are paid to a trust and distributed by the trustee to the
trust beneficiaries, where the plan-to-trust distribution and the trust-to-
beneficiary distribution occur *in the same taxable year of the trust*. If
the plan distribution is received by the trust in one taxable year, and
properly allocated to the charity's "separate share" of the trust under the
rules discussed in § 7.4.05, but nothing is distributed to the charity until
a later year, what happens?

If the amount is distributed to the charity in the year (Year 2)
following the year the income was received (Year 1), the trustee can
elect to treat the payment to the charity as if it had been made in Year
1 (and so can deduct it in Year 1). § 642(c)(1).

If the distribution to the charity does not occur until even later
than that, things get tougher. An *estate* can take a charitable deduction
for amounts "permanently set aside for" charity as well as for amounts
"paid to" charity. § 642(c)(2). Trusts, however, generally *cannot* take
a deduction for amounts that are merely "set aside for" charity; a trust
generally gets a deduction only for amounts *paid* to charity.

Therefore, if the distribution to the charity does not occur in the
same year the income is received by the trust, or in the immediately

following year, a trust will not get a charitable deduction for that amount, *unless* the trust is either: (1) subject to an election to be taxed as part of the decedent's estate under § 645 (see Prop. Reg. § 1.645-1(e)(2)(iii)(B), Example (iv); this election is not discussed in this book); or (2) eligible for a grandfather exception for certain pre-10/9/69 instruments (see § 642(c)(2)).

7.5 Types of Charitable Entities

7.5.01 *Overview of tax benefits of charitable giving*

So far we have been discussing "charity" as a potential recipient of retirement plan benefits as if all charities were the same. In fact there are many different types of entities that receive some special treatment in the Code because they dedicate all or part of their income or assets to charitable purposes, and each presents unique considerations as a potential beneficiary of retirement benefits.

This ¶ 7.5 examines various types of charitable entities from the point of view of their merits as potential beneficiaries of retirement benefits. This ¶ 7.5 does not cover every type of organization that may be eligible for one or another charitable deduction; it covers only the types most commonly encountered in estate planning. This section does not attempt to describe all the detailed requirements and attributes of these different types of charitable organization; for that information consult the sources in the Bibliography. Rather, the point of this ¶ 7.5 is to look at the principal distinguishing characteristics of each entity and describe the planning problems each presents with regard to bequests of retirement benefits.

In general, when considering the tax advantages of any type of charitable gift (not just gifts of retirement plan benefits), there are several different taxes to be concerned with. This ¶ 7.5.01 provides a brief overview of these various special charitable tax provisions, with a cross reference to a more detailed discussion of the particular tax provisions involved in charitable gifts *of retirement plan benefits*.

1.   Is the charitable entity exempt from income taxes (§ 501)? Since retirement plan distributions are generally includible in gross income (¶ 2.1.01), an important advantage of leaving such benefits to charity is avoidance of income tax. Public charities

(¶ 7.5.02), private foundations (¶ 7.5.03) and Charitable Remainder Trusts (¶ 7.5.04) are generally income tax-exempt, and therefore will not have to pay income tax on distributions they receive from a retirement plan. Pooled income funds (¶ 7.5.06) and charitable lead trusts (¶ 7.5.07) are not income tax-exempt.

2.　　　Do gifts or bequests to the entity qualify for the gift (§ 2522) or estate (§ 2055) tax charitable deduction? In the case of retirement plan benefits left to charity, the concern would be with the *estate tax* rather than the *gift tax* (but see also ¶ 7.6.01). The full value of retirement benefits left to a public charity (¶ 7.5.02) or private foundation (¶ 7.5.03) would be eligible for the estate tax charitable deduction. For benefits left to a Charitable Remainder Trust (¶ 7.5.04), pooled income fund (¶ 7.5.06) or charitable lead trust (¶ 7.5.07), only part of the total value (namely, the value of the charity's remainder or lead interest) would be deductible for estate tax purposes.

3.　　　Do gifts to the entity made by a living person qualify for an income tax deduction for such person, and if so what are the percentage limits on that deduction (see § 170)? Since this Chapter is concerned with naming charities as beneficiaries of retirement benefits *at death*, the individual income tax charitable deduction tax charitable deduction is not relevant (but see ¶ 7.6.01).

7.5.02 *Least-restricted or "public" charities*

§ 501 provides an income tax exemption for a lengthy list of organizations, including clubs, burial societies, employee benefit plans and, in § 501(c)(3), what people generally mean when they refer to "charities": "Corporations, and any community chest, fund, or foundation, organized and operated exclusively for religious, charitable, scientific, testing for public safety, literary, or educational purposes, or to foster national or international amateur sports competition (but only if no part of its activities involve the provision of athletic facilities or equipment), or for the prevention of cruelty to children or animals, no part of the net earnings of which inures to the benefit of any private shareholder or individual," and which does not engage in certain proscribed political activities.

Virtually this same definition is repeated in § 170(c)(2) (income tax deduction for gifts to any U.S. charity), § 2522(a)(2) (gift tax deduction for gifts by U.S. citizens or residents to charity), and § 2055(a)(2) (estate tax deduction for bequests to "charity"), except that:

1.   Unlike § 501(c)(3), none of these other sections includes "testing for public safety" in the list; and

2.   § 2522 and § 2055 (unlike the income tax sections) add "including the encouragement of art" to the list of charitable purposes; and

3.   § 170(c)(2)(A) limits the definition to *domestic* charities for purposes of the income tax charitable deduction (see ¶ 7.5.08).

These organizations are referred to in this Chapter as "public charities," meaning 501(c)(3) organizations that are not private foundations (¶ 7.5.03).

A public charity is totally exempt from income tax (except for the tax on "UBTI"; ¶ 7.6.02). § 501(a). Lifetime gifts to such charities are fully deductible for gift tax purposes. § 2522(a). Bequests to public charities qualify for the estate tax deduction, with no limit (other than that the deduction for the transferred property may not exceed the value of such property included in the gross estate). § 2055(a).

Lifetime gifts to all domestic charities qualify for the income tax charitable deduction under § 170(c). However, § 170(b) makes a further distinction, namely, between "50% charities" (i.e., charities gifts to which qualify for an income tax deduction of up to 50% of an individual donor's income), and "30% charities" (gifts to which qualify for an income tax deduction of only up to 30% of the individual donor's income). The latter (30%) group includes most "private foundations" (¶ 7.5.03), while the client's church, college, local community foundation and neighborhood non-profit hospital will normally all be in the "50%" group, as are such well-known major charities as the Red Cross, the United Way and the American Heart Association.

Making any type of gift (including a bequest of retirement plan death benefits) directly to a public charity presents the fewest problems.

The planner needs to verify that the organization is an exempt organization under § 501(c)(3) and, in the case of a major gift, the planner should review each of the Code sections under which a deduction will be claimed, to make sure that the organization in question meets the requirements. This is not generally a problem in the case of gift by a U.S. citizen to the typical charities mentioned above, but there are distinctions around the edges. For example, a *citizen's* gift to a charity organized "to foster national or international amateur sports competition" can qualify for the unlimited gift tax deduction, but the same gift by a *non-citizen* non-resident is subject to gift tax. Compare § 2522(a)(2) with § 2522(b)(2), (3).

7.5.03 *Private foundations*

In general, a private foundation is a "501(c)(3) organization" (see ¶ 7.5.02) that is primarily supported by contributions of one donor or family. However, the definition of a private foundation is notoriously convoluted (see § 509), especially since there are several different types and not all are subject to the same restrictions (see, e.g., § 170(b)(1)(E)). Untangling the various definitions and subsets of private foundations is beyond the scope of this Chapter. The discussion here will focus on how the special rules applicable to certain private foundations apply to retirement benefits payable to such an organization.

Certain private foundations, although exempt from "regular" income taxes (except on UBTI; ¶ 7.6.02), are subject to a 2% excise tax on net investment income. § 4940. PLR 9633006 ruled that a distribution from a Keogh plan to a foundation was subject to the 2% tax to the extent it represented investment income and gains accumulated inside the retirement plan, but not to the extent it represented contributions to the plan by the decedent or his employer. Timothy W. Mulcahy, CPA, criticized this ruling in "Is a Bequest of a Retirement Account to a Private Foundation Subject to Excise Tax?," Journal of Taxation, August 1996, page 108. Apparently the IRS agreed with his comments, and a later ruling, 9838028, held that the § 4940 tax "is a limited excise tax that applies only to the specific types of income listed in that section. Amounts from retirement accounts are deferred compensation income," not part of "the gross investment income" of a foundation, and therefore are *not* subject to the tax. PLR 2000-03055 came to the same conclusion.

7.5.04 *Charitable Remainder Trusts*

A "Charitable Remainder Trust" (CRT in this ¶ 7.5.04), as that term is used in this book, means a charitable remainder trust that meets the requirements of § 664.

The general idea of a CRT (for full details on these rules, see sources cited in the Bibliography) is that the trust pays out an annual income to one or more non-charitable beneficiaries (such as the donor and/or the donor's spouse or children) either for life or for a term of not more than 20 years. At the end of the life (or term) interest, the remaining trust assets are paid to charity.

A CRT must meet rigid requirements set forth in § 664. The annual payout to the non-charitable beneficiary (which is specified in the trust instrument) must be either a fixed dollar amount, in which case the trust is a "charitable remainder annuity trust" or CRAT, or a fixed percentage of the annually-determined value of the trust, in which case the trust is a "charitable remainder unitrust" or CRUT. The annual payout rate must at least 5% (but not more than 50%) of the initial trust value. A CRUT is slightly more flexible than a CRAT because it can provide that the annual payout to the non-charitable beneficiary is the unitrust percentage or the net income of the trust if less, and can even provide that there will be "makeup" distributions to the non-charitable beneficiary if in later years the trust's income exceeds the unitrust percentage. However, neither type of CRT can permit the non-charitable beneficiary to receive anything other than the unitrust or annuity payout amount.

A CRT pays no income tax itself because it is income tax-exempt (unless it receives "UBTI"; see ¶ 7.6.02). However, it has a unique internal accounting system called the "four-tier" system. Under this system, every dollar that the CRT receives is allocated to one of four tiers based on the federal income tax character of the receipt (ordinary income, capital gain, tax-exempt income, or principal). In effect, the CRT "remembers" what types of income it has received. Then, when the CRT makes a distribution to the non-charitable beneficiary, the distribution is deemed to come out of one of these tiers, and the federal income tax character of the amount is revived. If the distribution to the non-charitable beneficiary is deemed to come out of the ordinary income tier the beneficiary will have to include that distribution in his gross income as ordinary income.

Distributions to the non-charitable beneficiary are assigned to tiers on a "worst-first" basis, so (for example) the non-charitable beneficiary cannot receive any capital gain income from the CRT until the CRT has distributed everything it held in its ordinary income tier.

Some people mistakenly believe that, if they leave a retirement plan to a CRT, the CRT could take a distribution of the entire plan tax-free, reinvest the proceeds in municipal bonds, and pay tax-exempt municipal bond interest to the non-charitable beneficiary. This maneuver does not work, because the retirement plan distribution (to the extent it is "ordinary income"; see ¶ 2.1.01) all goes into the "ordinary income" tier. Even if the trustee *did* invest the proceeds in municipal bonds no distribution out to the non-charitable beneficiary would be treated as coming from the tax-exempt municipal bond interest "tier" until the ordinary income "tier" had been used up.

So, although the CRT pays no income tax when it receives a distribution from a retirement plan, the beneficiary of the CRT will have to pay income tax on the distributions *from* the CRT, to the extent those are deemed to represent the CRT's regurgitation of the retirement plan benefit under the four-tier system.

A *living person* who makes a gift to a CRT is entitled to an income and gift tax deduction equal to the actuarially determined value of the remainder (using IRS-prescribed actuarial tables and interest rates), which must be at least 10% of the value of the property given to the CRT. See ¶ 7.6.01.

When a *decedent* leaves a retirement plan or other asset to a CRT, the estate is entitled to an estate tax deduction equal to the actuarially determined value of the remainder (using IRS-prescribed actuarial tables and interest rates), which must be at least 10% of the asset's initial value.

The attraction of leaving retirement benefits plan death to a CRT is that the benefits are paid to the CRT with no income tax, meaning that the client's non-charitable beneficiaries can receive a life income generated by reinvestment of the *entire amount* of the retirement benefit. In contrast, if the non-charitable beneficiaries inherited the benefits as named beneficiaries under the plan, they would have to pay income taxes on the benefits as those were distributed to them, meaning that (once distribution of the benefits is complete) the amount left over for the beneficiaries to invest is vastly reduced. Thus they could expect a larger annual income from the CRT than they would receive by investing the after-tax value of any retirement benefits distributed to them directly.

This is not to suggest that the client's human beneficiaries will receive more money as life beneficiaries of a CRT that is named as beneficiary of the retirement plan than they would receive if they were named directly as beneficiaries of the plan. Normally the opposite is true, because an individual named directly as beneficiary of a retirement plan receives the *entire* retirement plan benefit, not just the income from the benefit. The income beneficiary of a CRT receives only the income from the reinvested plan proceeds; the proceeds themselves (the principal of the CRT) eventually go to the charity. Also, the economic advantage of deferral of distributions over the life expectancy of the beneficiary (¶ 2.1.02) reduces the negative effects of the fact that the distributions are taxable income to the beneficiary. Therefore, especially if a long-term life expectancy payout method is available, the human beneficiaries will normally do better financially by being named directly as beneficiaries of the retirement plan than by being life beneficiaries of a CRT that is named as beneficiary.

On the other hand, the payout from a CRT may be more attractive than naming the individual beneficiaries directly as beneficiaries of the retirement plan if long-term deferral is not available (for example, if the retirement plan in question does not offer a life expectancy payout; see ¶ 1.5.09), especially when the estate tax benefits of the charitable deduction are taken into account. For an example of how this mode of charitable giving may actually result in a "profit" to the family, see the Fallon case study in Chapter 11.

7.5.05 The "IRD deduction" and Charitable Remainder Trusts

Generally, when a human beneficiary of a retirement benefits receives a distribution from the plan, he must include such distribution in gross income as income in respect of a decedent (IRD) (¶ 2.2), but he is entitled to an income tax deduction for the federal estate taxes that were paid on those benefits. § 691(c); ¶ 2.2.07. If retirement benefits are paid to a Charitable Remainder Trust, that deduction for practical purposes disappears—nobody gets to use it.

Example: Participant leaves his $200,000 IRA payable to a charitable remainder unitrust (CRUT). The CRUT has no other assets. The CRUT is to pay a 10% unitrust payment each year to Participant's Child. On Child's death whatever is left in the CRUT is paid to the Red Cross. Child is 48 years old at Participant's death. Assume the value of

Child's unitrust interest is $180,000 for estate tax purposes and the federal estate tax attributable to this interest (¶ 2.2.07) is $83,000.

The first year after Participant's death the unitrust earns 7% ($14,000) but pays out 10% ($20,000) to Child. Clearly, $6,000 of the payment to Child is coming from the "principal" of the unitrust, and just as clearly this payment is coming out of IRD that the CRUT received. If the CRUT could pass out the deduction along with the IRD, Child would get a § 691(c) deduction of $83,000/$180,000 X $6,000 = $2,766. However, there is no mechanism by which a CRT can pass out such a deduction.

It appears that the 691(c) deduction would reduce the "taxable income" of the CRUT (i.e., the income assigned to the trust's "first tier"; see ¶ 7.5.04) in the year the distribution is received from the retirement plan. Reg. § 1.664-1(d)(2). All the distributions to Child would be deemed to come entirely out of the "net taxable income" of the CRT (first tier) until it had all been used up. The income of the CRT that was sheltered by the 691(c) deduction would effectively become "principal" that could be distributed to Child tax-free (fourth tier). However, the tax-free principal of the CRT is not deemed to be distributed to Child until after all net *taxable* income has been distributed. This point would never be reached in most CRTs, unless the unitrust payout rate substantially exceeds the anticipated income. In this example, if the trust continues to earn 7%, the 10% unitrust payments will not be coming out of the non-taxable funds until approximately year 26. Thus, some part of the unitrust payments Child receives after age 74 will be tax-free "return of principal" (distribution from the trust's "fourth tier") because of the § 691(c) deduction, but he gets no benefit from it for the first 26 years.

The IRS has confirmed this explanation of how § 691(c) applies to a CRT in PLR 1999-01023. Some practitioners disagree with the result in this ruling and argue that the unitrust distributions to the non-charitable beneficiary from the CRT should retain their character as IRD and therefore carry out the IRD deduction to the non-charitable beneficiary along with the taxable income, citing Reg. § 1.691(c)-1(d).

7.5.06 *Pooled income funds*

With a pooled income fund (see definition in § 642(c)(5)), the donor makes his gift to a fund maintained by the charitable organization that ultimately will receive the gift. The fund invests the gift collectively with gifts made by other donors, and pays back to the donor (or to another beneficiary named by the donor) a share of the fund's income corresponding to the relative value of the donor's gift. When the donor (and/or the beneficiary he nominated) dies, the share of the fund attributable to that donor's gift is removed from the fund and transferred to the charitable organization.

The pooled income fund has been called the "poor man's Charitable Remainder Trust," because it provides approximately the same benefits as a Charitable Remainder Trust (irrevocable gift of remainder interest to charity generates charitable gift (§ 2522(c)(2)(A)) or estate (§ 2055(e)(2)(A)) tax, and income (§ 170(f)(2)(A)) tax, deductions, while preserving a life income to the donor and/or the donor's chosen human beneficiaries), without the expense of creating and operating a stand-alone Charitable Remainder Trust.

Unlike Charitable Remainder Trusts, however, pooled income funds are not exempt from income tax. Reg. § 1.642(c)-5(a)(2); compare § 664(c). Thus, generally, a pooled income fund will file an income tax return, and include retirement plan distributions in its gross income, like any other trust would have to do (see ¶ 7.4.03). The fund can take a deduction for its *income* distributions to the non-charitable income beneficiaries (see § 661(a)), but the fund's receipt of retirement benefits is considered a receipt of *principal*, which the fund will not distribute to the non-charitable income beneficiaries. ¶ 6.1.07.

Can the pooled income fund take an offsetting charitable deduction for the amount of any retirement benefits included in its gross income? Generally, no. Like other (non-charitable) trusts, a pooled income fund is allowed an income tax deduction for amounts actually *paid* during the year (or in the following year) to charity (if paid pursuant to the governing instrument) (§ 642(c)(1)), but (like other trusts, and unlike an estate) a pooled income fund is generally *not* allowed a deduction for amounts that are merely permanently set aside for charity. ¶ 7.4.10.

Therefore, generally retirement plan death benefits paid to a pooled income fund will be subject to income tax in the year received by the fund to the same extent they would be taxable to an individual beneficiary (see ¶ 2.1.03). Accordingly a Participant who wants to leave his benefits in the form of a split gift, with life income to one or more human recipients and remainder interest to his favorite charity, can best do so by using a Charitable Remainder Trust (¶ 7.5.04), which is income tax-exempt.

7.5.07 *Charitable lead trusts*

A charitable lead trust (CLT) is the mirror image of a Charitable Remainder Trust (CRT) (¶ 7.5.04). Under a CLT, the charity receives either a fixed dollar amount (charitable lead annuity trust) or a fixed percentage of the value of the trust property (with such value being redetermined annually) (charitable lead unitrust) paid annually (or more often) for a fixed term of years, or for the life of an individual. At the end of the term of years (or upon the death of the individual who is the measuring life), the remainder interest is paid to individuals, such as the donor's children or grandchildren. (With a CRT, in contrast, the lead "unitrust" or annuity interest is paid to one or more individual beneficiaries for a term of years (or for life), and the remainder interest is paid to charity. § 664(d).)

The term "charitable lead trust" does not appear in the Code, but this type of entity is described in § 170(f)(2)(B).

Unlike a CRT, however, the CLT is not exempt from income taxes. Thus the CLT must include the retirement benefits when they are distributed from the retirement plan to the CLT. Because of this, leaving retirement plan death benefits to a CLT appears generally to be a disadvantageous way to fund such a trust.

Generally, the planning advantage of a CLT funded at death is that, in addition to satisfying the donor's charitable intentions, it may allow funds to pass to the donor's descendants (or other non-charitable beneficiaries) free of gift or estate taxes. This phenomenon occurs if the investment performance of the trust "beats" the IRS's § 7520 rate. When the initial bequest is made to the CLT, the IRS § 7520 tables are used to value the charity's and family's respective interests in the trust. The decedent's estate then pays estate tax on the value of the interest passing to the family. If the trust's investments outperform the § 7520 rate, all or part of the amount by which the investments outperform the § 7520 rate eventually passes to the family beneficiaries. Since the IRS rates did not predict that this value would exist, the excess value is never subjected to estate tax.

If the CLT is funded with retirement benefits, however, the CLT will generally start out at a disadvantage, since some of the principal that the IRS assumed the trust would have has in fact been used up paying income taxes. This makes it that much *less* likely that the trust will "beat" the IRS's § 7520 rate, because in effect the trust starts out with a loss. The client may well end up paying estate tax on *more* than the family beneficiaries eventually receive.

7.5.08 *Foreign charities*

Generally, an income tax charitable deduction is allowed only for gifts to charities that are "created or organized in the United States or in any possession thereof, or under the law of the United States, any State, the District of Columbia, or any possession of the United States...." § 170(c)(2)(A). The estate tax charitable deduction is not similarly limited to domestic organizations; compare § 2055.

7.6 Various Ideas and Issues

7.6.01 *Charitable gifts of retirement plan benefits during life*

How wonderful it would be if a Participant could transfer his retirement plan to a CRT, reserving the CRT income for himself and his spouse for life, never paying income tax on the underlying benefits, and even getting an income tax deduction for the value of his remainder gift. The author has seen this strategy recommended in print more than once, but it doesn't work. For one thing, qualified retirement plan benefits are non-assignable (with limited exceptions, but this isn't one of them). § 401(a)(13). For another, the income tax deduction for a charitable gift of ordinary income property is limited to the donor's basis, which, in the case of an IRA, is generally either zero or a relatively small amount. § 170(e)(1)(A); ¶ 2.1.04.

If the donor is willing to forego the income tax deduction part of the deal, can he assign an IRA to charity? An IRA is not *per se* non-assignable. One type of assignment is prohibited by the Code: if Participant pledges his IRA as security for a loan, it ceases to be an IRA and is treated as having been distributed to Participant. § 408(e)(4). The fact that one particular type of assignment is dealt with, and "punished," in § 408 implies that *other* assignments do *not* result in loss of IRA status. However, the IRS has made clear in various regulations that, in its view, the assignment of an IRA, although effective to transfer the account, causes it to lose its special tax characteristics. Reg. § 20.2056A, preamble, § E (dealing with the marital deduction for assets left to a non-citizen spouse), states that the assignment of an IRA to any assignee other than a 100% "grantor trust" would cause the assignor to be taxed immediately on the full value of the IRA. Similarly, the assignment of a Roth IRA by gift would be treated as a distribution of the account to Participant and the account would cease to be any kind of IRA after the assignment. Reg. § 1.408A-6, A-19; ¶ 5.5.07.

"The Charitable IRA Rollover Bill" has been a perennial proposal in Congress, though it has yet to become law. This proposal would allow individuals over age 70½ to transfer their IRAs to charity during life. While the donor would not be allowed an income tax deduction for the gift, he would also not have to recognize any income upon making the transfer. For comment on this proposal, see "Why Not Allow Lifetime Charitable Assignments of Qualified Plans and IRAs?" by Frank M. Burke, Tax Notes 7/7/97, page 121.

Until that legislation is passed, however, the only choice for someone who wishes to give his retirement plan to charity while he is still alive is to take a distribution from the plan and then give the same amount to charity. *Theoretically*, the charitable deduction should offset the income, so there would be no net income tax on the plan distribution; in real life, however:

A.　The percentage-of-income limits on the charitable deduction, the alternative minimum tax, state tax laws (which may not allow charitable deductions), and the limits on itemized deductions conspire to make it difficult in many cases to eliminate the income tax on large retirement plan distributions turned over to charity;

B.　Someone under age 59½ generally must pay the 10% penalty (see Chapter 9) if he takes a distribution even if the purpose of the distribution is to fund his charitable gift; and

C.　Someone who uses a retirement plan distribution to fund a CRT (¶ 7.5.04) to provide a lifetime income for himself and/or his spouse does not get an income tax deduction equal to the entire amount placed in the trust, since only part of it is a charitable gift.

7.6.02 *Unrelated business taxable income (UBTI)*

Although charities are generally exempt from income tax, they are taxed on their "unrelated business taxable income" (UBTI). § 511. If retirement plan distributions were considered UBTI, there would be no income tax advantage to leaving such benefits to charity.

The consequences would be even more drastic in the case of a Charitable Remainder Trust. A CRT is generally exempt from income tax if it meets all the requirements of § 664. However, a CRT is *not* income tax-exempt in any year that it has *any* UBTI. § 664(c). PLR 9253038 involved a CRT that was to be named as beneficiary of retirement benefits. The IRS ruled that the trust in question qualified as a Charitable Remainder Trust and thus was tax-exempt so long as it did not have any UBTI. Some practitioners take this ruling as implying that retirement plan distributions are *not* UBTI, although the ruling did not specifically say that.

7.6.03 *Gift of ESOP "qualified replacement property" to a CRT*

The Code allows a business owner, if various requirements are met, to sell stock of his company to an "employee stock ownership plan" (ESOP), then reinvest the proceeds in marketable securities ("qualified replacement property"), without paying income tax on the sale. § 1042. The untaxed gain carries over to the qualified replacement property and the capital gain tax thus deferred will be paid when the taxpayer "disposes of" the qualified replacement property.

A disposition of the qualified replacement property "by gift" does not trigger this "recapture" provision, but since the Code doesn't define "gift," there is some question whether transferring qualified replacement property to a Charitable Remainder Trust (which is not totally a "gift" if the donor retains an income interest) is considered a gift for this purpose.

PLR 9732023 answered this question favorably to the taxpayer involved in that ruling, concluding that "the contribution of the qualified replacement property to the charitable remainder unitrust will not cause a recapture of the gain deferred by the Taxpayers under section 1042(a) by operation of the provisions of section 1042(e)."

Unfortunately, even aside from the fact that a private letter ruling cannot be relied on as precedent, the language of the ruling is ambiguous and limited. It says: "In the present case, the transfer of the [qualified replacement property] to the charitable remainder unitrust constitutes a disposition of such property with the meaning of section 1042(e) of the Code. However under the facts of the present case, no gain is realized by the Taxpayers on the transfer...," with no indication of *why* no gain is realized. Presumably the rationale is that the transfer is a gift, and therefore excepted from the recognition of gain.

Assuming this ruling can be duplicated by other taxpayers, this approach represents a good way for some business owners to diversify their portfolios, and convert their closely held business into a lifetime income stream, without paying capital gain tax.

7.6.04 *Net unrealized appreciation of employer securities*

The Code gives special favorable treatment to distributions of employer securities from a qualified plan. Any growth in value of such securities which has occurred between the time the plan originally placed the securities in the employee's account and the time of the distribution is called "net unrealized appreciation" (NUA). Under certain circumstances, NUA is not taxed at the time of the distribution; rather, taxation is postponed until the stock is later sold. § 402(e)(4). When the stock is later sold, the NUA is taxed as long term capital gain; for full details, see ¶ 2.4.

A retired employee who holds stock with not-yet-taxed NUA has the same options that other individuals owning appreciated stock have when they wish to diversify their investments and/or increase the income from their portfolios: either sell the stock, pay the capital gain tax and reinvest the net proceeds; or, contribute the stock to a Charitable Remainder Trust (¶ 7.5.04) reserving a life income, thus avoiding the capital gain tax and generating an income tax deduction besides. See PLR 1999-19039.

7.6.05 *Charitable pledges (and other debts)*

If the client names a creditor as beneficiary of his retirement benefits, so that the benefits will be used to satisfy the client's debt to that creditor, the IRS would treat this as generating taxable income *to the client's estate.* Although generally retirement benefits are taxed to the person who "receives" them (in this case the creditor) (see ¶ 2.1.01), the IRS would say that the estate "received" the IRD, because the estate's debt was canceled when the benefits passed to the creditor.

A charitable pledge which remains unfulfilled at death may, depending on the facts and applicable state law, constitute a debt enforceable against the estate. See, *e.g.*, <u>Robinson v. Nutt</u>, 185 Mass. 345, 70 N.E. 198 (1904) (unpaid written charitable subscription enforced as a debt against the estate due to charity's reliance), and <u>King v. Trustees of Boston University</u>, 420 Mass. 52, 647 N.E. 2d 1196 (1995). However, a charitable pledge is *not* considered a debt for federal income tax purposes. Rev. Rul. 64-240 (1964-2 C.B. 172). Therefore, making retirement benefits payable to a charity as beneficiary, in fulfilment of a charitable pledge, will not cause the estate to realize income when the charity collects the benefits, regardless of whether the pledge was enforceable as a debt against the client's estate.

7.7 Summary of Planning Principles

1.   For a client who wishes to make charitable gifts upon his death, there are tax advantages to using retirement benefits to fulfill those gifts.

2.   Despite the tax advantages of funding charitable bequests with retirement benefits, such gifts have some pitfalls and complications, particularly if the benefits flow through a trust, or if part of the benefits will pass to individual beneficiaries.

3.   Making benefits payable to a Charitable Remainder Trust may maximize the value of the benefits to the family if the alternative is an immediate fully taxable distribution of the benefits at the Participant's death.

4.   The tax laws involved in charitable giving are just as complicated and technical as the rules dealing with retirement benefits, and when the two areas overlap the results are often unclear.

8

Disclaimers; Life Insurance; Grandfather Rules

Disclaimers have proven useful in post mortem planning for benefits. Life insurance held in a retirement plan poses unique challenges. Obscure "grandfather rules" can be beneficial to the few who qualify to use them.

8.1 Qualified Disclaimers of Retirement Benefits

8.1.00 *Overview of disclaimers of benefits*

A disclaimer is the refusal to accept a gift or inheritance. Federal tax law recognizes that a person cannot be forced to accept a gift or inheritance. Therefore, a disclaimer (provided it meets the requirements of § 2518; ¶ 8.1.01) is not treated as, itself, a taxable transfer. § 2518(a). Since the person making the disclaimer never accepted the property in the first place, the theory goes, he never owned it and therefore he could not have given it away.

Example: Mary dies, leaving her $100,000 IRA to Maureen as primary beneficiary. Maureen is already wealthy and does not want the money. Maureen disclaims the IRA by means of a disclaimer that meets all the requirements of § 2518 ("Qualified Disclaimer") and applicable state law. Under applicable state law, disclaimed property passes as though the disclaimant had predeceased the transferor (i.e., as if Maureen had predeceased Mary). Accordingly, the IRA passes as a result of Maureen's disclaimer to the contingent beneficiary of the IRA, who is Maureen's poor cousin Pat. Even though Maureen has voluntarily parted with her right to receive a substantial sum of money, an action that normally would be considered a gift, Maureen has *not* made a gift under the gift tax law. In contrast, if Maureen had "accepted" the IRA (for example, by withdrawing all the money from it and putting it in her bank account; see ¶ 8.1.05), and then written a check to Pat for

$100,000, she would have made a taxable gift.

Disclaimers can be very useful in post mortem planning for retirement benefits, as examples in ¶ 8.2 show. Unfortunately, many practitioners seem to have an oversimplified view of disclaimers; not every refusal to accept an inheritance is a *qualified* disclaimer, entitled to the blessings of § 2518. This ¶ 8.1 explains the critical *income tax* effects of disclaimers (¶ 8.1.02), and examines the requirements for a "qualified disclaimer," with emphasis on (i) how these requirements apply to disclaimers of retirement benefits and (ii) requirements that are often overlooked or misunderstood.

8.1.01 *Requirements of a Qualified Disclaimer under § 2518*

The following are the requirements for a Qualified Disclaimer under § 2518:

1. The disclaimer must be irrevocable, unqualified (unconditional) and in writing. § 2518(b), § 2518(b)(1). Yes that's right: in order to be qualified, the disclaimer must be unqualified! Verbal, revocable and conditional disclaimers are not Qualified Disclaimers.

Example: Harriet wants to disclaim two IRAs she has inherited. She writes to the first IRA provider that she disclaims IRA # 1, "provided such disclaimer will not make me ineligible for Medicaid." This disclaimer is not "unconditional," so it is not a Qualified Disclaimer. She telephones a representative of the custodian of IRA # 2 and tells him she refuses to accept IRA # 2 and wants no part of it. This is not a Qualified Disclaimer because it is not in writing.

2. The written disclaimer must be delivered to "the transferor of the interest, the transferor's legal representative, the holder of the legal title to the property to which the interest relates, or the person in possession of such property." Reg. § 25.2518-2(b)(2). See ¶ 8.1.12.

3. The disclaimer must be made within nine months after the transfer that created the interest that is being disclaimed (or, if later, nine months after the disclaimant attains age 21).

§ 2518(b)(2); ¶ 8.1.11. In the case of retirement plan death benefits, the date of the transfer is normally the date of death, but see ¶ 8.2.09.

4.   The disclaimant must not have "accepted the interest disclaimed or any of its benefits." § 2518(b)(3). See ¶ 8.1.05 through ¶ 8.1.10.

5.   The property must pass, as a result of the disclaimer, *to someone other than the disclaimant*. Exception: property can pass to the decedent's spouse as a result of the disclaimer, even if she is also the person making the disclaimer. § 2518(b)(4). See ¶ 8.2.05.

6.   The property must pass, as a result of the disclaimer, to whoever it passes to *without any direction on the part of the disclaimant*. Disclaimers in favor of the spouse are NOT excepted from this rule. § 2518(b)(4). See ¶ 8.2.06.

8.1.02 *Income tax treatment of Qualified Disclaimers*

§ 2518 recognizes Qualified Disclaimers "for purposes of this subtitle." § 2518 is part of Subtitle B of the Code, "Estate and Gift Taxes." Income taxes are governed by Subtitle A. Except for a minor provision dealing with disclaimers of powers by a trust beneficiary (§ 678(d)), there is no Code provision dealing with the effectiveness of disclaimers *for purposes of Subtitle A*.

The IRS Chief Counsel's office has filled the statutory gap, at least with respect to certain disclaimers of retirement benefits. GCM 39858 (9/9/81) ruled that a disclaimer of retirement benefits, if it met all requirements of § 2518 and applicable state law, is effective to shift the income tax on the benefits from the disclaimant (the person originally entitled to the benefits) to the person who receives the benefits as a result of the disclaimer. This GCM also held that such a disclaimer will not be deemed an "assignment or alienation" of plan benefits in violation of ERISA's anti-alienation provisions (§ 401(a)(13)).

Thus, at least for Qualified Disclaimers that are valid under applicable state law, we can be sure that a disclaimer will not be treated as an assignment of income or of plan benefits (either of which could cause disqualification of the plan and/or immediate taxation of the income in question).

8.1.03 *State law requirements of disclaimers*

It is very important for the disclaimer to comply with the applicable state law. The question of which state's law the disclaimer of a qualified plan benefit or IRA must comply with is beyond the scope of this book; leading candidates include the state of Participant's domicile and the state where the retirement plan is administered. If in doubt comply with both.

If the disclaimer is not valid under applicable state law, it may not be effective to transfer the ownership of the disclaimed property away from the disclaimant.

Example: Tanya files a purported disclaimer of an IRA she has inherited from her father. Although it is an unconditional written refusal to accept the property, and it is filed with the right person and within the required time frame, the applicable state law says that a disclaimer of an IRA is not valid unless it is notarized and Tanya's disclaimer is not notarized. The effect under the applicable state law is that Tanya still owns the IRA. Her disclaimer is not a Qualified Disclaimer (see ¶ 8.2.05).

Theoretically it is possible for a disclaimer to be qualified under § 2518 but not valid under state law; see § 2518(c)(3). However, under the IRS's interpretation of § 2518(c)(3), this could happen only if the state law dictates who will receive the disclaimer property in the event of an invalid disclaimer; compare § 2518(c)(3) and Reg. § 25.2518-1(c)(3), Examples 1 and 2. Thus, it would seem that this is rarely likely to actually occur. See also ¶ 8.2.08 regarding possible conflicts between disclaimers that are valid under state law and ERISA.

8.1.04 *Non-qualified disclaimers*

GCM 39858 did not purport to decide the income tax effects of a disclaimer that was either *not qualified* under § 2518 or *not valid under state law.*

The IRS has at least once treated a non-qualified disclaimer of a qualified retirement plan as effective to transfer the income tax burden of the retirement benefits to the person who took as a result of the disclaimer. See PLR 9450041. Nevertheless, a non-qualified disclaimer is clearly outside the safe harbor of GCM 39858.

This point is critical: there are cases when it does not really matter, for *gift tax purposes*, whether a disclaimer is qualified or not, but when the disclaimed property is income-taxable, as retirement plan distributions generally are (¶ 2.1.01), it is normally vital to have the disclaimer recognized for *income tax* purposes. See example at ¶ 8.2.05. If the disclaimer does not meet the requirements of § 2518, it may not be effective to shift the taxable income.

While the income tax effects of non-qualified disclaimers and disclaimers that are not valid under state law is uncertain, we have a safe harbor regarding the income tax treatment of a disclaimer that is valid under state law and qualified under § 2518. The rest of this ¶ 8.1 discusses how to meet the requirements of § 2518 in connection with disclaimers of retirement benefits. ¶ 8.2 discusses the planning uses (and pitfalls) of Qualified Disclaimers of retirement benefits.

8.1.05 *What constitutes "acceptance": overview*

One requirement of a Qualified Disclaimer is that the disclaimant must not "have accepted the interest disclaimed or any of its benefits." § 2518(b)(3). "Acceptance is manifested by an affirmative act which is consistent with ownership...." Examples of such an affirmative act include accepting "dividends, interest or rent from the property," "directing others to act with respect to the property" and "acceptance of any consideration in return for making the disclaimer." Reg. § 25.2518-2(d)(1). For exception for certain fiduciary actions, see ¶ 8.1.06.

Here are the easy clear examples of what does constitute acceptance. Assume Alpha dies and leaves 100 shares of Omega stock to each of his three children, Beta, Gamma and Delta. If a child predeceases Alpha, or disclaims the bequest of stock, that child's share passes to that child's issue if any, otherwise to the surviving children (or their issue).

A.   Beta receives a check for $10, representing the quarterly $.10-per-share dividend on his 100 shares of Omega stock. He endorses the dividend check, and deposits it in his bank account. Beta is deemed to have accepted *the stock* because he accepted *the income from it*, so he cannot later disclaim the stock. See Reg. § 25.2518-2(d)(4), Examples (6), (11). The proper way to disclaim an income payment in the form of a check is return the check uncashed along with a written disclaimer. Reg. § 25.2518-2(c)(5), Ex. (6).

B.   Gamma intends to disclaim all of his inheritance from Alpha, so it will pass to Gamma's children, but he thinks Omega stock is a terrible investment for them to own, so he calls his broker and instructs the broker to sell the 100 shares of Omega that were left to Gamma. Gamma has *exercised control* over the stock, and so cannot later make a Qualified Disclaimer of the stock (or of the proceeds of the sale of the stock). See Reg. § 25.2518-2(d)(4), Example (4), and ¶ 8.2.04.

C.   Delta neither accepts a dividend nor sells the stock, but Delta makes a deal with Beta that Delta will disclaim Delta's 100 shares of Omega stock if Beta disclaims some other property. By accepting *consideration* for his disclaimer, Delta is deemed to have exercised control over the property he is purporting to disclaim, and so he is deemed to have accepted the Omega stock. His disclaimer will not be qualified . Reg. § 25.2518-2(d)(1)(last sentence); Reg. § 25.2518-2(d)(4), Example (2).

On the other hand, certain actions do not constitute "acceptance." Acceptance must involve some action on the part of the beneficiary. Mere passive title-holding is not acceptance. For example, under many states' laws, if a decedent's real estate is bequeathed to a beneficiary, the title to that real estate automatically vests in the beneficiary on the death of the decedent. This automatic vesting does not constitute acceptance by the beneficiary, and does not prevent the beneficiary from making a Qualified Disclaimer of that real estate. Reg. § 25.2518-2(d)(1). See ¶ 8.1.07 and ¶ 8.1.08 for how this concept applies to retirement benefits.

8.1.06 *Limited exception for certain fiduciary actions*

This ¶ 8.1.06 discusses whether a person who is both a beneficiary and a fiduciary of the property can disclaim an interest *as beneficiary* despite having taken certain actions regarding the property in his capacity *as fiduciary*. For discussion of disclaimers by a fiduciary *in his capacity as fiduciary* see ¶ 8.2.07.

Actions by a person who is both a beneficiary and a fiduciary "in the exercise of fiduciary powers to preserve or maintain the disclaimed property" do not constitute acceptance *as beneficiary*. Reg. § 25.2518-2(d)(2).

Example: Mother dies and leaves her house to her three children A, B and C, and names C as executor. To fulfill his duties as executor under applicable state law, C arranges for insurance, security and maintenance for the house. These actions taken as executor would not preclude his disclaiming his interest as beneficiary.

This exception can easily lead practitioners astray. This is a very limited exception for which the IRS provides no examples in the regulations. The only fiduciary powers blessed are "to preserve or maintain the disclaimed property." Conspicuous by their absence from the list are such fiduciary powers as selling assets and allocating assets among beneficiaries' shares.

Also remember that any exercise of discretionary powers *to direct the enjoyment of the property*, even if exercised in a fiduciary capacity, would preclude a Qualified Disclaimer of the property by the individual in his personal capacity, unless the exercise of discretion is limited by an ascertainable standard. Reg. § 25.2518-2(e)(1)(next-to-last sentence). See ¶ 8.2.06.

ཟ⚬ཟ⚬ཟ⚬

Now we turn to how these rules apply to retirement benefits. No rulings or cases discuss what constitutes "acceptance" of a retirement plan death benefit, so we must analogize from cases, regulations and rulings involving other forms of property.

8.1.07 *Titling of the account does not determine acceptance*

The fact that a retirement plan account is retitled in the name of the beneficiary after the death of Participant does not in and of itself mean the beneficiary has accepted the account. See Reg. § 25.2518-2(d)(4), Example (6); PLR 8817061 (a surviving spouse's filing an election to take a statutory share of the decedent's estate did not constitute acceptance of the statutory share, so the surviving spouse could disclaim part of the statutory share); PLR 9214022.

<u>Example</u>: Rachel dies, leaving her IRA (which is held at Brokerage Firm X) to her husband Isaac. Isaac promptly calls Brokerage Firm X and informs them of Rachel's death. Brokerage Firm X retitles the account "Rachel, deceased, IRA, for the benefit of Isaac, beneficiary." Brokerage Firm X sends Isaac various paperwork explaining the account agreement, its fees, and his rights regarding rollover, investments and so forth. If this is all that happens, Isaac has not accepted the IRA. But: If Isaac gives Brokerage Firm X any instructions regarding the account, such as buying or selling investments, he has accepted the account (or at least those investments; see ¶ 8.1.09). If he names a successor beneficiary for his interest, see ¶ 8.1.10. If he takes a withdrawal from the account, see ¶ 8.1.09. If he elects, as surviving spouse of Rachel, to treat the inherited IRA as his own IRA (see ¶ 3.2.05) he has accepted it.

8.1.08 *Automatic deposit of benefits not acceptance*

It is common for a participant to arrange his IRA or other retirement plan so that periodic distributions are automatically deposited directly in his bank account. If the bank account is a joint account co-owned with the retirement plan beneficiary, the mere continuation of the automatic deposits after Participant's death would not, *in itself*, constitute acceptance of the retirement plan, or even of the amounts deposited, by the beneficiary, since there has been no action by the beneficiary.

<u>Example</u>: George receives monthly distributions of $2,500 from his IRA. These are automatically transferred, by the IRA provider, by electronic means, to the bank account he owns jointly with Martha, who is also named as beneficiary of the IRA. George dies on June 27. Two more monthly payments of $2,500 are transferred from the IRA to the bank account after George's death (on July 1 and August 1). When the IRA provider is notified of George's death, it ceases making the automatic transfers. Martha is not deemed to have accepted George's IRA just because of the continuation of the monthly automatic deposits, even though they were transferred into an account in her name, because she is not the one who directed that they be so transferred. These

deposits were initiated by George, not Martha.

Although the continuation of automatic distributions does not in and of itself create "acceptance" by the beneficiary, however, the waters quickly get muddied if the surviving account owner/beneficiary exercises control over the joint bank account funds after the Participant's death. For example, suppose Martha in the above example writes some checks on the (formerly) joint bank account, or withdraws some cash from it, after George's death, and later decides she wants to disclaim the IRA distributions that were placed in the account after George's death. (If she wants to keep those payments but disclaim the *rest* of the IRA, see ¶ 8.1.09.)

If she wants to say she never accepted the post-death automatic distributions from George's IRA, she presumably has to prove that the money she spent from that account after George's death did *not* come out of the post-mortem IRA distributions. If, after George's death and prior to the disclaimer, the balance in the account ever dipped below the then-cumulative total of the post-death transfers from the IRA, then Martha will not be able to argue that she did not accept the IRA distributions. So, for example, if in July, after the first $2,500 post-death automatic deposit came in from the IRA, the balance in the account dipped below $2,500, that would mean Martha must have spent some of the money from the IRA distribution. If she spent it, she accepted it.

On the other hand, if the account balance always stayed equal to or higher than the cumulative total of post-death IRA distributions, Martha should succeed in her claim that she never touched those distributions and so never accepted them. See PLR 2000-03023.

8.1.09 *Taking a distribution as acceptance of the entire plan*

If the beneficiary accepts a distribution from the plan, does that necessarily constitute an "acceptance" of the *entire* plan, precluding a Qualified Disclaimer of the rest of the plan? This problem becomes acute when a Participant who has passed his required beginning date (¶ 1.3) dies near the end of the year, not having taken his minimum required distribution (MRD) for the year. The beneficiary may feel rushed to take the MRD to avoid a penalty (¶ 1.5.03), but then, with more leisure to consider the matter, wish to disclaim the rest of the benefits. What the beneficiary would like to do in this situation is claim he has made only a partial acceptance of the inherited retirement plan.

The Code permits partial disclaimers. A person may disclaim "any interest" in property. § 2518(a). Reg. § 25.2518-3 is entirely devoted to disclaimers of "less than an entire interest." Several types of partial disclaimers are recognized, including a disclaimer relating to "severable property."

Severable property is "property which can be divided into separate parts each of which, after severance, maintains a complete and independent existence. For example, a legatee of shares of corporate stock may accept some shares of the stock and make a qualified disclaimer of the remaining shares." Reg. § 25.2518-3(a)(1)(ii).

When a beneficiary inherits an estate, or a joint securities account, the beneficiary has inherited in effect a collection of severable property. The beneficiary can take some assets from the inherited collection and refuse others. See Reg. § 25.2518-3(d), Ex. 17. The IRS has in rulings allowed beneficiaries to accept some assets from an estate, trust or joint investment account and later disclaim other assets. The favorable rulings (PLRs 8113061, 9036028 and 8619002) support the conclusion that a beneficiary may take a distribution from a typical self-directed IRA (which is, like an estate or a joint investment account, essentially a collection of severable property) without being deemed to have accepted the entire account and therefore without being precluded from disclaiming all or part of the rest of the account—unless possibly the distributions taken could somehow be construed as representing the income of the entire account. If the beneficiary thinks of this issue in advance, he can either execute a partial disclaimer before taking the distribution, or at least send in to the IRA provider, along with the request for a distribution, a written statement that the beneficiary is not accepting the entire account, just the amount of this distribution.

Taking a distribution *would* preclude a later disclaimer if the retirement benefit is not a collection of "severable" property. For example, suppose the retirement plan in question is a defined benefit plan, and the form of death benefit is a life annuity of $100 per month. As soon as the beneficiary accepts the first $100 check, he has accepted the entire benefit, because there is no way to "sever" the annuity.

8.1.10 *Naming a successor beneficiary as acceptance*

A beneficiary's designating a successor beneficiary for his interest in the account is probably not "acceptance." Reg. § 25.2518-

2(d)(1) provides that "The exercise of a power of appointment to any extent by the donee of the power is an acceptance of its benefits," but this apparently does not include an executory exercise; see Reg. § 25.2518-2(d)(4), Example (7), in which B is granted a testamentary power of appointment under A's trust and executes a will which would exercise the power, but then makes a Qualified Disclaimer of the power before he dies.

8.1.11 *Deadline for Qualified Disclaimer*

At one level the rule regarding the deadline for disclaimers of retirement benefits is simply stated ("nine months after Participant's death"), but when stated with all its exceptions and wrinkles the rule is more complicated: § 2518(b)(2) states that the disclaimer must be made "not later than the date which is 9 months after the later of--(A) the day on which the transfer creating the interest in such person is made, or (B) the day on which such person attains age 21." Now the wrinkles:

First, the deadline is measured from *the date of the transfer* which created the interest being disclaimed. Normally, in the case of retirement plan death benefits, the date of transfer is the date of Participant's death, but there are cases in which the transfer occurred or arguably occurred prior to Participant's death. For discussion of situations in which the time period may have started running *before* Participant died, see ¶ 8.2.09. *The rest of this ¶ 8.1.11 assumes the time period starts running at Participant's death.*

Second, if a beneficiary is under the age of 21 years at the time of Participant's death, the deadline for that beneficiary to complete a Qualified Disclaimer is nine months after the beneficiary reaches age 21. For the relation of this exception to the determination of Participant's "designated beneficiary" (for purposes of the minimum distribution rules discussed in Chapter 1) see ¶ 8.2.01.

Third, if the deadline for filing the disclaimer falls on a Saturday, Sunday or legal holiday (see Reg. § 301.7503-1(b) for definition), the deadline is extended to the next day which is not a Saturday, Sunday or legal holiday. Reg. § 25.2518-2(c)(2).

Fourth, in rules borrowed from the deadline for filing tax returns, the IRS provides that "a timely mailing of a disclaimer" to the correct person (¶ 8.1.12) "is treated as a timely delivery." Reg. § 25.2518-2(c)(2). Details of the requirements of "timely mailing" are found in Reg. § 301.7502-1(c)(1), (2), and (d).

8.1.12 *To whom is the disclaimer delivered?*

§ 2518(b)(2) requires that the disclaimer be received by "the transferor of the interest, his legal representative, or the holder of the legal title to the property to which the interest relates." Reg. § 25.2518-2(b)(2) adds one more candidate, "the person in possession of such property," but adds no further elucidation and no examples.

In the case of retirement benefits, the disclaimer cannot be delivered to "the transferor" (Participant) because he is dead, so that leaves "his legal representative" (i.e., the executor or administrator of Participant's estate), "the holder of the legal title to the property" and "the person in possession." The legal title to retirement benefits is generally held by the trustee (of a qualified plan or individual retirement trust) or custodian (of an individual retirement account or 403(b) mutual fund account), who also has "possession" of the retirement plan's assets.

The "or" in the Code and Regulation makes it appear that § 2518(b)(2) would be satisfied if the disclaimer is delivered either to the executor or administrator of Participant's estate or to the trustee or custodian of the retirement plan, in other words, that you have a choice of where to send the disclaimer. However, it is possible that, without specifically so stating, the government intends that the correct person to send the disclaimer to depends on the type of property; in other words, you can't just send it to any of the above, you have to send it to the right recipient. See Reg. § 25.2518-2(a)(3) and Reg. § 25.2518-2(c)(2), both of which speak of delivery to "*the person*" described in Reg. § 25.2518-2(b)(2), as though in the case of any particular asset there is only one possible recipient of the disclaimer and as though the menu of recipients in Reg. § 25.2518-2(b)(2) is only to accommodate different types of property, not to imply that for any type of property you can choose any of the foregoing.

Regardless of which destination would satisfy § 2518(b)(2), it is normally *also* necessary to comply with applicable state law requirements, which may have different or more specific requirements about where the disclaimer must be delivered (¶ 8.1.03). Also, in the case of a qualified retirement plan, check whether the plan has its own requirements about disclaimers and be sure to comply with those (see ¶ 8.2.08).

For what it's worth, in PLR 9016026 a qualified disclaimer of qualified plan benefits was filed with the employer and the plan trustee;

in PLR 9226058, a qualified disclaimer of an IRA was filed with the Probate Court. Other letter rulings discussing qualified disclaimers don't say where the disclaimers were filed.

8.2 Planning with Disclaimers

Disclaimers have proven to be of great value in "cleaning up" beneficiary designations where the deceased Participant named the "wrong" beneficiary. Disclaimers have been used to redirect benefits to the surviving spouse (so she can roll them over), and to create funding for a credit shelter trust that would otherwise have no assets. Under the proposed minimum distribution regulations, disclaimers will be increasingly important in establishing the life expectancy payout period; see ¶ 1.8.03. *Post mortem* planning flexibility can be increased if the possibility of disclaimers is planned for in the drafting stage, although excessive reliance on possible future disclaimers should be discouraged (¶ 8.2.04).

8.2.01 *Changing the "designated beneficiary"*

As explained in Chapter 1, § 401(a)(9)(B) requires that retirement benefits be distributed within a certain period of time after Participant's death. If the benefits are payable to a "designated beneficiary," that period of time is the life expectancy of the designated beneficiary. If the benefits are left to an individual ("Primary Beneficiary") who disclaims the benefits, and as a result of the disclaimer the benefits pass to a different individual ("Contingent Beneficiary"), which one of them is Participant's "designated beneficiary"?

The proposed minimum distribution regulations specify that disclaimers *are* given effect in determining who is the designated beneficiary. See Preamble, "Determination of the designated beneficiary." This result was in doubt under the pre-2001 version of the proposed regulations; see discussion at pages 308 *et seq.* of the 1999 edition of this book.

The proposed regulations provide that "the employee's designated beneficiary will be determined based on the beneficiaries designated as of the last day of the calendar year following the calendar year of the employee's death." That date is called in this book the

"Designation Date." See ¶ 1.8. "Consequently...any person who was a beneficiary as of the date of the employee's death, but is not a beneficiary as of that later date (e.g., because the person *disclaims entitlement to the benefit in favor of another beneficiary...*) *is not taken into account* in determining the employee's designated beneficiary for purposes of determining the distribution period for required minimum distributions after the employee's death." Prop. Reg. § 1.401(a)(9)-4, A-4(a) (emphasis added).

Thus, it is clear that an older beneficiary (such as a surviving spouse or child) can disclaim the benefits and allow them to pass to a younger contingent beneficiary (such as a child or grandchild) and the younger beneficiary will then be "the" designated beneficiary whose life expectancy becomes the Applicable Distribution Period, provided the disclaimer occurs prior to the Designation Date.

Note the following:

A.   Both of the proposed regulations' references use the term "disclaimers" rather than "Qualified Disclaimers." See ¶ 8.1.02, ¶ 8.1.04.

B.   If the beneficiary is under age 21 at the time of Participant's death, the deadline for such beneficiary's Qualified Disclaimer is nine months after his 21st birthday. ¶ 8.1.11. This could well be later than the Designation Date. A disclaimer (even if qualified) that does not occur until after the Designation Date is not effective to change the "designated beneficiary" for purposes of computing required distributions after Participant's death (see ¶ 1.8.01).

8.2.02 *Funding credit shelter trust*

In PLR 9442032, Participant named Spouse as primary beneficiary and his trust as contingent beneficiary. The trust provided that all IRA benefits had to be allocated to the marital trust, over which Spouse had a general power of appointment. No assets passed to the credit shelter trust. "To enable [the] estate to fully utilize the available unified credit," Spouse, as beneficiary of the IRA, disclaimed her interest in the IRA, and then, as beneficiary of the marital trust, disclaimed her general powers over the marital trust. As a result of these disclaimers, the IRA was now payable to a trust of which she was merely the life income beneficiary, with no general power of appointment. Then, as executor, she made a fractional QTIP election for the IRA and the trust. The non-elected portion of the IRA and marital trust became in effect the credit shelter trust.

8.2.03 *Salvaging spousal rollover*

If Participant dies having named the "wrong" beneficiary (typically, in published rulings, a trust), it may be possible to get the benefits to Spouse (so she can roll them over) by having the trust (or other "wrong" beneficiary) disclaim the benefits. This strategy works if, as a result of the disclaimer, the benefits pass outright to Spouse either as contingent beneficiary, or (more typically) as the "default" beneficiary under the plan (i.e., the person who, according to the governing provisions of the plan or IRA agreement, takes the benefits if Participant fails to name a beneficiary). If Participant's "estate" is the default beneficiary under the plan, this strategy still works *if* (as a result of the disclaimer) the benefits will pass outright to Spouse as residuary beneficiary under Participant's will or by intestacy. See ¶ 3.2.09. Unfortunately, this strategy doesn't work if Spouse will not get the benefits as a result of the disclaimer (for example, if the benefits will pass to the estate as a result of the disclaimer, and Participant's will or the state intestacy law would cause the estate to pass to Participant's children rather than to Spouse).

In PLR 9045050, Participant named a trust as his beneficiary. Spouse was a trustee of the trust. Upon Participant's death, Spouse, as trustee, made a Qualified Disclaimer of the benefits. As a result of the disclaimer, the benefits passed to Spouse outright rather than to the trust, and she rolled them over. PLR 199913048 was similar except that Spouse was not named as trustee of Participant's trust, but the named trustee declined to serve and the probate court appointed Spouse as "special trustee." Acting as special trustee, she disclaimed the benefits (with court approval) as did all other beneficiaries of Participant's trust, and the IRA passed to Spouse as the default beneficiary under the plan. Note that the IRS in this ruling did not regard the other trustees' refusal to serve, or the court's appointment of Spouse as special trustee, or the court's approval of the disclaimer by Spouse as trustee (which one guesses was required by local law to make the disclaimer effective) as constituting post mortem actions that made someone other than Participant the transferor of the benefits to Spouse.

In PLR 9450041, benefits were redirected from a marital trust to spouse via a chain of qualified and non-qualified disclaimers; the rollover was allowed.

8.2.04 *Building disclaimers into the estate plan: pitfalls*

It is wise, at the estate planning stage, to anticipate the possibility of disclaimers. For example, Participant may be trying to choose between naming Spouse as beneficiary, to achieve deferral of income taxes via a spousal rollover, on the one hand, and naming a credit shelter trust as beneficiary, on the other hand, to take full advantage of his unified credit. Each choice has its merits and a clear "winner" may not be apparent during the planning phase.

Participant may decide to make the benefits payable to Spouse as primary beneficiary, because his main goal is to provide for Spouse's financial security (for example), but provide that, if Spouse disclaims the benefits, the benefits will pass to the credit shelter trust. If funding the credit shelter trust appears to be the more attractive alternative at the time of Participant's death, Spouse can activate the credit shelter plan by disclaiming the benefits, which will then pass to the credit shelter trust as contingent beneficiary. PLR 9320015 contains an example of this type of planning. See also ¶ 10.5.

While it is wise to consider the possibility of disclaimers, the apparent flexibility of disclaimers can tempt planners to rely excessively on future disclaimers as a way of carrying out the estate plan. One justification for this approach is that it avoids the need to spend time analyzing the choices at the planning stage. Thus, professional fees are lower—at the planning stage. The estate plan relies on the fiduciaries and beneficiaries to make the decisions later, when a more informed choice can be made.

Before making important estate planning goals dependent on prospective disclaimers by beneficiaries or fiduciaries, the planner needs to weigh carefully the risks and drawbacks of relying on disclaimers. Contrary to the impression some practitioners have, disclaimers are not a simple solution. This ¶ 8.2.04 describes several issues that exist with disclaimers of any type of property. ¶ 8.2.05 and ¶ 8.2.06 explain two essential elements of a Qualified Disclaimer that are often misunderstood or overlooked. ¶ 8.2.08 and ¶ 8.2.09 discuss particular problems that arise with disclaimers of retirement benefits.

1.   One requirement of a Qualified Disclaimer is that the disclaimant must not have "accepted" the disclaimed property. Exercising investment control over the account would constitute acceptance; thus, if disclaimer is being considered by the beneficiary, the beneficiary must not make any investment changes in the account prior to the disclaimer.

2.   Disclaimers generally have an inexorable deadline of nine months after the date of death. ¶ 8.1.11. Thus, an estate plan which depends on disclaimers is extremely dependent on rapid action *post mortem*, especially if an IRS ruling is required.

3.   No matter how cooperative and disclaimer-friendly the proposed disclaimant may have been during the planning stage, the emotional turmoil caused by Participant's death, or other factors, could cause him or her to have a change of heart and not sign a disclaimer when the time comes.

4.   If estate taxes will be due on the disclaimed property, who will pay them? The decedent's will may contain a tax payment clause which may or may not operate correctly after the disclaimer.

8.2.05 *Property must pass to "someone other than" disclaimant*

§ 2518(b)(4) requires that the property must pass, as a result of the disclaimer, either to the *surviving spouse* or to *someone other than the disclaimant*.

Example: Donna is named as primary beneficiary of her brother's IRA. Within nine months of his death she disclaims the IRA. As a result of her disclaimer, the IRA passes to the contingent beneficiary of the IRA. The contingent beneficiary is a charitable remainder unitrust (¶ 7.5.04) of which Donna is the only non-charitable beneficiary. Since the IRA is not passing to "someone other than the disclaimant," and since Donna is not the spouse of the IRA owner, this disclaimer is not a Qualified Disclaimer (unless she also disclaims all interests in the charitable remainder unitrust). For *gift tax purposes* the fact that her disclaimer is not qualified makes no difference. Even though her disclaimer is treated as a gift for gift tax purposes there are no gift tax consequences, because the donee is a qualified charitable remainder trust (under § 664) of which the only beneficiaries are herself and a charity. Gifts to yourself or charity are not subject to gift tax. However, the fact that her disclaimer is not qualified means that the *income tax treatment* of the IRA is not within the safe harbor of GCM 39858. She may be liable for income taxes on the full value of the IRA (if the disclaimer is treated as an assignment of income in respect of a decedent under § 691; see ¶ 2.2.05).

This requirement is frequently overlooked, as planners cheerfully expect (e.g.) children to disclaim benefits that will then pass to a trust of which children are beneficiaries. Passing the benefits by disclaimer from the outright beneficiary to a trust only works if the outright beneficiary is (a) Spouse or (b) not a beneficiary of the trust.

8.2.06 *Property must pass "without direction" by disclaimant*

§ 2518(b)(4) also requires that the property pass, as a result of the disclaimer, to whoever it passes to *without any direction on the part of the disclaimant*. Disclaimers in favor of the spouse are NOT excepted from this rule.

Example: Emil disclaims an IRA left to him by his late wife, Emily. As a result of his disclaimer, the IRA passes to the contingent beneficiary of the IRA, which is a trust created by Emily. Although Emil is not a beneficiary of this trust, he is the trustee, and as such has the power to distribute principal, in his discretion as trustee (without any ascertainable standard), among the trust beneficiaries (Emily's children). Since the IRA is not passing "without direction on the part of the disclaimant," this disclaimer is not a Qualified Disclaimer (unless Emil disclaims his powers as trustee, or disclaims his right to be the trustee).

If the surviving spouse who is named as outright beneficiary of Participant's retirement benefits is to disclaim, she cannot thereafter retain any discretionary distribution powers over the disclaimed benefits (unless limited by an ascertainable standard). For example, if Spouse is disclaiming benefits which will then pass to a credit shelter trust for issue, she cannot be a trustee of that trust if the trustee has, say, discretionary power to "spray" the trust among Participant's issue; nor can she have a power of appointment enabling her to, *e.g.*, decide which issue of Participant will receive the trust after her death. Thus, taking advantage of the flexibility of disclaimers may eliminate the use of other, even more flexible *post mortem* planning tools, such as a spousal power of appointment.

8.2.07 *Disclaimers by fiduciaries of estates and trusts*

There is scant authority on the subject of disclaimers by fiduciaries (in their capacity as fiduciaries). There can be state law obstacles, such as a requirement of court approval or a requirement of specific language in the document authorizing disclaimers.

The requirement that property must pass "without any direction" on the part of the disclaimant (¶ 8.2.06) would presumably preclude a disclaimer from one discretionary trust to a second discretionary trust with the same trustees. The requirement that property must pass "to someone other than" the disclaimant (¶ 8.2.05) presumably bars a disclaimer by a trust in favor of another trust that has the same beneficiaries, or in favor of individuals (other than the spouse) who are also beneficiaries of the disclaiming trust.

The preceding statements deal with disclaimers by the trustee of a trust that is named as beneficiary of retirement benefits. When retirement benefits are payable to *Participant's own estate*, the IRS has ruled that Participant's executor may not disclaim the benefits (which in the case involved in the ruling would have allowed the benefits to pass to Spouse as default beneficiary under the plan) because Participant had "accepted" his own retirement benefits. PLR 9437042.

8.2.08 *Disclaimers and the plan administrator*

One concern is whether a plan administrator of a qualified retirement plan ("QRP") might cite ERISA requirements in refusing to recognize a disclaimer. A plan administrator might take the position that the plan requires the benefits to be paid to the beneficiary named by Participant, and the plan has no authority to pay the benefits to someone else if the named beneficiary is in fact living; that ERISA requires the plan to be administered in accordance with its terms; and that ERISA preempts state laws including disclaimer statutes.

In the author's view, this is not a correct interpretation of ERISA. QRP documents generally provide that the interpretation of the plan and administration of the trust are governed by state law to the extent not contrary to (or preempted by) ERISA. If the applicable state law permits disclaimers, the plan is required to give effect to them, in the author's view, unless the plan contains a specific provision to the contrary. All trustees, not just ERISA trustees, are required to administer their trusts in accordance with the terms of the trust instrument; most non-ERISA trust instruments say nothing one way or the other about disclaimers, but no one argues that trustees generally are entitled (let alone required) to ignore legally valid disclaimers. An ERISA trust is not different from any other trust except to the extent federal law requires it to be. In GCM 39858 (9/9/81), the IRS recognized that disclaimers do not violate ERISA. The IRS has blessed disclaimers of QRP benefits in numerous letter rulings; see, e.g., 9016026, 9247026 and 2001-05058.

In a similar vein, the IRS has recognized that a plan must conform to a state's "slayer" statute, and not pay benefits to the person who murdered the participant, even if that person is named as the beneficiary under the plan. See, *e.g.*, PLR 8908063.

On the other hand, the Supreme Court has upheld a QRP's refusal to follow a state statute that would have voided a beneficiary designation in favor of an ex-spouse. Egelhoff v. Egelhoff, 121 S. Ct. 1322, 532 U.S. 141 (2000). The Court cited ERISA's preemption and the need for uniform national rules for plan administration. Furthermore, in GCM 39858, while the IRS strongly endorsed the validity of disclaimers of QRP benefits, the approval was limited to disclaimers that satisfy the requirements of § 2518 and of state law (though the IRS has allowed the transfer of QRP benefits by *non-qualified* disclaimer at least once; see PLR 9450041). When confronted with a disclaimer, the administrator should consider obtaining an opinion of counsel that the disclaimer meets the requirements of applicable state law and § 2518.

Note that an employer who wanted to help (rather than frustrate) employees and their families could easily eliminate any possible ERISA-state law conflict by providing in the plan document that disclaimers would be given effect, and establishing reasonable procedures for verifying and implementing disclaimers.

These issues are of no concern to IRA administrators, since IRAs are not subject to ERISA and its pre-emption rule.

8.2.09 *REA and deadline for Qualified Disclaimers*

A Qualified Disclaimer must be made within a certain time period "after the ... date of the transfer creating the interest" being disclaimed. ¶ 8.1.11. The period is measured "with reference to the transfer creating the interest in the disclaimant." A transfer occurs when there is a "completed gift" (in the case of an inter vivos transfer), or (in the case of a transfer at death, or a transfer that becomes irrevocable at death) as of the date of death. Reg. § 25.2518-2(c)(3)(i).

So far, we have looked at retirement benefits under the assumption that the date of Participant's death is the starting point for measuring the time period during which a Qualified Disclaimer must be made. However, in any situation in which a beneficiary acquires rights in Participant's benefits earlier than the date of death we need to consider whether the time starts earlier.

Federal law gives married persons certain rights in each other's retirement benefits. See ¶ 3.4. Thus, under a qualified pension plan, Spouse acquires vested rights in Participant's benefits at the same moment Participant does (or upon their marriage, if the marriage occurred when Participant was already in the plan). If Spouse acquired rights in Participant's benefits more than nine months before the date of death, is it too late for her to disclaim these benefits when Participant dies?

§ 2503(f) provides that *certain* spousal waivers of retirement benefits are exempt from gift tax. Specifically, § 2503(f) says that, "If any individual waives, *before the death of a participant*, any survivor benefit, or right to such benefit, *under § 401(a)(11) or 417* [REA benefits, in other words], such waiver shall not be treated as a transfer of property by gift for purposes of this chapter" (emphasis added). Thus, the Code has a specific exemption from gift tax for *certain* spousal waivers, namely, waivers (1) of REA-guaranteed survivor benefits (2) that occur before the death of the participant. Does this mean that:

1.   <u>Waivers of *other* spousal plan benefits *are* taxable gifts?</u> Many plans, for administrative reasons, give spouses more benefits than REA strictly requires. Although the statutory exemption is limited to REA-guaranteed benefits, presumably the IRS would not attempt, in the case of a spousal waiver, to assess gift tax on the "enhanced" value of any plan spousal benefits over the strict

minimum guaranteed by REA. However, there is no authority on this question, yet, one way or the other.

2.   Spousal waivers that occur *after* the participant's death *are* taxable gifts? No. The IRS announced in GCM 39858 (9/9/81) that § 2503(f) does not imply Congressional intent to impose gift tax on spousal waivers that occur *after* Participant's death: "no inference should be drawn from § 2503(f) that a disclaimer of plan benefits *after* the participant's death should receive unfavorable tax treatment simply because Congress provided for favorable gift tax treatment if plan benefits are waived *before* the participant's death."

GCM 39858 involved a spousal disclaimer of REA-guaranteed benefits. The IRS stated that: "There is no evidence that Congress intended to preclude a spouse from disclaiming or renouncing benefits under a qualified plan payable after the participant's death." In view of the IRS's strong policy statement in this GCM, it appears the IRS has answered, for now, any questions that might exist about the disclaimer of REA-guaranteed benefits: such benefits can be the object of a Qualified Disclaimer, according to GCM 39858.

8.2.10 *Practical issues in disclaimers of retirement benefits*

If making a partial disclaimer, review Reg. § 25.2518-3, which discusses and gives examples of disclaimers of part of an inheritance by: disclaiming one or more separate interests in property while retaining others (Reg. § 25.2518-3(a)(1)(i); § 25.2518-3(d), Ex. (21)); disclaiming some "severable" property and accepting other severable property (see discussion at ¶ 8.1.09 and Reg. § 25.2518-3(a)(1)(ii); § 25.2518-3(d), Ex. (1), (3)); disclaimer of an undivided portion (Reg. § 25.2518-3(b); § 25.2518-3(d), Ex. (20)); and disclaimer of a pecuniary amount (or of everything except a pecuniary amount) (Reg. § 25.2518-3(c); § 25.2518-3(d), Ex. (16)-(19)). Follow the "successful" examples as closely as possible, and comply with state law requirements.

It's tempting to recite, in the disclaimer, who will receive the property as a result of the disclaimer, but it's not a good idea. Whenever you mention who the property is passing to, it looks like the disclaimant is either trying to direct who will receive the property or trying to make the disclaimer conditional on the property passing to those recipients. For an example of another type of extraneous language causing problems in a disclaimer, see TAM 8240012 (disclaimer of a pecuniary amount; disclaimant added the words "in cash or in kind"; IRS ruled this language did not sufficiently identify the assets disclaimed).

Investigate THOROUGHLY who will receive the property as a result of the disclaimer. A child (e.g.) may assume that if he disclaims an inheritance from father this will cause the inheritance to pass to mother only to find out later that the disclaimer caused the property to pass partly to mother and partly to some distant relatives of father. In the case of a retirement plan, normally a disclaimer by the primary beneficiary will cause the property to pass to the contingent beneficiary and a disclaimer by all named beneficiaries will cause the benefits to pass to the default beneficiary under the plan document.

If it is anticipated that a beneficiary might want to make a "formula" disclaimer (e.g., a surviving spouse as primary beneficiary disclaiming an amount sufficient to fully fund Participant's credit shelter trust), consider the practicalities of drafting such a formula, getting the plan administrator to accept it and then carrying out its terms all within a brief nine month window after Participant's death. If that looks like it might be difficult to accomplish, or if there is any other reason to anticipate the plan administrator may pose obstacles to the disclaimer (¶ 8.2.08), consider naming a trust as primary beneficiary, with the spouse as outright beneficiary under the trust. She can then disclaim interests in the *trust* as necessary to achieve the desired result. She will only need to deal with the (friendly, expert, understanding) trustee of Participant's trust and you sidestep the problems of dealing with the (cold, bureaucratic, non-knowledgeable) plan administrator.

Is it permissible to name one contingent beneficiary to take in case of disclaimer by the primary beneficiary, and a different contingent beneficiary to take in case of death of the primary beneficiary? The most common use of this dual designation of contingent beneficiary should not pose any problem to anyone, and that is where for example: (1) the primary beneficiary of an IRA is Spouse and (2) the contingent beneficiary of the IRA in case of Spouse's disclaimer is a trust of which Spouse is a life beneficiary ("Trust") and (3) the contingent beneficiary of the IRA in case of Spouse's death is the same person (or group of people) who is the remainder beneficiary of Trust at Spouse's death. The purpose of the dual contingent-beneficiary-designation on the IRA in this case is simply to allow Spouse to disclaim as outright beneficiary of the IRA, while keeping her interest as beneficiary of Trust; if she were *also* to disclaim her interest as beneficiary of Trust, the IRA would then pass to exactly the same people as would be the contingent beneficiaries of the IRA if Spouse had predeceased Participant.

In other words, even though it appears that Participant is naming "different" contingent beneficiaries on his IRA depending on whether Spouse predeceases him or disclaims the benefits, he really isn't. He's just allowing Spouse to decide what form she wants to take the benefits in (as outright beneficiary or as life beneficiary of a trust), which is perfectly alright under § 2518. It would be stupid to provide that Trust is also contingent beneficiary of the IRA *in case of wife's death*, because Trust won't even exist if Spouse predeceases Participant. In case of an IRA provider who refuses to accept the dual beneficiary designation in this situation, just name Trust as contingent beneficiary in both cases, then on Participant's death if Spouse predeceased the trustee of Trust will simply direct the IRA custodian to send the assets directly to the remainder beneficiaries of the trust (see ¶ 6.1.06).

8.2.11 *Disclaimers: summary of planning principles*

1.   Upon the death of a client, all plan and IRA beneficiary designations should be reviewed as soon as possible. Either: (a) no benefits should be distributed to any beneficiary until this review is completed or (b) if a beneficiary wants to take a distribution (or must do so to comply with the minimum distribution rules) the request for the distribution should be accompanied by a statement that the beneficiary is not thereby signifying his acceptance of the entire account (just the amount distributed). No beneficiary should exercise investment (or other) control over inherited plan benefits until this review is completed. If any beneficiary designation appears undesirable, consider the use of Qualified Disclaimers to redirect benefits to the "right" beneficiary.

2.   When preparing beneficiary designations as part of the estate planning process, be sure to name a contingent as well as a primary beneficiary. Consider whether different contingent beneficiaries should be named in case of a disclaimer by, as opposed to the death of, the primary beneficiary.

3.　　　When choosing among competing considerations in naming a primary beneficiary, the client should make the choice based on the relative priorities the client assigns to the choices (such as "financial security of spouse" versus "saving estate taxes for children"). To allow maximum flexibility after the client's death, name the second choice as contingent beneficiary.

4.　　　When a disclaimer is anticipated at the estate planning stage, take steps beforehand to facilitate that process, including: spousal waiver of REA rights, if needed; clear instructions to the beneficiaries regarding the choices that will be available to them and what considerations should be applied in making the choice; granting disclaimer authority to fiduciaries, along with guidelines for exercise of the power to disclaim; review the plan documents, § 2518 requirements, and state law to make sure these pose no obstacles to the proposed disclaimers; and make sure that there are no instructions for automatic benefit distributions which could create issues regarding "acceptance" of the benefits after Participant's death.

8.3　Plan-Owned Life Insurance: Income Taxes

This ¶ 8.2 explains the income tax consequences, to the plan participant ("Participant" or "employee") and his beneficiaries, of buying and holding life insurance in a qualified retirement plan ("QRP"). To enhance understanding, these consequences are contrasted with (a) the tax treatment of non-life insurance plan benefits and (b) the tax treatment of life insurance that is not held in a QRP. ¶ 8.3 discusses other planning considerations involved when dealing with plan-owned life insurance.

This Chapter discusses QRP-owned life insurance *from the perspective of the Participant*. Rules that are of concern only at the plan level (such as the limits on how much life insurance can be purchased in a QRP, and ERISA fiduciary investment rules) are beyond the scope of this book. For other sources, see the Bibliography. Similarly, the analysis of insurance products is beyond the scope of this book.

8.3.01　*Income tax consequences during employment*

Generally, an employee pays no income tax on his employer's

contributions to a retirement plan, or on plan earnings, until these are actually distributed to him. However, if the employer contributions (or plan earnings) are used to purchase *life insurance* on the employee's life, then the employee *does* become currently taxable on part of the retirement plan contributions or earnings.

§ 72(m)(3)(B) and Reg. § 1.72-16(b) govern the tax treatment of life insurance contracts purchased by QRPs when (a) the premium is paid with deductible employer contributions or with plan earnings and (b) the policy proceeds are payable to Participant or Participant's beneficiary. The amount "applied to purchase" such life insurance, as determined by IRS regulations, is includible currently in Participant's gross income (regardless of whether the amount is "vested").

The regulations provide that the amount of life insurance protection deemed purchased in any year is the difference between the death benefit payable under the policy and the cash surrender value of the policy at the end of the year. Reg. § 1.72-16(b)(3). Once the amount of life insurance protection provided is thus determined, the IRS next tells us how much of the employer contribution and plan earnings are deemed to have been "applied to purchase" this life insurance protection. The IRS has issued the following pronouncements on this subject:

1.   **Term Insurance**. When a QRP buys term insurance on the life of a Participant, the entire premium is includible in Participant's gross income. Rev. Rul. 54-52, 1954-1 C.B. 150.

2.   **Other Insurance: before Notice 2001-10.** If the policy provides more than "pure" death benefit protection (for example, if it also provides annuity benefits or if it has or will have a cash value), Rev. Rul. 55-747, 1955-2 C.B. 228 provided a table, called "P.S. 58," to be used to calculate the amount includible in Participant's gross income. This ruling was later modified by Rev. Ruls. 66-110, 1966-1 C.B. 12, and 67-154, 1967-1 C.B. 11, which provided that the insurer's lowest published rate for one-year term insurance available on an initial issue basis for "all standard risks" could be used if that rate was lower than the "P.S. 58 cost." Generally, the insurer's published term rates are considerably lower than the P.S. 58 Table rates.

3.   **Other Insurance: after Notice 2001-10.** In Notice 2001-10,
        2001-5 I.R.B. 459, the IRS took official notice of the fact that
        the P.S. 58 table rates are too high, revoked Rev. Rul. 55-747,
        and published a new table, "Table 2001," with considerably
        lower rates.

        Here are the options, going forward, for what the employee
must report as income each year due to non-term life insurance on his
life held in the retirement plan. After the amount of life insurance
protection is determined (see explanation above; this has not changed),
the amount reportable as the value of that insurance protection (which
the employee must include in gross income) is either taken from an IRS
table or from the insurer's actual rates. The choices are as follows,
"pending...further guidance" from the IRS:

A.   Table: For "taxable years ending on or before December 31,
        2001, taxpayers may continue to use the P.S. 58 rates set forth
        in Rev. Rul. 55-747 for purposes of determining the value of
        current life insurance protection provided to an employee
        under...a qualified retirement plan." Taxpayers may also use
        Table 2001 "to determine the value of current life insurance
        protection on a single life provided under a...qualified
        retirement plan for taxable years ending after the date of
        issuance of this notice" (January 2001). So for calendar 2001
        taxpayer can use either the P.S. 58 Table or Table 2001; after
        2001, only Table 2001 may be used. Notice 2001-10, Part
        IV(B)(1), (2).

B.   Insurer's published rates: "Taxpayers may continue to
        determine the value of current life insurance protection by using
        the insurer's lower published premium rates" as set forth in
        Rev. Rul. 66-110, subject to the following caveats about the
        future of this method: First, "for periods after December 31,
        2003" (not specified whether this means period ending after or
        beginning after 12/31/03), the IRS may require more
        substantiation from the insurer that these alleged premium rates
        are really in use (see Notice for details). Second, "no assurance
        is provided" that, "after the later of December 31, 2003, or
        December 31 of the year in which further guidance" is issued,
        the IRS will allow this method of determining the cost of

insurance protection *at all* for insurance contracts or certificates "issued after February 28, 2001." Notice 2001-10, Part IV(B)(3).

In the rest of this Chapter, "Current Insurance Cost" is used as shorthand for "the amount Participant is required to include in gross income because of the plan-held life insurance." In any particular case, this may be the rate from Table P.S. 58, the rate from Table 2001, or the insurance company's actual term rates if lower, whichever is applicable.

The amount of currently taxable income generated by a plan-owned policy rises as the employee gets older because term rates go up with age. If the cash surrender value of the policy increases over the years, this increase will reduce the "pure" death benefit (total face value of policy minus cash surrender value), which in turn would reduce the Current Insurance Cost.

The employee must find the cash elsewhere to pay the income tax on the Current Insurance Cost. For example, an employee in the 45% tax bracket (considering federal, FICA, state and local income taxes) must earn $818 of taxable salary to pay the income tax on $1,000 of Current Insurance Cost. For this individual, the tax on $1,000 of Current Insurance Cost is $450. He must earn $818 of taxable salary in order to have, after income taxes, the $450 of cash he needs to pay the income tax on the Current Insurance Cost. This income tax obligation continues even if the employer stops paying premiums on the policy (which can happen if the policy becomes "self-financing," meaning that the premiums are paid through policy dividends).

The amount included in Participant's gross income over the years on account of the Current Insurance Cost is considered his "investment in the contract" and in effect becomes his "basis" in the policy. See ¶ 2.1.04. Participant is entitled to recover this basis tax-free, but only if the policy itself is distributed to him. If the policy lapses, or is surrendered for its cash surrender value at the plan level, Participant's "basis" disappears and cannot be offset against other plan distributions. In other words, the payment of income taxes over the years on the Current Insurance Cost generates a "basis" that may or may not be recouped later. Reg. § 1.72-16(b)(4).

On the other hand, since the "Current Insurance Cost" is supposed to represent the annual cost of pure insurance protection, it is surprising the IRS allows it to be used as "basis" for any purpose; it is really an expense. An "owner employee" (see "Keogh plan," Glossary) does not get to treat even the Current Insurance Cost as an investment in the contract. Reg. § 1.72-16(b)(4).

8.3.02 *Issues at retirement: the "rollout"*

At retirement, Participant will typically face some thorny issues regarding the life insurance policy.

The IRS generally requires that life insurance policies be either converted to cash or distributed to Participant at "retirement." This is one of the constellation of plan qualification requirements known as the "incidental benefit rule," the gist of which is that a retirement plan is supposed to provide retirement benefits, and may provide only "incidental" other benefits. See Rev. Rul. 54-51, 1954-1 C.B. 147, as modified by Rev. Ruls. 57-213, 1957-1 C.B. 157, and 60-84, 1960-1 C.B. 159. If the life insurance policy is distributed, it cannot be rolled over to an IRA because an IRA cannot own life insurance (¶ 8.4.05). "Converting the policy to cash" would mean that the plan either sells the policy for cash, or terminates the policy by surrendering it to the insurance company (in exchange for which the insurance company would pay the plan an amount of cash equal to the policy's cash surrender value).

So, at retirement, Participant must either take the policy out of the plan as a distribution (thus losing further income tax deferral; see ¶ 8.3.03), or buy the policy from the plan (which requires coming up with cash; see ¶ 8.3.04), or terminate the policy by surrendering it to the insurance company (which means loss of the policy's insurance protection).

The unpleasant choices at retirement can be postponed *if* the plan is a profit sharing plan *and* the policy was paid for only with money held in the plan for more than two years, because this type of money is not subject to the "incidental benefit rule." Rev. Rul. 60-83, 1960-1 C.B. 157. In this situation, Participant can leave the policy in the plan along with his other benefits and withdraw it later (subject to the minimum distribution rules; Chapter 1). The annual taxable income to him from the existence of the policy in the plan will continue (¶ 8.3.01). The ability to keep the policy in the plan does not exist even for a profit sharing plan if the retirement plan is terminated altogether when the employee retires, as is often the case in a small business upon retirement of the business owner.

In contrast, if the employee buys his insurance *outside* of the retirement plan to begin with, the issues at retirement (which even an insurance agent has described as "the enormous gift and income tax consequences associated with a rollout to an insurance trust"; see ¶ 8.3.03-¶ 8.3.04 for details) simply do not arise. *All* retirement benefits can be cleanly rolled over to an IRA and taken out when Participant feels like it (subject to the minimum distribution rules); and the cash value build-up of the insurance policy is not subject to income tax at retirement or death or any other time.

8.3.03 *Rollout option #1: Plan distributes policy to Participant*

If the policy is distributed to Participant, Participant must include in gross income the "fair market value" of the policy (less his basis). Reg. § 1.402(a)-1(a)(1)(iii). The IRS has stated that the fair market value of a life insurance policy is its cash surrender value *unless* "the total policy reserves [established by the insurer to cover the death benefit, advance premium payments, etc.] ...represent a much more accurate approximation of the fair market value of the policy...." If the policy's reserves "substantially exceed" the policy's cash surrender value, the reserves represent a much "more accurate approximation of the fair market value of the policy," and Participant is required to include the amount of the policy reserves (minus his basis), not the cash surrender value (minus his basis), in gross income. Notice 89-25, Q&A 10, 1989-1 C.B. 662.

This is hardly a bright line test. How much larger than the cash surrender value must the reserves be before the reserves are deemed to "substantially exceed" the cash surrender value? In the Notice's example, the reserves were 3.8 times greater than, and were held to "substantially exceed," the cash surrender value. It appears that, if the policy is to be distributed *or sold* to Participant, the following steps are required:

1.   Determine the policy's cash surrender value.

2.   Obtain from the insurer a statement of the value of all policy reserves as of the proposed date of distribution of the policy.

3.   If (2) "substantially exceeds" (1), use (2) as the policy's value.

4.   If (2) does not "substantially exceed" (1), use (1) as the policy's value.

5.   If (2) exceeds (1), but it is unclear whether (2) "*substantially*" exceeds (1), obtain a ruling regarding which figure to use.

In determining his taxable income resulting from distribution of the policy a Participant who is not an "owner-employee" is entitled to offset, against the "fair market value" of the policy, his basis, i.e., the amounts includible in his gross income over the years on account of the plan's ownership of this policy (¶ 8.3.01), which are considered to be "premiums or other consideration paid" by Participant. Reg. § 1.72-16(b)(4).

A discrepancy between the cash surrender value and the "policy value" may create problems at the *plan* level, possibly affecting the plan's qualification, according to Notice 89-25. Those issues are beyond the scope of this book.

8.3.04 *Rollout Option #2: Plan sells policy to Participant*

If the policy is distributed to Participant (¶ 8.3.03), then all further opportunity to defer income taxes on the amount represented by the policy value is lost. For this reason, Participant may look at the possibility of purchasing the policy from the plan. Although this requires Participant to come up with some cash from other sources, it does allow him to continue deferring income tax on the amount represented by the policy value. Participant will own the policy (which he can transfer to an irrevocable trust, if he wants to remove the proceeds from his gross estate); and the plan will own cash, which can then be distributed to Participant and rolled over to an IRA for maximum continued deferral.

Buying the policy from the plan creates an ERISA problem. ERISA § 406(a) (29 U.S.C.§ 1106(a)) prohibits the sale of plan assets to a "party in interest." The definition of "parties in interest" includes categories one would expect, such as plan fiduciaries, the employer, and officers, directors and 10% owners of the employer. It also includes, surprisingly, any *employee* of the employer. ERISA § 3(14) (29 U.S.C. § 1002(14)). Thus, as an initial proposition, the sale of a life insurance policy from the plan to the insured employee is a "prohibited transaction."

The Department of Labor has issued a "Prohibited Transaction Class Exemption" (PTE 92-6, 2/12/92, 57 Fed. Reg. 5190; reproduced at RIA Pension Coordinator, page 94,456) which exempts such sales if certain requirements are met. Thus, if the desired approach is to have Participant buy the policy from the plan, there are two ways that this might be accomplished:

1.   Comply with PTE 92-6; or,

2.   If Participant does not have any connection with the employer or the plan except as an employee, it might be worth exploring the possibility that the sale is not a "prohibited transaction" once Participant retires and ceases to be an employee. Consult an ERISA specialist before embarking on this course.

To comply with PTE 92-6 when the insured employee is buying the policy from the plan, the following two requirements must be met:

1.   The contract would, but for the sale, be surrendered by the plan. PTE 92-6, I(3). This requirement is not a problem, if Participant is retiring, for the type of QRP that is *required* to sell or surrender the policy at that point (¶ 8.3.02).

2.   The price must be "at least equal to the amount necessary to put the plan in the same cash position as it would have been in had it retained the contract, surrendered it, and made any distribution owing to the participant of his vested interested [sic] under the plan." There is no offset for the Participant's basis mentioned in this formulation.

8.3.05 *Income tax consequences to beneficiaries*

§ 72(m)(3)(C) dictates that, in the case of a life insurance policy purchased by a retirement plan, the distribution of the cash surrender value is treated as a "payment under such plan," rather than as a distribution of life insurance proceeds (which is tax-exempt under § 101(a)). Thus, to the extent of the cash surrender value immediately before Participant's death, life insurance proceeds are treated the same as all other retirement plan distributions, which are normally subject to income tax when paid out to the beneficiaries after Participant's death.

Despite the fact that Participant might have been taxable on *more* than the cash surrender value if the policy had been distributed to him during life (¶ 8.3.03), the regulations state that only the cash surrender value is taxable to the beneficiaries after Participant's death. Also, the beneficiaries are entitled to deduct the amount of Participant's "basis" in the policy (¶ 8.3.01) from the amount otherwise includible in their gross income. See Reg. § 1.72-16(c)(3), Ex. 1.

This treatment of plan-owned life insurance compares unfavorably with the treatment of insurance policies purchased outside of retirement plans, proceeds of which are received by the beneficiaries 100% income tax-free. § 101(a).

8.4 Plan-Owned Life Insurance: Other Aspects

This ¶ 8.4 explains estate tax and other aspects of holding life insurance in a qualified retirement plan.

8.4.01 *Estate tax avoidance: the life insurance subtrust*

For the estate tax-conscious client, an important consideration in buying life insurance is to keep the insurance out of the insured's estate (and, in the case of a married person, his spouse's estate), to increase the value of the benefits for subsequent beneficiaries (who are referred to as the client's "children" in the following discussion, because that is the most commonly seen situation, but who could be any related or unrelated persons).

If the policy is purchased *outside* the retirement plan, it is easy to accomplish this goal. The client creates an irrevocable trust for the benefit of his intended beneficiaries; and the trustee buys the policy. The policy proceeds are never part of either spouse's estate. If the policy is bought through a retirement plan, on the other hand, it is not clear whether the proceeds can be kept out of the estate of the insured Participant.

Generally, the estate tax includability of retirement plan benefits is governed by § 2039. However, § 2042, not § 2039, governs estate tax treatment of life insurance even if the insurance is held inside a retirement plan. § 2039(a). Life insurance is subject to estate tax if it is payable to the insured's estate, or if the insured owns any "incident of ownership." § 2042. To keep plan-held life insurance out of the insured Participant's estate, therefore, it is necessary to deprive Participant of such "incidents of ownership" as the power to name the beneficiary of the policy, the power to surrender or borrow against the policy, and a reversionary interest (worth 5% or more) in the policy. § 2042(2); Reg. § 20.2042-1(c)(2).

Some practitioners believe this goal can be accomplished by establishing a "subtrust," which is defined as "an irrevocable life insurance trust slotted within the trust otherwise used to fund the pension or profit sharing plan" (definition from "The Qualified Plan as an Estate Planning Tool," by Andrew J. Fair, Esq., published by Guardian Life Insurance Company of America, New York, NY, 1995) (Pub. No. 2449).

The merits of the subtrust have been debated in numerous articles. See the Bibliography. Some writers conclude that the subtrust works to keep policy proceeds out of the estate, without disqualifying the underlying retirement plan. Other writers state that either the existence of the subtrust disqualifies the plan, or, if the plan *is* qualified, it is impossible for Participant not to have estate-taxable incidents of ownership in the policy.

It remains to be seen whether the subtrust device works as a way of keeping the policy proceeds out of the estate. To date, there is no published ruling or case upholding (or denying) the estate tax exclusion for life insurance held in a retirement plan subtrust. A loss on the estate tax issue could result in a tax of 40%-60% of the amount of the policy proceeds.

Even if the subtrust device does keep the death benefit out of the gross estate if Participant dies prior to retirement, new problems arise once Participant reaches retirement. If he then either buys the policy out of the plan (¶ 8.3.03) or receives it as a distribution (¶ 8.3.02), Participant is right back in the position of owning the policy. He will then have to contribute it to an irrevocable trust, and survive for three more years after the transfer, in order to get it out of his estate again. § 2035(a). See the next subsection for strategies people use to try to get the policy out of the plan, and into an irrevocable insurance trust, without triggering § 2035(a)'s three-year waiting period for estate tax exclusion.

8.4.02 *Avoiding estate tax inclusion at "rollout"*

As discussed at ¶ 8.3.02-¶ 8.3.04, the normal course is for the retirement plan to sell or distribute the policy to Participant at retirement. Participant may wish at that point to transfer the policy to his intended beneficiaries (or to an irrevocable trust for their benefit) to get the proceeds out of his estate for estate tax purposes. Since gifting the policy would not remove the proceeds from Participant's estate until three years have elapsed (§ 2035(a)), practitioners look for an alternative way to get the policy into the hands of the beneficiaries (or trust) without the three-year waiting period.

Since the plan cannot distribute benefits to anyone other than Participant during Participant's lifetime (because of ERISA's "exclusive benefit rule"), the only way out is for the plan to *sell* the policy to the intended beneficiaries (or trust), or else distribute or sell the policy to Participant, and have Participant sell it to the beneficiaries (or trust). Such sales raise several issues (in addition to the question of where the beneficiaries (or trust) will get the money to buy the policy):

The first problem is the "transfer for value" rule of § 101(a)(2). Life insurance proceeds (net of consideration paid for the policy) are taxable income to a recipient who acquired the policy in a transfer for value unless an exception applies. The purchase of the policy from Participant, or from the plan, by Participant's children (or a trust for their benefit) would be a "transfer for value," causing the eventual death benefit to be taxable income instead of tax-exempt income. However, the transfer for value rule does not apply if the policy is bought by the insured, a partner of the insured or a partnership in which the insured is a partner. § 101(a)(2)(B). Thus, the plan could sell the policy to a partnership in which Participant and his children are the partners, to avoid the transfer for value problem.

The next question is, whether life insurance owned by a partnership in which Participant is a partner is in or out of Participant's gross estate. As a partner, does Participant have "incidents of ownership" in a policy owned by the partnership (¶ 8.4.01)? A number of cases and IRS rulings have held that a partner does not have "incidents of ownership" in a policy on his life held by the partnership. It should be noted that these cases and rulings apparently involved arms' length, business partnerships, not family partnerships formed solely for the purchase of life insurance. Nevertheless, this is a promising route to explore when buying an insurance policy from a retirement plan. A discussion of partnership-owned life insurance is beyond the scope of this book. See Bibliography.

Another alternative is for Participant to sell the policy, for fair market value, to a "defective grantor trust," *i.e.,* a trust all of which is deemed to be "owned" by Participant under the "grantor trust rules" of §§ 671-677. The theory is that a transaction between Participant and his grantor trust is not treated as a sale (and therefore there is no transfer for value) because Participant and the trust are regarded as "one taxpayer" for income tax purposes. The trust could be structured so it would not be included in Participant's estate. Exploration of this idea is also beyond the scope of this book. See Bibliography.

The third problem is the prohibited transaction rules of ERISA (¶ 8.3.04). The Department of Labor's class exemption, PTE 92-6, exempts the sale of a life insurance policy by the plan to the insured participant *or his beneficiaries,* if various requirements are met. However, if the sale is to someone *other than* Participant, and would be a prohibited transaction if not specially exempted, the following requirements must be met, in addition to those discussed at ¶ 8.3.04:

1.   The buyer must be a "relative" of the insured participant. "Relative" means either a relative as defined in § 3(15) of ERISA (29 U.S.C. § 1002(15)) or § 4975(e)(6) (spouse, ancestor, lineal descendant or spouse of a lineal descendant), or a sibling or a spouse of a sibling.

2.   The buyer must be the beneficiary of the policy.

3.   The policy must first be offered for sale to Participant, who must give a written refusal to purchase, and must consent to the proposed sale to the beneficiary.

Note that the PTE's definition of "relative" does not include partnerships or trusts. If the strategy is to sell the policy from the plan directly to a partnership of Participant and Participant's children, the plan's ERISA counsel will have to determine whether (a) the transaction is a "prohibited transaction" and (b) if it is, whether the transaction is exempt under PTE 92-6. These issues can be avoided by having the plan sell or distribute the policy to Participant, and having Participant make the sale to the partnership or trust.

8.4.03 *Second-to-die insurance*

Buying a second-to-die ("joint and survivor life") policy inside a retirement plan raises additional problems. Trying to minimize estate taxes on a second-to-die insurance policy (insuring the lives of Participant and Spouse) owned by a QRP involves considerable complexity.

If the policy is purchased *outside* the plan, the only legal paperwork required to avoid estate and gift tax is one irrevocable trust to buy the policy, plus "Crummey" notices. If the policy is bought *inside* a retirement plan, on the other hand, one widely distributed booklet recommends a strategy that involves one trust, either three or four separate life insurance policies, and possibly a family partnership to deal with all the issues involved trying to keep the policy proceeds out of both spouses' estates.

An additional complexity with QRP-owned second-to-die insurance is that there are no IRS rulings or regulations indicating how to calculate the amount to be included in Participant's gross income for this form of coverage. Tables P.S. 58 and 2001 (¶ 8.3.01) cover only single life policies. See Notice 2001-10, 2001-5 I.R.B. 459, Part VI, requesting comments on "whether one or more premium rate tables should be prescribed" for second-to-die policies.

8.4.04 *Reasons to buy or not to buy life insurance inside the plan*

Here are reasons why people incur the complications of buying life insurance inside a retirement plan.

A.   The client is rated or uninsurable, and wants to buy insurance, and there is a policy available through the plan which the client can purchase without evidence of insurability.

B.   It is possible in some cases that the purchase of insurance, as an "incidental benefit," could increase permitted contributions to a defined benefit plan.

C.   The client needs insurance but has no money to pay for it outside the retirement plan. In this case, however, it is still advisable to look at the possibility of taking some money out of the plan to buy the insurance. Unless there is some reason the client cannot conveniently get money out of the plan (unacceptable level of tax on plan distributions; creditor or marital problems; plan doesn't permit it), the purchase of insurance outside the plan may be more tax-effective.

D.   Insurance is sometimes purchased inside a retirement plan as a way of (temporarily, it is hoped) depressing the value of the retirement plan, in order to reduce income taxes. For at least the first few years of the policy's existence, the cash surrender value of a whole life insurance policy is less than the amount of the premiums paid to purchase the policy, due to the commissions and other up-front costs involved. Thus, the value of this "investment" is less than the value of other investments that could have been made with the same amount of money. The vital second step of this approach is that, when the policy reaches its lowest point of value relative to what has been invested, the policy is distributed (¶ 8.3.03) or sold (¶ 8.3.04) to Participant. The distribution (or sale) transaction is less costly than it would have been had the plan invested in something other than life insurance, due to the depressed value of the policy. The vital third step of this approach is that, sometime after the "rollout," the policy increases rapidly in value so that at the end of the day the Participant still has a profitable investment. Obviously there is no guarantee that the life insurance policy (or any other investment) will increase in value at some future date. While this idea basically "works," it is not a reason to buy insurance the Participant otherwise doesn't want to buy. It might be a reason to buy an insurance policy the Participant does want to buy anyway inside the plan rather than outside the plan, if Participant is near the point at which he must start to take required distributions (Chapter 1).

E.   Sometimes a Participant is urged to buy life insurance inside his retirement plan because this mode of purchase enables him to "buy insurance with tax deductible dollars." This is not a reason to buy life insurance. *Any* investment bought inside a retirement plan is bought with "tax deductible dollars." There is nothing special about buying life insurance as opposed to stocks, bonds or money market funds with the tax deductible dollars inside the retirement plan. In fact, life insurance in a retirement plan makes the "dollars" in the retirement plan *less* "tax deductible" than they otherwise would be, because insurance necessitates Participant's paying income tax on the Current Insurance Cost (¶ 8.3.01).

8.4.05 *IRAs and life insurance*

A requirement of a valid IRA is that "No part of the [IRA's] funds will be invested in life insurance contracts." § 408(a)(3). When a Participant wants to buy life insurance and the only money he has available to use for this purchase is inside an IRA he has the following choices:

1.   One approach is to "roll" money from the IRA into a QRP, where it can be used to buy insurance (since QRP's aren't subject to the prohibition of § 408(a)(3)). The liberalized rules that apply after 2001 regarding what type of plan a distribution may be rolled into (¶ 2.5) should make it easier for Participants to roll IRA money into a QRP for purposes of purchasing life insurance.

2.   Another approach is for the IRA not to own the insurance directly, but rather to own an interest in an entity (such as a partnership) which in turn owns the insurance policy. Clearly, *at some point*, an entity shields the policy from being considered an asset of the IRA; for example, if the IRA owns a share of stock of General Motors, and General Motors owns an insurance policy on the life of the IRA owner, there is no reason to fear that the IRA has done something forbidden. On the other hand there is no guidance regarding what degree of control by the IRA or what other factors might be considered sufficient to cause an entity-held life insurance policy to be deemed held by the IRA, causing disqualification of the IRA. Disqualification of the IRA would cause the entire IRA value to be deemed distributed to the Participant. If Participant or his family have interests in the entity that owns the policy there are also prohibited transaction issues.

8.4.06 *Borrowing; premature distributions; MRDs*

If the QRP borrows against the policy, that may cause the plan to be subject to income tax on "unrelated business taxable income" (UBTI). See PLR 7918095.

The "Current Insurance Cost" that the employee must report each year on his income tax return is not considered a "distribution" to the employee for purposes of the 10% penalty on premature distributions (see Chapter 9). IRS Notice 89-25, 1989-1 C.B. 662, A-11.

Does the "Current Insurance Cost" income that the employee pays taxes on every year count towards the minimum distributions required under § 401(a)(9)? Nothing in the proposed regulations says that it does.

8.4.07 *Planning principles with plan-owned life insurance*

1.   If it is possible under the plan to designate a different death beneficiary for the life insurance policy proceeds, on the one hand, and any other plan death benefits, on the other, determine how much of the life insurance proceeds would be subject to income tax if the client died today, *i.e.*, the cash surrender value of the policy less Participant's basis. If the cash surrender value is relatively small, and the client has insufficient other assets to fully fund a credit shelter trust, consider naming the credit shelter trust as beneficiary of the plan-held policy. Since most of the proceeds would be income tax-free, the usual drawbacks of funding a credit shelter trust with plan benefits (see ¶ 10.5) would be minimized. The rest of the plan benefits, being fully income-taxable (¶ 2.1.01), could be left to the surviving spouse, who could roll them over to an IRA and continue to defer income taxes. See Form 3.1, Appendix B.

2.   Is it possible to further fine-tune the beneficiary designation for the life insurance policy, to the extent of directing that the income-taxable portion (pre-death cash surrender value, minus Participant's basis) will be paid to Spouse, and the "pure death benefit" portion and return of basis would pass to the credit shelter trust? It is not clear that such a beneficiary designation would be effective, as far as the IRS is concerned, to allocate the income-taxable portion to one beneficiary and the income-tax-free portion to the other. Although there

is no IRS pronouncement on the subject, the IRS might require the taxable and tax-free parts of the policy proceeds to be allocated among the recipients in proportion to what each receives from the contract.

3.   If a substantial portion of the life insurance proceeds will constitute taxable income to the beneficiary, consider making the life insurance proceeds payable to Spouse, who can then roll over the taxable portion tax-free to her own retirement plan (¶ 3.2). § 402(c)(2), (c)(9).

4.   In general, it is better to buy life insurance outside the retirement plan if estate taxes are a consideration. While the "subtrust" device may offer a chance of keeping plan-owned insurance out of Participant's estate, it is at best an unproven technique. *Definite* estate tax exclusion can be easily obtained for insurance owned outside the plan. With estate tax rates at 40%-60%, this factor will weigh heavily, especially for older and wealthier participants.

5.   If the client is not insurable at standard rates, investigate the availability of group insurance through his retirement plan (and elsewhere).

6.   If life insurance is owned by the client's retirement plan, investigate the "subtrust" as a way of keeping the policy proceeds out of the gross estate.

7.   When the time comes to remove the policy from the plan, investigate ways to get/keep the policy out of the client's gross estate without triggering the "three year rule" of § 2035, while avoiding a "transfer for value" or "prohibited transaction."

8.5 Grandfather Rules

Chapter 1 describes the "minimum distribution rules" of § 401(a)(9) as they are in 2001. Today's rules have evolved through a number of mutations over the years. At several stages of this evolution, "grandfather" exceptions were created, so that today some individuals have benefits that are wholly or partly exempt from the rules. The 1999 edition of this book (pages 376-386) contains a history of this evolution. This ¶ 8.5 discusses three grandfather rules which are exceptions to the minimum distribution rules of § 401(a)(9), the "TEFRA 242(b) election" (¶ 8.5.02), and two grandfather rules created by the Tax Reform Act of 1986 (¶ 8.5.03), but leaves out the history.

¶ 8.5.04 discusses another obscure grandfather rule, the continued availability of the estate tax exclusion for retirement benefits of certain individuals.

Other grandfather rules are discussed in Chapter 2: the former ability of non-spouse beneficiaries to roll over inherited benefits (¶ 2.5.04); and "10- year averaging" and "20% capital gain" income tax treatment for certain lump sum distributions (¶ 2.3.07-¶ 2.3.12).

8.5.01 *Why estate planners need to know the grandfather rules*

The grandfather rules are important for several reasons:

1. Although the grandfather rules affect few clients, significant tax savings can be achieved for some of those who are eligible for grandfather treatment. The planner needs to be aware of these opportunities.

2. A client may be postponing taking MRDs because he qualifies (or believes he qualifies) for a "grandfather" exception from the minimum distribution rules (Chapter 1). The planner needs to be able to verify that the client does or does not qualify for the exception he is claiming.

3. If a client qualifies for a beneficial grandfather rule, the planner should be aware of what actions would cause loss of entitlement to the benefits of the grandfather rule so that these actions can be avoided (or can be taken only if the benefits of the action outweigh the benefits of continued qualification for the grandfather rule).

4. The planner sometimes encounters a client who has not or may not have taken MRDs he was required to take in past years. The planner may conclude that the client will have to take catch-up distributions and/or be liable for a penalty (¶ 1.9.06). Before jumping to the conclusion that a penalty is owed, consider the possibility that for some or all of the years in question the client

may have qualified for a grandfather rule, and so may not have been required to take distributions.

8.5.02 *TEFRA 242(b) elections: validity and effect*

TEFRA (1982) significantly expanded the minimum distribution rules. For plan years beginning after 1983, § 401(a)(9) would apply to *all* qualified retirement plans (previously it had applied only to Keogh plans). Under the pre-TEFRA lifetime distribution rules, no distributions were required prior to retirement; TEFRA (and the Tax Reform Act of 1984, which "cleaned up" the TEFRA changes via many retroactive amendments) added a requirement that 5% owners would have to start distributions at age 70½ even if still employed. TEFRA also added requirements for distributions after the employee's death (there had been none previously).

TEFRA contained a grandfather rule, § 242(b)(2), which provided that a plan will not be disqualified "by reason of distributions under a designation (before January 1, 1984) by any employee of a method of distribution...(A) which does not meet the requirements of [§ 401(a)(9)], but (B) which would not have disqualified such [plan] under [401(a)(9)] as in effect before the amendment" made by TEFRA. Under TRA '84 the TEFRA grandfather rule was continued. Accordingly, the TRA '84 changes would not apply to "distributions under a designation (before January 1, 1984) by any employee in accordance with a designation described in section 242(b)(2) of [TEFRA] (as in effect before the amendments made by this Act)." TRA '84, § 521(d)(2)-5.

As a result of the many changes brought by TEFRA, there was a flurry of activity among sophisticated plan participants trying to make a "designation" by December 31, 1983 that would enable them to continue to use the older, more liberal rules. The benefits of a participant who made a proper and timely "designation" would not be subject to the new minimum distribution rules.

Theoretically, participants with "242(b) designations" can postpone the start of required distributions past age 70½, until retirement, even if they own more than 5% of the employer (¶ 1.3.02), and their death benefits are not subject to the "5- year rule" (¶ 1.5.04) or the "at-least-as-rapidly" rule (§ 401(a)(9)(B)(i)). In other words, theoretically, a Participant who has a TEFRA 242(b) election in place can enjoy more income tax deferral for his plan benefits than the usual minimum distribution rules would allow, especially if he is a 5% owner (¶ 1.3.05). Unfortunately, TEFRA 242(b) designations have not proved as useful as originally expected for several reasons:

(a)   The requirements for a valid "designation" (as set forth in IRS Notice 83-23, 1983-2 C.B. 418, 11/15/83) are quite restrictive: "The designation must, in and of itself, provide sufficient information to fix the timing, and the formula for the definite determination, of plan payments. The designation must be complete and not allow further choice." P. 419. This does not mean the designation may not be amendable or revocable. Rather, the designation must be self-executing, requiring no further actions or designations by Participant to determine the size and date of distributions. Many purported TEFRA 242(b) designations do not meet this test.

(b)   Also, Participant generally cannot carry over a 242(b) designation from one plan to another. Rolling over QRP benefits protected by a 242(b) designation into an IRA causes loss of the 242(b) protection. However, grandfather protection is not lost if benefits are moved to another QRP without any election on the part of Participant (*e.g.*, as a result of a plan merger), if the transferee plan accounts for such benefits separately. Prop. Reg. § 1.401(a)(9)-8, A-14, A-15.

(c)   TEFRA 242(b) designations generally attempted to defer distributions for as long as possible. This turned out to be counterproductive, because an unrealistically long proposed deferral made it more likely that an individual grandfathered from the minimum distribution rules by a 242(b) election would want to make withdrawals sooner than his "designation" indicates. However, "any change in the designation will be considered to be a revocation of the designation." Notice 83-23, p. 420 (next to last sentence).

(d)   If the 242(b) designation is revoked, drastic results ensue. In effect the grandfathered status is revoked retroactively, and Participant is required to take "make-up distributions"—withdraw from the plan all the prior years' distributions he had skipped. Prop. Reg. § 1.401(a)(9)-8, A-16.

Thus, a participant relying on a TEFRA 242(b) designation lives in a perilous state. The longer he defers his distributions, the larger becomes the "make-up" distribution which will be required if he ever changes his mind and modifies the designation.

8.5.03 Other MRD "grandfathers," including pre-1987 403(b) plans

Under the Tax Reform Act of 1986 , the minimum distribution rules were extended for the first time to 403(b) plans; and the exception permitting non-key or non-5% owner employees to postpone distributions until actual retirement was eliminated (only to be reinstated 10 years later; see ¶ 1.3.02). Two new grandfather rules were created to accommodate these changes; however for reasons explained in the next two paragraphs, these are of little significance, and accordingly they are not explained in depth here. The two grandfather rules created by TRA '86 are:

First, a non-5% owner who was *born on or before June 30, 1917*, would still be entitled to defer commencement of distributions until actual retirement, even though TRA '86 eliminated that right for non-5% owners born after June 30, 1917. Presumably nobody needs this grandfather rule anymore because in 1996 Congress reversed the rule *again* so that, now, as before 1986, *all* non-5% owners, whether born before, on or after June 30, 1917, can postpone distributions until actual retirement; see ¶ 1.3.02. If full explanation of this rule is needed, see pp. 381-382 of the 1999 edition of this book (or pp. 228-229 of the 1996 edition).

Second, TRA '86 made the minimum distribution rules applicable, for the first time, to all 403(b) plans, but made this rule prospective only by exempting pre-1987 403(b) plan balances from the new regime, provided such balance is accounted for separately. The pre-'87 account balance, while not subject to the full panoply of today's minimum distribution rules, is still subject to the more primitive predecessor of today's rules, the "incidental death benefit" rule. The significance of this grandfather rule has diminished over the years. The pre-1987 grandfather amount is a frozen, fixed-dollar amount; investment earnings and gains do not increase the grandfathered balance (though distributions in excess of required distributions *decrease* it). With the passage of time, additional contributions to the plan and investment growth make the pre-1987 balance an ever-smaller percentage of the overall plan balance. It is unlikely to be a significant planning factor. If full explanation of this rule is needed, see pages 382-386 of the 1999 edition of this book, or the even fuller explanation at pages 230-238 of the 1996 edition.

8.5.04 *The federal estate tax exclusion lives!*

Once upon a time IRC § 2039 provided an unlimited federal estate tax exclusion for most kinds of retirement benefits. The exclusion was limited to $100,000 by TEFRA '82 and repealed by TRA '84. However a grandfather clause was included in TRA '84 for both laws; then § 1852(e)(3) of TRA '86 made major substantive retroactive amendments to these grandfather clauses. The retroactive TRA '86 changes made it much easier to qualify for the exclusion than it was under the original grandfather provision in TRA '84.

However, no regulations were issued after the TRA '86 amendments. The casual researcher may find only the strict TRA '84 grandfather rules (as embodied in IRS Temp. Reg. § 20.2039-1T, 1/29/86) under which only participants who were "in pay status" and had "irrevocably elected a form of benefits" by 1982 or 1984 still qualified for the exclusion. But TRA '86 simply *repealed* those two requirements and substituted others. Thus Temp. Reg. § 20.2039-1T is nugatory.

The best explanation of this tangle appears in PLR 9221030. The current requirements for a decedent's estate to be eligible for a total (or $100,000) estate tax exclusion, as stated by the IRS in this ruling, are:

1.   A decedent who separated from service before 1983, and dies after 1984, without having changed the "form of benefit" before his death, will be entitled to 100% exclusion of the benefit. A change of beneficiary is fine; it is a change of the *form of payment* of the benefit that triggers loss of the exclusion.

2.   If the decedent separated from service after 1982 but prior to 1985, and did not change the form of benefit between the time of separation from service and the time of death, the estate is still entitled to the exclusion but it is limited to $100,000.

Both of these exclusions under the retroactive amended grandfather clause are available *regardless* of whether the election of form of benefits was irrevocable, and *regardless* of whether the benefits were "in pay status" on December 31, 1984 or any other particular date. See PLR 9221030.

Distributions Before Age 59½

*What distributions the 10% penalty
under § 72(t) applies to and how to
avoid it*

9.1 10% Penalty on Pre-Age 59½ Distributions

An individual who is under age 59½ and wants to withdraw money from his retirement plan faces a special obstacle: the 10% penalty imposed by § 72(t) on retirement distributions received prior to age 59½. This Chapter first describes various details of the penalty, then describes a highly useful and flexible exception to the penalty, the "series of substantially equal periodic payments," which can be used to help many clients get money out of their plans without paying the penalty. Finally, the Chapter explains the requirements of the other 11 exceptions to the penalty.

For application of the penalty in connection with Roth IRAs, see ¶ 5.6; in connection with spousal rollover, see ¶ 3.2.02.

9.1.01 § 72(t): penalty for "early" or "premature" distributions

§ 72(t) generally imposes a 10% additional tax on retirement plan distributions made before the participant attains age 59½. This additional tax is usually referred to as the "10% penalty" on "early distributions" or "premature distributions."

The § 72(t) penalty was added to the Code by the Tax Reform Act of 1986 and has been amended several times. The IRS has not issued regulations under § 72(t), presumably because it has given up trying to keep up with Congress's whims. The Service's position is revealed in IRS publications, IRS Notices, cases and private letter rulings. However, many aspects of the penalty (and its ever-growing list of exceptions) are not clear.

The 10% "additional tax" is not intended to be a punishment for wrongdoing, but merely a disincentive for early distributions (to encourage saving not only *for* but *until* retirement). The idea is to remove some of the benefits of tax-free accumulation if the accumulated funds are not used for their intended purpose.

9.1.02 *What types of plans the penalty applies to*

§ 72(t)(1) says that the penalty applies to any distribution from a "qualified retirement plan (as defined in § 4974(c))." § 4974(c)'s definition of "qualified retirement plan" includes 401(a) plans (true "qualified" retirement plans) as well as 403(b) arrangements and IRAs (both of which are not normally included in the term "qualified retirement plan"). (It also includes other types of plans not dealt with in this book.) *Although § 72(t) includes all of these plans in the term "qualified retirement plan," in this Chapter the term "qualified retirement plan" ("QRP") refers only to plans qualified under § 401(a), as distinguished from 403(b) arrangements and IRAs.*

Note that the plan in question does not have be "qualified" at the time of the distribution for the penalty to apply, as long as it was once a qualified plan. Powell v. Comm'r, 129 F.3d 321 (4th Cir. 1997).

9.1.03 *Distributions of employer stock*

An employee who receives employer stock in a lump sum distribution from a qualified plan is entitled to certain favorable tax treatment regarding the "net unrealized appreciation" in the stock. See ¶ 2.4. If the employee is under age 59½ at the time of the distribution, the 10% penalty will apply to the portion of the distribution that is includible in the employee's gross income at the time of the distribution. See ¶ 2.4.01.

9.1.04 *10% applies to amount included in gross income*

The penalty is not necessarily 10% of the total distribution. Rather, the 10% is calculated only with respect to "the portion of [the distribution] which is includible in gross income." § 72(t)(1); Notice 87-16, 1987-1 C.B. 446. To the extent the distribution is income tax-free because (for example) it represents the return of Participant's own after-tax contributions (¶ 2.1.04), or because it is rolled over to another plan or IRA in a qualifying rollover (¶ 2.5), it is also penalty-free. See, *e.g.*, PLR 9253049 (because a pre-age 59½ IRA distribution was excluded from the taxpayer's gross income by virtue of the U.S.-U.K.

tax treaty, it was also not subject to the 10% penalty); PLR 9010007 (tax-free rollover not subject to penalty).

Other than the fact that the penalty applies only to the portion of a distribution that is includible in gross income, the 10% penalty has nothing to do with the *income tax treatment* of the distribution. Nevertheless, the § 72(t) exceptions are a constant source of confusion to clients and practitioners who wrongly conclude that distributions that are *penalty-free* under § 72(t) are also *income tax-free*. Even Congress gets confused on this point; see § 72(t)(4)(B) (discussed at ¶ 9.2.12).

9.1.05 *IRA contributions withdrawn before tax return due date*

If an IRA contribution for which no deduction has been taken is withdrawn from the account (together with the net earnings on that contribution) before the due date (including extensions) of the participant's tax return for the year in which the contribution was made, the withdrawal of the contribution is not a taxable distribution (§ 408(d)(4)) and accordingly is also not subject to the penalty. However, "Generally, if an individual is not yet 59½ at the time of the withdrawal, upon withdrawing such amounts the individual will be required to pay the early withdrawal tax under section 72(t) on the earnings (if any) for the year for which the contribution was made." IRS Notice 87-16, 1987-1 C.B. 446; Hall v. Comm'r, T.C. Memo 1998-336. IRS Publication 590, "Individual Retirement Arrangements (IRAs)" (2000), at page 21, confirms that any income earned on the contribution that is included in the distribution "will be subject" to the early distributions penalty (unless it qualifies for one of the 12 exceptions; ¶ 9.2, ¶ 9.3).

9.1.06 *Enforcement of the penalty by IRS and courts*

The IRS eagerly seeks to collect the penalty wherever it applies. People who take money from their retirement plans apparently unaware that the penalty exists are of course caught by the penalty. A more sympathetic case (though not to the IRS) is presented by people who did not know they had received a distribution, or who had reason to believe the distribution in question was tax-free, and then find out the hard way that not only have they received a taxable distribution but it is subject to a penalty.

This can happen, for example, to a person who takes a loan

from a retirement plan but fails to meet the exact requirements of § 72(p), so that the loan is treated as a taxable distribution rather than a loan; Notice 87-13, 1987-1 C.B. 432, Q-20, confirms that the penalty applies to such "deemed distributions." It evidently happened to many under-age-59½ members of the Maryland State Teachers' Retirement System, when their pension plan was reorganized and they received distributions of their benefits that they were told (by their employer) could be rolled over tax-free to IRAs. Wrong. Each misled teacher had to pay the penalty. See, *e.g.*, Thompson v. Comm'r, 71 TCM 3160 (1996).

It happens to people whose attempts to roll over retirement plan distributions are held for one reason or another not to constitute "qualified rollovers"; see, *e.g.*, Rodoni v. Comm'r, 105 T.C. 29 (1995) (husband's distribution rolled over into IRA in the name of wife). It happened to Ben Moon who correctly rolled over his entire distribution check, but did not realize that 20% tax had been withheld from the distribution. Since he had therefore rolled over only 80% of the distribution, he was liable for income taxes and the 10% penalty on the part that had been paid directly to the IRS. The court had no sympathy for him, saying that the 20% withholding tax had been widely publicized (citing a Rutgers Law Journal article). Moon v. U.S., Kleinrock's Tax Cases 1997-193; U.S. Ct. Fed. Claims 95-702T, 7/9/97; CCH: 97-2 USTC 50,668.

Adding to the fun, the penalty may itself generate *another* penalty, if its existence means the taxpayer underpaid his estimated taxes. According to Notice 87-13, Q-20, "the taxpayer may have estimated tax liability with respect to such additional income tax."

The Tax Court impartially enforces the penalty, occasionally expressing sympathy for the taxpayers, but declining to modify the clear words of the statute. See, *e.g.*, Deal v. Comm'r, T.C. Memo 1999-352, in which the IRS erroneously told Ms. Deal by phone that the penalty did not apply to her distribution, so she did not roll it over; the IRS later assessed the penalty and the Tax Court upheld it.

Only on rare occasions has the penalty not been applied when the taxpayer did not fit into any of the exceptions. Certain involuntary distributions have escaped the penalty; see ¶ 9.3.10. In one case, Duralia v. Comm'r, T.C. Memo 1994-269, the IRS apparently forgot to assess the penalty.

The IRS's hard-and-fast attitude in penalty-collection cases changes completely, to soft-and-compliant, when it is presented with an advance ruling request regarding a *proposed* distribution. When a taxpayer seeks a letter ruling prior to commencing a "series of substantially equal periodic payments" (¶ 9.2), he is saying in effect "I will take these distributions from my retirement plan if you will rule that the distributions will not be subject to the 10% penalty," and the IRS sniffs revenue in the air. The IRS knows that, if it rules that the proposed distributions constitute a "series of substantially equal periodic payments," the taxpayer will take annual distributions for at least five years (¶ 9.2.13)—and that every year he will pay income taxes on those distributions. On the other hand, the IRS knows that if it refuses to rule favorably, the taxpayer will probably leave his benefits locked up in the plan until he reaches age 59½ and the IRS will receive no revenue until then. This dynamic causes the IRS to be quite flexible in approving proposed "SOSEPPs."

9.1.07 *Miscellaneous: bankruptcy, life insurance*

For a discussion of whether the penalty is dischargeable in bankruptcy, see In re Mounier, KTC 1998-464 (S.D. Cal. 1998).

When a qualified retirement plan purchases life insurance on the life of a plan participant, § 72(m)(3) generally requires that the cost of the insurance protection be included currently in the participant's gross income. ¶ 8.3.01. However, this deemed income is not treated as a distribution for purposes of § 72(t) and the 10% penalty does not apply. IRS Notice 87-16, 1987-1 C.B. 446, A-11.

9.1.08 *Overview of the exceptions to the penalty*

There are 12 exceptions to the penalty, with the result that many individuals are able to withdraw funds from their plans prior to age 59½ without paying the penalty. The exceptions are not the same for all types of retirement plans. For example, some exceptions that are available for qualified plans and 403(b) arrangements are *not* available for IRA distributions. Other exceptions apply *only* to IRAs. Some exceptions are available for all types of plans but apply differently depending on the type of plan involved.

Most of the exceptions have limited usefulness for planning purposes because they are triggered only in particular hardship situations (death, disability) or depend on a particular use of the funds distributed (college tuition, health insurance premiums, "first time" home purchase). However, there is no "hardship exception" *per se* to this penalty.

One of the exceptions stands out as an extremely useful planning tool: the "series of substantially equal periodic payments."

9.2 Exception: "Series of Equal Payments"

9.2.01 *Series of substantially equal periodic payments (SOSEPP)*

The penalty does not apply to a distribution which is "part of a series of substantially equal periodic payments (not less frequently than annually) made for the life (or life expectancy) of the employee or the joint lives (or joint life expectancies) of such employee and his designated beneficiary." § 72(t)(2)(A)(iv). While at first this appears to be a rather narrow window, in fact it is a wide open door, because:

1. Liberalized rollover rules introduced in 1992 (§ 402(c)) make it possible in many cases to create an IRA of the desired size to support the series (see ¶ 9.2.10) by taking that amount of money out of a profit sharing plan, even while still employed, and rolling the money over tax free to the IRA (see ¶ 2.5).

2. The payments do not in fact have to continue for the participant's entire life or life expectancy period, but only until the individual reaches age 59½, or until five years have elapsed, whichever occurs later. ¶ 9.2.13.

3. The IRS allows numerous methods for determining the size of the "equal payments." See ¶ 9.2.03 - ¶ 9.2.09.

This is the most significant exception for planning purposes. All the other exceptions are tied to a specific use of the money (home purchase, college tuition), or to some type of hardship situation (death, disability), or are otherwise narrowly limited. In contrast, everyone who has an IRA (or who can get one via a rollover from some other type of plan) can use the SOSEPP exception.

Participants in qualified plans can also use this exception to take a series of payments *from* the qualified plan, but only if they have separated from service. § 72(t)(3)(B). If Participant is still employed, he cannot take a SOSEPP from a QRP; but if the QRP permits in-service distributions Participant can roll a distribution over to an IRA and take the SOSEPP from the IRA. "Separation from service" is not required for a SOSEPP from an IRA.

There is one significant limitation on this exception: if the series of payments is "modified" before the five years are up (or before the participant reaches age 59½, if he started the SOSEPP more than five years before reaching age 59½), *all* payments in the series lose the shelter of the exception, and the penalty applies, retroactively and with interest, to all pre-age 59½ distributions. § 72(t)(4)(A). ¶ 9.2.12.

9.2.02 *How this exception works*

The SOSEPP exception starts from the premise that there is a fund of money (the retirement plan account) that will be gradually exhausted by a series of regular distributions over the applicable period of time. The "applicable period of time" is (i) the life expectancy of the participant or (ii) the joint life expectancy of the participant and his designated beneficiary. Thus, the SOSEPP must be designed so that, if it continued for that period of time, it would exactly exhaust the fund—even though the payments are required to be made for only five years (or until the participant reaches age 59½, if later). (¶ 9.2.13).

Note that § 72(t)(2)(A)(iv) itself does not say that the SOSEPP must be designed to *exhaust* the account over the applicable time period; it says only that the equal payments must be "made for" the applicable period of time. This wording clearly would preclude a series of equal payments that would exhaust the fund *before* the end of the applicable time period, but would not necessarily preclude a series of equal payments which would be too small to exhaust the fund. For example, if payments of $50,000 per year would exhaust the account over the taxpayer's life expectancy, why could he not take equal annual payments of any amount *up to* $50,000 per year? § 72(t)(2)(A)(iv)'s wording appears to permit him to take, say, $25,000 per year, so long as the payments were equal every year and continued for the required period of time.

However, the IRS's interpretation of this exception is that the SOSEPP must be designed to exhaust the fund over the applicable time period. See Notice 87-16, 1987-1 C.B. 446, A-12, and PLR 9805023. The participant cannot take annual distributions that are too small to exhaust the account, even if they are equal, regular, payments designed to continue over the applicable time period. Fortunately, if the individual's benefits are in an IRA, it is very easy to get around this problem; see ¶ 9.2.10.

9.2.03 How to determine the substantially equal payments

To determine the size of the required payments, you start with the current size of the fund as a given (see further discussion of adjusting the size of the fund as a way of adjusting the size of the payments, at ¶ 9.2.10), then apply several variables.

The first variable is the life expectancy measuring period. You can use the single life expectancy of the participant, which is what you should use if you want the largest possible payments. If for some reason you want smaller payments, you can use the joint life expectancy of the participant and his beneficiary, which may produce that result.

The next variable is how the life expectancy is to be determined: Which mortality table is used? Will a fixed life expectancy be used, or will life expectancy be redetermined annually? See ¶ 9.2.08

The final variable is an interest rate assumption. The size of the payments required to exhaust a fund will vary substantially depending on whether the assumed rate of return for the fund is high (larger payments required) or low (a low interest rate assumption produces smaller payments). See ¶ 9.2.07.

Note that the whole idea of the "series of substantially equal periodic payments" is fictional. In order for a SOSEPP to precisely exhaust a fund of money over the applicable time period, the fund would have to grow steadily at the specified rate of return. In reality, an investment fund rarely grows steadily over any period of time. Investments may even shrink in value. Therefore, in reality, if the equal payments program continued for the entire specified time period, it is likely that either the fund would be exhausted before the end of the period, or the payments would not exhaust the fund.

The IRS in Notice 89-25, 1989-1 C.B. 662, A-12, set forth three methods for calculating the periodic payments, saying that "Payments will be considered to be substantially equal periodic payments within the meaning of § 72(t)(2)(A)(iv) if they are made according to one of" these three methods. The distributions can be made annually or more frequently (monthly, quarterly, etc.). IRS Publication 590, "Individual Retirement Arrangements (IRAs)" (2000), page 20.

9.2.04 *First IRS method: minimum distribution*

"Payments shall be treated as satisfying § 72(t)(2)(A)(iv) if the annual payment is determined using a method that would be acceptable for purposes of calculating the minimum distribution required under § 401(a)(9). For this purpose, the payment may be determined based on the life expectancy of the employee or the joint life and last survivor expectancy of the employee and beneficiary."

Under this method, each year's distribution is determined by dividing the fund balance as of the preceding year end by the applicable life expectancy. One major difference, however, is that in the case of a SOSEPP under § 72(t)(2)(A)(iv), the resulting distribution amount is not merely the *minimum* distribution, it is also the *maximum* distribution.

This method is equivalent to assuming, for purposes of computing each year's payment, that *no* interest will be earned by the fund in the future. Then, each year, the payments are in effect adjusted to reflect the actual investment growth or decline since the prior year's distribution. As is true for "minimum required distributions" under § 401(a)(9), the payments will grow larger each year if there is a positive investment return. See ¶ 1.2.01.

The author has found no ruling or case in which the taxpayer used the minimum distribution method. Why is this method unpopular? Perhaps because it does not produce a steady predictable flow; the payments fluctuate depending on investment results.

When Notice 89-25 was issued, the IRS's proposed minimum distribution regulations promulgated in 1987 were the only official pronouncement on the subject of how to determine required distributions under § 401(a)(9). In January 2001, the IRS issued completely revised proposed minimum distribution regulations (¶ 1.1.03), replacing the 1987 version, but without specifying the impact on "Method 1" under IRS Notice 89-25.

Method 1 SOSEPPs that commenced prior to January 2001

Since a SOSEPP cannot be "modified" once it has begun (¶ 9.2.12), an individual who commenced a SOSEPP based on the method of determining required distributions set forth in the 1987 proposed regulations should continue to calculate his periodic payments in the same manner as before and not switch over to the new method described in the January 2001 proposed regulations because such a switch could well be considered a fatal modification of his SOSEPP. See Chapter 1 of the 1999 edition of this book for the details and variations of methods of computing minimum distributions under the old proposed regs.

Method 1 SOSEPPs that commence after January 2001

Under the proposed minimum distribution regulations issued in January 2001, all participants use the same table (called in this book the "Uniform Table") to calculate required distributions, regardless of who is named as the designated beneficiary and regardless of whether there even is a designated beneficiary. ¶ 1.4.01. The only exception is that a participant whose sole designated beneficiary is his spouse, and whose spouse is more than 10 years younger than he, uses the true joint life expectancy of participant and spouse rather than using the Uniform Table. ¶ 1.4.02. The Uniform Table is a table of joint and survivor life expectancies for a participant age 70 (or older) and a hypothetical designated beneficiary who 10 years younger than the participant. ¶ 1.2.04.

The IRS's issuance of the new proposed minimum distribution regulations, without any word as to the impact on Notice 89-25 Method 1, leaves participants in a bit of a vacuum. The statutory requirement of the SOSEPP is that it must be based on the life expectancy of the participant or joint life expectancy of participant and beneficiary, which makes it sound as though a participant cannot simply adopt the approach of assuming a hypothetical beneficiary 10 years younger than himself (as is the approach of the new proposed minimum distribution regulations). Of course the statute also required *minimum distributions* to be based on the participant's single life expectancy or the joint life expectancy of the participant and beneficiary, and the IRS is converting that to the new system under which everyone is assumed to have a 10-years-younger-beneficiary.

In the author's opinion, until the IRS makes some different pronouncement, the method of determining minimum distributions described in the 1987 proposed minimum distribution regulations should continue to be a safe harbor method to determine a "Method 1" SOSEPP at least through 2001 (since the "old proposed regulations" provide an "acceptable" method of determining required distributions through 2001; ¶ 1.1.04); and, for 2001 and later years, a SOSEPP based on the joint life expectancy of the participant and a hypothetical 10-years-younger beneficiary is protected in the Method 1 safe harbor because it is an "acceptable" method of determining required distributions for those years.

A participant may also, presumably, use his single life expectancy (using Table V from Reg. § 1.72-9, not recalculated) because (i) this is also an acceptable method of determining required distributions (albeit for beneficiaries, not participants) under the new proposed minimum distribution regulations and (ii) Notice 89-25 recognized that a participant is entitled to use his single life expectancy (even if the proposed minimum distribution regulations no longer use that particular table for calculating lifetime required distributions).

9.2.05 *Second IRS method: amortization*

"Payments will also be treated as substantially equal periodic payments within the meaning of § 72(t)(2)(A)(iv) if the amount to be distributed annually is determined by amortizing the taxpayer's account balance over a number of years equal to the life expectancy of the account owner or the joint life and last survivor expectancy of the account owner and beneficiary (with *life expectancies determined in accordance with proposed section 1.401(a)(9)-1* of the regulations) at an *interest rate that does not exceed a reasonable interest rate* on the date payments commence. For example, a 50 year old individual with a life expectancy of 33.1, having an account balance of $100,000, and assuming an interest rate of 8 percent, could satisfy section 72(t)(2)(A)(iv) by distributing $8,679 annually, derived by amortizing $100,000 over 33.1 years at 8 percent interest." (Emphasis added.)

This second method creates a predictable stream of payments that will in fact be equal. See, *e.g.*, PLR 9830042. The annual payment amount is determined at the beginning of the period in the same manner as the payments on a fixed-rate mortgage: a fixed dollar amount of principal (the retirement fund), plus a fixed rate of interest, are amortized over a fixed period of time (the life expectancy), with a series of level payments. The fixed payment so determined is paid out to the participant each year, regardless of the actual investment performance of the fund.

This method requires the taxpayer to come up with a "reasonable interest rate" (¶ 9.2.07), but life expectancy is determined as prescribed by the IRS tables V (single life expectancy) and VI (joint and survivor life expectancy) referenced in § 1.401(a)(9)-1 of both the old and the new proposed minimum distribution regulations.

The amortization method is the popular favorite, judging by private letter rulings where it outnumbers the annuity method (¶ 9.2.06) by five to one.

9.2.06 *Third IRS method: annuity*

"Finally, payments will be treated as substantially equal periodic payments if the amount to be distributed annually is determined by dividing the taxpayer's account balance by an annuity factor (the present value of an annuity of $1 per year beginning at the taxpayer's age attained in the first distribution year and continuing for the life of the taxpayer) with such annuity factor derived using a *reasonable mortality table* and using *an interest rate that does not exceed a reasonable interest rate* on the date payments commence. If substantially equal monthly payments are being determined, the taxpayer's account balance would be divided by an annuity factor equal to the present value of an annuity of $1 per month beginning at the taxpayer's age attained in the first distribution year and continuing for the life of the taxpayer. For example, if the annuity factor for a $1 per year annuity for an individual who is 50 years old is 11.109 (assuming an interest rate of 8 percent and using the UP-1984 Mortality Table), an individual with a $100,000 account balance would receive an annual distribution of $9,002 ($100,000/11.109 = $9,002)." (Emphasis added.)

This method allows more actuarial creativity, since any "reasonable mortality table" (not just the IRS's § 1.72-9 mortality tables) may be used. It also tends to produce the largest payments of any of the three methods, for reasons best known to actuaries. Also, despite the suggestion that the payments, once initially determined, must never vary in amount, the IRS has allowed taxpayers using this method to revalue their account balances and redetermine the interest factor annually. See PLRs 9021058 and 9531039.

We now turn to the questions that come up in designing and administering a SOSEPP:

9.2.07 *What is a reasonable interest rate?*

There is no IRS prescribed or safe-harbor interest rate.
Methods two and three allow any interest rate that "does not

exceed" a reasonable rate, so presumably an interest rate from as low as zero to as high as a reasonable rate is acceptable; method one assumes a zero interest rate. But, although sometimes the IRS states that it is opposed to use of an "unreasonably high" interest rate (which would produce excessive distributions) (see, *e.g.*, PLRs 9830042, 9604026 and 9601052), elsewhere the IRS says is it opposed to use of *any* "unreasonable interest rate," including perhaps one that is unreasonably *low*. See PLR 9747045.

Most private letter rulings state the interest rate the taxpayer is using, but do not explain the reasoning supporting use of that particular rate. The IRS has approved rates from as low as 5.6% (PLR 9514026) to as high as 8.2445% (PLR 9830042). As an illustration of the variability of "acceptable" interest rates, in seven rulings issued in 1995, the IRS approved programs based on interest rates of 5.6% (March), 5.95% (June), 6% (July), 7% (August), 8.8% (October), 6% (November) and "the Federal Mid-Term Applicable Rate" (May).

In some private letter rulings, the basis for picking a particular interest rate is revealed. For example, in PLR 9805023 the taxpayer's interest rate for determining a method two SOSEPP from her non-qualified annuity was chosen based on advice from an "investment advisor," who wrote that "based upon the investment performance of her annuity contract since it was purchased and allowing for the possibility of less favorable future market conditions" this particular rate would be reasonable. The IRS approved of this approach. (Note that this ruling involved a variable annuity contract, not a retirement plan; annuity contracts are subject, under § 72(q), to a similar 10% early distributions penalty, with a similar exception for a SOSEPP.)

The rest of the recent rulings which reveal the basis for selecting a particular interest rate used some variation of the applicable federal rate ("AFR") prescribed under § 1274(d). In PLR 9240042, the taxpayer used the long-term AFR (applicable, under § 1274(d), to obligations with a term of nine years or longer). The taxpayer in PLR 9531039 used the mid-term AFR (applicable, under § 1274(d), to obligations with a term of between three and nine years). In PLR 9747039 , the IRS approved use of "120% of the federal *mid*-term rate" for the last month of the year preceding the year the series commenced. Two days later, in PLR 9747045, the IRS approved use of the then-current "*Long* Term 120% AFR." In PLR 9812038, the IRS approved use of the long-term AFR.

These rulings suggest that any rate from the mid-term AFR up to 120% of the long-term AFR, and any other rate for which a valid justification can be presented, should be acceptable.

9.2.08 *What mortality table should be used?*

Most people who obtain private letter rulings are sticking to the life expectancy tables explicitly blessed in Notice 89-25.

Since methods one and two both specify that life expectancies will be determined in accordance with the proposed minimum distribution regulations, and since those proposed regulations specify use of the life expectancy tables in Reg. § 1.72-9, it is no surprise that all the rulings using method two use § 1.72-9's "Table V" for single life expectancy and "Table VI" for joint life expectancy. The life expectancies are determined based on attained age in the year distributions commence. Notice 89-25, Q&A 12. One daring taxpayer modified his Table V life expectancy to the extent of rounding it down to the next lowest whole number, with IRS approval. PLR 9747039.

Method three (annuity) allows the use of any "reasonable mortality table." The one example of method three in Notice 89-25 uses the UP-1984 Mortality Table, and most of the private letter rulings in which the annuity method was used also used this table. The exceptions were PLR 9021058, which used the 1983 IAM Male Mortality Table, and PLR 9824047, in which the IRS approved the use of Life Table 80 CNSMT.

What happens if a taxpayer is using a joint life expectancy factor under any of the three methods but then changes his designated beneficiary before the end of the no-modification period (¶ 9.2.13)? Is he required to change the life expectancy factor to reflect the new beneficiary? Is he forbidden to do so? The author has found no source addressing this question.

9.2.09 *Permitted variations in designing the SOSEPP*

Although IRS Publication 590, "Individual Retirement Arrangements (IRAs)" (2000) states at page 20 that you "must use an IRS-approved distribution method," in fact Notice 89-25 does not state that you are limited to the three methods described in the Notice. Several letter rulings have approved variations of the IRS-approved models. For example, in PLR 9816028, the participant's SOSEPP was based on the annuity method, but called for the payments to increase by

3% annually as a "cost of living adjustment." PLRs 9747045, 9723035 and 9536031 also involved regular payments that were to be "equal" except for an annual 3% cost of living adjustment.

In PLR 9531039, the taxpayer was allowed to redetermine the life expectancy factor, interest rate factor and account balance each year, rather than setting these factors once and for all at the beginning of the SOSEPP as method three requires. In PLR 9021058, the taxpayer was allowed to redetermine the interest rate factor and account balance each year.

9.2.10 *Applying the exception to multiple IRAs*

Must all IRAs be treated as one IRA for purposes of computing the payments? Or can one IRA be isolated from other IRAs owned by the same participant and used as a basis for these distributions?

§ 408(d)(1), which governs IRAs, provides that IRA distributions are includible in gross income "in the manner provided under § 72." § 408(d)(2) then provides that: "For purposes of applying section 72 to any amount described in paragraph (1)...(A) all individual retirement plans shall be treated as 1 contract, [and] (B) all distributions during any taxable year shall be treated as 1 distribution...." However, this provision states that it applies for the purpose of determining how much of any distribution is *included in gross income* (the subject of § 408(d)). There is no provision requiring that IRAs be aggregated for purposes of the *penalty* under § 72(t).

Similarly, the IRS, in Notice 89-25, at 665 (A-7), states that "For purposes of determining the taxation of IRA distributions, all IRAs maintained for an individual must be aggregated and treated as one IRA," but the IRS has never applied this *income tax* rule for purposes of the § 72(t) *penalty* and the SOSEPP exception.

For purposes of structuring a SOSEPP, the taxpayer has several choices: the series can be based on all of his IRAs, aggregated; or on some of the IRAs aggregated, with others excluded; or on one IRA to the exclusion of others. As the IRS said in PLR 9747039, "If a taxpayer owns more than one IRA, any combination of his or her IRAs may be taken into account in determining the distributions by aggregating the account balances of those IRAs. *The specific IRAs taken into account are part of the method of determining the substantially equal periodic payments....*" (Emphasis added.)

All IRAs aggregated: In each of the rulings PLR 9830042,

9824047, and 9545018, all of the taxpayer's IRAs were aggregated for purposes of computing the series payments. However, the rulings do not state that this aggregation was a requirement of the favorable rulings. The taxpayers may simply have wanted to aggregate all their IRAs.

Some IRAs aggregated, others excluded: In PLR 9816028 the taxpayer had numerous IRAs, seven of which were aggregated to form the basis of his proposed SOSEPP and the rest of which were not to be counted. In PLR 9801050 the taxpayer had several IRAs, three of which were aggregated to form the basis of his proposed SOSEPP and the rest of which were not to be counted. The IRS ruled favorably in both cases, requiring only that the series payments had to be made from the aggregated IRAs and not from the other accounts.

Take series from one IRA, not aggregated with others: In PLR 9818055 the taxpayer was taking a SOSEPP from one of her two IRAs. In PLR 9812038 the taxpayer was taking a SOSEPP from one of his three IRAs and wanted to start a second SOSEPP from a new, fourth, IRA, to be created by transfer of funds from one of the other IRAs (not the IRA that was already supporting the first SOSEPP). The IRS permitted this, and the ruling specifically stated more than once that the taxpayer's IRAs were not aggregated. In PLR 9747045 the taxpayer's IRS-approved SOSEPP was taken from one of her two rollover IRAs and not the other; the two were not aggregated.

These rulings indicate that the taxpayer must choose, at the beginning of his SOSEPP, either to aggregate or not to aggregate individual retirement accounts for purposes of designing and paying out the series. The SOSEPP can be based on one of several IRAs, on all of the taxpayer's IRAs on an aggregated basis, or on some IRAs aggregated with others excluded.

Whichever accounts are included in the initial design of the SOSEPP must be the sole source of payments in the series. Once the SOSEPP begins, funds should not be transferred *out of* the IRAs that are being used to support the series, except to make payments that are part of the series (or to be transferred to another one of the accounts that were aggregated to determine the series), or *into* any IRA that is part of the support for the series from an IRA or other plan that was not part of the support for the series.

The ability to pick and choose which IRAs will be aggregated in determining the size of the periodic payments gives the client tremendous flexibility:

Example: Rodney, age 56, has several IRAs. These are his only retirement plans. He wants to get the largest possible payments he can get for his SOSEPP. He aggregates all his IRA balances, and, working with an actuary, constructs the SOSEPP using only his own life expectancy, IRS method three, whichever commonly-used mortality table gives him the shortest life expectancy, and the highest possible "reasonable" interest rate.

Example: Sidney, age 53, has one big IRA. Sidney wants to take small annual payments from his IRA until he reaches age 59½. Even using the lowest possible "reasonable" interest rate, and the joint life expectancy of himself and his beneficiary, it is not possible, using the entire balance of his IRA, to come up with payments as small as he wants. So Sidney divides his IRA into two, one of which is just the right size to support a series of payments of the size that Sidney wants.

This tremendous flexibility afforded IRAs is not unlimited, however. Although it is acceptable to have two IRAs, and use only one of them to support the SOSEPP, for some unknown reason the IRS absolutely forbids using only *part* of an IRA to support a series. See PLR 9705033. Since the taxpayer can easily get to the same result by dividing one IRA into two, this prohibition is little more than a trap for the unwary.

The author has found no rulings or other sources dealing with the aggregation or disaggregation of 403(b) arrangements or qualified retirement plans for purposes of applying the SOSEPP exception.

9.2.11 *Starting a second series to run concurrently with the first*

A taxpayer receiving a SOSEPP from one or more IRAs may initiate a *second* series of equal payments from a different IRA. See, *e.g.*, PLR 9812038, discussed at ¶ 9.2.10, in which the taxpayer was receiving a SOSEPP from "IRA #1." After that SOSEPP had been under way for a while, he was allowed to begin a second SOSEPP from a different IRA, "IRA #4," that had been created just for the purpose. PLR 9747039 is another favorable ruling about starting a second SOSEPP from a different IRA.

However, the taxpayer may not start a second SOSEPP from the same IRA (or plan) that is already supporting the first SOSEPP; such a second series would constitute an impermissible "modification" of the first series (see ¶ 9.2.12).

9.2.12 *Modification of the series is prohibited*

If the participant "modifies" his series of payments before he has completed the required series duration (five years or until age 59½, whichever is longer; ¶ 9.2.13) he is severely punished. His qualification for the SOSEPP exception is retroactively revoked, and his "tax for the 1st taxable year in which such modification occurs shall be increased by an amount, determined under regulations, equal to the tax which (but for paragraph (2)(A)(iv)) would have been imposed, plus interest for the deferral period." § 72(t)(4)(A).

§ 72(t)(4)(B) defines the "deferral period" over which interest must be calculated, but its definition doesn't make much sense. It is: "the period beginning with the taxable year in which (without regard to paragraph (2)(A)(iv)) [which contains the SOSEPP exception] the distribution *would have been includible in gross income* and ending with the taxable year in which the modification" occurs. This shows that even Congress is confused between "penalty-free" (what the § 72(t) exceptions are all about) and "income tax-free" (which § 72(t) has no bearing on), since *any* distribution from the retirement plan "would have been includible" in the participant's gross income, regardless of whether it qualified under paragraph (2)(A)(iv).

The only exception to this tough rule is that if the series is modified "by reason of death or disability" there is no penalty. § 72(t)(4)(A). IRS Publication 590, "Individual Retirement Arrangements (IRAs)" (2000) echoes this, saying that a modification does not result in penalty if the "change from an approved distribution method is because of the death or disability of the IRA owner" (p. 20).

It is not clear whether death and disability *automatically* end the requirement of continuing the series, or whether the participant (or beneficiaries) must somehow demonstrate that the series could not have been continued *because* of the death or disability—for example, by showing that payments were suspended upon the participant's death because of a lawsuit about who was entitled to the benefits, or that the participant had to increase his distributions because of his disability.

9.2.13 *What is the period during which modification is prohibited?*

The beginning date of the no-modification period is the date of the first payment in the series. The ending date is the fifth anniversary of the date of the first payment in the series, or, *if later*, the date on which the participant attains age 59½. § 72(t)(4)(A). Once this ending date is passed, payments may be freely taken from the plan without penalty (or the series may be suspended—*i.e.*, the participant can STOP taking payments).

Note that the ending date of the five years is not simply the date of the fifth year's payment. The five years ends on the *fifth anniversary of the first payment*. In the case of <u>Arnold v. Commissioner</u>, 111 T.C. No. 250, the taxpayer, at age 55, took the first of a series of equal annual payments of $44,000 in December 1989. He took the second, third, fourth, and fifth payments in the series in January 1990, 1991, 1992, and 1993, respectively. In September 1993 he turned 59½, and, thinking he had now completed his greater-of-five-years-or-until-age-59½ requirement (because he had taken all five of the annual required payments and was over age 59½), he took another distribution of $6,776 in November 1993 from the same IRA.

The Tax Court, citing legislative history regarding how to calculate the five-year period, held that this $6,776 distribution was an impermissible modification of the SOSEPP because it occurred during the five years beginning on the date of the first distribution. Therefore, the taxpayer's qualification for the SOSEPP exception was retroactively revoked, and he owed the 10% penalty, plus interest, on all five of his $44,000 distributions!

9.2.14 *What changes constitute a modification?*

Examples of prohibited modifications of a SOSEPP include:

1.   Terminating the series (*i.e.*, ceasing to take the payments). See PLR 9818055.

2.   Taking an extra payment (*i.e.*, a payment that is over and above the payments required as part of the series) from the plan or IRA that is supporting the series (see <u>Arnold v. Commissioner</u>, discussed above).

3.   Possibly, changing from annual payments to quarterly or monthly payments (or vice versa), even if the total payments for the year add up to the right amount. There is no authority or

precedent for the proposition that the size of individual payments in the series does not matter so long as the annual total is the same each year. So, although the IRS has not explicitly ruled that such a switch would be a "modification," all payments should be equal (or otherwise exactly conform to the SOSEPP that was initially set up) unless a favorable ruling holding otherwise is obtained.

4.   Changing how the payments in the series are determined.

Example: In PLR 9821056, taxpayer retired at 47 and started a series of equal annual payments from his IRA. These payments were based on his then-life expectancy, existing account balance and projected rate of return. Five years later he wanted to recalculate the rest of the required payments, based on his new life expectancy and account balance and a new projected rate of return which reflected the actual investment experience of the account (which had been much more favorable than originally projected). He sought a ruling from the IRS that this would not be a "modification," on the theory that the change amounted to merely an adjustment to reflect actual experience, and the series was in fact continuing exactly as before. Unfortunately for him, the IRS ruled that "such a proposed change in payments...would be a modification."

Ironically, this taxpayer probably could have designed his series initially to build in the flexibility the IRS did not allow him to add later. For example, in PLR 9531039 the IRS approved an annuity-method SOSEPP which called for the annual redetermination of the so-called "equal payments" based on the individual's redetermined life expectancy, account balance and interest rate. Alternatively, this taxpayer could have kept some of his IRA money in another account, separate from the account supporting the SOSEPP, and used the second IRA to start a second SOSEPP later on. Especially with younger clients, it is highly desirable to build some flexibility into the program.

9.2.15 *What changes do not constitute a modification?*

The following changes in a SOSEPP have either been ruled not to be prohibited modifications, or have occurred without negative comment in cases or rulings involving other issues:

A.   When the paying agent, as part of a change in its computer systems, changed the date of monthly payments in a series to the first day of the month (instead of the last day of the preceding month), the change was ruled to be "ministerial," and not a "modification," even though the change meant that the recipient's income would include one fewer payment for the year the switch was made. PLR 9514026.

B.   The taxpayer in PLR 9221052 was receiving monthly payments from a money purchase pension plan. When that plan terminated in the middle of his SOSEPP, he sought to roll over the termination distribution to an IRA and continue paying himself the monthly payments from the IRA. The IRS ruled that this change would not constitute a modification.

C.   In PLR 9739044, a taxpayer got divorced after commencing his SOSEPP. The IRAs supporting the series were community property. The divorce court divided the IRAs and gave half of each to the taxpayer's ex-wife. Both spouses then apparently continued the SOSEPP, with each of them taking (from his or her respective share of the formerly unified IRAs) one half of the required annual distribution. The IRS ruled that, because the division of the IRA between the spouses was non-taxable under § 408(d)(6), and in view of the "continuous compliance with the requirements of § 72(t)(2)(A)(iv)," there was no modification.

D.   In the case of annual payments, it apparently does not matter exactly when during the year the payment is taken; in other words it does not have to be on the anniversary of the first payment to avoid having a "modification."

Examples: In PLR 9747039, the IRS ruled that the taxpayer would qualify for the exception "if [he] received at least five annual payments of $510,000 from IRA Y (at least one during each of the years 1997, 1998, 1999, 2000 and 2001) and does not otherwise modify his IRA distribution scheme." See also Arnold v. Commissioner, discussed above, where the taxpayer took his first annual payment in December of 1989 and his subsequent annual payments in January each year, and the opinion contains no negative comment on this procedure.

9.2.16 *How to construct a SOSEPP: software programs; actuary*

The Brentmark and Number Cruncher software programs (see Appendix D) do the calculations necessary to compute SOSEPP payments under IRS Notice 89-25 (among other calculations).

Although the IRS methods for calculating the equal payments appear easy, and software programs make them appear even easier, the author strongly recommends hiring an actuary to design the series, if the amounts involved are substantial, for several reasons. First, there is the comfort of a professional opinion that the interest rate and life expectancy tables being used are "reasonable." Second, actuarial calculations can easily be bungled by non-actuaries; see, *e.g.*, PLR 9705033 (penalty imposed because the required payments were improperly calculated by the client's "independent third-party financial advisor").

Finally, an actuary who is familiar with the ins and outs of § 72(t) can take the lead in designing a series that will most precisely achieve the client's goals—goals such as relatively small or large payments, the ability to add another series later, or payments that increase with cost of living or change to reflect investment results. Actuaries (at least the ones I deal with) are intelligent, knowledgeable and creative. A typical way in which I might pose a client's problem to an actuary would be, "This client wants to receive payments of $150,000 a year, plus cost of living adjustments, until age 59½ (he is now 53). What is the smallest amount he can place in a separate IRA, especially established for this purpose, to support such a series of payments?" See the Quentin case study, Chapter 11.

Even the IRS states that the amortization and annuity methods "generally require professional assistance." IRS Publication 590, "Individual Retirement Arrangements (IRAs)" (2000), page 20.

9.2.17 *How planning and investment professionals are using § 72(t)*

The flexibility of the SOSEPP exception to § 72(t) offers planning opportunities. The series of payments can help a client under age 59½ achieve financial, investment and estate planning goals.

For example, actuary and retirement expert Bruce Temkin suggests the following program for an under-age 59½ client who needs a substantial amount of money, for example to start a business: First, the client refinances his residence. He uses the loan proceeds to cover the immediate financial need. Then he takes from his IRA a SOSEPP (with the size of the payments matched to the mortgage payments) to repay the mortgage. There will be no penalty, and the tax-deductible mortgage interest will reduce the income tax on the IRA distributions.

A mutual fund firm's brochure for financial advisors suggests using familiarity with § 72(t) as a marketing technique. An advisor can "use 72(t) to generate sales" by helping clients who have taken early retirement set up a segregated IRA (to support a SOSEPP to pay for living expenses) and meanwhile preserve tax deferral for the rest of the retirement funds in another IRA (presumably invested by the advisor).

Individuals have used pre-age 59½ distribution programs to help finance early retirement, or just to achieve a better estate balance when IRA assets constituted a disproportionate share of the estate. One 45-year-old individual strongly believed that making capital gain-generating investments *outside* his IRA would be more favorable tax-wise than continuing to make tax-deferred ordinary income-generating investments *inside* the IRA. This client proceeded to take a series of equal payments to finance these capital gain investments. A § 72(t) series of equal payments may also be used to fund life insurance premium payments.

Another Temkin idea: Suppose your clients are a young couple. Right now, their estates consist mainly of large IRAs, but they expect to inherit substantial sums in the future from their parents. In view of their eventual expected estate tax problem, they would like to begin giving away $20,000 a year to their own children. § 72(t) allows them to take out enough from their IRAs each year to fund their annual gifting program, without penalty.

9.3 The Other Eleven Exceptions to the Penalty

We now turn to the other exceptions to § 72(t)'s penalty. Although these lack the broadly applicable planning possibilities of the SOSEPP, each can be useful in particular situations.

9.3.01 *Death benefits*

A distribution "made to a beneficiary (or to the estate of the employee) on or after the death of the employee" is exempt from the penalty. § 72(t)(2)(A)(ii). This exception applies to distributions from all types of plans. Thus death benefits may be distributed penalty-free from a qualified plan, 403(b) arrangement or IRA, regardless of whether the *beneficiary* receiving the benefits is over 59½ and regardless of whether the *participant* had attained age 59½ at the time of his death.

Despite the unique clarity of this exception, it generates confusion for the following reason: If a surviving spouse rolls over benefits inherited from the deceased spouse to the surviving spouse's *own* IRA, the funds rolled over lose the characteristic of "death benefits," and become simply part of the surviving spouse's own retirement account. Thus, distributions from the rollover IRA will once again be subject to the § 72(t) penalty rules if the surviving spouse is under age 59½—even if the deceased spouse was over age 59½ when he died. See ¶ 3.2.02.

9.3.02 *Distributions "attributable" to total disability*

A distribution that is "attributable to the employee's being disabled" is not subject to the penalty. § 72(t)(2)(A)(iii). "Disabled" is defined in § 72(m)(7): it means "unable to engage in any substantial gainful activity by reason of any medically determinable physical or mental impairment which can be expected to result in death or to be of long-continued and indefinite duration. An individual shall not be considered to be disabled unless he furnishes proof of the existence thereof [sic] in such form and manner as the Secretary may require."

Reg. § 1.72-17A(f)(1) & (2) (interpreting § 72(m) as it applies to lump sum distributions to self-employed persons) provides the following further elaboration on this definition: "In determining whether an individual's impairment makes him unable to engage in any substantial gainful activity, primary consideration shall be given to the nature and severity of his impairment. Consideration shall also be given to other factors such as the individual's education, training, and work experience. The substantial gainful activity to which section 72(m)(7) refers is the activity, or a comparable activity, in which the individual customarily engaged prior to the arising of the disability or prior to retirement if the individual was retired at the time the disability arose." Although the IRS's own regulation says that the "gainful activity" referred to is the individual's customary activity or a comparable one, IRS Publication 590, "Individual Retirement Arrangements (IRAs)" (2000) (at page 20) erroneously says you must be able to "furnish proof that you cannot do *any* substantial gainful activity because of your physical or mental condition" (emphasis added).

Another IRS requirement in Publication 590, "Individual Retirement Arrangements (IRAs)" (2000) is that "A *physician* must determine that your condition can be expected to result in death or to be of long continued and indefinite duration" (emphasis added). This requirement is not waived for those whose religious beliefs prohibit them from hiring physicians; the Tax Court points out that the regulation does not impair the free exercise of religion, it just makes such exercise more expensive in some cases. Fohrmeister v. Comm'r, 73 T.C.Memo 2483, 2486 (1997).

Reg. § 1.72-17A(f) also lists certain impairments, such as "Damage to the brain or brain abnormality which has resulted in severe loss of judgment, intellect, orientation, or memory," which are said to "ordinarily," but not "in and of themselves," result in the necessary impairment.

An individual suffering from depression was not "disabled" where he continued his normal occupation (securities trading). Dwyer v. Commissioner, 106 T.C. 337 (1996). Earning a salary and starting an engineering business are both activities that are "inconsistent with the exigencies of the statutory definition of disability." Kovacevic v. Comm'r, 64 TCM 1076 (1992) (another depression case).

What does it mean that the distribution must be "attributable" to the disability? Contrast this wording with § 402(d)/(e)(4)(A) (the definition of "lump sum distribution"), which gives lump sum distribution status to an otherwise-qualifying distribution made "after the employee has become disabled," without any requirement that the distribution be "attributable to" the disability.

If the distribution is from an employer plan, and is specifically triggered by a provision in the plan calling for distribution of benefits in case of total disability, then the distribution is clearly "attributable" to the employee's being disabled. If the plan does not specifically provide for disability benefits, but does provide for distribution of benefits upon termination of employment, and the cause of the termination of employment was the employee's disability, once again it would appear the distribution is "attributable" to the employee's being disabled.

But what if the termination of employment occurred long before the disability struck? Or what if the distribution is from an IRA, distributions from which can be taken at any time without regard to either disability or termination of employment? In Publication 590, "Individual Retirement Arrangements (IRAs)" (2000), the IRS reiterates (at page 19) that the distribution from an IRA must be "because" of the disability to qualify for this exception. Some commentators assume that any distribution to a totally disabled person is automatically exempt from the penalty. However, it is possible that the IRS will require the participant to demonstrate that the distribution was *necessitated* by the disability (*e.g.*, to substitute for employment income lost due to the disability).

9.3.03 *Distributions to pay deductible medical expenses*

Distributions after 1996 from any type of plan are penalty-free "to the extent such distributions do not exceed the amount allowable as a deduction under § 213 to the employee for amounts paid during the taxable year for medical care (determined without regard to whether the employee itemizes deductions for such taxable year)." § 72(t)(2)(B). "During the taxable year" presumably means "during the taxable year in which the distribution is received."

This exception may increase the medical problems of the participant by giving him a severe headache. Medical expenses are deductible under § 213 only to the extent such expenses exceed 7.5% of adjusted gross income. § 213(a). But the plan distribution *itself* is includible in gross income and thus decreases the "amount allowable as a deduction."

Example: Cathy's adjusted gross income for the year, before taking any distribution from her IRA, is $100,000. Cathy is 53. She has medical expenses of $10,000. Her medical expenses are deductible to the extent they exceed 7.5% of $100,000 or $7,500, so (again before considering any IRA distribution) she can deduct $2,500 of her medical expenses. She withdraws $2,500 from the IRA to help pay those medical expenses. However, the IRA distribution increases her adjusted gross income to $102,500, thus *decreasing* her permitted medical expense deduction to $2,312.50 ($10,000 of medical expenses minus [$102,500 X 7.5%=$7,687.50]=$2,312.50). So she owes the 10% penalty on $187.50 of the distribution (total penalty $18.75).

To avoid the penalty, while still taking advantage of the ability to withdraw from the plan to pay deductible medical expenses, the individual would have to perform a circular calculation, so that the distribution does not exceed [total medical expenses] minus 7.5% of [distribution plus other adjusted gross income]. Of course this assumes that the individual can determine his adjusted gross income and medical expenses to the penny on or before December 31 of the year in question, since a distribution must be matched with medical expenses incurred in the year of the distribution, not some preceding year.

9.3.04 *QRPs, 403(b) plans: separation from service after age 55*

A distribution from an employer plan made to an employee "after separation from service after attainment of age 55" is exempt from the penalty. § 72(t)(2)(A)(v). This exception is available for qualified plans and 403(b) plans, but not for IRA distributions. § 72(t)(3)(A).

The wording suggests that an employee who separates from the company's service *before* age 55 is not entitled to use this exception. In other words, an employee who quits, retires or is fired before he reaches age 55 cannot simply wait until age 55 and then take a penalty-free distribution. The IRS confirms this interpretation: The exception is available for distributions "made to you after you separated from service with your employer if the separation occurred during or after the calendar year in which you reached age 55." IRS Publication 575, "Pension and Annuity Income" (1997) (at page 32). Note that although IRS Publication 575 and Notice 87-13, 1987-1 C.B. 432, A-20, both state that the exception applies to separations from service occurring on or after *January 1* of the year the employee reaches age 55, § 72(t) itself limits the exception to distributions made after separations occurring after the actual 55th birthday.

Also, the distribution must occur after the separation from service, not before. <u>Humberson v. Comm'r</u>, 70 TCM 886 (1995).

9.3.05 *QRPs, 403(b) plans: QDRO distributions*

Distributions from a qualified retirement plan or 403(b) arrangement (but not from an IRA) made to an "alternate payee" under a qualified domestic relations order ("QDRO") (see § 414(p)(1)) are exempt from the early distributions penalty. § 72(t)(2)(C). This book does not cover QDROs.

9.3.06 *ESOPs only: certain stock dividends*

This Chapter generally does not cover special rules applicable to "employee stock ownership plans" ("ESOPs"). Under § 404(k), a company can take a tax deduction for dividends paid on stock that is held by an ESOP, and the ESOP can pass these dividends out to the plan participants, if various requirements are met. Such dividend payments are not subject to the 10% penalty. § 72(t)(2)(A)(vi).

9.3.07 *IRAs only: health insurance premiums for the unemployed*

In years after 1996, an unemployed individual can take penalty-free distributions from his IRA (but not from a qualified plan or 403(b) arrangement) to pay health insurance premiums. § 72(t)(2)(D). Here are the specific requirements for this exception:

The person must have separated from his employment, and, as a result of that separation, must have "received unemployment compensation for 12 consecutive weeks under any Federal or State unemployment compensation law." The distributions must be made during the year "during which such unemployment compensation is paid or the succeeding taxable year." Presumably this phrase does not imply that the 12 consecutive weeks' worth of unemployment compensation must all be received in the same taxable year, but presumably it does mean that the unemployed person does not become eligible until the year the 12 consecutive weeks are completed.

Does this clause mean that the unemployed person can take penalty-free distributions only in one year—*either* the year he completes the 12 weeks of unemployment benefits *or* the following year? Or does it mean that penalty-free distributions may be taken in both years? The IRS has offered no enlightenment.

The maximum distribution under this exception in any taxable year is the amount paid for "insurance described in § 213(d)(1)(D) [medical and long term care insurance] with respect to the individual and the individual's spouse and dependents." Also, the distribution must be made either while the individual is still unemployed or, if he becomes employed again, less than 60 days after he has been reemployed.

The IRS, in regulations, can permit a self-employed individual to use this exception "if, under Federal or State law, the individual would have received unemployment compensation but for the fact the individual was self-employed." No such regulations have yet been issued.

9.3.08 *IRAs only: distributions to pay expenses of higher education*

This is one of several exceptions added by the Taxpayer Relief Act of 1997. The 10% penalty will not apply to IRA distributions that do not exceed the taxpayer's "qualified higher education expenses" for the taxable year of the distribution. This exception is not available for distributions from qualified plans or 403(b) arrangements. § 72(t)(2)(E).

The distribution in question must be made after 1997 and be to pay for education provided in "academic periods" beginning after 1997; see IRS Notice 97-53, 1997-40 IRB 6, for full details. The distribution must be to pay for education furnished to the taxpayer or his spouse, or to any child or grandchild of either of them. (It's pretty fast work for a taxpayer under age 59½ to have college-age grandchildren.)

This exception borrows definitions from the Code section allowing various tax breaks to "qualified state tuition programs" (§ 529(e)(3)) for the type of expenses covered ("tuition, fees, books, supplies, and equipment required for the enrollment or attendance of a designated beneficiary at an eligible educational institution") and eligible institutions. "Eligible Institutions" include "virtually all accredited public, non-profit, and proprietary post-secondary institutions," according to Notice 97-60, 1997-46 IRB 1, § 4, A-2. Notice 97-60 provides many other details regarding this exception, including the fact that room and board are among the covered expenses if the student is enrolled at least half-time.

To the extent the education expenses in question are paid for by a scholarship, federal education grant, tax-free distribution from an Education IRA (§ 530), tax-free employer-provided educational assistance, or other payment that is excludible from gross income (other than gifts, inheritances, loans or savings), they cannot also be used to support a penalty-free IRA distribution. §§ 72(t)(7)(B), 25A(g)(2); Notice 97-60, § 4, A-1.

9.3.09 *IRAs only: distribution to help purchase someone's first home*

"Qualified first-time homebuyer distributions" from an IRA are not subject to the penalty. § 72(t)(2)(F). Beginning after 1997, an individual can withdraw from his or her IRA (but not from a qualified plan or 403(b) arrangement) up to $10,000, without paying the 10% penalty, if the distribution is used "before the close of the 120th day after the day on which such payment or distribution is received to pay qualified acquisition costs with respect to a principal residence of a first-time homebuyer who is such individual, the spouse of such individual, or any child, grandchild, or ancestor of such individual or the individual's spouse." § 72(t)(8)(A). For such a small exception, this one is quite complicated. Note the following:

The $10,000 is a lifetime limit. It applies to the person making the withdrawal (the IRA owner), not the person buying the home.

Example: Mom and Dad, both age 54, want to help Junior, age 27, buy his first home. All three of them have IRAs. Mom and Junior each withdraw $10,000 penalty-free from their respective IRAs, and Dad withdraws $5,000 from his IRA penalty-free, to help pay for Junior's new home. (Note each will have to pay *income taxes* on these withdrawals; only the 10% penalty is waived.) The following year, Sis, age 25, wants to buy *her* first home. But Mom and Junior can't dip into their IRAs penalty-free to help her out because they have already used up their $10,000 lifetime limit for such withdrawals. Dad still has $5,000 left that he can withdraw penalty-free to help Sis buy her home; otherwise, Sis is on her own.

"Principal residence" has the same meaning as in § 121 (exclusion of gain on sale of principal residence). § 72(t)(8)(D)(ii). § 121 itself does not contain a definition of "principal residence," but Reg. § 1.121-3(a) does, by cross reference to (now-repealed) § 1034 and Reg. § 1.1034-1(c)(3); refer to that regulation if there is doubt as to whether a particular residence is the homebuyer's principal residence.

"Qualified acquisition costs" are the costs of "acquiring, constructing, or reconstructing a residence", including "usual or reasonable settlement, financing, or other closing costs." § 72(t)(8)(C).

A "first-time homebuyer" is not someone who has literally never owned a home before, but just someone who hasn't owned a home in a while. It is a person who has had no "present ownership interest in a principal residence during the 2-year period ending on the date of acquisition of the" residence being financed by the distribution. If the homebuyer is married, both spouses must meet this test.

§ 72(t)(8)(D).

The "date of acquisition" is the date "a binding contract to acquire" the home is entered into, or "on which construction or reconstruction of such a principal residence is commenced"—but, if there is a "delay or cancellation of the purchase or construction" [what about *re*construction?] and, solely for that reason, the distribution fails to meet the 120 day test, the distribution can be rolled back into the IRA; AND the rollover back into the IRA will be a qualified tax-free rollover, even if it occurs more than 60 days after the distribution, so long as it occurs within 120 days of the distribution, AND the rollover back into the IRA will not count for purposes of the one-rollover-per-year limit of § 408(d)(3)(B). § 72(t)(8)(E). What could be simpler!

Finally, to the extent the distribution in question qualifies for one of the *other* exceptions (*e.g.*, a distribution under a QDRO, or to pay higher education or deductible medical expenses, or health insurance premiums for an unemployed person, or on account of death or total disability, or part of a SOSEPP), it will not count as a "first-time homebuyer" distribution even if it is used to pay expenses that would qualify it for the first-time homebuyer exception. § 72(t)(2)(F).

9.3.10 *IRS levy on the account*

Generally, even an involuntary distribution is subject to the penalty if received while under age 59½. See for example § 1011A(c)(13) of TAMRA, which provided that "§ 72(t) of the 1986 Code shall apply to any distribution without regard to whether such distribution is made without the consent of the participant pursuant to § 411(a)(11) or § 417(e)" (the Code provisions allowing plans to distribute small benefits immediately upon termination of employment, regardless of the employee's consent or lack thereof), and IRS Notice 87-13, 1987-1 C.B. 432, Q-20 to the same effect.

However, over the protests of the IRS, the Tax Court has excused certain taxpayers from the penalty when their benefits were seized by the government. See, *e.g.*, Murillo v. Comm'r, 75 T.C. Memo 1564 (1998); this case contains references to earlier cases on point.

For distributions after 1999, there is some statutory relief from this situation: If the retirement plan is taken by an IRS levy under § 6331, the forced "distribution" will not be subject to the 10% penalty. § 72(t)(2)(A)(vii).

9.3.11 *Return of certain excess contributions*

Certain excess contributions to "cash-or-deferred-arrangement" plans (such as 401(k) plans) may be distributed penalty-free if various requirements are met. See §§ 401(k)(8)(D) and 402(g)(2)(C).

9.4 Summary of Planning Principles

1.   Be aware that distributions (even inadvertent distributions) to a participant under age 59½ generally trigger a 10% penalty.

2.   If a client wants to take money from a retirement plan prior to age 59½, refer to this Chapter to determine whether he qualifies for an exception. Note carefully the requirements of any possibly applicable exception (*e.g.*, make sure it is available for the type of plan involved). Do not expect the exceptions to operate in a logical, fair and consistent manner.

3.   If a client has an IRA (or can create one by rollover from another type of plan), consider the highly flexible "SOSEPP" exception as a possible funding source for gifting programs, life insurance premium payments, tuition bills and other expenditures. Consider hiring an actuary to help design a substantial or creative SOSEPP. In general, create the smallest possible separate IRA to support the desired size of payment, and preserve as much flexibility as possible for future changes in the client's needs. See the Quentin case study, Chapter 11.

4.   The penalty does not apply to post-death distributions, but a surviving spouse who rolls over death benefits to her own retirement plan loses the exemption for death benefits.

10

The "How To" Chapter

*How to do "life and death planning" for
clients' retirement benefits in various
situations, and ideas for dealing with
some perennial problems in this field*

The preceding nine chapters explained what the law is. This
Chapter reassembles some of the information from the point of view of
what a practitioner might actually do with clients.

10.1 How to Take Lifetime Distributions

See Chapter 5 for considerations involved in converting to a
Roth IRA.

10.1.01 *Taking out extra: to reduce taxes*

If money could stay in the retirement plan long enough, the
economic benefits of tax-free investing would probably outweigh ANY
tax advantage that might accrue by taking the money out right now.
However, it may not be possible to leave the money in the plan long
enough, for many reasons, such as: the minimum distribution rules
(Chapter 1), which require distribution of the plan assets at a certain
point; or the plan doesn't offer a long-term payout option (¶ 1.5.09); or
the beneficiaries will have to withdraw the money right after
Participant's death to pay estate taxes, or to spend. Weigh the
advantages of whatever income tax deferral is *realistically* available
against the following possible tax advantages of Participant's taking out
of the plan, right now, more than is required:

Participant is in an unusually low tax bracket this year (in this
case consider Roth IRA conversion also; see ¶ 5.4).

Participant could take a distribution that would qualify for an
especially low tax rate, such as a distribution of employer securities
with "net unrealized appreciation" (¶ 2.4), or special averaging
treatment (¶ 2.3).

Participant wants to make gifts to reduce his future estate taxes and the only source of funds is the retirement plan. The estate tax savings may well outweigh the income tax advantages of leaving money in the plan. In view of the repeal of the estate tax now scheduled for 2010 (§ 2210) this strategy would appeal mainly to someone who does not expect to live that long.

If Participant's life expectancy is severely shortened (e.g., terminal illness), and it is expected that the estate will be subject to estate taxes, see ¶ 2.2.08, ¶ 2.4 and ¶ 5.5.06 for planning strategies.

If there are no non-retirement plan assets to fund a "credit shelter trust" in case of Participant's death, consider withdrawing funds now so such a trust could be funded with after-tax dollars (see ¶ 10.5 for more on this).

Match withdrawals to large charitable gifts to obtain charitable income tax deduction. In this situation, also keep an eye on the "Charitable Rollover Bill" (see ¶ 7.6.01).

If there is life insurance in the retirement plan, consider removing it so the policy can be transferred to an estate tax-free insurance trust; see ¶ 8.3.03-¶ 8.3.04. Also consider removing a life insurance policy (or any other plan asset) from a plan at any time that you believe its current value is relatively low. See ¶ 8.4.04 (#4).

If Participant has underpaid his estimated taxes and is coming up on the end of the year, consider taking a withdrawal from the retirement plan equal to the amount of the missing estimated taxes, and having the plan administrator withhold 100% of the distribution. The withholding is deemed to have been paid ratably throughout the year. This strategy can avert the penalty for underpayment of estimated taxes.¶ 2.1.05-¶ 2.1.06.

Whenever contemplating a tax-saving strategy that involves Participant's taking more out of a retirement plan than is required, keep financial planning in mind. If client's primary need is to have money to live on during retirement, leaving the money in the plan may be the best way to accomplish that goal, even if in the long run it may cost the surviving beneficiaries more taxes.

Consider also the other drawbacks of taking money out of a retirement plan, which may or may not apply in any particular case, such as: loss of creditor protection: (money inside a retirement plan may qualify for protection from claims of creditors; taking the money out of the plan may increase vulnerability); loss of future income tax deferral on the funds withdrawn; and loss of any special "grandfather" status that may be applicable (see ¶ 8.5).

10.1.02 *Taking out extra: non-tax reasons*

If Participant needs cash for living expenses or other goals, and must choose between selling appreciated assets that he holds outside the plan and taking the money out of a retirement plan, which should he do? Selling appreciated assets causes lower immediate taxes if the profit is taxed as long-term capital gain (because the tax is only 20% of the gain portion of the sale price) than taking a plan distribution (normally fully taxable as ordinary income; see ¶ 2.1.03 for exceptions). However, the appreciated assets, if held until Participant's death rather than being sold, will get a "stepped-up basis" at Participant's death (if he dies before 2010; or, in some cases, even if he dies after 2009), while the retirement benefits will not (¶ 2.2.01) —so taking the money from a retirement plan may result in lower income taxes over the long term.

If Participant is considering taking money out of the plan for living expenses or other goals, consider whether a home mortgage could be used instead. The mortgage interest payments would be tax deductible, while the plan investments would continue to accumulate tax-deferred.

Non-tax reasons to consider taking money out of a retirement plan include: balancing assets between retirement and non-retirement plan investments (in the interest of diversification); and, in a profit sharing plan, avoiding the necessity of obtaining spousal consent to Participant's choice of a death beneficiary (see ¶ 3.4.03).

If Participant is under age 59½, try to structure the distributions as a "series of substantially equal periodic payments" (¶ 9.2) or other form of distribution that is exempt from the 10% premature distributions tax (¶ 9.3).

Consider also the other drawbacks of taking money out of a retirement plan listed at ¶ 10.1.02 (last sentence).

10.1.03 *How to take MRDs*

Take minimum required distributions (MRDs) as late in the year as possible, to maximize income tax deferral. With late-in-the-year MRDs, consider having the plan administrator or IRA provider withhold the entire amount and use this withholding (which is deemed to have been paid ratably throughout the year) in lieu of paying estimated taxes (that would otherwise have to be paid in April, June and September). ¶ 2.1.05-¶ 2.1.06.

If using the late-in-the-year distribution strategy (especially if combining it with the withholding strategy), Participant must be careful not to die before taking the distribution. Death before taking the distribution would make the withholding strategy impossible, and also would set the beneficiaries up for a penalty because they might not have enough time before year-end to complete the MRD.

When commencing MRDs from an employer plan, if the employee has both an "employee contribution account" and an "employer contribution account" in the plan, use the former to satisfy the MRD requirement for both accounts, to maximize the tax-free portion of MRDs (see ¶ 1.9.03). This strategy does not work with IRAs (see ¶ 5.4.10-¶ 5.4.12).

If an IRA holds a hard-to-value asset such as a limited partnership, and Participant is concerned that the IRS might decide the asset is worth more than Participant thinks it is, Participant can be sure he will avoid the 50% penalty (¶ 1.9.06) by taking a proportionate share of that asset as part of his MRD. For example, if the MRD for the year is 1/26th of the prior year end value, Participant can be sure he is taking "enough" of that hard-to-value asset by distributing a 1/26th interest in the asset to himself shortly after the prior-year-end valuation date (and of course also taking out 1/26th of the other assets in the account). This will not avoid underpayment of income taxes if the IRS later decides the asset is undervalued on the IRA's books; it just avoids the § 4974 penalty (because, regardless of what the value of the asset turns out to be, Participant took the required proportion of it). To avoid costly annual appraisals and get the problem behind him, Participant could withdraw the hard-to-value asset entirely.

In general, consider taking distributions in kind to avoid commissions for selling securities.

As to which assets to take out of the plan to satisfy the MRD requirement, choose those you consider most likely to have capital gain-type appreciation in the future, e.g., choose a stock you think is temporarily depressed in price instead of a bond that generates taxable interest but is considered unlikely to increase in price. By removing the stock investment you consider "temporarily" undervalued, you pay tax on the current value (which you think is low), and enjoy capital gain treatment for the expected price rebound. Keep good records of the date of distribution value, as that will be your basis in the distributed securities going forward.

If Participant has multiple IRA accounts, consider taking all of each year's MRD just from one of them, using Notice 88-38 (¶ 1.9.01). This is administratively easier than taking MRDs from a multitude of accounts, and can be used as a painless way to close out smaller accounts.

The first year's MRD from a QRP can be combined with a special deal such as NUA (¶ 2.4) or special averaging treatment (¶ 2.3.07). If Participant is eligible for either of these, the deal should be reviewed as soon as possible, because once he has taken a MRD (or any other distribution) in one taxable year these special deals will no longer be available in subsequent years (unless there is a new triggering event), all as explained in ¶ 2.3.

10.2 How to Fix a Non-complying Trust

This ¶ 10.2 provides ideas for what to do with a trust that "flunks" the proposed minimum distribution trust rules (¶ 6.2, ¶ 6.3); see the "Trust Review Questionnaire" in Appendix C to test a trust for compliance with these rules.

10.2.01 *Fixing trust while Participant is living*

1.   Consider whether the trust can be amended without compromising other important objectives.

Example: Rose leaves all her assets including her $1 million IRA in trust for her sister, Susannah, for life and the trust provides that, on Susannah's death, $10,000 is to be paid to charity and the rest to Susannah's son, Morgan. Rose's trust flunks the rules because there is a non-individual beneficiary (¶ 6.2.11). Rose decides that she will take care of her charitable gift in some different way and amends the trust to delete the charitable remainder bequest.

2.   Consider creating a separate trust just for the retirement benefits. Because having two trusts is more complicated than having one trust, this approach will presumably make sense only if there are substantial assets both inside and outside the retirement plan.

Example: Cotton leaves her $1 million IRA and $2 million of other assets to a trust for her brother, Peter, for life. At Peter's death, half the trust's assets are to go to a charity and half to Peter's children. This trust flunks the rules because it has a non-individual beneficiary; ¶ 6.2.11. (Incidentally, it also does not qualify for an estate tax charitable deduction; see Chapter 7.) By creating two separate trusts for Peter's life benefit, one to receive the IRA and the other to receive Cotton's non-retirement assets, Cotton could cure this problem. For example, if Peter is young (so he has a long life expectancy) Cotton might decide to create one trust, to receive only the IRA, that would pass to Peter for life, then to his children. This trust would qualify for the life expectancy payout method. Then she could create a separate trust, to receive the other assets, that would pass on Peter's death partly to charity and partly to Peter's children. The amount passing to charity under this second trust could be determined by a formula that would take into account both trusts. Alternatively, if Peter is old (so that a long life expectancy payout will not be available for a trust of which he is the oldest beneficiary) she might want to leave the IRA to a separate Charitable Remainder Trust (CRT) (¶ 7.5.04) for Peter's life, and leave her non-retirement assets to a "regular" trust that would pay Peter income for life. The remainder interest under this second trust would pass to charity and to Peter's children, with the amount passing to the charity adjusted to reflect the amount the charity received from the CRT.

3.   Consider accepting the loss of the "life expectancy of oldest beneficiary" payout method.

Example: Wes is 72. He wants to leave his $1 million IRA to a discretionary trust for the benefit of a dozen of his old Army buddies, with remainder to a charitable organization that helps needy veterans. He does not want to use a CRT (¶ 7.5.04) because he expects that his buddies may need more than just the CRT income stream. He could create a conduit trust (¶ 6.3.08) for the buddies, but this would remove the trustee's discretion to accumulate distributions for use in later years. The oldest Army buddy, Denny, is older than Wes. So, having the benefits paid out over the life expectancy of the oldest human beneficiary of the trust (Denny) will provide even less deferral than the alternative (payout over the remaining life expectancy of Wes). Solution: Write the trust terms exactly as Wes wants them even though this will cause the trust to flunk the trust rules.

10.2.02 *After death, before Designation Date*

First, consider whether having the trust comply with the trust rules is an important goal (see the "Wes" example, # 3, ¶ 10.2.01). If it *is* an important goal, consider whether it is possible to fix the problem before the Designation Date by actions such as the following:

DISTRIBUTIONS:

If the problem is that the trust has one or more non-individual beneficiaries, consider whether these beneficiaries' interests could be eliminated prior to the Designation Date by distribution (¶ 1.8.05).

Example 1: Chrissy died, leaving her $1 million IRA to a trust. The trust provides that upon Chrissy's death the trustee is to pay $50,000 to Shore Country Day School, and hold the rest of the assets in trust for Chrissy's husband. The bequest to the school (a non-individual beneficiary) is the only "flaw" in the trust, which otherwise complies with the IRS trust rules. The trustee distributes the $50,000 bequest to Shore before the Designation Date. Thus the school is no longer a "beneficiary" of the trust at the time of the Designation Date and can be ignored. It makes no difference for this purpose whether the $50,000 paid to Shore came from the IRA benefits or from other trust assets.

Example 2: Mike left his $1 million IRA to his living trust. The only beneficiaries of the trust are Mike's children; however, the trust instructs the trustee to pay to Mike's estate "such amounts as my Executor shall request for payment of my debts, expenses of administration of my estate and taxes." The statute of limitations for filing claims against Mike's estate expires before the Designation Date. The Trustee, before the Designation Date, distributes to the estate sufficient assets to pay the known claims and estimated expenses and taxes. The executor, trustee and beneficiaries enter into an agreement (which is approved by the Probate Court and which is valid and binding, under applicable state law, on all parties including future fiduciaries and beneficiaries of the estate and trust), whereby the trustee is relieved of any obligation to pay any of the retirement benefits (or proceeds thereof) to the estate. The estate has been removed as a trust beneficiary prior to the Designation Date.

DISCLAIMER:

Example: Caleb dies at age 60, leaving his $1 million IRA and other assets to a trust to pay income to David for life, plus principal in the discretion of the trustee for David's health, support and happiness. On David's death, the trust is to distribute $25,000 to Harvard College, and the balance of the remaining principal to Rosemary and Gilbert (who are younger than David). Because of the bequest to a non-individual beneficiary (Harvard), the trust flunks and benefits will have to be distributed under the 5-year rule (¶ 1.5.04). If this bequest did not exist, the benefits could be distributed over the life expectancy of the oldest trust beneficiary, David, who is only 45. David, Rosemary and Gilbert have always been generous supporters of Harvard, and have named Harvard as beneficiary of substantial bequests in their own estate plans. They meet with Chuck from Harvard's Planned Giving Office and ask Chuck whether Harvard would like to disclaim the $25,000 remainder bequest under Caleb's trust. They do not compensate, or offer to compensate, Harvard for making the disclaimer, or make any threat or promise about what they will do or not do if Harvard does or doesn't disclaim. They simply point out a few facts. First, Harvard wouldn't be losing much by disclaiming (maximum $25,000, after life of a 45 year-old; the present value of this is much less than $25,000). Second, they remind Chuck that, if the life expectancy payout is not available to the trust, the trust will have less money in it overall, which will mean lower income for David, and less principal available for David, Gilbert and Rosemary. They point out that the less money these individuals have, the less they personally can afford to give to Harvard. Finally, they point out that Harvard's refusal to disclaim would leave them with a bad taste in their mouths as they see the IRS raid the IRA, and no longer would the name "Harvard" conjure only sweetness and light in their minds. Harvard disclaims the bequest. The trust uses the life expectancy payout method. David becomes Class Gift Chairman for his Harvard 25th Reunion Class and raises a record amount.

TRUST REFORMATION:

With proper proceedings in the Court having jurisdiction of the trust, it may be possible to have the trust reformed, settled, divided into separate trusts or otherwise re-engineered so that the trust that receives the benefits, as of the Designation Date, complies with the trust rules, even if the trust did not comply with such rules on the date of death. While post-death actions to modify a trust are normally *not* effective to accomplish such goals as, e.g. qualifying for the marital deduction, the proposed regulations specifically allow recognition of post-death changes for purposes of the minimum distribution rules. ¶ 1.8.01.

Example: Dolly left her $1 million IRA and other assets to a trust that provided life income to Brinley, and on Brinley's death provided a gift of $50,000 to charity and the balance to John or John's descendants. By an agreement of all beneficiaries and the trustee, including a guardian to represent the unborn descendants, approved by the Probate Court, the charity is paid a reduced sum immediately (equal to the present value of its remainder) and in exchange gives up its $50,000 remainder. In effect, the trust is reformed so that the charitable beneficiary can be removed before the Designation Date. This is presumably effective (assuming the trust meets all the other trust rules) to enable the trust to qualify for the life expectancy payout method. Whether it is effective to provide Dolly's estate with an estate tax deduction for this charitable gift is a totally separate question, since as of the date of death, that gift was in the form of a non-qualifying split interest.

10.2.03 *Other ideas*

1.   **Spousal rollover**. The IRS, in its rulings, has been liberal in permitting the spouse to roll over benefits even when Spouse was not named directly as beneficiary, so long as Spouse had the absolute right (as beneficiary of an estate or trust) to receive the benefits. ¶ 3.2.09.

2.   **Wait and see**. If Participant died before his RBD (¶ 1.3), and you believe that the trust should qualify for the life expectancy payout method but the result is not clear under the proposed regulations, use a "wait and see" approach. Begin distributions based on the assumption that the trust qualifies, and that the installments-over-life-expectancy method is available. This means making annual installment distributions, beginning by the end of the year after the year of Participant's death, based on the life expectancy of the oldest trust beneficiary. Once four years have elapsed, review the situation again. By then there may be final regulations, cases or other legal guidance

providing a definitive answer one way or the other. If the question has been answered unfavorably to your trust, or if it still is ambiguous and you do not want to seek an IRS ruling, you can still comply with the 5-year rule and distribute all benefits by December 31 of the year which contains the fifth anniversary of Participant's death.

3.   **Fight the IRS.** The IRS's proposed regulations do not have the force of law. See ¶ 1.1.06. Until final regulations have been issued, a taxpayer is entitled to act based on a "reasonable interpretation of the statute." So if the trust flunks the proposed regulations' test, but you can construct a "reasonable interpretation of the statute" under which you are ok, you may win. (However, if the current proposed regulations do not support you, final regulations can be passed later with retroactive effect and this may eliminate your victory.)

10.3 How to Plan for Disability

10.3.01 *Name a beneficiary for disability benefits*

Retirement plan documents should (but may not) permit Participant to direct the payment of lifetime benefits (disability and retirement) to his revocable living trust.

§ 401(a)(13) prohibits "assignment" of QRP benefits. Regulations provide that a voluntary, revocable assignment is not an "assignment" for purposes of § 401(a)(13). § 72(p)(1)(B) treats all "assignments" of plan benefits as loans from the plan, apparently taxable as distributions, and neither § 72(p) nor regulations thereunder suggests an exception for a voluntary revocable assignment of benefits. However, an "assignment" to a revocable trust should not be treated as an assignment for purposes of § 72(p) or § 401(a)(13) because Participant and his revocable trust are essentially treated as "one person" for income tax purposes under the grantor trust rules (§§ 671-677).

10.3.02 *Power of attorney*

The client's power of attorney should at a minimum enable the power holder to receive benefit checks and endorse them. It can go further and give the holder the power to make elections as to the form and timing of benefits (subject to the rights of client's spouse) but this would necessarily involve the power holder in making choices between the client and the beneficiary of death benefits under the plan. Giving the power to designate a beneficiary of plan death benefits gives even greater responsibility to the power holder. See Form 5.1, Appendix B.

10.4 How To Represent Beneficiaries

When advising a beneficiary who has inherited an IRA or other retirement plan, you need to cover five issues: the minimum distribution rules (planning opportunities and compliance); establishing separate accounts (if there are two or more beneficiaries); whether a plan-to-plan transfer is needed; the IRD deduction; and naming a successor beneficiary.

The following discussion assumes you are asked to help one or more non-spouse beneficiaries (for example, a deceased Participant's children) with an inherited IRA that offers the life expectancy payout method of distribution (¶ 1.2.01).

10.4.01 *MRDs: planning, compliance*

Minimum required distributions from an inherited retirement plan present both planning opportunities (helping the beneficiaries take advantage of the life expectancy payout method) and compliance challenges (making sure the beneficiaries take out the annual required distribution).

Planning: Explain the valuable income tax deferral opportunity offered by the "life expectancy payout method." See "Lena and Tina" example (¶ 1.2.01). Consider using software (Appendix D) to provide projections and illustrations of the financial rewards of this method.

Compliance: Once the beneficiaries sign up for the life expectancy payout method, be sure there is someone responsible to calculate the minimum distribution annually and make sure it gets paid. This could be a good occasion for an annual meeting with these clients.

Supervise the transition of the account from the decedent's ownership to the beneficiary's ownership with eagle eyes. The IRA provider's staff may or may not be aware of the critical issues involved in this step. If the IRA provider issues a check to the beneficiary (or transfers funds from the inherited account to the beneficiary's own

IRA), you are faced with a completed distribution (or a distribution followed by an illegal rollover).

Make sure that the IRA provider keeps the IRA titled as an "inherited" IRA. There is no particular required wording for this; the only requirement is that the account documentation must make clear that (even though the beneficiary now owns the account) this is not the "beneficiary's" IRA. The beneficiary cannot contribute to this account for example. Acceptable methods of titling include "John Doe, deceased, for the benefit of Richard Roe, beneficiary," and "Richard Roe, as beneficiary of John Doe, deceased." The name of the deceased Participant should appear somewhere, with indication that beneficiary owns this account merely as beneficiary of the original Participant.

The Social Security number on the account should be the beneficiary's, despite private letter rulings which say the decedent's number should be used. IRS Instructions for Form 1099-R (2000), p. R-5 ("Beneficiaries" section).

If the account was inherited from a Participant who died prior to issuance of the new proposed minimum distribution regulations in January 2001, see also ¶ 10.4.06.

10.4.02 *Establishing separate accounts*

If there are multiple beneficiaries, and their interests are fractional (e.g. "Equally to my four children"), they may want to treat the inherited benefit as "separate accounts" for MRD purposes, so that each beneficiary can use his or her own life expectancy to compute MRDs. See ¶ 1.7.06 and the Howard case study, Chapter 11. Separate accounts in this sense is just a bookkeeping concept—all the benefits stay in one commingled investment account, but someone keeps track of the proper allocation of the account's gains, losses and distributions among the different beneficiaries.

A conservative way to state the Separate Accounts rule would be as follows: If the client dies, leaving a particular plan or IRA to multiple beneficiaries, the respective shares going to the different beneficiaries constitute "separate accounts" within the meaning of the proposed regulations (so that each individual beneficiary can use his or her own life expectancy to measure required distributions, and so that the fact that some shares are payable to charities or other non-individual beneficiaries will not prevent the individual beneficiaries from using the life expectancy payout method) if:

A.   The shares of the respective beneficiaries are defined as fractional or percentage shares; AND

B.   There is "something extra" to establish "separate account" status.

That "something extra" could be either: (i) physical separation of the separate accounts prior to the Designation Date as was done in PLR 1999-31049; or (ii) language in the account agreement or beneficiary designation form specifying separate account treatment (see Section 3.05 of Forms 2.1, 2.2, Appendix B); or (iii) an agreement signed by all of the beneficiaries and (ideally) the IRA custodian or trustee after Participant's death but before the Designation Date specifying that the beneficiaries want to use the separate account method and confirming the acceptable accounting method they will use to account for gains and losses.

Also consider physical division of the IRA post mortem for reasons *other than* § 401(a)(9). Having "separate accounts within a single IRA" necessitates pro rata allocation of all investment gains and losses, and does not permit each beneficiary to "self-direct" the investment of his or her portion of the IRA. So, whether or not the beneficiaries are entitled to separate account treatment for minimum distribution purposes, they may well want the IRA "physically" divided up, after Participant's death, into actual separate inherited IRA accounts, one payable to each of the respective beneficiaries, so that each beneficiary can pursue his own investment objectives. This can easily be done with inherited IRAs by having the IRA provider divide the inherited IRA into several separate inherited IRAs, one for each beneficiary. The IRS has recognized the right of IRA beneficiaries to do this (by means of "custodian to custodian transfer," not by "rollover"). See, *e.g.*, PLR 9623037. As long as each beneficiary's separated inherited account is the right value (e.g., all accounts should initially be of equal value if the IRA was left equally to several children), they can even pick and choose which investments would go into which beneficiary's separated account.

10.4.03 *Plan-to-plan transfers*

The beneficiary of an inherited IRA may want to transfer it to a different IRA provider. This can be done by means of a direct transfer by one IRA custodian (or trustee) to another IRA custodian (or trustee), from one inherited IRA (the IRA that was actually inherited) to another "inherited IRA" (that isn't really inherited, it is a newly opened account in the name of the deceased participant). Even if there is no change of custodian or trustee, changing the account from one big account payable to multiple beneficiaries into multiple smaller accounts, each payable to one beneficiary, is considered a plan-to-plan transfer.

The IRS has no problem with these transfers PROVIDED: the transferee account is still titled as an inherited IRA, not the beneficiary's "own" IRA (see ¶ 10.4.01); and the assets go DIRECTLY from one IRA custodian (or trustee) to the other IRA custodian (or trustee). The WRONG way to do this is for the first IRA provider to give a check to the beneficiary, which he or she then deposits in the other IRA. This would be a "rollover," not a "plan-to-plan transfer," and (though the transactions look pretty much alike to most people) a non-spouse beneficiary CANNOT roll over an inherited IRA (¶ 2.5.04), so that procedure would be fatal.

Not all IRA providers will accept (or release) funds in beneficiary-initiated plan-to-plan transfers, but they should do so. Rev. Rul. 78-406, 1978-2 C.B. 157, provides the required legal authority allowing plan-to-plan transfers to take place even where a "rollover" would not be permitted. See, e.g., PLRs 2000-28040, 2000-28041.

10.4.04 *Don't forget the IRD deduction*

If Participant's estate was subject to federal estate tax, a beneficiary who has to pay income tax on distributions from Participant's retirement plan is entitled to an income tax deduction for the estate taxes paid on the inherited benefit. Calculation of this deduction is complex and uncertain (see ¶ 2.2.07-¶ 2.2.11), but the main problem with the deduction is (apparently) beneficiaries don't know about it and so don't take it. This is a big waste of money.

Surprisingly, the deduction goes to the person who receives taxable distributions from an inherited retirement plan (or other inherited "income" item); the deduction does not belong to the person who paid the estate tax. ¶ 2.2.09.

In an estate that was subject to a substantial estate tax, the effect of the "IRD deduction" is to lower the beneficiary's tax bracket on plan distributions. The beneficiary should take that into consideration when he needs some spending cash. If the beneficiary's choice is to take money from an inherited IRA or from his own IRA, the distribution from the inherited IRA may be subject to lower income taxes because of the IRD deduction. Also, a distribution from an inherited IRA is never subject to the 10% "premature distributions" penalty even if the beneficiary is under age 59½. ¶ 9.3.01. Before taking distributions from any IRA, however, the beneficiary should compare the financial effect of getting the money by taking out a mortgage on his/her home. The mortgage interest would be deductible, and the undepleted IRA could continue to grow tax-deferred.

10.4.05 *Naming a successor beneficiary*

Once the beneficiary has settled into a nice long-term life expectancy payout for the inherited IRA, he/she needs to consider what will happen to that account if he/she dies before the end of the life expectancy payout period. The IRS (and, now, most major IRA providers) recognize that a beneficiary can designate his or her own "successor beneficiary," to take over the account in case the original beneficiary dies before he or she has withdrawn all of the benefits. ¶ 1.9.02. Designating a successor beneficiary does not mean that the successor will be able to switch to such successor's life expectancy to measure distributions on the original beneficiary's death. ¶ 1.5.07. It just means that the successor can step into the shoes of the original beneficiary, and take distributions over the balance of the original beneficiary's life expectancy—without probate in most cases.

Designating a successor beneficiary should be part of a complete and coordinated estate plan for the beneficiary, and should be done as soon as possible after the beneficiary inherits the IRA.

10.4.06 *Beneficiaries of pre-2001 decedents*

The new proposed regulations (¶ 1.1.03) provide substantially increased income tax deferral opportunities for many individuals who are now taking required distributions from IRAs and other retirement plans they inherited from deceased participants—even for beneficiaries who inherited from decedents who died long ago, if the account is still in existence.

The proposed regulations "apply for purposes of determining required minimum distributions for calendar years beginning on or after January 1, 2002." Prop. Reg. § 1.401(a)(9)-1, A-2. Neither this statement of the effective date, nor the rule regarding the date for determining who is the designated beneficiary of a deceased participant (¶ 1.8.01), makes any distinction based on whether Participant died before or after any particular date. Thus it appears that all individuals now receiving required distributions from inherited retirement plans, *regardless of how long ago the original Participant died*, must switch to the new rules in 2002. IRS Notice 1270 (February 2001), which is a supplement to IRS Publication 590, indicates that all beneficiaries of inherited IRAs may use the new rules starting with the 2001 required distribution. There is no distinction between beneficiaries of IRA owners who died in 2000 and beneficiaries of IRA owners who died prior to 2000.

For beneficiaries of a Participant who died in the year 2000, the ability to use the new rules would mean that they would have until December 31, 2001, to finalize the decedent's beneficiary designation, and can take advantage of various post-mortem planning techniques. See ¶ 1.8. Even where there is no need (through post-mortem planning) to change the identity of the beneficiary who inherits the benefits, the switch from basing the Applicable Distribution Period for post-death distributions on the beneficiaries *as of the required beginning date* (RBD) (under the old rules) to basing it on the beneficiaries *as of the end of the year after the year of death* will help many beneficiaries.

Example 1: On her RBD back in 1996, Pearl named her estate as her IRA beneficiary, and thus was deemed to have no "designated beneficiary" (¶ 1.7.04). She started taking her distributions based on her single life expectancy (which was 15.3 years as of her first distribution year, 1995), not recalculated. She then died in 1999. By the time of her death, she had changed her beneficiary designation to her daughter, Ruby. Under the old rules, Ruby's MRD, as Pearl's beneficiary, for the year 2001 would be based on what was left of Pearl's single life expectancy, so Ruby would use a divisor of 9.3 (Pearl's original single life expectancy as of 1995, 15.3 years, minus 6 elapsed years). Under the *new* rules, since Ruby was Pearl's beneficiary at Pearl's death (and assuming she still is on the Designation Date), Ruby can switch over to using her own life expectancy. She determines that her life expectancy as of 2000 (the year after Pearl's death) was 31.3 years (because Ruby reached age 52 in 2000 and 31.3 years is the life expectancy from Table V for age 52). So her 2001 required distribution will be the 2000 year-end account value divided by 30.3—an increase of 21 years of income tax deferral for her inherited IRA.

Example 2: On his RBD in 1995, Dan named his wife Trish as primary (designated) beneficiary of his IRA, and elected to redetermine both life expectancies annually. His children were named as contingent beneficiaries. He never changed his beneficiary designation. Trish died in 1999 and Dan died in 2000. The children inherited the IRA. Under the old rules, the children would have to withdraw 100% of the benefits by December 31, 2001 (the "one year rule"). Under the new rules, they can use the oldest child's life expectancy to measure the MRDs (or even use each child's individual life expectancy, if they establish "separate accounts" by the Designation Date), because the applicable date for determining who are the "designated beneficiaries" of this account for purposes of post-death required distributions has shifted from *Dan's RBD* (back in 1995, when the beneficiary was Trish) to *the end of the year after the year of Dan's death* (by which time the children, not Trish, are the beneficiaries).

Example 3: Rich died in 1998, prior to his RBD. He left his $1 million IRA payable "$1,000 to my church and the rest to my son Randy." Randy paid out the charity's $1,000 bequest in 1999, meaning that Randy was the sole beneficiary as of 12/31/99 (the applicable date for determining the designated beneficiary under the new rules). As suggested under *"Cleanup strategies—death before the RBD,"* at page 20 of the 1999 edition of this book, Randy took minimum distributions from the account based on his life expectancy for the years 1999 and 2000, waiting to see if maybe (under some future interpretation of the minimum distribution rules) he could escape the 5-year rule. Under the old rules, Rich was deemed to have no designated beneficiary because of the multiple beneficiary rule. Under the new rules (¶ 1.8.05), Randy meets the requirements for a life expectancy payout.

10.5 How to Fund a Credit Shelter Trust

This ¶ 10.5 discusses the problem of "how to fund a credit shelter trust" when all or most of the client's assets are in the form of retirement plans. While in some cases the problem can be solved while still achieving all of the client's estate planning goals (see Solutions B and C), in other cases the client will have to choose between mutually exclusive competing objectives (see ¶ 10.5.03, Solutions A, D, H and J). Finally, some ideas that are advanced as solutions to this problem may not work as well as hoped (or at all) (see ¶ 10.5.03, Solutions E, F, G, I and K).

¶ 10.5.05 discusses the virtually identical drawbacks (and solutions) involved in funding a QTIP trust with retirement benefits.

10.5.01 *What the problem is and who has it*

There are significant income tax disadvantages to using retirement benefits to fund a credit shelter trust of which the surviving spouse ("Spouse") is a beneficiary. These income tax disadvantages (1) may reduce or eliminate the estate tax savings that is supposed to be obtained by using a credit shelter trust and/or (2) may reduce the amount of money Spouse has available to live on as compared with leaving the benefits outright to Spouse.

The problem arises when you have a married couple old enough and rich enough to care about estate taxes, but whose assets outside of retirement plans are less than the optimal credit shelter amount. For example, assume it is 2002 and the estate tax exemption (credit shelter amount) is $1 million. The couple's assets exceed $1 million. The "optimal credit shelter amount" is therefore $1 million. At least $1 million of the couple's assets consists of retirement benefits.

10.5.02 *Drawbacks of funding trust with benefits*

Here are the drawbacks of funding a credit shelter trust with retirement plan death benefits when Spouse is a beneficiary of the trust:

1. *Distributions start sooner after Participant's death (loss of income tax deferral, part 1).* Benefits paid to a credit shelter trust will have to be distributed, generally speaking, beginning within one year after Participant's death (but see Solution D). If Spouse received the benefits personally and rolled them over to an IRA, she wouldn't have to take any distributions until she reached age 70½. If Spouse received the benefits personally and did *not* roll them over, she wouldn't have to take any distributions until the year Participant would have reached age 70½. Thus, making benefits payable to a credit shelter trust often results in less income tax deferral because distributions

have to commence sooner than would otherwise be the case. This drawback is not a factor if both spouses are at, near or past age 70½.

2.   *Faster distributions during Spouse's life (loss of income tax deferral, part 2).* Benefits paid to a credit shelter trust will have to be distributed over the single life expectancy of the oldest beneficiary of the trust. This is the *best case* scenario for benefits paid to a trust, and assumes the IRS's "trust rules" (¶ 6.2) are complied with. This will produce a much more rapid distribution of the benefits than would be required if the benefits were payable to Spouse personally. If Spouse received the benefits personally and rolled them over to an IRA, she could withdraw the benefits gradually using the Uniform Table (¶ 1.4.01). Since the Uniform Table is equivalent to the joint life expectancy of Spouse and a hypothetical beneficiary 10 years younger than Spouse, the Uniform Table provides smaller required distributions than the single life expectancy of Spouse.

3.   *Faster distributions after Spouse's death (loss of income tax deferral, part 3).* If Spouse received the benefits personally and rolled them over to an IRA, she could name younger generation individuals as designated beneficiaries of the rollover IRA. After her death, the remaining benefits in the IRA could be paid out over the life expectancy of the younger-generation beneficiaries. In contrast, benefits paid to a credit shelter trust will have to be distributed over the single life expectancy of the oldest beneficiary of the trust (Spouse) even after that oldest beneficiary has died. Although the trust passes at that point to the younger generation beneficiaries, they will not be able to switch to their longer life expectancy to measure distributions (but see Solution D).

4.   *Higher income taxes on benefits paid to trust.* To the extent benefits are paid to the credit shelter trust and kept in the trust (i.e., not immediately distributed out to individual beneficiaries; see ¶ 6.1.03), they will be taxed at the *trust's* income tax rate. A trust moves into the highest federal bracket at a much lower level of taxable income ($8,900) than do human beings ($297,350) (2001 rates). Also, unlike human beings, trusts do

not get the benefit of the 10% bracket for any income. See § 1(i), as amended by EGTRRA 2001. Thus, for many families, making the benefits payable to a trust will cause them to be taxed at a higher rate than if the benefits were paid to individual beneficiaries.

5.   *"Wasting" part of the exemption paying income taxes.* If the credit shelter trust is funded with a $1 million retirement plan (other than a Roth IRA; see Solution G), the trust will have to pay income taxes on the retirement plan distributions as they are received. ¶ 2.1.01. Part of Participant's estate tax exemption will be "wasted" paying income taxes. In contrast, if the credit shelter trust is funded with non-income-taxable assets, the trust receives the full exemption amount, undiminished by income taxes. This factor may not be significant in the situation we are discussing because in the situation under discussion there is no choice: retirement benefits are the only asset available. However, it is certainly a serious consideration to very wealthy individuals whose total assets exceed the anticipated estate tax exemption levels. See Solution H.

6.   *Life expectancy payout may not be available except via spousal rollover.* The preceding drawbacks are inherent in the tax law. This drawback is not inherent in the law, but is a problem under some retirement plans: many (perhaps most) "qualified retirement plans" (such as pension plans, profit sharing plans and 401(k) plans) do not permit any form of death benefit other than a lump sum distribution. ¶ 1.5.09. With this type of plan, the only way to achieve the advantages of a life expectancy payout is to have the lump sum distribution paid outright to Spouse who rolls it over. If the lump sum is paid to the credit shelter trust, the trust will not even be able to use the "life expectancy of oldest beneficiary" to measure required distributions.

7.   *Spousal consent may be required to name a beneficiary other than Spouse.* Under virtually all qualified plans, Participant cannot designate a credit shelter trust (or any other beneficiary who is not Spouse) without Spouse's consent (see ¶ 3.4) as to either part or all of the plan benefit. IRAs and some 403(b)

plans are not subject to this requirement.

10.5.03 *Solutions: the good, the bad and the useless*

Here are the choices available to respond to the problem.

A. **Leave the benefits outright to spouse; underfund the credit shelter trust.** This eliminates drawbacks 1-7. The drawback of this solution is possibly increased estate taxes on the second death due to "wasting" the first spouse's estate tax exemption. This solution is appropriate if: Client cares more about Spouse's financial security than about saving estate taxes for future beneficiaries. Or, client believes that both spouses will probably live long enough so that increasing exemptions, decreasing assets and/or estate tax repeal will eliminate estate tax concerns, and therefore prefers reasonably definite income tax advantages over remote estate tax savings. Or, after running the numbers, client and planner conclude that the estate tax savings of a credit shelter trust would be wiped out by the income tax drawbacks, so the family will actually have more money than if they fund the credit shelter trust. If using this solution, the option of funding a credit shelter trust can be kept alive by naming the credit shelter trust as contingent beneficiary to the extent Spouse disclaims the benefit. Also, the couple could divide their non-retirement assets equally between them, so that, regardless of which spouse dies first, *some* assets will go into the estate tax-saving credit shelter trust of the first spouse to die.

The disclaimer non-solution. Many planners suggest that *the* solution to the problem is to name Spouse as primary beneficiary, and credit shelter trust as contingent beneficiary in case of Spouse's disclaimer; then expect that on Participant's death Spouse will disclaim a sufficient amount to fill up the credit shelter trust. This "disclaimer" estate plan does NOT eliminate the problem of funding a credit shelter trust with retirement benefits. If the situation hasn't changed when Participant dies, activating the credit shelter trust by having Spouse disclaim the retirement benefits will have EXACTLY the same drawbacks as naming the credit shelter trust as beneficiary in the first place (but now with all the added complications of carrying out a qualified disclaimer). The disclaimer plan is no more than a useful backstop, to be activated if (when Participant dies) something has changed: for example, if Spouse's financial situation has improved (she won the lottery?), or the tax laws, at the time of Participant's death, have changed so that having the retirement benefits pass to the credit shelter trust would no longer have a negative effect on the spouse's financial security.

B.   **Leave the benefits directly to the younger generation.** This does not eliminate drawback # 1; distribution of benefits will have to begin within one year after Participant's death. This solution does eliminate drawbacks 2 & 3 by going directly to the (long) life expectancy of the younger generation. This solution can eliminate drawback # 4 if the benefits go outright to the younger generation or go to a conduit trust (¶ 6.3.08) for them (so benefits are taxed at their individual rates rather than trust rates). It does not eliminate drawback 5, 6 or 7. This solution is appropriate if: Providing for Spouse's financial security is not a goal, or if Spouse's financial security is well provided for without this retirement benefit.

C.   **Community property solution.** This is an excellent solution that works perfectly (eliminates drawbacks 1-6) IF the couple have enough non-retirement assets to fund one credit shelter trust, but not both, AND the retirement plan in question is an IRA. The goal in such a situation is to have the non-retirement assets wind up in the estate of the first spouse to die (where they can be used, with none of the listed drawbacks, to fund decedent's credit shelter trust) and to have the retirement plan end up in the hands of Spouse (who can roll it over and get the advantages of longer term income tax deferral etc.). This goal can be achieved in non-community property states only if the couple can correctly guess which spouse is going to die first (see "Solution I"). In California and perhaps other community property states, such guessing is unnecessary. Participant and Spouse can sign a contract agreeing that all their assets (including the IRA) are "aggregate" community property, and assigning all their assets to a joint trust. The IRA is made payable to the joint trust. Then, on the first death, regardless of which spouse dies first, the survivor gets to choose which assets he (or she) will take from the joint pot as "his" (or "her") share of the community property, and can simply walk away with those assets, leaving the rest of the assets to constitute the deceased spouse's share of the community property (and to pass into the deceased spouse's credit shelter trust). So the survivor says "I'll take the IRA as my share" and keeps it (or, if it belonged originally to the deceased spouse, rolls it over to a new IRA in the survivor's name), and lets the non-IRA assets pass to the deceased spouse's credit shelter trust. This solution does not work even in community property states if the retirement plan is subject to ERISA, because the Supreme Court has held that ERISA's spousal protection rules (¶ 3.4) preempt community property law in plans subject to ERISA. Boggs v. Boggs, 520 U.S. 833 (1997). For more discussion of this approach and why and how it works, see PLR 1999-25033 (3/25/99) and "Practicalities of Post-Mortem Distribution Planning for Community Property Retirement Benefits and IRAs—Trusts as Beneficiaries, Separate Shares and Aggregate Theory Agreements," by Edward V. Brennan, Esq., California Trusts and Estates Quarterly, Vol. 5, No. 4 (Winter 1999). Non-community property state residents may be able to achieve the same advantages by transferring their property to an Alaska Community Property Trust. See "Alaska Enacts an Optional Community Property System Which Can Be Elected by Both Residents and Nonresidents," by David G. Shaftel and Stephen E. Greer, 25 ACTED Notes 206 (1999).

D.   **Conduit Trust: trust is required to pass out to Spouse all retirement plan distributions as they are received by the credit shelter trust.** The conduit trust (¶ 6.3.08) eliminates drawback # 4: the high trust income tax rates applicable to IRD distributions paid to the credit shelter trust as principal are avoided by having the credit shelter trust distribute out to Spouse all distributions the trust receives from the retirement plan, as the trust receives them. The result is that the retirement plan distributions will be taxed to Spouse at her (low) rate, rather than to the trust at its (high) rate. The trust terms would require that the Trustee distribute to Spouse all retirement plan distributions received by the trust, as and when they are received by the trust (regardless of whether these distributions are defined as income or as principal for trust accounting purposes;¶ 6.1.07). This is called a "conduit trust," and under the new proposed minimum distribution regulations, this trust could: postpone the commencement of required distributions until the decedent would have reached age 70½ (just as Spouse could have done had she been named directly as beneficiary) (which can provide substantial income tax deferral *if* Participant died well before reaching age 70½, thus eliminating drawback # 1); recalculate Spouse's life expectancy for purposes of MRDs to the trust (meaning that if the trustee takes only MRDs there is guaranteed to be something—not necessarily very much—left in the trust when Spouse later dies); and (if Participant and Spouse *both* die before the end of the year Participant would have reached age 70½) (not a very common scenario) the subsequent distributions to the younger generation remainder beneficiaries would be based on their life expectancy, not Spouse's (eliminating drawback # 3 in that unusual scenario). The first problem with this approach is that the bulk of the retirement plan will be distributed out over Spouse's life expectancy. If all plan distributions are distributed out to Spouse as the trust receives them, there will be little left in that retirement plan when Spouse dies, assuming she lives for all or most of her IRS-defined life expectancy. Few estate tax dollars will have been saved, because the retirement plan has been added to Spouse's estate just as if you had named her directly as beneficiary—but without the income tax deferral advantages of the spousal rollover. If you want to save estate taxes, you must provide that the credit shelter trust does NOT distribute the original value of Participant's retirement plan to Spouse. Keeping this money IN the credit shelter trust (and out of Spouse's estate) is the whole point of having a credit shelter trust. Thus this approach makes sense in only a very small number of situations where, for example, Spouse has a short life expectancy, but Participant does not want to cut her out entirely because she may need the money; and it is understood that the credit shelter trust device will save estate taxes only if Spouse dies prematurely. The second problem with this approach is that it totally solves only one of the drawbacks of using a credit shelter trust to receive Participant's retirement plan distributions—the high trust income tax rates (# 4) it partly solves Drawback # 1, and in rare cases Drawback # 3, but does not eliminate Drawbacks 2, 5, 6 or 7, or (in most cases) 3. The third problem with this approach is that it builds the whole trust on the assumption that the trustee will be able to and will want to take distributions from the retirement plan based on today's minimum distribution scheme. If the minimum distribution rules change, to require a faster payout than is required under today's rule, the credit shelter trust could end up with nothing in it in short order after Participant's death.

E.   **Spray trust for the benefit of Spouse and issue.** Another approach is to give the trustee discretion to distribute funds from the credit shelter trust to Spouse or issue to minimize overall income taxes paid. With this approach, the trustee could eliminate Drawback # 4 (high trust income tax rates) by passing retirement plan distributions out to Spouse and/or the issue, depending on who was in the lowest income tax bracket. This approach does not eliminate Drawbacks 1, 2, 3, 5, 6 or 7. Furthermore, to the extent income taxes are reduced by distributing the income to Spouse, her estate taxes are correspondingly increased (because she ends up owning assets that were supposed to stay in the credit shelter trust); this defeats the purpose of the credit shelter trust (as discussed under "Solution D"). On the other hand, to the extent income taxes are reduced by distributing the retirement plan distributions out to *issue*, the money is no longer available for Spouse's needs; and if she didn't need the money in this trust, why didn't you just make it payable to the issue in the first place and get the benefit of their long life expectancy? Again, this seems likely to be a realistic solution in very few cases, though there seems to be no harm in giving the trustee discretion to distribute to issue in a non-conduit credit shelter trust established for the primary benefit of Spouse.

F.   **Have Participant buy life insurance to replace the credit shelter trust.** This idea is apparently is that a $1 million life insurance policy placed in an irrevocable trust would replace the credit shelter trust, achieving the same estate tax savings, but this idea is false. The irrevocable insurance trust funded by lifetime gifts is a *different* way of transferring wealth estate tax-free. If Participant could figure out a way to fund his credit shelter trust, he could do both things—fund the credit shelter trust and *also* make lifetime gifts to an irrevocable insurance trust. Making lifetime gifts to an irrevocable insurance trust doesn't solve the problem we're looking at because at the end of the day *there is still nothing in the credit shelter trust*. A life insurance policy adds nothing to the solution to the credit shelter trust problem. However, a life insurance policy to pay the increased estate taxes generated by Solution A might be a nice addition for those adopting Solution A.

G.   **Converting to a Roth IRA, and using that to fund the credit shelter trust.** This eliminates drawback # 5 (wasting exemption paying income taxes): by paying the income taxes before death, Participant assures that the credit shelter trust can be funded with "after-tax dollars," namely the Roth IRA. Unfortunately, the Roth IRA does not eliminate the other drawbacks. It may alleviate drawback # 4 (high trust income tax rates), but only if the conversion itself can be done at a low income tax rate, which is unlikely. This idea does not solve the "loss of deferral" problems: The Roth IRA, if made payable to the credit shelter trust of which Spouse is the life beneficiary, would have to be distributed over Spouse's single life expectancy. Thus, Drawbacks 1, 2 and 3 are not eliminated. The way to maximize the value of a Roth IRA conversion is (i) do not withdraw from it during Participant's life; then either (ii) make it payable at death directly to children or grandchildren, so it is paid out over the (long) life expectancy of a young beneficiary or (iii) make it payable outright to Spouse, and she rolls it over and allows it to accumulate during *her* life, then *she* makes it payable at *her* death directly to children or grandchildren, so it is paid out (after her death) over the (long) life expectancy of a young beneficiary. A credit shelter trust that benefits Spouse for life can never use the younger beneficiaries' life expectancy; a Roth IRA payable to such a trust must be entirely distributed over the life expectancy of Spouse. So Participant would be paying the price of a Roth conversion (immediate loss of substantial amounts needed to pay income tax on the conversion) without getting the benefit (long term tax-free payout over younger beneficiary's life expectancy). Drawback # 7 does not apply to a Roth IRA.

H.   **Cash out enough of the IRA now to fund a credit shelter trust with after-tax dollars.** Participant could withdraw enough money from the retirement plan now, during life, to leave him with $1 million after paying the income tax on the withdrawal. If he is over 59½, he could make this withdrawal without paying a penalty. Then he could leave the $1 million non-retirement plan fund to the credit shelter trust and the remaining balance of the retirement plan to Spouse, who could roll it over to her own IRA. The major attraction of this option is that none of Participant's federal estate tax exemption would be "wasted" paying income taxes, because the credit shelter trust would be funded entirely with after-tax dollars, so Drawback # 5 is eliminated. This approach does not solve Drawbacks 1, 2 and 3 (loss of income tax deferral)—rather it totally sacrifices income tax deferral in favor of greater estate tax savings. This option may be attractive: if Participant is approaching his RBD (so he will have to begin taking large distributions soon anyway—by accelerating the distributions a few years, he would gain the peace of mind of having the credit shelter trust fully funded with non-retirement plan dollars); or if Participant is about to die (so he can be sure the benefits of the move—funding the credit shelter trust with after-tax dollars—would be realized soon); or if Participant has a strong propensity to invest in capital gain and growth-type investments which would be eligible for a stepped-up basis if held outside the retirement plan; or the family is way overweighted in retirement plan assets (for example Spouse also has a multi-million dollar retirement plan). This plan would be less attractive if Participant's major concern is creditors' claims (assets may be more easily protected inside the retirement plan); or if he is likely to be in a lower income tax bracket in later years (maybe he lives in a high income tax state now and is planning to move to a low tax state); or if this is the only asset in the family and there is major concern about whether Participant will have enough to live on during retirement; or if Participant has a tendency to spend any dollars that are not inside a retirement plan.

I.   **Put all non-retirement assets in the name of the spouse who will die first.** If there are sufficient assets to fund only one spouse's credit shelter trust, some planners believe they can easily predict which spouse will die first. Such a planner simply causes all the non-retirement assets to be put in that spouse's name, so they can be used to fund the credit shelter trust when that spouse dies; the retirement plan can then be left to (or kept by) the surviving spouse. Needless to say this plan can produce disastrous results if the "wrong" spouse dies first, especially if *all* the assets are in the other spouse's name. If the spouses die in the correct order, this plan eliminates drawbacks 1-7; but the community property solution (C) is a far better way to accomplish the result if it is available, and it doesn't require Tarot cards.

J.   **Leave the benefits to a traditional credit shelter trust.** If the best form of distribution of the benefits is a lump sum distribution, not rolled over (this could be the case if for example the entire plan balance consists of low-basis employer stock; see ¶ 2.4), it may not make much difference whether the distribution is paid to Spouse or a credit shelter trust. Similarly, if the alternative is leaving the benefits to a QTIP trust (not to the spouse outright), there's little difference in terms of drawbacks between leaving the benefits to a QTIP trust or a credit shelter trust. Also, if Spouse is not much older than the remainder beneficiaries, then Participant can name a credit shelter trust as beneficiary of the retirement plan, and have Spouse be a beneficiary of that trust, without suffering drawback # 3; however, drawbacks 1, 2, 4, 5, 6 and 7 still exist.

K.   **Make the credit shelter trust a 678 grantor trust.** This idea does not work. The approach that has been suggested by some practitioners is this: use § 678(a)(1) (see ¶ 6.3.09) to cause Spouse to be treated as the "owner" of the trust purposes for income tax purposes by making her the sole trustee with power to distribute principal to herself for health, education, maintenance and support ("HEMS" power). Since § 678(a)(1) says that a person who has power to pay funds to herself is treated as the "owner" of such funds for income tax purposes, and since § 678(a)(1) does not contain any apparent exceptions for a power limited by an ascertainable standard, Spouse would have to be treated as the owner of the trust principal by virtue of her power to pay such principal to herself (even though it is limited by an ascertainable standard). Yet this power is not broad enough to cause the trust principal to be included in Spouse's estate on her subsequent death because it meets the definition of a non-general (therefore non-taxable) power of appointment under § 2041. The problem with this idea is that, even though § 678 does not contain an *explicit* exception for powers limited by an ascertainable standard, the courts have not interpreted § 678 that broadly. When the IRS has sought to cause a surviving spouse to be taxable on trust income because of some right of lifetime withdrawal she holds, the courts have interpreted § 678 as applying only to a truly unrestricted right to withdraw from the trust. See *Blattmachr* [Bibliography], § 3:4.5, n. 159. In other words, the courts have interpreted § 678 just the opposite of the way it is interpreted by practitioners encouraging this approach. Accordingly, if Spouse's power to withdraw principal from the trust is limited by a HEMS standard, it is safe to conclude that she is *not* taxable on the trust's income from retirement plan distributions treated as principal merely by virtue of holding that power.

10.5.04 *Credit shelter trust of non-participant Spouse*

So far we have been looking at the problem of a married couple where one or both spouses have, as their only asset available to fund a credit shelter trust, a retirement plan. As the problem has been framed up to this point, both spouses have (or can have, if assets are rearranged slightly) sufficient assets to fund their respective credit shelter trusts, if retirement benefits are used for that purpose.

Now we turn the problem of a couple in which one spouse has *no* assets, and the other spouse's assets are entirely in the form of retirement benefits. This case poses an additional problem: how to fund a credit shelter trust if the non-participant Spouse dies first, since she has no assets in her name.

In a *non-community property state*, the only way to solve this problem is for Participant, while he and Spouse are both still living, to cash out (and pay tax on) enough of his retirement plan to give Spouse $1 million in cash (or else get divorced or legally separated, and have Spouse take part of Participant's retirement plan). Few clients are willing to pay enormous current income taxes (or get divorced) just to receive a speculative estate tax benefit down the road—especially since it would all be wasted effort if the non-participant Spouse does *not* die first!

In a *community property* state there is slightly more flexibility, if the retirement plan is an IRA. Since an IRA can be treated as community property, the parties could sign an agreement recognizing this asset as aggregate-basis community property, then the non-participant Spouse in her will could leave part of her share of Participant's IRA to her credit shelter trust (up to whatever amount is necessary to fully fund it) and the balance to Participant. Then, *if* the non-participant Spouse dies first, Participant could cash out as much of the non-participant Spouse's share of his IRA as necessary to fund non-participant Spouse's credit shelter trust, pay income tax on it, and transfer whatever's left to the credit shelter trust of the deceased non-participant Spouse.

Note that, even in a community property state that recognizes a non-participant Spouse's ownership of part of the IRA, there is *no way* that Participant can transfer any of the non-participant Spouse's share of *Participant's* IRA to *non-participant Spouse's* credit shelter trust without paying income tax on it. But at least if the IRA is community property Participant can, if, as and when non-participant Spouse predeceases him, transfer some of his IRA to her credit shelter trust without having the transfer be treated as a gift by him. In a non-community property state there is *no* way, even if Participant is *willing* to pay income taxes, to get funds from Participant's IRA to non-participant Spouse's credit shelter trust without gift tax consequences once non-participant Spouse has died.

10.5.05 *Funding QTIP trust with retirement benefits*

In a "second marriage" situation where a client wants to leave assets for the life benefit of Spouse, but ultimately have the funds pass to his children by a prior marriage; or any situation in which a client wants to leave assets in a life trust for Spouse's benefit rather than outright to Spouse for tax or non-tax reasons; the usual solution is a

"QTIP" trust. ¶ 3.3.04. However, leaving *retirement benefits* to a QTIP trust has exactly the same drawbacks as leaving benefits to a credit shelter trust for Spouse's life benefit (see ¶ 10.5.02, Drawbacks 1-7), except for #5 (wasting credit shelter amount paying income taxes) which doesn't apply to the QTIP trust. See ¶ 3.3.10 and the Koslow case study (Chapter 11).

The following discussion assumes Participant wants the trust to qualify for the federal estate tax marital deduction as a QTIP trust, *but the problems don't change even if the estate tax is repealed.*

Here are the solutions available to respond to the problem; some are similar to the "credit shelter trust" problem solutions listed at ¶ 10.5.03.

A.   **Leave the benefits outright to Spouse rather than to a QTIP trust.** This eliminates all the QTIP drawbacks. The drawback of this solution is whatever drawback the client perceived would exist if benefits were left outright to Spouse. For example, if Spouse has total control of the benefits, Spouse may not choose to leave the benefits to Participant's children of a prior marriage (see Solutions B and D). Or, client may perceive that Spouse cannot be expected to handle a large outright bequest properly (see Solution C). This solution is appropriate if: Client cares more about surviving spouse's financial security than about protecting the rights of future beneficiaries; or if, after running the numbers, client and planner conclude that the income tax drawbacks of the QTIP trust are so substantial that they outweigh whatever benefit client wanted to obtain from the QTIP trust.

B.   **Leave some benefits outright to spouse and some outright to the children.** With a QTIP trust, Spouse has a life interest and children have a remainder interest. The total value of their respective interests equals 100% of the value of the retirement plan. These relative values can be determined using the IRS's tables for valuing life estates and remainder interests (or some other set of actuarial tables). For example, it could be that the value of Spouse's life interest is 65% of the total value of the trust assets, and the children's remainder interest, at the outset, is worth 35% of the total trust value. (As the years go by, the relative value of Spouse's life estate declines and the value of the remainder interest increases to the same extent.) Participant in this example might consider leaving 65% of the benefits outright to Spouse and 35% outright to the children (or to a trust for their exclusive benefit). If Spouse takes full advantage of the spousal rollover and the children take full advantage of the life expectancy payout option, both Spouse and children should end up with substantially more dollars in their pockets than they would if they received theoretically the same relative amounts as life and remainder beneficiaries of a QTIP trust. Only the IRS loses. See Koslow case study, Chapter 11. The relative amounts left to the respective beneficiaries need not be exactly what their relative interests would have been in a QTIP trust—it can be whatever percentage Participant wishes. This solution can be appropriate if: Participant's reason for leaving benefits to a QTIP trust was to assure that each of his beneficiaries (Spouse and children) would receive a financial benefit from Participant's retirement plan; and Spouse's financial security is a goal, but Spouse's financial security can be provided for with less than all the retirement benefits; and Spouse is willing to consent to the arrangement, if her consent is required (¶ 3.4).

C.   **Conduit Trust: trust is required to pass out to Spouse all retirement plan distributions as they are received by the QTIP trust.** The advantages and problems of this solution are discussed at ¶ 10.5.03 (Solution D). This solution is not appropriate for someone whose goal in establishing a QTIP trust was to preserve principal for the children, because (unless Spouse dies prematurely) she ends up with 100% of the retirement plan, just as if you had named her directly as beneficiary—but without the income tax deferral advantages of the spousal rollover. This solution may be suitable if Participant wants a QTIP trust only because Participant believes that Spouse cannot suitably handle a substantial outright bequest, but Participant does not have the same concerns about Spouse's ability to handle a stream of distributions from a conduit trust.

D.   **Leave benefits outright to Spouse, leave other assets to (and**

maybe buy life insurance for) children. This eliminates all drawbacks and can be a good solution for a Participant whose reason for wanting a QTIP is to protect children by a prior marriage.

E.   **Converting to a Roth IRA, and using that to fund the QTIP trust.** The advantages and drawbacks of this solution are discussed at ¶ 10.5.03 (Solution G)

F.   **Name Spouse as outright beneficiary, but on the condition that she will name Participant's children as beneficiaries of her rollover IRA.** This frequently-advanced idea is a non-starter. First, the children are not at all protected by Spouse's assurance that she will name them as beneficiary of her rollover IRA. Unless they force Spouse into some kind of court proceedings, how will they know if she complied? But even if she complied, she has agreed to basically nothing, since she can withdraw all funds from that rollover IRA without anyone's consent or knowledge. Once the funds have been withdrawn from the IRA she can spend them and the children will get nothing. Once the funds have been withdrawn from the IRA she can leave them to anyone she chooses (if she does not spend them) and the children will get nothing. If Participant leaves the benefits to Spouse on the condition (enforced by some separate agreement, since no plan administrator or IRA provider would be able to accommodate such a condition) that she *not* spend them and that she will leave either the benefits themselves or the proceeds thereof to Participant's children, then he has created a terminable interest which will not qualify for the marital deduction (¶ 3.3.02).

G.   **Cash out the retirement plan and leave after-tax proceeds to a QTIP trust (or roll the benefits over to an IRA and leave that to a QTIP trust).** This would work to eliminate drawback # 7 in the case of some profit sharing plans (which require spousal consent in order to name a non-spouse beneficiary, but do not require spousal consent for Participant to withdraw funds from the retirement plan during life) (see ¶ 3.4.03). If Participant either is over 59½ or rolls the distribution over to an IRA, he could make this withdrawal without paying a penalty (see Chapter 9). This does not eliminate any other drawback.

H.   **Leave the benefits to a traditional QTIP trust.** If the best form of distribution of the benefits is a lump sum distribution, not rolled over (for example the entire plan balance consists of low-basis employer stock; ¶ 2.4), it may make no difference whether the distribution is paid to Spouse or a QTIP trust.

11

Case Studies

Case studies illustrating some typical situations in estate planning for retirement benefits

Dr. Della: Estate taxes on large retirement plan balance

Dr. Della is 68. She has a $5 million IRA, a home worth $800,000 and few other assets. Currently, her three children are named as beneficiaries of the IRA. She wants to leave all her assets to the three children, and name you, her estate planning attorney, as executor of her estate. She also want to save taxes. She is concerned about the large minimum distributions she will face in a few years when she reaches age 70½.

Before considering ways to *reduce* taxes, you first face the question of how estate taxes will be paid. Della's "estate" for estate tax purposes is $5.8 million, but her "probate estate" (the assets her executor would control) is only $800,000 (the value of the house), because the IRA would pass directly to her children as the named beneficiaries. The executor of the estate will be liable for $2 million of estate taxes, but most of Della's assets will be in the hands of the children, not the estate. The executor might have to sue the children to try to collect their share of the estate taxes. Whoever Della nominates as her executor might well refuse to accept the appointment if he/she/it figures out prior to accepting the position that the estate's liabilities (estate taxes on a $5.8 million taxable estate) exceed the value of the estate's only asset (the $800,000 house).

To avoid putting the executor in this difficult position, make sure the person who is primarily responsible for paying the estate taxes has control of the money. For example, make the IRA payable to a trust, and make sure the trustee is the same as the executor of the estate. That way, the executor can be sure the friendly trustee (himself) does not run away with the IRA money before taxes are paid. Or, make the three children co-executors as well as beneficiaries, so they are primarily as well as secondarily liable for the estate taxes.

Another approach is for Della to buy life insurance to assure the availability of funds to pay estate taxes. Again, she will need to be sure that the life insurance proceeds end up in the hands of the person who will need them to pay the estate tax.

Next Della invites everyone she knows to send her ideas for how to reduce the estate tax value of her IRA (and/or how to reduce the income tax impact of required minimum distributions). Here are the ideas she has received so far:

Roll the IRA back into a corporate retirement plan, then buy life insurance inside the plan, then distribute the policy out of the plan after a few years when the policy value is lower than the sum of premiums paid. The idea here is that, for the first several years of its existence, a life insurance policy is worth less than you paid for it; it takes many years for the cash value to catch up to what it would have been had you invested in (say) bonds rather than life insurance. An IRA cannot hold life insurance, so the possibility of using this scheme depends on having a qualified retirement plan (QRP) you can roll the IRA into. In Della's case, she would have to go to work for a company that had a plan that would permit her to roll her IRA into it and also would permit the purchase of life insurance in the plan. Prior to 2002, an IRA could be rolled into a QRP only if the IRA itself contained *only* funds rolled over *from* a QRP originally. After 2001 this restriction does not apply; any IRA can be rolled into a QRP that is willing to accept that type of contribution. ¶ 2.5.

Assuming she can take care of all these matters, is the life insurance idea a good one? Buying life insurance inside a retirement plan (and then "rolling the policy out" a few years later) is a very complicated proposition. To avoid surprises, review all the complications in advance; see ¶ 8.3.¶ 8.4.

Invest in a venture capital (or real estate development) partnership or other form of investment that temporarily reduces the value of the plan. This is a variation on the buy-life-insurance plan, but is more useful to the client who has no QRP available which can buy life insurance, or who does not want to buy life insurance. The idea is to invest the IRA in something that the client believes will be a profitable investment *over the long term*, but that *temporarily* declines in value right after the investment is made. The decline in value is due to a lack of transferability or lack of marketability of the investment during a lockup phase while the venture investments are still in the start-up stage (or while the real estate development is still just a hole in the ground). There are two essential ingredients to success with this approach. The first is that the client must either (a) die or (b) withdraw the investment from the plan while the investment is still in its reduced-value stage. The second is that the investment must later (after the client's death, or after the client has withdrawn the asset° from the retirement plan) grow in value sufficiently to make up for its initial decline.

Transfer IRA assets to family limited partnership. The idea here is to form a family partnership (FLP) among the IRA (which contributes all its investments to the FLP), the IRA owner (as general partner, perhaps) and (say) the client's children. The goal is to get the same "valuation discounts" for the investments inside the IRA as clients get for their outside-the-IRA investments by contributing same to FLPs. The main obstacle is whether having the IRA enter into a partnership with the IRA owner and other related parties constitutes a "prohibited transaction" under § 4975. This is a subject for analysis by an ERISA lawyer, not an estate planning specialist. Department of Labor Advisory Opinion # 2000-10a illustrates the analysis to be followed when determining whether a transaction of this type is a prohibited transaction. In that opinion the DOL stated that there were three separate prohibited transaction rules that could potentially be violated by investment of IRA assets in a FLP. The DOL found that the particular transaction in question was not a violation of *one* of those rules, but reserved judgment as to whether the later operation of the partnership might violate the other two rules. To read the opinion, go to the DOL website www.dol.gov./dol/pwba/public/programs/ori, and select opinion 2000-10a. For an excellent discussion of all the issues, see Bray, C.P., and Kearns, D.B., "The Family Limited Partnership As An Asset Of The IRA," Trusts & Estates 8/98 (page 93).

Felicia Fallon: Planning for post-death lump sum distribution

Felicia Fallon is 66. She has $8 million in total assets: $3 million in the qualified retirement plan (QRP) of her employer, and another $5 million of liquid investments and residential real estate.

She has two children, ages 46 and 44, and several grandchildren. The children are well provided for financially. While the children are to be the principal beneficiaries of her estate, Felicia has some interest in charitable giving. She has already used her estate tax and GST tax exemptions through lifetime gifts.

Under her employer's QRP, the only option for distribution of death benefits to a non-spouse beneficiary is a lump sum. ¶ 1.5.09. She does not plan to retire until she is age 75, but the plan prohibits her from taking any distributions prior to separation from service. Thus, if she dies prior to her projected retirement nine years from now, whoever receives her plan benefits will receive them in a lump sum. There is no possibility of a life expectancy payout to her designated beneficiaries.

In preparing Felicia's estate plan, we compare two possible scenarios. The first is making the benefits payable to the children. They withdraw all funds from the QRP within one year after Felicia's death, pay the income taxes on it, and invest what's left. The calculations show that after 44 years (which is the average joint and survivor life expectancy for two people age 46 and 44, according to IRS Table VI; see ¶ 1.2.04) the ultimate net value to family of this scenario is $11,083,390.

The other alternative is to have the benefits distributed to a charitable remainder unitrust (CRT) that would pay a 6% unitrust payout to the children for their joint lifetime and for the life of the survivor. The advantage of this scenario is that the CRT pays no income tax on the distribution it receives (¶ 7.5.04). The children would then receive, for life, the income from the entire $3 million IRA fund. They would have to pay income taxes on these distributions. On the death of the surviving child all funds remaining in the CRT would go to Felicia's favorite charity.

In addition to eliminating income taxes on the lump sum distribution, this approach produces a small estate tax charitable deduction to Felicia's estate for the value of the remainder interest that passes to charity. After 44 years, the accumulated value of the estate tax savings, and the accumulated value of distributions from the CRT, total $12,195,566—more than $1 million more, in terms of value to the children, than simply distributing the plan to them outright on Felicia's death.

These numbers suggest that leaving the benefits to a CRT does not "penalize" the children substantially or at all, making it an especially appealing approach to funding her charitable gifts. The calculations in this example are based on the following assumptions: Felicia Fallon dies, in December 1999. Felicia's other assets total $5 million, so her total estate is $8 million. All estate taxes are paid out of the non-retirement assets. The state death tax on her estate is exactly equal to the maximum credit for state death taxes allowed against her federal estate taxes. The two Fallon children are in the 39.6% tax bracket for all income. All the family's and CRT's investments earn 6% income, fully taxable.

While these projections are interesting (since they seem to show that the family makes a profit from a charitable gift), there are many limitations to such projections. For example, the calculations assume a 6% rate of income, year in and year out, on all investments. Actual investment return might be less or more than 6% in any particular year. Investments can also decline in value. Furthermore, the calculations assume that the entire 6% consists of interest and dividends taxable as ordinary income; in real life, it is probable that at least some of the investments *outside* the retirement plans would be invested for capital gain and that part of the return would therefore be capital gain. Capital gain is not taxed currently, but only when the asset is sold; and when it is sold, the tax rate on capital gain is lower than on other kinds of income.

The projections assume a 39.6% tax rate for all individuals. It is possible that some individuals would be in a lower bracket. A higher bracket could apply if state income taxes are figured in; and federal rates will probably change over the period of the projections.

The CRT scenario assumes that at least one child lives for 44 years. If both of them die before the 44 years are up, the entire trust at that point moves to the charity and they stop receiving any distributions. Thus, in case of premature death, the value to the family of the "CRT scenario" would probably be *lower* than the value of the "outright to children" scenario. The children can overcome this risk by buying decreasing term insurance on their lives; or, Felicia could simply decide that this risk is not of concern to her.

The CRT scenario assumes a 6% payout rate to the children and that the trust earns exactly 6% each year. The scenarios assume that there is a separate fund, outside the retirement plan, of $3,838,700. This would be the amount needed at Felicia's death to pay the estate taxes if all the benefits are paid to the family. If the benefits are paid to a CRT, the estate taxes would be reduced, so some of this fund would be available for the family, rather than going to pay estate taxes, and that has been figured into the value of the CRT scenario.

Howard: Naming multiple beneficiaries; "separate accounts"

Howard wants to leave 10% of his $1 million IRA to his favorite charity, the Salk Institute, and the balance equally to his two children Hanna and Hank. He would like each of the children to be able to use his or her own life expectancy to measure required distributions from the account after Howard's death.

The IRS's "multiple beneficiary rule" dictates that, when an IRA is left to multiple beneficiaries, then (unless the benefit is divided into "separate accounts," each of which is payable to a different beneficiary) all beneficiaries must be individuals or no beneficiary can use the "life expectancy payout method"; and even if all the beneficiaries are individuals, all must use the oldest beneficiary's life expectancy, unless the separate account rule applies. ¶ 1.7.06.

One possible approach to the problem is to create totally separate IRAs, one payable to each beneficiary. Howard rejects that approach because investing would be more cumbersome with three separate IRAs, and also he would have to keep switching money around each year to try to keep the accounts in the desired relative proportions despite varying investment results.

Next we look at how to get "separate account" treatment while keeping a single IRA. See discussion at ¶ 10.4.02.

The determination of whether separate accounts exist is made as of December 31 of the year after the year in which the participant dies (the "Designation Date"; ¶ 1.8). This means the subject of establishing "separate accounts" could be left up to the beneficiaries to take care of after Howard's death. However, to take some of the suspense out of that process, we can draft a beneficiary designation form that automatically creates separate accounts as of Howard's death. See Section 3.05, Forms 2.1, 2.2, Appendix B. With this approach the beneficiaries will be able to obtain the desired life expectancy payouts even if they somehow fumble the ball on establishing separate accounts after Howard's death.

Ken Koslow: QTIP trust (second marriage)

Ken Koslow is a 62-year-old executive, with two children by his first marriage, ages 36 and 33. His second wife, Karen, is also an executive; she is 54.

Ken wants to leave his life insurance to his children, his house to his wife, and all of his retirement benefits to a QTIP trust. The trust would pay income to Karen for life and on her death the balance would pass to his children.

Ken's assets consist of:

House - joint with spouse	$ 450,000
Qualified retirement plan	1,200,000
IRA	600,000
Non-plan investments	500,000
Life Insurance	500,000
Total	$3,250,000

The problem with this proposal is that paying his retirement benefits to a QTIP trust has many tax disadvantages; see ¶ 3.3.10, ¶ 10.5.05.

A non-tax disadvantage of leaving retirement benefits to QTIP trust is that Ken's children would have a long wait for a little money. Karen is only 18 years older than Ken's oldest child. Thus it is quite likely that Ken's children themselves will be "old" before they see anything from the marital trust. Karen's life expectancy is currently about 30 years under the IRS tables. Since the IRS tables do not reflect recent advances in longevity, and are "unisex" (so they do not reflect Karen's above-average life expectancy as female), they understate the average life expectancy of a female Karen's age. Thus the children can expect, based on average life expectancy, to wait *at least* 30 years before they get any benefits from their father's retirement plan. In the meantime Karen and the children are left competing with each other regarding the investment policies of the trust.

Using software, we project that the eventual value of the benefits to the family under the QTIP scenario (leaving all benefits to a QTIP trust) is $5,526,000 after 30 years. (Assumptions are discussed in more detail below.) Of this amount, assuming Karen dies in 30 years, $1,087,000 would pass to the children (being the then-remaining principal of the marital trust) and $4,439,000 would be held by Karen's estate (representing the accumulated distributions to her from the marital trust). There would be no dollars left inside the retirement plans.

This proposed scenario was compared with the "outright scenario," under which there would be no QTIP trust. The $1.2 million of QRP benefits would be made payable to Karen personally, and the

$600,000 IRA would be payable directly to Ken's children. Ken would make sure his life insurance and investments outside the plan were sufficient to pay the estate taxes on the benefits passing to the children.

This scenario has many advantages over the QTIP scenario. Each beneficiary would have total control of his or her own share of the benefits, without having to compete for the attention of the trustee of the QTIP trust. The children could use their long life expectancies to measure MRDs of their benefits.

Karen could roll over her share of the benefits to an IRA in her own name and defer the commencement of distributions until she reached age 70½. She would name her nieces as her designated beneficiaries on the rollover IRA. No benefits would be subject to the high income tax bracket of a trust.

Another advantage of this approach has to do with the practicalities of plan distribution options. QRPs very often do not permit an installment payout to any beneficiary other than a surviving spouse. ¶ 1.5.09. Thus, if QRP benefits are made payable to a marital trust, the plan may not permit the trust to draw those benefits out over the life expectancy of the oldest trust beneficiary. If the benefits are payable to Karen personally, by contrast, she can roll them to an IRA which has whatever payout distribution options she wants. ¶ 3.2.

Furthermore, QRPs are subject to "REA" (¶ 3.4), meaning that the benefits cannot be distributed to someone other than the spouse without her consent. By making the QRP benefits payable to Karen personally, Ken avoids the need for obtaining her consent, which would be required to make the benefits payable to a QTIP trust or some other beneficiary. Since REA does not apply to IRAs, Ken can make the IRA payable to his children without Karen's consent (subject to any requirements of state law or prenuptial agreements they may have signed). Last but definitely not least: both Karen and the children would end up with *substantially more dollars* in their pockets, as the following pages demonstrate.

The following projections assume that all investments earn 7% pre-tax, whether inside or outside a retirement plan, and that all plan distributions, net of income taxes, are accumulated rather than spent. The results compare values of the accumulated funds at the end of 30 years.

Scenario 1: All benefits ($1.8 million) left to a QTIP trust.

This *trust* distributes all of its income annually to Karen Koslow as required by the marital deduction rules. Each *plan* distributes to the *trust*, each year, the *greater* of the income for that year or the MRD required for that year based on the life expectancy of Karen Koslow (29.5 years). The trust then distributes the *income* portion of the distribution to Karen personally; *principal* distributions (*i.e.* the minimum distribution amount, to the extent it exceeds the income distribution; see ¶ 3.3.06) are retained in the trust fund as principal. It is assumed that the trust and Karen are both in the 39.6% bracket at all times (even though Karen's bracket might possibly drop after her eventual retirement). After 30 years here are the results:

Amount held in a retirement plan in Karen's name: $0.

Amount held in Karen's name personally (accumulated income distributions from the QTIP trust): $4,439,000.

Amount held in the QTIP trust (passing to children): $1,087,200 (gross of $1,800,000 paid to marital trust, minus 39.6% tax)

Total value to family: $5,526,000

Assuming Karen were to die at this point, the QTIP trust would pass to the children (actually, it would be subject to estate tax on Karen's death; however, for purposes of illustration, these scenarios assume that all estate taxes on both spouses' estates are paid by some other source of funds).

Scenario 2: QRP benefits paid to Karen, IRA to children.

Here are the assumptions used in Scenario 2:
One of Ken's children will probably be in the 31% bracket; the other would probably be in the 36% bracket. To compromise these differences, an overall tax rate of 33.5% on the children's benefits is used. The trust and Karen are always in the 39.6% bracket (even though Karen's bracket might drop after her eventual retirement).
The IRAs would be distributed gradually to the children over the 46.4-year life expectancy of the oldest child. This would call for

very small minimum distributions especially in the early years, but each child's income from this source would gradually increase. By the time the children reach their 60's, *each* would be receiving distributions of $40,000 per year (and growing) from the IRA fund. It would be a major source of retirement funding for them.

Karen would take the plans payable to her as a lump sum and roll them over to her own IRA. She would then defer all distributions until her age 70½, when she start withdrawing benefits using the Uniform Table (¶ 1.4.01).

Under this scenario here is what each beneficiary would have in 30 years: The children's accumulated personal funds (outside the IRA) would be, for both children together, $1,419,000, consisting of the accumulated after-tax MRDs from the inherited IRA. In addition, they would have $1.509 million *still inside* the IRA, to be distributed to them over the next 17 years. Contrast this with their having $1,087,000 outside of an IRA and *nothing* inside a retirement plan under Scenario 1. Increase in value to children: $1,841,000.

	Scenario 1: Benefits to Marital Trust	Scenario 2: QRP to Karen; IRA to Children	Increase:
Karen holds:			
In IRA	-0-	4,164,000	
Outside IRA	4,439,000	2,771,000	
Total	4,439,000	6,935,000	2,496,000
Children Hold:			
In IRA	-0-	1,509,000	
Outside IRA	1,087,000	1,419,000	
Total:	1,087,000	2,928,000	1,841,000
Total Value to Family:	5,526,000	9,863,000	4,337,000

Karen would have, in 30 years, accumulated $2.771 million *outside* of her rollover IRA from the accumulated MRDs, and would still have $4.164 million *inside* her rollover IRA. Thus her combined value would be $6.935 million, vs. $4.439 million under Scenario 1. Increase to Karen: $2,496,000.

Note: under Scenario 2 a substantial portion of Karen's and the children's money would still be inside an IRA and would not yet have been taxed, whereas under Scenario 1 all of the money would be after-tax. But, under Scenario 2, even if Karen totally liquidated her IRA 30 years from now (as opposed to continuing to distribute it gradually to herself over 15.3 more years), her after-tax value would be $5.286 million, which is still $847,000 *more* than under Scenario 1.)

Summary: If all benefits are left to a QTIP trust, all beneficiaries are *substantially worse off* than if some benefits are left to Karen outright and some to the children outright.

Quentin: Early retirement with "SOSEPP"

Quentin, age 56, is cutting back his workload. He is changing his position at his firm from full time managing director to part time consultant. He will still see a few clients, work on the marketing committee and drive a company car, but he will turn over the reins (and the nights and weekends work) to his successors.

To finance this plan, Quentin figures he needs an annual income of $150,000 over and above the paycheck he will receive from the firm. Since his profit sharing plan at the firm has $5 million in it, he figures he can afford his proposed agenda—*if* he can get money out of the retirement plan at a reasonable cost. He knows he has to pay income tax on the plan withdrawals but would like to avoid paying the 10% penalty.

First, Quentin looks at what would happen if he took money directly out of his company plan and put it in his bank account. *If* he were completely retiring now, he could withdraw from the company plan without penalty, because there is an exception to the 10% penalty for distributions from a qualified plan upon separation from service at age 55 or later (¶ 9.3.04). But this exception is not available to Quentin because he is not terminating his employment; he is just cutting back, not leaving.

The next thing he investigates is the possibility of taking a "series of substantially equal periodic payments" (SOSEPP) from the company plan. But this avenue, too, is blocked, because this exception is not available for distributions from a qualified plan unless there has been a "separation from service," and Quentin is not separating from service.

Quentin's solution is to (1) take a partial distribution of his benefits from the company plan, (2) roll the distribution over to an IRA, then (3) use the rollover IRA to support a SOSEPP to him that will satisfy the requirements of § 72(t). ¶ 9.2. He hires an actuary to determine what size fund would be needed to produce equal annual payments of $150,000 over his life expectancy, and generally to help him design the SOSEPP. The actuary suggests the following strategy to get Quentin his $150,000 per year:

First, create the *smallest possible* separate rollover IRA needed, within IRS guidelines, to support a $150,000 per year payout to Quentin. Unless there is a risk of totally depleting the entire account prior to the end of the age 59½/five year no-modifications period (¶ 9.2.12), it is desirable to use the smallest possible IRA because the less money that is tied up in this IRA (where it must remain untouched for five whole years, except for distributions required for the series), the more money is left in his company plan. The money that is still left in Quentin's *company* plan can be withdrawn freely after he reaches age 59½ in three years, without penalty, and without contaminating the series of equal payments Quentin is receiving from the IRA. Also, if it turns out that Quentin, before reaching age 59½, needs more money than the series is providing, he can always take *another* distribution from the company plan and use it to establish *another* rollover IRA, and use that second IRA to establish a new SOSEPP. ¶ 9.2.11.

In contrast to this, if all or most of his retirement plan money is tied up in the IRA that is supporting the SOSEPP, he will have little or no flexibility to increase his distributions if it turns out that he needs more money in the next five years than he now expects. Note that Quentin does not care whether this particular segregated IRA actually lasts for his entire life expectancy; it only has to last until the fifth anniversary of the first payment (the minimum no-modification period required, in Quentin's case, to avoid retroactive imposition of the 10% penalty; ¶ 9.2.13).

Now that we know the goal is to get level payments of $150,000 per year, for five years, using the smallest possible rollover IRA, several decisions become easy. First, it is necessary to decide which of the three IRS-approved methods (¶ 9.2.04-¶ 9.2.06) will be used to calculate the SOSEPP. The IRS's "minimum distribution" method (method 1; ¶ 9.2.04) is out; it does not produce the level, predictable payments Quentin is looking for. So the choice narrows down to methods two and three.

Second, as between a joint or a single life expectancy, Quentin should use the single life expectancy; the shorter the payout period, the smaller the fund needed to produce $150,000/year over that payout period. Third, for the same reason (achieving a shorter payout period) the actuary will use whatever "reasonable mortality table" produces the shortest life expectancy period for Quentin. For example, the actuary will not use the IRS's § 1.72-1 tables (¶ 1.2.04), because the IRS tables are "unisex," and a separate male mortality table will show a shorter life expectancy.

Fourth, the actuary will use IRS "method three," the annuity method, because that is the only one for which Notice 89-25 blesses the use of any "reasonable mortality table," as opposed to only the IRS mortality tables; use of other mortality tables can produce higher payments. Finally, the actuary will use the highest reasonable interest rate he can justify.

Note that Quentin's program for taking penalty-free early distributions is possible only because his company's profit sharing plan allows in-service withdrawals for employees who have attained age 55. Not all plans allow such withdrawals. If Quentin's plan did not permit any in-service withdrawals there would be no way he could access his retirement plan without quitting his job. This is a reminder that the flexibility of the IRA custom-made to support a SOSEPP is available only to participants who *have* IRAs to begin with, or who can get money from other types of retirement plans into an IRA.

Appendix A

Tables

1. <u>The Uniform Table for determining required lifetime distributions under Prop. Reg. § 1.401(a)(9)-5, A-4(a).</u>

Formerly known as: "Table for Determining Applicable Divisor for MDIB (Minimum Distribution Incidental Benefit)"			
Age	**Applicable divisor**	**Age**	**Applicable divisor**
70	26.2	93	8.8
71	25.3	94	8.3
72	24.4	95	7.8
73	23.5	96	7.3
74	22.7	97	6.9
75	21.8	98	6.5
76	20.9	99	6.1
77	20.1	100	5.7
78	19.2	101	5.3
79	18.4	102	5.0
80	17.6	103	4.7
81	16.8	104	4.4
82	16.0	105	4.1
83	15.3	106	3.8
84	14.5	107	3.6
85	13.8	108	3.3
86	13.1	109	3.1
87	12.4	110	2.8
88	11.8	111	2.6
89	11.1	112	2.4
90	10.5	113	2.2
91	9.9	114	2.0
92	9.4	115 and older	1.8

2.   Tax on Various Lump Sum Distributions
          (Chart prepared by Ed Slott, CPA)

If Your Lump Sum Distribution is:	10 Year Averaging Tax Is:
$100,000	14,471
150,000	24,570
200,000	36,922
250,000	50,770
275,000	58,270
300,000	66,330
318,833	72,733
350,000	83,602
375,000	93,102
400,000	102,602
450,000	122,682
500,000	143,682
550,000	164,682
600,000	187,368
650,000	211,368
700,000	235,368
750,000	259,368
800,000	283,368
850,000	307,368
900,000	332,210
1,000,000	382,210

Charts 2 and 3 are reproduced from the highly recommended newsletter, **Ed Slott's IRA Advisor**, with permission of the newsletter's author and publisher, Ed Slott, CPA. For subscription information or reprint permission, call 1-800-663-1340, or visit his website at **www.irahelp.com**.

3.　　Single Life Expectancy - Table V (ages 5-34)

Age	Life Expectancy	Age	Life Expectancy
5	76.6	20	61.9
6	75.6	21	60.9
7	74.7	22	59.9
8	73.7	23	59.0
9	72.7	24	58.0
10	71.7	25	57.0
11	70.7	26	56.0
12	69.7	27	55.1
13	68.8	28	54.1
14	67.8	29	53.1
15	66.8	30	52.2
16	65.8	31	51.2
17	64.8	32	50.2
18	63.9	33	49.2
19	62.9	34	48.3

4.   IRS "Table V": Single life expectancy (ages 35-110).
      From IRS Publication 590.

Age	Divisor	Age	Divisor
35	47.3	73	13.9
36	46.4	74	13.2
37	45.4	75	12.5
38	44.4	76	11.9
39	43.5	77	11.2
40	42.5	78	10.6
41	41.5	79	10.0
42	40.6	80	9.5
43	39.6	81	8.9
44	38.7	82	8.4
45	37.7	83	7.9
46	36.8	84	7.4
47	35.9	85	6.9
48	34.9	86	6.5
49	34.0	87	6.1
50	33.1	88	5.7
51	32.2	89	5.3
52	31.3	90	5.0
53	30.4	91	4.7
54	29.5	92	4.4
55	28.6	93	4.1
56	27.7	94	3.9
57	26.8	95	3.7
58	25.9	96	3.4
59	25.0	97	3.2
60	24.2	98	3.0
61	23.3	99	2.8
62	22.5	100	2.7
63	21.6	101	2.5
64	20.8	102	2.3
65	20.0	103	2.1
66	19.2	104	1.9
67	18.4	105	1.8
68	17.6	106	1.6
69	16.8	107	1.4
70	16.0	108	1.3
71	15.3	109	1.1
72	14.6	110	1.0

Appendix B
Forms

Table of Contents

INTRODUCTION; DRAFTING CHECKLIST

Introduction; Drafting Checklist

This Appendix contains sample forms which can be used by practitioiners as a starting point for drafting their own forms for various clients and situations. In drafting forms to dispose of retirement benefits, keep in mind the following points:

1.   Impress on the client that the "Designation of Beneficiary Form" is just as important a legal document as a will or trust. Often, more of the client's assets are controlled by this form than by his will. An improperly drafted (or missing) beneficiary designation form could cost the client's estate and family thousands of dollars in taxes, lost deferral opportunities and increased settlement costs.

2.   Read the applicable sections of the "Account Agreement" establishing the client's IRA or Roth IRA, to make sure the beneficiary designation and payout method the client desires are permitted. In the case of a qualified retirement plan (QRP) benefit, read the "Summary Plan Description" or the description of available benefit payout options in the employer-provided beneficiary designation form, then check conclusions with the Plan Administrator. In case of doubt read the actual plan documents.

3.   There are certain issues in the disposition of death benefits that need to be considered and covered. While some IRA providers now cover these matters in their printed IRA documents, others do not. If these matters are *not* covered in the IRA agreement or QRP documents, they can be covered in the beneficiary designation form:

A.   Who chooses the form of death benefits, the client-participant or the beneficiary? In the forms in this Appendix, the beneficiary chooses the form of death benefit (see Section 3 .01 in the Master Beneficiary Designation forms, 2.1 and 2.2).

B.   On the death of the Participant, the primary beneficiary is entitled to the benefits. If the beneficiary does not withdraw them immediately, what happens to benefits that are still in the IRA (or QRP) when the *primary beneficiary* dies? Will they pass to a new beneficiary designated by the primary beneficiary? Do they now belong to the primary beneficiary's estate, so they pass under his or her will? See

¶ 1.9.02. The Master Beneficiary Designation Forms in prior editions of this book specified that the beneficiary could name his or her own beneficiary. That part of the form has been dropped in this edition because experience showed that the provision doesn't help if the Plan doesn't allow beneficiaries to name their own beneficiaries, and is unnecessary if the Plan does allow beneficiaries to name their own beneficiaries.

C.   In the case of an IRA (or Roth IRA), can the beneficiary transfer the benefits to another IRA (or Roth IRA) still in the name of the deceased Participant? See Section 3.10 of the IRA/Roth IRA Master Beneficiary Designation Form (Form 2.1) and ¶ 2.5.01.

4.   Problems frequently arise with IRA providers when practitioners submit beneficiary designation forms that place unsuitable duties on the IRA provider. Most IRAs are custodial accounts, under which the IRA provider's duties are limited to custodial and tax reporting services, and the provider's fees are nominal. Administrators of most company retirement plans also are not set up to monitor and administer employees' retirement benefit accounts individually. There are IRA providers who offer "individual retirement trusts" (IRTs), which are identical in all tax attributes to IRAs, but are structured as trusts rather than custodial accounts. The IRT provider is the trustee of the IRT, and as such often provides a higher level of services than the typical IRA account contemplates. The IRT provider's fees would also typically be higher if it is providing trust services rather than just custodial services. Unless the client's particular IRA or IRT provider is set up to provide individual services customized for that client (with appropriate charges), the provider cannot be expected to do much more than send out benefit checks in specified proportions to beneficiaries whose names, addresses and Social Security numbers are listed in the beneficiary designation form. Here are some "do's and don't's" for avoiding problems with the plan or IRA administrator:

A.   Don't require the administrator to make legal judgments. A form that says "I leave the benefits to X unless he disclaims the benefits by means of a qualified disclaimer within the meaning of section 2518," appears to require the plan administrator to determine whether the disclaimer is qualified under § 2518 before it can decide who to pay the benefits to. Compare Form 3.1.

B. <u>Don't require the administrator to carry out functions of an executor or trustee</u>. For example, if you say "I designate my son as beneficiary, to receive only the minimum required distribution each year," you are requiring the plan administrator to control the beneficiary's withdrawals. Most IRAs have no mechanism for restricting the beneficiary's withdrawals. If you want to restrict the beneficiary's withdrawals or make them conditional in any way ("beneficiary can withdraw funds as needed for education"; "beneficiary can withdraw funds so long as she has not remarried") you must either (i) leave the benefits to a trust (so the trustee can enforce the conditions); or (ii) find an IRA provider that offers accounts which allow restricted withdrawal provisions (and probably charges accordingly).

C. <u>Don't make the administrator determine amounts dependent on external facts</u>. If it is necessary to include, in your beneficiary designation form, a formula that is dependent on external facts (for example, "I leave my grandchild an amount equal to my remaining GST exemption," or "I leave to the marital trust the minimum amount necessary to eliminate federal estate taxes"), do this in a way that does not make the IRA provider responsible to apply the formula. Provide that a beneficiary or fiduciary will certify the facts to the IRA provider, who can rely absolutely on such certification. See, e.g., Section II(B) of Form 3.3(A).

D. <u>Do avoid redundant or contradictory lists of definitions and payout options</u>. The list of definitions in Forms 2.1 and 2.2 are intended to be used with IRAs and retirement plans which have (as many do) no or incomprehensible defined terms. If the plan document already has suitable and clear definitions of "primary beneficiary," "death benefit," "the account" and other terms, using a different set of definitions may just create confusion.

5. Consider whether you wish to alter the applicable presumptions in case of simultaneous death. See ¶ 3.1.02.

6. If the disposition is intended to qualify for the marital deduction, include language to that effect. See Section 3.07 in the Master Beneficiary Designation forms (2.1 and 2.2); and several others, including Form 7.4; and ¶ 3.3.05, ¶ 3.3.14.

7.   Consider the extent to which you need to define any terms such as "issue *per stirpes*," or "income"; and/or specify which state's law shall be used to interpret terms you use in the form. It is highly likely that the QRP or IRA agreement specifies that the law of the sponsor's state of incorporation will be used. Since that may well not be the state in which your client lives (or dies), there is a potential for problems if the client's chosen disposition depends on a definition which varies from state to state. Although you cannot change the governing law of the "plan," a statement that the language *of the beneficiary designation* will be interpreted according to the laws of a particular state should be accepted in the sense that it will lead to the correct determination of the client's intent. See Section 3.04, Forms 2.1, 2.2.

8.   Follow the required formalities of execution. Most IRAs are simply custodial accounts. As such, they may be considered "probate" assets of Participant's estate in some states. Some states do not recognize a disposition of certain forms of retirement benefits unless executed with the formalities of a will.

9.   The choice of a contingent beneficiary should not be overlooked. For example:

A.   If benefits are being made payable to a trust, to take advantage of Participant's unified credit while providing life benefits for the surviving spouse, consider naming the trust as primary beneficiary only if the spouse survives. Consider naming the children (assuming that is Participant's choice as contingent beneficiary) directly as contingent beneficiaries if the spouse does not survive, to avoid the complications of running benefits through a trust (see Form 3.5A).

B.   Consider whether different contingent beneficiaries should be named depending on whether the primary beneficiary actually dies before Participant, or merely disclaims the benefits (see Form 3.6).

10.   Whenever a trust is named as beneficiary, see the Trust Drafting Checklist at ¶ 6.1.05, use the Trust Review Questionnaire in Appendix C to test compliance, and be sure to file the required documentation (see Forms 8.1 through 8.4). Some beneficiary designation forms in this Appendix in which benefits are left to a trust describe the trust as "the

[TRUST NAME] Trust [optional:, a copy of which is attached hereto]." The phrase "a copy of which is attached hereto" is optional, and would be used solely to <u>identify</u> the trust which is named as beneficiary. Attaching a copy of the trust to the beneficiary designation form does NOT satisfy the "documentation requirement." You could choose to identify the trust by other means (*e.g.*, "under agreement dated 1/1/98") instead of attaching a copy of the trust to the beneficiary designation form. No matter how you choose to identify the trust which is named as beneficiary, you ALSO must comply with the documentation requirement; see ¶ 6.2.09 and Forms 8.1 through 8.4.

11.   Finally, don't focus on taxes and minimum distributions to the exclusion of basic drafting issues. If the spouse is named as beneficiary, is that only if he/she is married to Participant at time of death?...or does divorce revoke the designation of spouse? If any beneficiary predeceases Participant, does his/her share pass instead to the surviving beneficiaries or to his/her own issue or to someone else?

1.   SIMPLE BENEFICIARY DESIGNATION FORM

Who might use this form: This form may be suitable for a client who wants to leave benefits outright to his spouse if living, otherwise to his children equally (and issue of deceased children). This form is included primarily for use with (1) retirement plans that are of relatively small value and (2) retirement plans which already contain, in the plan documents, the estate plan-friendly additional provisions included in the longer Master Beneficiary Designation forms (2.1 and 2.2). If the benefit is of substantial value, either absolutely or relative to the rest of the client's estate, and the plan documents do not have provisions dealing with the important estate planning issues covered in the longer forms, it would be advisable to use the longer forms.

1.1 Simple Beneficiary Designation: Spouse, Then Children (or Issue)

DESIGNATION OF BENEFICIARY

TO: [Name of IRA or Roth IRA Provider or Plan Administrator]
FROM: [Name of Participant]
RE: [IRA or Roth IRA No._____] or [or Name of Plan]

1.   I hereby designate as my beneficiary, my spouse, [SPOUSE NAME], whose date of birth is [SPOUSE BIRTHDATE], to receive all benefits payable under the above [account] [plan] in the event of my death.

2.   If my spouse does not survive me, I designate as my beneficiaries, in equal shares, such of my children as shall survive me; provided, that if any of my children does not survive me, but leaves issue surviving me, such issue shall take the share such deceased child would have taken if living, by right of representation. My children are:

Name   Address   Date of Birth   Social Security Number

[alt. 1: pay minor's benefits to a custodian]
3.   Any benefits becoming distributable to a person under the age of twenty-one (21) years shall be distributed to such person's surviving parent, if any, otherwise to my oldest then living child, as custodian for such person under the Uniform Transfers to Minors Act. Such custodian shall be entitled to act for the minor in all respects with regard to the benefits.

[alt. 2: pay minor's benefits to Participant's trust; make sure the trust instrument has suitable provision to receive this payment and hold it for the particular minor beneficiary who is entitled to it]
3.   Any benefits becoming distributable to a person under the age of twenty-one (21) years shall be distributed to the Trustee then serving as such under the [NAME OF TRUST] created by [Agreement/Declaration/Instrument/my Will] dated [date of trust

instrument] [optional:, a copy of which is attached hereto], to be held and administered for the benefit of such person as provided therein.

4.   Each beneficiary may choose the form and timing of distribution of his or her benefits, subject to limits imposed by the [plan] [Account Agreement] and applicable law.

Signed this _____ day of _____, 20 ___.

_____
Signature of Participant

2.   MASTER BENEFICIARY DESIGNATION FORMS: MORE COMPLEX PROVISIONS

How to use these forms: These Master Beneficiary Designation forms are meant to be used with all beneficiary designation forms provided in Sections 3 and 4 of this Appendix. Form 2.1 is meant to be used with IRAs (traditional and Roth). Form 2.2 is for QRPs. Make sure the IRA agreement does not contradict anything contained in these forms before using them. Some IRA providers now cover these matters in their printed IRA documents, making it unnecessary to repeat the provisions in the beneficiary designation form.

Other notes: Drafters will not use all of these provisions in every beneficiary designation form. Section 3.03 can be omitted if no minors can possibly become beneficiaries. Section 3.05 could be dispensed with if it is not likely there will be multiple beneficiaries. Section 3.07 can be omitted if Participant is not naming his spouse as beneficiary or contingent beneficiary. For discussion of the reason behind Section 3.07, see ¶ 3.3.14. These provisions, like all forms, are intended as examples only, and should be modified as necessary for individual clients. Also, note that a particular IRA provider or QRP administrator may not be willing to accept some of these provisions.

2.1   Master Beneficiary Designation: Traditional or Roth IRA

DESIGNATION OF BENEFICIARY
TO: _____

Name of Custodian or Trustee of the Account

FROM: _____

Name of Participant

RE: Account No. _____

I.   Definitions

The following words, when used in this form and capitalized, shall have the meaning indicated in this Section.

"Account" means the "Individual Retirement Account," "Individual Retirement Trust," "Roth Individual Retirement Account" or "Roth Individual Retirement Trust" referred to above, which is established and maintained under § 408 or § 408A of the Code.

"Administrator" means the IRA custodian or trustee named above, and its successors in that office.

"Agreement" means the account agreement between the Administrator and the undersigned establishing the Account.

"Beneficiary" means any person or entity entitled to ownership of all or part of the Account as a result of my death (or as a result of the death of another Beneficiary), whether such person or entity is a Primary, Contingent or Successor Beneficiary.

"Contingent Beneficiary" means the person(s) I have designated in this form to receive the Death Benefit if my Primary Beneficiary does not survive me (or disclaims the benefits).

"Death Benefit" means all amounts payable under the Account on account of my death.

"Primary Beneficiary" means the person or persons I have designated in this form to receive the Death Benefit in the event of my death.

"Successor Beneficiary" means a person entitled to receive the balance of another Beneficiary's benefits if such other Beneficiary dies before distribution of all of his or her share of the Death Benefit.

II.   Designation of Beneficiary

[Here insert the chosen designation of beneficiary provision, from Section 3 or 4 of this Appendix B, or elsewhere.]

III. Other Provisions [dispense with any of these that are not appropriate in view of the choice of beneficiary or that are not necessary because already covered in the IRA provider's documents governing the Account]

3.01 Form of Benefit Payments after my Death. Except as may be otherwise specifically provided herein, or in the Agreement, or by applicable law, each Beneficiary shall be entitled to elect the form and timing of distribution of benefits payable to him or her.

3.02 Instructions of attorney or personal representative. I direct the Administrator to comply with all instructions issued to it on my behalf by my duly appointed legal guardian, conservator or other personal representative, and/or, whether or not such a representative has been appointed, by my agent acting under a power of attorney executed by me which grants the authority the agent seeks to exercise.

3.03 Payments to Minors. If any Beneficiary becomes entitled to ownership of any part of the Account at a time when he or she is under the age of twenty-one (21) years, such ownership shall instead be vested in the name of such Beneficiary's surviving parent, if any, otherwise in the name of my oldest then living child if any, otherwise in the name of some other person selected by my Executor, as custodian for such Beneficiary under the Uniform Transfers to Minors Act of the state of my domicile at death, and such custodian shall have the power to act for such Beneficiary in all respects with regard to the Account.

3.04 Governing Law. The law of the State of _____ ____ shall apply solely for the purpose of interpreting my intent as expressed in this Designation of Beneficiary form. This provision is not intended to amend or supercede any governing law provision in the Agreement with respect to the interpretation and administration of the Agreement.

3.05 Multiple Beneficiaries. If there are multiple Beneficiaries entitled to ownership of the Account simultaneously, I direct that each such Beneficiary's proportionate share of the Account shall be treated as a separate account, payable solely to such

Beneficiary, within the meaning of Proposed Treasury Regulation § 1.401(a)(9)-8, A-3, and that the Account shall be deemed divided (as of the date of my death) into separate accounts, in proportion to the relative amounts payable to the respective Beneficiaries, with one such separate account payable to each of my Beneficiaries for purposes of determining the amount required to be distributed to each Beneficiary under § 401(a)(9) of the Internal Revenue Code. So long as the separate accounts remain commingled, all investment gains and losses incurred in the Account shall be allocated among the separate accounts pro rata, that is, in proportion to the relative values of the separate accounts. A distribution from the Account to any Beneficiary (or a transfer from the Account to a separate individual retirement account, still in my name, and payable to such Beneficiary) shall be charged to that Beneficiary's separate account (reducing its value for purposes of subsequent allocations of investment gains or losses). The Beneficiaries shall be entitled, by joint written instructions to the Administrator, to have the Account partitioned into multiple Accounts, corresponding to each Beneficiary's separate account, as of or at any time after my death, to the maximum extent such division is permitted by law to occur without causing a deemed distribution of the Account. Following such partition the newly created separated Accounts shall be maintained as if each were an Account in my name payable solely to the applicable Beneficiary, and no Beneficiary shall have any further interest in or claim to any Account other than the separate Account representing his or her interest.

3.06   Allowing Beneficiary to Appoint Investment Manager. The Beneficiary may designate an Investment Manager for the Account (or, if the Account has been partitioned pursuant to the preceding provisions hereof, such Beneficiary's separated Account). Upon receipt of written authorization from the Beneficiary, and until receiving notice that such authorization is revoked, the Administrator shall comply with investment instructions of the Investment Manager in accordance with the Beneficiary's authorization.

3.07   Preservation of marital deduction. If my spouse survives me, this paragraph shall apply to any portion (or all) of the Account as to which my spouse is the Beneficiary or as to which my spouse becomes the Beneficiary by virtue of the death of (or a disclaimer by) a prior Beneficiary. My spouse, as such Beneficiary, shall have the right, exercisable solely by my spouse, annually or more frequently (in my spouse's discretion), to require distribution to my spouse of all income of the Account, and also shall have the power, exercisable by my spouse alone and in all events, at any time or times and from time to time, to appoint all of the principal of the Account (including undistributed income) to my spouse. Rights given to my spouse under this paragraph shall be in addition to and not in limitation of any rights given to my spouse by law, by the Agreement or by other provisions hereof. My spouse shall have sole responsibility for determining the "income" and "principal" of the Account. The Administrator's responsibility under this section is limited solely to distributing to my Spouse any amounts my Spouse has instructed the Administrator to distribute to my Spouse.

3.08   Transferring Account. The Beneficiary shall have the right to have the Account (or, if the Account has been partitioned pursuant to the preceding provisions hereof, such Beneficiary's separated Account) transferred to a different individual retirement account or trust, of the same type ("traditional" or "Roth") as the Account, still in my name, with the same or a different custodian or trustee, if at the applicable time such transfer is permitted by law to occur without causing a deemed distribution of the Account.

Signed this _____ day of _____, 20 ___.

_____
Signature of Participant

Receipt of the above beneficiary designation form is hereby acknowledged this ___ day of _____, 20 ___.

_____
Name of Custodian or Trustee
By:_____
Title

2.2   Master Beneficiary Designation Form: Qualified Retirement Plan

WARNING: If Participant is married, spousal consent is required if anyone other than spouse is named as beneficiary. See ¶ 3.4.

DESIGNATION OF BENEFICIARY

TO: _____

        Name of Trustee or Plan Administrator

FROM: _____

        Name of Participant

RE: _____

        Name of Retirement Plan

I.   <u>Definitions</u>

        The following words, when used in this form and capitalized, shall have the meaning indicated in this Section.

        "Administrator" means the Plan Administrator or Trustee named above, and its successors in such office.

        "Beneficiary" means any person entitled to receive benefits under the Plan as a result of my death (or as a result of the death of another Beneficiary).

        "Contingent Beneficiary" means the person(s) I have designated in this form to receive the Death Benefit if my Primary Beneficiary does not survive me (or disclaims the benefits).

        "Death Benefit" means all benefits payable under the Plan on account of my death.

        "Plan" means the qualified retirement plan or other retirement arrangement described at the beginning of this form.

        "Primary Beneficiary" means the person designated in this form to receive benefits under the Plan on account of my death.

        "Successor Beneficiary" means a person entitled to receive the balance of another Beneficiary's benefits if such other Beneficiary dies before distribution of all of his or her share of the Death Benefit.

II.   <u>Designation of Beneficiary</u>

[Here insert the chosen designation of beneficiary provision, from Section 3 or 4 of this Appendix B, or elsewhere.]

III.   Other Provisions [dispense with any of these that are not appropriate in view of the choice of beneficiary or that are not necessary because already covered in the plan documents governing the benefits]

3.01   Form of Benefit Payments After My Death. Except as may be otherwise specifically provided herein, in the Plan, or by applicable law, each Beneficiary shall be entitled to elect the form and timing of distribution of any benefits payable to such Beneficiary.

3.02   Instructions of attorney or personal representative. I direct the Administrator to comply with all instructions issued to it on my behalf by my duly appointed legal guardian, conservator or other personal representative, and/or, whether or not such a representative has been appointed, by my agent acting under a power of attorney executed by me which grants the authority the agent seeks to exercise.

3.03   Payments to Minors. If any Beneficiary becomes entitled to benefits under the Plan at a time when he or she is under the age of twenty-one (21) years, such benefits shall be instead payable to such Beneficiary's surviving parent, if any, otherwise to my oldest then living child, if any, otherwise to some other person selected by my Executor, as custodian for such Beneficiary under the Uniform Transfers to Minors Act, and such custodian shall have the power to act for such Beneficiary in all respects with regard to the benefits to which such Beneficiary is entitled.

3.04   Governing Law. The law of the State of _____ shall apply solely for the purpose of interpreting my intent as expressed in this Designation of Beneficiary form. This provision is not intended to amend or supercede any governing law provision in the Agreement with respect to the interpretation and administration of the Agreement.

3.05   Multiple Beneficiaries. If there are multiple

Beneficiaries entitled to ownership of the Death Benefit simultaneously, I direct that each such Beneficiary's proportionate share of the Death Benefit shall be treated as a separate account, payable solely to such Beneficiary, within the meaning of Proposed Treasury Regulation § 1.401(a)(9)-8, A-3, and that the Death Benefit shall be deemed divided (as of the date of my death) into separate accounts, in proportion to the relative amounts payable to the respective Beneficiaries, with one such separate account payable to each of my Beneficiaries for purposes of determining the amount required to be distributed to each Beneficiary under § 401(a)(9) of the Internal Revenue Code. So long as the separate accounts remain commingled, all investment gains and losses shall be allocated among the separate accounts pro rata, that is, in proportion to the relative values of the separate accounts. A distribution to any Beneficiary shall be charged to that Beneficiary's separate account (reducing its value for purposes of subsequent allocations of investment gains or losses). The Beneficiaries shall be entitled, by joint written instructions to the Administrator, to have the Death Benefit partitioned into multiple Accounts, corresponding to each Beneficiary's separate account, as of or at any time after my death, to the maximum extent such division is otherwise permitted by the Plan and by law (without causing a deemed distribution of the Death Benefit). Following such partition the newly created separated Accounts shall be maintained as if each were a Death Benefit in my name payable solely to the applicable Beneficiary, and no Beneficiary shall have any further interest in or claim to any Death Benefit other than the separate account representing his or her interest.

   3.06   Allowing Beneficiary to Appoint Investment Manager. The Beneficiary may designate an Investment Manager for the Death Benefit (or, if the Death Benefit has been divided pursuant to the preceding provisions hereof, such Beneficiary's share of the Death Benefit). Upon receipt of written authorization from the Beneficiary, and until receiving notice that such authorization is revoked, the Administrator shall comply with investment instructions of the Investment Manager in accordance with the Beneficiary's authorization.

   3.07   Preservation of marital deduction. If my spouse survives me, this paragraph shall apply to any portion (or all) of the Death

Benefit as to which my spouse is the Beneficiary or as to which my spouse becomes the Beneficiary by virtue of the death of (or a disclaimer by) a prior Beneficiary. My spouse, as such Beneficiary, shall have the right, exercisable solely by my spouse, annually or more frequently (in my spouse's discretion), to require distribution to my spouse of all income of the Death Benefit, and also shall have the power, exercisable by my spouse alone and in all events, at any time or times and from time to time, to appoint all of the principal of the Death Benefit (including undistributed income) to my spouse. Rights given to my spouse under this paragraph shall be in addition to and not in limitation of any rights given to my spouse by law, by the Plan or by other provisions hereof. Rights given to my spouse under this paragraph shall be in addition to and not in limitation of any rights given to my spouse by law, by the Agreement or by other provisions hereof. My spouse shall have sole responsibility for determining the "income" and "principal" of the Death Benefit. The Administrator's responsibility under this section is limited solely to distributing to my Spouse any amounts my Spouse has instructed the Administrator to distribute to my Spouse.

Signed this _____ day of _____, 20 ___.

_____
Signature of Participant

Receipt of the above beneficiary designation form is hereby acknowledged this ___ day of _____, 20 ___.

_____
Name of Plan Administrator or Trustee
By:_____
Title

3.   SEVEN WAYS TO LEAVE BENEFITS TO THE MARITAL AND/OR CREDIT SHELTER SHARE

3.0   Explanation of the marital/credit shelter forms

Each of the following forms is a beneficiary designation designed to leave benefits to a marital or credit shelter share, or to split benefits between a marital and credit shelter share. These can be inserted into "Part II" of the appropriate "Master Beneficiary Designation Form" (Form 2.1 for a traditional or Roth IRA, Form 2.2 for a QRP) in the preceding section of this Appendix. Related provisions to be included in the client's trust instrument, when applicable, follow the beneficiary designation form.

In view of the changing exemption amounts under the federal estate tax, and the scheduled repeal (and reinstatement?) of that tax, formula clauses based on federal estate tax concepts may not work as intended (or at all). Under several of the marital/credit shelter formulas in this Appendix, if no "override" clause were added, nothing at all would go into the marital share if the estate tax were not in effect at the Participant's death. Because that result could be contrary to the client's intent, each of those forms includes an optional "**Minimum Marital Share Override**" provision, which provides that a certain minimum amount or percentage must be allocated to the marital share regardless of what the estate tax-based formula says.

This point must be discussed with the client before the estate plan is drafted: How much would you choose to leave to your spouse (or marital trust) if it is not necessary to leave *anything* to your spouse (or marital trust) to eliminate estate taxes on your estate? If the client is leaving assets to the spouse (or marital trust) only because that disposition is necessary to gain maximum federal estate tax deferral, the estate plan does not need a Minimum Marital Share Override. If, on the other hand, client wants the spouse (or the marital trust) to receive a certain minimum dollar or percentage amount regardless of what the federal estate tax happens to provide when client dies, it is necessary to include a Minimum Marital Share Override clause to carry out the client's intent. Each of the following forms includes such an optional clause if appropriate. The "Other Notes" at the beginning of each form explain whether that particular form includes an optional Minimum Marital Share Override clause and why or why not.

Needless to say, the client's estate plan must be reviewed regularly in light of all changes in the estate tax and other applicable laws that may affect it. Including a Minimum Marital Share Override in the trust instrument does not resolve all the possible issues concerning federal estate tax repeal or increased exemptions. The purpose of the Minimum Marital Share Override in these forms is simply to assure that a marital/credit shelter formula clause does not inadvertently, due to estate tax repeal or increased estate tax exemptions, leave to the spouse (or marital trust) less than the client intends the spouse (or marital trust) to receive.

3.1   Life Insurance to Credit Shelter Trust, Rest to Spouse

Who would consider using this form: Any client who holds life insurance inside his QRP, and wants the insurance proceeds payable to a trust (*e.g.,* to "fill up" a credit shelter trust), but wants the surviving spouse to be able to roll over the non-insurance portion of the benefits.

Warning: A client whose plan-held insurance is held in a "subtrust" (¶ 8.4.01) cannot designate the beneficiary for the policy.

Other notes: Under this form the amount each beneficiary receives is not dependent on an estate tax-driven formula. The credit shelter trust gets the insurance proceeds and the spouse gets the rest of the benefits, regardless of whether the federal estate tax exists or what the federal estate tax exemption amount is. Therefore, it is not necessary to include a Minimum Marital Share Override (Section 3.0).

3.1   Beneficiary Designation Form

II.   Designation of Beneficiary
A.   Primary Beneficiary
If my spouse, [SPOUSE NAME], survives me, the Death Benefit shall be distributed to the following Primary Beneficiaries:
1.   Any amount payable under any contract of life insurance on my life shall be paid to [TRUSTEE NAME], as Trustee of the [TRUST NAME] Trust, under Agreement of Trust dated [TRUST DATE] [optional:, a copy of which is attached hereto].
2.   The balance of the Death Benefit shall be paid to my spouse.
B.   Contingent Beneficiary
If my spouse does not survive me (or to the extent my spouse

disclaims any benefits otherwise distributable to my spouse under section A above), I direct that 100% of the Death Benefit (or the amount disclaimed as the case may be) shall be paid to [TRUSTEE NAME], as Trustee of the "Family Trust" of the said [TRUST NAME] Trust.

3.2   Benefits Payable to "Pourover" Trust, Under Which Assets Are Divided Between a Marital Share (Paid to Spouse Outright) and a Credit Shelter Trust by a Fractional Formula. Benefits Allocated to Marital Share

Who would consider using this form: Client who expects to need to use some or all of his retirement benefits to "fill up" a credit shelter trust, and wants any benefits not needed for that purpose paid to the spouse outright so she can roll them over. See ¶ 10.5.

Drawbacks of this form: Under this form and the related trust provision, the trustee is required to fund the marital share with retirement benefits to the maximum extent possible, and then is required to distribute the marital share outright to the spouse on her request. This approach is based on IRS private letter rulings, permitting the surviving spouse to roll over benefits which pass to her through a trust, if she has the unfettered right to withdraw the benefits. ¶ 3.2.09. Since this IRS policy has so far appeared only in private letter rulings, there is no guarantee the IRS will continue to recognize such rollovers, although it appears likely (and correct under the Code) that such rollovers will be allowed.

Other notes: This form names only the trust as beneficiary, regardless of whether the spouse survives. If the entire trust is to be distributed to Participant's issue outright on the death of the surviving spouse, consider naming the trust as primary beneficiary only if the spouse survives, and naming the issue directly as beneficiaries if the spouse does not survive. See form 3.5 for an example of this approach. Because this Form 3.2 has different dispositive provisions for the marital share (paid outright to spouse) and the credit shelter share (held in trust), an optional Minimum Marital Share Override provision (see Section 3.0) is included in the trust form.

3.2(A) Beneficiary Designation Form

II. Designation of Beneficiary

A. Primary Beneficiary

I hereby designate as my Primary Beneficiary, to receive 100% of the Death Benefit in case of my death, [TRUSTEE NAME] (hereinafter "my Trustee"), as Trustee of the [TRUST NAME] Trust, under Agreement of Trust dated [TRUST DATE] [optional:, a copy of which is attached hereto].

B. Distribution of Benefits to Spouse

My Trustee is directed under the said Agreement of Trust to allocate the Death Benefit, pursuant to a formula, between my spouse and the "Family Trust" established under said Agreement of Trust. My Trustee is further directed under said Agreement of Trust, if so requested by my spouse, to cause the part of the Death Benefit so allocated to my spouse to be (i) distributed outright to my spouse or (ii) transferred directly to an "individual retirement account" (or other eligible retirement plan) in my spouse's name. Accordingly, if the Administrator is so instructed by my Trustee, the Administrator shall, with respect to the amount indicated by my Trustee, (i) distribute such amount outright to my spouse or (ii) transfer such amount directly to an "individual retirement account" (or other eligible retirement plan) in my spouse's name.

3.2(B) Related Trust Provisions

__. Payments After My Death

Upon my death, the Trustee shall hold and administer all property of the Trust, including any amounts received or receivable then or later as a result of my death or otherwise, as follows:

.01 If my spouse does not survive me, the Trustee shall designate all of such property as the "Family Trust," to be held and administered as provided in Article __.

.02   If my spouse survives me, the Trustee shall divide the said property into two separate shares, to be designated respectively the Marital Share and the Family Trust. The two separate shares shall be funded pursuant to the following formula. If application of the formula results in assets being allocated to only one of the shares instead of both, the Trustee shall fund only such one.

.03   The Trustee shall allocate to the Marital Share a portion of the Remaining Trust Property determined by multiplying the Remaining Trust Property by a fraction. The numerator of the fraction shall be the smallest amount necessary, if allowed as a marital deduction, to eliminate the federal estate tax otherwise payable by reason of my death, reduced by the value of all other items included in my estate which qualify for the federal estate tax marital deduction and which pass or have passed to my spouse otherwise than under this provision. The denominator of the fraction is the value of the Remaining Trust Property. For purposes of this formula:

(i)   It shall be assumed with respect to property not passing under this trust that my Executor will elect to treat as "qualified terminable interest property" all property eligible for such treatment.

(ii)   The "values" of assets shall be their values as finally determined for purposes of the federal estate tax on my estate.

(iii)   The "Remaining Trust Property" means all property of this trust that is included in my federal gross estate, reduced by the amount of any debts, expenses of administration, specific and pecuniary bequests and death taxes payable out of such property.

(iv)   The federal estate tax credit for state death taxes shall be taken into account only to the extent its use does not increase the state death taxes otherwise payable on my estate.

[optional: **Minimum Marital Share Override** provision: either: "Notwithstanding the foregoing, the numerator of the fraction shall not be less than [here insert the minimum dollar amount the client wants the marital share to receive]" or "Notwithstanding the foregoing, the fraction applied to determine the portion of the Remaining Trust Property allocated to the Marital Share shall not be smaller than [here insert the minimum fractional or percentage amount the client wants the marital share to receive]."

.04   All property not allocated to the Marital Share pursuant to the preceding formula shall be designated as the Family Trust, and administered as provided in Article __.

.05   In selecting which assets shall be used to fund which share, the Trustee shall, to the maximum extent possible, allocate tax-favored retirement plans to the Marital Share and assets other than tax-favored retirement plans to the Family Trust. A "tax-favored retirement plan" means an individual retirement account (within the meaning of § 408 of the Internal Revenue Code (the "Code")), Roth individual retirement account (within the meaning of § 408A of the Code), qualified retirement plan (within the meaning of § 401(a) of the Code), "tax-sheltered annuity" (described in § 403(b) of the Code) and similar plans, accounts and arrangements; and shall, to the maximum extent possible, fund the Marital Share with .

.06   The Marital Share shall be distributed to my spouse, outright and free of trusts. To the extent that all or part of any tax-favored retirement plan is allocated to the Marital Share pursuant to the foregoing provisions, the Trustee may (and shall, if requested to do so by my spouse) cause such plan (or part thereof) to be paid directly from such plan to my spouse as beneficiary, or transferred (if so requested by my spouse) directly from such plan into an individual retirement account in my spouse's name, without the intervening step of transferring it to this Trust.

3.3   All Benefits Payable to a "Pourover" Trust, Under Which Assets are Divided Between a QTIP Marital Trust and a Credit Shelter Trust by a Fractional Formula; Drafter May Choose to Specify Allocation of Benefits to Marital Trust or Credit Shelter Trust

Who should consider this form: A client who does not want any benefits paid to the spouse outright and whose trust will be allocated between a marital trust and a credit shelter trust by a fractional formula. The related trust provisions contain two alternatives regarding funding these shares. One version requires benefits to be allocated to the marital share to the extent possible; the other requires benefits to be allocated to the credit shelter share to the extent possible. A third option is to omit both versions of paragraph .06 and allow the trustee to choose which assets to use to fund which share (but see ¶ 7.4.08).

Drawbacks of this form: No spousal rollover is possible under this form.

Other notes: If the trust named as beneficiary under this form has different dispositive provisions for the marital share and the credit shelter share (e.g., spouse is sole beneficiary for life of the marital share while the credit shelter trust is a "spray" trust for spouse and issue) determine whether including the optional Minimum Marital Share Override provision (see Section 3.0) would carry out the client's intent.

3.3(A) Beneficiary Designation Form

II.   Designation of Beneficiary

    A.   Primary Beneficiary

    I hereby designate as my Primary Beneficiary, to receive 100% of the Death Benefit, [TRUSTEE NAME] (hereinafter "my Trustee"), as trustee of the [TRUST NAME] Trust, under Agreement of Trust dated [TRUST DATE] [optional: , a copy of which is attached hereto].

    B.   Division of Benefit

    Under the terms of said Agreement of Trust, my Trustee is directed, if my spouse survives me, to divide the assets of said Trust into two separate trusts, to be designated the "Marital Trust" and the "Family Trust." If so instructed by my Trustee, the Administrator shall divide the Death Benefit into two separate accounts (within the meaning of Prop. Treas. Reg. § 1.401(a)(9)-8, A-3), both still in my name, one payable solely to the Marital Trust as Beneficiary and the other payable solely to the Family Trust as Beneficiary; or, in accordance with such instructions, shall designate the entire Death Benefit as payable to one of said trusts. The Administrator shall have no responsibility to determine the correctness of my Trustee's instructions regarding such allocation, and shall have no liability whatsoever to any person for complying with my Trustee's said instructions. The beneficiaries of the Marital Trust and Family Trust shall look solely to my Trustee for enforcement of their rights under the said Trusts.

    C.   Benefits Payable to Marital Trust

With regard to any portion of the Death Benefit so allocated to the Marital Trust, there must be distributed to the Marital Trust in each year, beginning with the year of my death, from the Marital Trust's portion of the Death Benefit, at least the net income of the Marital Trust's portion of the Death Benefit for such year accrued after my death. My Trustee, and not the Administrator, shall have sole responsibility for determination of the amount of such income, and directing the distribution of such amount to the Marital Trust.

3.3(B) Related Trust Provisions

__.   Payments Upon My Death

Upon my death, the Trustee shall hold and administer all property of the Trust, including any amounts received or receivable then or later as a result of my death or otherwise, as follows:

[here, copy sections .01 through .04 from form 3.2(B), including the optional **Minimum Marital Share Override** if appropriate, but change "Marital Share" to "Marital Trust", and add:]

.05   The Marital Trust shall be held and administered as provided in Article ___.

[Use one or the other of the following optional funding provisions, or neither, **but not both**]

[optional funding provision: alternative 1].

.06   Any death benefit under any "qualified retirement plan," individual retirement account, Roth IRA or similar tax-favored retirement arrangement that is payable to this Trust shall be allocated to the Marital Trust to the maximum extent possible within the limits of the preceding formula.

[optional funding provision: alternative 2].

.06   Any death benefit under any "qualified retirement plan," individual retirement account, Roth IRA or similar tax-favored retirement arrangement that is payable to this Trust shall be allocated to the Family Trust to the maximum extent possible within the limits of the preceding formula.

[here insert form 7.4, or otherwise take steps to qualify for the marital deduction; see ¶ 3.3.05]

3.4   Benefits Payable to Marital Trust Which Is Part of a "Pourover" Trust with a Pecuniary Marital Formula

Who should consider using this form: A client who wants to use a pecuniary marital formula for his marital/credit shelter share division because it is easier to administer; who wants his retirement benefits paid to a marital trust, and not outright to his spouse; and whose retirement benefits will probably not be needed to fund the credit shelter share. By making the benefits payable directly to the Marital Trust, the client avoids having the pecuniary formula applied to the benefits (see ¶ 2.2.05), avoids the complexity of transferring the retirement benefits from a "funding" trust into a Marital or Family Trust, and avoids having to use a fractional formula for any assets.

The preferred simplicity of administration which comes from using a pecuniary formula does not have to be sacrificed just because part of the trust will consist of retirement benefits. Under this form, the retirement benefits do not go through the pecuniary funding formula—the benefits bypass the formula and go straight into the Marital Trust.

Drawbacks: If the retirement benefits turn out to be a greater amount than is required to eliminate estate taxes, then this form would overfund the marital share. That problem can be solved easily post mortem by a fractional QTIP election, or, less easily, by a disclaimer by the marital trust. Also, no spousal rollover is possible under this form.

Other notes: If the trust named as beneficiary under this form has different dispositive provisions for the marital share and the credit shelter share (e.g., spouse is sole beneficiary for life of the marital share while the credit shelter trust is a "spray" trust for spouse and issue) determine whether including the optional Minimum Marital Share Override provision (Section 3.0) would carry out the client's intent.

Under this Form 3.4, the spouse is guaranteed to get at least the amount of the retirement benefits, because those are allocated to the marital trust *regardless* of what happens under the formula, so the question is whether the client wants the marital trust to be sure to receive the *greater* of (1) all the retirement benefits or (2) a specified dollar amount (even if that is more than the total value of the retirement benefits).

3.4(A) Beneficiary Designation Form

II.   Designation of Beneficiary

A.   Primary Beneficiary

I hereby designate as my Primary Beneficiary, to receive 100% of the Death Benefit, [TRUSTEE NAME], as trustee of the [MARITAL TRUST NAME] Marital Trust, established under Agreement of Trust dated [TRUST DATE] [optional:, a copy of which is attached hereto].

B.   Form of Distribution of Benefits

After my death, there shall be distributed to the Beneficiary, in each year, so long as my spouse is living, whichever of the following amounts is the greatest:

(a)   the net income of the Death Benefit for such year;

(b)   the Minimum Distribution Amount for such year; or

(c)   such amount as the Beneficiary shall direct by written instructions to the Administrator.

The Beneficiary, not the Administrator, shall have sole responsibility for determining the amounts under subparagraphs (a), (b) and (c).

3.4(B) Related Trust Provisions

___.   Payments After My Death

Upon my death, the Trustee shall hold and administer all property of the Trust, including any amounts received or receivable then or later as a result of my death or otherwise, as follows:

.01   If my spouse does not survive me, the Trustee shall

designate all such property as the "Family Trust" to be held and administered as provided in Article ___.

.02   If my spouse survives me, the Trustee shall divide the said property into two separate trust funds, to be designated the Marital Trust and the Family Trust, pursuant to the following formula. If application of the formula results in assets being allocated to only one of the trusts instead of both, the Trustee shall fund only such one.

(a)   The Trustee shall allocate to the Marital Trust all benefits payable under any "qualified retirement plan," "individual retirement account" (other than Roth IRAs), or similar retirement plan, annuity or arrangement, as well as any assets which are payable by the terms of my will, beneficiary designation form or otherwise directly to the Marital Trust.

(b)   The Trustee shall allocate to the Marital Trust such additional amount, if any, as is necessary to bring the total value of the Marital Trust up to the Optimum Marital Amount. To the extent there is a choice of assets, this gift to the Marital Trust shall be funded to the extent possible only with assets or the proceeds of assets which qualify for the federal estate tax marital deduction. The Marital Trust shall be held and administered as provided in Article ___.

[alt. 1: no Minimum Marital Share Override]

(c)   The "Optimum Marital Amount" means the smallest amount which, if it passed to my spouse in a manner qualifying for the federal estate tax marital deduction, would eliminate the federal estate tax on my estate (or minimize such tax, if it is not possible to eliminate it), reduced by the value of any property passing to my spouse otherwise than under this trust to the extent such property qualifies for the federal estate tax marital deduction (or would so qualify if my Executor so elected). In computing the Optimum Marital Amount, the federal estate tax credit for state death taxes shall be taken into account only to the extent its use in the foregoing formula does not increase the state death taxes otherwise payable on my estate. If the amount passing to my spouse would have no effect on the computation of the federal estate tax on my estate (for example, because such tax has been repealed) the Optimum Marital Amount shall be zero.

[alt. 2: includes Minimum Marital Share Override]

(c)   The "Optimum Marital Amount" means either (1) the smallest amount which, if it passed to my spouse in a manner qualifying for the federal estate tax marital deduction, would eliminate the federal estate tax on my estate (or minimize such tax, if it is not possible to eliminate it), or (2) $[here insert the minimum combined dollar amount the client wants to have pass to the spouse and the marital trust], whichever of the said two amounts is the greater, reduced by the value of any property passing to my spouse otherwise than under this trust. In computing the Optimum Marital Amount, the federal estate tax credit for state death taxes shall be taken into account only to the extent its use in the foregoing formula does not increase the state death taxes otherwise payable on my estate.

(d)   All property not allocated to the Marital Trust pursuant to the preceding formula (or, if no property is allocable to the Marital Trust pursuant to preceding formula, then all property of the Trust) shall be designated as the Family Trust, to be held and administered as provided in Article ____.

[here insert form 7.4, or otherwise take steps to qualify for marital deduction; see ¶ 3.3.05.]

3.5   Benefits Payable to "One Big QTIP Trust" if Spouse Survives; Trustee Can Divide the Trust; Issue are Contingent Beneficiaries

Who would use this form: The client who wants all income of his benefits paid to his spouse for life, but wants principal remaining at the spouse's death to pass to beneficiaries selected by client. This form leaves all the benefits to "one big QTIP trust," with the trustee having discretion either to make a fractional QTIP election, or to divide the trust into two separate trusts at the client's death, with the QTIP election being made for only one of them, whichever seems best at the time. Participant's issue are named directly as contingent beneficiaries if spouse does not survive Participant.

Drawbacks: See ¶ 10.5.05, and *Koslow* case study, Chapter 11.

Other notes: The trust form 3.5(B) allows the trustee to divide the trust into two or more separate trusts. Generation skipping transfer tax implications of division of a trust into two or more trusts are beyond the scope of this book. Since under this form the dispositive provisions are not affected either by federal estate repeal or by the amount of the federal estate tax exemption (because the dispositive terms of the marital and credit shelter shares are identical) it is not necessary to include a Minimum Marital Share Override (Section 3.0).

3.5(A) Beneficiary Designation Form

II.   Designation of Beneficiary

A.   Primary Beneficiary

I hereby designate as my primary Beneficiary, to receive 100% of the Death Benefit, if my spouse survives me, [TRUSTEE NAME], as Trustee of the [TRUST NAME] Trust under Agreement of Trust dated [TRUST DATE] [optional:, a copy of which is attached hereto].

B.   Form of Distribution of Benefits

After my death, there shall be distributed to the Beneficiary, in each year, so long as my spouse is living, whichever of the following amounts is the greatest:

(a)   the net income of the Death Benefit for such year;

(b)   the Minimum Distribution Amount for such year; or

(c)   such amount as the Beneficiary shall direct by written instructions to the Administrator.

The Beneficiary shall have sole responsibility for complying with these instructions as to the Form of Distribution of Benefits. The Administrator shall have no responsibility or liability to calculate the amounts specified above or to see that they are distributed. Any person who claims that the distributions called for above have not been properly made shall look solely to the Beneficiary for satisfaction of such claim.

C.   Contingent Beneficiary

I hereby designate as my Contingent Beneficiary, to receive 100% of the Death Benefit if my spouse does not survive me, my issue surviving me, by right of representation.

3.5(B) Related Trust Provisions

____.   Payments After My Death

Upon my death, the Trustee shall hold and administer all property of the Trust, including any amounts received or receivable then or later as a result of my death or otherwise, as follows:

.01   If my spouse does not survive me, the Trustee shall designate all of such property as the "Family Trust," to be held and administered as provided in Article ___.

.02   If my spouse survives me, the Trustee shall pay to my spouse the net income from the date of my death, at least quarter annually, for life.

.03   If this Trust is the beneficiary of death benefits under any "individual retirement account," "Roth IRA," "qualified retirement plan," or similar tax-favored retirement arrangement or annuity (the "Plan") the Trustee must withdraw from the Plan, in each calendar year, and deposit in this trust fund, at least whichever of the following amounts is the greater:

(a)   the Plan's net income for such year; or

(b)   the "minimum distribution amount" which is required to be withdrawn from such Plan under § 401(a)(9) of the Internal Revenue Code or other Code provisions or applicable law.

This paragraph .03 shall not be deemed to limit the Trustee's power and right to withdraw from the Plan in any year more than the greater of the said two amounts.

.04   Upon the death of my spouse, the principal, as it may then exist, shall be held, administered and distributed as provided for property of the Family Trust under Article ___.

.___   Division of the Trust

The Trustee in its discretion may divide the trust into two or more separate shares, each such separate share to be administered as a separate trust on all the same terms provided herein for the undivided trust fund. I anticipate that the Trustee will exercise its discretion under this Article for reasons of administrative convenience, or in order to recognize different characteristics the separate shares or trusts will have for purposes of certain taxes.

3.6   Benefits Payable to Spouse, "Disclaimable" to Credit Shelter Trust; Different Contingent Beneficiary Depending on Whether Spouse Predeceases or Disclaims

Who would consider using this form: A client who does not have sufficient non-retirement plan assets to fully fund a credit shelter trust, but wants nevertheless to leave the benefits to his spouse and allow the spouse to make the ultimate decision whether to (a) keep the benefits and roll them over to an IRA or (b) disclaim some or all of the benefits and allow them to flow to the credit shelter trust.

Drawbacks: See ¶ 8.2.04.

Other notes: Since under this form the surviving spouse is sole beneficiary of the benefits, and benefits pass to the credit shelter trust only to the extent the spouse chooses voluntarily to disclaim them, it is not necessary to include a Minimum Marital Share Override (Section 3.) to assure spouse receives a certain amount. How much spouse receives is entirely within spouse's own control.

3.6   Beneficiary Designation Form

II.   Designation of Beneficiary

A.   Primary Beneficiary

I hereby designate as my Primary Beneficiary, to receive 100% of the Death Benefit, my spouse, [SPOUSE NAME], if my spouse survives me.

B.   Contingent Beneficiary in Case of Disclaimer

If my spouse survives me, but disclaims the Death Benefit (or part of it), I hereby designate as my Contingent Beneficiary, to receive the part (or all) of the Death Benefit so disclaimed, [TRUSTEE NAME], as Trustee of the [TRUST NAME] Trust, under agreement dated [TRUST DATE] [optional:, a copy of which is attached hereto].

> C. Contingent Beneficiary in Case of Death
>
> If my spouse does not survive me, I hereby designate as my Contingent Beneficiary, to receive 100% of the Death Benefit, my issue surviving me, by right of representation.

3.7 Benefits Payable to Credit Shelter Trust, "Disclaimable" to Spouse

Who would consider using this form: A client who does not have sufficient non-retirement assets to fund a credit shelter trust, and expects to use his retirement benefits for that purpose, but wants to leave the door open for a spousal rollover because he thinks that (a) there might possibly be sufficient other assets to fund the credit shelter trust by the time he dies so the retirement benefits won't be needed after all or (b) even if there are not sufficient other assets to fund the credit shelter trust when he dies the rollover might appear at that time likely to produce a better overall tax and financial picture for his beneficiaries (see ¶ 10.5). This client does not want to make the benefits payable to the spouse and "disclaimable" to the credit shelter trust because he does not want to make the estate plan dependant on spouse's disclaimer.

Drawbacks of using this form: Do not use this form without first investigating applicable state law on disclaimers by fiduciaries.

Other notes: By using this form, the client has already decided that he is willing to have spouse receive no benefits (since under this form benefits pass to the surviving spouse only to the extent the credit shelter trust chooses voluntarily to disclaim them). Accordingly, it is not necessary to include a Minimum Marital Share Override (Sectcion 3.0) to assure spouse receives a certain amount. How much spouse receives is within the control of the trustee of the credit shelter trust.

3.7(A) Beneficiary Designation Form

> II. Designation of Beneficiary
>
> A. Primary Beneficiary
>
> I hereby designate as my Primary Beneficiary, to receive 100% of the Death Benefit [TRUSTEE NAME] (hereinafter "my Trustee"), as Trustee of the [TRUST NAME] Trust, under Agreement of Trust

dated [TRUST DATE] [optional:, a copy of which is attached hereto].

> B.   Alternative Primary Beneficiary
>
> If and to the extent that my Trustee disclaims any of the Death Benefit, I name as my Primary Beneficiary, for the portion (or all) of the Death Benefit so disclaimed, my spouse, [SPOUSE NAME], if my spouse survives me.

3.7(B) Related Trust Provisions

> .__   Disclaimers by Trustee
>
> .01   The Trustee shall have the power and authority, without the approval of any court, and without the consent of any beneficiary, to disclaim (refuse to accept) any property or interest in property that is payable to the trust by gift, devise, inheritance, bequest or otherwise, if the Trustee, in its discretion, determines that such disclaimer is in the best interest of beneficiaries of this Trust or will otherwise help achieve the objectives of this Trust.
>
> .02   In exercising its discretion under this Article, the Trustee shall be entitled to presume that any benefit conferred on an individual is likewise a benefit to the descendants of that individual, and shall bear in mind my objective of minimizing taxes for my family as a whole.

4.   OTHER BENEFICIARY DESIGNATION FORMS

4.1   Spouse is Primary Beneficiary; Children are Contingent

This is a designation of spouse if living otherwise children (or their issue), suitable for use with Forms 2.1 and 2.2.

> II.   Designation of Beneficiary
>
> A.   Primary Beneficiary
>
> I hereby designate as my Primary Beneficiary, to receive 100% of the Death Benefit, my spouse, [SPOUSE NAME], if my spouse survives me.

> **B.** <u>Contingent Beneficiary</u>
>
> If my spouse does not survive me, I hereby designate as my Contingent Beneficiary, to receive 100% of the Death Benefit, my children surviving me, in equal shares; provided, that if any child of mine does not survive me, but leaves issue surviving me, such issue shall take the share such deceased child would have taken if living, by right of representation.

4.2   Designating Children (Or Their Issue) as Beneficiaries

This is a designation of living children (and issue of deceased children) as the primary beneficiaries, suitable for use with the Master Beneficiary Designation forms (Forms 2.1 and 2.2).

II.   <u>Designation of Beneficiary</u>

I hereby designate as my Primary Beneficiary, to receive 100% of the Death Benefit, my children surviving me, in equal shares; provided, that if any child of mine does not survive me, but leaves issue surviving me, such issue shall take the share such deceased child would have taken if living, by right of representation.

5.   MISCELLANEOUS FORMS

5.1   Power of Attorney Dealing with Retirement Benefits

This clause could be added to the client's power of attorney or set up as a separate power of attorney just dealing with benefits:

> My Agent shall have the power to establish one or more "individual retirement accounts" or other retirement plans or arrangements in my name.
>
> In connection with any pension, profit sharing or stock bonus plan, individual retirement arrangement, Roth IRA, § 403(b) annuity or account, § 457 plan, or any other retirement plan, arrangement or annuity in which I am a participant or of which I am a beneficiary (whether established by my Agent or otherwise) (each of which is hereinafter referred to as "such Plan"), my Agent shall have the following powers, in addition to all other applicable powers granted by

this instrument:

     1.   To make contributions (including "rollover" contributions) or cause contributions to be made to such Plan with my funds or otherwise on my behalf.

     2.   To receive and endorse checks or other distributions to me from such Plan, or to arrange for the direct deposit of the same in any account in my name or in the name of [name of client's trust].

     3.   To elect a form of payment of benefits from such Plan, to withdraw benefits from such Plan, to make contributions to such Plan and to make, exercise, waive or consent to any and all elections and/or options that I may have regarding the contributions to, investments or administration, of, or distribution or form of benefits under, such Plan.

     4.   To designate one or more beneficiaries or contingent beneficiaries for any benefits payable under such Plan on account of my death, and to change any such prior designation of beneficiary made by me or by my Agent; provided, however, that my Agent shall have no power to designate my Agent directly or indirectly as a beneficiary or contingent beneficiary to receive a greater share or proportion of any such benefits than my Agent would have otherwise received unless such change is consented to by all other beneficiaries who would have received the benefits but for the proposed change. This limitation shall not apply to any designation of my Agent as beneficiary in a fiduciary capacity, with no beneficial interest.

5.2   Disclaimer of All Interests in an IRA

DISCLAIMER OF INDIVIDUAL RETIREMENT ACCOUNT

TO: [Name of IRA or Roth IRA Provider] and [Name(s) of deceased Participant's executor(s) or administrator(s)]

FROM: [Name of Beneficiary who is disclaiming]

RE: [Identify the IRA or Roth IRA being disclaimed; e.g., include account number and repeat name of the IRA provider firm]

IN THE NAME OF THE LATE: [Name of deceased Participant]

     I hereby unconditionally disclaim and refuse to accept any interest in the above-described individual retirement account left to me as beneficiary by the late [Name of deceased Participant]. This instrument is intended to be a "qualified disclaimer" within the meaning of § 2518 of the Internal Revenue Code. This instrument is intended to be effective as a disclaimer under the laws of the states of [Here insert name(s) of whichever state's (or states') law may apply; see ¶ 8.1.03]. I hereby certify that I have not accepted the interest hereby disclaimed or any benefits of such interest.

Signed this _____ day of _____, 20 ___.

_____

[Name of Beneficiary who is disclaiming]

[Include any formalities of execution, such as witnesses, notarization, etc. required by applicable state law or by the IRA provider.]

6. FORMS TO COMPLY WITH THE DOCUMENTATION REQUIREMENT OF IRS "TRUST RULES" WHEN TRUST IS NAMED AS BENEFICIARY OF RETIREMENT BENEFITS

6.1 Cover Letter: Post-Death Distributions: If Copy of Trust Is Given to the Plan

See ¶ 6.2.09. By the end of the year after the year of the death of Participant, the trustee of the trust that is named as beneficiary must send a copy of the trust (or the alternative "certification"; see Form 6.2) to the plan administrator. Although there is no requirement that any particular form accompany the copy of the trust, the following form can be used as a cover letter to accompany a copy of the trust sent to the plan administrator after the Participant's death:

To the Plan Administrator:
        Enclosed herewith is a copy of the actual trust document for the trust, of which the undersigned is the trustee, that is named as a beneficiary of [NAME OF DECEASED PARTICIPANT] under the [NAME OF RETIREMENT PLAN].

                        Signed:_____
                                Trustee

6.2   Certification Form: Post-Death Distributions: If Copy of Trust Is NOT Given to the Plan

See ¶ 6.2.09. By the end of the year after the year of the death of Participant, if the trustee does not send a copy of the trust itself to the plan administrator (see Form 6.1), the trustee of the trust that is named as beneficiary must send the plan administrator the following certification:

To the Plan Administrator:

The late [NAME OF DECEASED PARTICIPANT] named the [NAME OF TRUST] ("the Trust"), established under instrument of trust dated [DATE OF TRUST], of which the undersigned is the trustee, as beneficiary of his/her death benefits under the [NAME OF RETIREMENT PLAN] ("the Plan"). In accordance with Proposed Treasury Regulation § 1.401(a)(9)-4, A-6(b):

(i) I hereby certify that the following is a complete list of all beneficiaries of the Trust with respect to the trust's interest in the Plan (including contingent and remainderman beneficiaries, with a description of the conditions on their entitlement), as of the date hereof:

[The following is this author's interpretation of what the IRS is looking for when it requires "a complete list of all beneficiaries of the Trust"; this is not an official form. The following assumes a trust for the life benefit of Participant's spouse, with remainder to Participant's issue who are living at the death of the spouse; it assumes there are such issue living at Participant's death, and that no person has the power to vary the identity or relative shares of the beneficiaries.]

"Current beneficiary(ies): The participant's spouse, [NAME OF SPOUSE], who is entitled to all income of the trust for life, plus principal distributions if needed for medical expenses or support. If at any time during the spouse's life there is no child of the participant (and no issue of a deceased child of the participant) living, the trust terminates and is distributed to the spouse outright and free of trusts.

> **"Remainder beneficiary(ies)** (entitled to benefits upon the death of the participant's spouse, if they survive the spouse): The participant's children in equal shares, with issue of any deceased child to take the share such deceased child would have taken had he/she survived the participant's spouse; these beneficiaries take the trust property outright and free of trust on the death of the spouse. The names, addresses, Social Security numbers and dates of birth of the participant's currently living children are: [INSERT].
>
> **"Contingent beneficiary(ies)**: If at any time neither the participant's spouse nor any issue of the participant is living, and there is still money in this trust, the trust terminates and is distributed to the [NAME OF CONTINGENT BENEFICIARY].
>
> (ii) I certify that to the best of my knowledge: the above list is correct and complete; and that, within the meaning of P.R. § 1.401(a)(9)-4, A-5(b), paragraphs (b)(1), (2) and (3), the trust is valid under applicable state law, all beneficiaries of the trust are identifiable and the trust was irrevocable by its terms as of the participant's date of death.
>
> (iii) I agree to provide to you a copy of the Trust instrument upon demand.
>
> Signed:_____
>   Trustee

7.   TRUST PROVISIONS DEALING WITH BENEFITS

7.1   Administration During Donor's Life; Irrevocability

The purpose of including this language is to assure that the trust is a "grantor trust" as to the Participant and to make it clear to any plan administrator that the "Third rule" (irrevocability; ¶ 6.2.08) is complied with. This form is not suitable for a testamentary trust.

> ___. Administration During my Life

.01   The Trustee shall distribute to me such amounts of the principal or income of the trust (including all thereof) as I may request from time to time, or (if I am legally incapacitated) as my guardian, conservator or other legal representative may request on my behalf.

.02   I reserve the right to amend or revoke this trust by one or more written and acknowledged instruments delivered to the Trustee during my lifetime. This trust shall become irrevocable at my death.

7.2   Insulating Retirement Assets From Estate Claims

Notwithstanding any other provision hereof, except as provided in this paragraph, the Trustee may not, on or after December 31 of the year following the year of my death (the "Designation Date"), distribute to or for the benefit of my estate, any charity or any other non-individual beneficiary any Retirement Benefit payable to this trust under any qualified retirement plan, individual retirement account or other retirement arrangement subject to the "minimum distribution rules" of § 401(a)(9) of the Internal Revenue Code, or other comparable provisions of law. It is my intent that all such Retirement Benefits held by or payable to this trust on or after the Designation Date be distributed to or held for only individual beneficiaries, within the meaning of § 401(a)(9) and applicable regulations. Accordingly I direct that such benefits may not be used or applied on or after the Designation Date for payment of my debts, taxes expenses of administration or other claims against my estate; nor for payment of estate, inheritance or similar transfer taxes due on account of my death. This paragraph shall not apply to any bequest which is specifically directed to be funded with Retirement Benefits by other provisions of this instrument.

7.3   Excluding Older Adopted "Issue"

Notwithstanding any other provision hereof or of state law, the class of my (or any other person's) "issue" shall not include an individual who is my (or such person's) "issue" by virtue of legal adoption if such individual (i) was so adopted on or after December 31 of the year following the year of my death and (ii) is older than the oldest beneficiary of this trust who was a living member of said class

on said date.

7.4   Marital Deduction Savings Language

> If any marital trust created by this instrument becomes the beneficiary of death benefits under any "individual retirement account," "Roth IRA," "qualified retirement plan," or similar tax-deferred retirement arrangement or annuity (the "Plan") the Trustee must withdraw from the Marital Trust's share of the Plan, each year, at least whichever of the following amounts is the greater:
>
> A.   the net income of the Marital Trust's share of such Plan for such year; or
>
> B.   the "minimum distribution amount" which is required to be withdrawn from such share under § 401(a)(9) of the Internal Revenue Code or other applicable law.
>
> This paragraph shall not be deemed to limit the Trustee's power and right to withdraw from the Marital Trust's share of the Plan in any year more than the greatest of the said amounts.

7.5   Defining "Retirement Benefit"

The following definition is very broad and would encompass variable annuities and so-called "non-qualified" deferred compensation arrangements. It is not the only possible definition. If retirement benefits are a significant asset in your client's estate, review this definition to make sure that it includes all types of benefits your client has, and that it works properly with any other special provisions you intend to include to deal with the client's retirement benefits.

> In this instrument, the term "Retirement Benefit" means any benefit or amount that is owned by or payable to this trust under: an individual retirement account ("IRA") as defined in § 408; a Roth IRA as defined in § 408A; a "deemed" IRA or Roth IRA under § 408(q); an annuity or mutual fund custodial account under § 403(b); a pension, profit sharing, stock bonus or other retirement plan that is qualified under § 401(a); any other retirement plan or arrangement that is subject to the "minimum distribution rules" of § 401(a)(9), or equivalent rules under any other Code section; any annuity; or any plan or arrangement of deferred compensation for services. The plan, trust, account or

arrangement under which any Retirement Benefit is held for or payable to this trust is referred to as a "Retirement Plan."

7.6   Accounting for Retirement Benefits

.01   General Principles

This Article shall govern the Trustee's accounting for Retirement Benefits. In general, a Retirement Benefit shall be deemed an asset of the Trust, increases or decreases in its value shall be allocated to income or principal of the Trust as provided herein, and distributions from the Retirement Benefit shall be accounted for as provided herein.

.02   Certain Individual Account Plans.

With respect to a "self-directed" IRA or Roth IRA, or any other individual account Retirement Plan for which the Trustee receives such reporting of the investment activity in the Retirement Plan that the Trustee can readily determine the "income" and "principal" of the Trust's interest in the Retirement Plan in accordance with normal trust accounting principles, the Trustee shall account for the Trust's interest in the Plan as if the applicable Plan assets were owned by the Trust directly.

.03   Fixed Benefit Plans

With respect to any Retirement Benefit which consists of the right to receive one payment of a fixed amount on a certain date, or a series of fixed-amount payments on certain dates, the Trustee shall treat the inventory value of the Retirement Benefit as principal, and all subsequent increase in value shall be treated as income, accruing over the time between the date of the inventory value and the date of payment, at the rate of interest used to discount such payment to present value for purposes of determining its inventory value.

.04   All Other Plans

With respect to any other Retirement Benefit, the Trustee shall treat the inventory value of the Retirement Benefit as principal, and allocate any subsequent increases in value (or charge decreases in value) to income or principal in accordance with any reasonable method selected by the Trustee and consistently applied to the Trust's interest in such Plan, including:

1.   A method specified in any "Uniform Principal and Income Act" or other state law governing trust accounting for retirement benefits or deferred compensation.

2.   In the case of a plan similar to the type of plan specified in paragraph .02 (or .03) above, the method specified in said paragraph .02 (or .03) adapted as necessary.

3.   Any method used in the Internal Revenue Code or Treasury regulations to distinguish between "ordinary income" and "return of principal" (or corpus) with respect to similar assets.

.05   Treatment of Distributions from Plan

When a distribution is received from a Retirement Benefit, and, at the time of such distribution, under the foregoing rules, the Retirement Benefit is composed of both income and principal, such distributions shall be deemed withdrawn first from the income portion of the Retirement Benefit, until such income portion is exhausted, except to the extent the Trustee chooses to charge such distribution to the principal portion of the Retirement Benefit.

.06   Definition of Inventory Value

In the interpretation of this Article, the "inventory value" of a Retirement Benefit shall mean:

A.   In the case of a Retirement Benefit that becomes payable to (or is owned by) this trust as of the date of the donor's death, its "fair market value" determined in accordance with the rules applicable for valuing such interests for purposes of the federal estate tax (as in effect at the donor's death, or, if such tax does not then exist, as in effect on the date hereof). As is true under such rules, such value shall be determined without regard to any applicable restrictions that limit the ability to transfer such Retirement Benefit and without regard to the income taxability of future distributions from the Retirement Benefit; or,

B.   In the case of a Retirement Benefit that becomes payable to this trust as of a date after the date of the donor's death (for example, by transfer from another fiduciary), its "fair market value" shall be its value as of the donor's death determined as provided in the preceding subparagraph, adjusted as necessary for distributions, expenditures and receipts that occurred between the date of the donor's death and the date of transfer to this trust; or, if the trustee cannot determine its value in that manner, its "fair market value" shall be its value as of the date it becomes an asset of this trust, determined as provided in the preceding subparagraph, provided, in the case of a Retirement Benefit transferred to this Trust from another fiduciary (such as the donor's executor) accrued income so transferred shall be treated as income and shall not be included in "inventory value."

7.7 Establishing a "Conduit Trust" for One Beneficiary

From and after my death, this trust shall be held for the benefit of [Name of individual trust beneficiary] (hereinafter referred to as the "Beneficiary"). Each year, beginning with the year of my death, my Trustees shall withdraw from any Retirement Benefit the Minimum Required Distribution for such Retirement Benefit for such year, plus such additional amount or amounts as the Trustee deems advisable in its sole discretion. All amounts so withdrawn (net of expenses) shall be distributed to the Beneficiary, if the Beneficiary is then living. If the Beneficiary is then deceased, my Trustees shall instead distribute to [Name(s) of remainder beneficiary(ies)] the amount which would have been distributed to the Beneficiary had the Beneficiary been living.

The following definitions shall apply in administering this trust: The Minimum Required Distribution for any year shall be, for each Retirement Benefit, (1) the value of the Retirement Benefit determined as of the preceding year-end divided by (2) the Applicable Life Expectancy; or such greater amount (if any) as the Trustee shall be required to withdraw under the laws then applicable to this Trust to avoid penalty. The Applicable Life Expectancy means the life expectancy of the Beneficiary, determined in accordance with applicable Treasury regulations (or proposed regulations) under § 401(a)(9) of the Internal Revenue Code of 1986, as amended; provided, that the Minimum Required Distribution for the year of my death shall mean (a) the amount that I was required to take with respect to such Benefit during such year, minus (b) amounts actually distributed to me with respect to such Benefit during such year.

Appendix C

Trust Review Questionnaire

The purpose of this questionnaire is to help the attorney who is reviewing or drafting a trust agreement determine whether the trust complies with the "trust rules" of the IRS's proposed minimum distribution regulations § 1.401(a)(9)-0, *et seq.* (¶ 6.2, ¶ 6.3) so that the employee or plan owner ("Participant") who names such trust as beneficiary of his retirement benefits will be deemed to have a "designated beneficiary" (¶ 1.7) for purposes of post-death required distributions under § 401(a)(9). For explanation of these concepts (and for full explanation of matters described in summary fashion in the questionnaire) see Chapters 1 and 6.

Participant's surviving spouse is called "Spouse" in this questionnaire. To make the text easier to read, Participant is referred to as "he" and Spouse as "she"; the questionnaire applies identically to a female participant and her male spouse.

Section numbers refer to the Internal Revenue Code of 1986, unless preceded by "P.R.," in which case they refer to the IRS's proposed minimum distribution regulations.

See ¶ 6.2.05 regarding the date as of which these questions are applied.

Start at the beginning, with Question 1. Then follow to where your answer leads you. You will not be answering every question; answer only those which you are directed to answer by your answers to previous questions.

Eventually your answers will lead you either to a verdict, which is either ANSWER A, your trust "flunks"; ANSWER B or ANSWER E, your trust passes; or ANSWER C or ANSWER D, meaning there are reasons to believe, but no guarantee, that your trust passes; or into THE GRAY AREA, meaning there are reasons to believe that your trust flunks but it's not certain.

Note that you could come up with different answers for different retirement plans, if the trust contains different provisions for Participant's various retirement plans. For example, the trust might direct that Participant's profit sharing plan benefits, but not his IRA accounts, could be paid to non-individual trust beneficiaries; this would cause the trust to "flunk" the rules with regard to the profit sharing plan, but not with regard to the IRAs (see Question 5).

1.   Under the terms of the trust (or of Participant's beneficiary designation form), are the retirement benefits required to be paid only to one or more particular separate trust(s) or share(s) within the trust?

If yes, then the remaining questions should be answered ONLY with regard to the terms of the separate trust(s) or share(s) that could receive any part of the retirement benefits. Ignore provisions of any other trust(s) or share(s) that cannot possibly be funded with the benefits. Proceed to Question 2.

If no, then the remaining questions in the questionnaire should be answered with regard to all provisions of the trust. Proceed to Question 2.

Explanation: The regulations are concerned only with the provisions of the trust that affect the trust's interest in the retirement plan. ¶ 6.3.03. Provisions of the trust that can never apply to the retirement plan benefits can be ignored.

Examples:

1.   "Upon my death, if my spouse survives me, the trustee shall divide all property of the trust into two separate trusts, to be designated the Marital Trust and the Family Trust. Any retirement benefits that are payable to this trust shall be allocated exclusively to the Marital Trust. All other assets subject to this trust shall be divided between the Marital Trust and Family Trust pursuant to the following formula..." Because the retirement benefits are not allowed to pass to the Family Trust under this instrument, only the terms of the Marital Trust should be considered when answering the rest of the questions in this questionnaire. For example, the "oldest beneficiary of the trust" would mean the oldest person who could ever be a beneficiary of the Marital Trust. However, if the Marital Trust will be terminated on Spouse's death, and its assets will be added to the Family Trust at that time, all beneficiaries of both trusts need to be considered (unless the remainder beneficiary of the Marital Trust can be disregarded; see ¶ 6.3.04).

2.   "Upon my death, if my spouse survives me, the trustee shall

divide all property of the trust into two separate trusts, to be designated the Marital Trust and the Family Trust, pursuant to the following formula...." Because the retirement benefits could be allocated to either the Marital Trust or the Family Trust under this instrument, the terms of both trusts must be considered when answering the questions. For example, the "oldest beneficiary of the trust" would mean the oldest person who could ever be a beneficiary of either the Marital Trust or the Family Trust.

3. Trust terms are same as in "B," but prior to the Designation Date the Trustee irrevocably allocates all the retirement benefits to the Family Trust as permitted by the trust instrument. Only the terms of the Family Trust should be considered when answering the questions. For example, the "oldest beneficiary of the trust" would mean the oldest person who could ever be a beneficiary of the Family Trust.

2.   Will the trust be valid under applicable state law as of the Designation Date?

If yes, go to Question 3.
If no, go to ANSWER A.

Explanation: See ¶ 6.2.05 and ¶ 6.2.06.

3.   Is the trust irrevocable, or will it, by its terms, become irrevocable upon Participant's death?

If yes, go to Question 4.
If no, go to ANSWER A.

Explanation: ¶ 6.2.08.

4.   Did (or will) the trustee provide the required documentation to the plan administrator by the Designation Date?

If yes, go to Question 5.
If no, go to ANSWER A.

Explanation: ¶ 6.2.09.

5.   All individual beneficiaries, part 1: "The estate" as beneficiary of the trust: Does the trust contain a provision allowing or requiring the trustee to pay trust assets to Participant's estate (for example, to pay Participant's debts, administration expenses, funeral expenses, or estate taxes), and is it possible under the trust that, on or after the Designation Date, retirement benefits could be used by the trustee for these payments?

> If no, go to Question 6.
> If yes, go to THE GRAY AREA.

Explanation: All trust beneficiaries must be "individuals," and an estate is not an individual. ¶ 6.2.12.

Examples:

A.   The trust contains no provision permitting or requiring the trustee to make distributions to Participant's estate. The answer to Question 5 is "no."

B.   The trust contains a provision permitting or requiring the trustee to make distributions to Participant's estate, but the trust instrument says that retirement benefits may not be used for this purpose. The answer to Question 5 is "no."

C.   The trust contains a provision permitting or requiring the trustee to make distributions to Participant's estate. The trust instrument says that *IRA benefits* may not be used for this purpose, but benefits under *other types of retirement plans* may be used for this purpose. The answer to Question 5 is "no" with regard to any IRAs payable to the trust, but "yes" with regard to other retirement plans.

D.   The trust contains a provision permitting or requiring the trustee to make distributions to Participant's estate, but the trust instrument says that no such payments may be made on or after December 31 of the year after the year of Participant's death. The answer to Question 5 is "no."

E.   The trust contains a provision permitting or requiring the trustee to make distributions to Participant's estate, but the trust instrument says that retirement benefits may not be used for this purpose on or after December 31 of the year after the year of Participant's death. The answer to Question 5 is "no."

F.   The trust contains a provision permitting or requiring the trustee to make distributions to Participant's estate. The trust instrument does not prevent the trustee from using retirement benefits for this purpose on or after December 31 of the year after the year of Participant's death. The answer to Question 5 is "yes."

6.   All individual beneficiaries, part 2: Is all of the trust treated as a "grantor trust" with respect to an individual beneficiary under § 678(a)(1)?

If yes, go to Answer C.
If no, go to Question 7.

Explanation: Under § 678(a)(1) (part of the so-called "grantor trust rules" of the Code), a beneficiary who is a U.S. citizen or resident is treated for all purposes of the federal income tax as the "owner" of trust assets if such beneficiary has the sole unrestricted right to withdraw those assets from the trust. See ¶ 6.3.09.

Example of a "grantor trust" under § 678(a)(1):

"The trustee shall pay to my son such amounts of the income and principal of the trust (including all thereof) as my son shall request at any time and from time to time, and such additional amounts as the trustee deems advisable. On my son's death, the remaining principal shall be paid to his widow." The son, who is a U.S. citizen or resident, is treated as the owner of the principal and income of the trust under § 678(a)(1); the answer is "yes." Go to ANSWER C.

7.   All individual beneficiaries, part 3: Is the trust a "Conduit Trust" as to one or more individual beneficiaries?

If yes, go to Answer E.
If no, go to Question 8.

Explanation: Under a "conduit trust," the trustee is required to distribute out to the individual trust beneficiary (or beneficiaries) all distributions the trustee receives from the retirement plan. The trustee does not have the power to hold and retain inside the trust any plan distributions made during the lifetime of the beneficiary(ies). See ¶ 6.3.08.

Examples of Conduit Trusts:

1.   "With respect to any retirement plan payable to the trust, the trustee shall withdraw from such plan, in each year, the minimum required distribution under § 401(a)(9) for such year computed based on the life expectancy of my oldest grandchild who is living on the Designation Date, and immediately distribute such amount in equal shares per capita to my grandchildren living at the time of such distribution. If all my grandchildren die before the trust has been entirely distributed, the trust shall terminate and all property shall be distributed to the Berkshire-Taconic Community Foundation." The answer is "yes." The trust is a Conduit Trust as to the grandchildren. Go to ANSWER E.

2.   "With respect to any IRA or other retirement plan or arrangement payable to the trust, the trustee shall withdraw from such plan, in each year, and forthwith distribute to my spouse, the income of such plan for such year, or the minimum required distribution for such plan for such year under § 401(a)(9) (computed based on the life expectancy of my spouse), whichever amount is the greater; and such additional amount or amounts as the Trustee deems advisable." All plan distributions during Spouse's life are paid to Spouse outright, so this is a Conduit Trust as to Spouse. The answer is "yes." Go to ANSWER E.

8.   All individual beneficiaries, part 4: Under the trust terms, will the retirement benefits (and all proceeds thereof, i.e., amounts distributed from the plan and reinvested by the trustee) be distributed only to individuals *regardless* of who dies when?

> If yes, go to Question 10.
> If no, go to Question 9.

Explanation: Under the proposed minimum distribution regulations, the only trust (other than a "conduit trust"; see Question 5) that DEFINITELY passes the all-beneficiaries-must-be-individuals test is a trust under which the benefits must be distributed to individual beneficiaries in all events, i.e., regardless of whether any beneficiary lives to his or her IRS-defined life expectancy. See P.R. § 1.401(a)(9)-5, A-7(c)(3), Ex. 2 and ¶ 6.3.07.

Examples:

A. "The trust shall pay income to my spouse Ivan for life. At his death, the principal shall be paid in equal shares to such of our three children, Winken, Blinken and Nod, as are then living, or all to the survivor or survivors of them; provided that if any of them is not then living, but has left issue then living, such issue shall take the share such deceased child would have taken if living, by right of representation. If at any time during Ivan's lifetime none of our said three children is living, and no issue of any of them is living, the trust shall terminate and all property shall be distributed outright to Ivan." Under this trust, the benefits must pass to individual beneficiaries (either Ivan or one or more of the children or issue of the children) regardless of the order of deaths. This trust indisputably PASSES the all-beneficiaries-must-be-individuals test, so the answer to Question 8 is "yes."

B. "The trust shall pay income to my spouse Ivan for life. At his death, the principal shall be paid in equal shares to such of our three children, Winken, Blinken and Nod, as are then living, or all to the survivor or survivors of them; provided that if any of them is not then living, but has left issue then living, such issue shall take the share such deceased child would have taken if living, by right of representation. If none of our said three children nor any issue of theirs is then living, the principal shall be distributed to my favorite charity, the Northeast Animal

Shelter." Under this trust, the benefits will not pass to individual beneficiaries *if* all the children and their issue predecease Ivan. No matter how actuarially unlikely that event is, under the wording of the proposed minimum distribution regulations it is not *certain* (though it is probable; see explanations at Question 9 and ANSWER C) that this trust passes the all-beneficiaries-must-be-individuals test, so the answer to Question 8 is "No."

9.　　　　All individual beneficiaries, part 5: If all present and potential future individual beneficiaries of the trust who are living on the Designation Date live exactly as long as their predicted life expectancy (under IRS tables), will the trust assets *necessarily* be distributed entirely to individuals?

If definitely yes, go to Question 12.

If probably yes depending on the future fertility of the said individuals, go to THE GRAY AREA. If the answer is "No, but" the trust will stay in the family as long as there is a family (i.e., no non-individual beneficiaries unless there is a failure of issue) go to THE GRAY AREA.

Otherwise (i.e. "No"), go to Answer A.

Explanation: An essential element of complying with the trust rules is that all trust beneficiaries must be individuals. P.R. § 1.401(a)(9)-4, A-5(a). For this purpose both income and remainder beneficiaries count as "trust beneficiaries" (except in the case of a "conduit trust"—see Question 7). However, a contingent remainder beneficiary does not count (i.e. is disregarded) if he, she or it will receive a share of the benefits only if the prior (individual) beneficiaries die before their share of the plan benefits "has been distributed by the plan." P.R. § 1.401(a)(9)-5, A-7(c)(1).

Unfortunately, the meaning of this provision of the proposed regulations is subject to substantial doubt. See ¶ 6.3.10 for further explanation.

Examples:

1.　　　　"Income to my husband for his life, remainder to my issue, or, in default of issue, to charity," and Participant has issue living on the Designation Date who are younger than the husband. If those issue and the husband live exactly to their IRS-defined life expectancies, the trust will definitely be paid to individuals, so the answer is "yes"; proceed to Question 12.

2. "The Trustee shall withdraw from the Retirement Plan, each year, the Minimum Required Distribution computed based on the life expectancy of my son Bobby as 'designated beneficiary,' and such additional amounts as the Trustee deems advisable in its discretion. The Trustee shall pay to Bobby or apply for his benefit such amounts of the income and principal of the trust as the Trustee deems advisable in its discretion. When Bobby attains the age of 25 years (or upon his earlier death) the Trustee shall terminate the trust and distribute to Bobby (if he is then living, otherwise to the XYZ Charitable Foundation) outright and free of trust, all of the then undistributed income and all of the principal of the trust, including the Retirement Plan (as it may then exist) and all distributions from or other proceeds of the Retirement plan then held by the Trustee." If Bobby lives to his life expectancy, an individual (Bobby) will get all the trust assets, so the answer is "yes." The charity will get money only if the individual beneficiary dies before his life expectancy. Proceed to Question 12.

3. "Income to my wife, plus principal as needed for her health and support [or in the discretion of the trustee]; remainder to charity." Even if wife (the only individual beneficiary) lives to her life expectancy, she is not *guaranteed* to get all the trust property, so the non-individual beneficiary must be counted, and the answer is "no." The fact that the trustee MIGHT distribute all the principal to wife (because she needs it for her health or support) (or in the exercise of the trustee's discretion) makes no difference. Go to ANSWER A.

4. "Income to my issue per stirpes until 21 years after the death of my last descendant who is living at my death, then distribute the principal to my issue per stirpes, or, in default of issue, to charity." Because this trust extends beyond the life expectancy of all individuals who are living on the Designation Date, you

cannot demonstrate that the trust property must be distributed to individuals, even if all the individuals who are living on the Designation Date live to life expectancy. The ultimate distribution is *intended* to be to individuals (Participant's issue living at termination of the trust), but whether there will be any such issue living depends on the future fertility of the issue who are now living (not a contingency the proposed regulations state that you may ignore). Go to the GRAY AREA.

10.   Is it possible to identify with certainty the oldest individual who could ever possibly be a beneficiary of this trust?

If yes, go to Question 11.
If no, go to ANSWER A.

Explanation: Since minimum required distributions are paid out to a trust based on the life expectancy of the oldest trust beneficiary, you must be able to identify the oldest trust beneficiary with certainty on the Designation Date. P.R. § 1.401(a)(9)-4, A-5(b)(3), A-1; ¶ 6.2.07. If the trust is not a "Grantor Trust" or "Conduit Trust" (see Questions 6 and 7), all potential remainder beneficiaries must be considered in applying this test.

Examples:

A.   "Income to my husband for life, remainder to my issue surviving my husband and me, or, if none of our issue is then living, the trust shall terminate and be distributed to the Institute for Justice." New beneficiaries can come in after Participant's death, during period of husband's survivorship interest—for example, a child could die and be replaced by his or her own children in the class of "issue"—but such new beneficiaries must necessarily be *younger* than the existing beneficiaries (unless the trust would recognize the legal adoption of an older individual by a younger individual). So the answer is " yes"; it IS possible to identify with certainty the oldest beneficiary (husband). Proceed to Question 11.

B.   "The trustee shall pay all income of the trust to Husband for life. At Husband's death, the principal shall be distributed to such person or persons among the class consisting of our children and their spouses as Husband shall appoint by his last will. In default of such appointment, the principal shall be distributed to our issue then living by right of representation." Because any of the donor's children could, after the Designation Date, marry someone older than the donor's oldest child (and older than the oldest person who was a spouse of any of the children on the Designation Date), it is not possible, as of the Designation Date, to identify the oldest beneficiary of the trust. So the answer is "no." Go to ANSWER A.

11.   Does any person have a power of appointment over the benefits that could be exercised on or after the Designation Date?

If no, go to ANSWER B.

If yes, but such power is limited to a small, clearly-defined group of "identifiable" individuals, and does not include the power to appoint in further trust, go to ANSWER B.

If yes, but such power is limited to a small, clearly-defined group of "identifiable" individuals, and the power requires that the property must be appointed to them either outright or to a trust for their benefit that complies with the minimum distribution trust rules, go to ANSWER B.

Otherwise, go to THE GRAY AREA.

Explanation: P.R. § 1.401(a)(9)-5, A-7(d) provides that no person shall have the power to change the beneficiaries of the employee after the Designation Date. The IRS has never given an example of a forbidden power under this rule. See ¶ 6.2.13.

Examples:

A.   "Income to my husband for life, remainder to my issue surviving my husband and me, or, if all of our issue die prior to my husband's death, the trust shall terminate and be distributed outright to my husband." Definitely "no"; no person has any power of appointment in this example. Go to ANSWER B.

B.   "The trustee shall pay income to my spouse for life. Upon my spouse's death, the principal shall be paid to such persons among the class consisting of our issue as my spouse shall appoint by her will; provided that if all of our issue predecease my spouse, the trust shall terminate and be distributed outright to my spouse. Notwithstanding any contrary provision of state law, property may not be appointed in further trust under this power, but only outright." This is a "yes, but;" *yes*, there is a power of appointment, *but* such power is limited to a small, clearly-defined group of "identifiable" younger individuals (i.e., the donor's issue), with no power to appoint in further trust, so go to ANSWER B.

C. "The trustee shall pay income to my spouse for life, and on my spouse's death shall distribute the principal to such individuals born after my spouse as my spouse shall appoint by his last will; provided that if at any time there is no individual living in the entire world who was born after my spouse, the trust shall terminate and be distributed outright to my spouse." Although the power of appointment is limited to individual appointees who are younger than the spouse, the group of potential appointees is not small or narrowly defined. Go to THE GRAY AREA.

12.   Is it possible to identify with certainty the oldest individual who could ever possibly be a beneficiary of this trust?

If "definitely yes," go to Question 13.
If one or more older beneficiaries could be added later, *but* any such future-older-added-beneficiary could share in the trust ONLY if a prior, identifiable, individual beneficiary who is living on the Designation Date dies before his or her life expectancy, go to Question 13.
Otherwise (i.e., one or more older beneficiaries could be added later, and you cannot prove that any such future-older-added beneficiary could share in the trust ONLY if a prior, identifiable, individual beneficiary who is living on the Designation Date dies before his or her life expectancy), go to ANSWER A.

Explanation: Since minimum required distributions are paid out to a trust based on the life expectancy of the oldest trust beneficiary, you must be able to identify the oldest trust beneficiary with certainty on the Designation Date. P.R. § 1.401(a)(9)-4, A-5(b)(3), A-1. If the trust is not a " Grantor Trust" or "Conduit Trust" (see Questions 6 and 7), all potential remainder beneficiaries must be considered in applying this test, with one *probable* exception: a remainder beneficiary who will take only if a prior beneficiary dies before his or her life expectancy can probably be disregarded. (See explanation of Question 9 regarding this point.)

Examples:

1.   "Income to my husband for life, remainder to my issue surviving my husband and me." New beneficiaries can come in after participant's death, during period of husband's survivorship interest—for example, a child could die and be replaced by his or her own children in the class of "issue"—but such new beneficiaries must necessarily be *younger* than the existing beneficiaries (unless the trust would recognize the legal adoption of an older individual). So the answer is "definitely yes"; it IS possible to identify with certainty the oldest beneficiary (husband). Go to Question 13.

2.   "The trustee shall pay all income of the trust to Husband for life. At Husband's death, the principal shall be distributed to such person or persons among the class consisting of our children and their spouses as Husband shall appoint by his last will. In default of such appointment, the principal shall be distributed to our issue then living by right of representation." Because any of the donor's children could, after the Designation Date, marry someone older than the donor's oldest child (and older than the oldest person who was a spouse of any of the children on the Designation Date), it is not possible, as of the Designation Date, to identify the oldest beneficiary of the trust. So the answer is "no." Go to ANSWER A.

13.   Does any person have a power of appointment over the benefits which could be exercised on or after the Designation Date?

If definitely no, go to ANSWER D.

If yes, but such power affects only a remainder interest that can be disregarded (see explanations at ANSWERS C and E), go to ANSWER D.

If yes, but such power is limited to a small, clearly-defined group of "identifiable" younger individuals, and does not include the power to appoint in further trust, go to ANSWER D.

If yes, but such power is limited to a small, clearly-defined group of "identifiable" younger individuals, and the power requires that the property must be appointed to them either outright or to a trust for their benefits that complies with the minimum distribution trust rules, go to ANSWER D.

Otherwise, go to THE GRAY AREA.

Explanation: P.R. § 1.401(a)(9)-5, A-7(d) provides that no person shall have the power to change the beneficiaries of the employee after the Designation Date. The IRS has never given an example of a forbidden power under this rule. See ¶ 6.2.13.

Examples:

1.   "The trustee shall pay income to my spouse for life, remainder to my issue." There is no power of appointment. Definitely no; go to ANSWER D.

2.   "The trustee shall pay income and principal to or for the benefit of my minor children as needed for their support, medical expenses, care and education. When I have no living child under the age of 18 years, the trustee shall distribute the remaining income and principal to my issue then living, by right of representation." Participant has selected the beneficiaries *and* dictated the basis on which distributions are to be made to them. So this is a "definite no"; go to ANSWER D.

3.   "The trustee shall pay income to my spouse for life. Upon my spouse's death, the principal shall be paid to such persons among the class consisting of our issue as my spouse shall appoint by her will. Notwithstanding any contrary provision of state law, property may not be appointed in further trust under this power, but only outright." This is a "yes, but;" *yes*, there is a power of appointment, *but* such power is limited to a small,

clearly-defined group of "identifiable" younger individuals (i.e., the donor's issue), with no power to appoint in further trust, so go to ANSWER D.

4.   "The trustee shall pay income and principal to such of my issue as my trustee chooses in its discretion." This is a "Yes, but;" yes, there is a power of appointment, but such power is limited to a small, clearly-defined group of "identifiable" younger individuals, so go to ANSWER D.

5.   "The trustee shall pay income to my spouse for life, and on my spouse's death shall distribute the principal to such individuals born after my spouse as my spouse shall appoint by his last will." Although the power of appointment is limited to individual appointees who are younger than the spouse, the group of potential appointees is not small or narrowly defined. Go to THE GRAY AREA.

THE GRAY AREA

These are unresolved questions regarding the IRS's treatment of retirement benefits payable to trusts. If your trust is in THE GRAY AREA, it cannot be given an automatic "clean bill of health" as is, but that does not necessarily mean you must go to ANSWER A because: in most of these matters the IRS has not spoken clearly; or, if the IRS has spoken clearly, the IRS might change its mind or be held wrong in court. For ways to fix the problem, see ¶ 10.2

Since you have come to THE GRAY AREA, it means your trust has a problem; before looking into ways to cure that problem, you might want to pretend you've fixed it, and go back to the question that derailed your trust and complete the rest of the questionnaire. This process would reveal if the trust has other problems. Some trusts have more than one problem.

Issues that land you in THE GRAY AREA are:

Question 5: See explanation and suggestions at ¶ 6.2.12.

Question 9: Trust does not clearly vest in individuals who are living on the Designation Date even if they live to their life

expectancy: If the trust will be paid to individuals only *if* individuals who are living on the Designation Date produce issue, but there are non-individual beneficiaries who will take in case of default of issue, it is not clear whether the trust passes the "all beneficiaries are individuals" test. The IRS simply has not clarified the boundaries of this rule.

Planning mode: Revise the trust so that benefits are guaranteed to be distributed to individuals during the life expectancy of individuals who are living on the Designation Date if they live to their normal life expectancy, or get a ruling before proceeding.

Cleanup mode: If you are confident that your trust is payable to designated beneficiaries based on a "reasonable interpretation of the statute and proposed regulations," you could answer "yes" (see ¶ 1.1.06) (consider applying for an IRS ruling to back you up); or capitulate and go to ANSWER A.

Questions 11 and 13: No one knows the extent to which a power of appointment might be considered "the discretion to change the beneficiaries of the employee" after the Designation Date in violation of P.R. § 1.401(a)(9)-5, A-7(d). See ¶ 6.2.13.

ANSWERS. When you arrive here, you have reached the end of the questionnaire. Your answer is:

ANSWER A: If you have been directed to "Answer A," bad news: this trust "flunks" the minimum distribution trust rules of the IRS's proposed regulations. For ways to fix the problem, see ¶ 10.2.

Since you have come to ANSWER A, it means your trust has a problem; before looking into ways to cure that problem, you might want to pretend you've fixed the problem, and go back to the question that derailed your trust and complete the rest of the questionnaire. This process would reveal if the trust has other problems. Some trusts have more than one problem.

If your trust cannot be fixed (see ¶ 10.2), here are the results of flunking the test: If Participant died before his RBD, then all benefits must be distributed by December 31 of the calendar year that contains the fifth anniversary of the date of death. ¶ 1.5.02. If Participant died on or after his RBD, all benefits must be distributed over the remaining years of Participant's single life expectancy. ¶ 1.5.03.

ANSWER B: Congratulations! Your trust passes the test. All benefits must be distributed to individual beneficiaries in all events. Remember, however, that if Participant has not yet died, any amendment of the trust will necessitate another pass through this questionnaire, and that continued qualification will depend on providing required documentation to the "plan administrator" by the Designation Date (see Question 4). Also remember that, if the Designation Date has not yet passed, changes (such as death of one or more individual trust beneficiaries) could occur that would cause the trust to flunk (¶ 1.8.08) or would cause the rules to apply differently. If you reached Answer B, you are entitled to answer the **BONUS QUESTION**, below.

ANSWER C: Congratulations, maybe; it appears probable that your grantor trust passes the test.

If an individual beneficiary is deemed the owner of all of the trust's assets under § 678(a), then the retirement benefits should be deemed paid to such individual beneficiary for purposes of the minimum distribution rules, and the "all beneficiaries must be individuals" test is met. Because § 678(a)(1) requires that the individual beneficiary of a § 678(a)(1) grantor trust, if he or she is a U.S. citizen or resident (§ 672(f)(1)), must be treated as if he or she owned all the trust's assets personally for income tax purposes, it would appear that the IRS is required to recognize the trust beneficiary as the "sole beneficiary" of the retirement benefits for purposes of the minimum distribution rules. However, note the following:

1.   Although the IRS has seemed to recognize the § 678(a)(1) effect in private letter rulings allowing surviving spouses to roll over benefits left to this type of trust, the IRS has never mentioned § 678(a)(1) either in the private letter rulings or in the proposed minimum distribution regulations.

2.   If a trust beneficiary is deemed to be the "owner" (i.e., to be the sole beneficiary) of a retirement plan by virtue of § 678(a)(1), but then later releases or transfers any of his or her rights in the trust or in the retirement benefits, the IRS would probably (correctly) treat the beneficiary as having transferred an inherited retirement plan. This would trigger immediate

realization of the underlying income under § 691(a)(2)—even though, under § 678(a)(2), that beneficiary might *still* be treated as the owner of the trust's assets for income tax purposes. Accordingly, in order to qualify for (*and retain*) the favorable aspects of § 678 treatment, it is essential that the beneficiary not release or transfer any of his or her rights under the trust (otherwise than by death). Also note: the effect of the beneficiary's ceasing to be a U.S. resident or citizen is beyond the scope of this discussion.

If you reached Answer C, you are entitled to move on to the **BONUS QUESTION**, below.

ANSWER D: Congratulations, maybe. Under your trust, although the retirement benefits are not guaranteed to be paid only to individuals *in all events*, the benefits will be paid only to individuals if the assumption is made that all beneficiaries who are living on the Designation Date will live exactly to their IRS-defined life expectancy and then die. While this is one interpretation of what the IRS means by "only individual beneficiaries," and many practitioners believe the IRS intends these trusts to qualify, unfortunately the proposed regulations do not have specific language supporting this interpretation. Your trust probably passes the test, but there is uncertainty due to a lack of IRS guidance.

ANSWER E: Congratulations! Your trust is a MRD Conduit Trust and therefore passes the test.

Because all amounts distributed from the plan to the trust during the conduit beneficiary's lifetime must be distributed by the trust to the beneficiary, you are entitled to disregard remainder beneficiaries of the trust. ¶ 6.3.08. With a "conduit trust," the retirement benefits are deemed paid to the individual beneficiary of the trust for purposes of the minimum distribution rules, and the "all beneficiaries must be individuals" test is met; remainder beneficiaries can be disregarded.

Remember, however, that if Participant has not yet died, any amendment of the trust will necessitate another pass through this questionnaire, and also that continued qualification will depend on providing required documentation to the "plan administrator" by the Designation Date (see Question 4). Also remember that, if the

Designation Date has not yet passed, changes (such as death of one or more individual trust beneficiaries) could occur that would cause the trust to flunk (¶ 1.8.08) or would cause the rules to apply differently.

If you reached Answer E, and the sole "conduit beneficiary"of the trust is Participant's surviving spouse, you are entitled to answer "yes" to the **BONUS QUESTION**, below.

BONUS QUESTION. Is the surviving spouse the *sole* beneficiary of the trust?

If yes, then the special rules of § 401(a)(9)(B)(iii) and (iv) apply and the special method of computing the spouse's life expectancy applies. See ¶ 1.6 and ¶ 6.3.13.

If the answer is "no, these special rules do not apply.

Explanation: Yes: Spouse is the "sole beneficiary" of the trust if either: (a) she is treated as the sole owner of all of the trust's income and principal under § 678, which would be the case if she is a U.S. citizen or resident and has the unlimited right to withdraw all principal and income of the trust ("Grantor Trust") (see Question 6 and Answer C); or (b) distributions will be made from the plan to the trust over a period not exceeding Spouse's life expectancy *and* all distributions made from the plan during her life will be distributed outright to her from the trust ("Conduit Trust") (see Question 7 and ANSWER E).

No: If there are other beneficiaries of the trust who may receive distributions from the trust during Spouse's lifetime, the answer is "no." Similarly, if any funds distributed from the plan during Spouse's lifetime could be held in the trust for distribution to other beneficiaries after Spouse's death, the answer is "no."

Appendix D

Resources

This Appendix lists software, newsletters and other resources available to help professionals in planning for their clients' retirement plan benefits. For *books*, see the Bibliography. Because prices, ordering information and features change constantly, check with the vendor before placing an order.

Software

There are several software programs designed to assist professionals in evaluating retirement distribution options. The easiest way to compare is to visit the providers' websites, where most offer a downloadable demo. In alphabetical order:

Brentmark Pension & Roth IRA Analyzer (v. 6.10-6.11). $449. Includes 6 months' free maintenance; $129 annual update fee. This is probably the most powerful and feature-filled software available to help planners analyze proposed plan distribution strategies from QRPs, IRAs and Roth IRAs (comparing up to 4 scenarios simultaneously), including income tax, estate tax and spousal rollover aspects, and determine whether it is worthwhile to convert a traditional IRA to a Roth IRA, as well as making numerous other useful determinations regarding retirement plan distributions, such as pre-59½ distributions, impact of life insurance and annual gifting. While easy to use right out of the box, it would be best used by a sophisticated planner with training to understand the impact that changing assumptions has on outcome. I use Brentmark's "mini" program, Pension Distributions Calculator, for quick minimum distribution projections. Brentmark Software, Inc., 3505 Lake Lynda Drive #212, Orlando FL 32817-8327; 1-800-879-6665 or 407-679-6555; www.brentmark.com.

DistribuGuide. Developed by Natalie B. Choate, Esq., Michael Jones, CPA and Jonathan G. Blattmachr, Esq., this software tells you what minimum distributions are required from a decedent's retirement plan, and what options the beneficiaries have, under both the old and the new minimum distribution regulations. For details, visit www.ataxplan.com.

MRD-Determinator. This product of the outstanding brain of Guerdon Ely, the financial planner and math whiz, is designed to do all MRD calculations as well as projections comparing possible distribution scenarios. MRD-Determinator would provide more help than other programs in understanding the rules applicable in a particular case and is geared toward compliance and investment advice. $395, includes one-year support; $235 annual fee after that. Net Worth Strategies, 960 SW Disk Drive Suite B, Bend, OR 97702, (541) 383-3899, www.NetWorthStrategies.com or www.MRD-Determinator.com.

Numbercruncher 2001-11. $395 plus shipping (annual updates $99). This is not primarily a retirement distributions analysis product, but it does pre-59½ distribution calculations (Chapter 9). The program is fast and easy to use, like all Numbercruncher features. The printout shows the assumptions used in making the calculations, which is extremely helpful. Numbercruncher also does 51 other estate planning calculations. Indispensable tool for estate planners. Leimberg & LeClair Inc., PO Box 1332, Bryn Mawr, PA 19010, (610) 527-5216. Order at www.leimberg.com ("Estate Planning Software").

TigerTables. $199. An excellent, easy-to-use and inexpensive source of estate planning computations such as QPRT, CRUT, GRAT, etc. Developed by estate planning expert Larry Katzenstein, Esq., who says the IRS estate audit staff use this product. Tiger Tables Software 4529 Pershing Place, St. Louis, MO 63108. Visit www.tigertables.com (also find there the § 7520 rates updated monthly).

Newsletters and Other Resources

Ed Slotts IRA Advisor. When it comes to IRAs, Ed Slott, CPA, is smart, caring and knowledgeable. He also writes beautifully. Each month has in-depth discussion of practical retirement tax info by the most knowledgeable practitioners. Twelve 8-page issues per year sent by regular mail, $79.95. 800-663-1340 or subscribe (and find lots of other useful info) at www.irahelp.com.

Choate's Notes, by Natalie B. Choate. Published irregularly, free for now, sent by regular mail to customers of Ataxplan Publications and to professionals who request it by handing in business card at a Natalie Choate seminar (or sign up at www.ataxplan.com). Each issue contains a short article on some aspect of planning for retirement benefits, plus other info of interest to estate planning professionals.

Steve Leimberg's Employee Benefits and Retirement Planning. E-mail-only. Commentary and analysis of breaking news as it happens, such as new private letter rulings, cases, and legislation. Written by Bob Keebler, CPA, Noel Ice, Esq., Barry Picker, CPA, and other IRA gurus, edited by the incomparable Steve Leimberg. Includes "LawThreads," which summarizes recent exchanges on estate planning topics from various professional listservs; and 24-hr access to extensive database. Only $14.95 per month, it is indispensable. Sign on one-time free or subscribe at www.leimbergservices.com.

Laminated card, 9" X 11.5", with color charts summarizing the NEW minimum distribution rules: Lifetime distributions on one side, post-death on the other. $19.85 for one (includes shipping). For info, call 801-273-3310 or e-mail jackmcm@unidial.com

Barry Picker's Guide to Retirement Distribution Planning, by Barry Picker CPA/PFS, CFP. 40-pages. Clear, complete and accurate explanation of minimum distribution choices clients face. Includes checklist, worksheets and tables. Perfect to give to a client with substantial retirement assets. $24.95, plus $1.75 S&H (total $26.70); plus NY state & city tax if applicable. Call 718-934-4300 or order on line at www.BPickerCPA.com.

Who Should Be Beneficiary of Your IRA? A "turnkey" seminar for professionals to provide to clients and prospects. Schumacher Publishing, 800-728-2668. www.estateplanning.com.

For other "turnkey" seminar presentations, see www.power-presentations.net (Powerpoint seminars for professionals). Power Presentations, 8535 E. Hartford Dr. # 104, Scottsdale AZ 85255, (480) 325-8464.

Bibliography

Estate Planning is a magazine published by Warren Gorham & Lamont, 31 St. James Ave., Boston, MA 02116.

"TMP" refers to the "Tax Management Portfolio" series published by the Bureau of National Affairs, Inc., 1231 25th St., N.W., Washington, D.C. 20037. A publication date is not provided for books in this series because they are kept up to date by annual supplements.

"CCH" stands for Commerce Clearing House, Inc., 4025 W. Peterson Ave., Chicago, IL 60646-6085. www.cch.com or (800) 449-8114.

ACTEC Notes magazine is published by the American College of Trust and Estate Counsel, 3415 S. Sepulveda Boulevard Suite 330, Los Angeles, CA 90034, (310) 398-1888; www.actec.org.

References to "the old edition of this book" refer to *Life and Death Planning for Retirement Benefits* by Natalie B. Choate (Ataxplan Publications, 3d ed. 1999), which may be purchase for $39.95 plus shipping by calling 800-247-6553 (ask for the "1999 edition") or through the website www.ataxplan.com.

General note on sources: All statements in this book are based on the author's research using primary sources supplemented by secondary sources, with the exception of matters relating to the income tax treatment of trusts. Because the purpose of this book is only to highlight issues particularly involved when retirement plan benefits are paid to a trust, not to explain all the extremely complex rules of trust income taxation, I have relied on two secondary sources regarding this subject, namely, Blattmachr, J.G., and Michaelson, A.M., *Income Taxation of Estates and Trusts*, 14th Ed. (2000), (Practicing Law Institute Press, 810 Seventh Ave., New York, NY 10019) (cited as "*Blattmachr*") and Zaritsky, H. and Lane, N., *Federal Income Taxation of Estates and Trusts*, (third Edition, 2000; Warren, Gorham & Lamont) (cited as "*Zaritsky*"). I strongly recommend these books to those seeking information regarding the income taxation of trusts.

Information on topics not covered in this book: In addition to sources mentioned below under each particular Chapter (which may discuss topics related to, but not covered by, that Chapter), the following publications deal with topics related to the subject of, but not covered by, this book:

The best book for lawyers on tax-oriented estate planning is *Estate Planning Law and Taxation* (Fourth Edition, with 2001 Supplement) by Professor David Westfall and George P. Mair, Esq., published by Warren, Gorham & Lamont.

For discussion of retirement distribution choices when the prospective beneficiary needs to qualify for Medicaid, see "Retirement Plans: Naming a Beneficiary Who Is Receiving Public Assistance," by Richard A. Pagnano, Esq., <u>Oregon State Bar Estate Planning and Administration Section Newsletter, Vol XVII, No 3, July 2000</u>, PO Box 1689, Lake Oswego, OR 97035-0889.

For an excellent discussion of the status of retirement benefits as against claims of creditors, see Alson R. Martin, P.A., "Income and Estate Planning for Individuals with Qualified Retirement Plans and IRAs," in <u>How to Determine the Capital Necessary to Retire</u>, seminar materials published by ALI-ABA, 4025 Chestnut Street, Philadelphia, PA 19104-3099, 10/28/93, pages 116 to 122.

Introduction: Books and Other Resources on Retirement Plans and Estate Planning Generally

The best one-volume reference work for ERISA questions is *The Pension Answer Book,* by Stephen J. Krass, Esq. Mainly deals with "employer" issues such as the design, funding and qualification of retirement plans, but several chapters have material on distributions. Also covers prohibited transactions. A Panel Publication of Aspen Publishers, Inc., 7201 McKinney Circle, Frederick, MD 21704, (800) 638-8437; www.panelpublishers.com.

For 403(b) plans in general and TIAA-CREF plans in particular, the unsurpassed resource is *Understanding TIAA-CREF* (Oxford Univ. Press 2000; $27.50) by Irving S. Schloss, Esq., and Deborah V. Abildsoe.

Estate and Gift Tax Issues for Employee Benefit Plans, by Louis A. Mezzullo, Esq. (TMP 378) and *An Estate Planner's Guide to Qualified Retirement Plan Benefits* by the same author (American Bar Assoc., Section of Real Property, Probate and Trust Law, 1992) are excellent overviews of the subject. The former also covers subjects not covered in this book, including non-qualified deferred compensation plans, QDROs, and gift and estate tax issues.

For treatment of annuities, non-qualified plans, rollover details and many other distribution topics not covered in depth (or at all) in this book, I highly recommend CCH's *Retirement Benefits Tax Guide*, 2d ed. (in one volume) by Thomas F. Rutherford, J.D.

Chapter 1:   Minimum Distribution Rules

Practical Application of the Retirement Distribution Rules, by Seymour Goldberg, CPA, MBA, JD (IRG Publications, 2001) is the latest work from the MRD expert who started it all. $59 (includes shipping) plus NY state tax if applicable. (800) 808-0422.

Choate, N., "How to Create Separate Accounts Within a Single IRA for Purposes of the Minimum Distribution Rules," Trusts & Estates, Vol. 139, No. 9, page 38 (September 2000).

Chapter 2: Income Tax Matters

For more about IRD, see Alan S. Acker, *Income in Respect of a Decedent*, TMP 862.

For more discussion of lump sum distributions, see Frederick J. Benjamin, Jr., Esq., *Qualified Plans: Taxation of Distributions*, TMP 370-2d; *Taxation of Distributions from Qualified Plans*, by Diane Bennett *et al.*, Warren, Gorham & Lamont, ch. 5.1; and 2001 CCH *Standard Federal Tax Reporter,* ¶ 18,217A.082.

For more on what to do for clients who have company stock in their retirement plans, get the audiotape "Sophisticated Tax Planning Opportunities with Employer Securities Held Within Qualified Plans" (with written materials), by Robert Keebler CPA, $29.95 plus $4 shipping, plus WI tax if applicable; send check to Virchow Krause & Co., LLP, PO Box 11997, Green Bay, WI 54307-1997; call 920-490-5607 for further information.

Chapter 3: Marital Matters

For more information on spousal waivers under REA, see Lynn Wintriss, Esq. "Practice Tips: Waiver of Rights Under the Retirement Equity Act and Premarital Agreements," 19 ACTEC Notes, no. 2, Fall 1993.

"The 'Probate Law' of ERISA," by Mary Moers Wenig, Esq., in *Estate Planning Studies*, April 1996 issue (page 5), newsletter published for members of the bar by State Street Bank and Trust Company, 225 Franklin St., Boston MA 02101 (thoughtful and well written review of the background of REA and how it has been interpreted by the courts).

For more on community property issues regarding retirement benefits, see "Practicalities of Post-Mortem Distribution Planning for Community Property Retirement Benefits and IRAs—Trusts as Beneficiaries, Separate Shares and Aggregate Theory Agreements," by Edward V. Brennan, Esq., California Trusts and Estates Quarterly, Vol. 5, No. 4 (Winter 1999).

Chapter 4:   Retirement Benefits and the Non-Citizen Spouse

For requirements of the marital deduction when the surviving spouse is not a U.S. citizen, see CCH *Federal Estate and Gift Tax Reporter*, ¶ 7045 *et seq.*

Chapter 5:   Roth IRAs

Mervin M. Wilf, Esq., authored several articles regarding Roth IRAs in <u>Estate Planner's Alert</u> (newsletter published by Research Institute of America): "The Roth IRA: A New Estate Planning Opportunity,", October 1997, page 11; "Rith IRAs: Second Chance for Distribution Planning after Age 70½ (Nov. 1997, p. 9); "Roth IRA AGI Threshold: Per Spouse or Per Couple?" (Dec. 1997, p. 6); and "Roth IRA Rollover Amounts should be Limited" (Jan. 1998, p. 5). See also his "Innovative Estate Planning Strategies Using Roth IRAs," <u>Estate Planning</u> March/April 1998 (Vol. 25, No. 3) page 99.

Mervin M. Wilf, Esq., "Regs Ignore 'Repeal' of Incidental Death Benefit Rule for Roth IRAs," Pension & Benefits Week 10/5/98, p. 5.

Michael J. Jones, CPA, "Roth IRA Gifts May Terminate Income Tax Benefits," <u>Tax Notes</u>, 6/1/98, p. 1156,

For a discussion of the hidden pitfalls built into the assumptions used in financial and tax planning software, see *The Terrible Truth About Investing* by Bruce J. Temkin (Fairfield Press, 1998; 1-888-820-5958; $24.95 plus shipping), p. 223.

A thorough treatment of Roth IRAs in layman's language, complete with economic analysis and financial projections (both generally and to illustrate specific case studies) is the *Roth IRA Book: An Investor's Guide*, by Gobind Daryanani, Ph. D. (Digiqual Inc., Bernardsville, NJ, 1998; $34.95). Call toll-free 1 (877) Roth911, or visit <u>www.rothirabook.com.</u>

Another book with financial analysis of Roth IRAs is R.S. Keebler, CPA, MST, *A CPA's Guide to Making the Most of the New IRAs* (AICPA). Also visit <u>www.RothIRA.com</u> or read *Roth to Riches* by John D. Bledsoe (Legacy Press, $19.95).

Chapter 6:   Trusts as Beneficiaries of Retirement Benefits

For fiduciary income tax, see Blattmachr and Zaritsky books recommended at the beginning of the Bibliography, and *Preparing Fiduciary Income Tax Returns*, by Jeremiah W. Doyle IV, Esq., <u>et al.</u> MCLE, 10 Winter Place, Boston, MA 02108, 1997.

The problem of trust accounting for retirement benefits is the subject of "IRA Distributions to a Trust After the Death of the IRA Owner—Income or Principal?" by Jeremiah W. Doyle, Esq., Trusts & Estates, Vol. 139, No. 9, p. 38 (Sept. 2000).

Chapter 7:   Charitable Giving with Retirement Benefits

Books:

The Harvard Manual on Tax Aspects of Charitable Giving, by the late David M. Donaldson, Esq., Carolyn M. Osteen, Esq., et al.(8th edition, 1999) is a magnificent summary of sophisticated charitable giving techniques, replete with citations, written from the point of view of counsel for the charitable donee. The Harvard University Office of Planned Giving, Cambridge, MA 02138, 800-446-1277 (donation of $105, check only).

Conrad Teitell, Esq., is one of the country's top experts in the tax law of charitable giving, and fortunately for the rest of us he is also a prolific author and superb public speaker. For a complete catalogue of his books, newsletters and amazing seminars, call (800) 243-9122.

Articles and seminar outlines:

Blattmachr, J.G., "Income in Respect of a Decedent," 12 Probate Notes 47 (1986). This excellent article discusses numerous strategies for reducing taxes on retirement benefits and other IRD, including charitable dispositions.

Burke, F.M., "Why Not Allow Lifetime Charitable Assignments of Qualified Plans and IRAs?" Tax Notes 7/7/97.

Hicks, Z.M., "Charitable Remainder Trust may be more Advantageous than a Qualified Plan," Estate Planning (5-6/90, p. 158). This is not about estate planning for plan benefits, but rather about using a CRUT *instead of* a qualified plan as an accumulation/payout vehicle for retirement.

Hoyt, C.R., "How to Structure Charitable Bequests from a Donor's Retirement Plan Account"; seminar outline, 2000.

Mezzullo, L.A., "Using an IRA for Charitable Giving," March/April 1995 Probate & Property, the Journal of the ABA Section of Real Property, Probate and Trust Law, p. 41.

Mulcahy, T.W., "Is a Bequest of a Retirement Account to a Private Foundation Subject to Excise Tax?," Journal of Taxation, August 1996.

Newlin, Charles F., "Coping With the Complexity of Separate Shares Under the Final Regs.," Estate Planning, July 2000 (Vol. 27, No. 6, p. 243).

Shumaker, R.L., and Riley, M.G., "Strategies for Transferring Retirement Plan Death Benefits to Charity," 19 ACTEC Notes, no. 3, p. 162 (1993), and follow-up comments published in 20 ACTEC Notes, p. 22 (1994). Compares the economic effects of various ways of funding a $1 million charitable gift from a $4 million estate, including the use of retirement benefits.

Shumaker, R.L. (with Riley, M.G.), "Charitable Deduction Planning with Retirement Benefits and IRAs: What Can Be Done and How Do We Do It?," American Bar Association Section of Real Property, Probate and Trust Law meeting outline, Chicago, Illinois, August 1995.

Chapter 8:   Disclaimers; Life Insurance

See, generally, on disclaimers, the CCH *Federal Estate and Gift Tax Reporter;* or the RIA *Federal Tax Coordinator 2d;* or Mary Moers Wenig, Esq., *Disclaimers* (TMP 848).

For an excellent discussion of life insurance in the retirement plan, see Beverly R. Budin, Esq., *Life Insurance*, TMP 826.

Regarding "subtrusts," see: "The Qualified Plan as an Estate Planning Tool," by Andrew J. Fair, Esq., booklet distributed by Guardian Life Insurance Co. Of America, 201 Park Ave. South, New York, NY 10003; "Estate Tax on Life Insurance Held in Qualified Plans," by Mervin M. Wilf, Esq., in Retirement Plan Trio seminar 6/22/95, materials published by ALI-ABA, 4025 Chestnut St., Philadelphia, PA 19104-3099 (Publ. No. Q239); "IRS opens the way toward favorable estate and income tax treatment of plan distributions," by Kenneth C. Eliasberg, Esq., Estate Planning (7/83, p. 208); "Subtrusts and Reversionary Interests: A Review of Current Options," by I. Meyer Pincus, L.L.B., Journal of the American Society of CLU & ChFC (9/92, p. 64); "Excluding Qualified Plan Insured Incidental Death Benefits from the Participant's Gross Estate; Minority and Non-Stockholders," by Jonathan Davis, Esq., The Estates, Gifts and Trusts Journal (9-10/83, p.4); "Excluding Defined Benefit Plan Insured Death Benefits from the Gross Estate -- Sole and Majority Shareholders," by Jonathan Davis, Esq., Tax Management Compensation Planning Journal (5/84, p. 123).

Chapter 9:   Pre-Age 59½ Distributions

Toolson, Richard B., "Structuring Substantially Equal Payments to Avoid the Premature Withdrawal Penalty," Journal of Taxation, Nov 1990, page 276.

Glossary

This book assumes the reader is familiar with estate planning concepts and retirement plan terminology. This Glossary provides brief definitions of certain terms in these specialized fields to accommodate readers who do not have expertise in both fields. Terms that are an integral part of tax planning for retirement benefits (such as "rollover" and "IRD") are defined in the text dealing with that topic.

The Glossary is in two sections: the "Estate Planning Glossary" and the list of "Types of Retirement Plans."

Estate Planning Glossary

Credit shelter trust (sometimes also called "**Bypass Trust**"). The Code allows each person a tax credit which may be applied to gift or estate taxes otherwise due on transfers by that person. To the extent the credit is not used for lifetime transfers, it is available to shelter the person's estate from estate taxes. Because it may be applied to either gift or estate taxes, it is referred to as a "unified" credit.

The maximum credit allowed for deaths or gifts in 2002 is equal to the estate tax on a taxable estate of $1 million. Therefore, the effect of the credit is that each person can transfer up to $1 million free of gift or estate taxes to his children, or any other beneficiary who is not the person's spouse or a charity. (*Unlimited* amounts may be transferred tax-free to the spouse or charity.) The credit/exemption equivalent is scheduled to increase gradually over the years so that, for deaths in 2009 and later, the exemption is $3.5 million, leading to repeal of the estate tax altogether for deaths in 2010 (and reinstatement of the tax under the law as in effect in 2001, for deaths in 2011 and later).

Basic tax-oriented estate planning for a husband and wife involves making sure that each spouse takes full advantage of the federal estate tax exemption, most commonly by having the first spouse to die leave the exemption amount either to the children or grandchildren directly, or to a trust for their ultimate benefit. The surviving spouse may be a beneficiary of this trust, but does not have sufficient control over it to make it includible in his or her estate. Thus, this trust escapes estate tax at both deaths: it is not taxed in the first spouse's estate because it was sheltered by the decedent's unified credit; it is not taxed in the surviving spouse's estate because he or she does not own it. Because such a trust is "sheltered" by the first spouse's unified credit, this type of trust is called a "credit shelter trust." It is also called a "bypass trust" because it "bypasses" the surviving spouse's taxable estate and goes (eventually) to a younger generation tax-free.

Fractional bequest. A bequest or gift expressed as a fraction or percentage of a fund. A typical fractional bequest: "I bequeath my estate in equal shares to my children surviving me." A fractional bequest may be in the form of a formula, for example: "The Trustee shall pay to the Marital Trust a portion of the trust property determined by multiplying the value of the trust (as of my date of death) by a fraction, the numerator of which is the smallest amount necessary (if left to my spouse) to eliminate the estate tax on my estate, and the denominator of which is the total value of the trust." See forms in Appendix B for samples.

Generation Skipping Transfer (GST) Tax. The estate tax applies to all assets transferred by a decedent at death. The decedent's estate pays estate taxes, and then distributes whatever is left to the beneficiaries of the estate—typically the decedent's children. In the normal course of events, the children themselves die some decades later and the same assets are taxed *again* before being passed along to the children's own children.

To avoid having assets be subject to estate taxes in every generation, a grandparent might leave assets directly to grandchildren (to "skip" the estate taxes at the child's generation level), or to a trust which would benefit the children's generation for their lifetimes but not be included in the children's estates. Such "generation skipping trusts" are an important and valid way to reduce the estate tax burden on a family. The generation skipping transfer (GST) tax (Chapter 13 of the Internal Revenue Code) allows each person to transfer up to an exemption amount in the form of "generation skipping transfers," but imposes a tax, at a rate equal to the highest estate tax rate, on generation skipping transfers that exceed that limit. The amount of the exemption is $1,060,000 as of 2001. The exemption may increase through COLAs in 2002 and 2003; it is scheduled to increase in the years 2004-2009, leading to repeal of the GST tax in 2010 (and reinstatement in 2011 under EGTRRA's sunset provision).

Grantor Trust. Generally speaking, a trust is a separate taxpayer. It files its own tax returns and pays income tax on its income at special trust rates. (The only exception is that income distributed to the beneficiaries of the trust will normally be taxed at the beneficiary's rate rather than the trust's rate.)

However, in certain cases, the Code ignores the trust as a taxable entity and treats the income and deductions as belonging directly to the "grantor" (the person who contributed the money to the trust). The most common example is a "revocable living trust," under which the grantor can take the assets back any time he wants to. The Code ignores the trust during the grantor's life and treats its income and deductions as belonging directly to the grantor. There are many less obvious examples, and quite a number of complicated rules under §§ 671-677, under which part or all of a trust's income may be taxable directly to the grantor (or, under § 678, to the beneficiary). See ¶ 6.3.09. If a person is treated as the owner of all of a trust's assets under these rules, transactions between the trust and the deemed owner are ignored for tax purposes because in effect they are regarded as "one taxpayer."

Pecuniary bequest. A bequest or gift of a specific sum of money, for example: "I bequeath $10,000 to my son." A pecuniary gift may be in the form of a formula which produces a specific dollar amount, such as: "The Trustee shall pay to the Marital Trust an amount of money or other property equal in value to the smallest amount necessary, if taken as a marital deduction, to eliminate the federal estate tax on my estate." This is in contrast to a fractional bequest (*q.v.*).

Power of appointment. A power given by one person (the original transferor) to another person (the power holder) to decide who will receive property. Example: A trust which provides that Wife will receive the income of the trust during her life, and at her death the principal will be distributed among Husband's issue "as Wife shall appoint by her will." Wife has a power of appointment over the principal. In this book, "power of appointment" refers to a power exercisable by a beneficiary (*i.e.*, in a non-fiduciary capacity). See also "spray power."

Specific bequest. A bequest of a specific item of property, for example "I leave my Honda Civic automobile to my father" or "I give and bequeath to my spouse any retirement benefits payable to my estate."

Spray power. This is not an official term, but is used to describe a trustee's power to "spray" (or "sprinkle") income and/or principal of a trust among a class of beneficiaries. Example: "The Trustee shall pay the income and principal of the trust to my children for their health, education and welfare, in such amounts and proportions as the Trustee deems advisable." This is a type of "power of appointment."

Types of Retirement Plans

This section explains the different types of retirement plans discussed in this book.

What's most confusing about the various types of plans is that there is not one set of mutually exclusive categories; there are different overlapping classifications for different purposes. For example, "qualified retirement plans" are divided into two types (defined benefit and defined contribution) for purposes of the limits (under § 415) on what may be contributed or accrued for a Participant, but into three types (pension, profit sharing and stock bonus plans) for purposes of plan aggregation under § 402 (definition of lump sum distribution). Profit sharing and stock bonus plans must be defined contribution plans, but a pension plan may be either a Defined Contribution Plan or a Defined Benefit Plan. An ESOP can be either a profit sharing plan or a stock bonus plan; a Keogh plan can be any type of Qualified Retirement Plan other than a stock bonus plan or ESOP.

In general, the types of retirement plans this book deals with share the following universal characteristics:

1.   Each is a formal arrangement for accumulating capital for the primary purpose of financing the owner's retirement.

2.   The arrangement is funded with contributions from the owner's earnings (or from the owner's spouse's earnings), or with contributions made directly by the owner's employer.

3.   Investment earnings accumulated "inside" the arrangement are not subject to income tax so long as they remain "inside" (unlike capital accumulated outside a retirement plan, the earnings on which are taxed as they are realized).

4.   In order to receive this special tax benefit, the arrangement must comply with an array of tax rules and other requirements.

5.   One set of tax rules that all these plans must comply with (with some slight variations) is the minimum distribution rules of § 401(a)(9) (Chapter 1).

Beyond those universal characteristics, however, retirement plans come in a variety of flavors. The commonly-encountered types of retirement plans covered by this book vary widely in terms of the rules to which each type is subject, such as limits on contributions, tax treatment of distributions, when distributions are permitted, spousal rights, the likely availability of different planning devices, grandfather rules, creditors' rights, and so on.

An in-depth discussion of the rules applicable to the different types of retirement plans is beyond the scope of this Glossary. The purpose of this Glossary is to explain the differences among the various types of plans only to the extent such differences are likely to have an impact on planning choices.

403(b) arrangements or plans. These retirement plans are available only to tax-exempt employers. These plans are similar to Qualified Retirement Plans (QRP) in that the employee is not taxed currently on the plan contributions or earnings, but is taxed only as distributions are made to him. One difference is that the plan assets will be solely in the name of the employee, like an IRA. Another difference is that 403(b) money can be invested in only two types of investments: annuity contracts purchased by the employer and issued in the name of the employee; and "regulated investment companies" (mutual funds) held by a bank (or other approved institution) as custodian for the employee.

The main differences between 403(b) plans (also sometimes called in this book "403(b) arrangements") and other plans from a tax planning perspective are that a 403(b) plan distribution is never eligible for treatment as a "lump sum distribution" under § 402 (¶ 2.3) and the minimum distribution rules apply slightly differently; see ¶ 8.5.03.

Defined Benefit Plan. Under a Defined Benefit Plan, also called a "defined benefit pension plan," the employer promises to pay the employee a specific pension, starting at retirement, and continuing for the employee's life. Social Security is an example of a "Defined Benefit Plan" (although private pension plans, unlike Social Security, are not permitted to have cost-of-living adjustments).

Typically, the amount of the pension is based on a formula, such as "a monthly pension for life, beginning at age 65, equal to 1/12th of 1% of final average compensation times years of service, reduced by 10% for each year of service less than 10 if the employee has less than 10 years of service, and up to an annual maximum of 40% of career average compensation." The formula may be extremely elaborate, partly (inevitably) because it must include the "415 limits" (the limits under § 415 on what may be accrued for an individual employee) but also because, for example:

A.   The formula may award different percentages of compensation for different years (e.g., "1% of compensation for years 1965-1970, .75% of compensation for years 1971-1985 "); such a formula usually reflects changes in the benefit formula over the years.

B.   The formula may award a lower percentage for compensation below the FICA wage base than for compensation in excess of the FICA wage base.

C.   The formula will contain adjustments for early or late retirement. For example, if the annual pension promised is

"25% of average compensation, beginning at age 65," but the plan permits early retirement at age 55, there will be a reduction in the percentage amount for each year prior to age 65 that the employee retires. The two pension amounts will nevertheless be "actuarially equivalent" because a lower rate paid for more years is equivalent in value to a higher rate paid for fewer years.

Once the formula is established and the plan adopted, the employer then hires an actuary, who tells the employer, each year, how much must be contributed to the plan to amortize the employer's future obligations to retiring employees under the plan (and to the beneficiaries of deceased employees). The actuary is essentially required to predict the future: how many employees will stick around long enough to actually collect the promised pension? Along the way, how many wage increases will these employees have, that will boost the employer's obligations under the pension plan? How long will the retired employees live (and have to be paid by the plan) after retirement? How much will the plan's investments earn?

The law specifies some of the assumptions, such as a maximum and minimum interest rate that the actuary is permitted to use. Also, even if the employer designs the plan so that it starts off with a huge unfunded liability for past service, the employer is not permitted to pay off the entire unfunded liability at once. However, the law requires the employer to fund the plan to a specified extent each year. As a result, the actuary must produce not one but two contribution amounts for the employer's consideration each year—the legally required minimum contribution and the legally permitted maximum contribution.

The employee is guaranteed to receive the stated pension; a federal agency (the Pension Benefit Guaranty Corporation) insures employee pensions under Defined Benefit Plans. Any investment risk falls on the employer (and investment profits benefit the employer). Thus if the plan's investments do well one year, the employee's projected pension does not increase (but the employer may get by with a smaller contribution). Likewise, if the plan's investments decline in value, the employer may have to contribute more money to shore up the plan, but the employee is protected.

Defined Benefit Plans generally are of greater value to older employees (older than approximately age 50) than to young employees, just because of the time value of money. Even if their eventual projected pensions are the same amount, say $36,000 per year starting at age 65, the value is greater to the employee who will be receiving that sooner. $36,000 a year starting in 10 years (how the pension looks to the 55 year-old employee) is a more significant asset than $36,000 a year starting in 30 years (how the pension looks to a 35 year-old employee). The older employee's pension looks more valuable to the employer too, who has to contribute more for the older employee than for the younger.

Defined benefits plans were once the normal form of retirement plan for American businesses. Their overall popularity has declined (especially among small businesses) due to increasingly complex tax rules applicable to these plans and due to the lower cost and more easily understandable appeal of Defined Contribution Plans. However, Defined Benefit Plans remain attractive to the one-person business as a way of maximizing tax-deductible retirement contributions. If the business owner/sole employee is over age 50, approximately, a Defined Benefit Plan will give him a larger annual tax-deductible contribution than the limit under a defined contribution plan.

From an *estate planning perspective*, the Defined Benefit Plan has the following distinctive features:

First, the employee does not have an "account" in a Defined Benefit Plan the way he does in a Defined Contribution Plan. The employee's benefit statement for the Defined Benefit Plan will typically say the employee's "accrued benefit" under the plan is (e.g.) "$1,450 a month," of which (say) "80% is vested." What this means is that the employer has already obligated itself to provide for this employee (if the employee *keeps on working* until retirement age) a pension of $1,450 per month for life starting at the employee's "normal retirement age" under the plan (usually, 65); and if the employee *quits right now*, he's vested in 80% of that, meaning that at normal retirement age he would receive 80% of $1,450 per month.

The benefit statement may or may not contain more details such as: how much of a pension the employee would receive if he retired early (if the plan offers "early retirement"); and (of great significance in estate planning), whether the employee will be permitted upon retirement to withdraw the lump sum equivalent of the accrued pension, or what death benefit, if any, would be available for the employee's beneficiaries, which brings us to the second significant factor in planning for defined benefit pension benefits: Planners should be prepared for the fact that some Defined Benefit Plans do not offer the option of taking a lump sum equivalent in cash (or that the client may have already chosen an annuity option and foreclosed his ability to take a lump sum equivalent). Thus there will not be the ability to "roll over" benefits from this plan to an IRA.

Also, some Defined Benefit Plans provide no benefits at all after the death of the employee (or after the deaths of the employee and surviving spouse). Defined Benefit Plans are targeted purely at financing *retirement*, and (by law) may offer death benefits only "incidentally." Some Defined Benefit Plans are structured so that, if an employee dies prematurely, the money that was set aside to fund that employee's pension goes back into the general fund to finance the benefits of other employees, rather than passing to the deceased employee's heirs. There is nothing illegal or immoral about this; a plan structured this way is able to offer better retirement benefits to all employees. The employer may have encouraged the employee to provide for his heirs in some other way (such as by providing group life insurance).

Other Defined Benefit Plans *do* permit the employee, upon retirement, to take his benefits out of the plan in the form of a lump sum in cash, the value of which is "actuarially equivalent" to the value of the employee's vested pension under the plan. However, planning is not necessarily any easier in this situation. The employee in this type of plan will have to choose between a life annuity and a one-time cash distribution. If the employee is married the complexity of the decision is compounded by the spouse's rights to a survivor annuity (see ¶ 3.4).

This decision involves certain hazards. For example, remember that what is guaranteed to the employee is the monthly pension stated in the plan, *not* the equivalent lump sum value. The equivalent lump sum value is determined by discounting the projected stream of future pension payments back to its present cash value based on a certain discount rate (the interest rate that plan investments are assumed to earn in the future). If interest rates are rising as the employee approaches his retirement, the lump sum value of the pension will decline commensurately. This process can be extremely upsetting to an individual who is facing retirement and closely counting his available funds, and then finds out on the day he retires that the lump sum he is getting from the pension plan is smaller than it would have been if he had retired six months earlier, due to an increase in interest rates in the meantime. Thus employees should not regard the lump sum equivalent of their defined benefit pension plans as an asset in hand until it actually is in hand.

Furthermore, the employee's life expectancy and that of his/her spouse should influence the decision. If the employee's health is very poor, a life annuity may be a poor choice. On the other hand, if health is better than average, the annuity options may be attractive, especially if the plan in effect subsidizes certain annuity options (such as the joint and survivor annuity with the spouse). If the benefits in the plan are substantial, an actuary should be consulted to help the employee evaluate the choices under the plan; this is not a job for the estate planner.

Key points for the estate planner: expect a benefit statement that discusses a pension payable at retirement, rather than a current value;

determine whether the plan offers any death benefit beyond the legally-required spousal annuity; and, as the client approaches retirement, consider hiring an actuary to assist in the evaluation of benefit alternatives.

Defined Contribution Plan. A Defined Contribution Plan is, along with the "Defined Benefit Plan," one of the two broad categories of Qualified Retirement Plan. Defined Contribution Plans are also called "individual account plans." § 414(i). Under a Defined Contribution Plan, the employer may commit to making a certain level of contribution to the plan (such as "10% of annual compensation," an example of a money purchase pension plan formula), or (under a profit sharing plan) may make such contributions periodically on a discretionary basis or based on profit levels. Profit sharing plans, money purchase pension plans, 401(k) plans, target benefit plans and ESOPs are examples of Defined Contribution Plans.

Once the employer has contributed to the Defined Contribution Plan, the contributions are allocated among "accounts" for the individual employees who are members of the plan. What the employee will eventually receive from the plan is determined by (a) how much is allocated to his account under the contribution formula and (b) what is the subsequent investment performance of that account. The employer does not guarantee any level of retirement benefits. If the plan's investments do well, the profits will increase the employee's account value. If the plan's investments do poorly, the employee will receive less at retirement.

If the plan is "self-directed," each participant makes the investment decisions for his or her own account in the plan, from a menu of alternatives permitted by the plan. The menu may be very broad or may be limited to a small number of mutual funds. If the plan is not self-directed, the investments are determined at the plan level by the trustee of the plan.

Key points for estate planners: Participant's retirement benefits will normally be in the form of a lump sum distribution of the account balance, which Participant can then roll over to an IRA, although certain defined contribution plans offer annuities or instalment payouts.

ESOP (Employee Stock Ownership Plan). An ESOP is a Qualified Retirement Plan primarily designed to invest in stock of the sponsoring employer. Over the years, trying to head off the workers' revolution predicted by Karl Marx, Congress has tried to encourage employee ownership of the means of production, and one of its enticements is the ESOP. ESOPs have various liberalized rules compared with other retirement plans, most of which are of interest only to the employer-sponsor and not to estate planners.

Key points for estate planners: Distributions of company stock to an employee from an ESOP or any other retirement plan are eligible for certain favorable tax treatments if various requirements are met. See ¶ 2.4. Thus, if a client has a retirement plan that holds employer stock, all options should be carefully considered before that stock is disposed of. However, an ESOP is not required to distribute actual stock to the employee. An ESOP is allowed to permit only cash distributions. Thus the fact that an employee has a retirement account with employer stock in it does not mean the employee is going to be eligible for the special treatment.

Individual Account Plan. A retirement plan in which individual accounts are maintained on the plan's books for plan participants, with the result that each participant obtains the profits (or bears the losses) of his own account. IRAs, Roth IRAs, SEP-IRAs and Defined Contribution Plans are individual account plans, but a Defined Benefit Plan is not.

Individual Retirement Account (or Individual Retirement Trust) (IRA). This subsection describes "traditional" IRAs. For Roth IRAs, see Chapter 5. An IRA is not a Qualified Retirement Plan under § 401(a). Rather, it is a private "individual" retirement account created under § 408. An IRA can be structured as a trust (§ 408(h)) or as a custodial account (§ 408(a)); the tax treatment is exactly the same. An IRA can be funded in any of the following ways:

1.   With tax-free "rollovers" from other types of plans (see ¶ 2.5).

2.   With annual (non-mandatory) contributions by a Participant who is younger than age 70, up to a maximum of (a) a specified dollar limit (see ¶ 5.3.02) or (b) the individual's compensation income for such year, whichever is less.

3.   By annual (non-mandatory) contributions by Participant's spouse from the contributing spouse's earnings, if the contributing spouse's earnings are greater than those of Participant spouse.

4.   By direct contributions by Participant's employer.

Key points for estate planners:

1.   Annual (as opposed to rollover) contributions may be made only in cash. § 408(a)(1).

2.   The trustee or custodian must be a bank (or other organization which has gone through the formal IRS procedure for recognition of its similarity to a bank and therefore its worthiness to serve as custodian or trustee of an IRA). § 408(a)(2).

3.   "No part of the [IRA's] funds will be invested in life insurance contracts." § 408(a)(3). See ¶ 8.4.05.

4.   The Code contains a provision permitting tax-free division of an IRA between spouses in case of divorce or legal separation. § 408(d)(6).

5.   An IRA is income tax-exempt, but will lose its exemption if Participant engages in a "prohibited transaction" (see § 4975) with his IRA, and be treated for income tax purposes as if it were entirely distributed on the first day of Participant's taxable year. § 408(e)(2).

6.   Although it is generally income tax-exempt (see preceding item), an IRA is subject to the income tax on unrelated business taxable income of § 511; as a result, generally, holding a margin account or other leveraged investment inside an IRA will result in income tax. § 408(e)(1).

7.   If an IRA is pledged by Participant as security for a loan, the entire account is treated as being distributed to Participant. § 408(e)(4).

8.   Similarly, if an IRA invests in "collectibles," the amount so invested is treated as having been distributed (in other word, it is currently taxed). § 408(m).

9.   § 408 "shall be applied without regard to any community property laws." § 408(g).

Keogh Plan. A "Keogh plan" (or "H.R. 10 Plan") is a qualified retirement plan that covers one or more self-employed individuals. Thus, a "Keogh plan" is Qualified Retirement Plan established by an unincorporated employer (partnership or sole proprietor) for the benefit of the partners and employees of the partnership, or for the benefit of the sole proprietor and his or her employees. Any type of Qualified Retirement Plan other than an ESOP may be a "Keogh plan."

While this term (which never appears in the Code) is still used by self-employed persons to describe their retirement plans, almost all of the once-significant distinctions between plans adopted by corporations and plans adopted by the self-employed were eliminated by the Tax Reform Acts of 1984 and 1986, and the Unemployment Compensation Amendments of 1992. To read about what the differences used to be, see Reg. § 1.401(e).

There are still some differences of interest to planners, however. This summary gives an overview; for the nuances and exceptions, see the cited Code sections. Note that some of the differences are applicable to all "Self-employed persons" while others apply only to the "Owner-employee."

Definitions: A "Self-employed person" is an individual who has self-employment income. § 401(c)(1). In contrast, a "common law employee" (or, as the Code calls it, "an individual who is an employee without regard to§ 401(c)(1)") is an employee of someone else (not himself). An "Owner-employee" is the sole proprietor of an unincorporated business, or a partner "who owns more than 10 percent of either the capital interest or the profits interest" in the partnership. § 401(c)(3). So, all Owner-employees are Self-employed persons, but not all Self-employed persons are Owner-employees.

This author has not found a clear rule as to *when* the 10% test (for determining Owner-employee status) is applied; do we test only at the end of the plan year? Or must we determine whether the individual owned more than 10% of the capital *at any time during* the year? And is the test applied yearly? Or is the individual considered *forever* an Owner-employee if he was *ever* an Owner-employee?

Lump sum distributions: A lump sum distribution (LSD) may qualify for special tax treatment. See ¶ 2.3, ¶ 2.4. A LSD is a distribution of Participant's entire account balance within one calendar year following the most recent "triggering event." "Triggering events" are: for EVERYBODY, turning age 59½ or dying; for Self-employed persons ONLY, becoming disabled; and for common law employees ONLY, separation from service. § 402(d)(4)(A).

Premature distributions: A distribution from an employer plan made to an employee "after separation from service after attainment of age 55" is exempt from the 10% "premature distributions" penalty (see Chapter 9). Although § 72(t) does not specifically exclude the Self-employed from using this exception, it is not clear what would constitute "separation from service" for a sole proprietor.

Premature distributions, continued: In years after 1996, a person who has "received unemployment compensation for 12 consecutive weeks under any Federal or State unemployment compensation law" can take penalty-free distributions from his IRA to pay health insurance premiums. § 72(t)(2)(D). The IRS, in regulations, can permit Self-employed persons to use this exception. No such regulations have yet been issued.

Life insurance: Generally, if a Qualified Retirement Plan maintains a life insurance policy on the life of Participant, Participant must include the cost of the current insurance protection in his income each year; see ¶ 8.3.01. Unlike other Participants, however, an Owner-employee does not get to treat the accumulated cost (that he has paid tax on) as an "investment in the contract" (basis) for income tax purposes. Reg. § 1.72-16(b)(4); ¶ 8.3.02.

Pension Plan. A Pension Plan is a type of Qualified Retirement Plan under which the employer is *obligated* to make annual contributions, or, as the Code puts it, it is a plan "subject to the funding standards of section 412." The required annual contribution may be determined by an actuarial formula based on the promised benefits (Defined Benefit Plan), or may be simply a percentage of employees' compensation each year (Money Purchase Pension Plan), or may be derived from an actuarial formula involving benefits that are projected but not guaranteed (Target Benefit Plan). A pension plan is contrasted with a Profit Sharing Plan or Stock Bonus Plan, under which the employer's contributions are discretionary or linked to profits.

Key points for estate planners:

1. A pension plan may not permit "in-service distributions" (distributions of benefits prior to Participant's death, disability or separation from service), unless Participant has met the requirements for "retirement" (typically a minimum age and number of years of service). Even though a pension plan MAY permit in-service distributions if the employee has met the requirements for retirement, however, many do not permit any distributions until actual retirement.

2. Because pension plans may not permit in-service distributions, they may be more reluctant to permit participants to borrow from the plan while still employed.

3. Pension plans must offer the qualified joint and survivor annuity as the normal form of retirement benefit for most married employees, and the qualified pre-retirement survivor annuity as the normal form of pre-retirement death benefit for

most married employees, and these forms cannot be altered without spousal consent; see ¶ 3.4.

4.   All pension plans are considered "one plan" for purposes of determining whether there has been a distribution, within one calendar year of the recipient, of the employee's entire balance in "the" plan under § 402(d) (lump sum distributions; ¶ 2.3.04), even if they are not the same type of pension plan (e.g. a Defined Benefit Plan and a money purchase plan).

Profit Sharing Plan. A Profit Sharing Plan is a type of Defined Contribution Plan ("individual account plan") under which the employer's contributions are either entirely discretionary or are fixed to a certain percentage of profits. Most 401(k) plans and some ESOPs are profit sharing plans. The key differences between profit sharing plans, on the one hand, and pension plans, on the other, are as follows:

1.   A profit sharing plan MAY (subject to certain limits) permit "in-service distributions," that is to say, distributions to Participant prior to his separation from service and prior to his meeting the plan's requirements for "retirement." The significance of this for estate planning is that profit sharing funds may be available for certain planning purposes (such as rolling over some of the funds to an IRA, to support a "series of substantially equal periodic payments" under § 72(t); ¶ 9.2), even while the employee is still employed. However, it should be noted that most profit sharing plans do *not* in fact permit in-service distributions. This may be due to a historical accident: at one time, plans were very strict about when distributions were permitted because of concern about "constructive receipt"—the doctrine under which an individual is taxed on income he has a right to receive whether or not he actually takes the income. Although amendments to § 402 have eliminated the need for concern about constructive receipt (see ¶ 2.1.01), by providing that retirement benefits generally are taxed only when actually distributed, most plans still provide that there are no distributions prior to retirement. Another possible reason employers keep this requirement is that they want to encourage (or force) employees to leave the money in the plan and not dissipate it prior to retirement.

2.   While the "incidental benefit rule" (¶ 8.3.02) imposes limits on how much life insurance a QRP may buy, this limit does not apply to funds that have been in a profit sharing plan for more

than two years. Thus, if Participant wants to buy life insurance, the profit sharing plan may be a possible source of funds. A profit sharing plan, of course, may choose not to permit the purchase of life insurance even when the law allows it.

3.   Generally loan provisions are more liberal under a profit sharing plan than under a pension plan.

4.   While pension plans are *always* subject to REA's QJSA and QPSA requirements, profit sharing plans can qualify for a limited exemption. See ¶ 3.4.03.

Qualified Retirement Plan. A "Qualified Retirement Plan" (QRP) means a retirement plan that meets the requirements of § 401(a) (i.e., is "qualified" under § 401(a)). Since § 401(a) has more than 30 separate requirements, some of which cross reference other lengthy Code sections, it is no mean feat to be qualified under § 401(a). Most of the requirements (such as the requirement that the plan not discriminate in favor of highly compensated employees; requirements specifying which employees must be covered and how quickly their benefits must vest; limits on contributions prior to the employer's bankruptcy) are of little concern to the estate planner who is helping an employee plan for the distribution of his or her benefits. However, it is helpful to be aware of certain § 401(a) concepts that create the landscape in which all Qualified Retirement Plans must function. For example:

A.   A QRP is established and maintained by the "sponsor" of the plan. Normally, the sponsor of the plan is the employer of the employees who are covered by the plan, but it could also be a labor union or an association of employers. The employer could be a sole proprietor or partnership, in which case the plan is not only a QRP it is a "Keogh plan."

B.   The assets of the QRP generally must be kept in a separate trust for the "exclusive benefit" of the employees and their beneficiaries.

C.   If all the rules are complied with (including the § 415 limits on how much may be *contributed* to the plan each year, and the separate limits in § 404 on how much of each year's contribution may be deducted for income tax purposes), the employer gets a tax deduction for its contributions to the plan. However, the employee does not have to include the plan benefits in his or her gross income until he or she receives a distribution from the plan (¶ 2.1.01).

D.   The plan must prohibit the assignment or alienation of benefits by the employee. § 401(a)(13)(A).

E.   The plan must contain provisions required by REA. ¶ 3.4.

F.   The plan must not discriminate in favor of highly compensated employees, but:

1.   Contributions or benefits that bear a uniform relation to compensation are not considered discriminatory, even though higher-paid employees thereby receive greater contributions or benefits.

2.   The plan is actually required to discriminate *against* highly compensated employees, since contributions are generally based on compensation but compensation in excess of $170,000 per year (as of 2001) doesn't "count."

3.   Also, some discrimination against lower-paid employees is permitted, in that an employer may choose to "take credit" for the Social Security taxes it pays for employees.

There are several types of Qualified Retirement Plans (QRPs). The differences among the various types matter a great deal to the *employer*, because of the limits on what may be contributed to each type of plan and other aspects of the *employer*'s obligations to the plan. The differences also have some effect on planning options primarily because of the different distribution options likely (or required) to be available under different plans and the different spousal rights in different types of plans (¶ 3.4). Also, the different types of plans matter for purposes of the definition of lump sum distribution (¶ 2.3), since all plans of the same "type" (pension, profit sharing or stock bonus) are considered "one plan" for purposes of determining whether the employee has received a distribution of his entire benefit under "the" plan in one calendar year.

There are two overarching categories of QRP, "Defined Benefit Plan" and "Defined Contribution Plan." The primary effect of this distinction under the Code is different limits on how much the employer may contribute to each type of plan (§ 415). The effect of the distinction on *estate planning* is indirect, in that the forms of benefit likely to be offered are different.

INDEX

ORDER FORM
Save your book! Photocopy this form....

FORMS ON DISK

Now, all the forms in *Life and Death Planning for Retirement Benefits* plus several more that didn't fit into the book, are available ready to plug into your word processor and use in your practice. All beneficiary designation and election forms and related trust provisions, plus a "plan termination assignment" and all four IRS model spousal consent forms are included, in 8.5" x 11" page size. Provided for your convenience to save typing, meant to be used in conjunction with the book, so no instructions are included. Format: WordPerfect 8.0 and Word 2000, 3.5" disk.

Price: $49.95 (includes shipping and handling). Please add $2.50 Mass. sales tax for Mass. delivery.

Yes, please send me "Forms on Disk." $ 49.95
For Mass. delivery, add $2.50 Mass. sales tax $_____

TOTAL $_____

Photocopy this order form, fill out the copy, and mail it to:
Ataxplan Publications
P.O. Box 1093-F
Boston, MA 02103-1093

Name: _____
Company name: _____
Address: _____
City: _____ State: _____ Zip: _____ - _____
Telephone: (___) _____

Payment:
□ Check
□ Credit card: □ Visa □ Mastercard
Card number: _____
Name on card: _____ Exp. date_____ /__

Signature (required for credit card orders):

_____

NOTES

Order Form

Save your book! Photocopy this form....

Life and Death Planning for Retirement Benefits

✳   Fax order: (419) 281-6883   @   Web orders: **www.ataxplan.com**

☎   Telephone orders: Call Toll Free: 1(800) 247-6553. Have your
AMEX, Discover, VISA or MasterCard ready.

✉   Mail orders: Send check payable to "Book Masters" to:
BookMasters, Inc.
30 Amberwood Parkway
Ashland, OH 44805

**Please send me_____copies of Life and Death Planning for
Retirement Benefits (4th edition, 2002) at $89.95, plus $7.00 shipping,
each.** I understand that I may return any books for a full refund for any
reason, within 90 days.

Name: _____

Company name:_____

Address:_____

City: _____ State: _____ Zip: _____ - _____

Telephone: (___) _____

Sales tax:
Please add 5% sales tax for books shipped to a Massachusetts address.
Please add required sales tax for books shipped to an Ohio address.

Shipping: $7 charge is for UPS ground. For overnight service, inquire.

Payment:
☐ Check payable to "BookMasters"
Credit card: ☐ Visa, ☐ Mastercard, ☐ AMEX, ☐ Discover
Card number: _____
Name on card: _____Exp. date_____/__

Signature (required for credit card orders):

_____

Call *toll free* and order now

To order the "old edition," send $39.95 plus $7 shipping plus Mass. or Ohio
sales tax if applicable and specify "1999 edition."